CANADA YEAR BOOK
2007

Statistics Canada

Published by authority of the Minister responsible for Statistics Canada

© Minister of Industry, 2007

Available in Canada through authorized bookstore agents and other bookstores or from:

Statistics Canada
Finance Division
R.H. Coats Building., 6th Floor
100 Tunney's Pasture Driveway
Ottawa (Ontario) K1A 0T6
Phone (Canada and United States): 1-800-267-6677
Fax (Canada and United States): 1-877-287-4369
E-mail: *Infostats@statcan.ca*

September 2007
Catalogue no. 11-402-XPE
ISSN 0068-8142
ISBN 978-0-660-19747-0
Frequency: Annual
Ottawa
La version française de cette publication est disponible sur demande (no 11-402-XPF au catalogue).

Note of appreciation

Canada owes the success of its statistical system to a long-standing partnership between Statistics Canada, the citizens of Canada, its businesses, governments and other institutions. Accurate and timely statistical information could not be produced without their continued cooperation and goodwill.

The paper used in this publication meets the minimum requirements of American national Standard for Information Sciences – Permanence of Paper for Printed Library Materials, ANSI Z39.48 – 1984.
∞

Printed in Canada
Tri-Graphic (Ottawa) Limited

Library and Archives Canada Cataloguing in Publication Data
Canada year book
Issued also in French under title: Annuaire du Canada.
ISBN 978-0-660-19747-0 (paper)
CS11-402-XPE
1. Canada – Statistics. I. Statistics Canada. Communications and Library Services Division.
HA744 S81 2006   317.1

Foreword

Welcome to the 2007 edition of the
Canada Year Book

At Statistics Canada, we have a mandate to collect information about life in Canada, and to present it in a way that all Canadians may find accessible, useful and interesting.

This year's *Canada Year Book* introduces new chapters on Aboriginal peoples, ethnic diversity and immigration, families and housing, children and youth, languages, and seniors. The book's other 25 chapters have also been updated with the most current statistics and analysis.

As well, we mark a watershed event this year with the first phase of the *Canada Year Book* online collection, which digitizes Canada Year Books beginning with the first one published in 1867. This is a remarkable trove of archival material made accessible via the latest digital technology for all Canadians to explore and enjoy at any time. Please visit www.statcan.ca/canadayearbook

By studying the record of those who have gone before us, we can better understand how Canada grew and developed, and where it may be headed next. We hope our readers today and in the future will find the 2007 edition of the *Canada Year Book* to be a valuable record of our present time.

Ivan P. Fellegi
Chief Statistician of Canada

Acknowledgements

This *Canada Year Book* owes its existence to the work of dozens of people over many months. We would like to thank the Statistics Canada employees who helped to make this volume possible. Thanks also to the team members for their invaluable contributions:

Production manager
- Catherine Pelletier

Writers
- Andrew Bisson, Thérèse Brown, Peter Hammerschmidt, Susan Hickman, Elizabeth Hostetter, Laurel Hyatt, Catherine Pelletier, Tim Prichard, Dale Simmons, Tom Vradenburg, Nancy Zukewich

Senior editors
- Christine Duchesne (French), Tim Prichard (English)

Tables editor
- Brodie Fraser

Charts editor
- Brian Drysdale

Analyst
- Patricia Tully

Fact-checking
- Brian Drysdale

Editing and proofreading
- Thérèse Brown, Cailey Cavalin, Richard Drouin, Brodie Fraser, Paula Gherasim, Jennifer Kerr, Luc Moquin, Julie Morin

Design and composition
- Pamela Gendron-Moodie, Danielle Baum (Consultant)

Table and chart production
- Pamela Gendron-Moodie, Christian Massicotte, Paul McDermott

Cover Design
- Rachel Penkar

Mapping
- Allan Rowell

Indexing
- Patricia Buchanan (English), Monique Dumont (French)

Translation
- Official Languages and Translation Division

Printing procurement
- Johanne Beauseigle

Marketing
- Jeff Jodoin

Management
- François Bordé, Vicki Crompton, Bernie Gloyn, Eric St. John, Leila Ronkainen

Penny Stuart and Tom Vradenburg
Editors-in-Chief

Abbreviations and symbols

Provinces and territories

Newfoundland and Labrador	N.L.
Prince Edward Island	P.E.I.
Nova Scotia	N.S.
New Brunswick	N.B.
Quebec	Que.
Ontario	Ont.
Manitoba	Man.
Saskatchewan	Sask.
Alberta	Alta.
British Columbia	B.C.
Yukon	Y.T.
Northwest Territories	N.W.T.
Nunavut	Nvt.

Measurements

centimetre	cm
metre	m
kilometre	km
gram	g
kilogram	kg
litre	L
millilitre	mL
hour	h
watt	W
kilowatt	kW
degrees Celsius	°C

The symbols described in this document apply to all data published by Statistics Canada from all origins, including surveys, censuses and administrative sources, as well as straight tabulations and all estimations.

.	not available for any reference period
..	not available for a specific reference period
...	not applicable
0	true zero or a value rounded to zero
0^s	value rounded to zero where there is a meaningful distinction between true zero and the value that was rounded
p	preliminary
r	revised
x	suppressed to meet the confidentiality requirements of the *Statistics Act*
E	use with caution
F	too unreliable to be published

Note: In some tables, figures may not add to totals because of rounding.

When the figure is not accompanied by a data quality symbol, it means that the quality of the data was assessed to be 'acceptable or better' according to the policies and standards of Statistics Canada.

The statistics in this edition are the most up-to-date available at the time of its preparation. For more recent data, visit Canadian Statistics at www.statcan.ca

Contents

Aboriginal peoples

In 2001, just over 1.3 million Canadians reported that their ancestors belonged to at least one of the Aboriginal peoples defined by *The Constitution Act* (1982)—North American Indian, Inuit and Métis, each of which have unique heritages, languages, cultural practices and spiritual beliefs.

However, not everyone with Aboriginal ancestry reported that they were Aboriginal people. In the 2001 Census, 976,305 people identified themselves as members of at least one of these Aboriginal groups.

In 2001, North American Indians, also called First Nations peoples, made up 62% of the Aboriginal population, while 30% identified as Métis and 5% as Inuit. The remaining 3% could not be classified into just one Aboriginal group, or they were registered Indians or band members who did not identify as Aboriginal peoples. Eighty percent

of First Nations people also reported they were registered under the *Indian Act.*

Distribution of Aboriginal people

Aboriginal people accounted for a large share of the population in the territories in 2001: 85% in Nunavut, 51% in the Northwest Territories and 23% in Yukon. However, the largest absolute numbers lived in Ontario (188,000), followed by British Columbia (170,000), Alberta (156,000), Manitoba (150,000) and Saskatchewan (130,000).

Among metropolitan areas, Winnipeg is home to the largest Aboriginal population. Almost 56,000 were counted in 2001, or more than 8% of the city's residents. Winnipeg is also home to the largest Métis population (just over 31,000) and registered Indian population (19,000). Vancouver has

Chart 1.1
Non-Aboriginal and Aboriginal populations, by age group, 2001

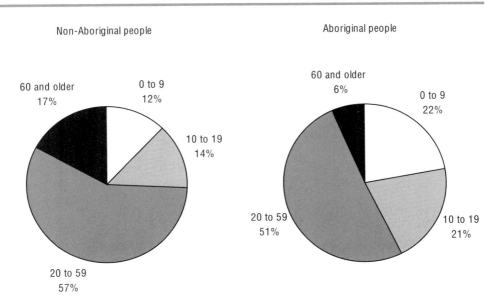

Non-Aboriginal people

- 60 and older 17%
- 0 to 9 12%
- 10 to 19 14%
- 20 to 59 57%

Aboriginal people

- 60 and older 6%
- 0 to 9 22%
- 10 to 19 21%
- 20 to 59 51%

Source: Statistics Canada, 2001 Census of Population.

the largest non-registered Indian population (8,000).

The Aboriginal identity population grew by 22% from 1996 to 2001, while the non-Aboriginal population grew 3%. About half of this Aboriginal population increase was the result of demographic or natural growth—higher fertility rates, for example. The other half was the result of non-demographic factors, such as better census coverage compared with previous years and a rising tendency for Aboriginal peoples to self-identify. Natural growth alone could increase the Aboriginal identity population to 1.4 million by 2017.

A young and growing population

From 1996 to 2001, the Métis population grew by 43%, First Nations people by 15% and the Inuit by 12%. Natural increase accounted for most of the growth among the First Nations and Inuit populations, whereas non-demographic factors explained most of the Métis population growth.

In 2001, half of all Aboriginal people were under 25. In sharp contrast, half of non-

Aboriginal population in Canada, the territories and selected provinces

	2001	2017
	% of population	
Canada	**3.4**	**4.1**
Nunavut	84.3	83.6
Northwest Territories	50.5	57.7
Yukon	23.8	35.3
Saskatchewan	13.8	20.8
Manitoba	13.8	18.4
Ontario	1.8	1.9
Quebec	1.3	1.6

Note: Data for 2001 are final estimates and data for 2017 are projections.
Source: Statistics Canada, Catalogue no. 91-547-XIE.

Aboriginal people were under 38. The Inuit have the youngest population in Canada (half are under 21), followed by First Nations (half are under 24) and Métis (half are under 27).

The number of Aboriginal people in their twenties is projected to increase dramatically. This may change the profile of job seekers in some parts of the country. Projections indicate that by 2017, Aboriginal people aged 20 to 29 will make up 30% of those in their 20s in Saskatchewan, 24% in Manitoba, 40% in Yukon and 58% in the

Chart 1.2
Aboriginal young adults without high school completion, not in school, by sex, selected census metropolitan areas

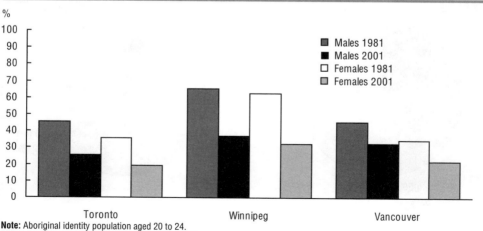

Note: Aboriginal identity population aged 20 to 24.
Source: Statistics Canada, Catalogue no. 89-613-MIE.

Northwest Territories. Already, 80% of Nunavut's population of 20- to 29-year-olds are Aboriginal people, and the proportion is expected to grow.

Quality of life gaps

Aboriginal people in Canada do not share the same quality of life as the general population. Their situation differs greatly by where they live, by Aboriginal group and by gender. For example, 1 in 3 Inuit living in the Arctic in 2001 reported there were times of the year when their water was contaminated.

In 2001, 14% of Aboriginal people were living in overcrowded housing conditions, compared with 4% of the general population. The highest percentage for overcrowded housing was found among Inuit, a rate of 32%. The overcrowding rate for First Nations people on reserves was also high at 25%.

Although the employment rate from 1996 to 2001 increased at a faster pace for Aboriginal people than for non-Aboriginal people, a gap remains. In 2001, 62% of non-Aboriginal people were employed, compared with

59% of Métis, 49% of Inuit and 45% of First Nations peoples.

Among the off-reserve population in Western Canada in 2005, the employment rate for Métis was similar to the non-Aboriginal population, 65%. The employment rate was far lower for First Nations peoples, 51%.

The share of Aboriginal people aged 20 to 24 who had not completed high school dropped substantially from 1981 to 2001, tumbling from 64% to 47% for men and from 61% to 40% for women. Aboriginal women are now more likely than Aboriginal men to have a college diploma or a university degree.

Nonetheless, from 1981 to 2001, the proportion of non-Aboriginal people with a university degree grew faster than the same proportion for Aboriginal people. This is important because education appears to reduce the employment gap between Aboriginal and non-Aboriginal Canadians. In 2001, for instance, the employment rates of Aboriginal and non-Aboriginal university graduates aged 20 to 64 were virtually identical.

Chart 1.3
Employment rates of non-Aboriginal and off-reserve Aboriginal people in Western Canada

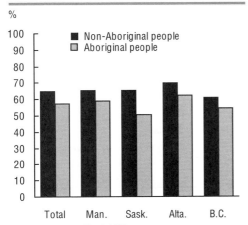

%

Non-Aboriginal people
Aboriginal people

100 90 80 70 60 50 40 30 20 10 0

Total   Man.   Sask.   Alta.   B.C.

Note: April 2004 to March 2005.
Source: Statistics Canada, Catalogue no. 71-587-XIE.

Selected sources

Statistics Canada

- *Aboriginal peoples of Canada: A demographic profile, 2001 Census.* Occasional. 96F0030XIE2001007

- *The Canadian Labour Market at a Glance.* Occasional. 71-222-XWE

- *Perspectives on Labour and Income.* Monthly. 75-001-XWE

- *A Portrait of Seniors in Canada.* Occasional. 89-519-XWE

- *Women in Canada: A Gender-based Statistical Report.* Occasional. 89-503-XIE

Other

- Health Canada

Aboriginal women face a paradox

The situation of Aboriginal women is paradoxical. Although they have more education than Aboriginal men, they are less likely to be part of the work force. And when they work for a wage, they earn less than Aboriginal men and non-Aboriginal women.

Family status may be a factor. Fertility rates were much higher from 1996 to 2001 among Aboriginal women, at 2.6 children on average over the course of their lifetime, than among non-Aboriginal women, at 1.5 children.

Among off-reserve Aboriginal women, 'family responsibilities' is the most common reason for not completing a postsecondary program, while 'pregnancy or the need to care for children' is the most common reason for dropping out of high school. However, Aboriginal women are also more likely than Aboriginal men or other women to return to school later in life.

In 2001, Aboriginal women were twice as likely as non-Aboriginal women to be lone parents (19% versus 8%). First Nations women were more likely to be lone parents (21%) than either Inuit (17%) or Métis (16%) women. As well, lone-parent families headed by Aboriginal women tend to be larger.

In 2001, 47% of Aboriginal women were employed, compared with 56% of non-Aboriginal women and 53% of Aboriginal men.

However, employment rates do not always reflect work for which no payment is received. Work of this type is common in many Aboriginal communities, especially in rural and remote ones, where much time is spent fishing, trapping, hunting, sewing, and providing care for children. Also, seasonal work is common in many Aboriginal communities.

Chart 1.4
Aboriginal women's living arrangements, by Aboriginal identity group, 2001

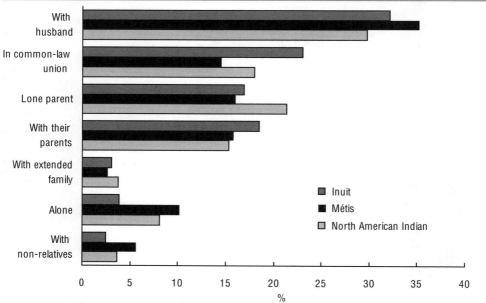

Note: Women aged 15 and older, Aboriginal identity population.
Source: Statistics Canada, Catalogue no. 89-503-XIE.

Seniors: Foundation of their communities

Seniors have influential and important roles in Aboriginal communities. As elders, Aboriginal seniors share their knowledge of traditions, culture and languages.

In 2001, 39,700 seniors aged 65 and older identified themselves as Aboriginal peoples. While Aboriginal peoples made up 3% of the total population, Aboriginal seniors made up only 1% of the total senior population.

Only 4% of Aboriginal peoples were aged 65 and older in 2001, compared with 13% of the non-Aboriginal population. Projections indicate that the number of Aboriginal seniors could climb to 7% of the total Aboriginal population by 2017, well below the 17% projected for non-Aboriginal seniors.

Aboriginal seniors have a lower median income than other seniors. In 2000, the median income of Aboriginal seniors was 83% that of non-Aboriginal seniors, or $14,259 compared with $17,123.

Seniors are especially vital in the retention of Aboriginal languages. The vast majority of Inuit seniors are able to carry on a conversation in Inuktitut; 78% of those aged 65 and older and 77% of those aged 45 to 64 can converse in Inuktitut. Among Métis seniors, 16% are able to carry on a conversation in an Aboriginal language.

First Nations seniors who live on reserve have very different characteristics from those who live off reserve. Among First Nations seniors living on reserve lands in 2001, 79% could converse in an Aboriginal language. That contrasts with 32% of First Nations seniors who lived off reserve lands.

Chart 1.5
Knowledge of Aboriginal languages, by Aboriginal identity group and selected age groups, 2001

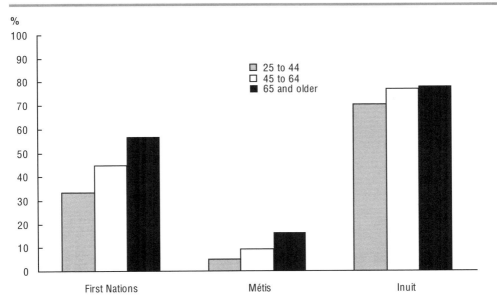

Note: Aboriginal identity population.
Source: Statistics Canada, 2001 Census of Population.

Where do Aboriginal people live?

According to the 2001 Census, 70% of 976,305 people with Aboriginal identity lived off reserves. Indian reserves are lands set aside for First Nations people, also referred to as North American Indians. In 2001, more than half (53%) of 505,000 First Nations people with legal Indian status lived on reserves. Because reserves are set aside for First Nations people, very few Métis or Inuit live on reserve lands.

In 2001, only 7,315 Métis—3% of Canada's 292,310 Métis—lived on reserves. Nearly 7 in 10 lived in cities: 4 in 10 in large cities, 3 in 10 in smaller cities.

The Inuit live predominantly in the North. In 2001, about half of Canada's 45,070 Inuit population was living in Nunavut, 21% in Nunavik (Northern Quebec), 10% in Nunatsiavut (Labrador) and 9% in Inuvialuit (Northwest Territories). With just 7% in large urban centres, the Inuit are the least likely of all Aboriginal people to live in large urban centres.

Among the 48% of First Nations peoples with legal Indian status who lived off reserves in 2001, most were in urban areas (21% in large cities and 17% in small cities), while the remaining 10% lived in rural non-reserve areas. Of First Nations peoples without legal Indian status, 73% lived in cities (both large and small).

Contrary to popular belief, Indian reserves are not losing population. Over the last 20 years, reserves have experienced small net gains in population with 3% of their population moving away, but 4% moving to reserves.

Chart 1.6
Area of residence of Aboriginal people, by Aboriginal identity and status group, 2001

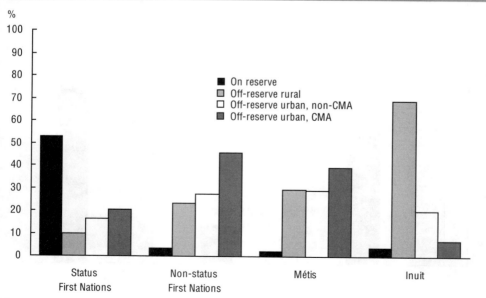

Note: Aboriginal identity population.
Source: Statistics Canada, 2001 Census of Population.

Aboriginal health and well-being

Two particularly pressing concerns for Aboriginal peoples today are access to adequate housing and their overall health. Compared with the general population, the percentage of Aboriginal peoples living in overcrowded housing is five to six times higher on reserves and in the North. Poor housing conditions allow diseases such as tuberculosis to spread.

In 2005, the tuberculosis rate was 27 active cases per 100,000 in Aboriginal peoples compared with 5 active cases per 100,000 in the Canadian population. Of the 1,600 active tuberculosis cases reported in Canada in 2005, 19% of the patients were Aboriginal peoples, 13% were non-Aboriginal Canadian-born and 63% were foreign-born.

HIV/AIDS rates among Aboriginal peoples is an ongoing concern, especially for Aboriginal women and youths. From 1998 to 2005, women made up 47% of all new HIV diagnoses among Aboriginal people, compared with 21% among non-Aboriginal people. Moreover, Aboriginal people receive a diagnosis of HIV at a younger age than non-Aboriginal people— one out of three Aboriginal persons newly diagnosed with HIV is under 30 years of age. By contrast, one out of five non-Aboriginal persons newly diagnosed is under 30.

Higher rates for diabetes mellitus among Aboriginal peoples is also of great concern. In 2001, 11% of Aboriginal adults on reserves had been diagnosed with diabetes, compared with 8% of First Nations adults off reserves, 6% of Métis, 2% of Inuit and 3% of the general population. High rates of diabetes are linked to key health determinants such as income, employment levels, education, social conditions and access to health care.

Chart 1.7
Population diagnosed with diabetes mellitus, by age group, 2001

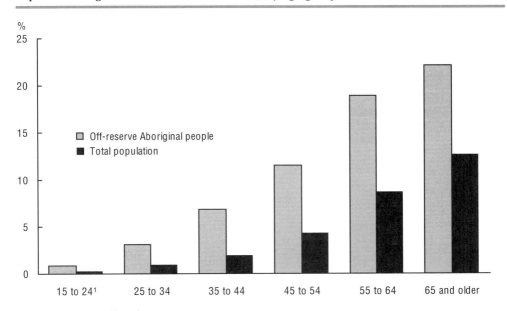

%

□ Off-reserve Aboriginal people
■ Total population

15 to 24[1]   25 to 34   35 to 44   45 to 54   55 to 64   65 and older

1. Data should be used with caution.
Source: Statistics Canada, Aboriginal Peoples Survey, 2001 and Canadian Community Health Survey, 2000/2001.

Table 1.1 Aboriginal origins population, by sex and by province and territory, 2001

	Canada	Newfoundland and Labrador	Prince Edward Island	Nova Scotia	New Brunswick
			number		
Both sexes	1,319,890	28,065	2,720	33,415	28,470
North American Indian	455,805	5,435	580	9,035	8,180
North American Indian and non-Aboriginal[1]	501,840	10,035	1,775	19,005	14,785
Métis	72,210	2,540	10	510	855
Métis and non-Aboriginal[2]	193,810	2,460	230	3,385	3,390
Inuit	37,030	3,135	20	135	105
Inuit and non-Aboriginal[3]	14,365	3,030	105	775	245
Multiple Aboriginal origins	44,835	1,425	10	575	910
Males	640,780	13,725	1,320	15,800	14,100
North American Indian	223,775	2,565	270	4,435	4,025
North American Indian and non-Aboriginal[1]	239,345	4,880	865	8,715	7,080
Métis	36,740	1,340	10	285	470
Métis and non-Aboriginal[2]	93,945	1,200	130	1,620	1,805
Inuit	18,560	1,535	10	50	75
Inuit and non-Aboriginal[3]	6,975	1,570	45	360	170
Multiple Aboriginal origins	21,445	635	0	330	490
Females	679,105	14,340	1,395	17,620	14,370
North American Indian	232,035	2,865	315	4,595	4,155
North American Indian and non-Aboriginal[1]	262,495	5,155	910	10,290	7,705
Métis	35,470	1,205	0	225	390
Métis and non-Aboriginal[2]	99,860	1,265	105	1,765	1,585
Inuit	18,465	1,600	10	85	35
Inuit and non-Aboriginal[3]	7,390	1,455	60	410	80
Multiple Aboriginal origins	23,390	790	10	245	420

1. The respondent reported having both North American Indian and non-Aboriginal origins.
2. The respondent reported having both Métis and non-Aboriginal origins.
3. The respondent reported having both Inuit and non-Aboriginal origins.
Source: Statistics Canada, 2001 Census of Population.

Quebec	Ontario	Manitoba	Saskatchewan	Alberta	British Columbia	Yukon	Northwest Territories	Nunavut
				number				
159,905	**308,105**	**160,250**	**135,035**	**199,015**	**216,110**	**6,990**	**18,955**	**22,860**
49,980	80,065	74,690	70,385	64,940	78,685	3,895	9,855	85
77,560	163,740	27,870	24,045	68,205	90,295	2,320	2,095	110
5,375	9,230	14,190	12,475	17,315	8,305	115	1,265	20
14,095	46,470	35,975	19,880	35,620	31,190	325	765	20
8,535	625	165	145	600	365	75	2,945	20,185
1,635	2,700	375	235	1,305	1,055	100	555	2,260
2,725	5,280	6,990	7,865	11,025	6,220	165	1,480	180
76,125	**148,195**	**78,155**	**65,460**	**97,080**	**106,335**	**3,415**	**9,470**	**11,600**
24,545	38,675	36,225	34,660	31,915	39,555	1,925	4,940	40
35,985	77,985	13,710	11,100	33,055	43,770	1,135	1,005	60
2,705	4,910	7,210	6,020	8,790	4,285	60	670	10
6,590	22,500	17,565	9,720	17,210	15,085	155	365	15
4,315	290	75	75	245	165	20	1,460	10,245
740	1,225	185	115	615	470	65	270	1,140
1,245	2,615	3,190	3,775	5,245	3,005	55	760	95
83,775	**159,910**	**82,095**	**69,570**	**101,935**	**109,775**	**3,570**	**9,485**	**11,255**
25,440	41,395	38,465	35,725	33,025	39,125	1,970	4,915	45
41,570	85,755	14,165	12,945	35,150	46,530	1,185	1,085	50
2,665	4,325	6,980	6,460	8,530	4,020	60	600	10
7,510	23,970	18,410	10,160	18,415	16,105	170	390	0
4,220	335	90	65	350	195	50	1,490	9,940
895	1,470	190	125	690	580	30	285	1,120
1,480	2,665	3,795	4,095	5,780	3,205	105	720	85

Table 1.2 Aboriginal origins population, by age group, sex and province and territory, 2001

	Canada	Newfoundland and Labrador	Prince Edward Island	Nova Scotia	New Brunswick
			number		
Both sexes, all ages	**976,305**	**18,780**	**1,345**	**17,015**	**16,990**
0 to 4	**102,610**	1,465	160	1,800	1,675
5 to 9	**113,075**	1,665	115	1,880	1,660
10 to 14	**108,270**	1,920	170	1,730	1,550
15 to 19	**92,985**	2,050	125	1,570	1,630
20 to 24	**76,080**	1,550	115	1,425	1,200
25 to 34	**148,550**	2,920	155	2,730	2,645
35 to 44	**145,855**	2,995	165	2,455	2,840
45 to 54	**96,365**	2,285	180	1,915	1,945
55 to 64	**52,830**	1,055	80	835	1,085
65 and older	**39,680**	875	80	675	755
Males, all ages	**476,700**	**9,395**	**635**	**8,320**	**8,655**
0 to 4	**52,375**	740	85	890	825
5 to 9	**57,905**	850	65	975	830
10 to 14	**55,060**	965	65	800	830
15 to 19	**47,020**	1,060	65	840	855
20 to 24	**36,585**	785	65	660	640
25 to 34	**70,275**	1,415	65	1,330	1,345
35 to 44	**68,405**	1,360	90	1,165	1,435
45 to 54	**45,800**	1,210	55	880	955
55 to 64	**25,140**	560	45	425	590
65 and older	**18,145**	450	35	360	355
Females, all ages	**499,605**	**9,380**	**710**	**8,690**	**8,330**
0 to 4	**50,235**	720	75	905	850
5 to 9	**55,170**	820	50	905	830
10 to 14	**53,210**	955	105	930	720
15 to 19	**45,970**	985	60	735	770
20 to 24	**39,500**	765	45	770	560
25 to 34	**78,275**	1,505	85	1,400	1,305
35 to 44	**77,450**	1,635	70	1,285	1,405
45 to 54	**50,565**	1,075	125	1,035	990
55 to 64	**27,690**	495	35	410	500
65 and older	**21,530**	425	45	315	405

Source: Statistics Canada, 2001 Census of Population.

Quebec	Ontario	Manitoba	Saskatchewan	Alberta	British Columbia	Yukon	Northwest Territories	Nunavut
				number				
79,400	**188,315**	**150,040**	**130,185**	**156,220**	**170,025**	**6,540**	**18,730**	**22,720**
7,580	17,160	18,000	16,785	16,890	15,445	635	1,880	3,135
8,090	20,165	18,985	17,885	18,675	17,900	665	2,245	3,150
7,840	18,320	17,085	16,855	18,130	18,650	675	2,245	3,100
6,700	16,575	14,400	13,395	15,535	16,315	575	1,800	2,330
6,085	14,150	11,615	10,570	13,145	12,415	450	1,485	1,880
11,780	28,745	22,890	18,870	25,190	25,470	900	2,705	3,535
12,130	31,710	20,820	16,355	22,330	27,555	1,230	2,685	2,585
9,240	20,925	13,305	9,890	14,005	18,860	665	1,675	1,480
5,405	11,935	7,410	5,375	7,185	10,170	405	985	895
4,555	8,630	5,540	4,210	5,135	7,240	345	1,025	625
38,995	**91,140**	**73,030**	**63,290**	**75,945**	**83,220**	**3,190**	**9,355**	**11,520**
3,935	8,660	9,325	8,515	8,680	7,835	320	945	1,630
4,150	10,500	9,720	9,085	9,415	9,210	330	1,190	1,600
4,055	9,370	8,510	8,360	9,355	9,680	350	1,135	1,590
3,345	8,390	7,255	6,700	7,895	8,220	295	900	1,200
2,975	6,810	5,305	4,910	6,490	6,045	220	725	945
5,665	13,385	10,710	8,535	11,935	12,375	435	1,335	1,740
5,720	14,910	9,765	7,790	10,290	12,770	570	1,275	1,260
4,530	9,940	6,470	4,695	6,280	8,950	310	795	735
2,570	5,505	3,540	2,735	3,220	4,770	205	525	450
2,055	3,675	2,435	1,975	2,390	3,365	150	535	375
40,405	**97,175**	**77,010**	**66,895**	**80,270**	**86,805**	**3,350**	**9,375**	**11,200**
3,645	8,500	8,675	8,270	8,210	7,615	310	935	1,510
3,935	9,665	9,265	8,805	9,260	8,685	340	1,055	1,550
3,785	8,950	8,575	8,500	8,775	8,975	325	1,110	1,505
3,355	8,185	7,140	6,695	7,645	8,095	280	895	1,130
3,110	7,340	6,305	5,655	6,650	6,370	230	755	935
6,115	15,360	12,185	10,335	13,255	13,100	465	1,370	1,800
6,410	16,800	11,055	8,565	12,040	14,790	655	1,410	1,325
4,710	10,985	6,840	5,190	7,730	9,915	355	885	750
2,840	6,435	3,870	2,645	3,965	5,400	200	460	445
2,495	4,955	3,110	2,235	2,740	3,875	195	490	250

Table 1.3 Population, by Aboriginal identity, highest level of schooling and sex, 2001

	All levels	Less than high school	High school only	Some post-secondary	Trade school[1]	College[1]	University[2]	University[3]
				number				
Both sexes	**23,901,360**	**7,476,900**	**3,367,900**	**2,590,165**	**2,598,925**	**3,578,400**	**601,425**	**3,687,650**
Aboriginal identity population	**652,350**	313,315	64,390	81,940	79,225	75,505	9,125	28,845
North American Indian	**395,325**	200,070	35,470	50,355	45,425	42,170	5,660	16,165
Métis	**207,610**	87,490	24,655	25,665	28,160	27,830	2,865	10,950
Inuit	**27,610**	15,940	1,700	3,550	3,070	2,610	230	515
Multiple Aboriginal identities	**4,535**	2,005	550	465	540	700	105	165
Other Aboriginal identity	**17,265**	7,805	2,010	1,910	2,030	2,200	260	1,050
Non-Aboriginal population	**23,249,015**	7,163,585	3,303,510	2,508,225	2,519,700	3,502,890	592,300	3,658,800
Males	**11,626,790**	**3,662,275**	**1,520,080**	**1,239,015**	**1,643,455**	**1,455,130**	**242,160**	**1,864,675**
Aboriginal identity population	**311,360**	157,520	30,660	35,305	47,290	26,730	3,060	10,795
North American Indian	**186,020**	99,290	16,775	21,175	26,655	14,860	1,745	5,525
Métis	**102,515**	45,800	12,035	11,490	17,380	9,920	1,165	4,725
Inuit	**13,650**	7,950	815	1,630	1,920	1,095	65	175
Multiple Aboriginal identities	**2,030**	1,045	205	175	285	240	20	55
Other Aboriginal identity	**7,155**	3,440	825	835	1,045	615	65	325
Non-Aboriginal population	**11,315,430**	3,504,755	1,489,420	1,203,710	1,596,165	1,428,400	239,100	1,853,880
Females	**12,274,570**	**3,814,625**	**1,847,820**	**1,351,150**	**955,470**	**2,123,275**	**359,265**	**1,822,975**
Aboriginal identity population	**340,985**	155,795	33,730	46,635	31,935	48,780	6,060	18,050
North American Indian	**209,300**	100,780	18,700	29,180	18,770	27,305	3,920	10,645
Métis	**105,100**	41,690	12,620	14,170	10,775	17,905	1,700	6,225
Inuit	**13,960**	7,990	885	1,915	1,155	1,515	160	345
Multiple Aboriginal identities	**2,510**	960	340	290	255	465	90	110
Other Aboriginal identity	**10,115**	4,370	1,185	1,075	980	1,585	200	720
Non-Aboriginal population	**11,933,585**	3,658,830	1,814,090	1,304,520	923,530	2,074,495	353,195	1,804,925

Note: Population aged 15 years and older.
1. Certificate or diploma.
2. Certificate or diploma below bachelor's degree.
3. Degree at the bachelor's level or higher.
Source: Statistics Canada, 2001 Census of Population.

Table 1.4 Population, by Aboriginal identity, labour force characteristics and sex, 2001

	All labour force status	In the labour force	Employed	Unemployed	Not in the labour force	Partici-pation rate	Employ-ment rate	Unemploy-ment rate
			number				%	
Both sexes	**23,901,360**	**15,872,070**	**14,695,135**	**1,176,940**	**8,029,290**	**66.4**	**61.5**	**7.4**
Aboriginal identity population	**652,350**	400,435	323,940	76,490	251,915	61.4	49.7	19.1
North American Indian	**395,325**	226,670	176,345	50,320	168,655	57.3	44.6	22.2
Métis	**207,615**	143,360	123,280	20,080	64,255	69.1	59.4	14.0
Inuit	**27,610**	17,260	13,425	3,830	10,345	62.5	48.6	22.2
Multiple Aboriginal identities	**4,535**	2,755	2,305	450	1,780	60.7	50.8	16.3
Other Aboriginal identity	**17,270**	10,390	8,585	1,805	6,880	60.2	49.7	17.4
Non-Aboriginal population	**23,249,010**	15,471,640	14,371,190	1,100,445	7,777,370	66.5	61.8	7.1
Males	**11,626,790**	**8,452,015**	**7,810,290**	**641,720**	**3,174,775**	**72.7**	**67.2**	**7.6**
Aboriginal identity population	**311,365**	207,920	163,490	44,425	103,450	66.8	52.5	21.4
North American Indian	**186,020**	116,655	87,445	29,210	69,365	62.7	47.0	25.0
Métis	**102,515**	76,335	64,575	11,760	26,180	74.5	63.0	15.4
Inuit	**13,650**	8,930	6,720	2,210	4,715	65.4	49.2	24.7
Multiple Aboriginal identities	**2,030**	1,220	985	235	810	60.1	48.5	19.3
Other Aboriginal identity	**7,150**	4,770	3,760	1,015	2,380	66.7	52.6	21.3
Non-Aboriginal population	**11,315,430**	8,244,100	7,646,805	597,290	3,071,330	72.9	67.6	7.2
Females	**12,274,570**	**7,420,055**	**6,884,840**	**535,220**	**4,854,515**	**60.5**	**56.1**	**7.2**
Aboriginal identity population	**340,985**	192,520	160,455	32,060	148,470	56.5	47.1	16.7
North American Indian	**209,305**	110,010	88,895	21,115	99,290	52.6	42.5	19.2
Métis	**105,100**	67,020	58,705	8,315	38,080	63.8	55.9	12.4
Inuit	**13,960**	8,330	6,705	1,620	5,630	59.7	48.0	19.4
Multiple Aboriginal identities	**2,505**	1,535	1,320	215	975	61.3	52.7	14.0
Other Aboriginal identity	**10,120**	5,620	4,830	795	4,495	55.5	47.7	14.1
Non-Aboriginal population	**11,933,580**	7,227,540	6,724,385	503,155	4,706,045	60.6	56.3	7.0

Note: Population aged 15 years and older.
Source: Statistics Canada, 2001 Census of Population.

Table 1.5 Population, by Aboriginal identity and selected labour force characteristics, Western Canada, 2005

	Western provinces	Manitoba	Saskatchewan	Alberta	British Columbia
	%				
Employment rate					
Aboriginal identity	**57.2**	58.9	50.7	62.6	54.5
North American Indian	**50.1**	48.6	42.1	57.4	49.8
Métis	**63.7**	65.6	57.9	66.4	62.5
Non-Aboriginal population	**65.2**	65.9	65.7	70.4	61.2
Unemployment rate					
Aboriginal identity	**13.6**	11.6	16.0	10.2	17.3
North American Indian	**17.7**	14.9	21.0	12.9	20.9
Métis	**10.5**	10.0	12.6	8.6	12.2
Non-Aboriginal population	**5.3**	4.8	4.5	4.2	6.6
Participation rate					
Aboriginal identity	**66.2**	66.6	60.3	69.7	65.9
North American Indian	**60.9**	57.0	53.3	65.8	62.9
Métis	**71.2**	72.9	66.2	72.7	71.2
Non-Aboriginal population	**68.9**	69.2	68.7	73.5	65.5

Notes: Non-reserve population aged 15 years and older.
Period from April 2004 to March 2005.
Source: Statistics Canada, Catalogue no. 71-587-XIE.

Table 1.6 Importance of keeping, learning and relearning an Aboriginal language, by Aboriginal identity group, age group and province and territory, 2001

	All age groups	15 to 24	25 to 44	45 to 64	65 and older
	% responding "very important" or "somewhat important"				
Aboriginal identity	**59.1**	**57.2**	**62.1**	**56.6**	**52.5**
Atlantic provinces	**58.3**	56.1	62.0	54.4	56.4
Quebec	**51.4**	51.1	60.2	44.1	34.0^E
Ontario	**57.7**	56.0	60.8	55.1	48.5
Manitoba	**54.7**	52.6	57.2	52.5	53.3
Saskatchewan	**64.5**	62.5	67.7	61.3	58.4
Alberta	**59.2**	57.1	61.3	59.6	49.6
British Columbia	**56.9**	52.4	58.8	58.8	54.2
Yukon	**77.5**	76.1	78.3	81.8	67.6
Northwest Territories	**75.2**	72.0	75.9	75.9	80.6
Nunavut	**95.0**	93.5	95.1	96.9	97.0
North American Indian	**63.8**	**62.0**	**66.9**	**61.2**	**55.9**
Atlantic provinces	**63.8**	60.7	69.7	58.4	60.4^E
Quebec	**47.6**	43.3	62.5	39.4	23.3^E
Ontario	**61.1**	61.6	62.8	59.8	50.4^E
Manitoba	**68.2**	65.4	70.0	66.7	73.5
Saskatchewan	**76.0**	69.5	79.7	77.1	77.6
Alberta	**66.5**	64.4	67.1	69.8	57.7
British Columbia	**61.6**	57.9	63.7	61.2	62.1
Yukon	**78.2**	76.5	78.7	82.0	66.6
Northwest Territories	**81.8**	77.6	83.0	82.1	84.6
Métis	**49.6**	**47.0**	**52.9**	**47.9**	**42.6**
Atlantic provinces	**48.8**	43.2	53.1	45.6	44.6^E
Quebec	**42.5**	39.9^E	44.5	42.1	42.6^E
Ontario	**47.7**	43.9	53.2	44.6	36.9^E
Manitoba	**46.3**	43.7	48.8	45.6	41.0
Saskatchewan	**53.4**	55.0	56.1	48.0	44.2
Alberta	**53.8**	52.1	56.9	52.7	43.2
British Columbia	**49.6**	42.9	51.8	53.8	45.4^E
Northwest Territories	**51.9**	48.1	56.1	50.0	57.1^E
Inuit	**86.9**	**86.8**	**87.6**	**85.1**	**87.9**
Newfoundland and Labrador	**74.1**	69.8	77.4	73.0	68.4
Quebec	**91.2**	91.6	95.2	80.5^E	100.0
Northwest Territories	**74.6**	71.4	72.5	82.6	81.2
Nunavut	**95.2**	93.7	95.3	96.4	97.0

Note: Non-reserve population aged 15 years and older.
Source: Statistics Canada, Catalogue no. 89-592-XIE.

Table 1.7 Population, by Aboriginal identity, income level and sex, 2001

	Total	Without income	With income	Under $5,000	$5,000 to $9,999
			number		
Both sexes	**23,901,360**	**1,178,305**	**22,723,050**	**2,945,715**	**2,477,270**
Aboriginal identity population	652,350	43,065	609,280	141,860	94,630
North American Indian	395,325	26,950	368,375	94,600	60,485
Métis	207,615	12,440	195,170	36,835	27,065
Inuit	27,610	2,380	25,230	5,860	3,970
Multiple Aboriginal identities	4,535	255	4,280	1,000	705
Other Aboriginal identity	17,270	1,040	16,225	3,565	2,400
Non-Aboriginal population	23,249,010	1,135,240	22,113,770	2,803,850	2,382,640
Males	**11,626,785**	**437,755**	**11,189,035**	**1,195,190**	**878,755**
Aboriginal identity population	311,365	18,665	292,690	66,840	39,170
North American Indian	186,020	11,765	174,250	45,465	25,405
Métis	102,515	5,205	97,310	16,575	10,800
Inuit	13,645	1,135	12,515	3,035	1,750
Multiple Aboriginal identities	2,030	145	1,880	415	315
Other Aboriginal identity	7,150	415	6,740	1,350	900
Non-Aboriginal population	11,315,430	419,085	10,896,340	1,128,350	839,580
Females	**12,274,570**	**740,555**	**11,534,015**	**1,750,520**	**1,598,520**
Aboriginal identity population	340,985	24,395	316,585	75,020	55,460
North American Indian	209,305	15,180	194,125	49,130	35,080
Métis	105,095	7,235	97,860	20,260	16,270
Inuit	13,960	1,240	12,715	2,825	2,220
Multiple Aboriginal identities	2,510	110	2,395	585	395
Other Aboriginal identity	10,115	625	9,490	2,215	1,500
Non-Aboriginal population	11,933,585	716,155	11,217,430	1,675,500	1,543,055

Notes: Population 15 years and older.
Income level of individuals in 2000.
Source: Statistics Canada, 2001 Census of Population.

$10,000 to $19,999	$20,000 to $29,999	$30,000 to $39,999	$40,000 to $49,999	$50,000 to $59,999	$60,000 and over	Median income
			number			$
5,008,265	**3,565,425**	**2,974,545**	**2,022,035**	**1,338,810**	**2,390,990**	**22,120**
151,135	85,580	58,910	33,455	19,155	24,555	13,525
93,310	49,740	32,445	17,000	9,595	11,200	12,263
46,700	29,800	22,035	13,680	7,960	11,100	16,342
6,175	3,295	2,365	1,400	895	1,270	13,699
1,020	585	405	220	140	200	13,573
3,930	2,165	1,665	1,150	570	785	14,535
4,857,130	3,479,840	2,915,635	1,988,585	1,319,655	2,366,440	22,431
1,931,575	**1,681,570**	**1,587,695**	**1,236,905**	**886,090**	**1,791,255**	**29,276**
63,075	40,830	31,055	20,470	12,705	18,545	15,512
39,375	23,400	16,025	10,000	6,185	8,390	13,173
19,165	14,635	12,825	8,960	5,615	8,740	20,767
2,725	1,710	1,250	730	500	810	14,902
345	250	190	135	95	140	14,824
1,465	835	770	645	305	465	16,859
1,868,500	1,640,735	1,556,645	1,216,430	873,385	1,772,710	29,730
3,076,690	**1,883,855**	**1,386,850**	**785,135**	**452,720**	**599,735**	**17,122**
88,065	44,750	27,855	12,985	6,445	6,010	12,311
53,940	26,340	16,420	7,000	3,405	2,805	11,844
27,535	15,160	9,215	4,725	2,340	2,360	13,592
3,455	1,585	1,110	670	390	460	12,987
675	340	220	90	45	60	12,971
2,465	1,325	890	505	260	320	13,055
2,988,625	1,839,100	1,358,995	772,150	446,275	593,725	17,273

Table 1.8 Commonly reported chronic conditions, by Aboriginal identity and by province and territory, 2001

	Arthritis or rheumatism	High blood pressure	Asthma	Digestive disorders[1]	Diabetes	Heart problems
			%			
Aboriginal identity	**19.3**	**12.0**	**11.6**	**10.2**	**7.0**	**6.5**
Atlantic provinces	20.5	15.2	9.9	10.4	5.9	6.1
Quebec	17.0	12.7	13.1	8.8	5.8	6.7
Ontario	25.7	14.6	15.8	12.6	9.4	9.3
Manitoba	17.3	12.6	10.7	8.7	7.6	4.8
Saskatchewan	17.1	11.0	9.5	9.5	7.9	5.5
Alberta	17.0	10.3	11.1	9.1	5.9	5.4
British Columbia	19.0	10.3	10.6	11.5	6.5	6.3
Yukon	15.6	12.7	9.8	10.7	5.4E	5.4
Northwest Territories	11.5	7.5	5.2	6.7	3.2	3.5
Nunavut	7.3	6.8	2.8	4.2	1.8E	5.1
North American Indian	**20.3**	**12.1**	**12.5**	**10.4**	**8.3**	**6.6**
Atlantic provinces	20.8	16.8	10.1	10.8	8.0E	5.1E
Quebec	18.7	13.8	15.8	8.4E	6.9E	8.0E
Ontario	26.7	14.9	16.6	12.0	11.0	8.1
Manitoba	17.7	12.8	11.4	8.7	10.3	5.5
Saskatchewan	17.3	9.9	9.2	9.5	8.7	5.8
Alberta	16.3	9.2	10.9	8.4	6.4	5.5
British Columbia	18.4	9.3	10.3	11.3	6.1	6.2
Yukon	15.0	12.5	9.4	11.7	5.3E	5.9
Northwest Territories	10.8	6.4	5.0	7.7	3.1	2.9
Métis	**19.5**	**12.7**	**11.7**	**10.5**	**5.9**	**6.8**
Atlantic provinces	21.2	15.2	8.9E	10.1E	3.6E	7.6E
Quebec	19.9	13.4	12.4	10.8	5.2E	5.9E
Ontario	24.0	14.7	14.9	13.2	6.0E	12.0
Manitoba	17.3	12.8	10.3	8.7	5.8	4.6
Saskatchewan	16.6	12.0	9.8	9.6	7.1	5.1
Alberta	17.4	11.4	11.2	9.5	5.3	5.4
British Columbia	21.1	11.8	11.7	11.4	6.7	6.3
Northwest Territories	14.2	7.3E	6.8E	6.4E	6.0E	4.3E
Inuit	**9.4**	**8.1**	**5.6E**	**5.8**	**2.3**	**4.8**
Newfoundland and Labrador	15.9	14.9	10.6E	8.6E	4.9E	4.9E
Quebec	4.2	4.3	2.9E	3.6E	2.4E	2.6E
Northwest Territories	11.0	11.4	3.5E	4.3E	x	4.7E
Nunavut	7.0	6.9	2.8	4.1	1.8E	5.0

Note: Non-reserve population aged 15 years and older.
1. Includes stomach problems or intestinal ulcers.
Source: Statistics Canada, Catalogue no. 89-592-XIE.

Agriculture

2

OVERVIEW

If you drive through some parts of rural Canada, such as the Prairies or southwestern Ontario, you might think every square metre is under cultivation and that everyone lives and works on a farm.

A century ago, most Canadians did live in rural areas and a large portion worked in agriculture. Compared with 50 years ago, agriculture today uses roughly the same amount of land but far less labour to produce more than enough to feed our population, which has more than doubled.

Don't be fooled by the huge fields of crops along our rural highways. Just 5% of Canada's land area is used for agriculture. That's still a large area—about 46 million hectares—but it's just 3% of the world's agricultural land.

As in most industrialized countries, farming here requires relatively few people. About 727,000 Canadians lived on farms in 2001, comprising 12% of Canada's rural population and just 2% of the overall population.

Who's working the farm?

Farming has become a way of life for just a few. Even in the most agriculture intensive areas, only a minority work in farming. Around Maple Creek, Saskatchewan, 45% of the labour force works in agriculture—the highest proportion in any census division; in southwestern Ontario's Huron County, the proportion is just over 15%.

In 2006, over 346,000 Canadians worked in agriculture, or 2% of the labour force. The next stage in the food production process—the food and beverage processing industry—employs another 270,000. Together, agriculture and food and beverage processing account for 3.4% of our economic output, as measured by gross domestic product.

Chart 2.1
Farm and non-farm populations

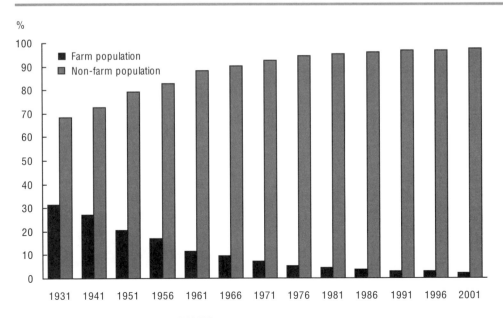

Source: Statistics Canada, Catalogue no. 95F0303XIE.

Farming is not all fields of green or gold grain swaying in the breeze. It's a tough, perennially difficult business: prices for most commodities have been declining for decades, and recent years have been particularly hard for certain agricultural commodities.

Pretty landscape, tough business

One measure of the prices farmers receive is Statistics Canada's Farm Product Price Index, whose base year is 1997. In 2006, the price index of all farm products was 96.1, down 9.6 percentage points from the most recent high in 2002. Prices in 2006 for some commodities, such as grains, oilseeds, hogs and poultry were well below their 1997 price levels. In contrast, prices for potatoes, other vegetables and dairy products in 2006 were well above their 1997 price levels.

For cattle farmers, market conditions have improved since the U.S. border reopened in mid-2005; for hog farmers, times are not so good. Farm cash receipts for cattle were 2% higher than in 2005, and producers shipped double the number of cattle. Although hog producers exported record numbers of hogs,

Percentage of experienced work force employed in agriculture, selected census divisions

	2001
	%
Division No. 4 (includes Maple Creek), Saskatchewan	45.2
Division No. 4 (includes Pilot Mound and Somerset), Manitoba	43.1
Division No. 4 (includes Hanna), Alberta	36.6
Les Jardins-de-Napierville, Quebec	16.2
Huron County, Ontario	15.4
Carleton County, New Brunswick	10.6

Source: Statistics Canada, custom tabulation using 2001 Census of Population data.

they earned 14% less than in 2005 because of lower prices, down 10.8 percentage points.

Grain prices have been in decline for much of the last two decades. From 1984 to 2006, grain prices dropped more than 33%, despite brief surges in the late 1980s, the mid-1990s and early 2000s. However, higher prices and sales pushed up farm cash receipts for wheat by 16% in 2006.

Net farm income is another indication of economic conditions for farmers. Statistics Canada gathers data on 'realized net income' for Canadian farms, a measure of the

Chart 2.2
Farm Product Price Index, selected commodities

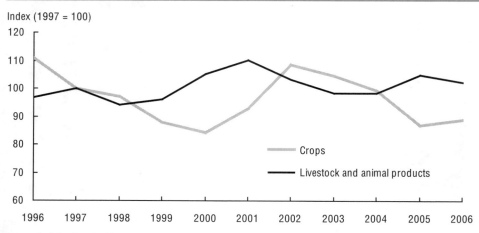

Index (1997 = 100)

Legend:
Crops
Livestock and animal products

Source: Statistics Canada, CANSIM table 002-0022.

difference between farmers' cash receipts and operating expenses, minus depreciation, and plus income-in-kind.

The 2005 net farm income data show the effects of two years of drought on the Prairies and the closing of the U.S. border to shipments of live Canadian cattle because of the bovine spongiform encephalopathy (BSE) scare. Canadian farmers' realized net income was down 14% to $1.9 billion from 2004 and at its lowest point since 2003, before the drought and BSE crisis began. Longer term, net farm income was 16% lower than the average of the years 2000 to 2004.

Agricultural program payments help to moderate the effect of market revenue fluctuations on farmers' incomes. In 2005, payments hit a record high of $4.9 billion, and represented 13% of total gross revenue.

Don't blame it all on BSE

It's not quite fair to blame 2005's poor financial showing completely on cattle, since shipments of live animals to the United States resumed at mid-year. Sales of exported live cattle and calves rebounded from zero in the first half of 2005 to $624 million, or about 10% of cattle and calf receipts. Cattle producers' overall receipts, including domestic sales, were up 25% from 2004.

Crops and hogs also contributed to the 2005 decline. Crop receipts were down 7% from 2004; hog receipts declined 8%. The reasons for fluctuations in receipts are usually a complex combination of factors, such as price changes, crop yields, and decisions by farmers to rush products to market or to hold them back.

Grain prices are a major factor in crop receipts. World grain supplies were ample in 2005, and so some prices were at near record lows. Cash receipts for wheat, excluding durum wheat, tumbled 21% from 2004, and were 28% below the 2000 to 2004 average. Prices for canola were down 24% from 2004, but increased deliveries by Canadian farmers moderated the dip in receipts to 14%.

Those swaying fields of gold might suggest a good harvest, but a host of factors that cannot be seen from the highway—prices, the size of grain stocks in storage from previous harvests, input costs, currency fluctuations, trade restrictions and shifting demand—all influence whether a good harvest translates into a good financial year for farmers.

Chart 2.3
Realized net income, value of inventory change and total net income

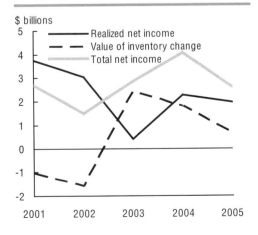

$ billions

- Realized net income
- Value of inventory change
- Total net income

Source: Statistics Canada, Catalogue no. 21-010-XIE.

Selected sources

Statistics Canada

- *Canada Food Stats.* Semi-annual. 23F0001XBB

- *Cattle Statistics.* 23-012-XIE. Semi-annual

- *Farm Product Price Index.* Monthly. 21-007-XIE

- *Food Statistics.* Semi-annual. 21-020-XIE

- *Hog Statistics.* 23-010-XIE. Quarterly

- *Net Farm Income—Agriculture Economic Statistics.* Semi-annual. 21-010-XIE

- *VISTA on the Agri-food Industry and the Farm Community.* Occasional. 21-004-XIE

Big upside for bioproducts

Ethanol and biodiesel are two of many new bioproducts already on the market or set to appear in the near future. Bioproducts are non-food products developed from biological or renewable material that comes from agricultural, food, forestry, marine, industrial or municipal sources.

Ethanol and biodiesel—collectively called biofuels—may present the biggest opportunity, given the huge quantities of gasoline and diesel fuel Canadians consume. Canada produced just 250 million litres of biofuels in 2004, whereas the United States produced 12.9 billion litres, according to the Canadian Renewable Fuels Association.

However, by 2010 Canadian production of biofuels could surpass 3 billion litres, or 5% of total gasoline consumption, just to keep up with government targets. Quebec, Ontario, Manitoba and Saskatchewan have

all mandated renewable fuel standards that call for a percentage of ethanol to be mixed with gasoline.

Other bioproducts that Canadian firms are developing include biological control agents for insects and weeds that may be less toxic for the environment than synthetic pesticides, new construction materials made from natural fibres (e.g., straw), and biodegradable plastics.

Quebec, Ontario and British Columbia, were home to 70% of the 232 firms surveyed in 2004 for the Bioproducts Development Survey. The firms tend to be small: only 16% have 150 or more employees.

Many of these firms also make other products: bioproducts account for just 25% of their total revenues. Of the $3 billion that the surveyed firms earned from bioproducts in 2003, about half came from exports.

Chart 2.4
Bioproducts firms in Canada, 2003

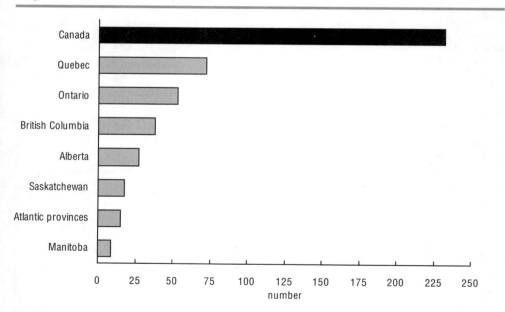

Source: Statistics Canada, Catalogue no. 21-004-XIE.

It has to be fresh!

Fresh fruits and vegetables are gaining popularity in the Canadian diet, with one exception: fresh potatoes.

Canadians consumed an average 39.4 kg of fresh fruit in 2005, up from 37.6 kg in 2004 and 36.0 kg in 1995, according to *Canada Food Stats*. Apples account for about one-fifth of fresh fruit consumption, or an average 7.6 kg per person in 2005, up from 6.8 kg in 2004. Bananas, oranges and grapes are perennial favourites, but mangoes, limes, papayas and pineapples are becoming new favourites.

Fresh vegetables—excluding potatoes—are on a similar track. Canadians consumed an average 40.5 kg in 2005, a slight increase from 39.8 kg in 2004.

Processed potatoes, in the form of french fries and potato chips, are still favourites.

Canadians averaged 2.5 kg of potato chips and 6.4 kg of french fries in 2005. About 44% of the potatoes Canadians consume are processed as chips and fries; the remaining 56% are served baked, boiled, roasted, mashed or scalloped.

Canadians averaged 15.8 kg of potatoes that had been purchased fresh, down from 21.8 kg in 1995.

Some of the trends in these data, which have been gathered for 30 years, may sound healthy, but the longer-term picture is more complex. From 1985 to 2005, average annual food energy consumption per person rose 9.4% to 2,581 kilocalories, but was down from a peak of 2,635 in 2001.

Canada Food Stats are estimates of the total amounts of various foods available to be eaten, adjusted for spoilage and waste.

Chart 2.5
Food energy consumed annually from the Canadian food supply

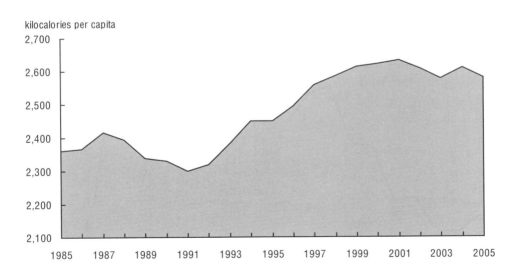

Note: Experimental data, use with caution.
The data have been adjusted for retail, household, cooking and plate loss.
Source: Statistics Canada, CANSIM table 003-0080.

Canada's beef industry after BSE

The worst effects of the BSE crisis have passed for Canada's cattle producers. The U.S. border is open again to live Canadian animals (but only those less than 30 months of age that are feeders and fed cattle). Producers are shipping hundreds of thousands stateside and shrinking their herds to more manageable levels. Older animals, however, still cannot be sent to the United States.

The border was reopened in July 2005. In the year following, the national herd declined from a peak of 17.1 million head to 16.2 million head in July. The herd shrank in all parts of the country, but three-quarters of the 2006 decline of 810,000 head occurred in the prairie provinces.

Before the border was closed in May 2003 because of a single case of BSE, more than 1 million head of live cattle, including many older cattle, were exported to the United States annually. After the U.S. and other

borders were shut, the national herd swelled. Canada lacked the slaughterhouse capacity to process those extra animals.

Cattlemen were stuck with tough choices: sell as many animals as possible in Canada at depressed prices, or hold onto them and pay for feed that added no value to their product.

In 2004 and the first half of 2005, producers sent a record number of cattle for processing. Canada's slaughter capacity was expanded, domestic beef demand held strong and some packaged meat was exported to the United States and other countries.

The age restrictions permit export of younger animals headed straight to slaughter or for a final month or two of feeding before slaughter. However, the ban on older animals, many of which are breeding stock, has hurt producers who used to sell breeder cattle south of the border.

Chart 2.6
Exports of live cattle and calves

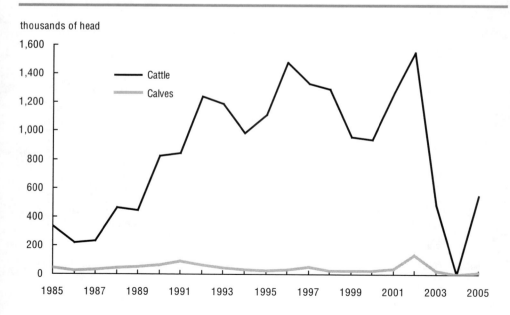

thousands of head

Source: Statistics Canada, CANSIM table 003-0026.

A big trader in food products

As a nation, we import about half of what we eat, and export about half the food we produce. This makes Canada one of the most trade dependent nations for agriculture and fish products. Other countries, especially the United States, are just as hungry for our agricultural exports.

Many of our imports are products we cannot grow. Grapes from Chile and oranges from Morocco are just two imports we now take for granted each winter. Our exports suggest a reputation as the world's bulk food store. Evidently, bulk food is good business for Canada: we posted a trade surplus of $8.2 billion in food and fish products in 2005.

Canada imported $22.0 billion of agricultural and fish products in 2005. Fruits and vegetables, either in whole form or in preparations, accounted for 29%. Another

29% was beverages and other prepared foods, 18% was fish, meat and live animals, and 24% was mainly cereal products, sugar, and fodder and feed for animals.

In 2005, our exports of agricultural and fish products totalled $30.2 billion. About 38% was fish, meat and live animals; 19% was grains and cereals; 9% was oilseeds and other vegetable products; and 34% were alcoholic and non-alcoholic beverages, other foods, animal feeds and tobacco. The United States is the destination for two-thirds of Canada's agricultural exports.

Greenhouse vegetables, as well as live cattle and hogs, became big export businesses in the 1990s, as a result of the 1988 Canada–U.S. Free Trade Agreement. To accommodate the increased export demand, greenhouses, feedlots and hog barns were built or expanded in the last 15 years.

Chart 2.7
Agricultural and fish products trade, 2005

Imports

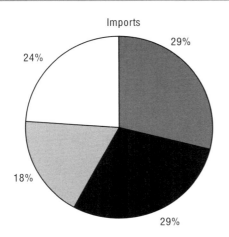

Exports

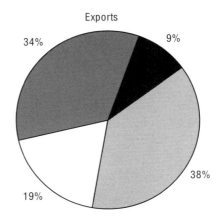

- Vegetables and fruit
- Beverages and other prepared foods
- Fish, meat and live animals
- Cereals, sugar, animal and other plant products

- Oilseeds and other vegetable products
- Fish, meat and live animals
- Grains and cereals
- Other food, feed, beverages and tobacco

Source: Statistics Canada, Catalogue no. 21-004-XIE.

Table 2.1 Livestock and poultry, 1992 to 2006

	1992	1993	1994	1995	1996	1997
	thousands					
Cattle	11,869	11,860	12,012	12,709	13,402	13,412
Bulls[1]	216	226	233	249	249	246
Milk cows	1,283	1,223	1,224	1,245	1,237	1,231
Beef cows	3,790	3,912	3,982	4,252	4,381	4,387
Dairy heifers[2]	599	537	532	528	524	531
Beef heifers[2]	1,150	1,226	1,182	1,290	1,418	1,388
For breeding	673	647	699	778	814	724
For market	476	579	484	512	604	664
Steers[3]	935	768	806	775	864	981
Calves	3,897	3,969	4,053	4,370	4,728	4,648
Pigs	10,784	10,566	10,888	11,522	11,490	11,740
Breeding stock	1,142	1,138	1,173	1,179	1,192	1,239
Boars,[4] six months and older	65	63	65	63	60	58
Sows[5] and gilts,[6] six months and older	1,077	1,075	1,108	1,115	1,132	1,181
All other pigs	9,641	9,427	9,715	10,344	10,299	10,501
Under 20 kilograms	3,234	3,137	3,233	3,339	3,349	3,433
20 to 60 kilograms	3,357	3,288	3,371	3,531	3,538	3,630
Over 60 kilograms	3,050	3,002	3,110	3,473	3,412	3,437
Sheep	465	469	466	441	456	447
Rams[7]	23	22	24	23	22	23
Ewes[8]	442	447	443	418	434	425
Lambs	183	164	173	176	187	180
Chickens	411,090	408,810	430,258	486,338	486,218	501,289
Turkeys	19,841	19,863	19,448	19,811	21,255	21,475

Note: Data reflect the annual average number of animals.

1. Uncastrated male bovines.
2. Female bovines that have never borne young.
3. Castrated male bovines.
4. Uncastrated male pigs.
5. Female pigs that have borne young.
6. Female pigs that have never borne young.
7. Male sheep.
8. Female sheep that have borne young.

Source: Statistics Canada, CANSIM tables 003-0004, 003-0018, 003-0031 and 003-0032.

1998	1999	2000	2001	2002	2003	2004	2005	2006
				thousands				
13,360	13,211	13,201	13,608	13,762	13,488	14,653	15,063	14,830
236	225	230	239	237	239	271	273	265
1,184	1,157	1,103	1,091	1,084	1,065	1,055	1,066	1,049
4,361	4,386	4,452	4,602	4,636	4,752	5,019	5,297	5,264
511	494	487	498	508	512	503	499	498
1,433	1,309	1,347	1,475	1,518	1,428	1,566	1,616	1,650
687	605	645	674	654	648	706	666	650
746	704	703	801	865	780	861	950	1,000
1,004	1,197	1,267	1,222	1,205	1,179	1,228	1,184	1,173
4,631	4,443	4,315	4,482	4,574	4,312	5,012	5,127	4,932
12,363	12,721	13,377	14,105	14,672	14,608	14,666	14,831	14,436
1,307	1,326	1,374	1,467	1,549	1,598	1,638	1,647	1,631
56	50	47	45	43	40	36	34	33
1,251	1,276	1,327	1,423	1,506	1,558	1,602	1,612	1,598
11,056	11,395	12,003	12,638	13,123	13,011	13,029	13,185	12,806
3,686	3,851	4,026	4,195	4,370	4,465	4,483	4,496	4,368
3,781	3,884	4,104	4,337	4,491	4,355	4,370	4,479	4,320
3,589	3,660	3,873	4,106	4,261	4,190	4,175	4,210	4,117
465	490	543	606	644	642	650	642	602
24	25	28	30	29	29	28	27	26
441	465	515	576	615	613	622	615	576
197	227	251	342	349	334	347	338	293
516,952	541,278	570,468	590,623	624,792	625,692	615,939	613,527	626,251
20,999	20,070	20,087	21,268	20,191	19,672	19,834	19,526	20,492

Table 2.2 Principal field crops, seeded areas, 1992 to 2007

	1992	1993	1994	1995	1996	1997	1998
				hectares			
All wheat	14,391,200	12,982,500	10,997,400	11,365,800	12,488,361	11,576,100	10,870,600
Spring wheat	12,532,300	11,240,300	8,298,100	8,822,500	9,983,447	9,016,600	7,533,200
Winter wheat	347,400	279,300	352,100	358,000	441,114	327,600	403,500
Durum wheat	1,511,500	1,462,900	2,347,200	2,185,300	2,063,800	2,231,900	2,933,900
Oats	1,663,400	1,728,800	1,840,400	1,579,400	2,060,342	1,876,300	2,062,600
Barley	4,086,700	4,559,200	4,329,600	4,654,300	5,238,025	5,021,500	4,632,300
All rye	226,900	241,400	239,200	215,300	218,265	208,000	267,300
Fall rye	192,500	217,100	204,800	197,100	202,065	191,800	249,100
Spring rye	34,400	24,300	34,400	18,200	16,200	16,200	18,200
Mixed grains	287,300	311,800	306,800	321,000	291,619	317,800	275,200
Corn for grain	1,081,300	1,035,900	987,900	1,006,500	1,130,775	1,052,500	1,126,500
Buckwheat	24,600	11,800	11,300	17,100	17,775	15,800	14,700
Dry field peas	273,100	505,800	696,100	819,400	544,300	848,500	1,084,500
Dry white beans	53,200	49,200	45,000	61,700	42,560	47,900	39,800
Coloured beans	19,800	37,200	38,600	43,200	43,144	43,900	54,100
Flaxseed	297,400	528,100	732,400	876,100	592,900	736,600	878,200
Soybeans	642,600	751,900	821,100	826,100	875,993	1,061,700	980,600
Mustard seed	119,400	190,200	323,600	267,000	239,100	292,200	283,200
Canola (rapeseed)	3,235,500	4,172,300	5,797,100	5,344,000	3,540,311	4,905,900	5,477,400
Sunflower seed	74,400	85,000	83,000	48,600	36,400	50,600	68,800
Sugar beets	22,600	22,200	25,500	24,900	23,800	14,200	18,200
Tame hay	6,414,200	6,514,700	6,738,800	6,577,600	6,395,660	6,349,500	6,578,600
Fodder corn	205,800	179,600	165,800	170,700	190,523	204,600	200,200
Lentils	279,200	372,300	398,600	333,800	303,500	329,000	378,400
Canary seed	94,300	126,300	204,300	147,600	248,800	113,300	210,400
Fababeans	5,600	3,600	2,800	4,000	1,840	2,400	5,600
Triticale	1,200	15,400	25,900	23,000	25,100	23,000	56,600
Safflower	..	4,000	2,000	2,000	800	..	1,200
Caraway seed	..	..	..	..	..	..	..
Coriander seed	..	..	..	..	..	..	..
Borage seed	..	..	..	..	..	..	..
Chick peas	..	..	..	..	..	10,500	38,800

Source: Statistics Canada, CANSIM table 001-0010.

1999	2000	2001	2002	2003	2004	2005	2006	2007
				hectares				
10,469,000	11,072,200	10,950,500	10,678,000	10,662,100	10,399,100	10,125,300	10,715,700	9,684,400
8,288,900	8,001,100	8,325,400	7,752,300	7,511,700	7,527,000	7,245,600	8,204,200	6,911,800
395,400	428,500	460,100	436,900	667,600	642,300	538,500	751,100	769,400
1,784,700	2,642,600	2,165,000	2,488,800	2,482,800	2,229,800	2,341,200	1,760,400	2,003,200
1,885,700	1,825,700	1,907,400	2,398,500	2,272,000	1,994,900	1,853,300	1,922,600	2,299,500
4,409,100	5,101,300	4,700,200	5,147,100	5,046,100	4,677,500	4,440,000	3,860,900	4,375,600
225,000	188,200	181,400	159,900	246,400	280,400	225,800	200,600	175,500
208,800	167,900	163,200	143,700	228,200	264,200	225,800	200,600	175,500
16,200	20,300	18,200	16,200	18,200	16,200	..	..	..
278,700	290,200	364,200	284,000	240,700	220,400	208,800	244,900	139,500
1,166,200	1,206,000	1,294,200	1,299,300	1,264,600	1,184,800	1,124,200	1,127,200	1,420,800
13,900	15,900	15,900	12,100	9,300	6,100	4,000	6,100	..
851,300	1,240,200	1,343,600	1,296,900	1,303,000	1,388,000	1,365,700	1,410,300	1,442,700
79,200	80,600	84,400	115,300	72,900	64,800	76,900	66,700	66,800
70,700	84,400	94,900	109,700	88,800	94,200	120,100	116,200	92,600
809,400	594,900	671,800	692,000	744,600	728,400	841,800	841,700	578,700
1,004,000	1,068,700	1,081,500	1,030,300	1,050,800	1,229,100	1,176,400	1,237,900	1,186,100
279,900	212,300	165,800	289,300	339,800	316,800	212,400	143,600	170,000
5,598,700	4,937,000	3,826,800	3,891,000	4,735,700	5,319,400	5,491,300	5,372,600	6,002,100
85,000	74,800	72,800	99,500	118,500	87,000	93,000	74,900	74,900
18,200	17,000	12,100	12,100	12,100	14,200	13,800	15,000	..
6,937,100	7,270,700	7,663,400	7,697,500	7,532,600	7,482,700	7,316,300	7,562,700	..
188,600	211,500	233,800	226,000	233,900	242,800	219,800	228,700	189,400
506,300	698,900	708,200	600,900	553,900	778,900	883,800	566,500	514,000
149,800	165,900	170,000	287,300	250,900	356,000	190,200	119,400	165,900
2,800	6,100	5,200	5,200	4,800	6,000	4,800	10,400	..
74,800	70,800	47,300	87,000	82,100	74,900	53,800	48,600	36,400
4,000	5,200	2,400	2,000	..	..	..	..	..
..	..	7,300	8,100	8,100	4,000	..	..	..
..	..	..	8,100	8,100	12,100	10,100	..	..
..	..	..	2,000	2,000	4,000	..	..	..
141,600	295,400	485,700	220,500	62,700	46,600	78,800	143,600	210,500

Table 2.3 Principal field crop production, 1991 to 2006

	1991	1992	1993	1994	1995	1996	1997
				tonnes			
All wheat	31,945,600	29,877,200	27,225,900	22,919,500	24,989,400	29,801,400	24,299,400
Spring wheat	26,603,400	25,360,400	23,100,000	16,944,400	18,847,100	24,146,900	19,032,400
Winter wheat	756,400	1,378,900	767,500	1,340,300	1,493,900	1,027,900	915,300
Durum wheat	4,585,800	3,137,900	3,358,400	4,634,800	4,648,400	4,626,600	4,351,700
Oats	1,793,900	2,828,500	3,556,800	3,640,500	2,872,800	4,361,100	3,489,300
Barley	11,617,300	11,031,500	12,972,100	11,692,000	13,032,500	15,562,000	13,533,900
All rye	338,700	281,100	318,600	399,700	309,600	309,400	320,000
Fall rye	310,800	243,000	280,500	348,900	291,800	291,100	303,400
Spring rye	27,900	38,100	38,100	50,800	17,800	18,300	16,600
Mixed grains	618,100	604,100	712,100	630,900	653,300	581,900	626,400
Corn for grain	7,412,500	4,882,600	6,755,200	7,189,900	7,280,900	7,541,700	7,179,800
Buckwheat	23,300	10,750	7,500	12,400	21,200	22,200	16,500
Dry field peas	409,700	504,800	970,200	1,441,000	1,454,700	1,173,000	1,762,300
Dry white beans	0	53,100	77,800	84,800	116,200	61,200	82,600
Coloured beans	0	20,100	53,000	85,900	86,900	71,800	85,400
Flaxseed	635,000	336,600	627,400	967,700	1,104,900	851,000	895,400
Soybeans	1,459,900	1,453,300	1,944,900	2,253,700	2,297,500	2,169,500	2,737,700
Mustard seed	121,100	133,300	215,900	319,300	244,300	230,800	243,400
Canola (rapeseed)	4,224,200	3,872,400	5,524,900	7,232,500	6,434,200	5,062,300	6,393,100
Sunflower seed	134,600	64,800	78,500	117,000	66,200	54,900	65,100
Sugar beets	1,085,000	775,700	782,900	1,091,300	1,026,900	1,034,200	635,000
Tame hay	29,192,400	27,694,600	29,703,700	31,141,300	26,851,400	28,025,000	21,137,500
Fodder corn	5,536,600	5,273,800	5,248,800	4,743,800	4,995,700	5,375,400	5,466,600
Lentils	342,800	349,000	348,700	450,400	431,900	402,500	378,800
Canary seed	100,300	124,100	127,800	240,400	154,600	284,600	115,000
Fababeans	18,800	11,200	5,200	6,800	5,800	5,520	4,300
Triticale	2,400	2,800	31,100	40,700	39,900	35,200	31,000
Safflower	..	..	500	1,100	2,000	700	..
Caraway seed	..	..	..	..	..	..	..
Coriander seed	..	..	..	..	..	..	..
Borage seed	..	..	..	..	..	..	..
Chick peas	..	..	..	..	..	..	14,500

Source: Statistics Canada, CANSIM table 001-0010.

1998	1999	2000	2001	2002	2003	2004	2005	2006
				tonnes				
24,082,300	26,959,900	26,535,500	20,630,200	16,197,500	23,552,000	25,860,400	26,775,000	27,276,600
16,564,600	20,900,800	19,027,000	16,010,200	10,767,400	16,440,300	18,451,000	18,788,100	20,052,100
1,475,800	1,718,200	1,800,000	1,570,500	1,553,200	2,832,100	2,447,400	2,072,300	3,403,400
6,041,900	4,340,900	5,708,500	3,049,500	3,876,900	4,279,600	4,962,000	5,914,600	3,821,100
3,957,500	3,641,300	3,403,300	2,690,700	2,910,700	3,691,000	3,683,100	3,432,300	3,602,300
12,708,700	13,196,000	13,228,600	10,845,600	7,489,400	12,327,600	13,186,400	12,481,200	10,004,500
408,200	386,600	260,300	227,800	133,800	327,100	417,900	358,600	301,500
391,700	366,800	247,000	215,600	129,400	307,800	403,900	358,600	301,500
16,500	19,800	13,300	12,200	4,400	19,300	14,000	..	..
540,000	462,800	434,900	446,500	358,900	384,400	318,000	303,100	290,700
8,952,400	9,161,300	6,953,700	8,389,200	8,998,800	9,587,300	8,836,800	9,460,800	9,268,200
14,800	12,500	13,600	16,300	12,200	9,900	1,500	4,600	6,500
2,336,800	2,251,900	2,864,300	2,044,800	1,365,500	2,124,400	3,338,200	3,099,800	2,806,300
73,900	149,100	119,300	136,200	209,700	151,000	72,100	117,900	137,600
111,200	135,400	142,100	153,000	197,100	193,300	141,500	201,100	235,100
1,080,900	1,022,400	693,400	715,000	679,400	754,400	516,900	1,082,000	1,041,100
2,736,600	2,780,900	2,703,000	1,635,200	2,335,700	2,268,300	3,048,000	3,161,300	3,532,800
238,600	306,400	202,200	104,800	154,300	226,100	305,500	201,400	116,100
7,643,300	8,798,300	7,205,300	5,017,100	4,520,500	6,771,200	7,728,100	9,660,200	9,105,100
111,800	121,900	119,300	103,800	157,400	150,300	54,400	89,300	153,200
880,000	743,900	821,000	544,300	344,700	680,400	743,900	607,800	870,900
21,825,000	25,032,900	23,921,600	20,373,500	18,140,900	22,360,400	25,614,500	26,629,400	27,617,300
6,425,600	6,611,500	5,890,300	6,079,000	6,355,800	7,213,000	7,908,700	7,469,000	8,382,400
479,800	723,800	914,100	566,300	353,800	519,900	962,000	1,277,900	692,800
235,300	166,000	170,800	113,900	185,700	226,400	300,500	227,200	117,300
13,700	6,500	15,400	10,200	9,100	8,400	15,300	9,800	18,000
85,300	126,200	89,700	31,200	26,000	68,600	80,000	43,200	26,900
1,400	3,800	6,700	2,900	1,100	..	..	..	..
..	..	..	2,000	2,400	3,200	2,500	..	..
..	..	..	..	5,200	4,800	7,900	8,900	..
..	..	..	..	800	500	700	..	..
50,900	187,200	387,500	455,000	156,500	67,600	51,200	103,900	182,300

Table 2.4 Principal field crop production, by province, 2006

	Canada	Newfoundland and Labrador	Prince Edward Island	Nova Scotia	New Brunswick
			tonnes		
All wheat	27,276,600	.	40,600	14,500	3,600
Spring wheat	20,052,100	.	32,400	2,700	3,000
Winter wheat	3,403,400	.	8,200	11,800	600
Durum wheat	3,821,100	.	.	.	.
Oats	3,602,300	.	10,900	2,900	16,000
Barley	10,004,500	.	91,100	5,400	27,400
Fall rye	301,500	.	..	..	.
Mixed grains	290,700	.	13,000	..	2,100
Corn for grain	9,268,200	.	.	19,000	.
Buckwheat	6,500	.	..	..	..
Dry field peas	2,806,300	.	..	..	..
Dry white beans	137,600	.	.	.	.
Coloured beans	235,100	.	.	.	.
Flaxseed	1,041,100	.	.	.	.
Soybeans	3,532,800	.	11,800	.	.
Mustard seed	116,100	.	.	.	.
Canola (rapeseed)	9,105,100	.	.	.	.
Sunflower seed	153,200	.	.	.	.
Sugar beets	870,900	.	.	.	.
Tame hay	27,617,300	28,100	257,600	365,600	344,700
Fodder corn	8,382,400	.	..	69,900	47,200
Lentils	692,800	.	.	.	.
Canary seed	117,300	.	.	.	.
Fababeans	18,000	.	.	.	.
Triticale	26,900	.	.	.	.
Coriander seed	..	.	.	.	.
Chick peas	182,300	.	.	.	.

Source: Statistics Canada, CANSIM table 001-0010.

Quebec	Ontario	Manitoba	Saskatchewan	Alberta	British Columbia
			tonnes		
163,500	2,642,700	4,084,600	12,482,300	7,818,100	26,700
153,000	247,700	3,543,600	9,076,800	6,966,200	26,700
10,500	2,395,000	541,000	275,700	160,600	..
.	.	..	3,129,800	691,300	.
270,000	98,200	979,000	1,526,800	670,900	27,600
310,000	298,300	1,145,900	3,470,500	4,624,500	31,400
4,400	50,000	81,300	134,600	31,200	..
52,000	156,000	7,100	13,300	43,900	3,300
2,730,000	6,096,300	406,400	.	16,500	.
..	..	6,500	..	..	.
..	..	91,000	2,126,900	586,100	2,300
..	85,000	52,600	.	..	.
14,700	64,600	93,000	.	51,900	.
..	..	193,000	805,200	42,900	..
540,000	2,721,600	259,400	.	.	.
.	.	..	90,500	25,600	.
11,800	11,300	1,826,800	3,962,100	3,265,900	27,200
.	.	153,200	..	..	.
..	..	..	.	870,900	.
4,005,200	5,796,900	3,147,900	4,413,500	8,019,500	1,238,300
1,670,100	4,535,900	957,100	..	517,100	585,100
.	.	..	692,800	..	.
.	.	4,500	112,800	..	.
.	.	9,500	2,000	4,800	.
.	.	..	11,900	15,000	.
.	.	.	..	.	.
.	.	.	159,500	22,800	.

Table 2.5 Farm cash receipts, 1992 to 2006

	1992	1993	1994	1995	1996	1997
	\$ thousands					
Farm cash receipts	**23,730,202**	**24,188,520**	**25,881,396**	**27,123,321**	**29,075,327**	**29,838,629**
Receipts from crops	8,551,035	9,045,654	11,542,606	13,114,105	14,016,229	14,102,990
Wheat	2,232,747	1,752,339	2,436,389	2,823,648	3,482,441	3,520,740
Oats	98,039	144,879	144,883	224,863	305,427	269,170
Barley	386,260	401,735	517,327	719,800	960,127	727,160
Canada Wheat Board payments[1]	489,336	1,057,920	1,367,430	1,432,766	1,123,878	725,720
Rye	21,173	20,540	24,310	30,776	38,989	34,242
Flaxseed	94,648	107,047	184,905	230,310	220,875	291,632
Canola (rapeseed)	999,392	1,194,351	2,111,164	1,906,362	1,968,956	2,127,750
Soybeans	324,342	438,744	506,678	661,659	626,673	814,222
Corn	514,863	419,255	505,789	704,294	808,128	696,106
Sugar beets	28,559	31,651	40,548	52,043	40,670	34,483
Potatoes	345,771	425,586	533,104	517,641	533,124	512,581
Vegetables	754,730	812,755	863,319	923,155	..	..
Greenhouse vegetables	..	..	..	..	218,473	270,361
Other vegetables	..	..	..	..	749,685	773,255
Tree fruits	193,872	183,157	207,773	252,265	241,440	234,840
Berries and grapes	190,296	186,764	219,213	240,738	254,740	251,236
Floriculture and nursery	866,160	861,662	883,978	941,540	999,335	1,095,216
Tobacco	311,914	277,994	373,946	296,647	345,332	353,267
Other crops	698,933	729,275	621,850	1,155,598	1,097,936	1,371,009
Receipts from livestock and their products[2]	11,388,328	12,300,208	12,513,891	12,703,800	13,857,294	14,626,880
Cattle and calves	4,452,356	4,924,284	4,812,930	4,607,189	4,730,759	5,285,317
Hogs	1,787,118	2,042,353	2,031,823	2,252,460	2,884,759	2,989,333
Sheep	2,498	3,047	2,908	3,206	3,026	3,494
Lambs	49,834	60,075	60,875	66,403	74,812	71,843
Dairy products	3,089,634	3,134,174	3,354,465	3,463,085	3,514,733	3,709,267
Hens and chickens	922,803	1,006,808	1,060,948	1,050,960	1,248,291	1,298,789
Turkeys	212,902	210,047	221,061	237,891	266,906	258,588
Eggs	522,041	534,455	559,998	590,826	644,956	482,874
Other livestock and products	244,394	263,730	289,745	305,781	364,527	404,631
Receipts from direct payments	3,790,839	2,842,658	1,824,899	1,305,416	1,201,804	1,108,759
Crop insurance payments[3]	355,954	723,721	414,825	306,725	256,832	302,721
Private hail insurance	54,888	47,078	198,180	174,738	81,613	71,068
Provincial stabilization payments	367,800	261,959	300,472	308,128	300,359	170,846
Dairy subsidy	230,979	229,930	222,304	213,553	170,657	146,610
Other payments	2,427,955	1,417,510	648,499	255,976	277,627	264,192
Net Income Stabilization Account payments	353,263	162,460	40,619	46,296	114,716	153,322
Income disaster assistance programs	..	..	..	..	..	..

1. Payments made directly to producers.
2. Data do not add to totals because data for horses and their products are suppressed for confidentiality.
3. As of 1992, data no longer include payments under private hail insurance plans.
Source: Statistics Canada, CANSIM table 002-0001.

1998	1999	2000	2001	2002	2003	2004	2005	2006
				$ thousands				
29,686,323	30,357,110	32,960,524	36,320,804	36,075,277	34,419,826	36,458,435	36,798,628	37,014,256
13,822,114	13,217,869	13,062,085	13,590,638	14,454,970	13,400,716	14,434,436	13,481,153	14,482,106
2,413,393	2,337,436	2,350,429	2,548,885	2,474,708	2,246,500	2,151,495	1,755,772	2,170,959
193,228	174,621	196,413	273,962	307,737	244,503	232,487	254,931	331,970
510,285	421,352	477,987	621,288	505,702	379,483	434,556	346,792	329,791
948,849	948,353	811,564	1,042,085	981,534	337,267	1,007,545		
19,743	17,212	15,285	16,210	12,182	12,440	28,857	13,050	16,358
262,858	138,965	148,743	162,780	239,835	192,160	198,714	170,117	154,294
2,663,207	1,771,010	1,560,025	1,723,047	1,778,264	1,889,576	2,149,436	1,855,278	2,501,609
800,348	618,194	677,947	534,483	587,657	758,345	630,898	761,031	680,063
642,363	742,902	676,073	630,884	819,169	786,685	794,416	625,675	753,497
39,838	30,527	32,899	19,333	20,072	22,732	30,921	32,140	38,180
612,166	700,669	679,916	722,879	917,617	846,378	820,292	779,593	899,242
..	..	..	..	..	..	..	..	..
376,949	438,491	504,713	589,710	593,763	637,136	716,726	722,312	758,243
787,818	779,893	796,238	873,847	844,869	876,876	907,683	889,923	925,278
231,839	252,633	260,280	258,050	233,864	244,591	222,914	207,056	210,874
254,377	320,013	286,441	280,447	294,783	312,930	375,083	344,320	381,583
1,220,579	1,322,114	1,588,698	1,665,576	1,828,717	1,902,346	1,925,250	1,887,211	1,950,488
358,610	356,706	348,427	240,007	274,150	222,256	231,181	194,942	178,521
1,485,664	1,846,778	1,650,007	1,387,160	1,735,689	1,523,641	1,648,376		
14,442,665	15,163,207	17,089,735	18,964,226	18,191,366	16,170,994	17,161,734	18,394,053	17,959,991
5,704,605	6,185,002	6,874,942	7,891,897	7,654,142	5,119,181	5,071,927	6,359,135	6,495,015
2,201,165	2,395,395	3,355,238	3,827,869	3,284,628	3,442,646	4,277,920	3,941,305	3,428,012
4,034	4,013	5,214	4,743	3,568	4,395	4,296	6,245	6,770
67,727	70,464	81,526	92,273	99,486	96,459	87,193	113,260	121,681
3,846,077	3,920,935	4,029,833	4,142,313	4,135,287	4,480,779	4,598,535	4,841,889	4,830,672
1,356,008	1,320,852	1,368,143	1,522,306	1,452,936	1,528,417	1,579,731	1,615,170	1,545,233
248,836	240,235	263,253	262,534	258,822	262,642	267,824	271,505	278,304
466,165	477,591	511,052	547,878	574,980	570,337	567,249	547,223	560,530
424,085	418,552	462,421	518,676	564,038	535,460	559,883		
1,421,544	1,976,034	2,808,704	3,765,940	3,428,941	4,848,116	4,862,265	4,923,422	4,572,159
318,356	239,544	451,382	917,589	1,407,047	1,707,485	755,810	820,072	600,268
55,855	68,628	159,254	123,657	86,071	104,507	108,718	116,304	138,832
507,947	572,776	411,180	516,476	395,673	711,321	626,336	390,763	542,136
132,113	103,652	72,666	41,885	8,758	..	..	..	..
138,549	209,689	836,148	1,097,940	528,782	1,161,404	1,421,290		
268,724	444,918	456,221	441,711	615,685	723,065	934,140	442,340	316,950
..	339,321	421,853	626,682	386,925	440,331	1,014,044	1,777,161	2,760,427

Table 2.6 Farm operators, by farm type and by province, 2006

	Canada	Newfoundland and Labrador	Prince Edward Island	Nova Scotia	New Brunswick
			number		
All operators[1,2]	**327,055**	**715**	**2,335**	**5,095**	**3,695**
Farm type[3]					
Dairy cattle and milk production	25,770	55	360	495	430
Beef cattle ranching and farming, including feedlots	86,000	60	475	905	670
Hog and pig farming	9,245	10	90	85	65
Chicken egg production	2,680	20	20	75	45
Broiler and other meat-type chicken production	2,935	5	15	90	15
Turkey production	445	0	5	15	5
Poultry hatcheries	70	0	0	5	0
Combination poultry and egg production	240	0	0	10	0
Other poultry production	390	0	0	0	0
Sheep farming	4,260	30	20	80	25
Goat farming	1,525	5	0	35	20
Apiculture	2,170	5	10	30	35
Horse and other equine production	22,905	15	115	260	195
Fur-bearing animal and rabbit production	535	25	15	125	20
Livestock combination farming	10,860	20	80	220	150
All other miscellaneous animal production	3,770	0	5	25	30
Soybean farming	8,390	0	10	0	5
Oilseed (except soybean) farming	13,505	0	0	0	0
Dry pea and bean farming	1,590	0	0	0	0
Wheat farming	15,480	0	15	5	10
Corn farming	4,880	0	0	10	5
Other grain farming	38,145	5	70	15	35
Potato farming	2,405	30	495	20	340
Other vegetables (except potato) and melon farming	5,315	95	70	175	100
Fruit and tree-nut farming	12,185	50	205	1,185	485
Mushroom production	235	0	0	5	5
Other food crops grown under cover	1,410	10	5	40	10
Nursery and tree production	6,895	60	25	500	215
Floriculture production	4,135	75	15	145	110
Tobacco farming	910	0	0	0	0
Hay farming	24,090	85	110	345	395
Fruit and vegetable combination farming	865	30	10	35	30
All other miscellaneous crop farming	12,815	20	90	165	245

Note: Each census farm is classified according to the commodity or group of commodities that accounts for 50% or more of the total potential receipts.

1. Figures may not add to totals because of rounding. Minor differences can be expected in figures appearing in other tables.

2. Farm operators are defined as those people responsible for the management decisions made in the operation of a census farm or agricultural operation. Up to three farm operators could be reported per farm.

3. The farm type is based on the North American Industry Classification System (NAICS) farm-typing categories. Although NAICS is revised periodically, the classifications for Canadian agriculture have remained the same and the data for the two census years are comparable.

Source: Statistics Canada, 2006 Census of Agriculture.

Quebec	Ontario	Manitoba	Saskatchewan	Alberta	British Columbia
			number		
45,470	**82,410**	**26,620**	**59,185**	**71,660**	**29,870**
12,545	8,540	820	360	1,050	1,115
6,375	15,000	9,240	16,795	30,115	6,365
2,975	3,395	1,155	315	950	200
225	935	180	75	220	880
555	1,260	135	110	295	455
70	165	35	15	50	85
10	20	10	5	10	10
30	70	15	5	25	85
100	135	15	10	35	85
930	1,515	195	260	615	590
235	555	105	80	265	225
215	530	350	350	395	255
1,200	6,560	1,265	1,600	7,095	4,600
95	170	25	0	10	45
885	3,665	660	1,285	2,365	1,535
270	445	180	725	1,605	485
475	7,665	225	5	5	0
20	35	1,940	7,130	4,270	115
0	195	170	1,085	130	5
100	1,225	1,645	8,730	3,680	70
2,535	2,270	35	0	10	15
1,580	6,155	5,050	16,110	8,945	185
435	345	240	130	250	110
1,240	2,250	145	60	185	1,000
1,840	2,835	185	230	360	4,815
25	105	0	0	10	80
395	510	10	35	135	260
910	2,080	215	115	820	1,960
740	1,525	210	220	415	690
5	900	0	0	0	0
2,360	7,965	1,655	2,470	5,855	2,850
160	255	15	20	60	250
5,935	3,115	510	845	1,435	460

Table 2.7 Farm operators, by sex and age group, census years 2001 and 2006

	2001		2006		2001 to 2006
	number	% of total	number	% of total	% change
All operators[1,2]	**346,195**	**100.0**	**327,055**	**100.0**	**-5.5**
Under 35	39,920	11.5	29,925	9.1	-25.0
35 to 54	185,575	53.6	164,160	50.2	-11.5
55 and older	120,705	34.9	132,975	40.7	10.2
Median age	49	…	51	…	4.1
Male operators	255,015	73.7	236,220	72.2	-7.4
Under 35	29,430	8.5	22,170	6.8	-24.7
35 to 54	132,060	38.1	114,695	35.1	-13.1
55 and older	93,530	27.0	99,360	30.4	6.2
Median age	49	…	52	…	6.1
Female operators	91,180	26.3	90,835	27.8	-0.4
Under 35	10,490	3.0	7,755	2.4	-26.1
35 to 54	53,510	15.5	49,465	15.1	-7.6
55 and older	27,175	7.8	33,615	10.3	23.7
Median age	48	…	50	…	4.2

1. Figures may not add to totals because of rounding. Minor differences can be expected in figures appearing in other tables.
2. Farm operators are defined as those people responsible for the management decisions made in the operation of a census farm or agricultural operation. Up to three farm operators could be reported per farm.
Source: Statistics Canada, Censuses of Agriculture, 2001 and 2006.

Table 2.8 Total farm area, land tenure and land in crops, census years from 1986 to 2006

	1986	1991	1996	2001	2006
			number		
Total number of farms	**293,089**	**280,043**	**276,548**	**246,923**	**229,373**
Total farm area					
Area in hectares[1]	67,825,757	67,753,700	68,054,956	67,502,446	67,586,739
Farms reporting	293,089	280,043	276,548	246,923	229,373
Average area in hectares per farm reporting	231	242	246	273	295
Total area owned					
Area in hectares[1]	43,218,905	42,961,352	43,060,963	42,265,706	41,377,673
Farms reporting	273,963	264,837	262,152	235,131	220,513
Average area in hectares per farm reporting	158	162	164	180	188
Total area rented or leased from others[2]					
Area in hectares[1]	24,606,852	24,792,348	24,993,993	25,236,740	26,209,066
Farms reporting	118,735	111,387	111,718	103,484	97,989
Average area in hectares per farm reporting	207	223	224	244	267
Land in crops (excluding Christmas tree area)					
Area in hectares[1]	33,181,235	33,507,780	34,918,733	36,395,150	35,912,247
Farms reporting	264,141	248,147	237,760	215,581	194,717
Average area in hectares per farm reporting	126	135	147	169	184

1. Conversion factor: 1 hectare equals 2.471 054 13 acres.
2. Total area rented or leased from others includes land; leased from governments, rented or leased from others and crop-shared from others.
Source: Statistics Canada, Census of Agriculture, 1986 to 2006.

Business, consumer and property services

3

OVERVIEW

Our mining, oil and natural gas industries may get all the headlines, but they will not displace service industries any time soon. The services sector dominates the economy, generating nearly $758.9 billion worth of output in 2006 and employing three-quarters of working Canadians.

Services make the economy run and save time for consumers. Canadian businesses rely heavily on the services sector for a wide range of activities, such as balancing their books, hauling their goods, building their corporate websites, and disposing of their industrial wastes. Consumers also depend on service providers such as banks, urban transit, hairdressers, dry cleaners and many others to help manage their busy days. Both businesses and consumers also turn to property service companies to manage the business of buying, selling and taking care of their real estate.

Significant long-term shift

Once known as "hewers of wood and drawers of water," Canada has undergone a significant long-term shift away from an economy based on natural resources. As industries diversified and Canadians took up or invented new technologies, the services sector grew to accommodate the changing economy.

After the Second World War, the services sector accounted for 49% of the Canadian economy; by 2006 it generated almost 70% of our gross domestic product (GDP).

The work force has adapted to the new economy. Today, more and more highly skilled Canadians provide world-class professional, technical and financial services. From 1991 to 2006, for example, the number of workers employed in professional,

Chart 3.1
GDP for goods- and services-producing industries

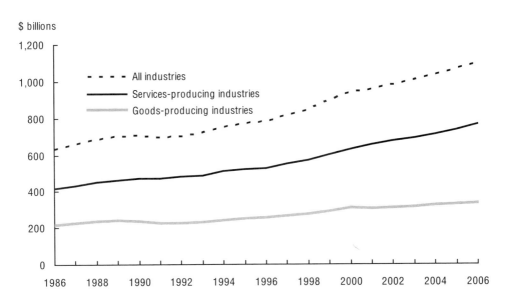

Source: Statistics Canada, CANSIM tables 379-0017 and 379-0020.

scientific and technical services grew 81%; the number of workers in primary industries, excluding agriculture, grew only 11%.

Mixed picture in the provinces and territories

All the provinces are now strongly oriented toward services, although how big a role services play depends to some extent on their economic strengths. In 2006, Nova Scotia, Prince Edward Island, Ontario and British Columbia saw 72% to 78% of their GDP generated by services. The continued strength of the natural resources sector in Newfoundland and Labrador, Saskatchewan and Alberta lower that proportion to 59% to 64% of those provinces' GDPs. Newfoundland and Labrador has actually seen its proportion of GDP from services drop almost 10% since 1999.

The three territories present a curious mix. The services sector plays a more significant role in both Yukon (83%) and Nunavut (74%) than in Canada overall. However, in the Northwest Territories, only 41% of GDP stems from services. The diamond boom

GDP at basic prices, selected industries

	1997	2006
	millions of chained (1997) dollars	
Wholesale trade	43,694	70,410
Retail trade	42,252	65,442
Finance and insurance	49,497	68,027

Source: Statistics Canada, CANSIM table 379-0017.

has transformed the Northwest Territories' economy, skewing it toward natural resources production, so that services' share of territorial GDP shrank by 20% from 1999 to 2006, even as the services sector there has been growing.

Fastest growing service industries

Although natural resource booms in our mines and oil fields have driven economic expansion on a regional basis, they have not changed the nationwide trend: in the decade from 1997 to 2006 alone, the services sector grew by 38%, compared with 26% growth for goods-producing industries.

The fastest growing service industries over this decade included administrative support,

Chart 3.2
Employment in professional, scientific and technical services, and in mining and oil and gas extraction industries

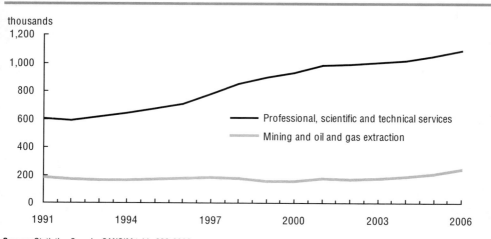

Source: Statistics Canada, CANSIM table 282-0008.

waste management and remediation services, wholesale trade, and professional, scientific and technical services.

Information and data processing services— Canada's news services, libraries and archives, online information service providers and data processors—also grew rapidly, up 73% over the decade. Broadcasting and telecommunications grew 71%, as Canadians signed up for new services, such as digital and satellite television, and bought cellphones. Still, all information and cultural industries combined remain a small component of the services sector, contributing $44.4 billion to GDP in 2006.

Whether for amusement or exercise, Canadians also regularly indulge in arts, entertainment and recreation services, to the tune of $9.3 billion in GDP in 2006. Good health appears to have been a major motivator in 2004, as fitness and recreational sports centres saw a 21% jump in revenue to more than $1.5 billion. Golf courses and country clubs surged by more than 15%, earning $2.3 billion.

Growing numbers of households have been devoting more and more of their budget

to entertainment services outside the home—attending movies, performing arts shows and sports events and visiting heritage institutions. From 1997 to 2005, spending on these activities climbed 37%. On average, each Canadian household spent $288 on entertainment services outside the home in 2005.

Canadians are increasingly pampering themselves, too. Personal care providers such as hair and aesthetics salons, spas and the like have seen their revenues steadily increase, reaching about $3.9 billion in 2004. Among personal services, sending the laundry and dry cleaning out has been popular: that industry generated revenues of $1.9 billion in 2004.

Canadians have also been spending more on services in the real estate market. The long-term upward trend in residential real estate prices has benefited agents, brokers and appraisers, whose total revenues surged by more than 9% to $9.2 billion in 2005.

Chart 3.3
Operating revenue of real estate agents, brokers and appraisers

$ billions

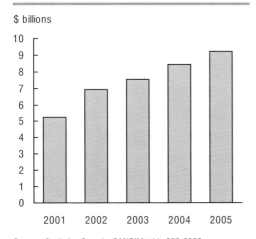

Source: Statistics Canada, CANSIM table 352-0005.

Selected sources

Statistics Canada

- *Canada's International Trade in Services.* Annual. 67-203-XWE

- *Employment, Earnings and Hours.* Monthly. 72-002-XIB

- *Gross Domestic Product by Industry.* Monthly. 15-001-XIE

- *Labour Force Information.* Monthly. 71-001-XWE

- *Provincial and Territorial Economic Accounts Review.* Semi-annual. 13-016-XWE

- *Service Industries Newsletter.* Irregular. 63-018-XWE

- *Trends and Conditions in Census Metropolitan Areas.* Occasional. 89-613-MIE

Trading services with the world

Canadians are major global traders. The value of what we sell has long been greater than what we buy from overseas. For the most part, this international trade surplus has stemmed from traditional exports such as natural resources and manufactured goods.

Canadian international trade in services recorded another in a long line of deficits in 2006. Companies bought $82.4 billion worth of services abroad and sold $67.2 billion. This record-high $15.2 billion services deficit was mainly the result of larger deficits in travel and transportation services.

Even though foreign tourists have always been drawn to Canada in large numbers, Canadian tourists abroad still outspent them in 2006, by $6.7 billion.

As more and more Canadians travelled abroad in 2006, their spending on

transportation provided by non-Canadian carriers really added up, driving the transportation services deficit to $7.1 billion. Higher fuel prices and stronger demand for transportation services contributed to the larger deficit in 2006.

Our international trade in commercial services posted a $2.2 billion deficit in 2006. The commercial services categories with the largest deficits were royalties and licensing fees, and insurance.

Architectural, engineering and technical services, computer and information services, and research and development services all generated surpluses within commercial services, as foreign companies sought out Canadian technological expertise and ingenuity.

Chart 3.4
Canada's balance of international transactions in services, selected regions, 2004

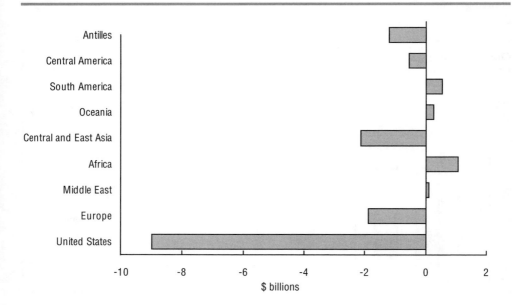

Source: Statistics Canada, CANSIM table 376-0036.

Rise of the services sector in our cities

Cities offer large concentrations of people, capital, knowledge and ideas. Hence, they are seen as natural hubs for the development of service industries. The services sector typically employs more workers in cities than in rural areas and small towns. In Canada's 27 largest cities in 2003, service jobs comprised 78% of the work force, compared with 75% in the country as a whole.

But these numbers mask some major differences among cities. Government is one of the largest providers of service sector jobs, which is why Canada's six most services-oriented cities are also capital cities with large public-sector work forces. In these capitals, service industries employ at least 85% of the work force. By contrast, other cities in Quebec and Southern Ontario have larger-than-average shares of workers employed in goods-producing industries.

Almost all Canadian urban areas became more services-oriented during the 1990s. From 1989 to 2003, the number of jobs in the services sector grew faster than in the goods sector in all but 4 of Canada's 27 largest urban areas. The share of workers in services grew faster in cities that had relatively low concentrations of services to start with.

The rise of service industries in our cities has coincided with a general decline in manufacturing and with an expansion of business services. Some of Canada's strongest production centres have seen large declines. In Montréal, for instance, the manufacturing work force lost 46,300 jobs from 1989 to 2003. Business services' fast growth has been largely the result of strong gains in professional, scientific and technical services: its share of total employment swelled from 5% in 1989 to 8% in 2003.

Chart 3.5
Employment in goods- and services-producing industries, selected census metropolitan areas, 2003

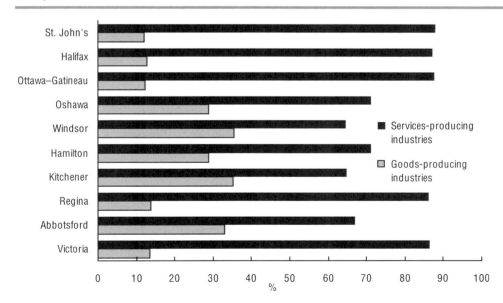

Source: Statistics Canada, Catalogue no. 89-613-MIE.

Making a living on the road

Canada's taxi and limousine drivers perform a crucial service. They take us across a congested city to a meeting, drive us to the airport, chauffeur our friends and family in style to graduations and weddings and get us home safely after a night on the town.

Taxi and limousine companies generated $1.3 billion in fares and other revenue in 2004, only slightly more than in the previous year, but 27% more than in 2000. Those who make their living on the road are particularly vulnerable to the price of fuel. Higher fuel costs in 2004 meant that operating expenses climbed faster than revenues. As a result, taxi and limousine services saw their operating margins shrink by about 4% from 2003.

The roughly 35,300 taxi and limousine firms are divided into two major categories: associations and companies, and self-employed drivers. A small number of

associations and companies—about 5% of all businesses in the industry—generate about 42% of the operating revenues. The more than 33,500 self-employed drivers, 95% of the industry, are responsible for the remaining 58%.

The larger companies operate on slim profit margins. In 2004, the operating revenue of taxi and limousine associations and companies was $530.3 million. Operating expenses consumed $523.6 million, leaving a profit margin of 3%. One-third of these expenses went to paying salaries, wages and benefits.

Self-employed drivers' operating revenues totalled $735.0 million and their expenses were $557.9 million, for a profit margin of 25%. Their profit margin is higher because they often report it as personal income.

Chart 3.6
Taxi and limousine service industry, revenues, expenses and carriers, 2004

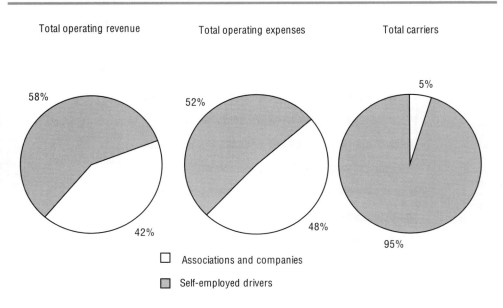

Total operating revenue   Total operating expenses   Total carriers

58%   42%   52%   48%   5%   95%

☐ Associations and companies
▨ Self-employed drivers

Source: Statistics Canada, CANSIM table 407-0001.

Are average wages higher in services?

Working the oil fields is where the money is. Average wages in the mining, oil and gas industry stood at $1,315 per week in August 2006—higher than the average in any other industry, even service industries that put a premium on education and high-tech skills.

Canadians working in goods-producing industries bring home paycheques that are, on average, 35% fatter than those in the services sector. However, earnings within the services sector vary greatly. For instance, average weekly earnings in service industries that require extensive training or education—such as management of companies and enterprises; professional, scientific and technical services; public administration; and finance and insurance—range from $941 to $965, compared with $937 in the goods-producing sector as a whole. Employees in other key service industries—including education, wholesale trade and transportation—make from $780 to $880 per week, somewhat more than the $696 average for the services sector overall. Average earnings across this sector are pulled down by the low wages paid in a few industries, i.e., accommodation and food services; arts, entertainment and recreation; and retail trade. Restaurant workers, who average $317 weekly, are among the lowest paid in the economy. Performing artists earn about $428 per week; retail salespeople, about $482.

From 1996 to 2006, wages in the services sector grew 29%, slightly faster than those in goods-producing industries, 25%. Workers in most service industries saw similar wage increases, but those in accommodation and food services, retail trade, and health care saw their earnings grow 32% to 39% over that decade.

Chart 3.7
Average weekly earnings of selected service industries

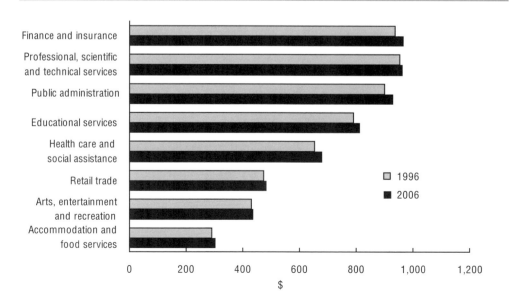

Source: Statistics Canada, CANSIM table 281-0028.

Table 3.1 Gross domestic product of goods- and services-producing industries, by province and territory, 2001 to 2005

	2001	2002	2003	2004	2005
	chained (1997) $ millions				
Canada					
Goods-producing industries	305,727.0	311,482.0	315,935.0	325,202.0	331,595.0
Services-producing industries	652,200.0	672,177.0	687,921.0	709,800.0	732,506.0
Newfoundland and Labrador					
Goods-producing industries	3,506.9	5,227.1	5,905.8	5,635.4	5,634.9
Services-producing industries	7,634.2	7,927.9	8,130.6	8,261.2	8,306.5
Prince Edward Island					
Goods-producing industries	682.3	746.4	733.9	787.3	785.0
Services-producing industries	2,130.0	2,201.3	2,258.1	2,307.1	2,364.4
Nova Scotia					
Goods-producing industries	5,250.4	5,586.0	5,609.2	5,511.4	5,499.8
Services-producing industries	16,287.5	16,899.2	17,274.3	17,542.9	17,927.7
New Brunswick					
Goods-producing industries	5,361.5	5,686.9	5,854.5	5,982.8	5,806.6
Services-producing industries	12,221.9	12,621.9	12,874.6	13,162.4	13,390.3
Quebec					
Goods-producing industries	70,015.6	71,095.8	70,903.6	72,345.6	72,916.1
Services-producing industries	134,223.1	138,578.6	141,548.1	145,585.2	149,345.2
Ontario					
Goods-producing industries	122,673.1	125,226.0	125,040.2	127,656.8	128,467.2
Services-producing industries	279,424.1	286,927.5	292,652.9	302,039.8	312,355.9
Manitoba					
Goods-producing industries	8,215.9	8,386.8	8,461.0	8,646.5	8,893.4
Services-producing industries	22,431.7	22,866.7	23,134.8	23,659.6	24,237.3
Saskatchewan					
Goods-producing industries	10,437.3	9,775.2	10,797.3	11,211.5	11,787.5
Services-producing industries	18,132.6	18,591.1	19,019.2	19,560.3	20,009.3
Alberta					
Goods-producing industries	47,534.9	47,005.6	48,225.3	50,909.0	53,330.5
Services-producing industries	71,529.6	74,393.2	77,440.1	80,764.8	84,734.7
British Columbia					
Goods-producing industries	30,037.9	30,966.9	31,574.8	33,217.2	34,326.9
Services-producing industries	85,130.7	87,937.4	90,218.3	93,612.8	96,851.4
Yukon					
Goods-producing industries	176.8	159.8	146.5	183.0	209.5
Services-producing industries	918.6	928.5	940.7	955.0	984.4
Northwest Territories					
Goods-producing industries	1,464.2	1,544.8	2,052.1	2,293.5	2,260.1
Services-producing industries	1,356.6	1,445.0	1,501.6	1,531.7	1,571.8
Nunavut					
Goods-producing industries	246.9	244.1	192.2	209.7	188.5
Services-producing industries	605.3	651.4	678.9	681.0	691.5

Note: North American Industry Classification System (NAICS), 2002.
Source: Statistics Canada, CANSIM tables 379-0020 and 379-0026.

Table 3.2 Average weekly earnings, by sector, 2002 to 2006

	2002	2003	2004	2005	2006
	\$				
All industries (excluding unclassified)	**679.32**	**688.31**	**702.87**	**725.51**	**747.08**
Goods-producing sector	854.02	868.28	886.22	914.82	938.95
Forestry, logging and support	852.47	867.64	887.54	925.75	966.70
Mining and oil and gas extraction	1,168.01	1,182.06	1,248.93	1,311.14	1,345.58
Utilities	1,058.31	1,068.89	1,061.59	1,065.65	1,087.82
Construction	810.87	831.35	841.22	872.81	895.21
Manufacturing	833.36	844.47	861.18	885.65	905.59
Services-producing sector	628.75	637.02	651.27	673.22	694.85
Trade	544.83	554.81	563.66	581.59	601.14
Transportation and warehousing	764.55	761.44	756.40	776.01	784.73
Information and cultural industries	821.36	822.71	833.69	881.23	933.13
Finance and insurance	852.81	879.82	903.02	935.96	964.93
Real estate and rental and leasing	610.78	606.52	626.72	650.96	675.10
Professional, scientific and technical services	901.63	914.98	928.59	951.99	963.06
Management of companies and enterprises	846.25	859.07	863.11	907.21	948.43
Administrative and support, waste management and remediation services	537.31	541.58	559.81	577.85	601.16
Educational services	715.27	735.43	761.02	787.81	813.02
Health care and social assistance	604.07	612.15	636.54	654.94	678.91
Arts, entertainment and recreation	444.63	427.29	422.60	429.47	436.62
Accommodation and food services	279.11	270.11	279.59	291.47	304.36
Public administration	829.33	855.15	872.05	899.05	930.85
Other services	530.24	527.67	546.85	565.48	583.52

Notes: North American Industry Classification System (NAICS), 2002.
  Data include overtime.
Source: Statistics Canada, CANSIM table 281-0027.

Table 3.3 Labour force employment, by job permanency, 2001 to 2006

	2001	2002	2003	2004	2005	2006
	thousands					
Permanent employees						
All industries	11,049.6	11,314.8	11,619.1	11,772.4	11,860.6	12,163.1
Goods-producing sector	2,831.7	2,894.1	2,946.9	2,968.7	2,946.5	2,944.1
Services-producing sector	8,217.9	8,420.7	8,672.2	8,803.7	8,914.1	9,219.0
Temporary employees						
All industries	1,619.8	1,681.2	1,651.3	1,721.2	1,797.6	1,823.2
Goods-producing sector	335.1	370.5	347.8	358.4	369.9	353.9
Services-producing sector	1,284.8	1,310.7	1,303.5	1,362.8	1,427.7	1,469.3

Note: North American Industry Classification System (NAICS), 2002.
Source: Statistics Canada, CANSIM table 282-0080.

Table 3.4 Operating statistics, selected services, 2001 to 2005

	2001			2002		
	Revenue	Expenses	Profit margin	Revenue	Expenses	Profit margin
	$ millions		%	$ millions		%
Personal and laundry services	7,133.7	6,529.9	8.5	7,640.3	6,861.5	10.2
Personal care	2,923.4	2,674.1	8.5	3,228.9	2,883.0	10.7
Funeral	1,227.4	1,110.0	9.6	1,313.8	1,178.2	10.3
Dry cleaning and laundry	1,770.0	1,630.7	7.9	1,885.3	1,707.9	9.4
Other personal services	1,212.9	1,115.0	8.1	1,212.3	1,092.4	9.9
Management consulting	6,514.8	5,278.3	19.0	6,710.0	5,410.0	19.4
Scientific and technical consulting	1,466.1	1,185.1	19.2	1,725.5	1,437.6	16.7
Offices of real estate agents and brokers	5,157.4	3,355.2	34.9	6,672.5	4,214.0	36.8
Offices of real estate appraisers	118.5	107.0	9.7	271.7	251.0	7.6
Automotive equipment rental and leasing	4,813.5	4,046.9	15.9	4,963.5	4,253.3	14.3
Consumer goods rental	1,861.8	1,759.7	5.5	1,940.8	1,820.5	6.2
General rental centres	265.0	233.2	12.0	271.8	238.6	12.2
Food services and drinking places	33,224.8	31,312.2	5.8	35,538.8	33,850.2	4.8
Full-service restaurants	14,756.5	13,930.4	5.6	15,993.2	15,283.4	4.4
Limited-service eating places	12,831.8	12,066.7	6.0	13,809.2	13,142.5	4.8
Special food services	2,754.0	2,635.4	4.3	2,915.3	2,775.1	4.8
Drinking places (alcoholic beverages)	2,882.6	2,679.8	7.0	2,821.2	2,649.2	6.1
Landscape architectural services	142.4	121.5	14.7	161.3	140.0	13.2
Specialized design services	1,919.2	1,747.5	8.9	2,042.4	1,799.2	11.9
Interior design	527.4	481.0	8.8	561.2	514.0	8.4
Industrial design	144.7	137.3	5.1	163.4	133.9	18.1
Graphic design	1,148.8	1,037.7	9.7	1,195.5	1,043.4	12.7
Other specialized design services	98.3	91.5	6.9	122.2	107.9	11.7
Advertising agencies	2,262.0	2,015.6	10.9	2,218.7	1,990.3	10.3
Other advertising and advertising-related services	2,681.2	2,467.1	8.0	2,675.4	2,480.8	7.3
Architectural services	1,539.3	1,306.6	15.1	1,824.7	1,553.4	14.9
Engineering services	10,446.0	9,324.3	10.7	10,866.3	9,679.0	10.9
Surveying and mapping services	1,792.1	1,593.5	11.1	1,833.1	1,676.8	8.5
Accounting, tax preparation, bookkeeping and payroll services	8,157.6	5,798.0	28.9	7,854.6	5,550.6	29.3
Employment services	5,125.0	4,933.9	3.7	5,420.7	5,227.4	3.6
Lessors of residential buildings and dwellings (except social housing projects)	18,043.8	14,616.0	19.0	18,704.0	15,123.3	19.1
Non-residential leasing	21,458.6	16,835.8	21.5	22,999.3	18,324.0	20.3
Real estate property managers	2,093.2	1,846.8	11.8	2,278.8	1,951.9	14.3

Note: North American Industry Classification System (NAICS), 2002.
Source: Statistics Canada, CANSIM tables 352-0003, 352-0005, 352-0008, 352-0010, 355-0005, 359-0001, 360-0001, 360-0002, 360-0004, 360-0005, 360-0006, 360-0007 and 361-0001.

2003			2004			2005		
Revenue	Expenses	Profit margin	Revenue	Expenses	Profit margin	Revenue	Expenses	Profit margin
$ millions		%	$ millions		%	$ millions		%
8,044.7	7,199.7	10.5	8,537.2	7,882.5	7.7	9,118.0	8,202.4	10.0
3,539.9	3,142.4	11.2	3,885.5	3,634.7	6.5	4,145.2	3,739.1	9.8
1,399.6	1,253.0	10.5	1,460.8	1,314.8	10.0	1,519.4	1,335.8	12.1
1,920.8	1,740.8	9.4	1,925.5	1,758.9	8.7	2,065.2	1,875.4	9.2
1,184.4	1,063.5	10.2	1,265.3	1,174.2	7.2	1,388.3	1,252.2	9.8
6,634.4	5,449.6	17.9	6,909.3	5,507.0	20.3	7,388.0	5,862.2	20.7
1,908.3	1,614.7	15.4	2,038.5	1,684.6	17.4	2,407.9	1,999.1	17.0
7,024.5	4,583.3	34.8	7,834.1	5,132.4	34.5	8,554.1	5,237.0	38.8
505.7	412.8	18.4	577.5	477.8	17.3	651.2	548.1	15.8
4,639.8	4,072.2	12.2	4,539.5	4,035.6	11.1	4,724.0	4,298.5	9.0
1,893.4	1,766.4	6.7	1,979.0	1,834.8	7.3	2,106.9	1,966.1	6.7
271.0	237.1	12.5	318.3	280.0	12.0	366.8	322.0	12.2
35,260.0	34,120.7	3.2	37,366.0	35,994.3	3.7	38,851.9	37,391.9	3.8
15,380.0	14,998.6	2.5	16,465.6	16,016.2	2.7	17,265.4	16,738.3	3.1
14,029.5	13,480.3	3.9	14,873.1	14,177.6	4.7	15,395.4	14,646.7	4.9
2,973.7	2,840.0	4.5	3,095.7	2,982.2	3.7	3,378.0	3,286.1	2.7
2,876.8	2,801.7	2.6	2,931.6	2,818.4	3.9	2,813.1	2,720.9	3.3
176.6	153.4	13.1	207.3	178.5	13.9	231.9	204.7	11.7
2,016.8	1,816.6	9.9	2,229.9	1,975.2	11.4	2,332.9	2,071.2	11.2
541.6	494.6	8.7	618.1	540.3	12.6	682.2	616.7	9.6
209.3	196.2	6.3	222.5	210.5	5.4	228.6	207.3	9.3
1,135.1	1,003.8	11.6	1,246.2	1,098.6	11.8	1,265.6	1,106.8	12.6
130.7	122.0	6.6	143.1	125.7	12.1	156.5	140.4	10.3
2,151.6	1,963.7	8.7	2,205.6	1,981.5	10.2	2,532.6	2,301.3	9.1
2,583.0	2,432.4	5.8	2,778.7	2,590.6	6.8	3,080.2	2,836.0	7.9
1,873.1	1,573.8	16.0	1,920.3	1,620.3	15.6	2,059.0	1,708.2	17.0
11,044.5	9,941.9	10.0	12,147.8	10,734.8	11.6	13,793.5	11,919.7	13.6
1,865.4	1,703.8	8.7	1,972.1	1,794.2	9.0	2,285.4	2,046.3	10.5
8,244.0	5,837.7	29.2	8,713.7	6,097.7	30.0	9,928.4	6,930.8	30.2
5,689.1	5,491.9	3.5	6,124.4	5,888.8	3.8	7,182.3	6,909.3	3.8
18,884.1	14,843.7	21.4	20,815.1	16,471.7	20.9	22,957.7	15,050.4	34.4
24,735.8	18,804.0	24.0	26,347.3	20,812.4	21.0	27,822.4	19,136.7	31.2
2,771.6	2,353.7	15.1	3,450.7	2,897.8	16.0	4,032.0	3,325.7	17.5

Table 3.5 Labour force employment, by sector and by province, 2006

	Canada	Newfoundland and Labrador	Prince Edward Island	Nova Scotia
		thousands		
All industries	**16,484.3**	**215.7**	**68.6**	**441.8**
Goods-producing sector	**3,985.9**	49.1	18.9	85.7
Agriculture	**346.4**	1.9	3.9	4.7
Forestry, fishing, mining, oil and gas	**330.1**	16.4	2.4	12.7
Utilities	**122.0**	2.2	0.3	1.8
Construction	**1,069.7**	12.9	5.7	27.3
Manufacturing	**2,117.7**	15.7	6.6	39.1
Services-producing sector	**12,498.4**	166.6	49.7	356.2
Trade	**2,633.5**	37.7	9.9	78.2
Transportation and warehousing	**802.2**	11.6	2.2	18.7
Finance, insurance, real estate and leasing	**1,040.5**	6.5	2.1	22.3
Professional, scientific and technical services	**1,089.9**	6.7	2.8	18.4
Business, building and other support services	**690.0**	8.5	2.8	28.8
Educational services	**1,158.4**	16.6	4.6	34.7
Health care and social assistance	**1,785.5**	30.1	7.9	59.1
Information, culture and recreation	**745.0**	8.8	2.6	16.3
Accommodation and food services	**1,015.0**	13.4	5.6	29.8
Public administration	**837.4**	15.3	6.3	29.2
Other services	**701.0**	11.3	2.9	20.7

Note: North American Industry Classification System (NAICS), 2002.
Source: Statistics Canada, CANSIM table 282-0008.

New Brunswick	Quebec	Ontario	Manitoba	Saskatchewan	Alberta	British Columbia
			thousands			
355.4	**3,765.4**	**6,492.7**	**587.0**	**491.6**	**1,870.7**	**2,195.5**
77.1	901.1	1,600.5	138.1	132.8	518.9	463.9
6.2	65.1	100.4	29.4	47.8	52.3	34.7
9.9	38.8	38.7	6.5	21.5	139.3	43.8
3.1	29.7	49.0	5.6	4.5	17.1	8.6
21.1	186.1	405.2	29.9	29.6	172.6	179.3
36.9	581.3	1,007.2	66.6	29.3	137.5	197.5
278.3	2,864.4	4,892.2	448.9	358.8	1,351.8	1,731.6
56.8	628.5	1,015.7	91.3	79.2	282.4	353.7
19.9	167.2	296.1	35.1	25.7	106.2	119.5
16.4	222.3	476.8	34.2	25.7	96.2	138.0
14.5	241.7	453.8	23.4	18.9	142.2	167.6
21.8	139.8	295.8	18.3	12.6	62.7	98.8
27.2	260.9	444.5	45.5	38.1	130.4	156.0
45.3	454.1	638.2	79.6	59.5	179.5	232.2
11.9	160.4	319.6	23.7	20.2	68.3	113.2
25.0	214.8	373.2	37.5	30.2	114.9	170.5
21.7	215.6	314.5	35.0	27.5	81.1	91.3
17.7	159.1	264.0	25.4	21.2	87.9	90.5

Table 3.6 Employment in goods- and services-producing industries, by census metropolitan area, 1989 and 2003

	1989		2003		Employment in services	
	Goods	Services	Goods	Services	1989	2003
	number				%	
Canada	**3,838,500**	**9,147,900**	**3,986,100**	**11,759,900**	**70.4**	**74.7**
All census metropolitan areas	2,199,800	6,390,800	2,320,700	8,273,200	74.4	78.1
St. John's	10,100	64,300	10,700	78,200	86.4	88.0
Halifax	24,200	134,900	24,200	163,800	84.8	87.1
Saint John	14,600	41,600	10,800	48,300	73.9	81.7
Saguenay	19,400	44,500	16,400	54,500	69.6	76.8
Québec	44,500	253,600	52,400	306,200	85.1	85.4
Sherbrooke	17,600	49,400	22,400	56,700	73.7	71.7
Trois-Rivières	18,500	43,000	17,000	48,900	70.0	74.2
Montréal	438,600	1,104,900	392,300	1,403,600	71.6	78.2
Ottawa–Gatineau	62,000	426,100	74,500	534,100	87.3	87.8
Kingston	8,400	46,700	8,500	46,900	84.7	84.6
Oshawa	47,000	79,400	49,300	122,500	62.8	71.3
Toronto	601,200	1,543,700	655,000	2,021,900	72.0	75.5
Hamilton	126,600	195,000	104,400	259,500	60.6	71.3
St. Catharines–Niagara	54,300	106,000	49,700	146,100	66.1	74.6
Kitchener	85,300	111,000	83,000	152,900	56.5	64.8
London	51,600	144,600	54,800	165,300	73.7	75.1
Windsor	50,300	81,800	57,200	104,200	61.9	64.6
Greater Sudbury / Grand Sudbury	19,800	50,400	15,900	56,600	71.8	78.1
Thunder Bay	14,200	47,500	13,100	51,100	76.9	79.6
Winnipeg	71,500	260,000	70,100	291,600	78.4	80.6
Regina	17,600	78,900	14,700	91,900	81.7	86.2
Saskatoon	21,500	80,600	20,000	101,100	78.9	83.5
Calgary	96,600	293,200	142,300	452,600	75.2	76.1
Edmonton	84,100	331,500	120,900	415,800	79.8	77.5
Abbotsford	16,000	33,800	24,500	49,600	67.9	67.0
Vancouver	162,800	636,400	195,400	915,400	79.6	82.4
Victoria	21,400	108,300	21,200	134,000	83.5	86.4
All non-census metropolitan areas	1,638,700	2,757,100	1,665,400	3,486,700	62.7	67.7

Note: Figures are rounded to the nearest 100.
Source: Statistics Canada, Catalogue no. 89-613-MIE.

Business performance and ownership

4

No matter how big or how small, every business enterprise in Canada started as an idea. At one time or another, an entrepreneur with some seed money and lots of energy decided to take a risk and set up shop—as a dry cleaner, computer manufacturer, trader, restaurateur, or even an emu farmer.

Their risk-taking and hard work has paid off: Canadian firms have more than doubled their overall operating profits from $112.1 billion in 1998 to $243.6 billion in 2006. Non-financial businesses, such as mining, theatre companies or Internet services, accounted for 72% of total operating profits; finance and insurance accounted for the rest.

Companies generating the biggest revenue are those supplying Canadians and the rest of the economy with goods—our manufacturers, wholesalers and retail stores. Together, they generated over $1,571.0 billion in

revenue and $73.3 billion in profit in 2006. Homebuilders and other construction companies garnered another $197.8 billion in revenue that year, followed closely by companies in the fast-growing oil and gas patch, at $157.4 billion. Banks and insurance companies together took in about $275.8 billion in revenue.

Bigger revenues, bigger profits?

Bigger revenues, however, do not always translate into bigger profits. In 2006, Canada's manufacturers, wholesalers and retailers were among the least profitable businesses, with an average profit margin of about 5%. Meanwhile, companies in the real estate, rental and leasing industry, in mining and in the oil and gas industries boasted profit margins ranging from 18% to 21% in 2006.

Chart 4.1
Operating profits, all industries

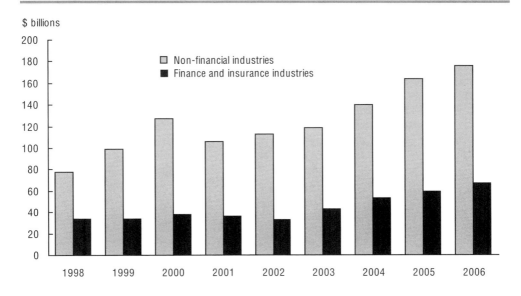

$ billions

Note: Seasonally adjusted data.
Source: Statistics Canada, CANSIM table 187-0002.

But financial institutions do the best: banks and credit card companies had profit margins of 26% and 41%, respectively.

Where's the growth?

Growth closely follows economic trends. Companies supporting the oil and gas boom in Western Canada saw considerable revenue growth from 2001 to 2006, as did real estate companies throughout the country. The rapid growth of the Internet has also been good for many companies. Information and cultural industries have seen their revenues jump over the same period.

Medium and large businesses tend to be best able to exploit new business trends and prosper. From 1991 to 2003, the number of medium-sized firms (20 to 99 employees) increased 25%, while the number of larger companies (100 to 499 employees) grew 33%. That compares with just an 11% increase in the number of small businesses (0 to 19 employees).

Yet small businesses are by far the most numerous. More than 9 out of 10 businesses in Canada in 2003 had fewer than 20

Business bankruptcies, selected industries

	2004	2006
	number	
All industries	**8,128**	**6,756**
Construction	1,344	1,152
Retail trade	1,204	989
Finance and insurance	118	81
Accommodation and food services	932	767

Source: Statistics Canada, CANSIM table 177-0006.

employees. Collectively, however, these small businesses employ about 21% of all Canadian workers. To put that into perspective, a minority of large firms—about 2,000 out of more than 1 million companies—provide paycheques to 43% of all employees. These proportions have changed little from 1993 to 2003.

Companies use capital investment to fuel their growth. Canada's small and medium-sized enterprises held debt totalling $377 billion in 2004. Without access to adequate capital, most small- to medium-sized companies cannot expand, launch new products or invest in research and development. Firms with 1 to 4 employees carried an average debt of $187,000. Those employing 5 to 19 people were $489,000

**Chart 4.2
Business bankruptcies**

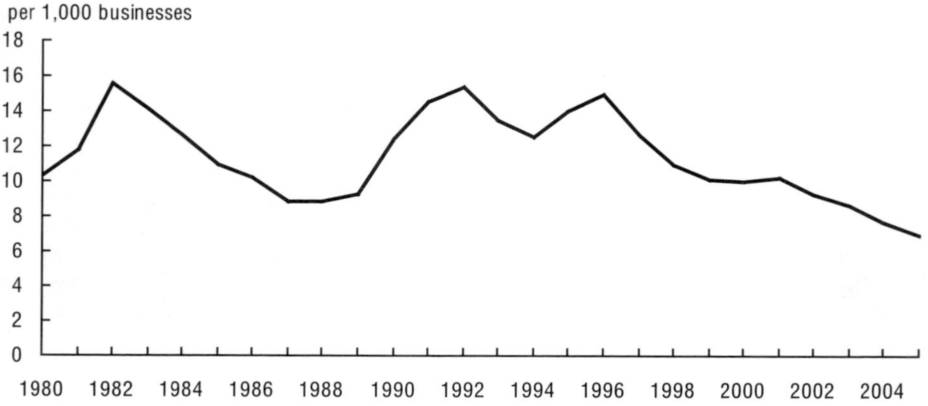

per 1,000 businesses

Source: Statistics Canada, Catalogue no. 11-621-MIE.

in debt, while businesses with 20 to 99 employees owed an average $2.2 million.

Business bankruptcies down to a 25-year low

Although business financing is the fuel of our economy, debts can pile up. And without strong operating profits to pay down the money owed, many businesses declare bankruptcy each year. However, a recent study showed that the rate of business bankruptcies in Canada in 2005 declined to a 25-year low. Just 7 firms out of 1,000 went bankrupt in 2005.

Indicators show that Canadian businesses today are healthier and better able to withstand difficult times. For instance, the recessions and economic restructurings of the early 1980s and 1990s were accompanied by sharply higher rates of business bankruptcy, which peaked in 1982 and 1992. The economic slowdown from 2001 to 2002, however, did not result in a comparable increase in business failures. Bankruptcy rates, as well as average financial losses

associated with bankruptcy, have declined significantly.

Share of business that are foreign-controlled remains stable

Some of the healthiest businesses in the Canadian economy are foreign-controlled and they have seen record profits in recent years. Despite their success, the share of foreign control among Canadian corporations remained stable in 2004—holding 22% of corporate assets in Canada and accounting for 30% of revenues. Aside from the odd fluctuation, these shares have remained fairly stable since the mid-1990s.

U.S.-controlled corporations are by far the biggest foreign players, accounting for 60% of foreign-controlled assets and revenues in 2004. After the United States, the biggest foreign players in the Canadian economy—as measured by both assets and revenues—are the United Kingdom, Germany, Japan, the Netherlands and France. In 2004, foreign control was highest in manufacturing (50% of total assets) and in oil and gas (45%).

Chart 4.3
Growth in number of businesses, by firm size, 1991 to 2003

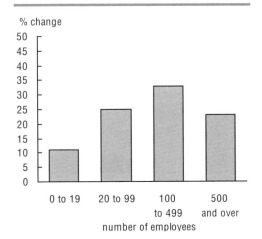

% change

Source: Statistics Canada, Catalogue no. 61-534-XWE.

Selected sources

Statistics Canada

- *Analysis in Brief.* Occasional. 11-621-MIE

- *Business Dynamics in Canada.* Occasional. 61-534-XIE

- *Corporations Returns Act.* Annual. 61-220-XIE

- *Environment Industry Survey: Business Sector.* Biennial. 16F0008XIE

- *Financial and Taxation Statistics for Enterprises.* Annual. 61-219-XIE

- *Public Sector Statistics.* Annual. 68-213-XIE

- *Quarterly Financial Statistics for Enterprises.* Quarterly. 61-008-XIE

Foreign banks raising their profile here

These days it is almost as easy to do business at a foreign bank as it is to walk into one of Canada's large chartered banks. Foreign banks have been raising their profile in Canada. From 1997 to 2004, foreign-controlled banks grew steadily and increased their share of the Canadian banking market to about 8%.

In 1999, the federal government allowed foreign-controlled banks to establish full-service branches in Canada, enabling international banking firms to offer a much wider range of financial services. Today, the Canadian banking industry includes 21 domestic banks, 26 foreign bank subsidiaries and 19 full-service foreign bank branches.

Foreign and domestic banks alike have been taking advantage of Canada's recent low interest rates, which have expanded the entire financial services market. Fuelled by increased consumer lending, the fastest growing foreign banks have been those offering credit card services and other electronic financial services, as well as those offering corporate and institutional finance.

But the foreign banks' expanding market share has been the work of a handful of companies. The operations of just six foreign banks accounted for 80% of the value of services provided: most of them grew at an annual average rate of 10% or more.

Still, home-grown banks continue to dominate Canada's financial services market. They have lost only a relatively small slice of market share to foreign banks, despite the latter's strong growth. Canadian banks are still seeing the total real value of their services expand by about 2% annually.

Chart 4.4
Market share, by type of financial institution, 2004

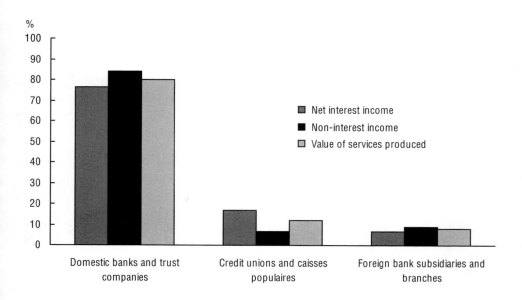

Source: Statistics Canada, Catalogue no. 11-621-MIE.

Green and growing

Canadians are recognizing the impact of human activity on the environment, and Canadian businesses have been responding to people's environmental concerns. Businesses are spending more on environmental protection and pollution-prevention activities. Research and development has contributed to the growing number of green businesses and has boosted their revenues.

Environmental goods and services measure, prevent, limit or correct damage to water, air and soil. Goods include recyclable materials and technologies that reduce greenhouse gas emissions. Services include waste management, environment-related construction projects and environmental consulting. Businesses providing these goods and services generated nearly $16 billion in revenue in 2002, up 8% from 2000. Several trends are driving the industry's growth. Our households and businesses are generating

more waste and the mining, oil, gas and coal industries are spending more on land reclamation and decommissioning. Waste management and remediation services firms saw revenues jump from $4 billion in 2000 to just over $5 billion in 2002.

Canadians are also looking for ways to be more energy efficient—by consuming less and recovering valuable by-products—so firms selling 'eco-efficiency' technologies are also growing fast. In 2002, environmental businesses earned $364 million selling technologies that reduce greenhouse gas emissions, such as fuel cells, alternative fuels, and solar and wind energy systems. Environmental consulting, engineering and analytical services generated $638 million; water and wastewater management services earned $470 million. Nearly 500 new green businesses were created from 2000 to 2002: most are consulting services firms.

Chart 4.5
Environmental services revenue, selected services, 2002

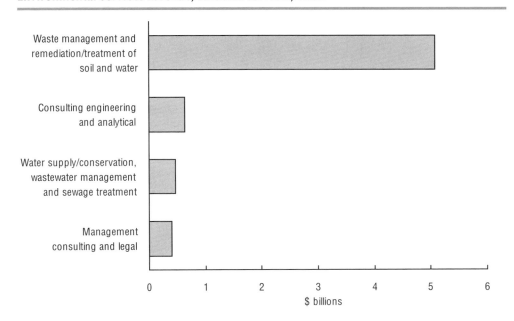

Source: Statistics Canada, Catalogue no. 16F0008XIE.

Business profits rolling in

One of the biggest stories in Canadian business over the past few years has been operating profits—they just keep growing. Growth slowed a bit in 2006, but firms still pushed operating profits up quarter after quarter, to a record $243.6 billion.

Corporate operating profits—pre-tax profits earned from normal business activities—have been climbing with only a few quarterly slips since 2002. The key factors sustaining the boom are low interest rates, which have fuelled consumer and business spending, and high commodity prices, which have swelled the bottom lines of mining, oil and gas firms.

The oil and gas industry has played a big part in the story. Operating profits have more than doubled from $14.7 billion in 2002 to $32.5 billion in 2006. But oil and gas firms were not the only star performers from 2002 to 2006. Mining companies'

operating profits soared 177%, buoyed by high prices for metals. Construction companies' operating profits jumped 126%, thanks to the hot housing and commercial construction markets. Transportation and warehousing, and banking profits jumped in this period, 62% and 139%, respectively. And the strong real estate market lifted real estate companies' operating profits by 24%.

Yet the profit tide has not raised all boats. Manufacturing industries, affected by higher fuel costs, a stronger Canadian dollar and a slowing U.S. economy, saw operating profits grow only 18% from 2002 to 2004 and drop 5% from 2004 to 2006.

Foreign-controlled companies have recorded some of the strongest growth in recent years. From 2002 to 2004, for example, operating profits of foreign-controlled corporations surged almost 39%.

Chart 4.6
Operating profits, selected industries

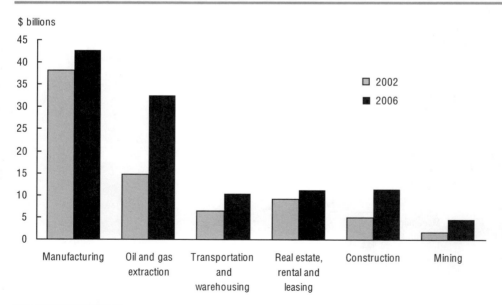

Note: Seasonally adjusted data.
Source: Statistics Canada, CANSIM table 187-0002.

Corporate taxes and tax credits

Big money-makers are also big taxpayers. Corporations generated $46.5 billion in tax payable to all levels of government in 2005. The lion's share is owed to the federal government, which assessed $31.5 billion in corporate taxes in 2005; provincial governments assessed $15.0 billion.

Like individuals, corporations use tax credits to reduce their taxable income and thus their taxes. For example, the total income tax payable by corporations in 2005 was $57.4 billion. But a federal tax credit for the income taxes corporations pay to provincial governments reduced that by $14.1 billion.

Another tax credit, the specific tax deduction that small businesses claim, was worth $5.3 billion in 2005, up from $4.7 billion in 2004. A deduction for manufacturing and processing profits was worth $1.4 billion, down from $1.7 billion in 2004.

Investment tax credits help corporations lower their tax burden when they post a loss. These accumulated credits are then paid as taxes when the company returns to profitability. Corporations claimed $1.6 billion of these credits in 2005, down from $2.0 billion the previous year.

Non-financial industries paid taxes of $35.5 billion, up $1.2 billion from 2004. More than half of this 3% increase came from the construction and real estate industries, which saw significant growth in 2005.

As the economy has grown, so too have government treasuries. The consolidated revenue from corporate taxes paid to all levels of government more than doubled from 1995 to 2005.

Chart 4.7
Corporate income taxes

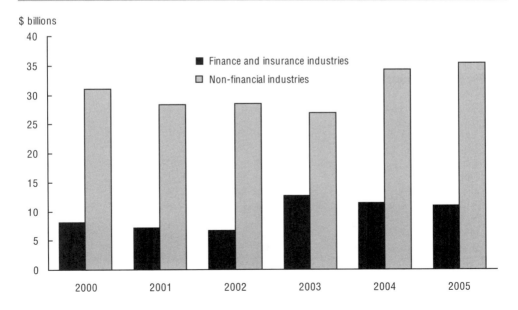

$ billions

Legend:
■ Finance and insurance industries
□ Non-financial industries

Source: Statistics Canada, CANSIM table 180-0003.

Table 4.1 Businesses, by province and territory, 1995 to 2003

	Canada	Newfoundland and Labrador	Prince Edward Island	Nova Scotia
		thousands		
1995	962.1	21.6	7.6	32.0
1996	963.8	20.5	7.5	31.4
1997	985.1	20.4	7.6	32.2
1998	1,005.0	20.4	7.7	32.4
1999	1,017.6	20.2	7.7	33.0
2000	1,021.6	19.8	7.3	32.3
2001	1,032.9	19.8	7.2	32.2
2002	1,044.7	19.6	7.2	32.0
2003	1,060.8	19.9	7.1	32.0

Note: A firm may exist in more than one province and, therefore, firm counts at the provincial and at the national levels may vary.

1. Includes data for Yukon, Northwest Territories and Nunavut.

Source: Statistics Canada, Catalogue no. 61-534-XIE.

Table 4.2 Bankruptcies, by sector and by province and territory, 2006

	Canada	Newfoundland and Labrador	Prince Edward Island	Nova Scotia
		number		
All sectors	**6,756**	**45**	**41**	**241**
Agriculture, forestry, fishing and hunting	358	3	8	13
Mining and oil and gas extraction	35	0	0	1
Utilities	14	0	0	1
Construction	1,152	8	5	44
Manufacturing	571	2	1	17
Wholesale trade	324	1	1	9
Retail trade	989	7	8	42
Transportation and warehousing	641	1	0	23
Information and cultural industries	136	1	1	4
Finance and insurance	81	0	1	3
Real estate and rental and leasing	149	0	1	10
Professional, scientific and technical services	431	1	3	12
Management of companies and enterprises	39	0	0	0
Administrative and support, waste management and remediation services	326	2	3	6
Educational services	60	0	1	3
Health care and social assistance	75	2	0	3
Arts, entertainment and recreation	156	1	2	4
Accommodation and food services	767	12	5	22
Public administration	11	1	0	1
Other services (excluding public administration)	441	3	1	23

Note: North American Industry Classification System (NAICS), 2002.

1. Includes data for Yukon, Northwest Territories and Nunavut.

Source: Statistics Canada, CANSIM table 177-0006.

New Brunswick	Quebec	Ontario	Manitoba	Saskatchewan	Alberta	British Columbia	Territories[1]
				thousands			
27.8	227.7	303.7	35.7	40.8	112.5	149.0	3.7
27.5	227.6	303.8	35.7	40.9	114.5	150.8	3.8
27.6	228.4	311.3	36.2	41.7	121.2	154.8	3.8
28.2	231.7	320.2	36.7	41.2	126.7	156.2	3.8
28.3	233.7	327.2	36.8	40.8	129.7	156.3	3.8
27.8	233.3	332.1	36.2	40.1	132.6	155.9	4.0
27.8	232.9	337.9	36.4	40.1	137.3	157.1	4.1
27.6	233.3	343.6	36.9	39.9	140.9	159.5	4.2
27.4	234.8	351.1	36.9	39.8	144.5	162.9	4.3

New Brunswick	Quebec	Ontario	Manitoba	Saskatchewan	Alberta	British Columbia	Territories[1]
				number			
193	1,837	2,677	160	301	666	587	8
19	70	52	37	90	19	47	0
0	3	6	0	3	19	3	0
0	3	3	0	0	1	6	0
22	183	496	16	39	223	115	1
20	213	221	13	4	38	42	0
4	130	130	1	7	22	19	0
34	271	424	20	34	67	80	2
31	154	231	16	44	90	50	1
0	44	64	4	1	5	12	0
2	28	31	1	1	10	4	0
5	46	63	1	2	12	9	0
8	136	170	3	14	35	49	0
2	12	16	0	2	1	6	0
9	89	144	2	10	26	35	0
0	22	25	0	3	4	2	0
3	21	25	0	5	8	8	0
8	44	69	6	2	14	6	0
11	241	316	31	25	42	59	3
1	3	5	0	0	0	0	0
14	124	186	9	15	30	35	1

Table 4.3 Businesses, by firm size, 1983 to 2003

	All businesses	0 to 19 employees	20 to 99 employees	100 to 499 employees	500 employees and over
			thousands		
1983	752.7	708.5	36.4	6.1	1.6
1984	779.8	732.0	39.6	6.6	1.7
1985	808.7	758.3	41.8	6.9	1.7
1986	834.3	781.3	44.1	7.2	1.8
1987	865.2	808.3	47.4	7.6	1.9
1988	889.0	828.9	50.1	8.0	1.9
1989	907.6	845.2	52.1	8.3	2.0
1990	917.4	855.7	51.5	8.2	2.0
1991	907.2	843.0	53.7	8.5	2.0
1992	907.8	845.7	52.1	8.1	1.9
1993	910.3	847.3	52.9	8.2	2.0
1994	918.0	853.8	53.7	8.5	2.0
1995	923.0	856.7	55.4	8.8	2.0
1996	925.2	857.7	56.5	8.9	2.1
1997	945.0	874.7	58.7	9.4	2.2
1998	957.9	886.2	59.8	9.7	2.2
1999	970.2	897.8	60.2	9.9	2.2
2000	980.8	905.5	62.4	10.5	2.3
2001	991.5	914.0	64.0	11.0	2.4
2002	1,003.0	923.2	66.2	11.2	2.4
2003	1,018.9	937.8	67.3	11.4	2.5

Note: Data prior to 1991 were backcasted from a model.
Source: Statistics Canada, Catalogue no. 61-534-XIE.

Table 4.4 Corporations carrying on activities in Canada, major financial statistics, by country of control, 2001 to 2005

	2001	2002	2003	2004	2005
	$ millions				
Canadian- and foreign-controlled corporations					
Assets	4,195,238	4,372,325	4,580,424	4,990,267	5,235,806
Operating revenue	2,401,139	2,430,061	2,514,887	2,671,764	2,848,520
Operating profit	170,466	170,455	188,832	217,529	249,887
	% change from previous year				
Assets	5.9	4.2	4.8	8.9	4.9
Operating revenue	4.0	1.2	3.5	6.2	6.6
Operating profit	-11.0	0.0	10.8	15.2	14.9
	$ millions				
Canadian-controlled corporations					
Assets	3,239,003	3,380,500	3,573,855	3,911,392	4,126,848
Operating revenue	1,672,272	1,713,607	1,767,131	1,869,121	1,997,197
Operating profit	119,264	121,675	133,262	149,758	173,643
Private corporations					
Assets	2,896,124	3,028,373	3,221,276	3,550,860	3,767,819
Operating revenue	1,583,575	1,627,343	1,677,966	1,766,939	1,890,670
Operating profit	93,702	95,835	105,873	126,014	148,033
Government business corporations					
Assets	342,879	352,127	352,578	360,531	359,028
Operating revenue	88,697	86,264	89,165	102,182	106,527
Operating profit	25,562	25,839	27,389	23,744	25,610
Foreign-controlled corporations					
Assets	956,235	991,825	1,006,570	1,078,875	1,108,959
Operating revenue	728,867	716,454	747,756	802,643	851,323
Operating profit	51,202	48,780	55,571	67,771	76,244
United States corporations					
Assets	609,557	637,457	622,361	657,637	659,809
Operating revenue	482,955	469,367	472,522	505,923	536,128
Operating profit	34,460	31,207	35,771	44,164	48,448
European Union corporations					
Assets	258,313	261,943	282,095	320,463	344,923
Operating revenue	155,760	155,996	179,360	191,724	207,331
Operating profit	11,850	12,666	14,090	16,739	19,737
Other foreign corporations					
Assets	88,365	92,425	102,114	100,776	104,227
Operating revenue	90,153	91,091	95,874	104,996	107,864
Operating profit	4,892	4,908	5,709	6,867	8,060

Source: Statistics Canada, CANSIM table 179-0004.

Table 4.5 Balance sheet for the banking sector, 2002 to 2006

	2002	2003	2004	2005	2006
	\$ millions				
Assets	**1,323,806**	**1,408,877**	**1,565,617**	**1,649,746**	**1,837,920**
Cash and deposits	14,545	22,446	44,520	39,752	31,435
Accounts receivable and accrued revenue	5,358	5,137	4,542	5,445	5,924
Investments and accounts with affiliates	70,196	81,370	91,455	85,559	98,900
Portfolio investments	242,364	257,589	277,946	316,894	373,708
Loans	844,373	869,138	970,474	1,041,953	1,152,766
Mortgage	411,648	436,101	477,267	515,631	556,806
Non-mortgage	432,725	433,037	493,207	526,321	595,960
Allowance for losses on investments and loans	-16,534	-10,765	-8,100	-7,433	-6,916
Bank customers' liabilities under acceptances	38,686	33,102	33,769	39,434	52,637
Net capital assets	8,830	8,877	8,796	9,214	9,680
Other assets	115,988	141,983	142,216	118,929	119,784
Liabilities	**1,233,500**	**1,315,616**	**1,466,510**	**1,536,865**	**1,709,660**
Deposits	907,694	965,529	1,064,463	1,141,786	1,242,769
Accounts payable and accrued liabilities	10,653	12,270	11,090	11,715	15,484
Loans and accounts with affiliates	4,466	17,962	19,115	11,465	11,776
Borrowings	23,298	25,934	29,588	33,407	37,374
Loans and overdrafts	2,999	5,012	6,897	7,802	8,994
From banks	935	283	608	574	763
From others	2,064	4,729	6,289	7,228	8,232
Bankers' acceptances and paper	97	0	0	0	0
Bonds and debentures	19,981	20,692	22,618	25,460	28,127
Mortgages	221	231	72	145	252
Future income tax	703	600	694	323	338
Bank customers' liabilities under acceptances	38,695	33,104	33,769	39,310	52,512
Other liabilities	247,990	260,216	307,792	298,859	349,406
Equity	**90,306**	**93,261**	**99,107**	**112,881**	**128,259**
Share capital	37,623	37,176	36,672	42,057	44,056
Contributed surplus	4,563	5,684	6,487	9,411	10,132
Retained earnings	48,120	50,401	55,949	61,413	74,071

Notes: North American Industry Classification System (NAICS), 2002.
Balance sheet values reflect the fourth-quarter levels.
Includes Canadian-only business of chartered banks; independent trust and mortgage companies; credit unions; and other depository credit intermediation.
Source: Statistics Canada, CANSIM table 187-0001.

Table 4.6 Balance sheet for the insurance sector, 2002 to 2006

	2002	2003	2004	2005	2006
	$ millions				
Assets	**303,682**	**325,419**	**345,653**	**362,002**	**392,596**
Cash and deposits	4,918	5,351	6,907	5,770	6,138
Accounts receivable and accrued revenue	18,590	21,195	21,613	19,467	19,412
Investments and accounts with affiliates	36,519	32,818	35,600	43,473	54,633
Portfolio investments	171,048	186,503	198,386	208,862	225,329
Loans	44,168	44,269	45,240	45,199	46,933
Mortgage	38,543	39,366	39,947	39,778	40,857
Non-mortgage	5,625	4,903	5,293	5,421	6,077
Allowance for losses on investments and loans	-138	-93	-126	-52	-54
Bank customers' liabilities under acceptances	0	0	0	0	0
Net capital assets	8,369	8,155	7,686	7,939	8,212
Other assets	20,209	27,220	30,346	31,344	31,993
Liabilities	**231,659**	**250,958**	**261,586**	**273,879**	**290,278**
Deposits	5,140	4,962	5,159	5,335	5,549
Actuarial liabilities of insurers	134,707	144,992	149,839	152,698	160,039
Accounts payable and accrued liabilities	49,571	55,533	60,248	60,503	61,886
Loans and accounts with affiliates	3,803	4,221	4,667	8,203	11,532
Borrowings	10,192	8,645	8,088	8,841	9,731
Loans and overdrafts	4,521	3,458	2,772	3,384	3,104
From banks	3,305	1,489	1,088	1,360	1,296
From others	1,216	1,970	1,684	2,024	1,807
Bankers' acceptances and paper	5	5	5	6	6
Bonds and debentures	5,492	4,979	5,104	5,215	6,304
Mortgages	175	202	206	237	317
Future income tax	-318	-93	-394	-499	-660
Other liabilities	28,562	32,699	33,978	38,798	42,203
Equity	**72,023**	**74,461**	**84,068**	**88,123**	**102,318**
Share capital	18,010	22,458	26,485	26,439	28,580
Contributed surplus	2,261	2,448	1,831	2,092	2,376
Retained earnings	51,753	49,555	55,752	59,593	71,362

Notes: North American Industry Classification System (NAICS), 2002.
Balance sheet values reflect the fourth-quarter levels.
Includes Canadian-only business of all insurers including reinsurers.
Source: Statistics Canada, CANSIM table 187-0001.

Table 4.7 Business credits, selected sources, 2002 to 2006

	2002	2003	2004	2005	2006
	annual average ($ millions)				
All business credits	**887,630**	**904,418**	**944,844**	**1,005,589**	**1,066,468**
Short-term business credits	263,086	255,399	253,297	270,550	305,960
Business loans					
Chartered banks	121,346	121,835	125,509	135,505	147,901
Other institutions	22,443	24,816	27,032	29,841	33,082
Chartered bank foreign currency loans to residents	22,825	18,534	18,064	17,870	20,196
Bankers' acceptances	44,883	39,308	35,929	37,878	48,362
Adjustment to short-term business credits	189	671	-1,322	-1,634	-1,121
Long-term business credits	624,544	649,019	691,547	735,038	760,508
Non-residential mortgages					
Chartered banks	16,443	16,965	17,731	18,621	19,629
Trust and mortgage loan companies	561	553	668	1,039	1,275
Credit unions and caisses populaires	10,967	11,698	12,263	13,785	15,856
Life insurance companies	23,880	24,800	26,178	27,499	28,242
Leasing receivables					
Chartered banks	5,124	4,807	5,070	5,555	6,384
Trust and mortgage loan companies	73	25	15	46	58
Other business credits					
Bonds and debentures	239,360	241,573	253,295	262,444	258,564
Equity and other	265,002	273,892	285,230	295,749	298,854

Source: Statistics Canada, CANSIM table 176-0023.

Children and youth

5

OVERVIEW

Canadian children are much healthier than earlier generations and most are reaching their teens in good or excellent health. Moreover, fewer infants are dying from illnesses, fewer children are growing up in low-income families, and more teens are finishing high school and pursuing postsecondary education. After graduation, job prospects are good.

In 2006, there were 10 million children, adolescents and young adults under age 25. Of those, 6 million were under 15 years of age, 2 million were aged 15 to 19 and 2 million were aged 20 to 24. The share of the population under 25 has fallen over the last three decades, from 48% in 1971 to 31% in 2006.

In older age groups, women outnumber men; however, there are slightly more young males than young females. In 2006, 51% of

Canadians under the age of 25 were male, and 49% were female.

Living arrangements

In 2004, 6 million people 19 and younger, or 75% of this age group, were living in a two-parent family, and 1.8 million children and adolescents, or 23%, were living with one parent, compared with 21% in 2000.

While it is not common, some children live with grandparents. According to the 2001 Census, 190,810 children under 15, or 3.3%, lived in the same household as one or more of their grandparents. Of these, 25,245 children, about 0.4%, lived in the same household as their grandparents and without their parents.

Few young people are parents themselves. In 2004, just 3% of young people aged 15 to

Chart 5.1
Population under 25, by sex

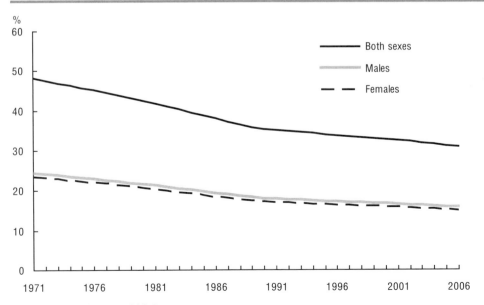

Note: Postcensal estimates as of July 1.
Source: Statistics Canada, CANSIM table 051-0001.

19 had children and were living as a couple or as a single parent. Another 7% in this age group lived alone or with non-relatives.

Young adults aged 20 to 24 live in a wider range of family types than those 19 and under. In 2004, 20% were living on their own or with non-relatives, and 25% were parents themselves. However, the majority, 55%, were living in a two-parent or a lone-parent family.

Health status

The health status of children and adolescents has improved in recent decades: infant mortality rates have decreased and several infectious diseases, such as diphtheria, acute poliomyelitis and scarlet fever, which used to kill many children, have been nearly eradicated. The majority of newborns have a healthy birth weight, above 2,500 grams.

Despite medical progress, 2,515 children aged 14 and younger died in Canada in 2004. More than 70% of these children died before age 1, primarily because of a condition or disease that occurred before or during birth. Injuries and accidents remain

Population under 25, by age group and sex

	2006		
	Both sexes	Males	Females
	number		
Total	10,075,694	5,159,304	4,916,390
0 to 4	1,712,848	877,078	835,770
5 to 9	1,844,308	944,083	900,225
10 to 14	2,087,453	1,069,711	1,017,742
15 to 19	2,170,044	1,111,764	1,058,280
20 to 24	2,261,041	1,156,668	1,104,373

Source: Statistics Canada, CANSIM table 051-0001.

the leading cause of death among children aged 1 to 14. Despite its rare incidence, cancer is the most common potentially fatal illness and the second leading cause of death in this age group.

A growing number of children and young people are overweight. In 2004, 26% of children and adolescents aged 2 to 17 were overweight or obese according to their body mass index, compared with 15% in 1979, a 73% increase. Data from 2004 show that 59% of children and adolescents ate fewer than five servings of fruits and vegetables per day, the recommended minimum number of servings according to the 2004 *Canada's Food Guide*. These young people were more

Chart 5.2
Living arrangements of adolescents and young adults, 2004

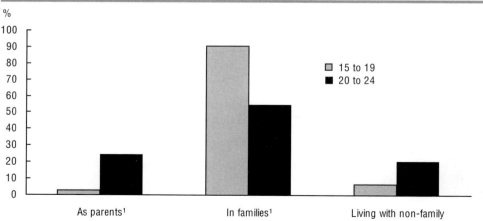

1. Includes couple and lone-parent families.
Source: Statistics Canada, CANSIM table 111-0010.

likely to be overweight or obese than those who ate fruits and vegetables more often.

Fewer adolescents are smoking today. In 2001, 14% of young people aged 12 to 17 smoked cigarettes every day or occasionally—in 2005, that was down to 8%. By contrast, 40% in that age group were exposed to second-hand smoke, compared with 23% for the Canadian population.

Among teenagers who drank alcohol regularly, 31% of drinkers aged 15 to 19 drank heavily—that is, consumed five or more glasses of alcohol on a single occasion at least 12 times a year in 2005. A higher proportion of boys than girls drank heavily: 38% of boys and 25% of girls.

Work and play

Just over half of preschool children attend some type of child care service. By age 4 or 5, most are enrolled in school, where they remain until at least age 16 or 17.

The number of young people pursuing postsecondary education has climbed, particularly university enrolment among those aged 18 to 24. From 1995/1996 to 2003/2004, the university student population in this age group grew 27%, reaching 990,400 students.

Even though the proportion of students who work while attending school has fallen since 1989/1990, 31% of high school students aged 15 to 17 were employed during the 2004/2005 school year. The percentage of students aged 18 to 24 who held a job during the school year was higher at 46%. Thanks to a vigorous economy, job creation for young people aged 15 to 24 grew 21% from 1997 to 2004—the equivalent of 428,000 new jobs.

Many young people spend part of their free time watching television, playing video games and using computers. In 2004, young people aged 12 to 17 spent an average of 10 hours each week watching television. If the time spent on a computer or playing video games is added, young people spend an average of 20 hours each week in front of a screen.

Selected sources

Statistics Canada

- *Canadian Social Trends.* Irregular. 11-008-XWE

- *Children and Youth Research Paper Series.* Occasional. 89-599-MIE

- *Education Matters: Insights on Education, Learning and Training in Canada.* Bi-monthly. 81-004-XIE

- *Health Indicators.* Semi-annual. 82-221-XIE

- *Income and the Outcomes of Children.* Occasional. 11F0019MIE2006281

- *Mortality, Summary List of Causes.* Annual. 84F0209XWE

Chart 5.3
Current smokers, by sex and selected age groups

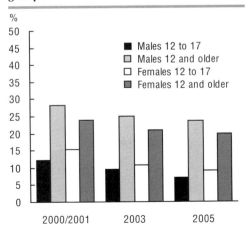

Legend:
- Males 12 to 17
- Males 12 and older
- Females 12 to 17
- Females 12 and older

(x-axis: 2000/2001, 2003, 2005; y-axis: % from 0 to 50)

Note: Includes daily or occasional smokers.
Source: Statistics Canada, Catalogue no. 82-621-XWE.

More parents using child care services

Over the past 30 years, some key trends have resulted in a greater demand for child care services—the number of single-parent families has increased and more women are working outside the home.

This increased demand coincides with a substantial rise in the number of spaces in licensed daycare centres. In 2003, licensed daycare centres had nearly 750,000 spaces, or 59% more than in 1998. The number of spaces is twice as high as in the early 1990s and almost seven times higher than in 1980.

The percentage of Canadian children in some type of child care has grown. In 2002/2003, 54% of children aged six months to five years received child care from someone other than their parents, compared with 42% in 1994/1995. Some children—including those from high-income households and those living with a single parent—are more likely than other children to be cared for by someone other than a parent.

Overall, there has been a decrease in the proportion of children cared for by a non-relative outside the home. The proportion of children receiving care in daycare centres and in their own homes by a relative have increased. In 2002/2003, child care provided outside the home by a relative was more common for children living in rural areas than for children in urban communities. A higher percentage of children of immigrants are cared for at home by a relative, compared with children whose parents were born in Canada. Children in low-income homes and children in Quebec are more likely to be cared for at daycare centres.

The average number of hours in care fell from 31 hours per week in 1994/1995 to 29 hours in 2002/2003.

Chart 5.4
Children in non-parental child care, by type of arrangement

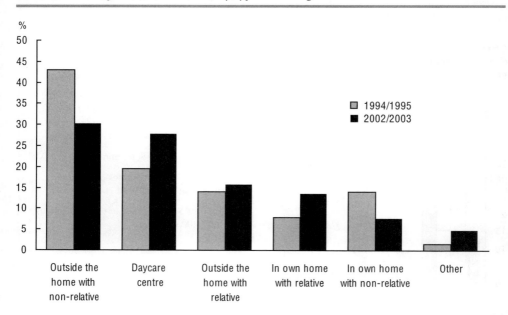

Source: Statistics Canada, Catalogue no. 89-599-MIE.

Positive relationships keep teens healthy

Adolescents, as a population, are generally healthy, but the teen years are a period of rapid change. During this time, young people may try things that could be harmful to their health and well-being—such as taking drugs, consuming alcohol, smoking or engaging in risky sexual behaviour. However, only focusing on risky behaviours and indicators of poor health does not give a complete picture of their health and development.

The 2000/2001 National Longitudinal Survey of Children and Youth (NLSCY) focused on the link between the quality of adolescents' relationships—at home, at school, in the community and with friends—and their health status and behaviour. These relationships are considered positive assets.

The NLSCY results show that teens who feel valued by their parents and who are involved with their school are also healthier and have greater self-worth. As well, they are less likely to adopt unhealthy behaviours. Adolescence is a time of growing independence from parents, but families still play an important role.

Adolescents who have a higher number of positive assets are generally less likely to adopt risky behaviours. They are more likely to report a good health status, higher self-worth and a lower level of anxiety than adolescents who have fewer positive assets.

Young people who have four to five positive assets report higher levels of self-worth and good health than young people who have only two to three. Among the adolescents surveyed, self-worth and health status were both better among young people who had two to three assets than among those who had no assets or only one.

Chart 5.5
Adolescents' psychological and health status and behaviours, by their positive assets, 2000/2001

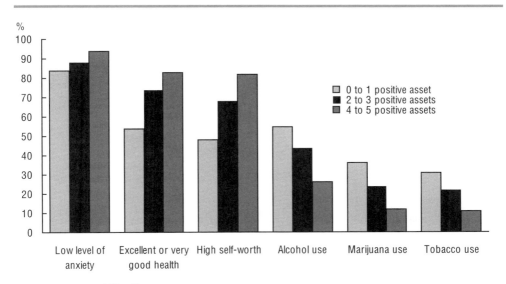

Notes: Adolescents aged 12 to 15.
A positive asset is defined as a high level of parental nurturing; parental monitoring; school engagement; peer connectedness reported by a child; or as participation in a volunteer activity by a child in the past 12 months before the survey.
Source: Canadian Institute for Health Information, analysis of data from Statistics Canada's National Longitudinal Survey of Children and Youth.

Children's behaviour linked to home life

Most Canadian children are in good physical and emotional health and have no social or behavioural problems. However, some experience social and academic difficulties.

According to the 2002/2003 NLSCY, 4% of children aged 8 to 11 had learning disabilities in 2002. These children were slightly more likely to suffer from anxiety and emotional disorders than children without learning disabilities. Children with learning problems also scored higher on a scale of aggression and other conduct disorders. A child's age and sex did not affect these results.

Slightly different results were observed with regard to altruism or positive social behaviour. Children with learning disabilities scored lower on average than other children, but the gap narrowed when age and sex were taken into consideration.

A positive home life can partly compensate for the difficulties faced by children with learning problems. For example, children from homes where parenting styles are ineffective have higher levels of aggressive behaviours and conduct disorders, anxiety, and emotional disorders. They also obtain lower scores for altruism and positive social behaviour.

The bonds with their parents also influence a child's mental well-being. The 2000/2001 NLSCY shows that young people who report greater degrees of closeness, affection and understanding with their parents exhibit fewer symptoms of depression.

Chart 5.6
Measures of selected behaviours of children aged 8 to 11, 2002/2003

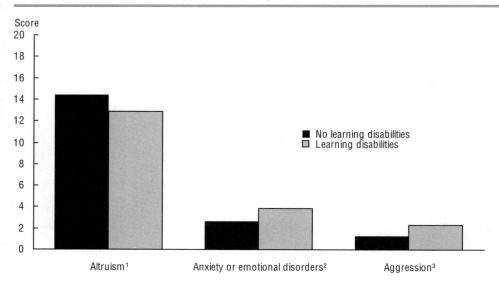

1. Indicates the presence of prosocial behaviours on a scale of 1 to 20.
2. Indicates the presence of behaviours associated with anxiety and emotional disorder on a scale of 1 to 14.
3. Indicates the presence of behaviours associated with conduct disorders and physical aggression on a scale of 1 to 12.
Source: Statistics Canada, Catalogue no. 11-008-XIE.

Fewer children living in low income

Over the past few years, the number and share of children living in low-income homes has declined. Some 865,000 children under 18 lived in low-income families in 2004, compared with 1.3 million in 1996. The percentage of children in low-income families fell from a peak of 19% in 1996 to 13% in 2004.

Of the 550,000 lone-parent families headed by women in 2004, 36% lived in low income, down from 56% in 1996. However, these families still include a disproportionately high percentage of the children who live in low-income situations. In 2004, the percentage of children living in low-income families was 40% for lone-parent families headed by women, compared with 8% for two-parent families.

According to a 2006 study based on the NLSCY, children's well-being is almost always linked to the family's household income. Regardless of the child's age or the way the household income was measured, higher income is associated with better physical, social, emotional, cognitive and behavioural well-being in children.

Although the degree of this association varies depending on the characteristics of well-being used, children from higher income households have better outcomes than children from lower income households. This association holds for all children aged 4 to 15.

The study could not establish the degree of the causal relationship between household income and children's well-being: income might be a proxy for other family characteristics that affect children.

Chart 5.7
Children in low income, by family type

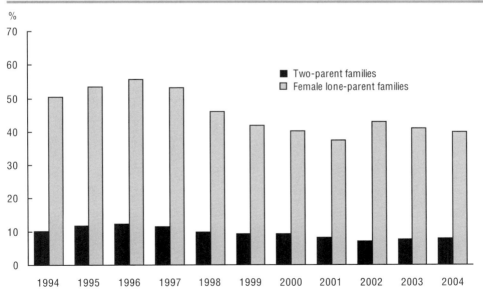

Notes: Low-income cut-offs after tax, 1992 base.
      Children under 18 years.
Source: Statistics Canada, CANSIM table 202-0802.

Table 5.1 Population of children and youth, by age group, selected years from 1971 to 2006

	1971		1976		1981	
	number	%	number	%	number	%
Both sexes, less than 25 years	**10,574,502**	**48.1**	**10,602,398**	**45.2**	**10,378,549**	**41.8**
Under 1 year	360,298	1.6	353,161	1.5	367,393	1.5
1 to 4 years	1,475,835	6.7	1,406,373	6.0	1,436,167	5.8
5 to 9 years	2,267,863	10.3	1,909,468	8.1	1,794,559	7.2
10 to 14 years	2,328,801	10.6	2,290,924	9.8	1,934,296	7.8
15 to 19 years	2,164,210	9.9	2,389,105	10.2	2,368,997	9.5
20 to 24 years	1,977,495	9.0	2,253,367	9.6	2,477,137	10.0
Males, less than 25 years	**5,380,361**	**24.5**	**5,404,881**	**23.0**	**5,299,180**	**21.4**
Under 1 year	184,138	0.8	181,003	0.8	188,084	0.8
1 to 4 years	754,678	3.4	721,493	3.1	736,714	3.0
5 to 9 years	1,159,505	5.3	978,516	4.2	921,586	3.7
10 to 14 years	1,190,029	5.4	1,171,796	5.0	991,714	4.0
15 to 19 years	1,100,199	5.0	1,217,755	5.2	1,211,105	4.9
20 to 24 years	991,812	4.5	1,134,318	4.8	1,249,977	5.0
Females, less than 25 years	**5,194,141**	**23.7**	**5,197,517**	**22.2**	**5,079,369**	**20.5**
Under 1 year	176,160	0.8	172,158	0.7	179,309	0.7
1 to 4 years	721,157	3.3	684,880	2.9	699,453	2.8
5 to 9 years	1,108,358	5.0	930,952	4.0	872,973	3.5
10 to 14 years	1,138,772	5.2	1,119,128	4.8	942,582	3.8
15 to 19 years	1,064,011	4.8	1,171,350	5.0	1,157,892	4.7
20 to 24 years	985,683	4.5	1,119,049	4.8	1,227,160	4.9

Note: Percentage of the total population of Canada.
Source: Statistics Canada, CANSIM table 051-0001.

Table 5.2 Population of children and youth, by age group and by province and territory, 2006

	Canada	Newfoundland and Labrador	Prince Edward Island	Nova Scotia	New Brunswick
			%		
Both sexes, less than 25 years	**30.9**	**28.5**	**31.7**	**29.3**	**28.9**
Under 1 year	1.1	0.9	1.0	0.9	0.9
1 to 4 years	4.2	3.7	4.0	3.7	3.7
5 to 9 years	5.7	5.0	5.7	5.2	5.1
10 to 14 years	6.4	5.8	6.7	6.0	6.0
15 to 19 years	6.7	6.6	7.4	6.7	6.5
20 to 24 years	6.9	6.6	7.0	6.8	6.6
Males, less than 25 years	**15.8**	**14.5**	**16.1**	**14.9**	**14.9**
Under 1 year	0.5	0.4	0.5	0.5	0.5
1 to 4 years	2.1	1.9	1.9	1.9	1.9
5 to 9 years	2.9	2.6	3.0	2.6	2.6
10 to 14 years	3.3	3.0	3.5	3.0	3.1
15 to 19 years	3.4	3.3	3.7	3.4	3.4
20 to 24 years	3.5	3.3	3.5	3.5	3.4
Females, less than 25 years	**15.1**	**14.0**	**15.6**	**14.4**	**14.1**
Under 1 year	0.5	0.4	0.5	0.5	0.4
1 to 4 years	2.1	1.8	2.1	1.8	1.8
5 to 9 years	2.8	2.4	2.7	2.5	2.5
10 to 14 years	3.1	2.8	3.2	3.0	2.9
15 to 19 years	3.2	3.2	3.7	3.3	3.1
20 to 24 years	3.4	3.3	3.5	3.3	3.2

Note: Percentage of the total population of Canada, the province or the territory.
Source: Statistics Canada, CANSIM table 051-0001.

1986		1991		1996		2001		2006	
number	%	number	%	number	%	number	%	number	%
9,918,782	38.0	9,806,045	35.0	9,997,399	33.8	10,081,766	32.5	10,075,694	30.9
368,442	1.4	406,662	1.5	379,242	1.3	332,343	1.1	342,735	1.1
1,472,517	5.6	1,551,465	5.5	1,581,906	5.3	1,426,853	4.6	1,370,113	4.2
1,829,350	7.0	1,933,794	6.9	2,015,912	6.8	2,016,678	6.5	1,844,308	5.7
1,814,538	7.0	1,897,903	6.8	2,008,491	6.8	2,078,664	6.7	2,087,453	6.4
1,987,685	7.6	1,928,056	6.9	2,009,812	6.8	2,116,904	6.8	2,170,044	6.7
2,446,250	9.4	2,088,165	7.4	2,002,036	6.8	2,110,324	6.8	2,261,041	6.9
5,081,116	19.5	5,020,195	17.9	5,119,696	17.3	5,165,165	16.7	5,159,304	15.8
187,943	0.7	208,374	0.7	193,891	0.7	170,286	0.5	175,987	0.5
755,641	2.9	793,917	2.8	810,960	2.7	729,929	2.4	701,091	2.1
939,112	3.6	991,319	3.5	1,032,563	3.5	1,032,352	3.3	944,083	2.9
927,874	3.6	973,082	3.5	1,031,057	3.5	1,064,560	3.4	1,069,711	3.3
1,020,740	3.9	991,252	3.5	1,033,058	3.5	1,088,667	3.5	1,111,764	3.4
1,249,806	4.8	1,062,251	3.8	1,018,167	3.4	1,079,371	3.5	1,156,668	3.5
4,837,666	18.5	4,785,850	17.1	4,877,703	16.5	4,916,601	15.8	4,916,390	15.1
180,499	0.7	198,288	0.7	185,351	0.6	162,057	0.5	166,748	0.5
716,876	2.7	757,548	2.7	770,946	2.6	696,924	2.2	669,022	2.1
890,238	3.4	942,475	3.4	983,349	3.3	984,326	3.2	900,225	2.8
886,664	3.4	924,821	3.3	977,434	3.3	1,014,104	3.3	1,017,742	3.1
966,945	3.7	936,804	3.3	976,754	3.3	1,028,237	3.3	1,058,280	3.2
1,196,444	4.6	1,025,914	3.7	983,869	3.3	1,030,953	3.3	1,104,373	3.4

Quebec	Ontario	Manitoba	Saskatchewan	Alberta	British Columbia	Yukon	Northwest Territories	Nunavut
				%				
28.9	31.4	33.7	34.5	33.8	29.7	33.2	40.5	52.9
1.0	1.0	1.2	1.2	1.2	0.9	1.2	1.6	2.5
3.9	4.3	4.7	4.8	4.9	3.8	4.2	6.1	9.6
5.1	5.9	6.4	6.2	6.1	5.2	5.8	7.9	11.2
6.1	6.6	7.1	7.0	6.6	6.0	6.9	8.6	10.6
6.2	6.7	7.2	7.7	7.1	6.5	7.7	8.2	10.3
6.4	6.9	7.2	7.5	7.9	7.1	7.5	8.1	8.8
14.8	16.1	17.3	17.8	17.4	15.2	16.9	20.7	27.3
0.5	0.5	0.6	0.6	0.6	0.5	0.6	0.8	1.3
2.0	2.2	2.4	2.5	2.5	2.0	2.2	2.9	5.0
2.6	3.0	3.3	3.2	3.1	2.7	2.7	4.1	5.9
3.1	3.4	3.6	3.6	3.4	3.1	3.4	4.5	5.4
3.2	3.4	3.7	4.0	3.7	3.3	4.1	4.1	5.2
3.3	3.5	3.7	3.9	4.0	3.7	3.9	4.2	4.4
14.1	15.4	16.4	16.7	16.4	14.4	16.3	19.8	25.7
0.5	0.5	0.6	0.6	0.6	0.5	0.6	0.8	1.2
1.9	2.1	2.3	2.3	2.4	1.9	2.0	3.2	4.6
2.5	2.9	3.1	3.0	3.0	2.5	3.0	3.7	5.3
3.0	3.2	3.5	3.4	3.2	2.9	3.5	4.1	5.2
3.0	3.3	3.5	3.7	3.5	3.2	3.5	4.1	5.0
3.1	3.4	3.5	3.6	3.8	3.5	3.6	3.9	4.3

Table 5.3 Children and youth, by family structure, 2004

	Total children and youth	Family structure		
		In couple families	In lone-parent families	Non-family persons
		number		
Age of child				
0 to 4 years	**1,669,740**	1,350,240	319,410	90
5 to 9 years	**1,898,020**	1,465,490	432,260	260
10 to 14 years[1]	**2,208,420**	1,657,540	549,730	1,150
15 to 19 years[1]	**2,265,890**	1,573,560	534,040	158,290
20 to 24 years[1]	**1,467,400**	888,820	175,520	403,060

1. Excludes young people who are parents.
Source: Statistics Canada, CANSIM table 111-0010.

Table 5.4 Young parents, by family structure, 2000 to 2004

	2000	2001	2002	2003	2004
	number				
Parents aged 15 to 19 years					
Couple families	59,000	59,690	52,080	55,690	57,720
Lone-parent families	14,400	13,850	13,210	12,680	11,750
Parents aged 20 to 24 years					
Couple families	426,400	421,950	380,840	407,700	409,740
Lone-parent families	74,510	73,840	73,040	73,080	71,340

Source: Statistics Canada, CANSIM table 111-0010.

Table 5.5 Deaths and death rates of children, by age group, 1994, 1999 and 2004

	1994		1999		2004	
	number	rate per 100,000 population	number	rate per 100,000 population	number	rate per 100,000 population
All ages[1]	**207,077**	**7.1**	**219,530**	**7.2**	**226,584**	**7.1**
Males	109,742	7.6	113,669	7.6	114,513	7.2
Females	97,335	6.6	105,861	6.9	112,071	6.9
Under 1 year	**2,417**	**6.3**	**1,776**	**5.3**	**1,775**	**5.3**
Males	1,374	6.9	985	5.7	953	5.5
Females	1,043	5.6	791	4.8	822	5.0
1 to 4 years	**518**	**0.3**	**387**	**0.3**	**286**	**0.2**
Males	293	0.4	214	0.3	154	0.2
Females	225	0.3	173	0.2	132	0.2
5 to 9 years	**318**	**0.2**	**284**	**0.1**	**195**	**0.1**
Males	185	0.2	169	0.2	126	0.1
Females	133	0.1	115	0.1	69	0.1
10 to 14 years	**408**	**0.2**	**330**	**0.2**	**259**	**0.1**
Males	246	0.2	213	0.2	157	0.1
Females	162	0.2	117	0.1	102	0.1

1. Total number of deaths for all Canadians in all age groups.
Source: Statistics Canada, CANSIM table 102-0504.

Table 5.6 Causes of death of children, by age group, 2001 to 2003

	2001		2002		2003	
	number	rate per 100,000 population	number	rate per 100,000 population	number	rate per 100,000 population
Under 1 year						
Perinatal conditions	925	277.2	918	279.2	981	292.7
Congenital conditions	436	130.6	427	129.9	423	126.2
Sudden infant death syndrome	112	33.7	111	33.9	96	29.1
1 to 4 years						
Accidents (unintentional injuries)	97	6.9	85	6.0	86	6.3
Malignant neoplasms	45	3.2	33	2.3	29	2.1
Congenital conditions	41	2.9	41	2.9	35	2.5
5 to 9 years						
Accidents (unintentional injuries)	87	4.3	83	4.2	69	3.5
Malignant neoplasms	57	2.8	50	2.5	45	2.3
Congenital conditions	18	0.9	17	0.9	12	0.6
10 to 14 years						
Accidents (unintentional injuries)	102	4.9	131	6.2	110	5.2
Malignant neoplasms	44	2.1	42	2.0	40	1.9
Suicide (intentional self-harm)	27	1.3	35	1.7	27	1.3
15 to 19 years						
Accidents (unintentional injuries)	472	22.6	454	21.4	444	20.9
Suicide (intentional self-harm)	207	9.9	215	10.1	216	10.2
Malignant neoplasms	77	3.7	56	2.6	83	3.9

Source: Statistics Canada, CANSIM tables 102-0538, 102-0551 and 102-4502.

Table 5.7 Current daily or occasional smokers among children and youth, by age group, selected years from 2000 to 2005

	2000 to 2001		2003		2005	
	number	%	number	%	number	%
12 to 19	**605,558**	**18.7**	**490,404**	**14.8**	**405,109**	**12.1**
Males	292,307	17.6	244,134	14.4	204,113	11.9
Females	313,250	19.8	246,270	15.2	200,996	12.3
12 to 14	69,203	6.0	43,731	3.4	30,923	2.5
Males	30,483	5.1	19,594	2.9	10,439	1.6
Females	38,720	7.0	24,137	4.0	20,485	3.5
15 to 19	536,354	25.7	446,673	21.9	374,185	17.7
Males	261,824	24.7	224,540	21.7	193,674	18.1
Females	274,530	26.7	222,133	22.1	180,511	17.2
20 to 24	**745,446**	**35.0**	**718,612**	**33.2**	**682,127**	**30.5**
Males	403,213	37.3	393,206	35.4	378,655	32.4
Females	342,232	32.6	325,406	30.8	303,472	28.3

Note: Household population aged 12 and older.
Source: Statistics Canada, CANSIM tables 105-0027, 105-0227 and 105-0427.

Table 5.8 Alcohol consumption among children and youth, by age group, 2005

	Never 5 or more drinks on one occasion		Five or more drinks on one occasion, less than 12 times a year		Five or more drinks on one occasion, more than 12 times a year	
	number	%	number	%	number	%
12 to 19 years	**659,167**	**38.3**	**540,132**	**31.4**	**475,980**	**27.7**
Males	288,123	32.7	275,922	31.3	292,601	33.2
Females	371,045	44.2	264,210	31.5	183,379	21.9
12 to 14 years	169,247	71.8	42,273	17.9	10,690	4.5
Males	89,190	73.0	20,755	17.0	6,262E	5.1E
Females	80,057	70.6	21,518	19.0	4,428E	3.9E
15 to 19 years	489,920	33.0	497,860	33.5	465,290	31.3
Males	198,933	26.2	255,167	33.6	286,339	37.7
Females	290,987	40.1	242,693	33.5	178,951	24.7
20 to 24 years	**445,266**	**22.6**	**619,617**	**31.4**	**878,119**	**44.5**
Males	157,258	15.1	293,335	28.1	576,782	55.3
Females	288,007	31.0	326,282	35.1	301,337	32.4

Note: Household population aged 12 and older who are current drinkers.
Source: Statistics Canada, CANSIM table 105-0431.

Table 5.9 Measured child obesity, by age group, 2004

	Neither overweight nor obese		Overweight		Obese	
	number	%	number	%	number	%
2 to 11 years	**2,780,278**	**75.8**	**619,039**	**16.9**	**270,416**	**7.4**
Males	1,426,706	76.8	288,868	15.5	142,186	7.7
Females	1,353,572	74.7	330,172	18.2	128,230	7.1
2 to 5 years	1,058,739	78.5	204,534	15.2	85,152	6.3
Males	551,625	80.6	89,872	13.1	42,829E	6.3E
Females	507,114	76.4	114,662	17.3	42,323E	6.4E
6 to 11 years	1,721,539	74.2	414,505	17.9	185,264	8.0
Males	875,081	74.6	198,996	17.0	99,357	8.5
Females	846,458	73.7	215,510	18.8	85,907	7.5
12 to 14 years	**911,624**	**70.6**	**264,893**	**20.5**	**114,075**	**8.8**
Males	473,031	66.8	156,447	22.1	78,647	11.1
Females	438,593	75.3	108,446	18.6	35,428E	6.1E
15 to 17 years	**869,471**	**71.0**	**232,908**	**19.0**	**121,721**	**9.9**
Males	421,070	68.8	122,648	20.0	68,240E	11.2E
Females	448,400	73.3	110,260	18.0	53,482	8.7

Notes: Obesity categories based on measured body mass index.
　　　Household population aged 2 to 17, excluding pregnant females and residents of the territories.
Source: Statistics Canada, CANSIM table 105-2002.

Table 5.10 Measured child obesity, by province, 2004

	Neither overweight nor obese		Overweight		Obese	
	number	%	number	%	number	%
Canada	**4,561,372**	**73.8**	**1,116,840**	**18.1**	**506,213**	**8.2**
Newfoundland and Labrador	59,575	64.4	17,544	19.0	15,392E	16.6E
Prince Edward Island	20,075	69.8	6,457	22.4	2,242E	7.8E
Nova Scotia	116,716	68.0	38,875	22.6	16,053E	9.4E
New Brunswick	91,044	65.8	29,270	21.1	18,151E	13.1E
Quebec	1,058,652	77.4	211,533	15.5	97,444	7.1
Ontario	1,821,819	72.5	476,704	19.0	214,102	8.5
Manitoba	161,657	69.2	51,084	21.9	20,917	9.0
Saskatchewan	139,947	70.9	37,103	18.8	20,356	10.3
Alberta	523,224	78.2	95,785	14.3	50,376E	7.5E
British Columbia	568,663	73.6	152,484	19.7	51,180E	6.6E

Notes: Obesity categories based on measured body mass index.

Household population aged 2 to 17, excluding pregnant females and residents of the territories.

Source: Statistics Canada, CANSIM table 105-2002.

Table 5.11 Measured child obesity rates, by selected health behaviours and age group, 2004

	Estimated population	Overweight	Obese
	thousands	%	
Total population aged 2 to 17	**6,184**	**18.1**	**8.2**
Daily fruit and vegetable consumption (ages 2 to 17)			
Fewer than 3 servings	1,307	18.7	10.2
3 to 4 servings	2,310	19.0	9.0
5 servings or more	2,552	16.8	6.4
Weekly physical activity (ages 6 to 11)			
Less than 7 hours	359	16.7	9.3E
7 to 13 hours	982	18.4	8.2
14 hours or more	957	18.0	7.5E
Leisure-time physical activity (ages 12 to 17)			
Boys			
Active or moderately active	974	24.0	9.3
Sedentary	346	13.0	16.3E
Girls			
Active or moderately active	709	18.5	6.3
Sedentary	486	18.0	9.2E
Daily screen time (ages 6 to 11)			
1 hour or less	484	12.5E	5.3E
1 to 2 hours	1,013	15.3	7.1E
More than 2 hours	824	24.1	10.6
Weekly screen time (ages 12 to 17)			
Less than 10 hours	614	13.9	9.1E
10 to 19 hours	699	21.9	6.6
20 to 29 hours	728	20.2	11.2
30 hours or more	466	23.8	11.2E

Notes: Obesity categories based on measured body mass index.

Household population aged 2 to 17, excluding pregnant females and residents of the territories.

Source: Statistics Canada, Catalogue no. 82-620-MWE.

Construction

6

OVERVIEW

The banging hammers and swinging cranes at construction sites across Canada are telling indicators of economic and social trends in this country. The most obvious recent example is the enormous demand for residential and commercial construction in Alberta's booming economy, which has created jobs and attracted thousands of migrants from across the country and from around the world.

But construction is hot all over Canada. Lower interest rates have encouraged more Canadians to buy new houses or to renovate older homes. And increased wholesale and retail sales have businesses scrambling to build more offices, retail stores and warehouses, boosting non-residential construction.

All told, contractors took out a record $66.3 billion in residential building permits

in 2006, up 9% from $60.8 billion the previous year. Municipalities across Canada authorized building 233,200 new homes that year, down slightly from 2005, but still the third highest figure since 1988. Moreover, the value of residential permits increased in 20 of 28 census metropolitan areas in 2006.

Renovations

Meanwhile, Canadians undertook $32.0 billion worth of renovations in 2006, accounting for 40% of all residential construction investment, a 9% increase from 2005.

The value of non-residential building permits also increased. Investment in the construction of non-residential buildings reached $35.5 billion in 2006, up 12% from 2005. This was the largest gain on record, and

Chart 6.1
Value of non-residential building permits, by province

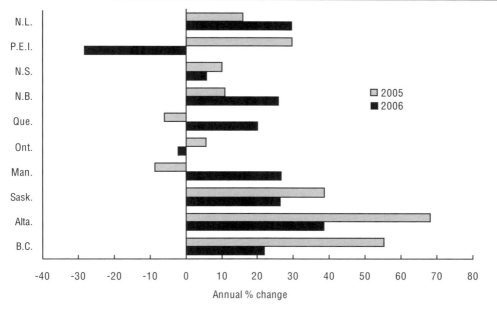

Source: Statistics Canada, CANSIM table 026-0005.

a sign of a strong economy and thriving industry.

In 2006, the entire construction industry added $67.7 billion to Canada's gross domestic product (GDP): this industry first crossed the $60-billion threshold in 2005. However, employment in the industry stabilized in 2006 after several years of growth.

Investment in new homes

The healthy economy and low interest rates kept the housing market hot in 2006. Despite the ongoing availability of new homes, investment continued to rise. The strongest growth in new home investment was in single-family homes, which rose 9% to $25.5 billion, and in apartments and condominiums, which rose 13% to $9.3 billion. Higher prices played a big role in the increase; while the number of housing starts remained almost unchanged, each new home cost more.

The main drivers of growth in new home investment—particularly in Western Canada—were the dynamic economy,

Chart 6.2
New Housing Price Index

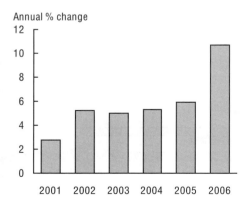

Annual % change

Note: Index base period 1997=100.
Source: Statistics Canada, CANSIM table 327-0005.

GDP for the construction industry

	2002	2006
	\$ millions (1997) constant	
Construction	**54,620**	**67,657**
Residential building construction	18,307	22,193
Non-residential building construction	11,189	11,649
Engineering, repair and other construction activities	25,124	33,815

Source: Statistics Canada, CANSIM table 379-0017.

interprovincial migration, rising employment, international immigration and relatively low mortgage rates.

The Canada Mortgage and Housing Corporation (CMHC) tracks the average price of new single- and semi-detached homes. In the summer of 2006, the average price nationally was $381,000, up from $342,000 a year earlier, an increase of 11%. In Toronto, the average price was $631,585. In Calgary and Edmonton, prices rose to averages of $359,286 and $284,521, while the average price in Vancouver hit $763,076. The lowest average price of a new single- and semi-detached home in a metropolitan area was in Trois-Rivières, at $159,250.

At the end of 2006, Statistics Canada's New Housing Price Index (NHPI)—which measures changes over time in contractors' selling prices of new houses—was 147.5. This means that the price of new homes has risen 47.5% since 1997, the base year of the index. Unsurprisingly, the NHPI shows that the cost of new homes in Calgary shot up an incredible 42.4% since December 2005. Edmonton followed closely with a 41.5% increase in the same period, and Saskatoon was third at 16.1%. The national average increase was 10.7%.

Non-residential construction

Construction activity on non-residential properties was high for a sixth consecutive year in 2006, due in large part to the booming economy of Western Canada. Among the nine provinces seeing growth in non-residential construction, Alberta showed the largest gain, at 40%, followed by British Columbia at 27%. Together, Alberta and British Columbia accounted for about 80% of the total increase in Canada's non-residential investment.

Much of the increase in non-residential construction was due to higher investment in commercial buildings, which rose 14% to $20.4 billion. The main factor behind this was the strong increase in office building construction, up 23% to $7.6 billion.

Warehouse construction also jumped— almost 29% to $2.7 billion. The increase likely stemmed from declining vacancy rates for office buildings in large urban centres, and the strong performance by retailers and wholesalers, which was supported by growth in consumer spending and international trade. Investment in hospitals and health clinics rose 16%, the sixth consecutive annual increase in this category.

Mortgage approvals

Low interest rates have been motivating many Canadians to seek mortgages to finance the

purchase of a home. Indeed, the value of mortgage loans approved by CMHC and approved lenders rose to $182.1 billion in 2005, up 11% from the previous year. Loan approvals rose 2%, and the average loan amount in 2005 was 11% higher than in 2004.

In 2005, lenders approved loans on 135,500 new dwelling units, down slightly from 135,700 in 2004. The most dramatic increase occurred from 2001 to 2002, when the number of approved units jumped from 111,700 to 139,900.

The number of approvals on existing residential properties in 2005 remained relatively stable from 2004, at 1.1 million dwelling units. In 2001, 812,300 units were approved. New and existing single-detached dwellings received the bulk of approvals in 2005.

The jump in the value of mortgages approved also led to an increase in mortgage credit— the total mortgage debt that Canadians hold—which grew to $687 billion by 2006, up from $628 billion in 2005.

Chart 6.3
Mortgage loan approvals for new homes

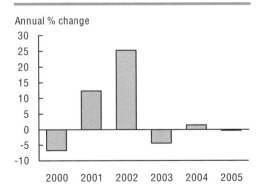

Annual % change

Notes: Data are limited to fully documented loans approved by CMHC or by approved lenders.
Excludes Nunavut.
Source: Statistics Canada, CANSIM table 027-0017.

Selected sources

Statistics Canada

- *Between the Producer and Retailer: A Review of Wholesale Trade for 2005.* Occasional. 11-621-MWE2006040

- *Building Permits.* Monthly. 64-001-XWE

- *Canadian Economic Observer.* Monthly. 11-010-XWB

Other

- Canadian Institute of Mortgage Brokers and Lenders

- Canada Mortgage and Housing Corporation

- U.S. Census Bureau

The greying of construction

Construction, like many industries, has an aging work force. More baby boomers are working beyond 55 or are re-entering the job market after retirement. In addition, fewer young people are pursuing careers in the building trades.

Employment in construction grew steadily from 824,000 in 2001 to just over 1 million in 2005. By July 2006, it reached a peak of 1.2 million employees. Most of these employees—including salespeople, managers and administrative support workers—were aged 25 to 45, with an average age of 39.7 years. The accommodation and food services industry had the lowest average age, 31.8, and agriculture had the highest, 43.9.

In all industries, the number of workers aged 55 and older rose 6.2% from 2004 to 2005, compared with a 0.7% increase in workers under 55. In 2001, there were 2.7 labour force participants aged 20 to 34 for every participant aged 55 and older, down from 3.7 in 1981.

In 1976, 66,000 people working in the Canadian construction industry were aged 55 and older. By 2005, that number had more than doubled to 137,000. Construction workers aged 15 to 24 numbered 143,400 in 1976, but they declined by almost half to 72,000 during the early 1990s recession. In 2005, this age group in construction rebounded to almost the 1976 levels, reaching 141,900 workers.

Despite this rebound, the skilled trades are viewed as a less viable career option for young people. Since the end of the Second World War, Canada has relied on immigrants to fill skilled trade jobs. A shortfall in workers may hit the construction trades as baby boomers enter their retirement years.

Chart 6.4
Average age of employees, selected industries

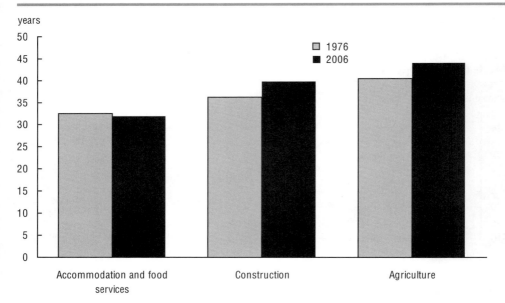

Source: Statistics Canada, Labour Force Survey.

Slowdown in building materials industry

Homeowners who take on small renovations tend to buy their building materials from big box retailers or from dealers who specialize in one product, such as lumber. Construction companies that build housing developments purchase their lumber, steel and other products from wholesalers.

In 2005, wholesalers of building materials recorded sales of more than $66 billion, up 8.5% from 2004. However, this growth was less than half the 20.0% seen in 2003.

Sales of lumber rose 2.5% to $13 billion, a fraction of the 23.8% growth in 2004. Part of this slowdown was lumber prices, which fell 5.0%. Overcapacity in North America, combined with greater world competition, also contributed to the trend. These sales numbers also reflect changes in the housing markets in the United States and Canada. First, U.S. builders are building more

multi-family homes, which use less lumber. Second, housing starts in Canada fell 3.4% in 2005, also crimping demand for lumber.

Metal products, such as wiring and structural steel, showed less growth than lumber in 2005. Wholesalers of metal products had sales of $14 billion, up only 7.1% compared with a 33.3% gain in 2004. Prices began to level out in 2005 after China's entry into steel production.

Wholesalers of building supplies, such as paint and hardware, continued to post strong results, with sales of more than $39 billion in 2005. This was an 11.2% increase, a slight slowdown compared with a 14.7% gain in 2004. This group of wholesalers has experienced virtually uninterrupted growth since the fall of 2003, driven in large part by the strong renovation and construction markets in Canada.

Chart 6.5
Wholesale trade sales growth of building materials

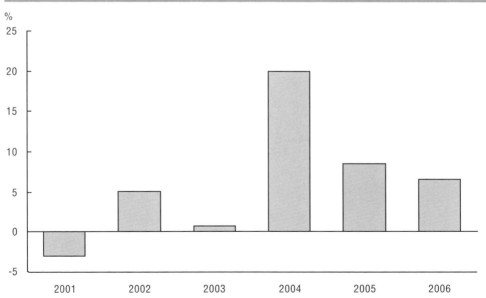

Note: North American Industry Classification System 2002 special aggregation.
Source: Statistics Canada, CANSIM table 081-0010.

Building in North America: Boom or bust?

Are these boom or bust times for North America's construction industry? It depends where you look and which sector you consider.

In 2006, Canada's housing sector benefited from low mortgage rates, a robust job market, strong consumer confidence and a huge demand for housing in Western Canada. From 2005 to 2006, the value of residential construction increased 8.5% to $79.8 billion, although the number of new units approved by municipalities decreased 2.4%.

In the United States, by contrast, the housing sector slowed—despite favourable mortgage rates, steady growth in consumer spending, gains in real disposable income and high consumer confidence. From 2005 to 2006, the value of U.S. residential construction declined just 1.9%, whereas building permits for privately-owned housing dropped 14.9%,

as above-average decreases hit the Midwest (–19.3%) and the West (–19.0%). The drop in housing was the major reason behind the slowdown in U.S. economic growth.

The Canadian economy remained fertile ground in 2006 for non-residential construction. The value of non-residential permits surged 14.5% from 2005, owing to strong retail sales, lower office vacancy rates, low interest rates and record corporate profits. The value of U.S. non-residential construction increased 13.3%, a sign that this sector was not being dampened by the cooler housing market and housing oversupply.

The twin stars of Canada's construction boom were Alberta and British Columbia. Alberta has been in the midst of the strongest period of economic growth ever recorded by a province, thanks to the huge inflow of money from higher oil prices and capital investment.

Chart 6.6
Building permits for housing units, Canada and the United States

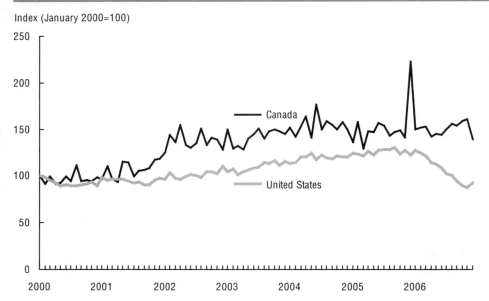

Index (January 2000=100)

Sources: Statistics Canada, CANSIM table 026-0010; United States Census Bureau; and Department of Housing and Urban Development.

Western boom in construction

The economies of the two biggest western provinces, Alberta and British Columbia, continued to expand in 2006. The booming natural resources sector and trade with Asia boosted economic activity in British Columbia, which posted its lowest unemployment rate in 30 years. In Alberta, the population grew by more than 98,000 people from 2005, thanks to an abundance of jobs in natural resources. Coupled with low interest rates, this activity boosted demand for new housing in both provinces.

In British Columbia, new home construction entered its sixth consecutive year of growth in 2006, the longest since the 1985-to-1989 expansion. Housing starts soared from 14,400 units in 2000 to 36,400 units in 2006.

In Alberta, housing starts hit 48,962 in 2006—the highest number since 1978.

Calgary had the largest increase, up 25% compared to 2005. Increases in residential and non-residential construction led to a shortage of workers in the building trades. However, new opportunities in construction began to draw people from other industries, such as farming, manufacturing, and accommodation and food services.

In 2006, wages continued to rise to reflect the demand for construction workers. The basic union wage for a carpenter in Calgary in 2001 was $27.50 per hour; that climbed to $31.04 by the end of 2006.

In Winnipeg, where the demand for new construction was not as intense as in other cities, the average wage for a carpenter at then end of 2006 was $24.07 per hour, up just slightly from $23.70 in 2001.

Chart 6.7
Housing starts, Alberta and British Columbia

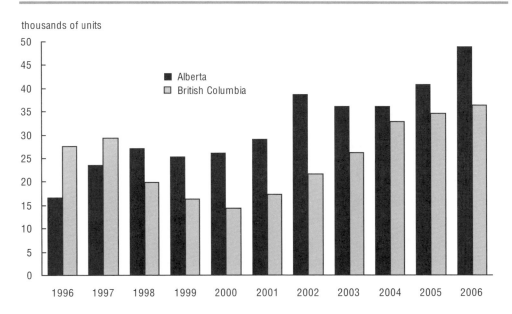

Source: Statistics Canada, CANSIM table 027-0008.

Table 6.1 Housing starts, by province, 1992 to 2006

	1992	1993	1994	1995	1996	1997
	number					
Canada	168,271	155,443	154,057	110,933	124,713	147,040
Newfoundland and Labrador	2,271	2,405	2,243	1,712	2,034	1,696
Prince Edward Island	644	645	669	422	554	470
Nova Scotia	4,673	4,282	4,748	4,168	4,059	3,813
New Brunswick	3,310	3,693	3,203	2,300	2,722	2,702
Quebec	38,228	34,015	34,154	21,885	23,220	25,896
Ontario	55,772	45,140	46,645	35,818	43,062	54,072
Manitoba	2,310	2,425	3,197	1,963	2,318	2,612
Saskatchewan	1,869	1,880	2,098	1,702	2,438	2,757
Alberta	18,573	18,151	17,692	13,906	16,665	23,671
British Columbia	40,621	42,807	39,408	27,057	27,641	29,351

Source: Statistics Canada, CANSIM table 027-0009.

Table 6.2 Value of building permits, by province and territory, 1992 to 2006

	1992	1993	1994	1995	1996	1997
	$ millions					
Canada	26,957.1	25,586.3	27,636.7	24,589.3	26,155.4	30,838.2
Newfoundland and Labrador	242.5	255.4	262.7	201.7	224.1	213.6
Prince Edward Island	132.1	112.5	112.7	95.2	95.8	110.0
Nova Scotia	604.9	594.9	669.2	619.6	689.0	630.7
New Brunswick	453.7	427.4	440.5	487.9	441.1	459.0
Quebec	5,207.2	5,375.6	5,898.5	4,947.4	4,938.0	5,133.2
Ontario	9,962.9	8,774.7	10,001.3	9,192.2	9,597.6	12,888.7
Manitoba	541.2	528.6	685.3	525.4	592.3	689.6
Saskatchewan	323.1	326.8	372.3	478.2	543.0	626.8
Alberta	3,105.6	2,713.5	2,740.5	2,506.6	2,883.1	4,446.3
British Columbia	6,255.5	6,389.2	6,317.9	5,401.4	6,053.1	5,543.8
Yukon	71.2	42.2	51.0	74.0	51.8	49.6
Northwest Territories (including Nunavut)	57.1	45.7	84.9	59.6	46.6	46.9
Northwest Territories	..	..	..	..	..	..
Nunavut	..	..	..	..	..	..

Source: Statistics Canada, CANSIM table 026-0003.

1998	1999	2000	2001	2002	2003	2004	2005	2006
				number				
137,439	149,968	151,653	162,733	205,034	218,426	233,431	225,481	227,395
1,450	1,371	1,459	1,788	2,419	2,692	2,870	2,498	2,234
524	616	710	675	775	814	919	862	738
3,137	4,250	4,432	4,092	4,970	5,096	4,717	4,775	4,896
2,447	2,776	3,079	3,462	3,862	4,489	3,947	3,959	4,085
23,138	25,742	24,695	27,682	42,452	50,289	58,448	50,910	47,877
53,830	67,235	71,521	73,282	83,597	85,180	85,114	78,795	73,417
2,895	3,133	2,560	2,963	3,617	4,206	4,440	4,731	5,028
2,965	3,089	2,513	2,381	2,963	3,315	3,781	3,437	3,715
27,122	25,447	26,266	29,174	38,754	36,171	36,270	40,847	48,962
19,931	16,309	14,418	17,234	21,625	26,174	32,925	34,667	36,443

1998	1999	2000	2001	2002	2003	2004	2005	2006
				$ millions				
33,340.8	35,736.1	36,950.1	40,856.1	47,262.1	50,772.0	55,578.6	60,750.7	66,265.8
252.7	296.8	282.9	298.3	383.3	421.0	501.2	494.1	538.4
116.1	140.9	98.8	217.2	146.2	178.1	223.8	244.0	207.0
637.1	907.2	878.5	699.9	877.3	1,014.1	1,125.8	1,188.0	1,291.4
481.0	481.2	484.6	535.1	663.8	696.3	797.3	829.0	933.3
5,897.4	5,939.6	6,272.0	7,571.1	8,628.4	10,090.9	11,629.6	11,288.0	11,878.3
13,839.8	16,732.5	17,556.5	19,069.3	22,281.4	23,235.2	23,905.3	24,129.6	23,292.2
1,031.8	879.4	853.9	739.2	888.9	1,065.0	1,150.4	1,128.5	1,378.8
672.9	721.6	609.0	703.3	708.6	772.6	770.0	905.7	1,138.6
5,552.2	4,801.9	5,296.4	5,911.7	6,846.5	6,667.2	7,327.1	10,201.7	13,875.7
4,739.6	4,695.5	4,492.0	4,954.8	5,659.4	6,394.2	7,938.7	10,182.9	11,541.5
39.9	48.8	55.5	49.8	31.3	52.6	75.9	77.3	95.6
80.2	..	90.6	..	..	..	..	..	..
..	..	23.0	76.0	91.6	86.2	105.3	68.7	37.7
..	..	47.2	30.4	55.4	98.6	28.1	13.2	57.4

Table 6.3 Investment in non-residential building construction, by census metropolitan area, 2002 to 2006

	2002	2003	2004	2005	2006
	$ millions, not seasonally adjusted				
All census metropolitan areas	**19,163.6**	**19,475.6**	**20,810.9**	**22,498.5**	**25,350.2**
St. John's	156.2	167.5	188.2	244.3	222.5
Halifax	179.0	233.9	306.1	461.0	601.3
Saint John	57.5	70.4	95.3	72.6	103.4
Saguenay	119.6	135.6	97.3	91.3	124.3
Québec	508.7	494.0	546.7	624.3	637.2
Sherbrooke	133.2	131.7	124.6	111.8	150.0
Trois-Rivières	109.6	168.4	145.9	103.1	131.3
Montréal	3,059.1	2,742.9	2,868.4	2,889.9	2,756.4
Ottawa–Gatineau	1,544.8	1,522.1	1,348.5	1,280.0	1,580.0
Quebec part	171.0	225.7	185.6	242.7	187.4
Ontario part	1,373.8	1,296.4	1,162.9	1,037.3	1,392.7
Kingston	120.9	163.6	141.5	162.3	116.0
Oshawa	263.9	411.8	485.2	488.2	387.5
Toronto	4,772.7	5,034.4	6,188.3	6,435.6	6,252.9
Hamilton	693.3	698.6	741.1	571.8	621.2
St. Catharines–Niagara	405.2	407.4	356.5	281.7	275.1
Kitchener	693.2	584.2	534.5	635.7	503.2
London	547.2	614.3	535.8	561.5	424.3
Windsor	393.2	403.7	303.7	279.8	328.2
Greater Sudbury / Grand Sudbury	174.8	170.5	91.8	132.5	115.9
Thunder Bay	173.6	148.5	118.8	94.6	112.8
Winnipeg	420.4	557.7	659.9	684.7	884.5
Regina	180.0	233.4	226.7	232.0	316.7
Saskatoon	270.9	230.0	219.8	258.3	404.0
Calgary	1,222.1	1,234.4	1,357.8	1,828.7	2,653.2
Edmonton	942.0	898.5	1,002.5	1,248.3	1,683.1
Abbotsford	153.5	103.9	80.3	140.2	261.1
Vancouver	1,619.5	1,628.4	1,685.1	2,327.3	2,807.7
Victoria	249.4	285.8	360.4	257.0	341.0

Source: Statistics Canada, CANSIM table 026-0016.

Table 6.4 Capital expenditures for construction, by sector, 2003 to 2007

	Actual			Preliminary actual	Intentions
	2003	2004	2005	2006[1]	2007[2]
			$ millions		
Canada	**136,763.6**	**154,125.2**	**171,964.8**	**193,276.3**	**202,392.2**
Agriculture, forestry, fishing and hunting	1,471.0	1,476.2	1,359.4	1,330.2	1,342.6
Mining and oil and gas extraction	24,588.2	29,942.4	39,397.4	45,938.8	43,714.6
Utilities	8,534.4	8,843.5	9,861.4	12,357.2	15,218.0
Construction	444.1	500.5	531.0	571.0	618.3
Manufacturing	2,870.6	2,611.6	2,235.7	2,326.8	2,484.2
Wholesale trade	983.4	900.8	1,106.7	1,281.3	1,433.1
Retail trade	2,894.4	4,063.5	3,665.8	3,918.5	4,194.1
Transportation and warehousing	3,543.1	3,510.7	3,966.3	5,483.5	6,454.9
Information and cultural industries	2,243.1	2,411.1	2,693.5	2,238.4	2,216.5
Finance and insurance	580.0	525.9	809.0	637.5	871.3
Real estate and rental and leasing	2,713.4	3,308.3	3,550.1	4,739.9	5,601.6
Professional, scientific and technical services	332.9	358.2	330.8	441.8	450.4
Management of companies and enterprises	25.1	43.4	26.5	22.2	32.0
Administrative and support, waste management and remediation services	205.2	214.2	248.8	248.8	325.7
Educational services	4,358.4	4,355.1	4,707.7	5,088.0	5,496.3
Health care and social assistance	3,371.2	3,061.0	3,708.7	4,099.4	4,459.7
Arts, entertainment and recreation	518.3	901.7	692.6	610.1	1,336.4
Accommodation and food services	1,099.1	1,231.5	1,508.6	1,750.2	1,820.5
Housing	61,607.5	70,060.2	73,574.9	79,857.2	80,971.1
Public administration	13,978.2	15,316.1	17,511.6	19,851.5	22,857.6
Other services (excluding public administration)	402.0	489.1	478.4	483.9	493.6

Notes: The Capital Expenditures Survey collects data on the intentions for capital investment and the expenditures for the previous two years.
North American Industry Classification System, 2002.
1. Data reflect the preliminary actuals for capital expenditures for 2006.
2. Data reflect the intentions for capital expenditures for 2007.
Source: Statistics Canada, CANSIM table 029-0005.

Table 6.5 Labour force employed in construction, by province, 2001 to 2006

	2001	2002	2003	2004	2005	2006
	thousands					
Canada	**824.3**	**865.2**	**906.0**	**951.7**	**1,019.5**	**1,069.7**
Newfoundland and Labrador	10.5	9.3	9.5	11.7	12.4	12.9
Prince Edward Island	4.5	4.3	4.2	4.1	4.7	5.7
Nova Scotia	24.6	24.0	24.5	28.2	27.7	27.3
New Brunswick	18.7	19.7	19.2	19.4	18.6	21.1
Quebec	137.6	153.4	162.9	164.5	179.2	186.1
Ontario	336.3	344.5	369.1	367.6	394.8	405.2
Manitoba	27.1	26.0	26.9	27.7	28.2	29.9
Saskatchewan	23.1	24.8	23.3	24.0	26.3	29.6
Alberta	131.3	141.4	146.6	160.5	159.7	172.6
British Columbia	110.7	118.1	119.8	144.0	168.0	179.3

Note: Annual data.
Source: Statistics Canada, CANSIM table 282-0008.

Table 6.6 Production of building materials, 2002 to 2006

	2002	2003	2004	2005	2006
	thousands of cubic metres				
Dry sawn lumber	79,803.7	79,319.3	84,589.6	82,888.9	80,870.4
	thousands of metric bundles				
Asphalt shingles, all sizes	43,391.0	39,747.0	43,639.0	40,284.7	44,590.3
	thousands of metric tonnes				
Cement	13,081.0	13,418.0	13,862.9	14,179.4	14,335.5
Steel pipe and tubing	2,220.1	2,431.6	2,647.2	2,837.1	2,948.5

Note: Standard Classification of Goods.
Source: Statistics Canada, CANSIM tables 303-0001, 303-0003, 303-0006, 303-0009, 303-0046, 303-0052 and 303-0060.

Crime and justice

7

Enforcement of laws affects all Canadians—whether a police officer is arresting someone in a small town or the Royal Canadian Mounted Police are monitoring security on Parliament Hill. It is also a big-ticket item for governments: federal, provincial, territorial and municipal governments spent more than $12 billion on policing, courts, legal aid, prosecutions and adult corrections in 2002/2003. (Calculating the total cost is difficult because all levels of government help pay the justice bill.) Policing accounted for 61% of justice costs; adult corrections, 22%; courts, 9%; legal aid, 5%; and criminal prosecutions, 3%.

The amount of crime taking place is measured by the crime rate—the number of reported incidents per 100,000 population in a year. Canada's crime rate in 2005 was 7,761 offences per 100,000, down 5% from 2004.

The decrease was primarily driven by a lower rate of non-violent crimes, such as counterfeiting, break-ins and auto thefts. Police services reported a 6% decrease for property crimes, a 7% drop each for motor vehicle thefts and break-ins, and a 6% drop for thefts under $5,000.

Violent crime accounted for 12% of *Criminal Code* offences. The homicide rate rose in 2005 to its highest level in nine years, but the overall rate of violent crime, which also includes attempted murder, assault, robbery, sexual assault, other sexual offences and kidnapping, was unchanged.

Provincial crime rates ranged from a low of 5,780 incidents per 100,000 population in Ontario to a high of 14,320 incidents in Saskatchewan.

Saskatchewan's violent crime rate was the highest among the provinces for an

Chart 7.1
Violent crimes, by province

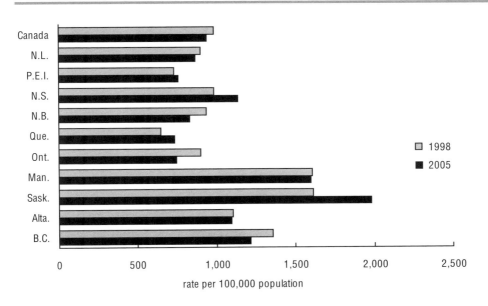

Source: Statistics Canada, CANSIM table 252-0013.

eighth year in a row and was 24% higher than the next highest, Manitoba. Although Quebec's violent crime rate rose 2% in 2005, it reported the lowest rates among the provinces over the past decade.

Homicide rate rises

Police services reported 658 homicides in 2005, or about two victims per 100,000 population. After reaching a 30-year low in 2003, Canada's homicide rate climbed 4% in 2005 to its highest point in a decade. The most substantial increases in the number of homicides were reported in Ontario, where 31 more homicides occurred than in 2004; the next highest, Alberta, had 23 more than in 2004.

Homicide victims are more likely to be killed by someone they know than by a stranger. In the 478 solved homicides in 2005, about 50% of the victims were killed by an acquaintance, about 30% by a family member and about 20% by a stranger.

Most homicide victims in 2005 were male—480 males versus 178 females. The victimization rate for males peaked at 25

Chart 7.2
Homicides in Canada

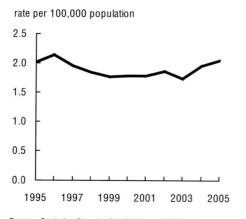

rate per 100,000 population

Source: Statistics Canada, CANSIM table 252-0013.

Violent crimes

	2004	2005
	% of violent crime	
Total	100.0	100.0
Homicide	0.2	0.2
Attempted murder	0.2	0.3
Assaults (level 1 to 3)[1]	77.5	77.1
Sexual assault	7.6	7.7
Other sexual offences	0.9	0.9
Robbery	9.1	9.4
Other crimes of violence[2]	4.5	4.4

1. Constitutes intentional application of force without consent, attempt or threat to apply force to another person, or openly wearing a weapon (or an imitation) while accosting or impeding another person.
2. Includes unlawfully causing bodily harm, discharging a firearm with intent, abduction, assault against police officers or other peace or public officers, as well as other assaults.

Source: Statistics Canada, CANSIM table 252-0013.

to 29 years; for females, it peaked at 30 to 39 years. Ninety percent of persons accused of homicide were male, and the rate of accused peaked at 18 to 24 years of age for both males and females.

Since the mid-1980s, firearms have been used in about one out of three homicides each year. Firearms were used to kill 222 Canadians in 2005, 49 more than in 2004. Homicides committed with a firearm increased in all regions except Manitoba, British Columbia and the territories. Since the early 1970s, however, the type of firearm used in homicides has changed. Rifles and shotguns have steadily become less common, handguns have become more so.

Homicides aside, firearms are rarely used in most other crimes in Canada.

Gang-related homicides

Data about the extent of gang activity in Canada are very limited. And while it is generally accepted that organized crime exists in Canada, the full extent of it is unknown. Gang-related homicides—which stem from the activities of organized crime groups and street gangs—gained steadily from 4% of all homicides in 1994 to 15% in 2003, then fell back to 11% in 2004. In 2005, however, the number of gang-related homicides rose to 107, or 16% of all homicides. The largest increase was in Ontario, where gang-related homicides more than doubled from 14 in 2004 to 31 in 2005.

In 2005, the highest numbers of gang-related homicides occurred in Toronto (23), Edmonton (16), Montréal (15) and Calgary (9). Of all gang-related killings, 69% were committed with a firearm, usually a handgun, compared with 27% of non gang-related homicides.

Youth crime rate declines

The youth crime rate fell 6% from 2004 to 2005, and youth violent crime declined 2%. During the same period, the rate of youths—those aged 12 to 17 years—who were charged decreased 6%, and those cleared otherwise fell 7%. Changes in legislation—such as the *Youth Criminal Justice Act* (YCJA), which came into force in 2003—can significantly affect the number of youths who

are diverted from further exposure in the justice system. The YCJA contains provisions that are designed to allow youth who have committed less serious offences to be diverted from courts and custodial facilities; serious offenders serve longer sentences.

Since the introduction of the YCJA, the proportion of apprehended youths who are formally charged has dropped, from 56% in 2002—when the *Young Offenders Act* was still in effect—to 43% in 2005.

Youths accused of crimes are not always formally charged, even though police might have sufficient evidence to do so. Police have a range of alternatives to laying formal charges, mainly taking no further action, issuing an informal warning, referring the youth to community programs or issuing a formal police caution.

Selected sources

Statistics Canada

- *Child and Spousal Support: Maintenance Enforcement Survey Statistics.* Annual. 85-228-XIE

- *Family Violence in Canada: A Statistical Profile.* Annual. 85-224-XIE

- *Juristat.* Irregular. 85-002-XIE

- *Measuring Violence Against Women: Statistical Trends.* Occasional. 85-570-XIE

- *Police Resources in Canada.* Annual. 85-225-XIE

Chart 7.3
Youths charged with crimes

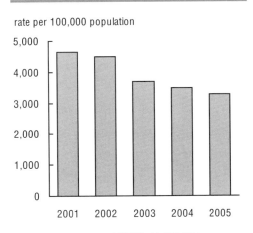

rate per 100,000 population

Source: Statistics Canada, CANSIM table 252-0014.

Child and spousal support enforcement

People who are separated or divorced can find it difficult to collect court-ordered spousal and child support payments. Federal guidelines on child support emphasize the need for children to benefit from the financial means of both spouses after a separation.

About one-half of all support obligations for spousal and child support payments in Canada—court-ordered and voluntary—are now registered with 'maintenance enforcement programs' (MEPs). Although MEPs are intended to help people collect these payments, more difficult cases may still end up in court. More than 90% of MEP cases involve support for children.

Nearly 407,800 cases were enrolled in MEPs in March 2006—data are excluded for Newfoundland and Labrador, Manitoba and Nunavut. The types of clients and

their obligations, enforcement powers and practices, enrolment procedures and payments processes all differ from one province or territory to another. And not all cases are automatically enrolled in an MEP.

Most MEP cases with monthly support payments involve amounts of $400 or less. Fewer than 5% require a monthly payment over $1,000. Most cases—anywhere from 56% to 78%—are in compliance with their regular monthly payments.

As of March 31, 2006, from 46% to 72% of support cases had payments in arrears when the parties enrolled, be it months or years earlier. However, many of these cases have paid all or some of the amounts owed. MEPs in seven provinces collected $604 million in regular payments, excluding arrears, in the year ending March 31, 2006. Most of the money was for the benefit of children.

Chart 7.4
Cases enrolled in maintenance enforcement programs, by regular monthly payment, selected provinces, 2006

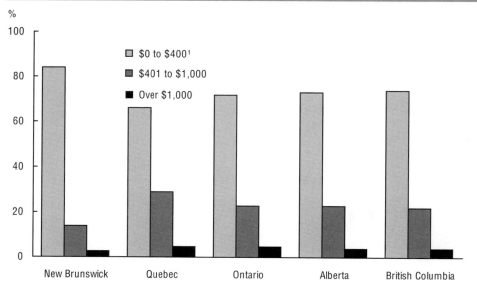

%

Legend:
- $0 to $400[1]
- $401 to $1,000
- Over $1,000

Provinces: New Brunswick, Quebec, Ontario, Alberta, British Columbia

Note: Payment due at March 31.
1. Cases may have a $0 monthly payment because they have no regular ongoing obligation, they only have arrears, or they have a different payment schedule, such as quarterly.
Source: Statistics Canada, Catalogue no. 85-228-XIE.

Violence against women

Women are at greater risk than men of being the victims of the most severe forms of spousal violence, including being killed by a spouse, sexual assault and criminal harassment (also called stalking). Although men are more likely than women to be killed, physically attacked and robbed by strangers and acquaintances in a public place, women are at greater risk of being victims of violence in their homes from an intimate partner.

From 1975 to 2004, over three times more women than men were victims of spousal homicide—2,178 women compared with 638 men. In this period, men were twice as likely as women to be charged with first degree murder in spousal homicide cases.

According to the 1999 and 2004 General Social Surveys (GSS), fewer than one-third of self-reported female and male victims of spousal violence seek police help. Reasons

for not reporting the abuse are similar for both men and women, but significantly more male (44%) than female victims (27%) say they do not want anyone to find out about the violence.

In 2004, 86% of victims of police-reported sexual offences were female. Data consistently show that women under 25 are at greatest risk of being sexually assaulted. In 2005, police reported over 23,000 sexual assault incidents—this rate was little changed from 2004. However, the 2004 GSS showed that 88% of sexual assaults go unreported.

Women are more likely than men to be victims of stalking. Data from 68 police departments show incidents of criminal harassment rose steadily from 1998 to 2004. This increase may indicate a rise in stalking, but it may also reflect a rise in reporting or changes in the application of the law.

Chart 7.5
Victims of violence, by type of violence and sex, 2004

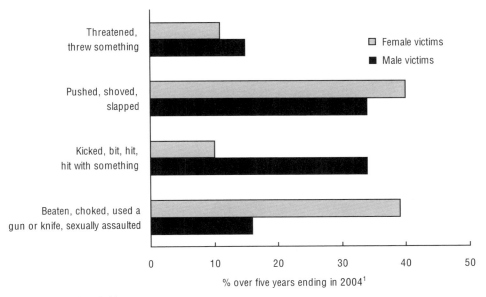

% over five years ending in 2004[1]

1. Population aged 15 and older.
Source: Statistics Canada, Catalogue no. 85-570-XIE.

Shifts in the adult custodial population

Since the 1980s, the profile of Canada's adult custodial population in the provincial/territorial correctional system has shifted dramatically. For the first time, the number of adults held on remand or other temporary detention and the number of sentenced offenders were virtually equal.

On an average day in 2005, about 9,800 adults were in provincial/territorial custody serving a sentence, while another 9,900 adults were in remanded custody or in another form of temporary detention. Only a decade earlier, offenders serving a prison sentence made up 72% of the provincial/territorial custodial population; the remand population accounted for the remaining 28%.

This represents an 83% increase in remand counts from 1995 to 2005. During the same period, sentenced custody dropped 31%. Several factors may be contributing to the rising number of remanded individuals. For example, bail might be more frequently denied because of changing practices and policies. Also, processing cases in criminal courts has become more lengthy and complex, keeping adults in remand longer.

From 1995 to 2005, the proportion of remanded adults who served between one week and one month rose from 20% to 25%, and adults who were held in remanded custody for more than a month increased from 14% to 22%.

The conditional sentence, introduced as a punitive option in 1996, is likely contributing to the decreasing number of adults who serve their sentence in custody. The number of admissions to conditional sentences nearly doubled from 1997 to 2005—offenders who would have been admitted to a detention facility may instead be serving a conditional sentence in the community.

Chart 7.6
Adult correctional population, by status

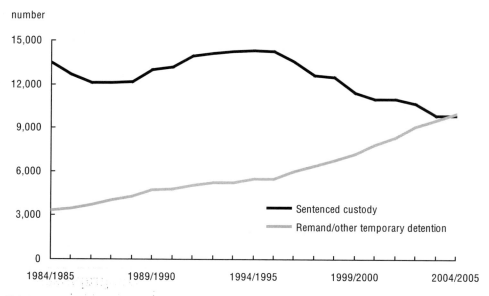

number

Note: Average annual actual in-counts in provincial/territorial custody.
Source: Statistics Canada, CANSIM table 251-0005.

Police services: size and spending

Canada had almost 62,500 police officers in May 2006—or one officer for every 520 Canadians—as the number of police reached its highest level in over a decade. However, for the past 30 years, police strength has remained relatively stable.

The national rate of 192 officers per 100,000 population in 2006 was 7% below the peak of 206 reached in 1976. Saskatchewan, which has had the highest provincial crime rate since 1997, had the highest police strength in Canada for a sixth consecutive year, at 205 officers per 100,000 population in 2006. Quebec reported the next greatest police strength and had one of the lowest crime rates in the country. The lowest levels of police strength in 2006 were in Newfoundland and Labrador—156 police officers per 100,000—and in Prince Edward Island, 159 per 100,000. Crime rates in the two provinces are relatively low.

From 1996 to 2006, the number of women working as police officers grew three times faster than the number of men. In 2006, 11,200 women worked as police officers, 6% more than in 2005. With these increases, almost one out of five police officers were women. In 2006, the highest proportions of female officers were in British Columbia, 21%, and in Quebec, 20%. Prince Edward Island, New Brunswick and Manitoba had the lowest shares, about 14% each.

Policing expenditures totalled $9.3 billion, or $288 per person, in 2005. Adjusted for inflation, this was a 4% increase from 2004. For every dollar spent in all justice sectors, 61 cents goes to policing. The federal, provincial/territorial and municipal governments share the responsibility and costs for policing.

Chart 7.7
Police officers, by sex

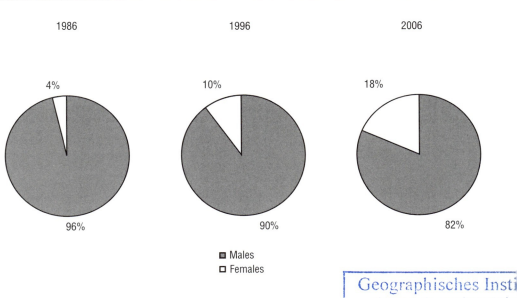

1986   1996   2006

4%   10%   18%

96%   90%   82%

☐ Males
☐ Females

Source: Statistics Canada, CANSIM table 254-0003.

Table 7.1 Crimes, by type of offence and by province and territory, 2005

	Canada	Newfoundland and Labrador	Prince Edward Island	Nova Scotia	New Brunswick
	rate per 100,000 population				
All offences	**8,512.6**	**6,603.8**	**8,625.6**	**8,963.5**	**7,449.5**
Criminal Code offences (excluding traffic offences)	**7,761.1**	6,088.8	7,985.5	8,345.2	6,755.5
Crimes against the person	**942.9**	868.7	761.7	1,138.2	834.0
Homicide	**2.0**	1.7	0.0	2.1	1.2
Attempted murder	**2.4**	0.6	0.0	4.2	1.5
Assault (level 1 to 3)[1]	**727.4**	728.5	648.7	935.1	685.6
Sexual assault	**72.2**	84.5	64.4	82.6	68.0
Other sexual offences	**8.5**	4.1	7.2	6.9	14.0
Robbery	**88.8**	28.9	12.3	75.4	32.7
Other crimes against the person[2]	**41.5**	20.3	29.0	31.9	31.1
Property crimes	**3,737.6**	2,534.7	3,468.2	3,625.7	2,722.9
Break and enter	**804.2**	813.6	611.8	778.1	647.6
Motor vehicle theft	**496.1**	150.2	165.8	280.6	191.5
Theft over $5,000	**54.2**	22.9	26.1	40.7	45.5
Theft $5,000 and under	**1,985.5**	1,296.2	2,331.4	2,009.4	1,518.6
Possession of stolen goods	**104.9**	35.9	55.8	213.9	52.5
Fraud	**292.7**	215.9	277.3	302.9	267.2
Other *Criminal Code* offences	**3,080.7**	2,685.5	3,755.6	3,581.3	3,198.6
Criminal Code traffic offences	**368.0**	231.0	472.8	339.6	359.3
Impaired driving	**234.3**	169.0	399.0	278.8	283.2
Other *Criminal Code* traffic offences[3]	**133.6**	62.0	73.9	60.8	76.1
Federal statute offences	**383.5**	283.9	167.3	278.7	334.7
Drugs[4]	**285.9**	164.0	134.7	214.7	239.4
Other federal statute offences	**97.6**	120.0	32.6	64.0	95.3

1. Constitutes the intentional application of force without consent, the attempt or threat to apply force to another person or openly wearing a weapon (or an imitation) while accosting or impeding another person.
2. Includes unlawfully causing bodily harm, discharging firearms with intent, abductions, assaults against police officers, assaults against other peace or public officers and other assaults.
3. Includes dangerous operation of a motor vehicle, boat, vessel or aircraft; dangerous operation of a motor vehicle, boat, vessel or aircraft causing bodily harm or death; driving a motor vehicle while prohibited; and failure to stop or remain.
4. Includes possession, trafficking, importation and production.
Source: Statistics Canada, CANSIM table 252-0013.

Quebec	Ontario	Manitoba	Saskatchewan	Alberta	British Columbia	Yukon	Northwest Territories	Nunavut
			rate per 100,000 population					
6,744.9	**6,336.7**	**12,554.1**	**15,956.2**	**10,841.4**	**13,104.4**	**24,183.6**	**44,037.0**	**34,292.5**
6,032.1	5,779.8	11,743.1	14,319.5	10,023.4	11,946.6	22,399.0	41,245.2	32,782.1
739.3	747.8	1,599.7	1,983.4	1,096.0	1,214.5	3,088.3	6,614.4	7,041.9
1.3	1.7	4.2	4.3	3.4	2.3	3.2	0.0	6.7
3.5	1.7	1.6	5.4	1.7	2.5	6.5	4.7	16.7
524.7	558.1	1,253.0	1,625.9	877.2	977.9	2,765.6	5,942.0	5,974.9
65.0	62.2	111.9	131.5	69.0	80.3	180.7	407.2	796.9
14.1	4.8	7.5	16.4	6.5	8.9	19.4	23.3	26.7
88.9	79.1	170.4	125.0	91.3	108.6	51.6	34.9	20.0
41.9	40.2	51.0	74.8	47.0	34.1	61.3	202.4	200.1
3,132.8	2,807.7	4,994.7	5,483.6	4,874.0	6,234.5	6,028.1	6,484.1	5,554.8
857.7	545.0	1,122.5	1,468.2	891.6	1,166.1	1,603.9	2,284.7	2,844.1
507.3	314.8	1,205.9	621.4	651.9	818.0	477.6	639.8	546.8
66.7	46.3	58.4	52.1	67.8	52.6	113.0	76.8	46.7
1,425.7	1,523.5	2,315.2	2,772.4	2,669.3	3,677.6	3,475.5	3,029.2	1,830.5
38.3	100.8	85.9	193.6	177.0	160.3	116.2	153.6	66.7
237.1	277.4	206.8	375.9	416.3	360.0	242.0	300.1	220.1
2,160.0	2,224.2	5,148.8	6,852.6	4,053.5	4,497.7	13,282.6	28,146.7	20,185.4
394.9	253.2	328.7	998.4	486.3	434.8	1,232.7	1,277.3	596.8
216.9	141.6	252.5	520.2	364.4	335.6	1,013.3	1,056.3	480.1
178.0	111.6	76.2	478.2	121.9	99.2	219.4	221.0	116.7
317.9	303.8	482.2	638.4	331.6	723.0	551.8	1,514.6	913.6
252.4	225.1	163.2	310.2	258.2	606.7	309.8	1,019.0	816.9
65.5	78.7	319.0	328.1	73.4	116.3	242.0	495.6	96.7

Table 7.2 Crimes, by type of offence, 2000 to 2005

	2000	2001	2002	2003	2004	2005
	rate per 100,000 population					
All offences	**8,432.6**	**8,453.7**	**8,504.0**	**8,902.5**	**8,954.9**	**8,512.6**
Criminal Code offences (excluding traffic offences)	7,666.5	7,655.4	7,705.6	8,144.1	8,165.8	7,761.1
Crimes against the person	984.4	983.8	968.8	965.2	945.0	942.9
Homicide	1.8	1.8	1.9	1.7	2.0	2.0
Attempted murder	2.5	2.3	2.2	2.2	2.1	2.4
Assault (level 1 to 3)[1]	761.6	763.9	751.3	747.7	732.7	727.4
Sexual assault	78.2	77.5	78.1	74.3	72.1	72.2
Other sexual offences	10.2	8.7	8.8	8.1	8.2	8.5
Robbery	88.1	88.0	85.0	89.8	86.0	88.8
Other crimes against the person[2]	42.1	41.7	41.6	41.4	42.1	41.5
Property crimes	4,080.9	4,003.5	3,973.2	4,121.5	3,971.9	3,737.6
Break and enter	955.9	900.9	878.4	899.7	862.8	804.2
Motor vehicle theft	522.4	543.5	516.1	550.1	531.6	496.1
Theft over $5,000	69.6	67.2	63.2	61.3	53.1	54.2
Theft $5,000 and under	2,160.5	2,126.3	2,127.1	2,212.3	2,107.9	1,985.5
Possession of stolen goods	93.0	86.9	95.8	104.7	111.8	104.9
Fraud	279.6	278.8	292.7	293.4	304.8	292.7
Other *Criminal Code* offences	2,601.2	2,668.1	2,763.6	3,057.5	3,248.9	3,080.7
Criminal Code traffic offences	366.4	387.6	374.8	369.8	377.3	368.0
Impaired driving	258.2	266.7	255.1	245.2	251.3	234.3
Other traffic offences[3]	108.2	120.9	119.6	124.7	126.0	133.6
Federal statute offences	399.8	410.7	423.6	388.6	411.7	383.5
Drugs[4]	287.0	288.2	295.7	274.1	305.3	285.9
Other federal statute offences	112.7	122.5	127.9	114.5	106.4	97.6

1. Constitutes the intentional application of force without consent, the attempt or threat to apply force to another person or openly wearing a weapon (or an imitation) while accosting or impeding another person.
2. Includes unlawfully causing bodily harm, discharging firearms with intent, abductions, assaults against police officers, assaults against other peace or public officers and other assaults.
3. Includes dangerous operation of a motor vehicle, boat, vessel or aircraft; dangerous operation of a motor vehicle, boat, vessel or aircraft causing bodily harm or death; driving a motor vehicle while prohibited; and failure to stop or remain.
4. Includes possession, trafficking, importation and production.
Source: Statistics Canada, CANSIM table 252-0013.

Table 7.3 Persons charged, by type of offence, 1995 and 2005

	1995			2005		
	Youth and adults charged	Youths charged	Adults charged	Youth and adults charged	Youths charged	Adults charged
	rate per 100,000 population					
All offences	**2,781.2**	**5,402.4**	**2,498.9**	**2,196.5**	**3,297.9**	**2,084.8**
Criminal Code offences (excluding traffic offences)	**2,158.8**	5,060.8	1,846.3	**1,698.4**	2,864.2	1,580.2
Crimes against the person	**570.2**	941.2	530.3	**492.1**	782.4	462.6
Homicide	**2.3**	2.6	2.3	**2.0**	2.5	1.9
Attempted murder	**3.3**	3.6	3.3	**2.0**	1.8	2.0
Assault (level 1 to 3)[1]	**437.1**	666.8	412.4	**384.7**	549.0	368.1
Sexual assault	**44.1**	66.5	41.7	**28.4**	48.2	26.4
Other sexual offences	**4.9**	8.0	4.5	**2.6**	5.6	2.2
Robbery	**40.9**	148.3	29.3	**38.0**	128.5	28.8
Other crimes against the person[2]	**37.7**	45.5	36.8	**34.3**	46.7	33.1
Property crimes	**926.5**	2,856.4	718.7	**533.4**	1,045.1	481.5
Break and enter	**190.5**	782.4	126.8	**92.9**	316.9	70.1
Motor vehicle theft	**63.2**	288.4	38.9	**36.4**	127.4	27.1
Theft over $5,000	**18.6**	38.4	16.5	**6.8**	8.3	6.7
Theft $5,000 and under	**433.7**	1,377.7	332.1	**229.6**	372.9	215.1
Possession of stolen goods	**94.6**	273.1	75.3	**88.2**	175.9	79.3
Fraud	**126.0**	96.6	129.2	**79.5**	43.6	83.2
Other *Criminal Code* offences	**662.0**	1,263.2	597.3	**673.0**	1,036.7	636.1
Criminal Code traffic offences	**403.0**	0.0	446.4	**267.4**	0.0	294.6
Impaired driving	**342.8**	0.0	379.8	**215.0**	0.0	236.8
Other Criminal Code traffic offences[3]	**60.2**	0.0	66.6	**52.5**	0.0	57.8
Federal statute offences	**219.4**	341.7	206.3	**230.6**	433.7	210.0
Drugs[4]	**174.7**	212.5	170.6	**185.4**	221.2	181.7
Other federal statute offences	**44.8**	129.1	35.7	**45.3**	212.5	28.3

1. Constitutes the intentional application of force without consent, the attempt or threat to apply force to another person or openly wearing a weapon (or an imitation) while accosting or impeding another person.
2. Includes unlawfully causing bodily harm, discharging firearms with intent, abductions, assaults against police officers, assaults against other peace or public officers and other assaults.
3. Includes dangerous operation of a motor vehicle, boat, vessel or aircraft; dangerous operation of a motor vehicle, boat, vessel or aircraft causing bodily harm or death; driving a motor vehicle while prohibited; and failure to stop or remain.
4. Includes possession, trafficking, importation and production.
Source: Statistics Canada, CANSIM table 252-0014.

Table 7.4 Homicides, by province and territory, 2003 to 2005

	2003		2004		2005	
	number	rate per 100,000 people	number	rate per 100,000 people	number	rate per 100,000 people
Canada	**549**	**1.7**	**624**	**2.0**	**658**	**2.0**
Newfoundland and Labrador	5	0.1	2	0.4	9	1.7
Prince Edward Island	1	0.7	0	0.0	0	0.0
Nova Scotia	8	0.9	14	1.5	20	2.1
New Brunswick	8	1.1	7	0.9	9	1.2
Quebec	99	1.3	111	1.5	100	1.3
Ontario	178	1.5	187	1.5	218	1.7
Manitoba	43	3.7	50	4.3	49	4.2
Saskatchewan	41	4.1	39	3.9	43	4.3
Alberta	64	2.0	86	2.7	109	3.4
British Columbia	94	2.3	113	2.7	98	2.3
Yukon	1	3.3	7	22.7	1	3.2
Northwest Territories	4	9.5	4	9.3	0	0.0
Nunavut	3	10.3	4	13.5	2	6.7

Note: Homicide includes murder, manslaughter and infanticide.
Source: Statistics Canada, CANSIM table 253-0001.

Table 7.5 Homicides, by method, 2003 to 2005

	2003		2004		2005	
	number	%	number	%	number	%
All methods	**549**	**100.0**	**624**	**100.0**	**658**	**100.0**
Shooting	161	29.3	173	27.7	222	33.7
Stabbing	142	25.9	205	32.9	198	30.1
Beating	121	22.0	136	21.8	145	22.0
Strangulation	64	11.7	63	10.1	45	6.8
Fire (burns/suffocation)	12	2.2	13	2.1	7	1.1
Other methods	27	4.9	21	3.4	24	3.6
Not known	22	4.0	13	2.1	17	2.6

Note: Homicide includes murder, manslaughter and infanticide.
Source: Statistics Canada, CANSIM table 253-0002.

Table 7.6 Solved homicides, by type of accused–victim relationship, 2000 to 2005

	2000	2001	2002	2003	2004	2005
	number					
Total accused–victim relationship	**420**	**453**	**468**	**430**	**476**	**478**
Total family relationships	132	187	184	142	163	156
Spouse	69	89	84	78	75	74
Parent	31	43	36	31	36	20
Other family relationship	32	55	64	33	52	62
Other intimate relationship	24	13	17	11	24	16
Acquaintance	187	185	188	207	214	217
Stranger	72	62	72	61	73	86
Accused–victim relationship unknown	5	6	7	9	2	3

Source: Statistics Canada, CANSIM table 253-0006.

Table 7.7 Homicides, by census metropolitan area, 1995 to 2005

	Average from 1995 to 2004		2005[1]		
	number	rate per 100,000 population	population of census metropolitan area[2]	number	rate per 100,000 population
Population of 500,000 or more					
Toronto	81	1.7	5,306,912	104	2.0
Montréal[3]	70	2.0	3,675,155	48	1.3
Vancouver[4]	53	2.6	2,156,509	62	2.9
Calgary	15	1.6	1,061,524	26	2.5
Edmonton[3]	24	2.5	1,024,946	44	4.3
Ottawa[5]	10	1.2	876,798	11	1.3
Québec	8	1.2	720,787	5	0.7
Winnipeg	21	3.1	698,791	26	3.7
Hamilton[6]	11	1.7	697,239	11	1.6
Population from 100,000 to 499,999					
Kitchener	5	1.0	485,248	7	1.4
London	5	1.0	471,033	14	3.0
St. Catharines–Niagara	6	1.4	434,347	14	3.2
Halifax	7	2.0	380,844	10	2.6
Victoria	6	1.9	336,030	2	0.6
Oshawa	2	0.8	333,617	1	0.3
Windsor	6	2.0	333,163	5	1.5
Gatineau[7]	4	1.3	284,963	3	1.1
Saskatoon	6	2.5	244,826	9	3.7
Regina	6	3.2	201,435	8	4.0
St. John's	2	1.1	181,527	2	1.1
Abbotsford[8]	5	3.0	162,907	4	2.5
Greater Sudbury / Grand Sudbury	3	1.6	160,912	2	1.2
Kingston[8,9]	3	1.6	154,389	5	3.2
Sherbrooke	2	1.1	148,225	0	0.0
Saguenay	1	0.8	147,071	1	0.7
Trois-Rivières	2	1.0	145,567	0	0.0
Saint John	1	0.9	145,363	0	0.0
Thunder Bay	2	1.8	124,262	3	2.4

1. Thirteen homicides included in the 2005 totals occurred in previous years: two in Montréal, one in Toronto, one in Kitchener, one in Edmonton, three in Vancouver and five in areas with a population less than 100,000.
2. Estimates have been revised and adjusted by the Canadian Centre for Justice Statistics to correspond with police boundaries.
3. Includes one homicide that occurred in a correctional institution in 2005.
4. As a result of ongoing investigations in Port Coquitlam, British Columbia, there were five homicides reported in the Vancouver total for 2004 that occurred in previous years, since homicides are counted according to the year in which police file the report.
5. Ottawa refers to the Ontario part of Ottawa–Gatineau.
6. Includes one homicide that occurred in a correctional institution in 2004.
7. Gatineau refers to the Quebec part of Ottawa–Gatineau.
8. Abbotsford and Kingston became census metropolitan areas in 2001. Average number and rate are calculated from 2001 to 2004.
9. Includes one homicide that occurred in a correctional institution and one that occurred in a halfway house in 2005.
Source: Statistics Canada, Catalogue no. 85-002-XIE.

Table 7.8 Adult criminal court, cases sentenced to prison, 1999 to 2003

	1999	2000	2001	2002	2003
			number		
All offences	**74,309**	**74,941**	**86,399**	**88,990**	**83,077**
Criminal Code offences	68,713	69,494	80,197	82,624	77,326
Crimes against the person	17,045	17,491	20,352	20,803	18,736
Homicide	89	100	142	129	105
Attempted murder	50	36	38	69	35
Robbery	969	766	939	876	738
Sexual assault	482	480	466	436	398
Other sexual offences	4,819	5,036	5,704	6,037	5,387
Major assault	5,227	5,516	6,254	6,398	5,615
Common assault	2,865	2,999	3,615	3,661	3,327
Uttering threats	343	399	508	502	497
Criminal harassment	1,847	1,757	2,188	2,192	2,173
Other crimes against the person[1]	354	402	498	503	461
Property crimes	20,843	19,859	23,659	24,447	23,601
Theft	5,106	4,659	4,920	5,021	4,795
Break and enter	7,224	6,901	9,099	9,477	9,405
Fraud	1,041	1,100	1,328	1,368	1,207
Mischief	3,767	3,536	4,345	4,467	4,343
Possession of stolen property	3,505	3,495	3,789	3,898	3,641
Other property crimes	200	168	178	216	210
Administration of justice	17,806	19,600	22,708	24,049	23,075
Other *Criminal Code* offences	4,533	4,456	5,003	5,213	4,736
Criminal Code traffic offences	8,486	8,088	8,475	8,112	7,178
Impaired driving	5,249	5,035	5,143	4,950	4,167
Other *Criminal Code* traffic offences[2]	3,237	3,053	3,332	3,162	3,011
Federal statute offences	5,596	5,447	6,202	6,366	5,751
Drug possession	945	945	1,182	1,193	1,104
Drug trafficking	2,214	2,227	2,841	3,011	2,520
Youth Criminal Justice Act	426	458	507	480	253
Residual federal statute offences	2,011	1,817	1,672	1,682	1,874

Notes: Adult Criminal Court Survey data are not reported by Manitoba and Nunavut. The Northwest Territories last participated in the survey in 1999/2000. The survey's data for 2002/2003 were revised because of a data processing error. Revisions primarily affected the 2002/2003 case count for Quebec. Since 2001/2002, adult criminal courts in nine provinces and one territory reported to the survey. Reporting jurisdictions include Newfoundland and Labrador, Prince Edward Island, Nova Scotia, New Brunswick, Quebec, Ontario, Saskatchewan, Alberta, British Columbia and Yukon. These jurisdictions represent approximately 90% of the completed adult criminal court caseload in Canada. New Brunswick and British Columbia began reporting to the survey in 2001/2002.

Excludes cases where the length of the prison sentence was not known and cases where the length was specified as indeterminate.

1. Includes unlawfully causing bodily harm, discharging firearms with intent, abductions, assaults against police officers, assaults against other peace or public officers and other assaults.

2. Includes dangerous operation of a motor vehicle, boat, vessel or aircraft; dangerous operation of a motor vehicle, boat, vessel or aircraft causing bodily harm or death; driving a motor vehicle while prohibited; and failure to stop or remain.

Source: Statistics Canada, CANSIM table 252-0021.

Table 7.9 Youth court, sentenced cases, by outcome, 2003

	Cases sentenced to custody		Cases sentenced to probation	
	number	median days of sentence	number	median days of sentence
All offences	**9,084**	**33**	**25,261**	**360**
Criminal Code offences	7,433	40	21,727	360
Crimes against the person	2,774	60	8,806	360
Homicide	11	720	3	360
Attempted murder	4	450	8	360
Robbery	119	180	481	540
Sexual assault	46	120	241	540
Other sexual offences	732	65	2,076	360
Major assault	841	30	3,594	360
Common assault	335	33	1,120	360
Uttering threats	22	52	88	360
Criminal harassment	615	112	1,071	360
Other crimes against the person[1]	49	120	124	360
Property crimes	2,834	45	9,788	360
Theft	1,087	60	3,385	360
Break and enter	865	30	3,191	360
Fraud	105	28	969	360
Mischief	625	40	1,565	360
Possession of stolen property	120	40	506	360
Other property crimes	32	60	172	360
Administration of justice	1,383	20	1,590	360
Other *Criminal Code* offences	378	40	1,221	360
Criminal Code traffic offences	64	60	322	360
Impaired driving	3	40	111	360
Other *Criminal Code* traffic offences[2]	61	60	211	360
Federal statute offences	1,651	20	3,534	360
Drug possession	32	18	343	360
Drug trafficking	114	60	726	360
Youth Criminal Justice Act / Young Offenders Act	1,411	20	2,369	360
Other federal statute offences	94	9	96	207

1. Includes unlawfully causing bodily harm, discharging firearms with intent, abductions, assaults against police officers, assaults against other peace or public officers and other assaults.

2. Includes dangerous operation of a motor vehicle, boat, vessel or aircraft; dangerous operation of a motor vehicle, boat, vessel or aircraft causing bodily harm or death; driving a motor vehicle while prohibited; and failure to stop or remain.

Source: Statistics Canada, CANSIM table 252-0041.

Table 7.10 Composition of the adult correctional population, 2002 to 2005

	2002	2003	2004	2005
	number			
All correctional services	**154,653**	**159,013**	**154,351**	**152,618**
Custodial supervision	32,012	32,523	31,747	32,117
All provincial/territorial custody	19,262	19,685	19,368	19,816
Provincial/territorial custody, sentenced	10,931	10,607	9,863	9,830
Remand	7,980	8,727	9,163	9,640
Other temporary detention, provincial/territorial	351	351	342	346
Federal custody, sentenced	12,750	12,838	12,380	12,301
Community supervision	122,641	126,490	122,604	120,500
All provincial community supervision	115,243	119,268	115,510	113,546
Probation	101,915	105,061	100,993	98,805
Provincial parole	1,388	1,014	885	810
Conditional sentences	11,941	13,193	13,632	13,931
Community releases[1]	7,397	7,222	7,094	6,954

Note: Data refer to the average daily midnight count of offenders who are legally required to be at a facility and are present at the time a head count is taken.

1. Movement from custody to federal conditional release and includes provincial/territorial and federal offenders on day parole and full parole, and federal offenders on statutory release. Offenders released on warrant expiry and other release types are excluded.

Source: Statistics Canada, Catalogue no. 85-002-XIE.

Table 7.11 Adult correctional services, incarceration and probation rates in federal, provincial and territorial programs, selected years from 1994 to 2004

	1994	1996	1998	2000	2002	2004
	rate per 100,000 adults					
Incarceration rates[1]						
Canada[2]	**155**	**150**	**141**	**134**	**133**	**129**
Provinces and territories[3]	91	87	84	80	81	79
Federal jurisdiction[4]	64	63	57	54	52	49
Probation rates						
Canada[2]	**462**	**462**	**444**	**438**	**433**	**396**
Provinces and territories[3]	462	462	444	438	433	396
Federal jurisdiction[4]	.	.	.	.	.	.

Note: Not all variables are applicable to or available for all jurisdictions. Interjurisdictional comparisons of the data should be made with caution.

1. Based on total actual-in counts.

2. Represents the total or weighted average of provincial, territorial and federal jurisdiction figures.

3. Represents the total for all reporting jurisdictions and therefore does not represent a complete provincial and territorial total where data for some jurisdictions are incomplete or not available. The sentenced and other actual-in counts for 1999/2000 and 2000/2001 were revised in 2003/2004.

4. Federal values represent the total of the five Correctional Service Canada regions.

Source: Statistics Canada, CANSIM table 251-0004.

Culture and leisure

8

Canada has a long and proud tradition of arts, culture and sport. We are recognized worldwide for quality musical productions, unique film-making, award-winning fiction, and sports such as hockey. The country also boasts a rich array of art galleries, historic sites and museums that attract millions of visitors.

Performing arts, like theatre and musical events, remain popular. However, movie-going is Canadians' preferred entertainment activity outside the home. In 2005, we spent an average $106 per household going to the movies. People in the Northwest Territories spent the most, an average $132 per household.

Spectator sports have wide appeal as well. In 2005, households spent an average of $44 on live sports events: British Columbians spent the most, $70 per household. Both for

fun and to stay healthy, Canadians also take part in games such as golf and soccer and in recreational activities such as running and swimming.

Canadians also devote significant time to reading books and magazines, watching television and listening to music. More and more are using the Internet to play and download movies, television shows, songs and radio programs. Online video games and gambling are also popular, particularly among young people.

The economic benefits of culture and leisure

Culture and leisure businesses contributed $54 billion to Canada's economy in 2005, up a substantial 19% from 2000, faster than the 13% growth of total gross domestic product

Chart 8.1
Annual household spending on entertainment

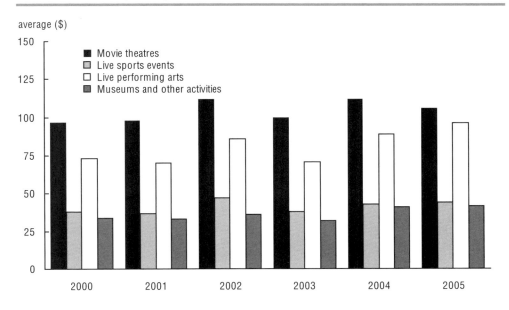

average ($)

Legend:
- Movie theatres
- Live sports events
- Live performing arts
- Museums and other activities

Source: Statistics Canada, CANSIM table 203-0010.

(GDP) over the same period. Information and cultural industries—including publishing, movie and sound recording, broadcasting and telecommunications, news services and libraries—showed the most stellar growth by far over the period, 22%; these industries contributed $44 billion to GDP in 2005.

Arts, entertainment and recreation industries—including performing arts, spectator sports, museums, heritage sites, zoos, amusement parks, gambling, golf courses, ski hills, fitness centres and bowling centres—contributed $9 billion to the economy in 2005, an increase of 9% since 2000.

In 2005, the publishing industry contributed nearly $8.8 billion to the Canadian economy, up from $8.3 billion in 2004.

The magazine industry prospered in 2003/2004, producing 2,383 titles and selling 758 million copies. Ten years earlier, Canadian magazine publishers produced 1,678 titles and sold 575 million copies.

Book publishers produced 16,776 new book titles in 2004, up almost 7% from 2000, and reprinted 12,387 existing titles, a

Chart 8.2
Gross domestic product, all industries and culture and leisure industries

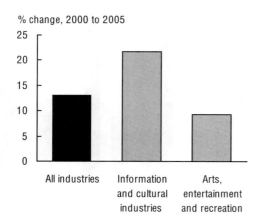

% change, 2000 to 2005

Source: Statistics Canada, CANSIM table 379-0017.

Books published in Canada

	2004		
	Titles published	Titles reprinted	Titles in print
		number	
Total	**16,776**	**12,387**	**121,524**
Educational	3,412	6,644	49,919
Children's books	2,228	1,961	16,933
Other trade, all formats[1]	8,833	2,635	36,952
Other[2]	2,304	1,148	17,721

1. Includes mass-market paperbacks, trade paperbacks, and trade hardcover books.
2. Includes scholarly, general reference, professional and technical books.
Source: Statistics Canada, Catalogue no. 87F0004XIE.

19% increase from four years earlier. More than half the new titles in 2004 were adult fiction and non-fiction. Canadian publishers printed 2,228 children's book titles in 2004 and reprinted 1,961 titles. In 2004, book publishers had a total industry profit of $235 million.

Rising incomes, interest in wellness push recreation spending

A renewed interest in well-being, especially among baby boomers, as well as rising personal incomes, led to more spending on health and fitness in 2005. This prompted an expansion in the number of fitness and recreation centres across the country. Golf courses also enjoyed renewed success, as the sport increased in popularity, possibly the result of retiring baby boomers heading to the links.

In 2005, households spent an average $3,918 on recreation, up slightly from $3,678 in 2004. Items included in the 2005 figure are: an average $166 on sports and athletic equipment; $665 to buy and operate recreational vehicles such as snowmobiles, bicycles and trailers; and $299 for the use of sports and recreation facilities.

In 2005, Canadians aged 15 and older spent on average 1.1 hours per day on active sports and leisure activities; males reported

1.3 hours per day, whereas females reported 0.9 hours.

Spectator sports—including professional and semi-professional sports clubs and teams, as well as horse racing—also remain big draws. In 2005, Canadians spent an average of $44 on spectator sports, a slight increase from the previous year.

Support for performing arts remains strong

Public support for Canada's performing arts remained strong in 2004, both at the box office and in the form of grants, subsidies and donations from various government and private sector sources.

Live performances accounted for almost half the revenue of for-profit and not-for-profit performing arts companies in 2004, unchanged from 2001. In total, companies' revenues surpassed $1.2 billion in 2004, up 4% over 2003 and about 26% higher than in 2001. The for-profit companies generated just over half the total.

Theatre, the predominant segment, accounted for 28% of total revenue, while music groups—everything from orchestras to rock groups—accounted for 25%. The remaining 47% was split among musical theatre (including opera), dance, and a miscellaneous category that includes circuses and ice skating shows.

Grants, subsidies and donations from various government and private sector sources made up 27% of total revenue, down slightly from 28% three years earlier. In the not-for-profit sector, grants, subsidies and donations increased 6% over 2003. Contributions from government increased 7%, more than twice the 3% growth seen in donations from the private sector.

Provincial governments were the biggest backers of not-for-profit companies in 2004. They accounted for $75 million in revenue, or 46% of total public sector support.

Selected sources

Statistics Canada

- *Annual Demographic Statistics.* Annual. 91-213-XIB

- *Births.* Semi-annual. 84F0210XIE

- *Canadian Social Trends.* Quarterly. 11-008-XIE

- *Population Projections for Canada, Provinces and Territories.* Occasional. 91-520-XWE

- *Quarterly Demographic Statistics.* Quarterly. 91-002-XWE

Chart 8.3
Sources of operating revenue, performing arts, 2004

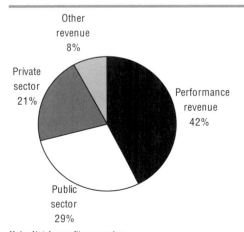

Other revenue 8%

Private sector 21%

Performance revenue 42%

Public sector 29%

Note: Not-for-profit companies.
Source: Statistics Canada, Catalogue no. 87F0003XIE.

Heritage institutions see record crowds

Canada's heritage institutions posted record attendance in 2004. Heritage institutions include museums, historic sites, zoos and aquariums, art galleries and botanical gardens in urban and rural areas across the country. These sites saw more than 35 million visitors in 2004, compared with close to 32 million in 2002. Most of these visits, 86%, took place in not-for-profit institutions.

Museums of all types—including exhibition centres, planetariums and observatories—drew the most visitors: 45% of total attendance at heritage institutions. Households spent an average of $42 on admission to museums and other heritage institutions in 2005.

Culture industries—such as the visual arts and heritage institutions—employ more people in urban centres than in rural areas. In 2003, less than 3% of Canada's rural work force was employed in culture. However, rural residents fill many of the jobs in culture. From 1996 to 2003, rural residents held about 25% of heritage institution jobs and 20% of jobs in the visual arts. Many employees were part-time: 37% of the rural residents working in culture were part-time employees; nationally, 22% working in culture were part-time.

Not-for-profit heritage institutions also rely on volunteers. In 2004, 85% of workers in art museums and galleries were volunteers, the highest share among heritage institutions. Reliance on volunteers was also high for historic sites: almost 74% of the work force worked without pay.

Not-for-profit institutions were the primary beneficiaries of government grants and subsidies in 2004. Most of this support (43%) was federal funding; provincial governments contributed 41% and other governments, primarily municipal and regional, provided the remaining 16%.

Chart 8.4
Employment in heritage institutions, 2004

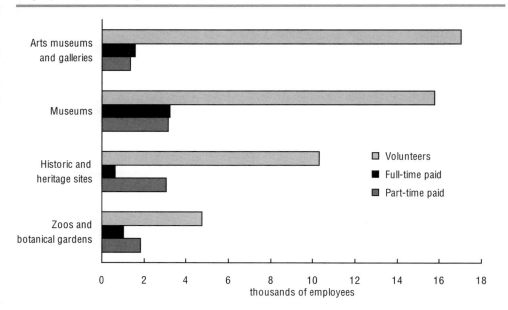

Source: Statistics Canada, Catalogue no. 87F0002XIE.

Canada's trade in culture goods

China has emerged as one of Canada's significant trading partners in culture goods. In 2000, China became the second largest exporter of these goods to Canada, displacing the United Kingdom and France. However, most cultural products imported to Canada still come from the United States.

Canadian companies imported $278 million in culture goods from China in 2005, and exported $13 million to China, down from the record $15.5 million exported in 2004.

Writing and published works accounted for 58% of the value of culture goods we imported from China in 2005, while visual arts represented 32%.

Canada's imports of culture goods increased in 2005, continuing a generally upward trend that began in 1996. In recent years, this has been at least partly driven by a strong Canadian dollar. By contrast, Canada's export market for culture goods fell for a second consecutive year in 2005.

The United States accounted for 76% of Canada's culture goods imports in 2005, down from 82% in 1999. At the same time, more than 89% of our culture goods exports went to the United States in 2005, compared with 94% in 1999; the peak for U.S. exports was close to 96% in 2002. In 2005, Canada imported $3.1 billion in culture goods from the United States and exported $2.1 billion.

In 2005, writing and published works made up 75% of all culture goods imported from the United States, down from 77% in 1997. Three-quarters of our culture goods imports from the United States were books, newspapers and periodicals; film, advertising and books made up half of our culture goods exports to the United States.

Chart 8.5
Trade in culture goods with the United States

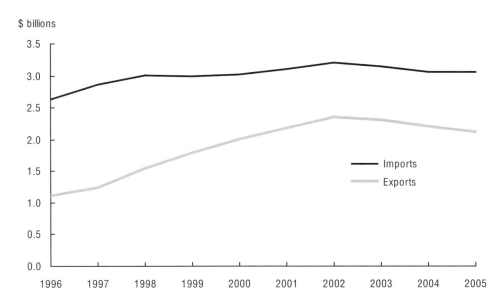

$ billions

Source: Canada, Catalogue no. 87-007-XIE.

Commercial radio listening stabilizes

Technologies such as file-sharing, streaming audio, and radio and music downloading are changing the way people listen to the radio and purchase and collect music. Compact disc sales declined sharply from $794 million in 1998 to $687 million in 2003. By contrast, traditional radio listening was stable in 2005 for a third year in a row.

Canadians tuned in to radio on average for 19.1 hours per week in 2005, which was more than one hour less per week than the peak of 20.5 hours in 1999.

Teenage males aged 12 to 17, a group that is likely to download music and other entertainment from the Internet, reduced their listening time the most from 2000 to 2005. They reported listening for an average of 8.6 hours per week in 2005, down from 10.1 hours in 2001. However, their listening time has apparently stabilized. Alberta teens listened to the radio for 10.0 hours a week, the highest of any province.

Contemporary music is the first choice of teens—26% of their listening time was devoted to this format in 2005, the same as in 2004. The increase in listening time for contemporary music is wholly attributable to adults aged 18 and older.

The gap between adult and teen listening times remains very wide, since adult listening is more than double that of teens, although it has stopped expanding. Adults aged 18 and older are the core audience for commercial radio in Canada.

Prince Edward Islanders were the most avid radio listeners in 2005, at 21.2 hours per week.

Chart 8.6
Radio listening, by selected radio station format and audience characteristics, 2005

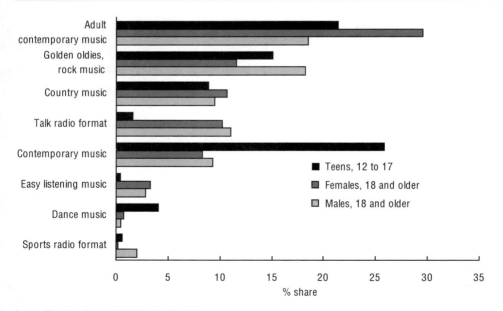

Source: Statistics Canada, CANSIM table 503-0003.

Household spending on leisure

How much money do you spend on entertainment and leisure? Do you buy tickets for the movies or the ballet? Do you purchase books or collect artwork? Canadian households spend most of their income on taxes, food, shelter and transportation. Culture goods and services such as books and museum admissions make up a small part of total household spending.

From 1999 to 2004, average household spending on culture goods and services rose 12%, comparable to the rate of inflation, which rose 13%. In the same period, overall household spending climbed 21%.

Canadian households spent an average $1,450 on culture goods and services in 2004, compared with $1,290 in 1999. After accounting for inflation, however, average household spending on culture was virtually unchanged.

Cable and satellite television took up the largest portion (32%) of household spending on culture goods and services—an average of $462 in 2004 compared with $332 in 1999. DVD, CD, and audio and video cassette purchases accounted for the next biggest expenditure at 8%, or $116 per household; movie theatre admissions were close behind at $112 per household.

In 2004, households spent an average $111 on textbooks, and $106 on other types of books. Households averaged $99 on newspapers in 2004, down from $108 in 1999.

Couple households with children—the largest share of the entertainment market—led in spending on textbooks, pre-recorded audio and video, books, photographic services, and admissions to museums and other venues.

Chart 8.7
Annual household spending on selected culture goods and services

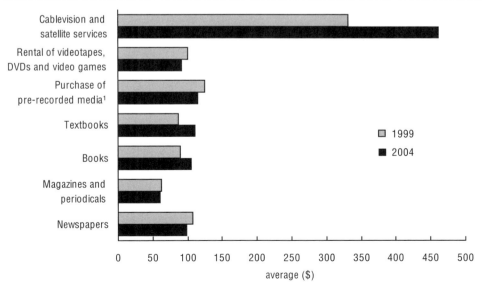

1. DVDs, CDs, videocassettes, audiocassettes and downloads.
Note: 2004 constant dollars.
Source: Statistics Canada, Catalogue no. 87-004-XWE.

Table 8.1 Federal government expenditures on culture, by cultural activity and by province and territory, 2003/2004

	Canada[1]	Newfoundland and Labrador	Prince Edward Island	Nova Scotia	New Brunswick
			$ thousands		
All cultural activities	**3,499,568**	**45,048**	**19,023**	**117,397**	**56,009**
Libraries	**43,289**	0	2	15	15
Heritage resources	**937,218**	20,917	8,809	50,067	14,654
Arts education[3]	**18,263**	0	0	0	2
Literary arts	**162,144**	555	128	1,653	813
Performing arts	**184,503**	1,896	2,613	5,428	5,711
Visual arts and crafts	**23,226**	261	187	921	435
Film and video	**386,183**	1,032	578	14,307	3,163
Broadcasting[4]	**1,605,488**	17,122	4,625	42,667	27,474
Sound recording	**28,507**	4	78	50	86
Multiculturalism	**14,317**	234	108	303	304
Multidisciplinary activities[5]	**81,474**	2,969	1,866	1,842	2,887
Other culture activities	**14,956**	59	30	145	466

Note: Figures may not add to totals because of rounding.

1. Total expenditures at the national level exclude intramural (operating and capital) expenditures by Human Resources Development Canada directly related to training and employment development in the culture sector.
2. Includes national organizations, foreign countries and unallocated expenditures.
3. Refers to the fine, applied and performing arts rather than to strictly academic fields such as language, history, literature, etc. The term 'arts,' as used here, includes theatre, music, dance, painting, drama, photography and any other area of arts study reported by arts education institutions.
4. The Canadian Broadcasting Corporation distributes its program costs by location of production activities. Station transmission and network distribution costs are related to the geographic location of the transmitter except for land lines and satellite channels, which are paid by Ottawa, but transferred to Toronto and Montreal network centres. Payments to private station affiliates are charged to the responsible network centres and relate also to the province where these centres are located. Administration costs and capital expenditures are distributed according to the province where the administration function is located geographically and the location of capital assets.
5. Includes financial support given to cultural facilities, centres, festivals, municipalities, cultural exchange programs and arts organizations for various cultural activities.

Source: Statistics Canada, CANSIM table 505-0001.

Quebec	Ontario	Manitoba	Saskatchewan	Alberta	British Columbia	Yukon	Northwest Territories	Nunavut	Other national organizations and foreign countries[2]
				$ thousands					
1,171,180	1,463,715	85,078	45,762	152,848	203,084	16,425	30,471	11,125	82,402
28,165	14,809	28	7	53	66	10	7	7	105
267,773	339,321	34,281	15,534	74,823	73,414	10,172	15,210	9,055	3,188
7,484	8,024	703	0	1,562	488	0	0	0	0
40,004	81,108	1,653	1,080	3,718	8,095	108	76	17	23,136
37,967	90,970	8,256	2,942	9,442	14,679	672	754	131	3,042
6,011	7,943	1,581	980	1,043	3,373	60	33	70	330
173,930	129,526	7,696	2,129	13,191	36,712	106	37	230	3,548
555,195	749,519	28,201	21,108	43,288	58,211	5,059	14,100	1,490	37,428
18,670	9,216	36	45	63	238	11	0	0	10
3,571	2,624	487	642	1,629	903	0	58	0	3,453
28,543	20,613	2,008	1,257	3,997	6,837	173	196	124	8,162
3,868	10,041	147	38	38	68	54	0	0	0

Table 8.2 Federal government expenditures on culture, by cultural activity, 1998/1999 to 2003/2004

	1998/1999	1999/2000	2000/2001	2001/2002	2002/2003	2003/2004
	$ thousands					
All cultural activities[1]	2,817,086	2,809,375	2,954,793	3,216,927	3,425,691	3,499,568
Libraries	45,079	36,794	39,896	51,218	45,285	43,289
Heritage resources	654,391	638,856	709,491	739,495	786,199	937,218
Arts education[2]	7,489	11,404	10,881	11,996	14,227	18,263
Literary arts	123,486	129,158	160,038	174,679	183,357	162,144
Performing arts	112,001	126,093	131,787	164,477	207,858	184,503
Visual arts and crafts	17,023	17,520	18,423	21,227	21,351	23,226
Film and video	292,547	294,072	305,945	328,585	397,786	386,183
Broadcasting[3]	1,455,905	1,435,663	1,475,316	1,585,541	1,600,551	1,605,488
Sound recording	9,279	9,777	10,210	18,606	22,977	28,507
Multiculturalism	1,744	3,635	3,520	888	11,720	14,317
Multidisciplinary activities[4]	79,142	97,217	80,453	108,259	102,671	81,474
Other culture activities	19,000	9,185	8,832	11,954	31,709	14,956

Note: Figures may not add to totals because of rounding.

1. Total expenditures at the national level exclude intramural (operating and capital) expenditures by Human Resources Development Canada directly related to training and employment development in the culture sector.
2. Arts education refers to the fine, applied, and performing arts rather than to strictly academic fields such as language, history, literature, etc. The term 'arts' as used here includes theatre, music, dance, painting, drama, photography and any other area of arts study reported by arts education institutions.
3. The Canadian Broadcasting Corporation distributes its program costs by location of production activities. Station transmission and network distribution costs are related to the geographic location of the transmitter except for land lines and satellite channels, which are paid by Ottawa, but transferred to Toronto and Montreal network centres. Payments to private station affiliates are charged to the responsible network centres and relate also to the province where these centres are located. Administration costs and capital expenditures are distributed according to the province where the administration function is located geographically and the location of capital assets.
4. Includes financial support given to cultural facilities, centres, festivals, municipalities, cultural exchange programs and arts organizations for various cultural activities.

Source: Statistics Canada, CANSIM table 505-0001.

Table 8.3 Attendance of cultural performances, by cultural activity, 2004

	Total attendance[1]	Performances at home	Performances on tour	Performances for youth[2]	Average attendance per performance
	number				
All cultural activities	14,199,261	10,868,597	3,187,010	3,358,709	325
Theatre	7,820,079	5,910,478	1,886,489	2,086,254	261
Musical theatre, dinner theatre, opera	1,147,858	1,087,723	55,174	140,472	340
Dance	1,583,245	977,083	554,794	332,292	461
Musical group or artist	3,185,490	2,676,518	468,459	630,012	644
Other performing arts companies	462,589	216,795	222,094	169,679	232

Note: Figures may not add to totals because of rounding.

1. Total attendance at performances is greater than the sum of attendance at home and on tour performances because some performances are classified as 'other,' and attendance at these does not appear separately here.
2. Includes performances for youth at home and on tour.

Source: Statistics Canada, Catalogue no. 87F0003XIE.

Table 8.4 Attendance of cultural performances, by province, 2004

	Total attendance[1]	Performances at home	Performances on tour	Performances for youth[2]	Average attendance per performance
			number		
Canada	**14,199,262**	**10,868,598**	**3,187,011**	**3,358,708**	**325**
Newfoundland and Labrador	**318,519**	287,860	30,256	25,584	147
Prince Edward Island	**x**	x	x	x	x
Nova Scotia	**377,806**	125,026	252,780	51,591	431
New Brunswick	**227,817**	136,703	88,714	61,545	299
Quebec	**3,914,295**	2,611,611	1,247,952	989,106	311
Ontario	**5,071,897**	4,361,684	682,968	995,218	379
Manitoba	**509,657**	340,019	165,438	114,950	371
Saskatchewan	**293,210**	235,544	46,666	59,599	343
Alberta	**1,386,596**	1,143,238	201,914	301,413	298
British Columbia	**2,082,265**	1,610,438	469,598	758,619	302

Note: Figures may not add to totals because of rounding.

1. Total attendance at performances is greater than the sum of attendance at home and on tour performances because some performances are classified as 'other,' and attendance at these does not appear separately here.
2. Includes performances for youth at home and on tour.
Source: Statistics Canada, Catalogue no. 87F0003XIE.

Table 8.5 Government expenditures on culture, by level of government and by province and territory, 2003/2004

	Total gross expenditures	Federal government	Provincial and territorial governments	Local governments[1]
			$ thousands	
Total expenditures	**7,706,675[2]**	**3,499,568**	**2,200,067**	**2,007,040**
Newfoundland and Labrador	**96,057**	45,048	39,006	12,003
Prince Edward Island	**33,486**	19,023	11,753	2,710
Nova Scotia	**209,243**	117,397	57,007	34,839
New Brunswick	**131,943**	56,009	52,082	23,852
Quebec	**2,317,653**	1,171,180	726,842	419,631
Ontario	**2,969,512**	1,463,715	628,228	877,569
Manitoba	**262,407**	85,078	111,832	65,497
Saskatchewan	**206,349**	45,762	87,733	72,854
Alberta	**537,275**	152,848	198,518	185,909
British Columbia	**777,259**	203,084	264,668	309,507
Yukon	**29,885**	16,425	12,779	681
Northwest Territories	**41,942**	30,471	9,620	1,851
Nunavut	**11,262**	11,125	0	137
Other[3]	**82,403**	82,403	0	0

1. Calculated on a calendar-year basis.
2. Includes intergovernmental transfers of about $365 million.
3. Includes national organizations, foreign countries and unallocated expenditures.
Source: Statistics Canada, Catalogue no. 87F0001XIE.

Table 8.6 Periodical publishing, financial and employment information, by region, 2003/2004

	Canada	Atlantic	Quebec
	$ thousands		
Revenue	**1,553,196**	**30,114**	**418,137**
Advertising	993,589	16,670	231,874
Single-copy sales	117,745	1,890	62,899
Subscription sales	291,330	8,286	94,319
Government grants	35,095	741	11,550
Website/e-commerce	11,856	121	1,340
Ancillary products	37,708	429	5,544
Other revenues	65,874	1,977	10,612
Expenses	**1,401,904**	**29,217**	**365,184**
Editorial and design	248,139	5,731	67,187
Production and printing	439,922	9,219	123,580
Fulfillment and invoicing	142,772	2,006	34,894
Marketing and promotion	188,377	3,763	40,783
Distribution	119,353	2,053	28,788
Administration and general	216,495	5,855	62,450
Website/e-commerce	15,045	107	1,832
Ancillary products	31,800	482	5,669
Profit or loss before taxes	**151,293**	**897**	**52,953**
	%		
Profit margin	**9.7**	**3.0**	**12.7**
	number		
Periodicals with profit/loss	**2,383**	**123**	**551**
With profit	**1,490**	79	346
With loss	**893**	44	205
Employment			
Full-time employees	**6,462**	286	1,448
Part-time employees	**3,018**	106	773
Volunteers and unpaid staff	**4,956**	369	1,247
	$ thousands		
Total remuneration	**411,716**	**11,773**	**92,742**
Full-time employees	298,793	9,734	67,204
Part-time employees	39,743	1,063	8,129
Freelance fees	73,180	976	17,408
	thousands		
Circulation			
Total annual circulation	**758,160**	13,946	178,753
Circulation per periodical	**318**	113	324
	number		
Circulation per issue	**26,908**	8,561	26,113

1. Includes Yukon, the Northwest Territories and Nunavut.
Source: Statistics Canada, Catalogue no. 87F0005XIE.

Ontario	Manitoba	Saskatchewan	Alberta	British Columbia	Territories[1]
\$ thousands					
918,756	32,057	20,068	32,848	99,474	1,741
610,982	22,203	14,100	25,439	71,032	1,289
45,917	1,241	478	206	5,067	46
161,700	4,790	4,681	3,753	13,530	270
18,426	1,190	315	648	2,156	70
10,071	x	27	121	175	x
30,004	x	x	429	1,172	x
41,656	x	x	2,252	6,342	x
833,112	30,082	14,664	31,264	96,480	1,900
144,378	5,944	3,190	6,343	14,837	529
248,770	9,541	5,433	10,056	32,815	507
96,522	2,391	1,234	1,064	4,412	248
117,532	4,417	2,055	4,026	15,529	272
71,992	2,898	1,042	3,215	9,318	49
117,159	4,684	1,663	5,900	18,489	295
12,431	102	x	320	244	x
24,327	105	x	340	837	x
85,645	1,975	5,404	1,585	2,994	-159
%					
9.3	6.2	26.9	4.8	3.0	-9.1
number					
1,162	104	40	157	240	6
728	56	24	99	154	4
434	48	16	58	86	x
3,481	215	107	269	647	9
1,456	120	63	169	315	16
2,282	260	50	256	488	x
\$ thousands					
243,496	10,564	5,626	12,109	34,674	732
174,700	7,711	5,020	8,297	25,730	397
22,824	1,370	458	1,951	3,734	214
45,972	1,484	148	1,861	5,211	121
thousands					
465,709	12,424	6,852	23,509	56,677	289
401	119	171	150	236	48
number					
32,746	15,670	8,537	16,779	24,910	7,785

Table 8.7 Heritage institutions, 2004

	Total	Museums	Arts museums and galleries	Historic and heritage sites	Zoo and botanical gardens
			number		
Total heritage institutions	**613**	**299**	**109**	**173**	**33**
			$ thousands		
Total operating revenues	**897,402**	**435,485**	**235,335**	**90,755**	**135,827**
Unearned operating revenues	**581,851**	313,460	172,535	51,360	44,496
Federal government	**202,283**	126,702	x	x	1,146
Provincial government	**192,706**	109,126	60,439	14,270	8,871
Other government	**74,074**	24,863	x	x	21,427
Institutional/private	**112,788**	52,769	x	x	13,052
Earned operating revenues	**329,683**	132,981	64,930	39,915	91,858
Admissions	**134,547**	56,546	12,609	14,610	50,782
Memberships	**14,680**	6,013	4,320	589	3,759
Other earned revenues	**180,456**	70,422	48,001	24,716	37,317
Total operating expenditures	**921,519**	**450,063**	**243,591**	**93,535**	**134,330**
Wages	**431,674**	206,362	105,190	50,717	69,405
Artifacts	**26,081**	6,247	19,027	711	96
Other operating expenses	**463,765**	237,453	119,374	42,108	64,830
Operating profit	**-24,117**	**-14,578**	**-8,256**	**-2,780**	**1,497**
			number		
Employment					
Full-time	**6,466**	3,231	1,557	640	1,038
Part-time	**9,384**	3,156	1,350	3,053	1,826
Volunteers	**47,856**	15,771	17,033	10,310	4,743

Note: Figures may not add to totals because of rounding.
Source: Statistics Canada, Catalogue no. 87F0002XIE.

Table 8.8 Music releases, by language and category, 1998, 2000 and 2003

	1998	2000	2003
		number	
Language of lyrics			
Canadian artists	1,023	1,034	904
English lyrics	452	457	429
French lyrics	159	189	205
Other[1]	412	388	270
Non-Canadian artists	5,705	5,620	4,715
English lyrics	3,950	4,093	3,698
French lyrics	125	144	107
Other[1]	1,630	1,383	910
Musical categories[2]			
Canadian artists	1,023	1,034	904
Popular music/rock	379	363	300
Classical music	159	131	97
Jazz and blues	62	52	73
Country and folk music	99	126	120
Children's music	31	38	31
Other	293	324	283
Non-Canadian artists	5,705	5,620	4,715
Popular music/rock	2,099	2,022	2,039
Classical music	1,508	1,338	912
Jazz and blues	533	767	441
Country and folk music	367	266	196
Children's music	121	68	84
Other	1,077	1,159	1,043

Note: Data exclude singles (any sound recording that contains up to three cuts, including compact disks and cassettes).

1. Instrumental (no lyrics) or lyrics other than English or French.
2. Musical categories are assigned by the survey respondents.
Source: Statistics Canada, CANSIM tables 507-0004 and 507-0005.

Table 8.9 Sound recording industry, revenue from sales of recordings, 1998, 2000 and 2003

	1998	2000	2003
	\$ thousands		
All formats	**891,645**	**861,402**	**708,723**
Singles	3,784	1,523	2,845
Vinyl albums	807	913	608
Compact discs	794,244	805,451	686,967
Cassettes	x	53,403	x
Other[1]	x	112	x
All musical categories[2]	**891,645**	**861,402**	**708,723**
Popular music/rock	651,533	622,893	472,661
Classical music	59,653	52,528	55,551
Jazz and blues	37,816	54,993	48,888
Country and folk music	51,930	43,912	47,892
Children's music	20,059	13,040	13,944
Other	70,655	74,036	69,787

Note: Figures may not add to totals because of rounding.
1. Other formats including multi-media.
2. Musical categories are assigned by the survey respondents.
Source: Statistics Canada, CANSIM tables 507-0001, 507-0006 and 507-0007.

Table 8.10 Selected financial statistics of the sound recording industry, 1998, 2000 and 2003

	1998	2000	2003
	number		
Canadian and foreign-controlled companies	**280**	**331**	**300**
Canadian	263	315	287
Foreign	17	16	13
New releases	**6,728**	**6,654**	**5,619**
	\$ thousands		
Revenue	**1,323,880**	**1,319,264**	**1,153,205**
Revenue from industry-related activities	1,137,758	1,193,423	985,430
Sales of recordings by Canadian artists	154,047	137,969	110,366
Sales of recordings by non-Canadian artists	737,598	723,433	598,357
Sales of masters, licensing fees and other royalties[1]	70,297	56,997	53,401
Other revenue from industry-related activities	175,815	275,024	223,305
Revenue from non-industry-related activities	186,122	F	167,775
Expenses	**1,134,042**	**1,161,698**	**1,122,662**
Cost of goods sold	638,465	578,604	530,249
Interest	4,186	76,792	73,306
Depreciation	10,907	15,602	19,684
Other operating expenses	480,484	490,700	499,424
Profit before taxes	**189,838**	**157,566**	**30,542**

Note: Figures may not add to totals because of rounding.
1. All types of royalties are included. In 2003, neighbouring rights were added.
Source: Statistics Canada, CANSIM table 507-0001.

Table 8.11 Film and video distribution and videocassette wholesaling industry, 2000/2001 to 2004/2005

	2000/2001	2001/2002	2002/2003	2003/2004	2004/2005
	$ thousands				
Revenue	**2,813,116**	**3,036,646**	**3,278,386**	**3,437,629**	**3,539,617**
All domestic market and exports (foreign clients)	1,293,115	1,416,325	1,551,737	1,515,513	1,588,673
Domestic market, film, video and audio-visual distribution revenue	1,070,860	1,211,661	1,292,707	1,194,539	1,256,764
Theatrical	390,584	403,066	462,583	382,666	446,338
Pay television	81,212	110,528	112,340	105,633	134,592
Conventional television	409,576	465,504	471,317	433,576	404,353
Home video	165,746	212,966	227,018	244,916	246,564
Non-theatrical	23,742	19,598	19,449	27,749	24,916
Exports (foreign clients)	222,256	204,664	259,030	320,975	331,909
Videocassettes wholesaling	1,399,383	1,508,251	1,607,954	1,816,057	1,817,096
Other revenue	120,618	112,070	118,695	106,059	133,848
Expenses	**2,465,884**	**2,707,572**	**2,837,886**	**2,687,072**	**2,737,531**
Salaries and benefits	144,578	172,005	147,565	153,203	166,939
Licensing (rights, royalties and other fees)	806,685	856,954	965,709	837,587	846,967
Depreciation and amortization	48,765	56,511	66,484	36,512	15,697
Interest	15,381	18,314	20,170	14,949	18,368
Other expenses	1,450,475	1,603,788	1,637,958	1,643,621	1,689,560
	number				
Canadian and foreign-controlled companies	**216**	**217**	**211**	**215**	**207**
Canadian	193	195	192	193	184
Foreign	23	22	19	22	23
Employment	**3,592**	**3,900**	**4,033**	**3,972**	**4,152**
Full-time employees	3,045	3,551	3,699	3,468	3,481
Part-time employees	518	335	320	490	660
Working proprietors	29	14	14	14	11
	%				
Profit margin[1]	**12.3**	**10.8**	**13.4**	**21.8**	**22.7**

1. Total revenue less total expenses (profit or loss) shown as a percentage of total revenue.
Source: Statistics Canada, CANSIM tables 501-0001, 501-0002, 501-0003 and 501-0005.

Table 8.12 Movie theatres and drive-ins, by selected characteristics, 1999/2000 to 2004/2005

	1999/2000	2000/2001	2002/2003	2003/2004	2004/2005
			number		
Theatres					
All movie theatres and drive-ins	712	744	645	628	641
Movie theatres	644	677	587	574	583
Drive-ins	68	67	58	54	58
Screens					
All movie theatres and drive-ins	2,926	3,258	2,979	2,980	2,933
Movie theatres	2,820	3,152	2,890	2,896	2,842
Drive-ins	106	106	89	84	91
			thousands		
Paid admissions					
All movie theatres and drive-ins	119,291	119,271	125,358	119,637	120,275
Movie theatres	117,352	117,574	123,815	118,161	118,498
Drive-ins	1,940	1,696	1,543	1,477	1,778
			$ thousands		
Operating expenses					
All movie theatres and drive-ins	904,994	1,048,127	1,171,463	1,169,184	1,137,033
Movie theatres	887,804	1,032,069	1,155,535	1,153,627	1,119,828
Drive-ins	17,190	16,058	15,928	15,557	17,206
			$		
Average ticket prices					
All movie theatres and drive-ins	5.78	6.30	7.27	7.45	7.47
Movie theatres	5.77	6.29	7.27	7.45	7.47
Drive-ins	6.30	6.55	7.29	7.54	7.02
			%		
Profit margin					
All movie theatres and drive-ins	4.4	-2.7	5.3	4.5	8.7
Movie theatres	4.2	-2.9	5.2	4.4	8.7
Drive-ins	12.5	9.4	10.0	11.5	9.2

Note: Data for 2001/2002 are not available.
Source: Statistics Canada, CANSIM table 501-0010.

Economic accounts

How is Canada's economic health? It may seem a question better left to statisticians and economists, but it affects every Canadian. Almost everything we do every day is linked to the economy—we go to work, buy goods and services, pay taxes, accumulate wealth and make investments. And if Canada's major economic accounts—the tools that statisticians and economists use to measure the economy's size and performance—are any indication, our economy has been good to us over the past decade.

A long boom

From 1996 to 2006, Canada's gross domestic product (GDP), which reflects the total value of all goods and services produced by a nation, did not stop growing. In real terms (adjusted for inflation), GDP expanded 23% during the first half of the past decade, and

then another 14% during the second half. In nominal terms, the value of all goods and services produced in Canada in 2006 was $1.45 trillion—or just over $44,000 for every man, woman and child in the country.

The services sector dominates the economy—it accounted for more than two-thirds of GDP in 2006. Services have also been the driving force of Canada's economic growth, expanding nearly 17% over the last five years—or almost twice as fast as the goods-producing sector, which grew just over 9%.

In addition to measuring production by industry, GDP can also be calculated using other approaches that measure economic performance. For example, income-based GDP measures the returns to the factors of production, including labour income of individuals and earnings of corporations. Adding up all of Canada's income, such as

Chart 9.1
Gross domestic product, income-based

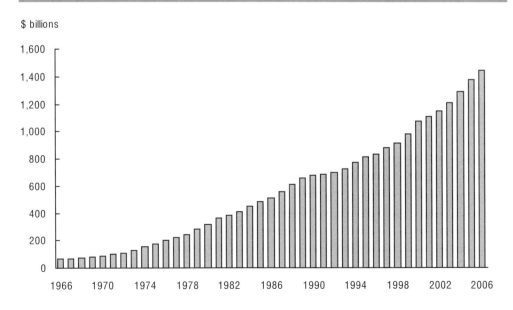

$ billions

Source: Statistics Canada, CANSIM table 380-0016.

labour income, profits and taxes, shows that the economy grew more than 25% from 2002 to 2006 (not adjusted for inflation). Rapid growth in corporate profits and advances in labour income accounted for much of that increase.

Another method called expenditure-based GDP tracks economic performance from a spending perspective—final spending on production—which includes consumer spending, business investments and government purchases. Of all the money spent in 2006, 56% (not adjusted for inflation) came from the wallets of individual Canadians shopping for goods and services. Among the other big-spending sectors, our three levels of government accounted for about 20% of all spending on goods and services. In 2006, expenditure-based GDP in real terms grew 2.8% for Canada.

Growing national wealth

The economy has grown considerably over the last decade, and Canadians have benefited from this expansion. The national balance sheet accounts—another of the economist's tools—show that economic

National balance sheet

	2002	2006
	$ millions	
Assets	12,155,289	16,713,938
Liabilities	8,386,110	11,594,704
Net worth	3,769,179	5,119,234

Source: Statistics Canada, CANSIM table 378-0004.

growth and appreciation of assets have stimulated Canada's overall net worth to grow significantly. By 2006, the economy had accumulated $16.7 trillion in assets and $11.6 trillion in liabilities, for a total net worth of $5.1 trillion—a jump of almost 35% since 2002.

National net worth surged 10% in 2006 alone, thanks to a significant drop in net foreign indebtedness combined with a strong increase in non-financial assets. The gains in non-financial assets were led by business investment in non-residential structures and by the continuing growth in the value of residential real estate.

Most of the wealth in the economy belongs to individuals through their ownership of non-financial assets and their substantial investments in corporations—via equities held in pensions and investment funds. The lion's share of household assets is financial, and these assets have seen robust growth over the last four years. Pensions, investment funds and equities account for 76% of household financial assets of $3.7 trillion. Another $0.7 trillion is made up of cash and deposits socked away in banks and other financial institutions.

For many Canadians, the most striking growth has occurred in the value of their home and their consumer durable goods. By 2006, the total value of household non-financial assets reached $2.6 trillion, about 45% higher than in 2002, with residential real estate leading the way.

Accompanying the real estate boom has been a lending boom. Household liabilities—particularly mortgages and consumer credit—have grown 37% since 2002.

Chart 9.2
National net worth

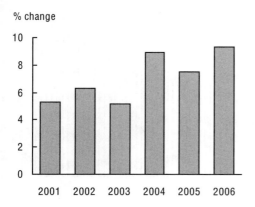

% change

Source: Statistics Canada, CANSIM table 378-0004.

Trading with the world

Since Canada is a trade-dependent nation, economic health has as much to do with activity outside our borders as it does with activity inside them. The economist's toolbox also contains some economic accounts tools for tracking this activity.

One is Canada's balance of international payments. It's a summary of economic transactions between Canada and the rest of the world. On its current account side—which tracks the export and import of goods and services, as well as other international activity—the value of goods exported to other countries in 2006 rose for a third consecutive year, to $455.7 billion. Also in 2006, Canadians imported $404.4 billion worth of goods. Together, these exports and imports created a trade surplus of $51.3 billion—the smallest in seven years, but a large surplus nonetheless.

Meanwhile, there is Canadians' international trade in services. We consistently import more services than we export, creating a trade deficit in services year after year. In 2006, the services trade deficit was

$15.2 billion—the largest deficit in services ever.

On the other side of the ledger, Canada's capital and financial account are comprised mainly of transactions in financial instruments. In 2006, these transactions led to a net outflow of $18.5 billion. In other words, Canada's international assets grew faster than its liabilities to the rest of the world, which has been the norm over the last eight years. However, this was the lowest net outflow since 2003.

The growth in assets in 2006 came largely from Canada's portfolio investment, mainly foreign bonds. The increase in liabilities was concentrated in foreign direct investment— the largest increase in foreign direct investment in six years.

Selected sources

Statistics Canada

- *Canada's Balance of International Payments.* Quarterly. 67-001-XWE

- *Canada's International Transactions in Securities.* Monthly. 67-002-XWE

- *Canadian Economic Accounts Quarterly Review.* Quarterly. 13-010-XWE

- *Gross Domestic Product by Industry.* Monthly. 15-001-XIE

- *National Balance Sheet Accounts, Quarterly Estimates.* Quarterly. 13-214-XWE

- *National Income and Expenditure Accounts, Quarterly Estimates.* Quarterly. 13-001-XIB

- *Provincial and Territorial Economic Accounts Review.* Semi-annual. 13-016-XIE

- *Provincial Economic Accounts, Annual Estimates - Tables and Analytical Document.* Semi-annual. 13-213-PPB

Chart 9.3
Balance of international payments

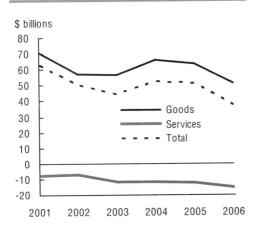

$ billions

Goods
Services
Total

2001 2002 2003 2004 2005 2006

Source: Statistics Canada, CANSIM table 376-0001.

Economic growth shifts from east to west

The continuing resources boom has shifted economic growth from east to west. Since 2003, Alberta and British Columbia have outpaced the nation.

Alberta led the provinces in growth for a third consecutive year in 2006, rising 6.8%, adjusted for inflation. Oil prices are the main driver, but the effects are rippling throughout the province's economy—and beyond.

British Columbia, at 3.6%, outpaced the national average for a fifth consecutive year in 2006. The construction industry benefited from demand for housing and investment for the 2010 Olympics. And Yukon's economy continued its three-year surge, up 2.9% from 2005, as high prices for metals and minerals spurred exploration.

Machinery and equipment manufacturing for the Alberta market benefited Saskatchewan, but the province's economic output rose just

0.4% in 2006, down from 3.1% growth in 2005. Ideal growing conditions led to strong exports of canola and wheat: thus, Manitoba outpaced the national average in 2006 for the first time since 1998.

The same factors lifting Western Canada have dampened growth east of Manitoba. High commodity prices have pushed up the loonie and fuel prices, which makes manufacturing more expensive and slows exports. Ontario and Quebec, the traditional manufacturing centres, have fallen short of the national average from 2003 to 2006.

Newfoundland and Labrador grew 2.8% in 2006, thanks to the first full year of production at a new nickel mine and oilfield. New Brunswick gained 2.6% with the re-opening of two pulp and paper mills. Prince Edward Island's economy grew 2.0%, helped by an improved potato harvest and construction of a wind farm.

Chart 9.4
Real GDP, by province and territory, 2006

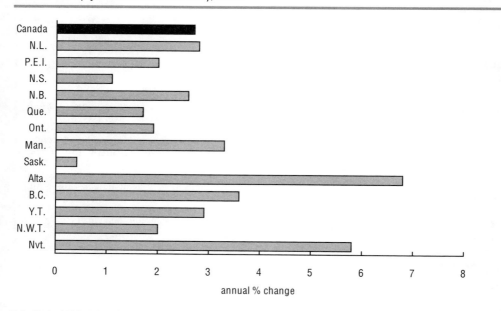

annual % change

Note: Chained 1997 dollars.
Source: Statistics Canada, CANSIM table 384-0002.

The industries driving the growth

With all the talk about the resurgence of resource-based industries, you might think that Canadian economic growth is being driven by oil, mining and natural gas producers. While this industry and its related economic activities have driven big growth in recent years, other industries also play a major role in our economic well-being.

The overall economy advanced 2.8% in 2006, a slight slowdown from 2005 (all figures are adjusted for inflation). Canadian shoppers accounted for the largest part of this growth, with consumer spending advancing 4.2%.

The construction industry posted the strongest growth rate in the entire economy in 2006, 7.4%. Much of this growth was thanks to engineering projects and construction related to the oil patch, although home and commercial building also contributed.

The retail and wholesale trade industries were busy in 2006 keeping store shelves stocked and cash registers ringing. Retailers saw their industry advance 5.2% in 2006, outdoing their already impressive growth from the previous year. Wholesalers saw a second straight year of nearly 7% growth.

Another strong performer is the white-collar world of finance, insurance and real estate, which grew 3.8% in 2006 and more than 18% since 2001. On a less positive note, activity in the manufacturing sector decreased 1.3%, with manufacturing of non-durable goods showing the biggest decline.

Despite the construction industry's strong showing and the continued visibility of our energy sector, Canada's economic growth has been largely driven by service industries, which generate more than two-thirds of our GDP and employ 3 in 4 Canadians. While goods-producing industries as a group crept up 0.8% in 2006, services grew 3.6%.

Chart 9.5
GDP, by selected industries, 2006

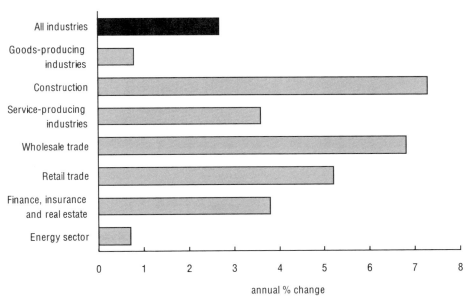

annual % change

Note: Chained 1997 dollars.
Source: Statistics Canada, Catalogue no. 15-001-XIE.

Business investment still stoking growth

Consumers led economic growth in 2006, but business investment also helped to stoke the growth. Canadian shoppers spent 4.2% more in 2006 than in the previous year—their strongest shopping spree since 1997. Still, business investment to construct homes, infrastructure, and commercial and industrial buildings grew even faster, 7.1%, although less money was involved than in consumer expenditures.

Fixed capital investment—mainly the real estate boom—has accounted for a considerable share of the annual gains in GDP since 2003. Climbing prices and greater demand for homes have created strong annual growth for homebuilders since 2000—14.1% in 2002 alone.

Handy Canadians have also helped to fuel the boom in residential investment. Home renovation outlays had their eighth consecutive year of robust growth in 2006, at 7.1%.

However, as the overall pace of investment in residential construction slowed in the last two years to 2.1% growth by the end of 2006, business investment in non-residential structures, machinery and equipment quickened and topped 9.9%.

Big-spending consumers are partly responsible. As more shoppers flock to stores, companies often invest in building more stores, malls and warehouses to meet demand. But clearly the oil and gas boom in Western Canada is also a major factor in non-residential investment. The boom has spurred large-scale infrastructure expansion—particularly in and around Alberta's oil sands: investment nearly doubled in 2005.

Chart 9.6
Real GDP, business gross fixed capital formation

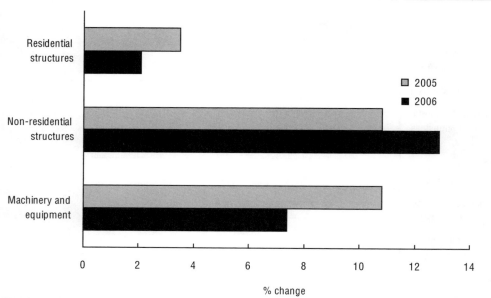

Note: Chained 2002 dollars.
Source: Statistics Canada, Catalogue no. 13-010-XWE.

Investing overseas

Canadians have never been shy about investing money overseas. Recently, this trend has intensified. By the end of 2006, strong global markets had helped push Canadian investment in foreign securities to record levels.

By December 2006, Canadians had been adding foreign stocks, bonds and money market instruments to their portfolios for 23 straight months. In 2006 alone, this investment abroad reached a record $78.7 billion—64% went into debt instruments such as bonds, while the rest was invested in equities, such as stocks.

Foreign bonds, which companies or governments issue to raise money and are repaid at a fixed price and date, have been a hot investment choice. The Canadian government removed restrictions on foreign holdings in 2005. That shifted investors'

focus away from slow-growth domestic bonds to faster-growth foreign bonds. To diversify holdings toward stronger growth, many investors have turned to 'maple bonds'—bonds that foreign companies issue in Canadian dollars. As a result, the amount invested in foreign bonds has multiplied over five-fold since 2003.

Canadians' investment in foreign stocks can vary widely month to month—for instance, investment swung from $5.2 billion purchased in August 2006 to $952 million sold in September—but it has been very strong overall. In 2006, Canadians bought $28.3 billion of foreign stocks, the most since 2001. Of this total, 69% went into U.S. shares. Overseas mining, oil and gas, banking and insurance firms were popular stock picks for Canadian investors.

Chart 9.7
Canadian portfolio investment in foreign securities

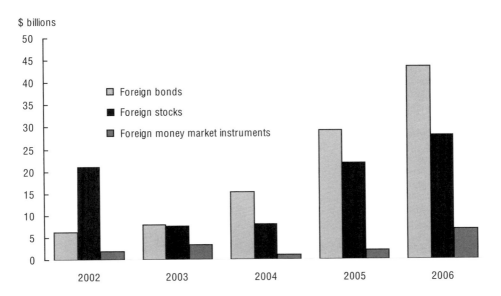

Note: Net flows; reverse of balance of payment signs.
Source: Statistics Canada, CANSIM table 376-0018.

Table 9.1 Gross domestic product, expenditure-based, by province and territory, 1992 to 2006

	1992	1993	1994	1995	1996	1997
	$ millions					
Canada	700,480	727,184	770,873	810,426	836,864	882,733
Newfoundland and Labrador	9,549	9,771	10,264	10,652	10,417	10,533
Prince Edward Island	2,345	2,471	2,521	2,662	2,823	2,800
Nova Scotia	18,094	18,343	18,667	19,296	19,512	20,368
New Brunswick	14,038	14,693	15,286	16,380	16,626	16,845
Quebec	158,362	162,229	170,478	177,331	180,526	188,424
Ontario	286,493	293,405	311,096	329,317	338,173	359,353
Manitoba	24,434	24,590	25,958	26,966	28,434	29,751
Saskatchewan	21,220	22,928	24,480	26,425	28,944	29,157
Alberta	74,936	81,179	88,041	92,036	98,634	107,048
British Columbia	87,242	94,077	100,512	105,670	108,865	114,383
Yukon	1,086	882	910	1,047	1,128	1,107
Northwest Territories (including Nunavut)	2,174	2,267	2,387	2,400	2,525	2,691
Northwest Territories	..	..	..	..	..	..
Nunavut	..	..	..	..	..	..
Outside Canada	507	349	273	244	257	273

Note: Dollar amounts in current prices.
Source: Statistics Canada, CANSIM table 384-0002.

Table 9.2 Gross domestic product, income-based, 1992 to 2006

	1992	1993	1994	1995	1996	1997
	$ millions					
Gross domestic product at market prices	700,480	727,184	770,873	810,426	836,864	882,733
Net domestic product at basic prices	557,995	576,833	613,352	644,818	664,294	700,063
Wages, salaries and supplementary labour income	387,788	394,816	404,918	418,825	428,792	453,073
Corporation profits before taxes	32,648	41,102	65,464	76,270	80,335	87,932
Government business enterprise profits before taxes	5,993	4,694	5,827	6,709	6,143	6,653
Interest and miscellaneous investment income	52,742	52,381	52,000	50,981	50,477	48,881
Accrued net income of farm operators from farm production	1,727	2,017	1,255	2,702	3,825	1,663
Net income of non-farm unincorporated business, including rent	39,406	42,068	44,931	46,363	49,278	54,663
Inventory valuation adjustment	-3,285	-3,122	-5,372	-2,473	-1,596	-623
Taxes less subsidies on factors of production	40,976	42,877	44,329	45,441	47,040	47,821
Taxes less subsidies on products	51,378	54,350	56,721	59,758	61,126	66,025
Capital consumption allowances	89,573	94,035	99,631	105,021	110,818	116,574
Statistical discrepancy	1,534	1,966	1,169	829	626	71

Note: Dollar amounts in current prices.
Source: Statistics Canada, CANSIM table 380-0016.

1998	1999	2000	2001	2002	2003	2004	2005	2006
				$ millions				
914,973	982,441	1,076,577	1,108,048	1,152,905	1,213,408	1,290,788	1,371,425	1,439,291
11,176	12,184	13,922	14,179	16,457	18,186	19,473	21,486	24,897
2,981	3,159	3,366	3,431	3,701	3,806	4,027	4,169	4,332
21,401	23,059	24,658	25,909	27,082	28,801	29,859	31,344	31,966
17,633	19,041	20,085	20,684	21,169	22,346	23,487	24,162	25,221
196,258	210,809	224,928	231,624	241,448	250,626	262,988	273,588	284,158
377,897	409,020	440,759	453,701	477,763	493,219	517,608	537,657	556,282
30,972	31,966	34,057	35,157	36,559	37,420	39,825	41,681	44,757
29,550	30,778	33,828	33,127	34,343	36,583	40,021	42,897	45,051
107,439	117,080	144,789	151,274	150,594	170,300	188,865	218,433	235,593
115,641	120,921	131,333	133,514	138,193	145,763	157,540	168,855	179,701
1,087	1,085	1,190	1,259	1,254	1,302	1,404	1,521	1,596
2,652	..	..	..	..	..	..	..	..
..	2,292	2,515	2,972	3,033	3,691	4,245	4,121	4,103
..	747	834	876	951	992	1,073	1,113	1,213
286	300	313	341	358	373	373	398	422

1998	1999	2000	2001	2002	2003	2004	2005	2006
				$ millions				
914,973	982,441	1,076,577	1,108,048	1,152,905	1,213,175	1,290,828	1,375,080	1,446,307
723,487	780,786	863,254	884,203	912,615	967,051	1,032,534	1,104,917	1,164,344
475,335	502,726	545,204	570,008	593,307	621,003	654,957	694,041	737,382
86,132	110,769	135,978	127,073	135,229	144,501	169,151	189,357	198,859
7,080	8,401	11,329	10,787	11,661	12,604	12,923	14,578	13,823
47,134	47,249	55,302	52,579	46,693	49,989	54,109	61,070	65,310
1,724	1,819	1,243	1,675	1,101	1,439	3,106	1,321	344
57,936	61,466	64,944	68,857	74,292	77,181	81,037	83,636	85,980
-753	-2,317	-2,439	574	-3,584	4,262	-1,747	-933	-1,775
48,899	50,673	51,693	52,650	53,916	56,072	58,998	61,847	64,421
68,439	72,747	76,647	75,871	84,139	84,380	89,838	94,334	97,161
122,659	128,999	137,425	147,536	155,567	161,817	168,274	176,338	184,750
388	-91	-749	438	584	-73	182	-509	52

Table 9.3 Gross domestic product, expenditure-based, 1992 to 2006

	1992	1993	1994	1995	1996	1997
	\$ millions					
Gross domestic product at market prices	**700,480**	**727,184**	**770,873**	**810,426**	**836,864**	**882,733**
Personal expenditure on consumer goods and services	411,167	428,219	445,857	460,906	480,427	510,695
Durable goods	48,808	50,170	54,116	56,169	59,197	67,988
Semi-durable goods	38,129	39,263	41,104	42,304	42,766	44,939
Non-durable goods	108,307	111,863	112,287	115,024	118,697	123,143
Services	215,923	226,923	238,350	247,409	259,767	274,625
Government current expenditure on goods and services	168,787	171,163	171,590	172,459	171,161	171,756
Government gross fixed capital formation	19,959	19,805	21,634	21,406	20,587	20,104
Government inventories	-40	-4	-1	30	-2	5
Business gross fixed capital formation	111,272	111,269	123,321	121,592	129,351	154,737
Residential structures	39,903	39,666	42,422	36,136	39,538	43,519
Non-residential structures and equipment	71,369	71,603	80,899	85,456	89,813	111,218
Non-residential structures	29,654	30,192	34,002	34,669	36,360	43,872
Machinery and equipment	41,715	41,411	46,897	50,787	53,453	67,346
Business investment in inventories	-6,522	-1,294	528	8,999	2,271	8,174
Non-farm	-5,810	-2,153	775	8,705	1,577	9,174
Farm	-712	859	-247	294	694	-1,000
Exports of goods and services	189,784	219,664	262,127	302,480	321,248	348,604
Goods	163,464	190,213	228,168	265,334	280,079	303,379
Services	26,320	29,451	33,959	37,146	41,169	45,225
Imports of goods and services	192,393	219,673	253,014	276,618	287,553	331,271
Goods	154,428	177,121	207,875	229,938	237,689	277,727
Services	37,965	42,552	45,139	46,680	49,864	53,544
Statistical discrepancy	-1,534	-1,965	-1,169	-828	-626	-71
Final domestic demand	**711,185**	**730,456**	**762,402**	**776,363**	**801,526**	**857,292**

Note: Dollar amounts in current prices.
Source: Statistics Canada, CANSIM table 380-0017.

1998	1999	2000	2001	2002	2003	2004	2005	2006
				$ millions				
914,973	**982,441**	**1,076,577**	**1,108,048**	**1,152,905**	**1,213,175**	**1,290,828**	**1,375,080**	**1,446,307**
531,169	560,884	596,009	620,614	655,722	686,552	720,401	760,701	803,502
71,325	77,693	81,958	84,930	92,085	93,793	95,479	100,014	105,716
47,262	49,548	52,115	54,565	57,052	58,485	60,608	63,055	66,818
126,253	132,959	143,264	150,305	158,399	168,144	176,939	187,836	195,572
286,329	300,684	318,672	330,814	348,186	366,130	387,375	409,796	435,396
179,317	186,054	200,084	211,706	224,428	238,416	248,868	262,650	279,806
20,046	23,039	24,524	27,287	28,589	30,107	32,082	36,296	40,336
-27	-3	24	13	-45	15	21	27	-41
161,790	171,431	181,748	189,978	196,585	208,090	229,434	253,074	277,885
42,497	45,100	48,572	55,133	65,651	72,714	82,918	89,791	98,386
119,293	126,331	133,176	134,845	130,934	135,376	146,516	163,283	179,499
45,177	47,229	49,826	52,966	50,659	54,545	62,081	72,674	85,698
74,116	79,102	83,350	81,879	80,275	80,831	84,435	90,609	93,801
4,733	4,990	11,505	-4,740	-2,674	4,305	5,589	9,642	7,824
5,409	4,951	11,355	-3,745	-1,094	2,982	4,098	9,038	8,369
-676	39	150	-995	-1,580	1,323	1,491	604	-545
379,203	424,258	490,688	482,463	479,185	462,473	495,347	520,379	524,706
327,160	369,037	429,375	420,733	414,034	399,122	429,064	451,779	455,696
52,043	55,221	61,313	61,730	65,151	63,351	66,283	68,600	69,010
360,871	388,303	428,754	418,836	428,301	416,856	440,732	468,197	487,660
303,395	327,026	362,337	350,067	356,728	342,711	363,307	388,282	404,391
57,476	61,277	66,417	68,769	71,573	74,145	77,425	79,915	83,269
-387	91	749	-437	-584	73	-182	508	-51
892,322	**941,408**	**1,002,365**	**1,049,585**	**1,105,324**	**1,163,165**	**1,230,785**	**1,312,721**	**1,401,529**

Table 9.4 Gross domestic product at basic prices, by sector, 1992 to 2006

	1992	1993	1994	1995	1996	1997
	\$ millions 1997 constant					
All sectors[1]	**703,485**	**720,700**	**753,118**	**772,843**	**783,810**	**816,763**
Goods-producing sectors						
Agriculture, forestry, fishing and hunting	19,054	20,397	20,683	20,993	21,228	20,427
Mining and oil and gas extraction	28,917	30,158	31,479	32,601	32,948	33,935
Manufacturing	110,926	117,004	125,812	132,123	133,569	142,282
Construction	41,072	39,621	40,831	39,310	40,713	42,995
Utilities	22,950	23,533	24,123	25,010	25,455	26,685
Services-producing sectors						
Transportation and warehousing	32,773	33,561	36,219	37,640	38,774	40,337
Information and cultural industries	22,206	22,269	22,985	23,786	24,130	27,979
Wholesale trade	34,542	35,296	38,193	38,781	40,402	43,694
Retail trade	37,813	38,989	41,192	42,755	43,521	42,252
Finance and insurance, real estate and renting, and leasing and management of companies and enterprises	134,790	138,688	146,423	150,679	154,435	161,052
Professional, scientific and technical services	19,962	21,137	22,590	23,837	24,317	30,289
Administrative and support, waste management and remediation services	14,920	15,662	16,267	17,783	18,503	15,386
Educational services	42,825	43,276	43,469	43,827	43,938	42,314
Health care and social assistance	51,723	51,699	51,941	52,031	51,072	51,403
Arts, entertainment and recreation	6,330	6,205	6,647	6,809	6,935	7,405
Accommodation and food services	17,298	17,705	18,324	18,982	19,084	19,652
Public administration	50,000	50,031	50,437	50,374	49,117	49,482
Other services	14,608	15,000	15,281	15,564	15,689	19,194

Note: North American Industry Classification System (NAICS), 2002.

1. Aggregates are not always equal to the sum of their components from 1981 to 1996. This is caused by changing the set of relative prices when a new base year is adopted.

Source: Statistics Canada, CANSIM table 379-0017.

1998	1999	2000	2001	2002	2003	2004	2005	2006
				$ millions 1997 constant				
848,963	**896,577**	**946,025**	**960,658**	**985,873**	**1,006,985**	**1,039,166**	**1,069,661**	**1,100,363**
21,696	23,322	22,904	20,811	19,721	21,632	23,047	23,777	23,391
34,461	34,399	35,459	35,507	36,345	38,287	39,469	39,750	40,173
149,390	161,526	179,564	170,761	172,130	171,499	174,992	176,497	174,946
44,348	46,415	48,833	52,367	54,620	56,274	59,764	63,108	67,658
26,140	26,409	26,502	25,533	26,982	27,221	27,366	28,562	28,045
41,036	43,604	45,764	46,741	46,638	47,176	49,494	51,403	52,782
29,866	33,658	36,356	39,232	41,017	41,924	42,534	44,258	45,310
47,202	50,467	53,696	55,858	57,846	60,252	63,510	68,040	73,508
45,442	47,497	50,291	53,371	56,771	58,533	60,732	63,627	67,275
166,070	174,007	181,064	187,897	193,595	197,828	205,480	212,385	220,522
34,032	37,549	41,462	42,631	43,729	45,610	46,838	48,284	49,736
16,418	18,328	19,083	19,988	21,799	22,531	23,351	24,187	25,668
42,575	43,565	43,757	43,972	44,712	45,252	46,293	47,055	47,969
51,901	53,411	55,113	56,134	56,933	58,369	59,477	60,305	61,561
7,603	7,984	8,499	8,913	9,130	9,117	9,223	9,283	9,523
20,779	21,630	22,319	22,661	23,063	22,533	22,983	23,223	24,136
50,249	51,828	53,208	54,693	56,346	57,882	59,084	59,902	61,533
19,755	20,978	22,151	23,588	24,496	25,065	25,529	26,015	26,627

Table 9.5 Canada's balance of international payments, 1992 to 2006

	1992	1993	1994	1995	1996	1997
			$ millions			
Current account						
Receipts	**205,455**	**235,576**	**285,601**	**330,978**	**351,038**	**385,415**
Goods and services	188,585	218,444	260,917	301,130	319,965	347,134
Goods	163,464	190,213	228,167	265,334	280,079	303,378
Services	25,122	28,230	32,750	35,796	39,886	43,755
Investment income	13,770	13,787	21,100	25,898	26,176	33,252
Transfers	3,100	3,346	3,584	3,951	4,897	5,029
Payments	**230,815**	**263,670**	**303,331**	**337,078**	**346,438**	**396,812**
Goods and services	191,674	218,964	252,285	275,869	286,650	330,346
Goods	154,430	177,123	207,873	229,937	237,689	277,727
Services	37,245	41,840	44,413	45,933	48,961	52,619
Investment income	34,903	40,619	46,990	57,089	55,571	62,133
Transfers	4,237	4,088	4,056	4,120	4,217	4,333
Balance	**-25,360**	**-28,093**	**-17,730**	**-6,099**	**4,600**	**-11,397**
Goods and services	-3,089	-520	8,632	25,261	33,315	16,788
Goods	9,034	13,090	20,295	35,397	42,391	25,652
Services	-12,123	-13,610	-11,663	-10,136	-9,076	-8,864
Investment income	-21,133	-26,832	-25,889	-31,191	-29,395	-28,882
Transfers	-1,137	-742	-472	-169	680	697
Capital account, net flow	**8,574**	**10,704**	**10,241**	**6,784**	**7,957**	**7,508**
Financial account, net flow[1]	**13,316**	**23,763**	**7,520**	**-5,489**	**-20,191**	**8,256**
Canadian assets, net flow	-14,411	-26,943	-49,029	-38,394	-73,306	-62,546
Canadian direct investments abroad	-4,339	-7,354	-12,694	-15,732	-17,858	-31,937
Canadian portfolio investments	-11,749	-17,881	-8,927	-7,331	-19,317	-11,849
Foreign portfolio bonds	-1,401	-5,071	435	-1,085	-2,070	-6,642
Foreign portfolio stocks	-10,348	-12,811	-9,362	-6,247	-17,247	-5,207
Foreign money market	..	..	..	..	..	..
Other Canadian investments	1,677	-1,707	-27,408	-15,331	-36,132	-18,760
Loans	-877	-1,139	123	-3,438	-4,208	-18,923
Deposits	1,604	10,214	-19,889	-7,162	-18,015	-2,898
Official international reserves	5,750	-1,206	489	-3,778	-7,498	3,389
Other assets	-4,800	-9,576	-8,131	-952	-6,411	-328
Canadian liabilities, net flow	27,727	50,706	56,550	32,905	53,116	70,803
Foreign direct investments in Canada	5,708	6,103	11,206	12,703	13,137	15,958
Foreign portfolio investments	24,701	52,799	23,312	25,233	18,668	16,181
Canadian portfolio bonds	18,766	31,446	15,995	30,730	17,953	6,166
Canadian portfolio stocks	1,036	12,056	6,412	-4,242	8,034	7,645
Canadian money market	4,898	9,296	905	-1,254	-7,319	2,369
Other foreign investments	-2,682	-8,196	22,032	-5,032	21,311	38,664
Loans	792	-325	-137	1,129	5,994	1,873
Deposits	-4,037	-8,180	21,005	-6,009	16,863	34,106
Other liabilities	564	310	1,165	-151	-1,546	2,685
Statistical discrepancy	3,470	-6,374	-32	4,805	7,633	-4,367

1. A minus sign denotes an outflow of capital resulting from an increase in claims to non-residents or a decrease in liabilities to non-residents.

Source: Statistics Canada, CANSIM tables 376-0001 and 376-0002.

1998	1999	2000	2001	2002	2003	2004	2005	2006
				$ millions				
414,777	461,219	531,961	513,754	514,913	496,899	539,081	575,151	594,207
377,385	422,670	489,090	480,795	477,522	460,903	493,757	518,762	522,926
327,162	369,035	429,372	420,730	414,039	399,122	429,067	451,783	455,696
50,223	53,636	59,718	60,065	63,483	61,781	64,690	66,979	67,230
32,338	32,905	36,755	25,990	30,502	29,253	38,169	48,213	61,599
5,054	5,644	6,116	6,968	6,890	6,743	7,155	8,176	9,682
426,140	458,649	502,692	488,649	495,135	482,250	510,030	547,208	570,629
359,947	387,298	427,836	417,945	427,434	416,011	439,988	467,423	486,789
303,399	327,026	362,337	350,071	356,727	342,710	363,308	388,282	404,395
56,549	60,272	65,500	67,874	70,707	73,302	76,680	79,141	82,394
61,965	66,518	69,863	65,320	60,799	59,284	62,468	70,735	73,446
4,228	4,834	4,992	5,384	6,902	6,955	7,574	9,051	10,394
-11,363	2,570	29,269	25,104	19,778	14,649	29,051	27,943	23,578
17,438	35,373	61,254	62,850	50,088	44,892	53,769	51,340	36,137
23,763	42,009	67,036	70,659	57,311	56,413	65,759	63,501	51,302
-6,325	-6,636	-5,782	-7,809	-7,224	-11,521	-11,990	-12,162	-15,165
-29,627	-33,613	-33,109	-39,330	-30,297	-30,031	-24,299	-22,522	-11,847
826	810	1,124	1,584	-12	-212	-419	-875	-712
4,934	5,049	5,314	5,752	4,936	4,225	4,466	5,940	4,201
-405	-17,531	-27,070	-21,375	-22,144	-19,935	-37,295	-38,287	-22,741
-67,161	-41,946	-142,039	-113,930	-83,631	-67,724	-87,448	-116,081	-165,339
-50,957	-25,625	-66,352	-55,800	-42,015	-32,118	-56,841	-40,645	-51,322
-22,497	-23,101	-63,927	-37,573	-29,319	-19,054	-24,369	-53,279	-78,693
-7,064	-2,477	-3,963	-1,920	-6,229	-7,974	-15,290	-29,238	-43,602
-15,433	-20,623	-59,965	-35,653	-21,253	-7,699	-8,092	-21,951	-28,291
..	..	..	..	-1,837	-3,381	-987	-2,089	-6,800
6,292	6,780	-11,759	-20,556	-12,297	-16,553	-6,238	-22,157	-35,325
12,637	2,680	-5,126	-8,051	-8,587	7,614	3,558	8,217	-12,201
-6,225	10,592	3,973	-2,172	5,844	-19,286	-10,661	-15,817	-8,183
-7,452	-8,818	-5,480	-3,353	298	4,693	3,427	-1,653	-1,013
7,332	2,326	-5,125	-6,980	-9,851	-9,574	-2,561	-12,903	-13,927
66,757	24,415	114,969	92,555	61,487	47,789	50,153	77,793	142,598
33,828	36,762	99,198	42,844	34,769	10,483	-474	35,046	78,317
24,779	3,738	14,598	37,779	18,599	19,714	54,762	9,577	32,544
10,337	2,602	-21,458	41,002	18,297	7,870	19,449	-78	18,015
14,311	14,346	35,232	4,125	-1,531	13,491	35,742	9,133	10,814
130	-13,209	824	-7,349	1,833	-1,646	-429	522	3,715
8,149	-16,086	1,173	11,932	8,119	17,592	-4,135	33,171	31,737
3,181	6,641	3,396	-5,941	1,400	2,192	-2,013	3,496	11,873
3,375	-24,103	-962	23,716	13,565	18,304	-531	28,951	20,724
1,593	1,377	-1,261	-5,843	-6,846	-2,904	-1,591	723	-860
6,833	9,912	-7,514	-9,481	-2,570	1,062	3,778	4,404	-5,038

Table 9.6 National balance sheet, assets, 1992 to 2006

	1992	1993	1994	1995	1996	1997
			\$ millions			
All assets	**6,436,779**	**6,836,021**	**7,261,081**	**7,621,198**	**8,105,253**	**8,682,898**
Non-financial assets	2,546,805	2,654,584	2,783,847	2,852,877	2,942,186	3,077,380
Residential structures	667,367	707,914	739,526	749,702	770,434	798,876
Non-residential structures	697,122	709,197	737,311	759,734	788,612	818,984
Machinery and equipment	255,061	266,244	280,939	291,852	295,130	316,413
Consumer durables	212,657	218,930	227,097	231,167	236,360	246,692
Inventories	121,723	124,483	131,535	146,976	151,010	158,782
Land	592,875	627,816	667,439	673,446	700,640	737,633
Financial assets	3,889,974	4,181,437	4,477,234	4,768,321	5,163,067	5,605,518
Official reserves	15,135	16,881	17,487	20,769	28,204	25,705
Currency and bank deposits	346,096	386,748	414,558	442,188	464,682	504,193
Deposits in other institutions	211,405	183,650	173,614	177,209	181,106	168,562
Foreign currency and deposits	41,662	43,663	51,390	60,940	80,699	83,313
Consumer credit	99,752	104,551	111,166	116,713	124,054	132,826
Trade receivables	130,487	139,379	145,109	156,170	164,913	171,371
Bank loans	150,209	146,588	152,733	156,407	155,890	165,433
Other loans	91,638	92,441	103,787	108,681	116,467	132,026
Government of Canadashort-term paper	138,696	139,687	129,356	133,524	117,851	95,038
Other short-term paper	54,139	63,370	66,829	69,965	80,505	103,581
Mortgages	398,735	417,936	433,497	443,906	459,879	478,715
Canada bonds	147,180	160,497	196,841	211,323	236,162	257,268
Provincial bonds	168,367	172,593	174,398	185,059	189,232	196,566
Municipal bonds	30,771	32,413	33,240	32,896	33,851	33,669
Other Canadian bonds	95,287	105,496	118,813	121,893	127,457	146,112
Life insurance and pensions	470,799	526,636	562,116	606,231	655,736	716,423
Corporate claims	436,091	462,841	503,729	545,557	576,758	645,998
Government claims	119,113	115,210	118,551	116,629	128,318	127,675
Shares	402,959	464,964	514,889	551,957	641,383	747,558
Foreign investments	65,302	80,452	96,910	104,850	127,767	150,569
Other financial assets	276,151	325,441	358,221	405,454	472,153	522,917

Source: Statistics Canada, CANSIM table 378-0004.

1998	1999	2000	2001	2002	2003	2004	2005	2006
				$ millions				
9,236,089	9,885,481	10,555,419	11,160,760	11,737,908	12,194,457	13,046,496	14,048,355	15,231,434
3,218,515	3,382,306	3,564,334	3,737,307	3,965,790	4,167,500	4,483,592	4,794,042	5,157,467
829,677	871,382	906,034	958,361	1,031,276	1,122,515	1,215,119	1,314,745	1,465,798
845,979	875,800	920,032	946,214	976,364	1,015,034	1,084,323	1,131,290	1,165,960
343,059	362,083	387,713	408,142	421,169	401,783	403,433	413,633	429,636
258,923	277,357	292,519	308,021	330,846	345,088	359,248	374,978	386,824
170,248	179,202	194,775	190,419	192,381	187,661	194,972	206,397	215,949
770,629	816,482	863,261	926,150	1,013,754	1,095,419	1,226,497	1,352,999	1,493,300
6,017,574	6,503,175	6,991,085	7,423,453	7,772,118	8,026,957	8,562,904	9,254,313	10,073,967
35,920	41,463	47,801	53,327	56,230	45,689	40,314	38,029	40,960
500,298	540,982	605,648	637,910	678,791	707,792	782,036	856,234	919,320
174,625	185,072	147,525	160,118	164,536	180,135	193,269	210,475	225,308
93,760	106,853	68,843	86,488	99,598	89,391	94,779	107,659	137,908
144,189	158,245	172,093	187,131	204,792	225,221	248,691	273,869	302,103
177,799	193,695	211,106	214,873	220,682	226,005	232,658	254,173	263,727
181,953	179,536	187,401	183,646	188,161	186,216	204,636	216,670	233,352
145,558	163,978	170,401	176,959	194,674	192,815	209,452	219,123	233,575
77,955	85,482	72,775	92,290	97,163	108,420	110,734	120,159	113,158
128,194	160,587	173,781	169,597	171,604	156,627	154,342	175,390	214,354
497,928	519,765	544,082	571,944	601,957	640,838	687,882	748,525	816,121
272,808	270,424	275,418	265,727	252,269	256,616	241,593	239,769	233,402
194,756	212,204	223,209	229,529	243,154	249,110	269,554	279,833	277,287
30,354	28,140	31,248	31,468	32,827	34,068	35,633	36,067	38,557
165,706	197,381	223,714	244,926	275,042	307,390	349,091	414,970	476,637
788,892	861,409	940,531	955,577	979,100	1,012,979	1,080,258	1,165,390	1,262,798
734,715	748,271	868,874	976,178	1,063,854	1,075,689	1,168,054	1,217,074	1,308,610
138,481	178,467	194,366	206,288	211,297	208,916	209,713	209,243	217,751
835,134	925,606	1,030,985	1,083,434	1,112,494	1,146,388	1,201,121	1,313,995	1,463,863
172,303	193,275	225,148	256,414	280,438	263,886	265,695	295,396	367,418
526,246	552,340	576,136	639,629	643,455	712,766	783,399	862,270	927,758

Table 9.7 National balance sheet, liabilities, 1992 to 2006

	1992	1993	1994	1995	1996	1997
	\$ millions					
Liabilities and net worth	**6,436,779**	**6,836,021**	**7,261,081**	**7,621,198**	**8,105,253**	**8,682,898**
All liabilities	4,188,088	4,505,176	4,810,317	5,092,511	5,474,432	5,895,740
Currency and bank deposits	352,489	393,728	423,528	450,727	471,893	513,500
Deposits in other institutions	211,662	183,874	173,741	177,332	181,229	168,672
Foreign currency and deposits	74,342	72,791	85,759	82,751	94,066	110,575
Consumer credit	99,752	104,551	111,166	116,713	124,054	132,826
Trade payables	130,709	141,647	147,728	158,491	165,026	171,156
Bank loans	144,312	138,914	146,186	149,012	150,255	155,889
Other loans	121,007	120,616	126,871	130,736	138,149	149,057
Government of Canada short-term paper	160,396	172,479	165,199	164,230	142,128	116,782
Other short-term paper	68,542	76,391	78,504	83,360	94,351	122,071
Mortgages	399,140	418,319	433,889	444,326	460,199	479,026
Canada bonds	214,358	236,552	271,078	297,160	330,359	348,389
Provincial bonds	268,362	294,409	321,003	335,365	339,388	342,060
Municipal bonds	35,534	37,553	39,007	38,947	39,858	39,432
Other Canadian bonds	161,012	179,281	200,766	212,669	226,424	262,779
Life insurance and pensions	470,799	526,636	562,116	606,231	655,736	716,423
Corporate claims	183,583	194,280	211,810	229,417	244,039	288,752
Government claims	119,113	115,210	118,551	116,629	128,318	127,675
Shares	699,599	779,751	843,824	906,591	1,027,530	1,157,537
Other liabilities	273,377	318,194	349,591	391,824	461,430	493,139
Net worth	**2,248,691**	**2,330,845**	**2,450,764**	**2,528,687**	**2,630,821**	**2,787,158**

Source: Statistics Canada, CANSIM table 378-0004.

1998	1999	2000	2001	2002	2003	2004	2005	2006
				$ millions				
9,236,089	9,885,481	10,555,419	11,160,760	11,737,908	12,194,457	13,046,496	14,048,355	15,231,434
6,317,237	6,746,853	7,199,917	7,626,890	7,980,810	8,243,656	8,743,026	9,420,744	10,172,955
510,176	552,014	618,480	654,150	692,773	722,022	798,264	872,473	940,210
174,732	185,186	147,525	160,118	164,536	180,135	193,269	210,475	225,308
120,232	124,102	93,582	110,309	120,120	107,519	103,666	116,274	132,089
144,189	158,245	172,093	187,131	204,792	225,221	248,691	273,869	302,103
175,277	191,070	211,065	219,593	227,139	227,310	231,656	251,353	265,928
174,593	171,523	177,246	173,216	178,433	180,701	196,762	207,364	217,241
163,928	182,862	185,987	187,799	199,182	196,217	206,014	217,614	222,459
97,253	98,203	84,362	99,729	107,050	118,941	118,762	129,632	126,307
149,783	175,332	189,948	183,283	186,542	166,356	165,240	185,764	223,451
498,252	520,095	544,397	572,266	602,323	641,194	688,233	748,873	816,467
360,273	359,966	355,308	339,262	331,079	315,027	295,423	285,530	278,641
352,913	351,666	354,263	362,379	376,886	368,899	383,642	391,666	392,391
36,277	33,410	36,071	35,926	36,389	37,202	39,080	39,827	42,664
310,331	343,500	371,832	452,086	498,611	519,113	568,588	627,889	710,072
788,892	861,409	940,531	955,577	979,100	1,012,979	1,080,258	1,165,390	1,262,798
331,966	324,638	356,884	399,148	440,710	427,029	429,373	478,062	513,323
138,481	178,467	194,366	206,288	211,297	208,916	209,713	209,243	217,751
1,285,010	1,397,217	1,599,601	1,705,341	1,791,515	1,886,844	2,019,868	2,167,565	2,380,209
504,679	537,948	566,376	623,289	632,333	702,031	766,524	841,881	903,543
2,918,852	3,138,628	3,355,502	3,533,870	3,757,098	3,950,801	4,303,470	4,627,611	5,058,479

Table 9.8 Canada's international investment position, assets, 2001 to 2006

	2001	2002	2003	2004	2005	2006
	\$ millions					
All assets	**921,976**	**979,184**	**921,148**	**961,998**	**1,013,424**	**1,190,429**
Canadian direct investments abroad	399,253	435,494	412,217	448,975	459,606	523,260
Canadian portfolio investments	239,762	270,775	253,788	265,374	292,412	364,664
Portfolio foreign bonds	38,870	45,392	45,809	58,549	82,276	128,505
Portfolio foreign stocks	200,892	216,307	197,025	195,745	197,082	216,194
Other Canadian investments	282,962	272,915	255,143	247,649	261,405	302,504
Loans	68,402	71,731	50,695	49,392	45,957	72,360
Allowances	-11,851	-11,918	..	..	..	..
Deposits	108,929	99,056	103,583	109,442	120,813	131,427
Official international reserves	53,327	56,230	45,690	40,315	38,030	40,959
Other assets	64,155	57,817	55,174	48,500	56,605	57,758

Note: Data are as of December 31.
Source: Statistics Canada, CANSIM table 376-0037.

Table 9.9 Canada's international investment position, liabilities, 2001 to 2006

	2001	2002	2003	2004	2005	2006
	\$ millions					
All liabilities	**1,125,414**	**1,187,876**	**1,137,847**	**1,142,120**	**1,179,855**	**1,289,417**
Foreign direct investments in Canada	340,429	356,819	373,685	383,498	407,610	448,858
Foreign portfolio investments	526,178	554,975	507,150	520,432	507,419	541,677
Portfolio Canadian bonds	427,228	449,072	401,050	398,090	380,818	404,590
Portfolio Canadian stocks	77,487	80,617	84,712	102,721	105,818	112,571
Portfolio Canadian money market instruments	21,463	25,285	21,388	19,621	20,783	24,515
Other foreign investments	258,806	276,082	257,012	238,190	264,826	298,882
Loans	56,035	58,772	52,398	40,237	41,645	49,508
Deposits	181,055	195,036	183,125	175,978	201,025	227,149
Other liabilities	21,716	22,275	21,489	21,975	22,156	22,225
Canada's net international investment position	**-203,437**	**-208,692**	**-216,699**	**-180,122**	**-166,431**	**-98,988**

Note: Data are as of December 31.
Source: Statistics Canada, CANSIM table 376-0037.

Education, training and learning

10

OVERVIEW

For the past 20 years, the proportion of students who graduate from high school has continued to grow. In addition, an increasing number of young people go on to postsecondary education, and girls are now more likely than boys to do undergraduate university studies full-time. At the graduate level, university enrolment among women was also almost equal to that among men.

The school-age population should decline in the coming year because of the drop in the birth rate. This decline could, in some areas, result in underutilized facilities, overstaffing and fewer program offerings. Conversely, areas where enrolment has been rising may feel pressure to spend more to maintain per-student expenditure.

The increasing cultural diversity of Canada's school-age population can also have repercussions on the school system. For example, some provinces have school boards or commissions that reflect religious and language preferences. Moreover, students who have difficulty in the language of instruction, be it English or French, usually take additional language training.

Student population

The number of students enrolled in public elementary and secondary schools in Canada has slipped compared with the 1997/1998 school year. Nearly 5.3 million children were enrolled in public schools in 2003/2004, down 1.2% from 1997/1998.

During this period, enrolment in public elementary and secondary schools, measured in full-time equivalents, rose only in Ontario and Alberta. In Ontario, enrolment reached 2.1 million students in 2003/2004, up 1.6%

Chart 10.1
Elementary and secondary public school enrolment, by province, 1997/1998 to 2003/2004

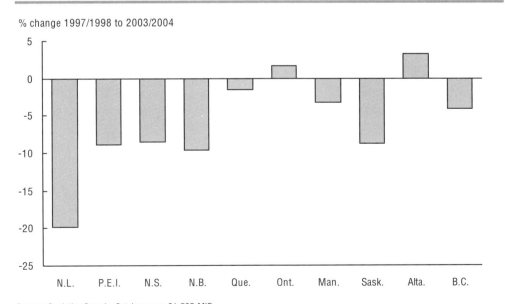

% change 1997/1998 to 2003/2004

Source: Statistics Canada, Catalogue no. 81-595-MIE.

from 1997/1998, while in Alberta, enrolment rose to 549,500 students, a 3.2% increase. In Ontario, the increase is essentially the result of immigration; in Alberta, it is the result of migration from other provinces.

The biggest drop was in Newfoundland and Labrador, where enrolment has fallen 19.9% since 1997/1998 to 81,545 in 2003/2004. Net migratory loss to the other provinces largely explains this situation.

The number of students enrolled in Canadian universities reached the 1 million mark for the first time in the 2004/2005 school year, the result of the double cohort in Ontario, an increase in the number of foreign students, and an increase in the number of young adults in school. This was the seventh consecutive year that enrolment peaked. However, the increase compared with the previous year was only 2.1%, the lowest since 2000.

Graduates

Just over 335,000 students in public elementary and secondary schools graduated

Chart 10.2
University degrees granted, by program level and sex

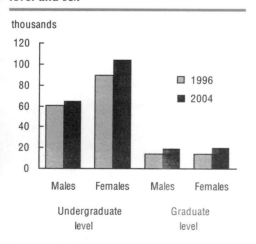

thousands

Source: Statistics Canada, CANSIM table 477-0014.

Elementary and secondary public school indicators

	1997/1998	2003/2004
	number	
Students	5,354,706	5,289,031
Graduates	204,745	335,286
Teachers	327,538	338,787

Source: Statistics Canada, Catalogue no. 81-595-MIE.

in the 2003/2004 school year, up 3.0% over 1999/2000. The main reason for this increase is the elimination of Grade 13 (OAC) in Ontario. If graduates from the double cohort in Ontario are excluded, the total number of graduates in Canada was relatively stable from 1999/2000 to 2003/2004.

Since the early 1990s, the high school drop-out rate has fallen considerably. In the 1990/1991 school year, 16.7% of youth aged 20 to 24 did not attend school and had not graduated from high school. In 2004/2005, this rate had dropped to 9.8%. Almost two-thirds of the 212,000 drop-outs in Canada in 2004/2005 were boys.

In 2004, university students earned an unprecedented number of bachelor's and master's degrees. In fact, universities awarded a record 209,100 degrees, diplomas and certificates in 2004, up 5.3% from 2003, and over 30,000 more than in 2001.

From 1996 to 2004, the number of bachelor's and first professional degrees increased 15.8%, offsetting the 6.4% decline in the number of undergraduate diplomas and certificates granted in this period.

Nearly 31,600 students earned a master's degree in 2004, up 9.0% from 2003, the seventh consecutive annual increase. For the first time, master's degrees comprised more than 15% of all degrees awarded.

Once again, more women graduated than men. In 2004, 124,800 women received a degree. Women made up approximately 60% of graduates for the third year in a row.

The number of degrees, diplomas and certificates rose in all fields of study in 2004, except agriculture, natural resources and conservation. The fields with the greatest increases were health, parks, recreation and fitness, visual and performing arts, and communications technologies.

Education funding

From 1997/1998 to 2003/2004, the total expenses of public elementary and secondary schools in Canada increased by 22%, from $34.5 billion to $42.2 billion. In comparison, inflation was 14% during the same period. Public administrations fund basic elementary and secondary education.

The total expenses of universities and colleges reached $31.3 billion in 2006. This is up from a total of $23.5 billion in 2002. Universities and colleges are mostly funded from public funds, but other sources of revenue, such as own-source revenue, sales of goods and services and tuition fees, also provide funding.

The average tuition fees of undergraduate university students have increased since the early 1990s. On average, undergraduate students paid $4,347 in tuition for the

2006/2007 school year, up from $4,211 the previous year. This amount is almost three times the average of $1,464 in 1990/1991.

For the 2006/2007 school year, the biggest tuition fee increases were for architecture and commerce students. The most expensive programs are still dentistry and medicine.

University tuition fees vary from province to province. For example, the average tuition of undergraduate students in Nova Scotia is the highest in the country. Undergraduate students in Quebec continue to pay the lowest fees because of a freeze on tuition for Quebec residents that has kept fees at less than half the national average since the late 1990s.

Selected sources

Statistics Canada

- *Analytical Studies Branch Research Paper Series.* Occasional. 11F0019MIE
- *Culture, Tourism and the Centre for Education Statistics - Research Papers.* Occasional. 81-595-MIE
- *Education Indicators in Canada: Report of the Pan-Canadian Education Indicators Program.* Occasional. 81-582-XIE
- *Education Matters: Insights on Education, Learning and Training in Canada.* Bi-monthly. 81-004-XIE
- *Perspectives on Labour and Income.* Monthly. 75-001-XIE

**Chart 10.3
University tuition fees**

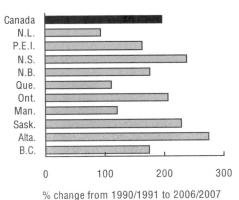

% change from 1990/1991 to 2006/2007

Source: Statistics Canada, Tuition and Living Accommodation survey.

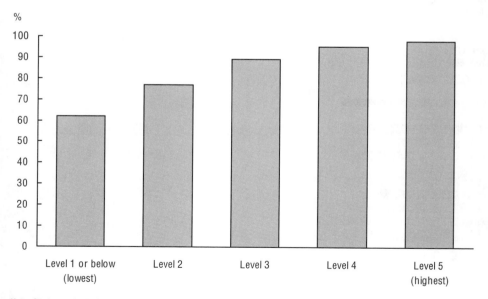

Reading literacy fosters achievement

Reading literacy at the age of 15 plays an important role in completing high school and attending postsecondary institutions. According to 2004 data, youth with good reading literacy are more likely to obtain their high school diploma, while those who have difficulties are more likely to drop out or still be in high school at the age of 19.

Eighty-seven percent of students had graduated from high school at the age of 19. However, only 62% of the students with the lowest reading literacy had finished high school. Almost all students who attained the highest levels of reading literacy had graduated by age 19.

Students who had not pursued postsecondary studies at the age of 19 posted reading literacy results that were, on average, more than one level below the results of those who had gone on to postsecondary studies. In

addition, only 28% of youth with the lowest reading literacy level had done some type of postsecondary education.

Reading literacy affects obtaining a high school diploma, even when factors such as sex, mother tongue, parents' level of education, family income, place of residence, school involvement and social involvement are considered. It also affects participation in postsecondary studies, given the known factors associated with it: sex, mother tongue, parents' education level and family income.

Neither the quality of reading literacy nor academic qualifications guarantee success in life. However, without them, Canadians face higher risk of encountering barriers to employment, enjoying less financial security and fewer positive social outcomes.

Chart 10.4
High school completion rates, by reading proficiency at age 15, 2004

Note: Students who had completed high school by age 19.
Source: Statistics Canada, Catalogue no. 81-595-MIE.

Smart, skilled, and some are very mobile

Some of Canada's doctoral graduates choose to move to other countries, but the majority stay here. However, the effect of every one who leaves Canada seems significant because there are relatively few doctoral graduates.

According to the Survey of Earned Doctorates, about 3,600 students graduated with doctoral degrees from Canadian universities from July 2003 to June 2004. Of the 3,300 graduates who completed the survey, 20% planned to leave Canada after graduation. Among those planning to leave, two-thirds were headed to the United States. Of those intending to leave Canada, 40% were graduates of life sciences programs such as agriculture, biology and health sciences.

Of the doctoral graduates planning to leave, however, about one-half intended to return to Canada at some point in the future. Another one-third were uncertain about returning.

Canada also attracts many of the brightest from other countries. About 23% of 2004 doctoral graduates surveyed were foreign students: over 60% of them planned to stay here after graduation. About three-quarters of these foreign students graduated in research and development-intensive fields such as engineering and physical and life sciences.

Many doctoral graduates saw the prospect of a good research and development job after graduation as a big draw. Of those with firm job plans, whether in Canada or overseas, 30% said their job would be related to research and development. Another 30% said they would be teaching.

According to the Organisation for Economic Co-operation and Development, Canada's proportion of the population with graduating with doctoral degrees puts us in the middle of the pack internationally.

Chart 10.5
Primary activity for doctoral graduates, 2003/2004

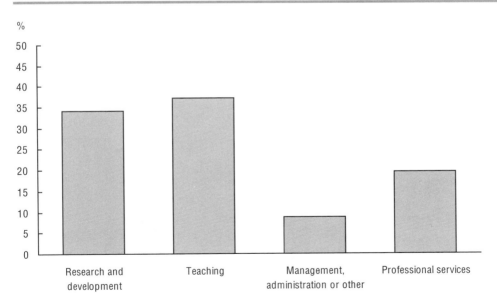

Note: Graduates from July 1, 2003 to June 30, 2004 with firm employment for the next year.
Source: Statistics Canada, Catalogue no. 81-595-MIE.

Does it pay to go back to school?

The notion that education is something one completes before entering the labour market has become outdated. Rapid technological change, a lack of new qualified workers and other factors mean more and more adults are returning to school to update their knowledge and skills or to acquire new ones.

In a study conducted from 1993 to 2001, 14% of men and 15% of women were adult students and more than half earned a postsecondary certificate. Young educated workers were more likely to take part in adult education than older, less educated workers.

Most adult workers who earned a postsecondary certificate saw their earnings jump. For example, all groups of men who obtained a postsecondary certificate posted higher growth in their hourly earnings than those who did not participate in adult

education. The returns ranged from 6% for men whose initial level of education was college or higher to 10% for those who started with high school or less. All groups of men saw strong gains in their annual earnings, except those aged 35 to 59.

Only women aged 17 to 34 enjoyed high returns in both hourly and annual earnings—11% and 15%, respectively—on obtaining a postsecondary certificate. Less educated women who obtained a postsecondary certificate also netted significant returns in hourly, but not annual, earnings.

Younger and older adult workers took different paths to return to school. Older workers only saw gains if they stayed with the same employer. For younger workers, earning a postsecondary certificate was associated more with getting a new, better-paying job than with getting higher pay at their old job.

Chart 10.6
Adult education participation rates, by age and sex, 1993 to 2001

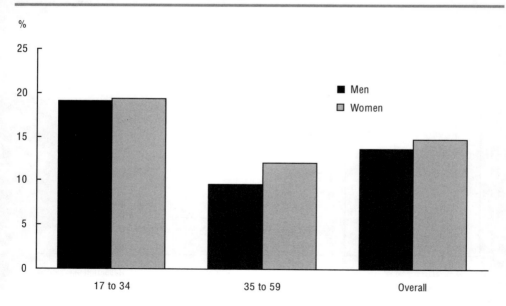

Source: Statistics Canada, Catalogue no. 75-001-XIE.

Fewer low-income youth at university

Canada's economically disadvantaged students are less likely to go to university than students from well-off families. In a 2007 study, just over half of the young people from families at the top of the income distribution attended university at age 19, compared with fewer than one-third of young people from families in the lowest 25%.

The study found only weak evidence that financial constraints were a direct barrier to attending university. Instead, it found that the gap is almost entirely associated with differences in academic performance and parental influences.

About 84% of the gap was related to the characteristics of youth from different economic backgrounds, such as their academic performance, parents' level of education, parental expectations and high school attended. In contrast, only 12% of

the gap in university attendance was related to the higher incidence of being "financially constrained" among lower-income youth.

Weaker academic performance among lower-income youth accounted for just over one-third of the gap. Specifically, young people from more disadvantaged backgrounds had a poorer performance on a standardized reading test and reported lower school marks at age 15.

An additional 30% of the gap was related to the lower levels of education of the parents of lower-income youth. About 12% was associated with the lower educational expectations that parents placed on lower-income youth.

The study concluded that the income divide in university participation is largely the result of factors that are present well before most youth begin to consider university.

Chart 10.7
University participation rate, by parental income quartile, 2003

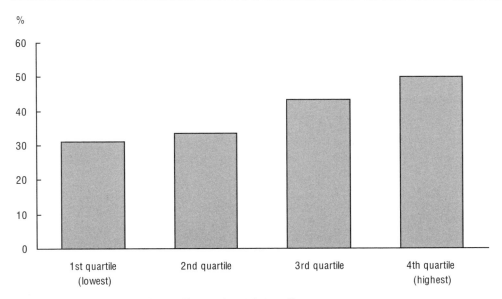

Note: University attendance at age 19; parental income when student was 15.
Source: Statistics Canada, Catalogue no. 11F0019MIE.

Table 10.1 Educational attainment of working-age population, by sex, 1996 to 2006

	Working-age population	0 to 8 years of study		Some high school		High school graduate	
	thousands	thousands	%	thousands	%	thousands	%
Both sexes							
1996	**22,967**	2,825	12.3	4,521	19.7	4,552	19.8
1997	**23,256**	2,747	11.8	4,423	19.0	4,362	18.8
1998	**23,523**	2,646	11.2	4,444	18.9	4,460	19.0
1999	**23,787**	2,588	10.9	4,395	18.5	4,570	19.2
2000	**24,094**	2,502	10.4	4,293	17.8	4,719	19.6
2001	**24,444**	2,371	9.7	4,272	17.5	4,740	19.4
2002	**24,797**	2,322	9.4	4,205	17.0	4,811	19.4
2003	**25,107**	2,262	9.0	4,015	16.0	4,810	19.2
2004	**25,443**	2,223	8.7	3,988	15.7	4,906	19.3
2005	**25,806**	2,163	8.4	3,918	15.2	5,121	19.8
2006	**26,185**	2,122	8.1	3,954	15.1	5,208	19.9
Males							
1996	**11,260**	1,347	12.0	2,282	20.3	2,094	18.6
1997	**11,404**	1,287	11.3	2,217	19.4	2,013	17.7
1998	**11,549**	1,249	10.8	2,226	19.3	2,076	18.0
1999	**11,683**	1,227	10.5	2,210	18.9	2,134	18.3
2000	**11,843**	1,181	10.0	2,160	18.2	2,210	18.7
2001	**12,024**	1,110	9.2	2,166	18.0	2,230	18.5
2002	**12,201**	1,092	9.0	2,132	17.5	2,260	18.5
2003	**12,352**	1,056	8.5	2,053	16.6	2,266	18.3
2004	**12,515**	1,031	8.2	2,041	16.3	2,319	18.5
2005	**12,693**	1,012	8.0	2,016	15.9	2,432	19.2
2006	**12,883**	983	7.6	2,022	15.7	2,496	19.4
Females							
1996	**11,707**	1,479	12.6	2,239	19.1	2,459	21.0
1997	**11,852**	1,459	12.3	2,205	18.6	2,349	19.8
1998	**11,974**	1,397	11.7	2,218	18.5	2,385	19.9
1999	**12,104**	1,361	11.2	2,185	18.1	2,436	20.1
2000	**12,252**	1,321	10.8	2,134	17.4	2,508	20.5
2001	**12,420**	1,261	10.2	2,106	17.0	2,510	20.2
2002	**12,596**	1,230	9.8	2,072	16.5	2,551	20.2
2003	**12,755**	1,206	9.5	1,962	15.4	2,545	20.0
2004	**12,928**	1,192	9.2	1,948	15.1	2,587	20.0
2005	**13,113**	1,151	8.8	1,902	14.5	2,690	20.5
2006	**13,303**	1,140	8.6	1,932	14.5	2,712	20.4

Note: Population aged 15 and older based on Labour Force Survey estimates.
Source: Statistics Canada, CANSIM table 282-0004.

Some postsecondary		Postsecondary certificate or diploma		All university degrees		Bachelor's degree		Above bachelor's degree	
thousands	%	thousands	%	thousands	%	thousands	%	thousands	%
2,031	8.8	5,932	25.8	3,106	13.5	2,115	9.2	991	4.3
2,121	9.1	6,357	27.3	3,247	14.0	2,214	9.5	1,033	4.4
2,120	9.0	6,513	27.7	3,340	14.2	2,304	9.8	1,036	4.4
2,116	8.9	6,597	27.7	3,522	14.8	2,402	10.1	1,119	4.7
2,275	9.4	6,584	27.3	3,722	15.4	2,507	10.4	1,215	5.0
2,241	9.2	6,916	28.3	3,905	16.0	2,661	10.9	1,244	5.1
2,274	9.2	7,124	28.7	4,061	16.4	2,790	11.3	1,271	5.1
2,453	9.8	7,261	28.9	4,306	17.2	2,969	11.8	1,337	5.3
2,478	9.7	7,458	29.3	4,390	17.3	3,070	12.1	1,320	5.2
2,221	8.6	7,692	29.8	4,690	18.2	3,227	12.5	1,464	5.7
2,117	8.1	7,832	29.9	4,952	18.9	3,445	13.2	1,507	5.8
979	8.7	2,897	25.7	1,662	14.8	1,051	9.3	611	5.4
1,019	8.9	3,132	27.5	1,735	15.2	1,105	9.7	630	5.5
1,018	8.8	3,197	27.7	1,784	15.4	1,159	10.0	625	5.4
1,020	8.7	3,247	27.8	1,847	15.8	1,170	10.0	676	5.8
1,107	9.3	3,259	27.5	1,926	16.3	1,208	10.2	718	6.1
1,088	9.0	3,406	28.3	2,025	16.8	1,295	10.8	730	6.1
1,117	9.2	3,505	28.7	2,095	17.2	1,351	11.1	744	6.1
1,189	9.6	3,586	29.0	2,203	17.8	1,430	11.6	773	6.3
1,229	9.8	3,675	29.4	2,220	17.7	1,463	11.7	758	6.1
1,106	8.7	3,783	29.8	2,345	18.5	1,519	12.0	827	6.5
1,060	8.2	3,857	29.9	2,466	19.1	1,612	12.5	853	6.6
1,052	9.0	3,035	25.9	1,444	12.3	1,063	9.1	380	3.2
1,102	9.3	3,225	27.2	1,512	12.8	1,109	9.4	403	3.4
1,103	9.2	3,316	27.7	1,556	13.0	1,145	9.6	411	3.4
1,096	9.1	3,351	27.7	1,675	13.8	1,232	10.2	443	3.7
1,168	9.5	3,325	27.1	1,796	14.7	1,299	10.6	497	4.1
1,152	9.3	3,510	28.3	1,881	15.1	1,366	11.0	515	4.1
1,158	9.2	3,619	28.7	1,967	15.6	1,439	11.4	528	4.2
1,264	9.9	3,675	28.8	2,103	16.5	1,540	12.1	563	4.4
1,249	9.7	3,783	29.3	2,170	16.8	1,608	12.4	562	4.3
1,116	8.5	3,909	29.8	2,345	17.9	1,708	13.0	637	4.9
1,057	7.9	3,975	29.9	2,487	18.7	1,833	13.8	654	4.9

Table 10.2 School board revenue and expenditures, 1992 to 2006

	1992	1993	1994	1995	1996	1997
			$ thousands			
Revenue	**31,779,197**	**31,603,451**	**32,064,138**	**32,224,966**	**31,899,333**	**32,042,472**
Own-source revenue	11,383,409	11,779,777	11,312,396	11,359,580	11,640,998	12,157,134
Property and related taxes	10,226,228	10,615,606	10,126,998	10,180,707	10,433,594	10,926,304
Real property taxes	8,920,373	9,304,047	8,862,895	8,913,431	9,152,598	9,617,759
Grants in lieu of taxes	164,648	164,130	150,483	145,988	148,583	152,255
Federal government	45,748	41,180	40,222	40,870	39,173	44,341
Federal government business enterprises	2,279	1,815	1,900	1,815	1,843	1,962
Provincial and territorial governments	101,502	109,377	101,001	96,656	100,548	99,793
Provincial and territorial government business enterprises	12,297	9,103	5,732	5,109	5,223	4,054
Local governments	0	318	362	383	407	457
Local government business enterprises	2,822	2,337	1,266	1,155	1,389	1,648
Business taxes	956,251	958,475	976,084	1,006,023	1,015,806	1,047,918
Miscellaneous property and related taxes	184,956	188,954	137,536	115,265	116,607	108,372
Other taxes	2,113	596	566	930	619	651
Sales of goods and services	1,083,530	1,094,451	1,107,931	1,094,804	1,130,374	1,157,659
Intergovernment	467,215	450,263	426,572	409,886	395,245	382,141
General	616,315	644,188	681,359	684,918	735,129	775,518
Rentals	49,015	49,479	54,413	40,309	41,443	43,403
Other sales of goods and services	567,300	594,709	626,946	644,609	693,686	732,115
Investment income	54,233	49,400	55,135	61,675	53,049	46,592
Other interest income	5,261	5,711	5,161	4,802	4,857	5,270
Other investment income	48,972	43,689	49,974	56,873	48,192	41,322
Other revenue from own sources	17,305	19,724	21,766	21,464	23,362	25,927
Specific-purpose transfers from other government subsectors	20,395,788	19,823,674	20,751,742	20,865,386	20,258,335	19,885,338
Federal government	76,242	89,919	98,538	132,051	92,000	81,580
Provincial and territorial governments	20,165,582	19,584,064	20,502,833	20,585,449	20,015,657	19,650,260
Education transfers	19,440,044	18,856,849	19,761,317	19,860,652	19,253,989	18,960,162
Debt charges (interest)	725,538	727,215	741,516	724,797	761,668	690,098
Local governments	153,964	149,691	150,371	147,886	150,678	153,498
Expenditures	**31,666,395**	**31,215,122**	**32,133,862**	**31,738,443**	**31,754,347**	**32,212,258**
Education	30,787,056	30,283,658	31,112,930	30,642,856	30,687,738	31,169,335
Debt charges	879,339	931,464	1,020,932	1,095,587	1,066,609	1,042,923
Interest	879,140	931,302	1,020,779	1,095,385	1,066,523	1,042,534
Other debt charges	199	162	153	202	86	389
Surplus/deficit (-)	**112,802**	**388,329**	**-69,724**	**486,523**	**144,986**	**-169,786**

Note: Data not available for New Brunswick, Yukon and Nunavut.
Source: Statistics Canada, CANSIM table 385-0009.

1998	1999	2000	2001	2002	2003	2004	2005	2006
				$ thousands				
35,590,628	32,933,191	34,049,949	35,230,651	36,895,015	39,085,203	39,348,228	41,328,799	45,457,819
9,186,870	9,593,045	9,696,626	9,851,322	10,121,370	10,349,619	10,435,931	10,907,645	11,315,980
7,801,048	8,009,046	7,999,391	8,105,789	8,197,216	8,355,012	8,483,512	8,902,057	9,233,020
7,602,321	7,814,361	7,803,833	7,907,445	8,013,090	8,163,446	8,293,159	8,702,948	9,033,628
96,439	89,993	90,908	84,244	78,233	82,718	81,214	84,155	82,172
40,772	36,637	36,802	32,480	30,971	31,887	32,509	33,603	33,001
2,330	2,116	1,447	876	469	376	308	322	313
48,405	46,928	47,941	44,850	40,749	44,254	41,924	43,433	42,144
3,148	3,026	3,367	3,758	4,322	4,228	4,243	4,452	4,369
484	483	469	510	527	525	536	543	574
1,300	803	882	1,770	1,195	1,448	1,694	1,802	1,771
26,780	28,381	29,054	31,123	32,065	33,432	34,535	36,010	34,671
75,508	76,311	75,596	82,977	73,828	75,416	74,604	78,944	82,549
599	650	708	723	695	692	715	746	718
1,304,790	1,492,498	1,590,727	1,644,381	1,822,908	1,878,446	1,839,105	1,888,136	1,963,120
457,962	483,870	547,924	519,393	515,877	512,769	527,331	540,674	562,263
846,828	1,008,628	1,042,803	1,124,988	1,307,031	1,365,677	1,311,774	1,347,462	1,400,857
49,226	56,675	58,919	66,368	105,892	117,929	119,779	124,752	129,212
797,557	951,953	983,884	1,058,620	1,201,139	1,247,748	1,191,995	1,222,710	1,271,645
54,598	65,691	78,818	74,635	71,844	83,865	81,960	84,756	86,023
4,641	5,892	5,574	6,324	6,985	5,322	5,498	5,733	5,520
49,957	59,799	73,244	68,311	64,859	78,543	76,462	79,023	80,503
25,835	25,160	26,982	25,794	28,707	31,604	30,639	31,950	33,099
26,403,758	23,340,146	24,353,323	25,379,329	26,773,645	28,735,584	28,912,297	30,421,154	34,141,839
82,258	90,975	84,721	89,923	104,689	98,705	86,519	89,211	93,242
26,161,478	23,088,695	24,103,915	25,120,176	26,494,344	28,459,642	28,650,516	30,151,637	33,867,134
25,637,572	22,688,501	23,723,258	24,701,947	26,089,163	28,059,578	28,240,574	29,734,232	33,433,957
523,906	400,194	380,657	418,229	405,181	400,064	409,942	417,405	433,177
160,022	160,476	164,687	169,230	174,612	177,237	175,262	180,306	181,463
32,091,168	32,700,627	34,142,482	35,368,073	36,873,300	38,264,627	39,479,158	41,439,144	45,033,800
31,309,610	31,955,580	33,416,048	34,624,407	36,150,312	37,528,221	38,759,210	40,735,347	44,356,765
781,558	745,047	726,434	743,666	722,988	736,406	719,948	703,797	677,035
781,414	737,104	721,368	734,845	712,633	729,472	712,874	696,623	669,470
144	7,943	5,066	8,821	10,355	6,934	7,074	7,174	7,565
3,499,460	232,564	-92,533	-137,422	21,715	820,576	-130,930	-110,345	424,019

Table 10.3 Enrolment in public elementary and secondary schools, by province and territory, 1997/1998 to 2003/2004

	Canada	Newfoundland and Labrador	Prince Edward Island	Nova Scotia	New Brunswick
		number			
1997/1998	5,354,706	101,768	24,397	162,359	131,586
1998/1999	5,359,724	97,557	24,146	160,011	129,131
1999/2000	5,372,346	94,118	24,089	158,205	127,003
2000/2001	5,358,545	90,287	23,153	155,873	124,942
2001/2002	5,367,314	87,019	22,843	153,450	122,792
2002/2003	5,349,725	84,397	22,615	150,599	120,600
2003/2004	5,289,031	81,545	22,239	148,514	118,869
		% change			
1997/1998	..	..	..	..	..
1998/1999	0.1	-4.1	-1.0	-1.4	-1.9
1999/2000	0.2	-3.5	-0.2	-1.1	-1.6
2000/2001	-0.3	-4.1	-3.9	-1.5	-1.6
2001/2002	0.2	-3.6	-1.3	-1.6	-1.7
2002/2003	-0.3	-3.0	-1.0	-1.9	-1.8
2003/2004	-1.1	-3.4	-1.7	-1.4	-1.4

1. Until 1998/1999, data for the Northwest Territories include Nunavut; from 1999/2000 on, data for the Northwest Territories exclude Nunavut.

Source: Statistics Canada, Catalogue no. 81-595MIE2006004.

Table 10.4 Graduates of public elementary and secondary schools, by province and territory, 1997/1998 to 2003/2004

	Canada	Newfoundland and Labrador	Prince Edward Island	Nova Scotia	New Brunswick
		number			
1997/1998	204,745	7,365	1,735	10,387	8,754
1998/1999	207,177	6,896	1,628	10,151	8,798
1999/2000	325,688	6,810	1,798	9,914	8,912
2000/2001	324,230	6,109	1,717	10,064	8,552
2001/2002	334,274	6,079	1,667	10,124	8,574
2002/2003	354,566	5,956	1,753	10,387	8,291
2003/2004	335,286	5,631	1,734	10,445	7,996
		% change			
1997/1998	..	..	..	..	..
1998/1999	1.2	-6.4	-6.2	-2.3	0.5
1999/2000	57.2	-1.2	10.4	-2.3	1.3
2000/2001	-0.4	-10.3	-4.5	1.5	-4.0
2001/2002	3.1	-0.5	-2.9	0.6	0.3
2002/2003	6.1	-2.0	5.2	2.6	-3.3
2003/2004	-5.4	-5.5	-1.1	0.6	-3.6

Note: Canada totals exclude Ontario.

Source: Statistics Canada, Catalogue no. 81-595MIE2006004.

Quebec	Ontario	Manitoba	Saskatchewan	Alberta	British Columbia	Yukon	Northwest Territories[1]	Nunavut[1]
				number				
1,260,513	2,095,630	194,798	196,013	532,301	631,445	6,333	17,563	...
1,250,268	2,111,622	195,091	194,797	543,387	629,544	6,102	18,068	...
1,245,022	2,131,626	199,419	192,885	546,402	628,265	5,975	9,753	9,584
1,237,981	2,143,599	192,299	190,711	549,633	625,073	5,764	9,672	9,558
1,244,689	2,163,108	191,102	186,518	548,122	622,837	5,608	9,678	9,548
1,245,339	2,164,940	189,217	182,687	551,375	613,235	5,610	9,747	9,364
1,241,071	2,129,742	188,498	178,932	549,533	605,517	5,520	9,689	9,362
				% change				
..	..	..	..		..	..	..	...
-0.8	0.8	0.2	-0.6	2.1	-0.3	-3.6	2.9	...
-0.4	0.9	2.2	-1.0	0.6	-0.2	-2.1	-46.0	...
-0.6	0.6	-3.6	-1.1	0.6	-0.5	-3.5	-0.8	-0.3
0.5	0.9	-0.6	-2.2	-0.3	-0.4	-2.7	0.1	-0.1
0.1	0.1	-1.0	-2.1	0.6	-1.5	0.0	0.7	-1.9
-0.3	-1.6	-0.4	-2.1	-0.3	-1.3	-1.6	-0.6	0.0

Quebec	Ontario	Manitoba	Saskatchewan	Alberta	British Columbia	Yukon	Northwest Territories	Nunavut
				number				
90,884	..	11,970	10,969	25,743	36,360	245	242	91
91,680	..	11,829	11,218	26,561	37,740	290	258	128
90,051	114,404	13,433	11,682	28,321	39,716	258	255	134
87,468	115,599	12,508	11,512	29,303	40,703	283	284	128
86,708	124,783	12,424	11,449	29,877	41,923	280	250	136
85,817	143,187	13,354	11,429	31,155	42,534	282	282	139
87,713	123,238	13,952	11,083	32,159	40,571	332	302	130
				% change				
..	..	..	..	..	..	..	..	...
0.9	..	-1.2	2.3	3.2	3.8	18.4	6.6	40.7
-1.8	..	13.6	4.1	6.6	5.2	-11.0	-1.2	4.7
-2.9	1.0	-6.9	-1.5	3.5	2.5	9.7	11.4	-4.5
-0.9	7.9	-0.7	-0.5	2.0	3.0	-1.1	-12.0	6.3
-1.0	14.7	7.5	-0.2	4.3	1.5	0.7	12.8	2.2
2.2	-13.9	4.5	-3.0	3.2	-4.6	17.7	7.1	-6.5

Table 10.5 University and college revenue and expenditures, 1992 to 2007

	1992	1993	1994	1995	1996	1997	1998
	\$ thousands						
Revenue	**15,777,481**	**16,369,729**	**16,419,382**	**16,759,086**	**17,260,407**	**16,729,056**	**17,389,686**
Own-source revenue	4,775,098	5,232,539	5,612,258	5,889,502	6,277,982	6,653,193	7,447,138
Sales of goods and services	3,581,381	4,036,333	4,349,760	4,567,345	4,843,608	5,187,833	5,699,797
Tuition fees	1,888,817	2,137,148	2,339,171	2,507,056	2,690,708	2,889,160	3,179,565
Other sales of goods and services	1,692,564	1,899,185	2,010,590	2,060,289	2,152,900	2,298,673	2,520,232
Investment income	372,453	376,157	367,552	366,970	427,658	408,272	556,419
Other revenue from own sources	821,264	820,049	894,945	955,187	1,006,716	1,057,088	1,190,922
Transfers from other levels of government	11,002,382	11,137,190	10,807,124	10,869,584	10,982,425	10,075,863	9,942,548
Federal government	1,036,574	1,079,685	1,095,690	1,110,639	1,090,080	1,022,516	980,566
Provincial and territorial governments	9,959,687	10,049,264	9,701,848	9,746,774	9,877,178	9,028,729	8,932,862
Local governments	6,121	8,241	9,586	12,171	15,167	24,618	29,120
Expenditures	**15,677,144**	**16,314,392**	**16,749,070**	**16,917,362**	**17,192,872**	**16,804,525**	**17,194,597**
Postsecondary education	15,390,167	16,034,061	16,451,698	16,559,462	16,747,684	16,381,240	16,762,116
Administration	2,986,317	3,073,970	3,103,484	3,157,017	3,361,662	3,205,490	3,251,008
Education	8,750,877	9,127,476	9,320,107	9,304,767	9,249,982	9,176,367	9,253,953
Support to students	375,646	404,958	428,626	447,082	453,669	307,665	347,649
Other	3,277,326	3,427,656	3,599,481	3,650,595	3,682,371	3,691,718	3,909,506
Special retraining services	..	..	..	..	..	..	..
Debt charges	286,977	280,331	297,372	357,900	445,189	423,285	432,481
Surplus/deficit (-)	**100,337**	**55,337**	**-329,689**	**-158,276**	**67,535**	**-75,469**	**195,089**

Notes: Fiscal year ending March 31.
Excludes Yukon College for confidentiality purposes.
Source: Statistics Canada, CANSIM table 385-0007.

1999	2000	2001	2002	2003	2004	2005	2006	2007
				$ thousands				
20,064,718	**20,380,239**	**21,732,604**	**23,262,806**	**25,359,135**	**28,096,412**	**29,484,455**	**30,990,494**	**33,847,597**
7,887,522	8,791,925	9,630,461	10,339,207	11,244,357	12,752,007	13,336,261	13,976,578	15,413,521
6,044,702	6,715,382	7,371,133	8,132,232	9,026,491	9,906,500	10,520,144	11,024,426	12,168,566
3,506,275	3,881,521	4,144,097	4,486,787	5,085,897	5,766,539	6,152,681	6,453,724	7,147,470
2,538,427	2,833,861	3,227,036	3,645,445	3,940,594	4,139,962	4,367,463	4,570,702	5,021,096
476,694	592,797	604,613	396,046	370,231	821,830	645,905	678,871	747,924
1,366,126	1,483,746	1,654,715	1,810,929	1,847,635	2,023,677	2,170,212	2,273,281	2,497,031
12,177,196	11,588,314	12,102,143	12,923,599	14,114,778	15,344,405	16,148,194	17,013,916	18,434,076
1,112,046	1,352,613	1,624,714	1,922,197	2,270,560	2,564,931	2,678,489	2,819,458	3,073,356
11,049,246	10,221,834	10,451,811	10,947,140	11,817,345	12,750,006	13,444,014	14,167,730	15,330,445
15,904	13,867	25,618	54,262	26,873	29,468	25,691	26,728	30,274
18,022,802	**19,478,054**	**21,278,479**	**23,454,251**	**25,590,341**	**27,690,208**	**29,609,613**	**31,262,977**	**34,107,650**
17,679,221	18,800,032	20,569,831	22,717,330	24,820,214	26,804,032	28,699,579	30,277,775	33,044,907
3,438,931	3,826,107	4,267,373	4,662,921	4,717,093	4,759,180	5,377,969	5,737,298	6,257,850
9,724,860	9,806,404	10,447,939	11,372,063	12,485,313	13,748,442	14,250,885	15,003,320	16,351,516
407,889	513,845	603,597	718,845	818,445	961,623	1,031,730	1,080,572	1,197,408
4,107,541	4,653,676	5,250,922	5,963,501	6,799,363	7,334,787	8,038,995	8,456,584	9,238,132
..	240,451	243,966	272,106	271,758	284,984	277,324	288,372	318,114
343,581	437,571	464,682	464,815	498,369	575,652	606,483	669,187	716,182
2,041,916	**902,185**	**454,125**	**-191,445**	**-231,206**	**406,204**	**-125,158**	**-272,484**	**-260,053**

Table 10.6 University enrolment, by instructional programs, 1993/1994 to 2004/2005

	1993/1994	1994/1995	1995/1996	1996/1997
	number			
All instructional programs	**874,605**	**858,972**	**846,408**	**829,767**
Personal improvement and leisure	..	..	..	..
Education	80,010	77,472	73,290	70,428
Visual and performing arts and communications technologies	25,479	25,494	25,704	24,882
Humanities	143,907	139,254	144,522	135,750
Social and behavioural sciences and law	148,179	147,720	143,607	136,992
Business, management and public administration	130,134	123,222	120,414	121,188
Physical and life sciences and technologies	77,472	77,112	78,525	76,842
Mathematics, computer and information sciences	32,607	32,454	32,133	32,622
Architecture, engineering and related technologies	65,364	63,657	62,259	62,088
Agriculture, natural resources and conservation	14,301	14,067	15,135	15,831
Health, parks, recreation and fitness	71,730	73,131	73,884	74,694
Personal, protective and transportation services	258	210	183	189
Other instructional programs	85,167	85,173	76,752	78,255

Source: Statistics Canada, CANSIM table 477-0013.

Table 10.7 University enrolment, by program level, 1993/1994 to 2004/2005

	1993/1994	1994/1995	1995/1996	1996/1997
	number			
All program levels	**874,605**	**858,972**	**846,408**	**829,767**
Trade/vocational and preparatory training certificate or diploma	..	..	..	..
Community college certificate or diploma and other community college	3,015	2,016	2,409	2,457
Undergraduate level	668,535	658,284	648,972	639,588
Bachelor's and other undergraduate degree	596,274	586,116	580,185	575,886
Other undergraduate level	72,261	72,168	68,787	63,702
Graduate level	112,047	112,947	112,524	112,068
Master's degree	69,942	69,783	69,300	69,093
Earned doctorate	26,475	27,147	27,306	27,198
Other graduate levels[1]	15,633	16,017	15,918	15,777
Other program levels[2]	91,008	85,722	82,503	75,651

1. Includes master's qualifying year, university graduate level certificate or diploma, PhD. (Doctor of Philosophy) qualifying year or probationary, internship (Postgraduate Medical Education known as post-MD.) and residency (medical, dental, veterinary).

2. Includes program levels not applicable and non-program (taking non-credit courses or taking courses without seeking a credit).

Source: Statistics Canada, CANSIM table 477-0013.

1997/1998	1998/1999	1999/2000	2000/2001	2001/2002	2002/2003	2003/2004	2004/2005
			number				
822,774	826,362	847,503	850,572	886,605	933,870	993,246	1,014,486
..	..	..	0	66	69	51	30
67,623	65,673	66,279	66,879	69,747	72,216	76,839	72,561
24,984	25,359	25,413	26,922	27,900	29,862	33,984	35,514
130,038	127,392	119,358	123,744	129,738	136,083	147,918	145,146
132,135	129,795	132,498	136,659	140,247	151,671	164,832	178,146
124,626	128,556	134,367	134,517	141,165	151,695	160,539	162,849
76,536	75,537	79,272	79,140	80,553	83,616	91,719	96,441
34,407	37,473	41,574	43,527	46,377	45,897	44,190	40,929
63,438	65,223	67,434	70,023	74,817	81,087	85,776	86,451
16,731	16,362	16,416	15,420	14,841	14,487	14,613	14,640
74,781	74,826	74,847	74,268	80,589	84,810	91,908	97,950
351	345	372	1,047	1,185	1,317	1,299	1,683
77,118	79,821	89,673	78,426	79,374	81,063	79,575	82,152

1997/1998	1998/1999	1999/2000	2000/2001	2001/2002	2002/2003	2003/2004	2004/2005
			number				
822,774	826,362	847,503	850,572	886,605	933,870	993,246	1,014,486
..	..	147	204	90	159	168	105
2,352	2,232	2,811	2,295	2,088	2,268	2,946	2,367
633,018	633,495	650,367	657,189	680,619	719,058	770,391	785,757
572,331	571,161	583,146	589,695	613,473	648,321	696,720	716,982
60,687	62,337	67,221	67,497	67,146	70,737	73,671	68,775
112,692	113,481	116,304	118,152	124,605	134,952	142,644	148,776
69,852	71,292	74,331	75,195	79,533	85,800	89,385	92,148
27,003	26,505	26,493	26,598	27,390	29,340	32,004	34,527
15,834	15,681	15,483	16,356	17,679	19,815	21,249	22,101
74,712	77,154	77,868	72,738	79,206	77,433	77,103	77,478

Table 10.8 University degrees, diplomas and certificates granted, 1993 to 2004

	1993	1994	1995	1996
	number			
All instructional programs	**173,850**	**178,074**	**178,065**	**178,113**
Personal improvement and leisure	..	..	..	..
Education	26,628	26,304	26,454	25,713
Visual and performing arts and communications technologies	5,127	5,310	5,241	5,199
Humanities	22,623	23,058	22,386	22,377
Social and behavioural sciences and law	38,334	39,423	39,678	38,988
Business, management and public administration	31,428	31,623	30,252	30,054
Physical and life sciences and technologies	12,015	13,119	13,662	14,631
Mathematics, computer and information sciences	6,762	6,825	7,194	6,996
Architecture, engineering and related technologies	12,135	12,999	13,293	13,341
Agriculture, natural resources and conservation	2,400	2,616	2,754	3,036
Health, parks, recreation and fitness	15,801	16,197	16,563	16,734
Personal, protective and transportation services	63	78	54	75
Other instructional programs	534	525	537	966

Source: Statistics Canada, CANSIM table 477-0014.

Table 10.9 University degrees, diplomas and certificates granted, by province, 1993 to 2004

	1993	1994	1995	1996
	number			
Canada	**173,850**	**178,074**	**178,065**	**178,113**
Newfoundland and Labrador	2,649	2,718	2,571	2,907
Prince Edward Island	498	573	585	528
Nova Scotia	7,806	8,103	7,887	7,725
New Brunswick	3,945	4,005	4,149	4,428
Quebec	56,334	57,852	56,856	56,253
Ontario	64,803	66,189	66,861	67,668
Manitoba	5,958	6,285	6,315	6,030
Saskatchewan	6,216	5,415	5,784	5,715
Alberta	11,637	12,282	12,270	12,240
British Columbia	13,998	14,652	14,784	14,616

Source: Statistics Canada, CANSIM table 477-0014.

1997	1998	1999	2000	2001	2002	2003	2004
			number				
173,934	172,074	173,577	176,556	178,101	186,153	198,525	209,076
..	..	..	..	..	..	..	3
23,742	21,636	22,290	22,542	22,395	23,754	24,942	25,428
5,205	5,256	5,202	5,373	5,904	5,949	6,654	7,320
20,988	20,364	19,593	20,064	19,809	20,463	22,095	22,350
37,872	37,899	36,702	36,315	36,096	37,398	39,120	41,757
29,916	30,492	31,629	33,213	34,728	37,485	40,785	43,170
15,183	15,552	14,607	14,730	14,808	14,283	14,685	15,186
6,867	6,966	7,710	8,448	9,060	10,008	10,647	11,079
12,912	13,026	12,798	13,305	13,839	14,766	16,380	17,460
3,240	3,258	3,825	4,008	3,885	3,654	3,765	3,576
16,746	16,497	16,920	16,518	16,215	17,220	18,129	20,136
102	81	90	81	228	270	270	360
1,158	1,047	2,211	1,959	1,131	903	1,053	1,254

1997	1998	1999	2000	2001	2002	2003	2004
			number				
173,934	172,074	173,577	176,556	178,101	186,153	198,525	209,076
2,952	3,000	3,114	2,931	2,862	2,898	2,976	3,168
570	405	540	534	606	555	624	672
7,785	7,812	7,824	7,638	7,680	7,878	8,766	9,579
4,311	4,032	3,975	4,032	4,101	4,395	4,557	4,944
53,589	51,066	50,958	50,847	51,153	54,009	57,786	61,212
65,562	65,898	65,697	67,221	68,286	70,749	75,864	80,436
5,895	5,640	5,442	5,340	5,397	5,580	5,871	6,309
5,337	5,445	5,547	5,793	5,694	5,739	5,865	5,835
12,816	13,002	13,560	14,052	15,087	16,344	17,199	18,012
15,117	15,780	16,917	18,171	17,238	18,000	19,017	18,906

Table 10.10 Employment in educational and related services, by province and territory, 2002 to 2006

	2002	2003	2004	2005	2006
			number		
Canada	**983,699**	**996,387**	**1,010,814**	**1,031,380**	**1,055,465**
Newfoundland and Labrador	16,398	16,612	16,504	15,813	16,127
Prince Edward Island	4,168	4,255	4,464	4,462	4,466
Nova Scotia	37,042	36,449	36,537	36,025	37,134
New Brunswick	24,129	24,206	23,834	24,285	24,952
Quebec	234,962	237,454	238,454	236,586	241,182
Ontario	351,465	362,346	370,804	387,460	397,519
Manitoba	42,403	43,166	44,584	46,156	45,841
Saskatchewan	37,061	37,202	37,977	38,603	38,818
Alberta	104,655	104,806	105,655	107,756	109,537
British Columbia	127,102	125,536	127,590	129,927	135,680
Yukon	1,118	1,146	1,156	1,200	1,234

Notes: Excludes owners or partners of unincorporated businesses and professional practices, the self-employed, unpaid family workers, people working outside Canada, military personnel, and casual workers for whom a T4 is not required
Data for Northwest Territories and Nunavut are not available.
Source: Statistics Canada, CANSIM table 281-0024.

Table 10.11 Undergraduate tuition fees for full-time students, by discipline, 2002/2003 to 2006/2007

	2002/2003	2003/2004	2004/2005	2005/2006	2006/2007
			average ($)		
Average undergraduate tuition fees	**3,749**	**4,018**	**4,140**	**4,211**	**4,347**
Agriculture	3,301	3,495	3,618	3,643	3,712
Architecture	3,524	3,587	3,599	3,610	3,805
Arts	3,617	3,813	3,962	3,982	4,104
Commerce	3,743	3,985	3,790	3,806	3,989
Dentistry	9,703	11,681	12,239	13,033	13,463
Education	3,019	3,149	3,252	3,277	3,334
Engineering	3,865	4,400	4,591	4,740	4,887
Household Sciences	3,486	3,669	3,816	3,914	4,037
Law	5,021	5,995	6,577	6,904	7,221
Medicine	8,063	9,137	10,139	10,318	10,553
Music	3,586	3,759	3,754	3,936	4,092
Science	3,728	3,957	4,093	4,219	4,353

Note: Using the most current enrolment data available, average tuition fees have been weighted by the number of students enrolled by institution and field of study. Fees at both public and private institutions are included in the weighted average calculations.
Source: Statistics Canada, Centre for Education Statistics.

Table 10.12 Undergraduate tuition fees for full-time students, by province, 2002/2003 to 2006/2007

	2002/2003	2003/2004	2004/2005	2005/2006	2006/2007
	average ($)				
Canada	3,749	4,018	4,140	4,211	4,347
Newfoundland and Labrador	2,729	2,606	2,606	2,606	2,606
Prince Edward Island	3,891	4,133	4,374	4,645	4,947
Nova Scotia	5,214	5,556	6,003	6,323	6,571
New Brunswick	4,186	4,457	4,719	5,037	5,328
Quebec	1,851	1,865	1,888	1,900	1,916
Ontario	4,665	4,911	4,831	4,933	5,160
Manitoba	3,144	3,155	3,236	3,333	3,338
Saskatchewan	4,286	4,644	5,062	5,063	5,063
Alberta	4,165	4,511	4,940	4,838	4,828
British Columbia	3,176	4,098	4,735	4,867	4,960

Note: Using the most current enrolment data available, average tuition fees have been weighted by the number of students enrolled by institution and field of study. Fees at both public and private institutions are included in the weighted average calculations.
Source: Statistics Canada, Centre for Education Statistics.

Table 10.13 Public and private elementary and secondary education expenditures, by province and territory, 1997/1998 to 2002/2003

	1997/1998	1998/1999	1999/2000	2000/2001	2001/2002	2002/2003
	$ thousands					
Canada	37,163,556	38,758,819	39,401,683	40,285,311	42,294,686	43,237,551
Newfoundland and Labrador	564,714	569,287	573,908	577,319	608,376	626,352
Prince Edward Island	127,047	143,263	142,211	150,277	156,399	154,311
Nova Scotia	920,575	1,027,450	1,080,247	996,439	1,006,261	1,145,116
New Brunswick	847,354	866,150	885,836	843,565	864,441	891,580
Quebec	7,600,775	7,772,687	8,554,451	8,860,058	9,628,481	9,616,102
Ontario	15,502,879	16,191,535	15,786,513	15,842,478	16,390,755	16,722,053
Manitoba	1,616,574	1,690,214	1,756,112	1,821,560	1,853,923	1,956,411
Saskatchewan	1,335,093	1,375,143	1,387,902	1,453,208	1,490,336	1,631,892
Alberta	3,528,301	3,882,363	3,922,073	4,139,444	4,401,026	4,504,733
British Columbia	4,802,043	4,907,057	5,005,492	5,294,063	5,552,127	5,617,944
Yukon	82,838	76,779	81,178	81,289	87,159	91,247
Northwest Territories (including Nunavut)	211,662	208,959	..	..	..	..
Northwest Territories	..	..	118,246	117,625	140,288	156,824
Nunavut	..	..	85,416	85,439	91,986	98,458
Foreign and undistributed[1]	23,701	47,932	22,098	22,547	23,128	24,528

Note: Data are estimates for the most recent year, budgetary for the second most recent year, and preliminary for the third most recent year.
1. Foreign and undistributed expenditures by the federal government that cannot be attributed to a particular province or territory.
Source: Statistics Canada, CANSIM table 478-0014.

Table 10.14 Private college enrolment, by major field of study and sex, 1993 and 2003

	1993			2003		
	Both sexes[1]	Males	Females	Both sexes[1]	Males	Females
			%			
Total[1]	100.0	17.5	82.5	100.0	30.7	69.3
Secretarial science	39.0	0.4	38.6	18.3	1.0	17.3
Business and finance	13.8	4.0	9.8	23.5	7.1	16.4
Computer science	13.9	6.1	7.8	13.7	7.1	6.6
Health professions	3.9	0.3	3.6	5.0	0.3	4.7
Others	29.3	6.7	22.6	39.5	15.2	24.3

1. Components might not add up to the total because of rounding.
Source: Statistics Canada, Survey of Labour and Income Dynamics.

Energy

11

OVERVIEW

Energy plays a central role in Canadian life. Canadians are among the world's biggest consumers of energy, relying heavily on it for transportation, heating, industrial production and economic growth. Canada is also one of the world's leading producers of energy, exporting huge quantities annually. The environmental impact of energy use has become one of the major issues of our day, forcing many Canadians to rethink how they consume energy.

At the individual level, some hard facts about energy supply and demand hit almost all Canadians in 2006, when gasoline prices soared above $1.00 a litre. Crude oil prices have risen significantly—from $US20 in 2002 to US$77 in the fall of 2006—because of increased demand for oil, political change in Venezuela, the war in Iraq, other conflicts in the Middle East, production cuts by the Organization of Petroleum Exporting

Countries (OPEC), and supply disruption after hurricanes in the Gulf of Mexico.

Even though production volume fell slightly in 2005, the value of crude oil exports increased 21%, partly the result of a 30% gain in prices. From 1990 to 2004, the average price for regular unleaded gasoline at Canadian gas stations climbed about 44%, and then jumped another 15% in 2005 alone. Meanwhile, fuel oil for heating households rose 126% from 1990 to 2005.

But rising energy prices aren't turning Canadians off energy: we continue to consume more than ever. Energy consumption per capita has increased an average 1% a year over the past 20 years. In 2004, we used 363 gigajoules of energy per capita, compared with 302 gigajoules in 1984. One gigajoule is the equivalent of a 30-litre tank of gasoline, and will keep a

Chart 11.1
Energy production, by primary energy source

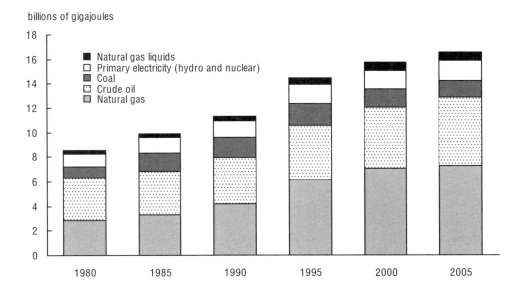

billions of gigajoules

Legend:
- Natural gas liquids
- Primary electricity (hydro and nuclear)
- Coal
- Crude oil
- Natural gas

Source: Statistics Canada, CANSIM tables 128-0002 and 128-0009.

60-watt incandescent light bulb lit for six months.

The energy machine

In 2004, driven by an increase in gas and oil production, 16.6 billion gigajoules of primary energy were generated in Canada, more than double the amount in 1978. Gas and oil accounted for 78% of the total production. Electricity (including primary steam) comprised 12% of energy production in the late 1970s, but less than 10% in 2004. Coal production has consistently accounted for about 9%.

Quebec and British Columbia are major generators of hydroelectric power, whereas Alberta and Ontario lead the way in thermal-electric energy production. Ontario produces 89% of Canada's nuclear power.

Less than one-half of one percent of the country's generating capacity comes from wind or tidal power—non-polluting, renewable energy sources. Though still a very minor part of the energy industry, wind energy is the fastest-growing form of renewable energy in the world. Canada's

Chart 11.2
Production of crude oil, 2006

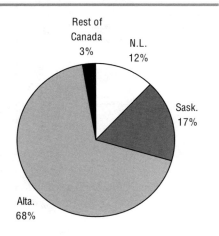

Rest of
Canada
3%

N.L.
12%

Sask.
17%

Alta.
68%

Source: Statistics Canada, CANSIM table 126-0001.

Energy production by fuel type, 2005

	terajoules
Coal	1,400,510
Crude oil	5,632,426
Natural gas	7,249,864
Natural gas liquids	655,787
Primary electricity, hydro and nuclear	1,608,679
Refined petroleum products	4,698,812

Source: Statistics Canada, CANSIM table 128-0009.

leader in wind energy generation is the town of Pincher Creek, Alberta, which harnesses the chinook winds on the Rocky Mountains' eastern slopes. Combined, Pincher Creek and Quebec's Gaspé Peninsula generate almost 87% of all of Canada's wind power.

Keeping pace with demand

Canada is one of the world's largest energy producers, and exports virtually all its surplus energy to the United States, primarily via pipelines and power lines. Global demand and high oil prices have pushed Canada's energy exports upward over the last 25 years. Energy exports have more than quadrupled from 2.1 billion gigajoules in 1980 to 8.8 billion gigajoules in 2004.

Canada's oil industry is currently booming. In 2005, a 30% surge in prices pushed the value of oil exports up to $30 billion, from $25 billion the previous year. Two-thirds of all oil produced was exported in 2005, with 99% of it going to the United States. Overall, oil accounted for 6.7% of all goods and services exported in 2005, more than twice the proportion 10 years earlier.

Two-thirds of the crude oil produced in Canada in 2005 came from Alberta. About one million barrels a day, or 42% of the province's total production, was extracted from the massive oil sands alone. Most of Canada's 180 billion barrels of crude oil reserves—a total second only to Saudi Arabia—is found in the oil sands of northern Alberta. As the most productive fields of natural gas are exhausted, the industry is turning toward developing non-conventional natural gas from coal—otherwise known as coal bed methane—in the Western Canada Sedimentary Basin.

Energy efficiency

As the extent of our impact on the environment becomes more clear, many Canadians have been looking for ways to improve energy efficiency and reduce greenhouse gas (GHG) emissions. Since 1990, energy efficiency in Canada has increased an estimated 14%. In 2004, efforts to conserve energy lowered consumption by more than 900 million gigajoules, reducing GHG emissions by 53.6 megatonnes— roughly equivalent to removing 13 million cars and light trucks from the roads.

The introduction of new appliances, vehicles, machines and production methods have been part of the solution. From 1990 to 2004, energy efficiency in the home increased by 21%, and the transportation industry increased its efficiency by 18%. Industrial users boosted their energy efficiency by 12%.

Selected sources

Statistics Canada

- *Analysis in Brief. Occasional.* 11-621-MIE
- *Canadian Social Trends.* Irregular. 11-008-XWE
- *The Consumer Price Index.* Monthly. 62-001-XIB
- *Energy Statistics Handbook.* Quarterly. 57-601-XIE
- *Human Activity and the Environment:* Annual Statistics. Annual. 16-201-XIE
- *Innovation Analysis Bulletin.* Irregular. 88-003-XIE

Other

- Canadian Centre for Energy
- Canadian Wind Energy Association
- National Energy Board
- Natural Resources Canada

Chart 11.3
Research and development spending on alternative sources of energy

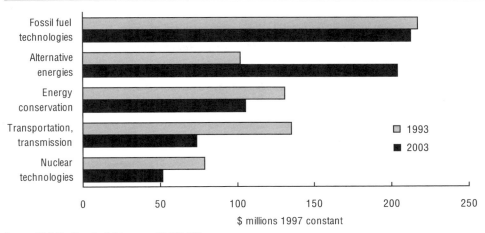

Source: Statistics Canada, Catalogue no. 11-621-MIE.

Soaring oil prices

Canadians are paying more for gas at the pump and for higher heating oil bills thanks to international factors, such as geopolitical instability, natural disasters and a growing industrial and consumer demand for crude oil—especially from India and China.

In 2001, the price of oil was at a low US$15.95 a barrel. Over the next couple of years, oil prices climbed significantly and rapidly, as the Organization of Petroleum Exporting Countries cut production, the Chavez government in Venezuela changed the oil industry there, and war began in Iraq.

Then hurricanes hit the U.S. Gulf Coast in 2004 and 2005, damaging offshore drilling rigs and closing refineries. Hurricane Katrina in August 2005 significantly disrupted oil and natural gas production and delayed deliveries. By the fall of 2006, the price of oil had climbed to US$77 a barrel.

This has translated into higher prices for Canadians. From 1990 to 2006, the consumer price of household heating fuel oil increased 123%. Retail prices have more than doubled in every urban centre since 1990. Prince Edward Islanders in Charlottetown and Summerside paid the lowest average annual price in 2006, at 78 cents a litre, whereas residents of Victoria, British Columbia were paying the highest heating oil prices in 2006, an annual average of 94 cents a litre.

Gasoline prices rose 57% from 1990 to 2006. The annual average retail price of regular unleaded gasoline in 2006 was $1.00 per litre or more in urban centres in all provinces and territories, except Ontario, Manitoba and Alberta. Drivers in Yellowknife, Northwest Territories paid the highest average retail price in 2006, almost $1.10 per litre; Edmonton, Alberta's drivers paid the lowest price, $0.91 per litre on average.

Chart 11.4
Household heating fuel, average retail prices, selected urban centres

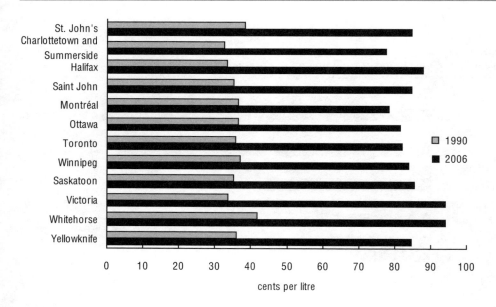

cents per litre

Source: Statistics Canada, CANSIM table 326-0009.

Winds of change

Canadians have long taken advantage of geography to generate electricity from water: hydroelectricity is our leading renewable energy source. Now Canada's governments and businesses are investing in new sources of renewable energy.

Our fastest-growing renewable energy sources are wind and tidal energy—clean and abundant sources that are economical to produce and fairly reliable where winds and climate are suitable. In 2000, Canada's winds and tides were harnessed to produce 971,873 megawatt hours of electricity, more than triple the output in 2000. However, this comprised only 0.2% of the electricity generated in Canada that year. Hydroelectric generators produced 58% of our electricity.

Alberta, already a star in fossil fuels, also generates the majority of Canada's electricity produced from wind and tide—64% in 2004.

Quebec is second, accounting for 19%. Quebec also produces half the country's hydroelectricity.

Wind and tidal electricity made up 1% or less of the electricity produced in each province and territory in 2004, with one exception: Prince Edward Island generated 73% of its electricity production from wind and tide.

Other renewable energy sources are being developed. Canadian businesses spent $204 million on research and development (R&D) of alternative energy sources and technologies in 2003. More than 40% of that spending went to technologies to store energy or to alternative fuels, such as ethanol and biodiesel. Improvements to hydroelectric generation accounted for 14% of R&D spending, and solar energy, 11%. Only 7% of alternative energy R&D spending went to biomass energy, carbon dioxide capture and wind power technologies combined.

Chart 11.5
Wind and tidal electricity generated

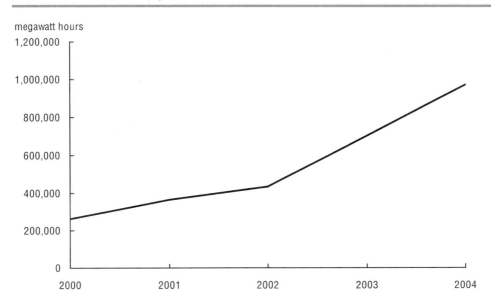

megawatt hours

Sources: Statistics Canada, Catalogue no. 57-202-XIE.

The ways we heat our homes

Where we live in Canada—and the mix of energy sources, distribution networks and local prices in that province—determines to a large extent how we heat our homes.

Hydroelectricity, for example, is abundant in Quebec, Manitoba, British Columbia and Newfoundland and Labrador, so it is an important source of energy for heating households in these provinces.

In Quebec, where electricity rates are among the lowest in Canada, more than two out of three households use electricity to heat their homes. More than one-third of dwellings in Quebec are apartments and about 80% of these buildings are electrically heated. This usage rate is much higher than the national average of 56%.

Half of all households in New Brunswick and Newfoundland and Labrador rely on electricity as their leading source. In Nova Scotia, electricity heats only one-quarter of homes. Instead, 50% of families in Nova Scotia turn to oil for home heating. In Prince Edward Island, oil heats 81% of households.

Wood is a popular heating alternative in Atlantic Canada: about one in seven households use wood and other solid fuels like coal. In Newfoundland and Labrador, it is as high as nearly one in five households.

Virtually no homes are heated with natural gas in Atlantic Canada, where natural gas has only been on the market since 2004. In all provinces west of Quebec, natural gas has emerged as the dominant home heating fuel, and has been the only fuel whose use has grown in the last decade.

Fully 97% of Alberta's households heat with natural gas. Natural gas pipelines are plentiful in Manitoba and British Columbia, so about 60% of households there heat with natural gas. Ontarians also use natural gas as their principal energy source for heating.

Chart 11.6
Principal home heating fuel

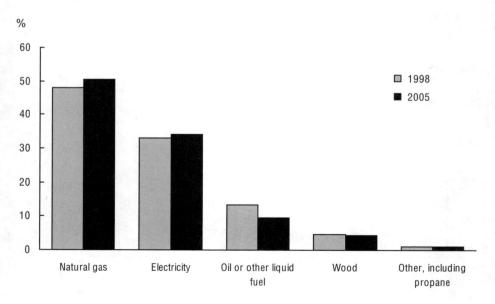

Source: Statistics Canada, CANSIM table 203-0019.

Natural gas heats up

Over the last 50 years, more Canadians have come to rely on natural gas to heat their homes and commercial spaces. By 2005, half of all Canadian dwellings were heated primarily with natural gas. The new TransCanada natural gas pipeline in the 1950s allowed 26% of homes to heat with gas. The oil shocks of the 1970s and government policies favouring natural gas in Ontario and the Western provinces encouraged wider gas use to heat homes.

In 2005, more than 5.1 million homes were heated with natural gas, at an average annual cost of $1,400. Canadian homes and businesses consumed 2.3 billion gigajoules of natural gas in 2005.

Canada produced 7.2 billion gigajoules in 2005, and exported half of it to the United States: most went to utilities, industries and consumers in the Midwest and Northeast.

Expanding in the 1990s, by 2005 gas made up 44% of the country's primary energy production.

Alberta, British Columbia and Saskatchewan produce 97% of Canada's natural gas. According to Natural Resources Canada, these three provinces alone account for one-quarter of the natural gas produced in all of North America. Another 2% of Canada's production comes from Nova Scotia's and Newfoundland and Labrador's offshore reservoirs.

Employment in the oil and gas industry rose 65% from 1997 to 2006. About 75% of jobs in the industry were in Alberta. These workers are much more likely to work full-time, 95% to 97%, compared with 82% in other industries. They were also less likely to be unionized (9% versus 32%). Their earnings in 2006 averaged $30.36 per hour, compared with $16.73 in the labour market as a whole.

Chart 11.7
Natural gas reserves and value

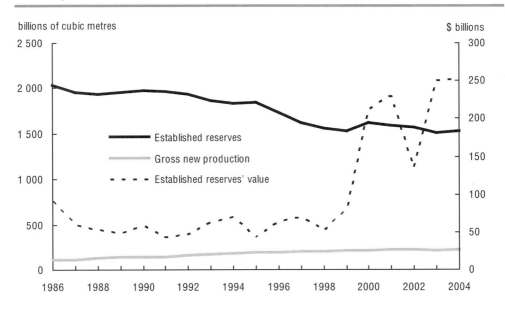

Source: Statistics Canada, CANSIM tables 131-0001, 153-0001 and 153-0014.

Table 11.1 Energy supply and demand, 1991 to 2005

	1991	1992	1993	1994	1995	1996
			petajoules			
Primary energy supply[1]						
Availability	9,091.0	9,176.3	9,314.1	9,564.3	9,695.2	10,097.2
Production	11,887.9	12,196.2	13,077.8	13,913.3	14,489.2	14,800.3
Exports	4,998.0	5,246.8	5,653.8	6,348.6	6,878.6	6,950.2
Imports	1,628.9	1,625.0	1,644.9	1,749.7	1,682.5	1,977.2
Primary and secondary energy supply						
Net supply[2]	7,842.4	8,015.7	8,165.2	8,412.4	8,583.6	8,899.6
Producer consumption	937.2	978.8	988.3	1,017.2	1,039.8	1,059.1
Non-energy use	696.4	709.2	729.5	740.6	758.8	800.0
Primary and secondary energy demand[3]	**6,208.8**	**6,327.6**	**6,447.4**	**6,654.7**	**6,785.0**	**7,040.4**
Industrial	1,977.8	1,961.6	1,973.2	2,053.4	2,105.6	2,180.5
Transportation	1,795.1	1,885.8	1,918.2	2,021.3	2,065.1	2,124.7
Agriculture	195.2	196.9	198.8	195.8	209.2	222.9
Residential	1,183.1	1,216.3	1,256.7	1,286.7	1,259.1	1,358.2
Public administration	134.4	133.7	132.1	143.1	143.3	134.1
Commercial and other institutional	923.1	933.4	968.6	954.4	1,002.6	1,020.4

1. Primary energy sources are coal, crude oil, natural gas, natural gas liquids, hydro, and nuclear electricity.
2. Primary and secondary sources.
3. Final demand.
Source: Statistics Canada, CANSIM tables 128-0002 and 128-0009.

Table 11.2 Consumer Price Index, energy, 1992 to 2006

	1992	1993	1994	1995	1996	1997
			1992=100			
Electricity	100.0	104.2	104.9	104.4	105.6	106.8
Natural gas	100.0	103.8	112.5	105.6	104.4	112.2
Fuel oil and other fuel	100.0	101.7	100.4	99.0	105.8	112.3

Source: Statistics Canada, CANSIM table 326-0002.

1997	1998	1999	2000	2001	2002	2003	2004	2005
				petajoules				
10,200.1	10,194.9	10,518.3	10,831.0	10,950.4	11,163.5	11,478.5	11,527.5	11,310.2
15,284.4	15,368.7	15,358.2	15,768.4	15,894.9	16,171.0	16,170.9	16,553.7	16,547.3
7,496.4	7,818.3	7,824.0	8,328.4	8,443.8	8,561.9	8,499.0	8,822.7	8,662.2
2,231.8	2,385.3	2,518.5	2,852.2	3,013.4	2,923.6	3,459.8	3,107.6	3,007.4
8,927.6	8,841.3	9,190.7	9,423.7	9,303.5	9,623.1	9,829.9	10,014.0	9,990.1
999.2	1,073.3	1,229.3	1,257.4	1,264.9	1,344.1	1,340.0	1,303.2	1,354.9
833.0	811.8	828.9	790.3	863.2	894.3	903.4	1,029.3	981.8
7,095.5	**6,956.2**	**7,132.5**	**7,376.0**	**7,175.4**	**7,384.7**	**7,586.5**	**7,681.6**	**7,653.5**
2,196.9	2,149.0	2,177.3	2,268.6	2,166.3	2,229.5	2,318.6	2,343.2	2,283.1
2,182.9	2,256.6	2,307.3	2,279.8	2,240.4	2,250.1	2,266.3	2,347.3	2,388.8
230.0	224.7	229.9	231.9	218.1	206.8	211.8	208.9	208.7
1,295.1	1,183.5	1,232.3	1,287.8	1,240.0	1,286.7	1,338.2	1,313.0	1,296.1
135.9	130.3	124.5	131.3	126.8	125.2	128.1	131.9	136.6
1,054.8	1,012.3	1,061.4	1,176.4	1,184.1	1,286.7	1,323.8	1,337.5	1,340.2

1998	1999	2000	2001	2002	2003	2004	2005	2006
				1992=100				
107.8	108.5	109.2	111.1	119.6	117.2	122.0	125.4	132.5
119.1	130.7	158.9	206.0	168.7	219.5	214.9	229.9	237.1
100.8	101.3	143.2	143.5	131.8	151.5	166.7	209.2	218.0

Table 11.3 Gasoline prices, by selected urban centres, 1991 to 2006

	1991	1992	1993	1994	1995	1996
	cents per litre					
St. John's	63.6	60.8	57.0	58.6	62.8	61.4
Charlottetown and Summerside	63.3	60.8	56.8	55.0	59.3	59.2
Halifax	..	..	50.7	52.0	54.3	54.8
Saint John	..	..	54.7	53.6	56.0	55.1
Québec	64.2	61.1	59.0	56.7	58.2	60.6
Montréal	64.3	60.2	57.4	55.2	56.8	60.6
Ottawa	59.2	57.3	54.2	52.5	53.8	55.1
Toronto	53.8	52.4	51.1	49.8	52.4	56.1
Thunder Bay	58.8	57.2	56.5	56.2	56.6	61.2
Winnipeg	52.8	49.5	52.1	52.3	54.6	56.9
Regina	47.4	49.4	53.6	55.6	57.5	59.3
Saskatoon	52.7	51.6	55.7	55.3	57.8	60.8
Edmonton	49.8	47.6	45.7	45.4	47.6	49.6
Calgary	50.5	46.6	47.3	47.4	50.0	51.7
Vancouver	57.8	53.8	54.8	55.6	58.4	59.2
Victoria	58.2	52.1	51.0	51.8	54.8	57.9
Whitehorse	62.1	58.4	58.0	58.1	63.4	67.0
Yellowknife	66.1	64.4	65.2	65.7	70.2	73.2

Note: Average annual price of regular unleaded gasoline at self-service filling stations.
Source: Statistics Canada, CANSIM table 326-0009.

Table 11.4 Household heating fuel prices, by selected urban centres, 1991 to 2006

	1991	1992	1993	1994	1995	1996	1997
	cents per litre						
St. John's	41.0	39.7	39.6	36.3	36.5	39.8	44.3
Charlottetown and Summerside	38.9	35.5	36.0	34.4	36.1	37.5	39.2
Halifax	37.2	36.5	36.5	33.8	34.0	38.5	42.8
Saint John	38.6	38.2	38.7	36.2	35.2	41.7	46.4
Québec	40.3	39.2	39.2	39.6	39.0	41.8	40.9
Montréal	38.9	37.7	37.0	36.5	33.4	34.6	36.7
Ottawa	39.0	37.3	37.4	37.3	37.3	39.6	42.8
Toronto	38.0	36.4	38.0	38.3	38.3	40.6	43.4
Thunder Bay	43.9	40.9	41.0	40.2	42.0	45.2	43.8
Winnipeg	42.5	41.0	42.5	41.8	41.9	44.4	47.8
Regina	38.2	36.1	35.7	35.6	36.9	39.7	42.7
Saskatoon	40.3	37.6	38.0	39.3	40.9	41.9	44.1
Vancouver	41.7	40.4	41.4	41.5	41.5	42.5	43.9
Victoria	39.8	39.0	39.5	39.6	39.6	40.5	44.2
Whitehorse	45.0	41.8	42.5	42.5	41.9	43.3	46.0
Yellowknife	39.5	37.1	38.7	38.7	37.9	39.6	38.9

Note: Average annual price.
Source: Statistics Canada, CANSIM table 326-0009.

1997	1998	1999	2000	2001	2002	2003	2004	2005	2006
				cents per litre					
67.7	64.4	66.2	83.0	79.1	77.0	82.8	91.7	102.1	107.6
60.6	53.6	52.9	70.1	71.9	68.2	74.0	84.1	96.4	103.0
60.6	57.1	60.8	76.1	72.8	73.4	78.0	87.5	97.9	103.7
60.2	55.4	59.2	73.3	70.0	72.5	78.8	88.0	97.9	102.2
61.3	55.2	61.5	71.9	74.0	72.1	77.8	87.0	97.5	102.4
61.9	56.3	63.0	77.2	73.8	71.4	76.7	85.8	96.4	100.8
56.0	51.3	56.2	69.0	66.0	65.9	70.2	77.2	88.5	92.2
56.1	51.6	57.5	70.8	67.8	67.3	70.9	76.6	89.0	93.4
62.6	54.0	58.0	72.6	72.5	71.0	76.9	82.8	94.0	98.5
57.4	53.3	57.3	66.7	65.0	63.2	67.6	76.7	90.0	96.6
60.0	55.6	60.5	71.7	72.2	72.7	76.0	82.5	92.7	99.6
60.6	56.7	59.8	71.7	72.2	73.0	75.9	82.8	93.5	99.8
52.1	47.0	51.4	63.5	61.3	63.4	67.4	75.9	85.1	91.0
53.2	48.9	52.6	64.0	64.5	64.6	66.3	74.8	85.8	92.3
58.8	50.6	54.3	69.1	68.9	70.4	76.8	86.0	97.1	103.8
59.0	52.7	59.2	73.5	73.9	73.9	81.1	89.9	99.2	105.4
67.9	66.9	67.3	81.4	81.7	80.8	83.6	93.9	105.5	107.6
73.9	72.1	73.6	85.4	88.2	88.5	92.2	96.8	105.0	109.5

1998	1999	2000	2001	2002	2003	2004	2005	2006
				cents per litre				
35.1	38.6	56.1	54.5	50.1	54.8	62.4	78.6	84.8
32.4	32.8	48.8	51.3	46.5	53.4	56.8	73.8	77.6
36.9	38.9	56.1	54.7	53.3	61.4	68.5	83.6	87.9
41.5	40.9	59.4	58.7	54.9	62.4	66.0	83.2	84.7
37.0	38.2	50.2	49.1	48.8	56.3	61.3	77.2	79.0
32.8	33.6	51.3	49.9	46.3	54.3	58.6	75.0	78.6
39.2	39.3	53.4	56.8	49.2	57.2	62.9	77.4	81.6
41.2	39.1	54.3	55.9	50.8	57.9	64.0	78.0	82.2
37.7	39.1	54.3	54.6	47.9	57.1	62.9	81.4	85.5
47.0	45.6	56.1	60.2	53.0	60.8	64.4	81.6	84.0
40.9	41.4	53.3	55.2	51.8	55.7	62.4	82.0	82.6
42.1	41.7	54.0	56.5	54.6	59.3	65.3	80.0	85.5
41.4	42.2	57.1	58.1	54.2	59.2	69.4	88.1	89.0
40.7	42.9	57.9	58.0	53.6	62.9	72.3	90.8	94.1
42.4	41.6	57.0	63.1	57.5	64.5	72.3	88.4	94.1
35.0	37.1	52.3	51.9	49.0	56.5	62.0	81.3	84.8

Table 11.5 Established crude oil reserves, 1990 to 2004

	1990	1991	1992	1993	1994	1995
	millions of cubic metres					
Canada	**657.3**	**614.9**	**590.4**	**582.2**	**544.5**	**553.0**
Newfoundland and Labrador	..	..	..	..	..	..
Ontario	1.4	1.3	1.2	1.2	2.0	1.9
Manitoba	7.4	7.2	6.7	6.5	6.3	5.6
Saskatchewan	119.8	120.2	122.6	130.2	141.9	150.1
Alberta	510.5	468.5	442.0	426.8	374.8	374.1
British Columbia	18.2	17.7	17.9	17.5	19.4	21.3

Note: Data are for closing stock of established crude oil reserves.
Source: Statistics Canada, CANSIM table 153-0013.

Table 11.6 Established natural gas reserves, 1990 to 2004

	1990	1991	1992	1993	1994	1995
	billions of cubic metres					
Canada	**1,978.6**	**1,965.2**	**1,929.1**	**1,859.9**	**1,832.7**	**1,840.9**
Nova Scotia	..	..	..	..	..	..
Ontario	16.9	16.7	16.9	17.2	13.4	12.0
Saskatchewan	83.9	82.1	78.4	84.7	86.7	86.6
Alberta	1,647.4	1,626.2	1,594.7	1,534.9	1,490.3	1,488.8
British Columbia	230.4	240.1	239.2	223.1	242.2	253.5

Note: Data are for closing stock of established natural gas reserves.
Source: Statistics Canada, CANSIM table 153-0014.

Table 11.7 Established reserves of natural gas liquids, 1990 to 2004

	1990	1991	1992	1993	1994	1995
	thousands of cubic metres					
Canada	**649,718**	**639,935**	**636,588**	**621,645**	**593,278**	**599,569**
Manitoba	72	65	61	56	52	46
Saskatchewan	1,976	1,862	1,724	2,035	2,207	2,155
Alberta	637,300	626,600	623,700	603,200	574,300	580,600
Propane	124,800	121,400	121,100	118,100	111,600	109,400
Ethane	320,000	316,000	312,000	305,000	290,000	300,000
Butane	71,700	69,900	70,600	67,100	63,900	62,900
Pentanes plus	120,800	119,300	120,000	113,000	108,800	108,300
British Columbia	10,370	11,408	11,103	16,354	16,719	16,768

Note: Data are for closing stock of established reserves of natural gas liquids.
Source: Statistics Canada, CANSIM table 153-0015.

1996	1997	1998	1999	2000	2001	2002	2003	2004
millions of cubic metres								
526.7	532.2	673.5	642.5	667.3	644.7	606.1	590.0	603.8
..	..	144.3	138.0	159.6	151.0	134.4	121.3	138.7
1.9	1.8	1.9	1.9	2.0	1.9	1.8	1.9	1.9
5.1	4.7	4.2	4.3	4.5	4.0	3.4	4.6	3.9
156.8	176.6	180.9	169.1	182.1	184.9	183.9	184.7	187.9
342.0	326.8	315.2	301.6	291.4	278.3	260.3	253.9	249.2
20.9	22.3	26.9	27.7	27.6	24.7	22.3	23.6	22.2

1996	1997	1998	1999	2000	2001	2002	2003	2004
billions of cubic metres								
1,725.9	1,620.4	1,562.2	1,526.8	1,614.5	1,590.8	1,569.7	1,504.1	1,532.2
..	..	..	..	67.1	61.7	56.2	23.2	19.3
12.5	12.5	12.2	12.0	11.6	11.5	11.3	11.5	11.5
81.8	76.5	71.5	68.6	75.6	81.7	76.2	87.4	85.0
1,378.1	1,284.0	1,239.9	1,207.2	1,210.7	1,184.4	1,171.4	1,122.2	1,127.0
253.5	247.4	238.6	239.0	249.5	251.5	254.7	259.9	289.4

1996	1997	1998	1999	2000	2001	2002	2003	2004
thousands of cubic metres								
546,580	502,751	487,525	487,339	486,977	476,429	370,919	310,651	307,546
91	0	..	..	..	..	..	..	..
2,086	1,632	1,482	1,306	1,010	981	1,000	1,029	888
527,500	483,400	468,900	469,700	473,900	463,600	359,100	298,500	295,000
103,000	91,400	88,600	82,600	85,500	84,100	79,300	69,400	71,300
264,000	245,000	238,000	256,000	252,000	252,100	165,100	124,000	122,900
58,500	51,900	51,100	48,600	50,400	49,900	46,900	41,900	41,500
102,000	95,100	91,200	82,500	86,000	77,500	67,800	63,200	59,300
16,903	17,719	17,143	16,333	12,067	11,848	10,819	11,122	11,658

Table 11.8 Energy fuel consumption of the manufacturing sector, by subsector, 2000 to 2005

	2000	2001	2002	2003	2004	2005
	terajoules					
All manufacturing	**2,597,020**	**2,511,331**	**2,511,322**	**2,521,077**	**2,614,696**	**2,526,174**
Food	94,607	89,116	88,765	89,041	90,928	91,666
Beverage and tobacco products	13,113	12,196	12,896	12,237	12,266	12,018
Textile mills	9,993	8,634	8,238	8,050	8,058	7,287
Textile product mills	4,053	4,275	4,303	3,554	3,545	3,498
Clothing	5,107	5,174	4,985	4,978	3,997	2,504
Leather and allied products	1,137	1,071	966	768	568	372
Wood products	129,434	118,511	122,595	120,183	124,853	128,877
Paper	883,378	834,855	830,779	835,318	850,894	800,071
Printing and related support activities	9,668	8,754	8,548	8,765	8,521	8,656
Petroleum and coal products	325,858	345,471	366,241	368,429	405,491	358,016
Chemicals	294,962	275,596	252,056	254,575	278,149	272,827
Plastic and rubber products	32,172	33,972	32,592	35,045	37,011	39,090
Non-metallic mineral products	121,203	115,198	118,845	117,924	126,049	124,494
Primary metals	536,431	524,957	519,559	521,073	521,069	529,160
Fabricated metal products	33,678	38,542	41,361	39,784	41,647	41,982
Machinery	13,893	14,070	13,819	15,223	16,042	17,529
Computer and electronic products	6,636	3,682	3,931	4,563	5,100	5,556
Electrical equipment, appliances and components	7,046	6,318	6,011	6,708	7,107	7,180
Transportation equipment	59,592	54,249	57,134	56,725	56,267	57,524
Furniture and related products	10,063	11,058	11,308	11,521	10,908	11,660
Miscellaneous manufacturing	4,997	5,633	6,391	6,610	6,226	6,205

Note: North American Industry Classification System (NAICS), 2002.
Source: Statistics Canada, CANSIM table 128-0006.

Table 11.9 Energy fuel consumption of the manufacturing sector, by fuel type, 2000 to 2005

	2000	2001	2002	2003	2004	2005
	terajoules					
Energy consumed	**2,597,020**	**2,511,331**	**2,511,322**	**2,521,077**	**2,614,696**	**2,526,174**
Coal	49,055	47,572	46,775	50,841	55,381	50,285
Coal coke	103,429	96,338	93,299	92,236	93,389	92,150
Coke oven gas	27,120	27,036	26,824	28,019	28,333	29,552
Electricity	690,247	684,234	696,960	705,419	700,993	723,778
Heavy fuel oil	139,163	139,351	114,653	138,696	150,234	126,039
Middle distillates	24,885	22,736	19,838	18,166	19,896	20,603
Natural gas	782,775	721,897	726,312	672,564	694,866	662,989
Petroleum coke and coke from catalytic cracking catalyst	68,417	75,647	84,085	88,419	94,986	84,468
Propane	13,239	15,358	12,640	11,634	9,448	8,238
Refinery fuel gas	151,392	173,033	175,149	178,996	207,558	186,407
Spent pulping liquor	319,683	288,942	290,859	292,635	299,806	283,722
Steam	37,394	40,076	41,336	47,956	48,029	48,764
Wood	190,220	179,109	182,594	195,495	211,777	209,178

Note: North American Industry Classification System (NAICS), 2002.
Source: Statistics Canada, CANSIM table 128-0006.

Environment

12

The 2006 Canadian Environmental Sustainability Indicators—air quality, greenhouse gas (GHG) emissions and freshwater quality—provide evidence of growing pressures on Canada's environmental sustainability and Canadians' health and well-being, as well as evidence of potential consequences for our long-term economic performance.

Trends for air quality and GHG emissions point to greater threats to human health and the planet's climate. The water quality indicator shows that guidelines are being exceeded, at least occasionally, at many selected monitoring sites across the country.

The three indicators provide key information about environmental sustainability, health and well-being, and the consequences of our economic growth and lifestyle choices. Some of the same social and economic forces drive the changes in all three indicators, some of the same substances affect all three and some of the same regions show up as stressed according to all three indicators.

Air quality indicator

Many air pollutants—nitrogen oxides, ground-level ozone, volatile organic compounds (VOCs) and fine particulate matter, to name a few—have adverse effects on the environment and on human health. Smog, for example, is mainly composed of ground-level ozone and fine particulate matter—two pollutants used as national indicators of air quality.

From 1990 to 2004, the ground-level ozone exposure indicator increased an average 0.9% yearly. In 2004, values were highest at monitoring stations in southern Ontario,

Chart 12.1
Ground-level ozone, 1990 to 2004

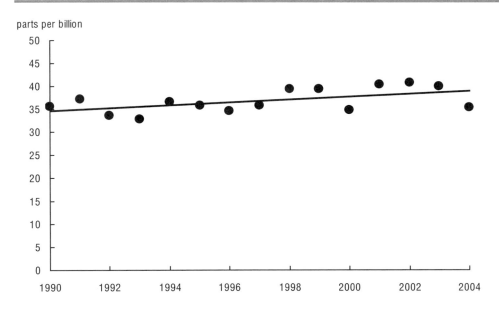

parts per billion

Source: Statistics Canada, Catalogue no. 16-251-XWE.

followed by Quebec and eastern Ontario. Ground-level ozone in southern Ontario has been on an upward trend since 1990. Other regions show no discernable trend.

Produced by human activities, ground-level ozone is formed by chemical reactions involving increases in both nitrogen oxides and VOCs in the presence of sunlight. We contribute to VOCs in the air mainly by producing oil and gas, by driving vehicles, and by burning wood. Most nitrogen oxides come from human actitivies, such as burning fossil fuels.

The highest levels of fine particulate matter for 2004 were primarily in southern Ontario, although some areas in southern Quebec and eastern Ontario also posted high levels.

Exposure to ground-level ozone and fine particulate matter is of concern because there are no established thresholds below which these pollutants are safe. Fine particulate matter especially threatens health because it can travel deep into the lungs. Both these substances can aggravate asthma, emphysema and other respiratory conditions. Children are especially sensitive to the effects of air pollution.

Chart 12.2
Greenhouse gas emissions, 1990 to 2004

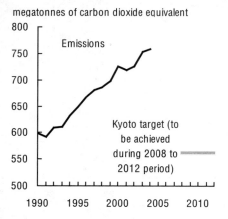

megatonnes of carbon dioxide equivalent

Source: Statistics Canada, Catalogue no. 16-251-XWE.

Households influenced by advisories of poor air quality in 2005, by selected province

	Aware of advisory	No change in routine or behaviour
	%	
Canada	**32**	**61**
P.E.I.	7	70
Que.	25	69
Ont.	56	56
Sask.	5	71
Alta.	9	73
B.C.	21	77

Source: Statistics Canada, Households and the Environment Survey, 2006.

In 2005, 32% of Canadian households were aware of poor air quality advisories in their area. Of those households, 39% made changes to their activity or routine. For example, at least one individual in the household may have used an asthma inhaler, curtailed outdoor physical activity or used public transit instead of their motor vehicle.

Greenhouse gas emissions indicator

Although GHG occurs naturally to help regulate the planet's climate, human activities result in GHG emissions that contribute to global climate change. In 2004, Canada's GHG emissions reached 758 megatonnes, 27% higher than in 1990. This rate of increase outpaced population growth, which was 15%. In other words, GHG emissions per person increased 10% over this period—this makes Canada one of the highest per capita GHG emitters in the world.

The geographic distribution of emissions corresponds to the location of natural resources, population and heavy industry— 31% of Canada's GHG emissions came from Alberta in 2004; 27% originated in Ontario.

The rise in GHG emissions from 1990 to 2004 was driven mainly by the oil, gas and coal industries (32% of the overall increase), road transportation (24%) and thermal electricity and heat production (22%).

GHG emissions declined for the chemical, pulp and paper, and construction industries.

Canada's GHG emissions per unit of gross domestic product fell 14% from 1990 to 2004—more economic activity occurred for each tonne of GHG emitted. A key contributor was efficiency improvements in the energy industry itself, without which total emissions would have been significantly greater. Nonetheless, rapid economic growth has translated into greater GHG emissions.

Water quality indicator

The water quality indicator assesses surface freshwater's capacity to protect aquatic life such as fish, invertebrates and plants. It does not assess the quality of water for human consumption. To evaluate the potential for adverse effects, experts measure specific substances in water and compare them against scientifically established thresholds.

Primary manufacturers, service industries, institutions and households discharged at least 110,000 metric tonnes of pollutants into Canada's surface waters in 2004. The largest quantities of pollutants were nitrate ion and

ammonia. More highly toxic pollutants, such as mercury, are also released in smaller but still significant amounts. Many pollutants also make their way into water after having been released into the air or onto the land.

Freshwater quality was monitored at 340 selected monitoring sites across southern Canada. It was rated 'good or excellent' at 44% of the sites, 'fair' at 34% and 'marginal or poor' at 22% from 2002 to 2004. At 30 monitoring sites across northern Canada, freshwater quality was rated 'good or excellent' at 67% of the sites, 'fair' at 20% and 'marginal or poor' at 13%.

Water quality in the Great Lakes region is assessed differently from other sites because of the large area of the lakes—about 92,200 square kilometres in Canadian territory—and the nature of the surface water and bottom sediment monitoring program.

In 2004 and 2005, freshwater quality measured in the Great Lakes was rated 'good or excellent' for Lake Superior, Lake Huron, Georgian Bay and eastern Lake Erie. For central Lake Erie, it was rated 'fair,' while for the western basin of Lake Erie and for Lake Ontario it was 'marginal.'

Chart 12.3
Status of freshwater quality at sites in southern Canada, 2002 to 2004

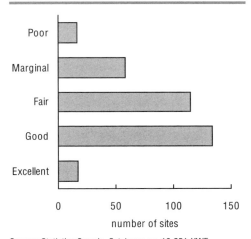

number of sites

Source: Statistics Canada, Catalogue no. 16-251-XWE.

Selected sources

Statistics Canada

- *Canada's Mineral Production, Preliminary Estimates.* Annual. 26-202-XIB

- *Canadian Economic Observer.* Monthly. 11-010-XIB

- *Canadian Environmental Sustainability Indicators.* Annual. 16-251-XIE

- *Human Activity and the Environment: Annual Statistics.* Annual. 16-201-XIE

- *Waste Management Industry Survey: Business and Government Sectors.* Biennial. 16F0023XIE

Transportation's effects on air quality

Canadians are dependent on vehicles for almost everything we do. At the same time, transportation is a major emitter of pollutants that contribute to poor air quality, especially in and around urban areas. From 1990 to 2004, transportation accounted for 28% of the growth in GHG emissions.

In 2004, transportation was the source of nearly 75% of carbon monoxide, more than 50% of nitrogen oxides, and more than 25% of VOCs and 17% of fine particulate matter in the air we breathe. As well, 86% of the rise in greenhouse gas emissions was from road vehicles, particularly light trucks, such as vans, sports utility vehicles and pickup trucks, and heavy-duty vehicles, such as transport trucks.

Nonetheless, Canadians are not changing their buying patterns—48% of the vehicles sold in 2005 were trucks. About half of these

sales were to businesses, reflecting economic conditions in the country.

Businesses keep costs down by minimizing inventories and using 'just-in-time' delivery of parts and products. This has contributed to a booming trucking industry, but it also means trucks are making more trips.

The number of motor vehicles registered in Canada increased 14% from 1999 to 2006. Light vehicle (weighing less than 4,500 kilograms) registrations increased 13% over the same period. In 1951, Canada had five people registered per vehicle; by the mid-1980s, there were two people per vehicle.

Cleaner burning fuels and catalytic converters have helped curb output of air pollutants. Nevertheless, nitrogen oxides and VOCs still contribute to smog and acid rain, and carbon monoxide remains a serious threat to human health.

Chart 12.4
Transportation greenhouse gas emissions, by selected mode or vehicle type

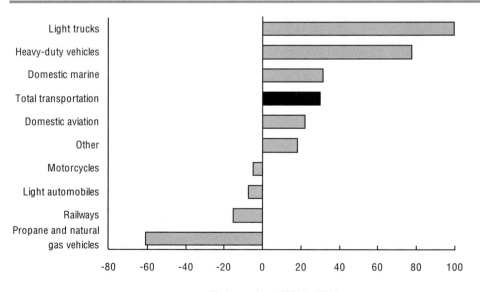

% change from 1990 to 2004

Note: Greenhouse gas emissions in carbon dioxide equivalents.
Source: Statistics Canada, Catalogue no. 16-201-XWE.

Protecting and managing the environment

Protecting the environment means more than preventing pollution and cleaning up our messes. For most businesses, it also requires continuing improvements in product design, technology and operations. Many businesses can reduce their pollutants while also cutting costs and improving productivity.

Primary and manufacturing industries spent $6.8 billion on environmental protection in 2002—24% more than in 2000. This increase was partly driven by new environmental regulations and industries' efforts to reduce pollutants like GHG emissions.

Businesses spent just over $1 billion to reduce GHG emissions in 2002. The oil and gas industry led the spending at $245 million, followed closely by the pulp, paper and paperboard industry, at $242 million.

The private sector invested $428 million in 2002 for prevention and control of water

pollution. It also spent $1.5 billion to protect air quality—75% of that spending was by the oil and gas, electric power, and petroleum and coal products industries. Businesses invested $1.4 billion in pollution prevention equipment, as well as $907 million in pollution abatement and control systems for treating wastes.

In 2002/2003, the Canadian government spent $6.9 billion on pollution abatement and control systems, of which $2.9 billion went to sewage collection and disposal and $2.0 billion went to waste collection and disposal. Local governments spent 92% of these allocated expenditures.

The federal government spent another $349 million, in 2003/2004, on research and development for pollution prevention and environmental protection—$200 million more than it spent in 1995/1996 for this purpose.

Chart 12.5
Environmental protection expenditures, all industries, 2002

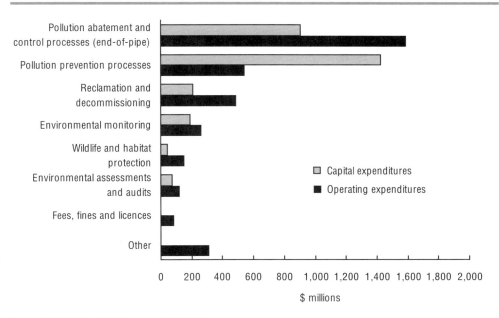

Source: Statistics Canada, Catalogue no. 16F0006XIE.

Solid waste: Managing our garbage

Because nearly every aspect of our lives generates some form of garbage, managing our waste is a challenge. In 2004, municipalities and businesses that provided waste management services handled a total of 33.2 million tonnes of non-hazardous solid waste in Canada, 8% more than in 2002. That is four times the 2% growth rate of Canada's population over the same period.

Industrial, commercial and institutional sources—as well as construction, renovation and demolition projects—accounted for 15.5 million tonnes, 61% of the non-hazardous waste that was not recycled. Household sources accounted for 39%. Canadian households disposed of 9.8 million tonnes of waste—that is 306 kg per capita and 1.6% more per capita than in 2002.

Ontario and Quebec, with 62% of Canada's population, accounted for 66% of the residential waste generated nationwide in 2004. By weight, our residential waste consists mainly of organic materials from kitchens and yards. Newspapers and other paper fibres account for the second highest portion.

More and more household wastes are being recycled. About 27% of residential waste was diverted away from landfill sites and incinerators in 2004, an increase of four percentage points from 2002. In 2004, 7.9 million tonnes of non-hazardous waste were recycled. Non-residential sources accounted for 54% of the materials prepared for recycling; households accounted for 46%.

Centralized facilities across the country composted 1.7 million tonnes of organic wastes in 2004. This amount excludes backyard composting and on-site composting by industry.

Chart 12.6
Waste diversion rate, by province, 2004

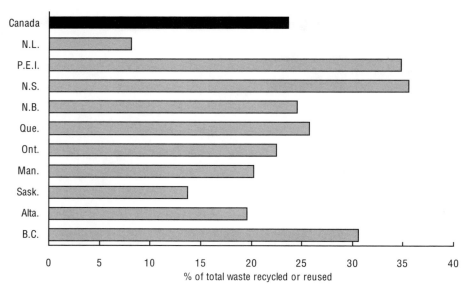

% of total waste recycled or reused

Note: Non-hazardous waste disposed of in public and private waste disposal facilities.
Source: Statistics Canada, Catalogue no. 16F0023XIE.

Mining is booming

Canada's mineral resources are contributing to our booming economy. A 67% increase in mining profits in 2005, representing $2.7 billion, stemmed from increasing global demand for mining products.

This has been a surprising reversal for Canada's mineral resources. Since 1990, investment in mining had been weak and jobs had fallen 53%. But in 2005, employment in mining industries jumped 16% and investment surged 20%.

From 2004 to 2005, the value of metallic minerals production increased 7.7%, led by nickel, copper, gold, iron ore, uranium and zinc. The value of non-metallic minerals production rose 3.6%—led by potash, with a 31.3% increase.

Canada is the world leader in uranium production: it is a $500-million industry. Canada accounts for about one-third of the global yield. Besides supplying about 15% of our electricity, uranium is exported to several countries for use in nuclear power plants.

With 33% of global production, Canada is also the world leader in potash mining. Canada has the largest known potash deposit—estimated at 56 billion tonnes. Potash mining occurs primarily in Saskatchewan, but also in New Brunswick.

The word 'spectacular' describes Canada's rise in diamond mining. Prior to 1998, diamond mining in Canada was virtually non-existent. In 2004, Canada ranked third globally in value of diamond production.

With mining comes an impact on the environment. In 2005, mining added 15,600 kilotonnes of GHGs to the environment. The industry spent $194 million on pollution prevention programs and pollution control and abatement in 2002.

Chart 12.7
Canadian mineral production value

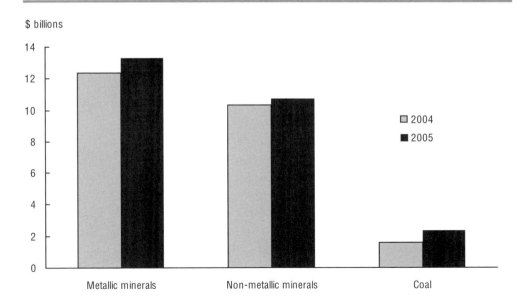

$ billions

Source: Statistics Canada, Catalogue no. 26-202-XIE.

Table 12.1 Greenhouse gas emissions, by source, 1990 and 2004

	1990	2004	1990	2004	1990	2004
	Carbon dioxide		Methane		Nitrous oxide	
	kilotonnes					
Total[1]	460,000	593,000	3,900	5,200	150	140
Energy	430,000	553,000	2,000	3,000	30	30
Stationary combustion sources	277,000	352,000	200	200	7	9
Electricity and heat generation	94,700	129,000	1.8	4.7	2	2
Fossil fuel industries	51,000	75,000	80	100	1	2
Petroleum refining and upgrading	23,000	29,000	0.4	0.6	0.4	0.5
Fossil fuel production	28,100	46,200	80	100	0.7	1
Mining	6,160	15,300	0.1	0.3	0.1	0.3
Manufacturing industries	54,400	50,300	3	3	2	2
Iron and steel	6,420	6,480	0.2	0.3	0.2	0.2
Non ferrous metals	3,210	3,220	0.07	0.07	0.05	0.05
Chemical	7,060	6,250	0.15	0.13	0.1	0.1
Pulp and paper	13,400	8,990	2	2	0.8	0.9
Cement	3,570	4,310	0.07	0.09	0.05	0.05
Other manufacturing	20,700	21,100	0.4	0.4	0.4	0.4
Construction	1,860	1,340	0.03	0.02	0.05	0.03
Commercial and institutional	25,700	37,700	0.5	0.7	0.5	0.8
Residential	41,300	40,700	100	90	2	2
Agriculture and forestry	2,400	2,080	0.04	0.04	0.05	0.06
Transportation[2]	142,000	185,000	30	30	20	30
Domestic aviation	6,220	7,590	0.5	0.4	0.6	0.7
Road transportation	103,000	140,000	16	12	12	16
Light-duty gasoline vehicles	51,600	47,800	9	3.5	6.3	6.0
Light-duty gasoline trucks	20,300	41,000	4	4.5	4.2	8.3
Heavy-duty gasoline vehicles	2,990	4,010	0.42	0.57	0.44	0.60
Motorcycles	225	214	0.18	0.17	0.00	0.00
Light-duty diesel automobiles	657	750	0.02	0.02	0.05	0.05
Light-duty diesel trucks	578	873	0.02	0.02	0.04	0.06
Heavy-duty diesel vehicles	24,300	44,400	1	2	0.7	1
Propane and natural gas vehicles	2,160	837	2	1	0.04	0.02
Railways	6,320	5,350	0.3	0.3	3	2
Domestic marine	4,730	6,260	0.4	0.5	1	1
Others	22,000	26,000	10	10	4	6
Off-road gasoline vehicles	5,000	4,000	6	4	0.1	0.08
Off-road diesel vehicles	10,000	14,000	0.5	0.7	4	5
Pipelines	6,700	8,280	6.7	8.3	0.2	0.2
Fugitive sources	11,000	16,000	1,600	2,400	...	0.1
Coal mining	...	...	90	50	...	...
Oil and natural gas	11,000	16,000	1,500	2,300	...	0
Oil	1,910	3,650	230	300	...	...
Natural gas	4,200	7,200	640	1,000	...	...
Venting	110	160	...	1,000	...	0.1
Flaring	4,340	5,350	2.61	3.91	...	0.00

See notes and source at the end of this table.

	1990	2004	1990	2004	1990	2004
	Carbon dioxide		Methane		Nitrous oxide	
	kilotonnes					
Industrial processes	30,300	39,600	...	...	37.1	12.7
Mineral products	8,300	9,500	...	...	...	...
Cement production	5,400	7,100	...	...	...	...
Lime production	2,000	2,000	...	...	...	...
Mineral product use[3]	1,100	630	...	...	...	...
Chemical industry	3,900	5,700	...	...	37.1	12.7
Ammonia production	3,900	5,700	...	...	...	...
Nitric acid production	...	...	...	...	2.5	2.7
Adipic acid production	...	...	...	...	34.6	9.98
Metal production	9,800	12,000	...	...	...	...
Iron and steel production	7,060	8,160	...	...	...	...
Aluminum production	2,700	4,200	...	...	...	...
Sulfur hexafloride used in magnesium smelters and casters	...	...	...	...	...	...
Consumption of halocarbons and sulfur hexafloride	...	...	...	...	...	...
Other and undifferentiated production	8,300	12,000	...	...	...	...
Solvent and other product use	...	...	...	...	1.3	1.6
Agriculture	...	...	1,000	1,290	77	89
Enteric fermentation	...	...	877	1,140	...	...
Manure management	...	...	120	150	13	17
Agricultural soils	...	...	...	...	63	72
Direct sources	...	...	...	...	35	37
Pasture, range and paddock manure	...	...	...	...	10	14
Indirect sources	...	...	...	...	20	20
Waste	270	200	1,100	1,300	3	3
Solid waste disposal on land	...	...	1,100	1,300	...	...
Wastewater handling	...	...	11	12	3	3
Waste incineration	270	200	0.4	0.06	0.4	0.2
Land use, land use change and forestry	-87,000	59,000	160	640	7	27
Forest land	-110,000	51,000	150	640	6.4	27
Cropland	13,000	-140	...	5	...	0.3
Grassland	.	.	.	.	.	.
Wetlands	6,000	1,000	...	0.1	...	0.01
Settlements	8,000	7,000	...	3	...	0

Note: Figures may not add to totals because of rounding.
1. National totals exclude all greenhouse gas emissions from the Land use, land use change and forestry sector.
2. Emissions from ethanol fuel are reported within the gasoline vehicle sub-categories.
3. The category Mineral product use includes carbon dioxide emissions from the use of limestone and dolomite, soda ash and magnesite.
Source: Environment Canada.

Table 12.2 Substances released to the land, 2004

	Releases[1]	Share of total
	tonnes	%
Hydrogen sulphide	226,578.4	81.5
Zinc and its compounds	9,560.5	3.4
Asbestos (friable form)	7,447.6	2.7
Ammonia[2]	6,985.6	2.5
Methanol	5,751.0	2.1
Manganese and its compounds	5,565.2	2.0
Phosphorous (total)	3,601.5	1.3
Ethylene glycol	2,703.8	1.0
Lead (and its compounds)	2,038.5	0.7
Vanadium and its compounds (except when in an alloy)	1,507.7	0.5

Note: Top 10 substances only.
1. Data include disposals.
2. Refers to the total of both ammonia (NH_3) and ammonium ion ($NH_4{}^+$) in solution.
Source: Statistics Canada, Catalogue no. 16-201-XIE.

Table 12.3 Waste disposal and diversion, by province, 2000, 2002 and 2004

	2000	2002	2004	2000	2002	2004
	Total waste disposed			Total materials diverted		
	tonnes					
Canada	**23,168,870**	**23,829,009**	**24,674,855**	**6,500,684**	**6,907,956**	**7,836,497**
Newfoundland and Labrador	398,818	376,593	400,048	38,386	30,386	35,308
Nova Scotia	391,827	389,194	399,967	169,724	215,349	231,526
New Brunswick	415,058	413,606	442,173	122,724	144,661	149,804
Quebec	5,806,200	5,543,800	55,438,002	1,743,000	1,743,376	1,743,376
Ontario	8,931,600	9,645,633	10,053,154	2,415,498	2,515,498	2,900,125
Manitoba	914,511	896,556	928,118	160,671	188,480	207,116
Saskatchewan	821,946	795,124	833,511	133,380	127,235	142,763
Alberta	2,750,004	2,890,294	3,077,311	589,642	690,517	768,408
British Columbia	2,581,336	2,738,180	2,841,361	1,105,121	1,214,475	1,324,166

Note: Data for Prince Edward Island and the territories suppressed to meet the confidentiality requirements of the *Statistics Act.*
Source: Statistics Canada, Catalogue no. 16-253-XIE.

Table 12.4 Capital expenditures on pollution prevention, by environmental milieu and by industry, 2002

	All environmental milieu	Air	Surface water	On-site contained solid and liquid waste	Noise, radiation and vibration	Other
				$ millions		
All industries	**1,427.2**	**950.5**	**224.7**	**138.3**	**12.9**	**100.8**
Logging	**0.6**	0.0	0.1	0.5	0.0	0.0
Oil and gas extraction	**243.7**	184.0	34.6	19.0	3.5	2.7
Mining	**31.1**	x	20.5	7.6	0.0	x
Electric power generation, transmission and distribution	**228.2**	164.9	27.7	x	x	x
Natural gas distribution	**x**	x	x	x	0.0	0.0
Food	**46.4**	23.8	9.4	4.3	0.0	8.8
Beverage and tobacco products	**6.4**	1.8	0.4	2.8	0.0	1.3
Wood products	**29.0**	x	5.4	15.6	x	0.4
Pulp, paper and paperboard mills	**152.9**	65.3	x	3.8	x	x
Petroleum and coal products	**499.9**	425.0	48.6	x	x	x
Chemicals	**x**	x	16.9	12.9	0.6	x
Non-metallic mineral products	**24.4**	3.5	2.0	1.2	0.2	17.5
Primary metals	**31.1**	15.5	7.2	7.2	0.0	1.2
Fabricated metal products	**x**	x	x	0.3	0.2	2.1
Transportation equipment	**27.3**	18.5	3.5	3.9	0.2	1.3
Pipeline transportation	**32.0**	5.3	x	20.5	x	x

Source: Statistics Canada, Catalogue no. 16-201-XIE.

Table 12.5 Capital expenditures on pollution abatement and control, by environmental milieu and by industry, 2002

	All environmental milieu	Air	Surface water	On-site contained solid and liquid waste	Noise, radiation and vibration
				$ millions	
All industries	**907.7**	**580.6**	**203.3**	**104.8**	**18.9**
Logging	**x**	x	x	x	x
Oil and gas extraction	**85.9**	48.4	21.2	13.7	2.7
Mining	**36.3**	7.5	22.9	5.7	0.2
Electric power generation, transmission and distribution	**218.3**	166.8	36.5	14.9	0.3
Natural gas distribution	**x**	x	0.0	x	0.1
Food	**59.5**	15.0	37.6	x	x
Beverage and tobacco products	**1.9**	0.2	0.8	0.8	0.1
Wood products	**x**	x	x	x	x
Pulp, paper and paperboard mills	**57.4**	32.3	16.5	8.1	0.5
Petroleum and coal products	**226.7**	155.8	35.1	28.5	7.3
Chemicals	**26.4**	15.8	5.0	3.4	2.2
Non-metallic mineral products	**38.7**	27.8	2.0	7.9	1.0
Primary metals	**87.4**	66.1	13.9	7.2	0.2
Fabricated metal products	**x**	1.3	1.5	x	0.1
Transportation equipment	**29.7**	x	x	4.4	0.1
Pipeline transportation	**x**	x	0.1	x	x

Source: Statistics Canada, Catalogue no. 16-201-XIE.

Table 12.6 Production of selected mineral commodities, 2004 and 2005

	2004	2005ᴾ
	carats	
Diamonds	12,679,910	12,299,733
	kilograms	
Gold	130,727	120,061
Platinum group	27,541	22,585
	tonnes	
Zinc	791,373	667,964
Copper	562,795	592,393
Nickel	186,694	188,749
Lead	76,730	79,252
Uranium	11,599	11,627
Molybdenum	9,519	7,910
Cobalt	5,060	5,533
Silver	1,337	1,127
Cadmium	848	671
Bismuth	217	193
Antimony	105	96
Gemstones	292	67
Tantalum	91	63
	kilotonnes	
Sand and gravel	252,609	246,337
Stone	161,975	160,384
Iron ore	28,405	32,210
Salt	13,903	13,632
Potash	10,109	10,886
Gypsum	9,904	8,581
Quartz	1,681	1,980
Peat	1,320	1,247
Nepheline syenite	712	740
Soapstone, talc, pyrophyllite	72	76
Barite	20	23

Note: Canadian mines only.
Source: Statistics Canada, Catalogue no. 26-202-XIB.

Table 12.7 Mining, production workers and value of production, 2000 to 2005

	2000	2001	2002	2003	2004	2005
	number					
Mining (except oil and gas)	**39,443**	**37,724**	**36,811**	**35,829**	**34,786**	**35,342**
Coal mining	4,759	4,531	4,331	3,923	3,731	3,822
Iron ore mining	3,680	2,923	3,085	3,275	2,663	2,811
Gold and silver ore mining	6,002	5,323	5,386	5,134	4,832	4,622
Diamond mining	419	485	762	992	1,032	763
Potash mining	2,513	2,525	2,544	2,720	2,981	3,051
	$ millions					
Mining (except oil and gas)	**17,019.5**	**16,564.8**	**16,556.8**	**16,641.6**	**20,753.0**	**24,635.5**
Coal mining	1,485.9	1,704.4	1,666.4	1,285.4	1,552.7	2,828.6
Iron ore mining	1,599.8	1,377.2	1,326.1	1,403.6	1,424.4	2,600.1
Gold and silver ore mining	2,118.6	2,261.8	2,490.6	2,460.3	2,494.1	2,319.3
Diamond mining	647.8	718.4	780.1	1,587.7	2,096.7	1,762.1
Potash mining	1,703.2	1,669.6	1,681.6	1,623.5	2,197.3	2,553.4

Source: Statistics Canada, CANSIM table 152-0005.

Ethnic diversity and immigration

13

OVERVIEW

Over the past 100 years, more than 13 million immigrants have arrived to forge a new life here, making Canada one of the world's most ethnically diverse countries. Most came from Europe during the first half of the twentieth century. Later on, non-Europeans started arriving in larger numbers as economic immigrants or refugees, or as family members of previous immigrants.

By 1970, half of all immigrants were coming from Caribbean nations, Asia and South America. In the 1980s, a growing number were arriving from Africa.

In the 1990s, 58% of Canada's immigrants were born in Asia (including the Middle East); 20% were from Europe; and 22% came from the Caribbean, Central and South America, Africa and the United States. Most (73%) settled in Toronto, Montréal and Vancouver, transforming the ethno-cultural

composition and socioeconomic dynamics of these cities.

In 2001, 10.3 million people—nearly half of Canada's population aged 15 and older, not including Aboriginal peoples—reported British, French or Canadian ethnic origins, or some combination of the three, reflecting the long history of British and French peoples in Canada. Meanwhile, 4.3 million Canadians reported other European origins, 2.9 million reported non-European origins, while 3.3 million reported mixed ethnicity.

Visible minority population growing fast

Canada's visible minority population is growing much faster than its total population: 25% growth from 1996 to 2001 versus 4% growth in the general population. This is due

Chart 13.1
Recent immigrants to Canada, by region of origin

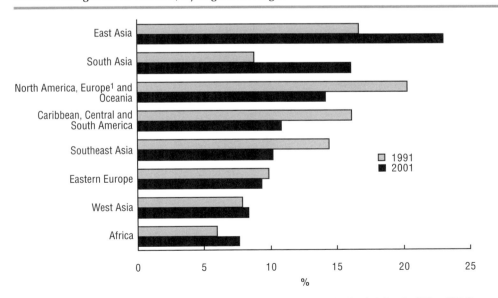

Note: Recent immigrants are individuals born outside Canada who immigrated here in the decade before the 1991 or 2001 Census.
1. Northern, Western and Southern Europe.
Source: Statistics Canada, Catalogue no. 89-613-MIE.

largely to increased immigration from Asia, Africa, the Caribbean, Central and South America and the Middle East. In 2001, about 70% of the visible minority population was born outside Canada.

From 1981 to 2001, the number of visible minorities increased more than threefold from 1.1 million people, or nearly 5% of the population, to 4.0 million people, or 13% of the population. Chinese made up the largest visible minority group in 2001, followed by South Asians and Africans.

By 2017, about 20% of Canada's population could be visible minorities, or anywhere from 6.3 million to 8.5 million people. Close to half are projected to be South Asian or Chinese. The highest growth rates are projected for West Asian, Korean and Arab groups, whose populations could more than double by 2017 but remain small relative to the South Asian, Chinese and African populations. In 2017, 95% of the visible minority population will live in a census metropolitan area (CMA), virtually unchanged from 2001.

Canada's population is highly urban: 64% of Canadians lived in a CMA in 2001. The proportion of recent immigrants settling in a

Recent immigrants, by region of origin and selected CMAs, 2001

	Montréal	Toronto	Vancouver
	%		
North America, Europe[1] and Oceania	12.5	8.4	9.8
Eastern Europe	10.8	10.7	4.6
Caribbean, Central and South America	19.1	12.6	3.2
Africa	18.2	6.0	3.0
South Asia	10.9	22.9	11.1
Southeast Asia	6.8	9.7	12.0
East Asia	9.2	21.5	51.0
West Asia	12.5	8.3	5.4

Note: Includes individuals who were born abroad and immigrated to Canada during the years from 1991 to 2001.
1. Includes countries in Northern, Western and Southern Europe.
Source: Statistics Canada, Catalogue no. 89-613-MIE.

CMA rose from 84% in 1981 to 94% in 2001. The share of Canadian-born people residing in a CMA grew from 53% to 59%.

Recent immigrants prefer CMAs for many reasons: 41% cite a spouse, partner or family in the area; 18% cite proximity to friends. Others cite job prospects, educational opportunities, lifestyle and housing.

Chart 13.2
Growth of visible minorities in Canada

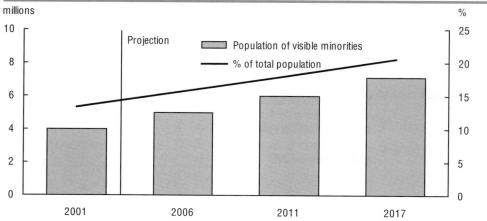

Note: Projections are based on a scenario that uses trends observed in the 2001 Census and preceding years.
Source: Statistics Canada, Catalogue no. 91-541-XIE.

From 1981 to 2001, Canada's five largest cities—Toronto, Montréal, Vancouver, Ottawa–Gatineau and Calgary—received much smaller shares of immigrants from North America, Western Europe and Oceania, but received larger shares from West Asia, South Asia and East Asia.

In Montréal, most recent immigrants have arrived from Haiti, Algeria, France and Lebanon. In Vancouver, more than half of recent immigrants in 2001 were from East Asia, with 62% of them coming from just five countries: China, Hong Kong, Taiwan, India and the Philippines.

By 2017, fully 49% of Toronto's population could be immigrants, up from 44% in 2001. In Vancouver, the proportion is projected to rise from 38% to 44%.

Recent immigrants have strong ethnic ties

The strength of immigrants' attachment to an ethnic group is related to their length of time in Canada. Recent immigrants often settle close to family and friends, who are more

likely of similar ethnic background, which may contribute to a strong sense of belonging to their ethnic group.

Of immigrants who arrived here from 1991 to 2001, 71% rated at least one of their ancestral origins as important to their identity. This compares with 57% of second-generation Canadians (those born in Canada with at least one foreign-born parent) and with 44% of the third generation (those born in Canada to two Canadian-born parents).

Sense of belonging also varies by ethnic group. For instance, 78% with Filipino ancestry report a strong connection to their ethnic group, as do 65% of East Indians and 65% of Portuguese. But just 36% of Dutch, 33% of Germans and 33% of Ukrainians report a strong connection to their ethnic group. This likely reflects the longer time these latter groups have been in Canada.

Regardless of length of time here, immigrants are more likely than people born here to participate in ethnic or immigrant associations. Recent immigrants, however, are less likely to participate in other types of organizations in Canada.

Chart 13.3
Recent immigrants, selected census metropolitan areas

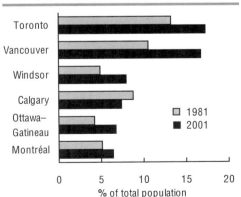

Note: Recent immigrants are individuals who were born outside of Canada and immigrated here in the decade preceding the 1981 or 2001 Census.
Source: Statistics Canada, Census of Population, 1981 and 2001.

Selected sources

Statistics Canada

- *Canadian Social Trends.* Irregular. 11-008-XWE

- *Ethnic Diversity Survey: Portrait of a Multicultural Society.* Occasional. 89-593-XIE

- *Immigrants in Canada's Census Metropolitan Areas.* Occasional. 89-613-MWE2004003

- *Population Projections of Visible Minority Groups, Canada, Provinces and Regions.* Occasional. 91-541-XIE

- *Ten Things to Know About Canadian Metropolitan Areas: A Synthesis of Statistics Canada's Trends and Conditions in Census Metropolitan Areas Series.* Occasional. 89-613-MWE2005009

More mixed couples

Marriages and common-law unions involving spouses from different population groups increased in the 1990s. In 2001, of the 14.1 million people living in a marriage or common-law union, 452,000 individuals were in a couple with a visible minority spouse and a non-visible minority spouse, or in a couple with spouses from two different visible minority groups. In 2001, such mixed unions represented 3% of individuals in couples, slightly higher than in 1991.

Japanese-Canadians are the most likely visible minority to marry or live common-law with a non-Japanese person. Next most likely are people of Latin American origin and black people. Among the least likely to marry outside their group are South Asians and Chinese.

Mixed unions account for 7% of all married or common-law couples in Vancouver, 6% in Toronto and 3% in Montréal. However, among people aged 20 to 29, the proportions are almost double: 13% in Vancouver, 11% in Toronto and 6% in Montréal.

Mixed couples are younger—5% of couples aged 20 to 29 versus 1% of couples aged 65 and over in 2001—and are more likely to be foreign-born and to live in a large city. They tend to be better educated than couples in the general population. For example, 6% of people with a university degree are in a mixed union, versus 2% of people with high school or less.

Mixed union couples are more likely to have children. In the general population in 2001, 57% of all couples had children, compared with 59% of couples with a visible minority spouse and a non-visible minority spouse, and 69% of couples with spouses from two different visible minorities.

Chart 13.4
Persons in mixed-union couples, by age group

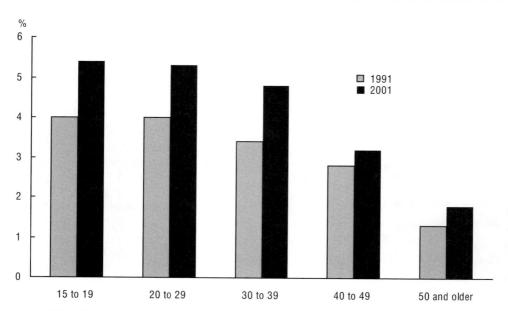

Source: Statistics Canada, Census of Population, 1991 and 2001.

Immigrants' home ownership slips

Home ownership declined markedly among immigrant families in some cities from 1981 to 2001, particularly among families with a main wage earner aged 25 to 54.

Some of the decline is linked to immigrants' poorer fortunes in the labour market. Length of time in Canada is also a factor: in 2001, 37% of immigrants had lived here 10 or fewer years, compared with only 30% in 1981. Age is another factor: immigrants aged 45 to 54 had higher home-ownership rates from 1981 to 2001 than the Canadian-born population in the same age group. In this period, immigrants aged 35 to 44 saw their home-ownership rates fall. By 2001, the rate for immigrants 35 to 44 had dropped below that of Canadian-born in the same age group.

In Montréal, 52% of immigrant families owned their own home in 1981, compared with 46% of Canadian-born families. In

Toronto, 65% of immigrant families owned homes, compared with 55% of Canadian-born families. In Vancouver, 70% of immigrant families owned their homes; 58% of Canadian-born families did so.

By 2001, the situation had reversed in Montréal (42% of immigrant families owned homes versus 54% of Canadian-born families) and in Toronto (61% versus 64%). The picture in Vancouver did not change (64% versus 55%).

Housing was a particular problem for immigrants who arrived from 1996 to 2001. Some of these immigrants found quality housing to be out of their reach. They ended up in 'core housing need.' In other words, they were living in rented dwellings that needed major repairs, were overcrowded or that required them to spend 30% or more of their before-tax income on rent.

Chart 13.5
Home ownership, immigrant and Canadian-born heads of families, selected census metropolitan areas

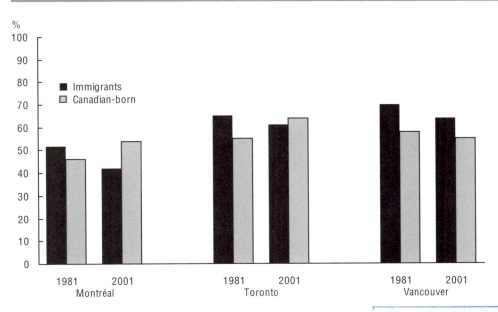

Sources: Statistics Canada, Census of Population, 1981 and 2001, and Catalogue no. 11F0019MIE.

Becoming Canadian

Naturalization—acquiring citizenship—may be the final step of a newcomer's migration and a declaration of commitment to Canada. Citizenship grants people the right to vote, hold public office, be employed in the public service and carry a Canadian passport.

Most people residing in Canada are Canadian citizens—81% by birth and 14% by naturalization. The remaining 5% are not eligible, are eligible but have not taken the steps to naturalize, or are not permanent residents. According to the 2001 Census, 84% of all eligible immigrants—those who have resided in Canada for at least three years—are Canadian citizens.

Refugees and people from developing countries or from countries with political, economic or social systems different from ours, such as some in Asia and Africa, are most likely to naturalize. In 2001, 93% of immigrants from Vietnam and 89% from the People's Republic of China who were eligible had become Canadians. More than 80% of the newcomers from Africa, in Canada for more than five years, had done so. The longer newcomers stay, no matter where they come from, the more likely they are to become Canadian citizens.

Younger immigrants are more likely to take up citizenship than older immigrants. About 85% of those under 20 at the time of entry become citizens, versus only 72% of those aged 70 and older.

Factors influencing a newcomer's decision to naturalize include expected length of stay, dual citizenship rules, attachment to the home country and to Canada, the source country's tax laws and rules on asset transfers, as well as the time, cost and knowledge required to become a citizen.

Chart 13.6
Immigrants who are Canadian citizens, by length of residence in Canada

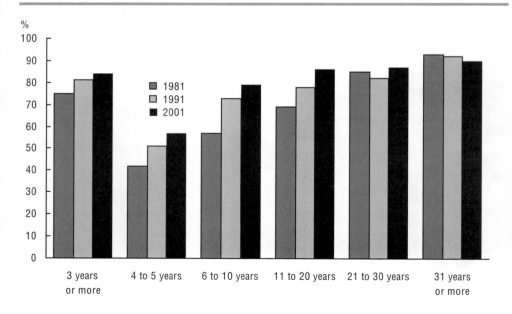

Source: Statistics Canada, Census of Population, 1981, 1991 and 2001.

Children of immigrants doing well

Second-generation Canadians are doing well—many are doing better than third-generation Canadians—according to a study of people who were born in Canada to at least one immigrant parent. In general, second-generation Canadians are more educated and earn more on average than Canadians of a similar age whose parents were both born here.

Second-generation Canadian men born from 1964 to 1976 are more likely to hold a university degree than Canadians of the same age whose parents were born in Canada. They also have an earnings advantage—about 6% higher average weekly earnings in 2000—except if their father was born in the Caribbean, Central America, South America or Oceania; those second-generation Canadian men had earnings 14% below the average. On the other hand, if his father came

from North America, Northern or Western Europe, the second-generation man's earnings were 14% above the average.

The picture is similar for second-generation Canadian women, except a father's country of birth has less impact on his daughter's education level or earnings. These women earned on average just over $27,000 in 2000, whereas women with two Canadian-born parents made less than $25,000. Women with Asian-born fathers earned 27% above the average, while women with African-born fathers had an earnings advantage of 26%.

In 2001, more than one-third of Canadians aged 16 to 65 were immigrants or the children of immigrants. About 7% were second-generation Canadians with both parents born in another country, while a further 7% to 8% had one parent who was born outside Canada.

Chart 13.7
Educational attainment of children of immigrants living in Canada for two generations or more, by sex, 2001

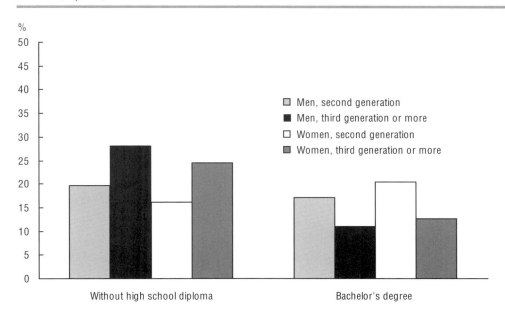

Source: Statistics Canada, Catalogue no. 11F0019MIE.

Table 13.1 Foreign-born population, by province and territory, census years 1991 to 2001

	1991	1996	2001
		% of total population	
Canada	**16.2**	**17.5**	**18.5**
Newfoundland and Labrador	1.5	1.6	1.6
Prince Edward Island	3.2	3.3	3.1
Nova Scotia	4.4	4.7	4.6
New Brunswick	3.4	3.3	3.1
Quebec	8.7	9.5	10.0
Ontario	24.1	25.8	27.1
Manitoba	12.9	12.4	12.2
Saskatchewan	5.9	5.4	5.0
Alberta	15.2	15.2	15.0
British Columbia	22.5	24.7	26.4
Yukon	10.8	10.4	10.6
Northwest Territories	4.9	4.8	6.4
Nunavut	..	..	1.7

Source: Statistics Canada, Census of Population, 1991 to 2001.

Table 13.2 Foreign-born population, by census metropolitan area, census years 1991 to 2001

	1991	1996	2001
		% of total population	
St. John's	2.8	2.9	2.9
Halifax	6.4	7.0	6.9
Saint John	4.3	4.0	3.8
Saguenay (formerly Chicoutimi)	0.7	0.7	0.9
Québec	2.2	2.6	2.9
Sherbrooke[1]	3.8	4.3	4.6
Trois-Rivières	1.3	1.6	1.5
Montréal	16.4	17.8	18.4
Ottawa–Gatineau (formerly Ottawa–Hull)	14.7	16.3	17.6
Kingston[2]	13.5	12.8	12.4
Oshawa	17.2	16.5	15.7
Toronto	38.0	41.9	43.7
Hamilton	23.5	23.6	23.6
St. Catharines–Niagara	18.9	18.3	17.8
Kitchener	21.5	21.8	22.1
London	18.8	19.2	18.8
Windsor	20.6	20.4	22.3
Greater Sudbury / Grand Sudbury (formerly Sudbury)	8.1	7.5	7.0
Thunder Bay	13.1	12.2	11.1
Winnipeg	17.4	16.9	16.5
Regina	8.4	8.0	7.4
Saskatoon	8.2	7.6	7.6
Calgary	20.3	20.9	20.9
Edmonton	18.3	18.5	17.8
Abbotsford[2]	19.8	20.3	21.8
Vancouver	30.1	34.9	37.5
Victoria	19.5	19.3	18.8

Note: Census metropolitan areas are based on the 2001 Census geography.
1. Sherbrooke became a census metropolitan area in 1986.
2. Kingston and Abbotsford became census metropolitan areas in 2001.
Source: Statistics Canada, Census of Population, 1991 to 2001.

Table 13.3 Selected ethnic origins, 2001

	Total responses	Single response[1]	Multiple responses[2]
		number	
Total population	**29,639,035**	**18,307,545**	**11,331,490**
Canadian	11,682,680	6,748,135	4,934,545
English	5,978,875	1,479,525	4,499,355
French	4,668,410	1,060,760	3,607,655
Scottish	4,157,210	607,235	3,549,975
Irish	3,822,660	496,865	3,325,795
German	2,742,765	705,600	2,037,170
Italian	1,270,370	726,275	544,090
Chinese	1,094,700	936,210	158,490
Ukrainian	1,071,060	326,195	744,860
North American Indian	1,000,890	455,805	545,085
Dutch (Netherlands)	923,310	316,220	607,090
Polish	817,085	260,415	556,665
East Indian	713,330	581,665	131,665
Norwegian	363,760	47,230	316,530
Portuguese	357,690	252,835	104,855
Welsh	350,365	28,445	321,920
Jewish	348,605	186,475	162,130
Russian	337,960	70,895	267,070
Filipino	327,550	266,140	61,405
Métis	307,845	72,210	235,635
Swedish	282,760	30,440	252,325
Hungarian (Magyar)	267,255	91,800	175,455
American (United States)	250,005	25,205	224,805
Greek	215,105	143,785	71,325
Spanish	213,105	66,545	146,555
Jamaican	211,720	138,180	73,545
Danish	170,780	33,795	136,985
Vietnamese	151,410	119,120	32,290

1. The respondent reported having only one ethnic origin.
2. The respondent reported having more than one ethnic origin.
Source: Statistics Canada, 2001 Census of Population.

Table 13.4 Visible minority population, by province and territory, 2001

	Total population	Visible minority population	Black	South Asian	Chinese
			number		
Canada	**29,639,035**	**3,983,845**	**662,210**	**917,075**	**1,029,395**
Newfoundland and Labrador	**508,075**	3,850	840	1,005	925
Prince Edward Island	**133,385**	1,180	370	115	205
Nova Scotia	**897,570**	34,525	19,670	2,890	3,290
New Brunswick	**719,710**	9,425	3,850	1,415	1,530
Quebec	**7,125,580**	497,975	152,195	59,505	56,830
Ontario	**11,285,550**	2,153,045	411,095	554,870	481,505
Manitoba	**1,103,695**	87,110	12,820	12,880	11,930
Saskatchewan	**963,150**	27,580	4,165	4,090	8,085
Alberta	**2,941,150**	329,925	31,390	69,585	99,095
British Columbia	**3,868,870**	836,440	25,465	210,295	365,485
Yukon	**28,520**	1,025	115	210	225
Northwest Territories	**37,105**	1,545	170	190	255
Nunavut	**26,665**	210	65	30	35

Source: Statistics Canada, 2001 Census of Population.

Table 13.5 Visible minority population, by census metropolitan area, 2001

	Total population	Visible minority population	Black	South Asian	Chinese
			number		
St. John's	**171,105**	2,310	350	745	520
Halifax	**355,945**	25,085	13,085	2,345	2,440
Saint John	**121,340**	3,160	1,440	305	490
Saguenay	**153,020**	985	325	40	290
Québec	**673,105**	11,075	3,640	340	1,275
Sherbrooke	**150,385**	3,835	1,040	225	245
Trois-Rivières	**134,645**	1,240	515	50	90
Montréal	**3,380,645**	458,330	139,305	57,935	52,110
Ottawa–Gatineau	**1,050,755**	148,680	38,185	22,275	28,810
Kingston	**142,765**	6,735	850	1,525	1,605
Oshawa	**293,550**	20,690	7,180	4,630	2,355
Toronto	**4,647,960**	1,712,535	310,500	473,805	409,530
Hamilton	**655,055**	64,380	12,855	14,285	9,000
St. Catharines–Niagara	**371,400**	16,845	3,840	2,535	2,665
Kitchener	**409,770**	43,770	7,345	11,190	5,895
London	**427,215**	38,300	7,610	4,925	4,660
Windsor	**304,955**	39,330	8,125	6,530	5,710
Greater Sudbury / Grand Sudbury	**153,890**	3,125	1,075	535	715
Thunder Bay	**120,365**	2,690	440	330	420
Winnipeg	**661,725**	82,565	11,440	12,285	10,930
Regina	**190,020**	9,880	1,580	1,665	2,370
Saskatoon	**222,635**	12,410	1,520	1,850	3,960
Calgary	**943,310**	164,900	13,665	36,855	51,850
Edmonton	**927,020**	135,770	14,095	29,065	41,285
Abbotsford	**144,990**	25,755	595	18,660	1,610
Vancouver	**1,967,480**	725,655	18,405	164,360	342,665
Victoria	**306,970**	27,185	2,180	5,775	11,245

Source: Statistics Canada, 2001 Census of Population.

Korean	Japanese	Southeast Asian	Filipino	Arab/West Asian	Latin American	Visible minority, not included elsewhere	Multiple visible minority
				number			
100,660	73,315	198,880	308,575	303,965	216,975	98,920	73,875
105	70	120	260	350	85	45	45
20	80	45	40	180	75	30	20
585	420	790	655	4,000	520	1,170	535
105	130	305	355	770	425	265	275
4,410	2,830	44,115	18,550	85,760	59,520	7,555	6,705
53,955	24,925	86,410	156,515	155,645	106,835	78,915	42,375
1,040	1,665	5,480	30,490	2,100	4,775	2,070	1,860
635	435	2,600	3,030	1,475	2,005	420	640
7,800	9,950	23,740	33,940	24,550	18,745	4,220	6,910
31,965	32,730	34,970	64,005	28,985	23,880	4,195	14,465
0	35	105	235	30	45	10	15
20	40	190	465	105	55	20	35
10	0	10	35	15	10	0	0

Korean	Japanese	Southeast Asian	Filipino	Arab/West Asian	Latin American	Visible minority, not included elsewhere	Multiple visible minority
				number			
50	60	80	115	280	55	35	20
475	335	715	480	3,355	410	980	465
40	10	75	125	190	240	155	90
25	10	50	0	10	220	15	0
140	145	1,650	60	1,515	2,005	210	95
50	50	315	90	695	1,050	45	30
0	15	235	10	130	175	10	10
3,760	2,295	39,570	17,890	79,410	53,155	6,785	6,115
1,590	1,575	9,535	5,205	28,285	7,660	2,735	2,825
345	165	365	445	525	630	125	135
610	465	560	905	985	965	1,355	680
42,615	17,415	53,565	133,680	95,820	75,910	66,455	33,240
2,030	1,165	4,910	4,950	6,850	4,945	2,000	1,390
905	625	1,280	1,200	1,460	1,535	295	505
1,135	460	5,450	1,050	3,545	4,850	1,875	975
1,705	525	3,165	1,615	7,545	4,470	1,205	875
390	145	2,805	2,955	8,920	2,235	1,225	290
45	75	70	115	170	220	65	40
30	190	275	295	230	240	70	170
955	1,585	5,030	30,095	1,960	4,550	1,990	1,745
225	165	1,185	1,010	480	800	185	215
185	140	1,130	1,460	825	845	175	320
3,885	3,845	12,560	16,380	11,395	8,605	2,250	3,610
2,830	1,845	9,690	14,170	10,845	7,510	1,675	2,760
760	540	1,180	640	170	995	205	390
28,850	24,025	28,465	57,025	27,330	18,715	3,320	12,495
680	1,740	1,245	1,810	685	1,160	210	455

Table 13.6 Visible minority population, by age group, 2001

	All age groups	0 to 14	15 to 24	25 to 44	45 to 64	65 to 74	75 and older
				number			
Total population	**29,639,030**	**5,737,670**	**3,988,205**	**9,047,175**	**7,241,135**	**2,106,875**	**1,517,975**
Visible minority population	**3,983,845**	942,195	634,685	1,351,310	794,510	171,230	89,925
Black	**662,210**	195,120	110,615	207,895	116,005	21,485	11,095
South Asian	**917,075**	228,345	139,805	310,470	182,735	39,355	16,370
Chinese	**1,029,395**	195,255	157,730	342,650	231,950	65,000	36,810
Korean	**100,660**	19,525	21,110	33,870	21,575	2,730	1,855
Japanese	**73,315**	12,735	10,980	23,780	15,990	5,360	4,470
Southeast Asian	**198,880**	50,125	32,775	74,200	32,420	6,250	3,105
Filipino	**308,575**	68,795	44,485	108,895	68,110	10,745	7,545
Arab/West Asian	**303,965**	76,580	50,840	111,055	52,780	9,055	3,650
Latin American	**216,980**	48,450	38,550	81,985	40,745	4,860	2,385
Visible minority, not included elsewhere	**98,915**	21,705	14,890	35,145	21,125	4,280	1,765
Multiple visible minority	**73,875**	25,570	12,895	21,355	11,070	2,105	875

Source: Statistics Canada, 2001 Census of Population.

Families, households and housing

14

OVERVIEW

Canada's families and households have undergone major changes since the late 1960s. Common-law unions, lone-parent families, smaller households and people living alone are all on the rise. Behind the shifts are diverse factors such as a falling birth rate, delayed marriage and childbearing, and the rise in divorces.

Yet the family is alive and well in Canadian society. In 2001, 25.6 million people lived in a family household, representing 87% of the population living in private households. There were nearly 8.5 million census families, up from 5.0 million in 1971.

The proportion of families with mom, dad and kids—still the largest group—is declining, whereas the proportion with no children at home is on the rise. In 2001, married or common-law couples with children aged 24 and under living at home represented 44% of all families, down from 55% in 1981. The proportion of couples with no children at home was 41% in 2001, up from 34% in 1981.

Common-law unions increasingly popular

More and more couples are living in common-law arrangements. From 1981 to 2001, the proportion of common-law families more than doubled from 6% to 14%.

The trend toward common-law unions is strongest in Quebec—30% of all couples in 2001. This percentage is close to that in Sweden, a country known for having one of the highest rates of non-marital unions.

Canadians are now more likely to start their conjugal life through a common-law relationship. Even so, most couples are

Chart 14.1
Census families, by presence of children

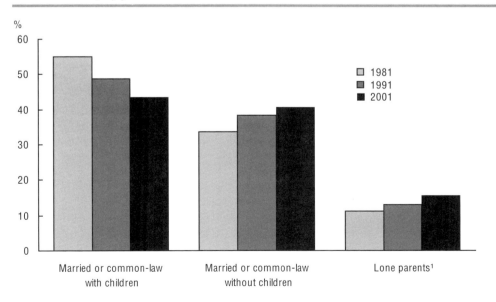

1. Changes to the census family definition in 2001 make comparisons with previous years difficult for lone-parent families.
Source: Statistics Canada, Catalogue no. 96F0030XIE.

married. In 2006, an estimated 84% of couples were legally married.

Nevertheless, a growing number of children live in other types of family structures. In 2001, around 732,900 children 14 and under, or 13%, were living with parents who have a common-law relationship—more than four times the 3% in 1981. Blended families accounted for 12% of all couples with children in 2001, compared with 10% in 1995.

In 2001, 1.1 million children 14 and under, or 19%, were not living with both their parents. Most of these children were living with a lone parent, in most cases their mother. Also, 190,810 children in this age group were living in the same household as their grandparents. However, they accounted for only 3% of all children 14 and under.

Several provinces began to register same-sex marriages in 2003 and 2004. Then on June 28, 2005, Canada became the third country after Belgium and the Netherlands to recognize same-sex marriages. In 2003, 774 same-sex marriages were registered in British Columbia, the only province that published data on same-sex marriages at that time. Just over half of those couples were not

Family characteristics, 2005

	number
Families with no children	3,446,960
Families with one child	2,554,820
Families with two children	2,051,520
Families with three or more children	888,790

Source: Statistics Canada, CANSIM table 111-0011.

residents of Canada, and a greater proportion of women than men married a person of the same sex. Nearly 28% of the women had been married before, versus 14% of the men.

Households are smaller

Households have been shrinking over the past two decades. Fewer people are living in large households, and more people are living alone. In 1981, households had 2.9 persons on average. By 2001, the average household size was 2.6 persons.

The proportion of one-person households has increased—from 20% of all households in 1981 to 26% in 2001. Meanwhile, the proportion of households with four or more persons shrank from 33% of all households to 26%.

Chart 14.2
Household size, by number of persons

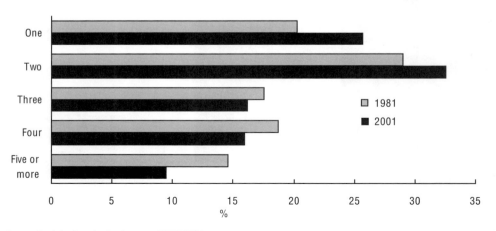

Source: Statistics Canada, Catalogue no. 96F0030XIE.

The decline in household size stems partly from the much lower fertility rates in recent decades—on average, couples are having fewer children. The number of childless couples and couples with no children still residing with them has climbed significantly. Also dissolutions of marriages and common-law unions often result in smaller households, as does the death of a spouse.

A growing number of elderly persons are living alone, which is also contributing to the rise of the one-person household. In 2001, among Canadians aged 65 and older, 35% of women and 16% of men were living alone, compared with 32% of women and 13% of men in 1981. Women have a longer life expectancy and are more likely to be widowed, so a larger proportion of women than men live alone in their later years.

Most households own their home

Most Canadians own their home. In 2005, 67% of households were homeowners, whereas the other households rented. Just under half of those who owned had no mortgage. The average age of mortgage-free owners was 60, compared with 44 for those with a mortgage.

The proportion of households owning their home has been stable for more than 10 years. However, the proportion varies from one province or territory to another. In 2005, the proportion of homeowner households ranged from 59% in Quebec to 80% in Newfoundland and Labrador. Nunavut has the highest share of households that rent.

Canadians' houses are getting bigger, even though families are getting smaller. In 1997, 38% of households lived in a dwelling with at least seven rooms; by 2005, that proportion had risen to 41%. Over the same period, the proportion of households inhabiting a home with one to four rooms remained stable.

Most dwellings in Canada are in good shape. In 2005, 77% of households lived in a home needing no repair. Only 7% of households lived in a structure needing major repairs, down from nearly 9% in 1997.

Chart 14.3
Couple families, by legal marital status

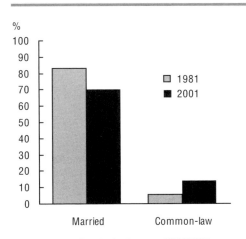

%

☐ 1981
■ 2001

Married   Common-law

Source: Statistics Canada, Catalogue no. 96F0030XIE.

Selected sources

Statistics Canada

- *Canadian Social Trends. Semi-annual.* 11-008-XIE

- *Changing Conjugal Life in Canada.* Occasional. 89-576-XIE

- *Marriages.* Annual. 84F0212XIE

- *Perspectives on Labour and Income.* Monthly. 75-001-XIE

- *Spending Patterns in Canada.* Annual. 62-202-XIE

All the modern conveniences

Most Canadian households are well equipped with time-saving appliances and high-tech gadgetry to benefit from today's telecommunications networks. For example, just 40% of households owned a computer in 1997, whereas 72% did in 2005. As a result, the proportion of households using the Internet shot up from 17% to 64%.

Though the familiar appliances—refrigerator, electric range, colour TV, automatic washer and dryer, land line telephone—seem like they have been fixtures in Canadian homes for decades, these conveniences were not so common before the 1950s. In the years since then, Canadians' expectations of the necessities of life have risen substantially.

Television was one of the first appliances to rapidly become a household fixture. In 1954, 20% of households had a TV set; in 1960, 80% had one. The automatic washer was present in just 20% of households in 1964. It was not until 37 years later, in 2001, that 80% of households had an automatic washer. Microwave ovens were more quickly adopted. In 1979, barely 5% of households had microwaves—by 1997, the share had risen to 88%. And that proportion continued to expand during the 2000s, so that 94% of households had a microwave in 2005.

DVD players have become the most rapidly adopted new technology since television in the 1950s. They were first reported by 20% of households in 2001; by 2005, 77% of households owned a DVD player.

The popularity and convenience of cell phones are undeniable—22% of households had one in 1997 and that shot to 64% by 2005. This figure is higher than the percentage of households owning a dishwasher, which stood at 57% in 2005.

Chart 14.4
Elapsed time to 80% household saturation, selected appliances

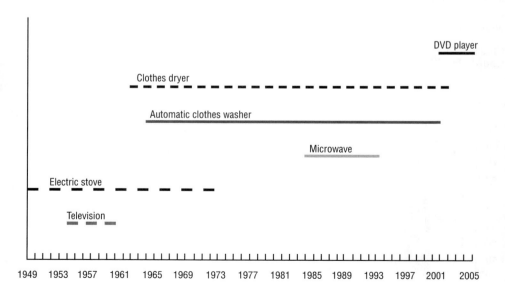

Note: Chart illustrates the elapsed time from 20% to 80% of households owning an appliance.
Source: Statistics Canada, Survey of Household Spending and Household Facilities and Equipment Survey.

Marrying more than once

In the past 30 years, the number of couples divorcing has risen sharply, and more and more couples are choosing common-law unions. Yet most Canadians continue to marry—some more than once in their lives.

In 2001, just over 16.6 million people aged 25 and older had been legally married at some point in their life. Of this group, 89% had married once; 10% had married twice. Less than 1% of Canadians had tied the knot more than twice during their lifetime.

The likelihood that a marriage will succeed is generally higher for those who marry in their thirties, do not live common-law before the wedding, have children, attend religious services, are university-educated and believe that marriage is important for their happiness.

The longer a couple has been married, the greater their chances of staying together,

both in a first marriage and in subsequent marriages. For example, someone who married for the first time in the 1960s is at 13% lower risk of breaking up than someone who married in the 1970s. However, the risk is 67% higher for someone who married in the 1990s.

The chances of a breakup are even higher for couples in a second marriage. People who remarried in the 1980s have a 43% greater risk of breaking up than those who remarried in the 1970s.

Among adults whose first marriage ended in divorce, 43% were remarried at the time of the 2001 General Social Survey. Research indicates that the support of family and friends plays a key role in the quality of the marital relationship, especially in couples where both partners are remarried.

Chart 14.5
Legally married population, by number of marriages, 2001

Note: Population age 25 and older.
Source: Statistics Canada, Catalogue no. 11-008-XIE.

Parents and their adult children

Advertising, movies and TV programs often portray parents as wanting their adult children to leave home. Despite some friction, however, many parents appreciate having their adult children live with them. The General Social Survey found that 32% of parents whose youngest child was aged 20 to 34 had at least one adult child still living with them in 2001.

A minority of parents with two or more adult children living at home expressed frustration. These parents were twice as likely as parents whose adult children had left home to be frustrated by how much time they had to devote to their children (8% versus 4%).

Despite these drawbacks, most of the parents are happy to have their adult children living with them. Fully 64% of parents with adult children aged 20 to 34 at home were 'very satisfied' with the amount of time they spent together, compared with 54% of parents whose children had moved out.

One-quarter of the parents living with an adult child had a 'boomerang kid'—an adult child who had returned to the nest after living outside it for a time. Parents who were living with at least one boomerang kid were more likely than those whose adult children had never left home to express frustration over the amount of time they had to devote to their adult children.

Parents who lived in a large census metropolitan area, who owned a single-family home and who were born in Asia, South America or Europe were more likely to have at least one of their adult children living with them.

Chart 14.6
Probability of living with an adult child, by parent's place of birth, 2001

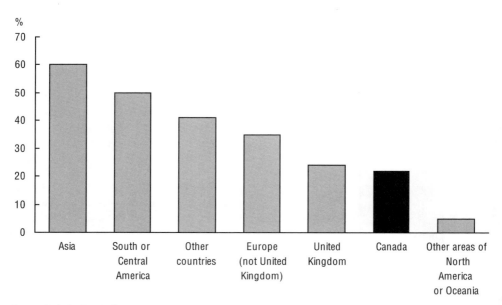

Source: Statistics Canada, Catalogue no. 11-008-XIE.

For lone mothers, education pays off

Raising children is hard work, even with two parents. So when it's up to one parent only, every little advantage helps. In the two decades since 1981, the signs have been encouraging. Notably, the average lone parent in 2001 was older, had fewer children and was much more educated than in 1981. As a result, many more lone mothers today hold a job, and more are employed full time.

Average employment earnings, adjusted for inflation, among lone parents climbed 35% over these two decades, and their low-income rate declined nine percentage points to 43%.

Education was key: the improved demographic profile for the average lone parent was not mirrored among lone mothers aged 25 to 34 who had not finished high school. This group saw its average employment earnings decline and its low-income rate rise substantially over the same two decades.

Higher levels of education, however, did not produce the same results for lone fathers. The proportion of lone fathers who were employed part time or full time was lower in 2001 than in 1981. Moreover, their employment earnings declined, especially among the younger and less educated.

Full-time work can protect lone parents against low income. In 2000, just 14% of lone mothers working full time for the whole year had low income, compared with 62% of those with a different work pattern or not in the labour market. For lone fathers, the proportions were 7% and 38% respectively.

Low income is associated with problems in other aspects of life such as health, work and friendships.

Chart 14.7
Low-income rate of lone mothers working full time, full year

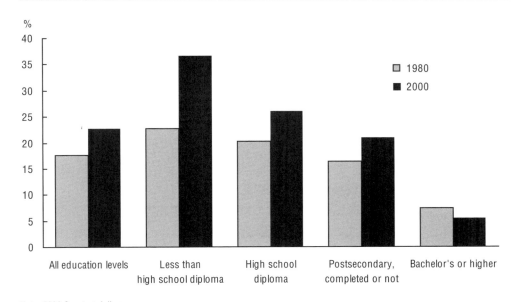

Note: 2000 Ccnstant dollars.
Source: Statistics Canada, Catalogue no. 75-001-XIE.

Table 14.1 Population, by marital status and sex, 2002 to 2006

	2002	2003	2004	2005	2006
	number				
Total marital status	31,372,587	31,676,077	31,989,454	32,299,496	32,623,490
Males	15,538,572	15,688,977	15,842,787	15,995,582	16,155,454
Females	15,834,015	15,987,100	16,146,667	16,303,914	16,468,036
Single	13,092,573	13,231,209	13,365,440	13,499,845	13,636,581
Males	6,999,555	7,078,089	7,153,823	7,229,446	7,306,199
Females	6,093,018	6,153,120	6,211,617	6,270,399	6,330,382
Married[1]	15,340,377	15,438,972	15,554,963	15,669,374	15,793,063
Males	7,659,734	7,701,393	7,751,256	7,800,470	7,855,431
Females	7,680,643	7,737,579	7,803,707	7,868,904	7,937,632
Widowed	1,520,850	1,532,940	1,544,635	1,553,989	1,564,356
Males	282,218	288,816	294,876	300,417	305,640
Females	1,238,632	1,244,124	1,249,759	1,253,572	1,258,716
Divorced	1,418,787	1,472,956	1,524,416	1,576,288	1,629,490
Males	597,065	620,679	642,832	665,249	688,184
Females	821,722	852,277	881,584	911,039	941,306

Note: Population estimates as of July 1.
1. Includes people who are legally married, legally married and separated, and living in common-law unions.
Source: Statistics Canada, CANSIM table 051-0010.

Table 14.2 Marriages, by province and territory, 2002 to 2006

	2002	2003	2004p	2005p	2006p
	number				
Canada	146,738	147,391	148,585	151,047	149,236
Newfoundland and Labrador	2,959	2,876	2,850	2,806	2,750
Prince Edward Island	901	823	827	828	831
Nova Scotia	4,899	4,742	4,729	4,696	4,660
New Brunswick	3,818	3,724	3,708	3,687	3,646
Quebec	21,987	21,138	21,279	22,250	22,150
Ontario	61,615	63,485	64,114	64,668	65,115
Manitoba	5,905	5,659	5,710	5,733	5,747
Saskatchewan	5,067	4,977	5,011	5,000	4,982
Alberta	17,981	17,622	17,909	18,376	19,102
British Columbia	21,247	21,981	22,080	22,634	19,887
Yukon	143	158	160	160	160
Northwest Territories	144	139	141	140	136
Nunavut	72	67	67	69	70

Source: Statistics Canada, CANSIM table 053-0001.

Table 14.3 Divorces, by province and territory, 1999 to 2003

	1999	2000	2001	2002	2003
			number		
Canada	**70,910**	**71,144**	**71,110**	**70,155**	**70,828**
Newfoundland and Labrador	892	913	755	842	662
Prince Edward Island	291	272	246	258	281
Nova Scotia	1,954	2,054	1,945	1,990	1,907
New Brunswick	1,671	1,717	1,570	1,461	1,450
Quebec	17,144	17,054	17,094	16,499	16,738
Ontario	26,088	26,148	26,516	26,170	27,513
Manitoba	2,572	2,430	2,480	2,396	2,352
Saskatchewan	2,237	2,194	1,955	1,959	1,992
Alberta	7,931	8,176	8,252	8,291	7,960
British Columbia	9,935	10,017	10,115	10,125	9,820
Yukon	112	68	91	90	87
Northwest Territories (including Nunavut)	83	..	..	..	..
Northwest Territories	..	94	83	68	62
Nunavut	..	7	8	6	4

Source: Statistics Canada, CANSIM table 053-0002.

Table 14.4 Census families, selected years from 1971 to 2004

	All families		Husband–wife families		Lone-parent families	
	thousands	average number of family members	thousands	average number of family members	thousands	average number of family members
1971	**5,042.6**	3.7	4,566.3	3.8	476.3	3.1
1976	**5,714.5**	3.5	5,156.7	3.5	557.9	2.9
1981	**6,309.2**	3.3	5,597.2	3.3	712.0	2.7
1986	**6,864.2**	3.1	5,995.0	3.2	869.2	2.6
1991	**7,482.1**	3.1	6,511.8	3.1	970.3	2.6
1996	**7,975.0**	3.1	6,818.5	3.1	1,156.5	2.6
2001	**8,481.4**	3.0	7,149.1	3.1	1,332.3	2.5
2004	**8,701.7**	3.0	7,335.3	3.1	1,366.4	2.5

Source: Statistics Canada, Catalogue no. 91-213-XIE.

Table 14.5 Family structure, by province and territory, 2001

	Canada	Newfoundland and Labrador	Prince Edward Island	Nova Scotia	New Brunswick
			number		
All families	8,371,020	154,385	38,425	262,910	215,105
No children at home	3,059,225	53,820	13,400	101,190	81,205
Children at home	5,311,795	100,565	25,020	161,720	133,895
Families of married couples	5,901,430	116,435	28,490	188,805	152,765
No children at home	2,431,720	46,155	11,475	83,930	66,420
Children at home	3,469,700	70,285	17,015	104,870	86,340
Families of common-law couples	1,158,410	14,900	3,630	29,960	27,730
No children at home	627,505	7,665	1,925	17,260	14,790
Children at home	530,900	7,230	1,705	12,705	12,940
Lone-parent families	1,311,190	23,055	6,305	44,140	34,615
Male parent	245,825	4,115	1,060	7,440	6,535
Female parent	1,065,365	18,935	5,245	36,700	28,075

Note: Census families in private households.
Source: Statistics Canada, 2001 Census of Population.

Table 14.6 Family structure, by census metropolitan area, 2001

	All families			Families of married couples		
	All families	No children at home	Children at home	Families of married couples	No children at home	Children at home
				number		
St. John's	49,515	15,850	33,655	35,480	12,500	22,980
Halifax	100,670	37,720	62,950	71,405	29,575	41,825
Saint John	35,210	12,480	22,730	25,285	10,520	14,770
Saguenay	44,800	16,280	28,520	27,265	11,175	16,095
Québec	189,430	72,670	116,760	104,170	44,655	59,520
Sherbrooke	41,725	17,015	24,710	22,685	10,780	11,905
Trois-Rivières	38,570	15,145	23,430	21,350	10,160	11,195
Montréal	935,255	331,510	603,740	550,285	220,485	329,795
Ottawa–Gatineau	293,705	104,515	189,190	203,020	79,120	123,910
Oshawa	83,860	26,185	57,675	61,905	21,875	40,030
Toronto	1,280,960	381,710	899,245	974,350	320,725	653,625
Hamilton	186,480	66,570	119,905	141,370	56,925	84,445
St. Catharines–Niagara	107,510	42,340	65,170	81,020	36,945	44,080
Kitchener	115,955	40,015	75,940	87,595	33,385	54,205
London	119,455	44,330	75,125	87,405	36,640	50,765
Windsor	85,890	29,095	56,795	64,210	24,860	39,350
Greater Sudbury / Grand Sudbury	45,560	17,645	27,915	32,710	14,675	18,040
Thunder Bay	34,300	12,595	21,700	24,765	10,535	14,240
Winnipeg	182,190	64,925	117,265	131,720	53,935	77,785
Regina	52,540	18,650	33,890	37,435	15,560	21,875
Saskatoon	60,245	21,710	38,530	43,820	18,225	25,595
Calgary	259,465	92,980	166,485	191,570	72,990	118,575
Edmonton	255,000	89,330	165,670	186,250	72,210	114,040
Vancouver	535,255	189,915	345,340	401,385	152,540	248,845
Victoria	86,295	39,450	46,850	61,875	32,010	29,865

Note: Census families in private households.
Source: Statistics Canada, 2001 Census of Population.

Quebec	Ontario	Manitoba	Saskatchewan	Alberta	British Columbia	Yukon	Northwest Territories	Nunavut
				number				
2,019,555	3,190,985	302,855	265,620	811,285	1,086,030	7,810	9,700	6,355
751,735	1,110,100	111,185	103,260	297,655	429,485	2,755	2,555	885
1,267,820	2,080,890	191,670	162,360	513,630	656,550	5,055	7,145	5,480
1,175,440	2,406,340	224,055	198,300	600,995	797,490	4,465	5,115	2,735
505,190	936,430	94,870	89,895	241,740	351,875	1,825	1,510	410
670,255	1,469,910	129,185	108,400	359,250	445,610	2,645	3,605	2,325
508,525	298,545	29,635	25,255	93,765	120,125	1,795	2,555	1,990
246,550	173,670	16,315	13,360	55,910	77,605	930	1,045	470
261,970	124,875	13,320	11,890	37,855	42,520	865	1,510	1,520
335,590	486,105	49,160	42,065	116,520	168,420	1,550	2,035	1,635
68,025	84,865	9,065	7,910	23,575	31,960	325	505	445
267,570	401,245	40,100	34,155	92,945	136,455	1,220	1,530	1,190

	Families of common-law couples			Lone-parent families		
Families of common-law couples	No children at home	Children at home	Lone-parent families	Male parent	Female parent	
			number			
5,050	3,355	1,700	8,980	1,470	7,515
12,550	8,140	4,405	16,715	2,390	14,325
3,540	1,960	1,575	6,385	950	5,435
10,870	5,110	5,765	6,660	1,460	5,205
54,045	28,015	26,035	31,205	6,525	24,680
12,165	6,240	5,930	6,870	1,615	5,255
10,450	4,985	5,465	6,770	1,305	5,460
215,780	111,025	104,760	169,185	30,430	138,755
42,555	25,400	17,155	48,125	8,825	39,310
8,990	4,310	4,685	12,965	2,440	10,525
96,610	60,985	35,630	209,995	34,350	175,645
16,570	9,650	6,930	28,535	4,815	23,715
9,625	5,400	4,230	16,855	3,005	13,850
11,710	6,630	5,080	16,650	2,660	13,990
12,690	7,685	4,995	19,360	3,105	16,255
7,290	4,235	3,050	14,390	2,340	12,050
5,340	2,975	2,365	7,510	1,280	6,230
3,670	2,065	1,605	5,860	1,070	4,790
18,155	10,990	7,165	32,315	5,630	26,685
5,205	3,090	2,115	9,900	1,715	8,180
5,815	3,490	2,325	10,610	1,570	9,040
29,740	19,985	9,760	38,155	7,300	30,855
27,705	17,120	10,580	41,055	7,810	33,240
52,005	37,370	14,635	81,860	14,810	67,050
10,620	7,435	3,185	13,800	2,435	11,365

Table 14.7 Population, by living arrangements and by province and territory, 2001

	Total population in private households	People in family households	Spouses, common-law partners or lone parents	Children in census families
	number			
Canada	**29,522,300**	**25,586,660**	**15,430,855**	**9,582,615**
Newfoundland and Labrador	**507,245**	463,185	285,715	167,590
Prince Edward Island	**133,070**	118,110	70,545	45,565
Nova Scotia	**895,310**	777,715	481,680	279,785
New Brunswick	**717,540**	633,475	395,595	224,885
Quebec	**7,097,855**	5,993,305	3,703,515	2,190,140
Ontario	**11,254,730**	9,941,520	5,895,870	3,809,265
Manitoba	**1,090,630**	936,825	556,545	362,115
Saskatchewan	**956,635**	821,035	489,175	316,680
Alberta	**2,918,920**	2,532,540	1,506,050	962,450
British Columbia	**3,858,730**	3,287,350	2,003,650	1,187,490
Yukon	**28,165**	23,940	14,075	9,165
Northwest Territories	**36,955**	32,915	17,370	14,450
Nunavut	**26,525**	24,755	11,080	13,040

Note: Population in private households.
1. Non-relatives may be present.
Source: Statistics Canada, 2001 Census of Population.

Table 14.8 Household equipment, 1997 to 2005

	1997	1998	1999	2000
	%			
Washing machine	81.1	81.4	80.3	80.9
Clothes dryer	77.4	78.9	77.6	78.5
Dishwasher	48.8	50.9	49.4	51.2
Refrigerator	99.8	99.8	99.6	99.8
Freezer	59.3	58.9	57.6	57.9
Microwave oven	88.0	88.5	89.4	91.0
Air conditioning	32.0	33.1	34.1	34.4
Telephone (regular or cellular)	98.4	98.5	98.7	98.8
Cellular telephone	21.9	26.2	31.9	41.8
Compact disc (CD) player	63.9	65.7	70.2	74.1
Cablevision	74.8	72.9	73.3	72.4
Satellite dish	..	..	..	..
Digital video disc (DVD) player	..	..	..	..
Compact disc (CD) writer	..	..	..	..
Digital video disc (DVD) writer	..	..	..	..
Video cassette recorder	87.1	87.7	88.5	89.9
Home computer	39.8	45.0	49.8	54.9
Internet use from home	17.4	24.7	33.1	42.3
Colour television	98.6	98.7	98.8	98.9
Vehicle (owned or leased)	..	82.4	82.4	83.5
Owned vehicles (automobiles, trucks, vans)	78.8	78.5	78.1	79.3
Leased vehicles (automobiles, trucks, vans)	..	8.6	8.7	9.1

Notes: All data refer to December 31 of the reference year.
Every second year starting with 2001, statistics for Canada include the territories. For the other years, Canada-level statistics include only the 10 provinces.
Source: Statistics Canada, CANSIM table 203-0020.

Non-family people living with relatives[1]	Non-family people living with census families other than their own	People in non-family households	Living with relatives[1]	Living with non-relatives only	Living alone
		number			
332,085	**241,105**	**3,935,640**	**222,390**	**736,375**	**2,976,880**
6,545	3,340	44,055	3,195	6,805	34,060
1,185	815	14,960	1,005	2,370	11,580
9,585	6,660	117,595	6,460	22,125	89,005
7,435	5,560	84,065	5,340	15,140	63,585
57,960	41,685	1,104,545	59,770	164,010	880,765
149,515	86,870	1,313,215	77,830	245,220	990,160
9,955	8,210	153,805	9,175	22,870	121,760
7,550	7,635	135,595	8,495	21,950	105,150
30,955	33,095	386,380	23,675	107,330	255,375
50,170	46,040	571,380	26,805	126,440	418,135
250	455	4,225	180	780	3,265
545	555	4,040	270	990	2,785
435	190	1,775	195	330	1,250

2001	2002	2003	2004	2005
		%		
80.4	80.5	81.2	81.9	82.2
79.3	78.4	78.8	79.5	80.4
52.1	54.6	55.0	56.0	57.2
99.7	99.9	99.7	99.8	99.7
56.1	56.8	56.1	55.2	56.3
91.3	92.4	93.0	93.8	94.1
35.8	37.5	39.6	41.7	44.2
98.6	98.7	98.8	98.9	98.9
47.6	51.7	54.0	58.9	64.2
71.1	73.9	76.2	79.7	80.4
68.1	66.1	64.8	66.3	65.4
..	..	..	22.0	22.6
..	..	..	68.3	77.1
..	..	..	38.3	43.5
..	..	..	16.0	24.5
91.6	92.1	90.2	90.0	89.1
59.8	64.1	66.6	68.7	72.0
49.9	54.5	56.9	59.8	64.3
99.2	99.1	99.0	99.2	99.0
83.0	84.0	83.1	83.8	83.6
78.2	79.3	78.2	79.1	79.0
9.8	9.8	9.8	9.9	10.1

Table 14.9 Owned dwellings, by province and territory

	2000	2001	2002	2003	2004	2005
				%		
Canada	**64.2**	**64.4**	**64.8**	**65.6**	**65.8**	**67.1**
Newfoundland and Labrador	74.8	76.4	76.5	77.0	76.6	79.6
Prince Edward Island	71.0	71.3	69.8	73.2	72.7	68.5
Nova Scotia	69.7	72.4	69.5	69.9	71.1	71.2
New Brunswick	75.0	72.6	71.7	73.8	76.9	76.8
Quebec	55.6	57.7	56.8	57.1	56.6	59.2
Ontario	65.2	64.8	66.7	68.0	67.6	68.8
Manitoba	71.1	70.9	68.7	70.6	68.9	73.0
Saskatchewan	71.6	71.3	73.1	72.5	73.9	74.5
Alberta	71.5	70.4	71.1	72.1	72.2	74.0
British Columbia	64.5	63.7	63.3	64.0	66.6	65.3
Yukon	..	63.2	..	62.2	..	62.1
Northwest Territories	..	48.8	..	51.9	..	60.9
Nunavut	..	20.8	..	26.9	..	F

Notes: All data refer to December 31 of the reference year.

In every second year starting with 2001, statistics for Canada include the territories. For the other years, Canada-level statistics include only the 10 provinces.

Includes owned dwellings with or without a mortgage.

Source: Statistics Canada, CANSIM table 203-0019.

Table 14.10 Average number of rooms per dwelling, by household size and by province and territory, 2001

	All households	One person	Two people	Three people	Four people	Five people	Six people or more
				number			
Canada	**6.3**	**4.7**	**6.1**	**6.8**	**7.5**	**7.9**	**8.1**
Newfoundland and Labrador	7.0	5.6	6.8	7.3	7.8	8.3	8.3
Prince Edward Island	6.7	5.2	6.5	6.9	7.7	8.5	8.6
Nova Scotia	6.5	5.1	6.4	7.0	7.7	8.1	8.6
New Brunswick	6.5	5.2	6.4	6.9	7.5	8.0	8.6
Quebec	5.8	4.5	5.8	6.4	7.0	7.5	7.8
Ontario	6.4	4.8	6.2	6.8	7.5	7.9	8.0
Manitoba	6.1	4.6	6.0	6.7	7.3	7.6	7.5
Saskatchewan	6.6	5.1	6.6	7.2	7.8	8.1	7.9
Alberta	6.6	4.9	6.4	7.1	7.8	8.2	8.3
British Columbia	6.2	4.5	6.1	6.9	7.7	8.3	8.6
Yukon	5.9	4.5	5.6	6.4	7.3	7.6	7.9
Northwest Territories	5.7	4.3	5.4	5.9	6.5	6.6	6.8
Nunavut	5.2	4.1	4.7	5.1	5.4	5.6	6.1

Source: Statistics Canada, Catalogue no. 95F0323XCB.

Geography

15

OVERVIEW

Geography influences so much in our lives—where we work, how we live and what we do. In measuring all these activities, Statistics Canada relies on a framework of well-defined geographic areas in collecting, organizing, analyzing and presenting the vast economic and social data the Agency produces about Canada's people and places. Defining these geographic areas—a process called geocoding—is fundamental to how Statistics Canada measures trends in Canadian society.

Geocoding is so fundamental because it links data about Canadians to their geography. Together with census data, geographers can find out how cities are growing, where people are settling, the median age or income of the inhabitants.

By using software to link with postal codes, policy makers can study school districts or commuting patterns, and governments can use data to determine, for example, transfer payments, or the need for more hospitals or services for seniors.

Growing more urbanized

The 2006 Census showed that Canada's population continues to grow and gravitate toward larger urban centres. Reflecting this trend, geographers have added six new census metropolitan areas (CMAs) to Canada's list of large urban areas—Moncton, N.B.; Barrie, Brantford, Guelph and Peterborough, Ont.; and Kelowna, B.C.

With these six cities, Canada now has 33 CMAs, which include 68% of the population. This is up from 27 CMAs in 2001 and 25 CMAs in 1996.

Map 15.1
Greater Golden Horseshoe population change from 2001 to 2006, by 2006 census subdivision

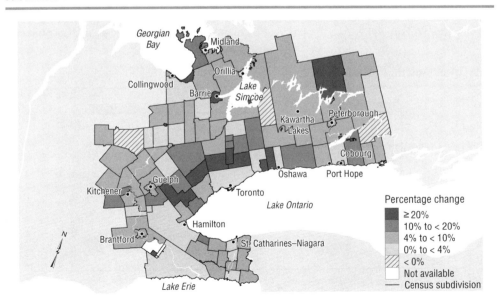

Source: Statistics Canada, Census of Population.

Smaller urban areas are known as census agglomerations (CAs). A CA is defined when an urban core population reaches at least 10,000. For the 2006 Census, there are 111 CAs in Canada, compared with 112 in 1996. Six CAs became CMAs, seven new CAs were defined and two—Gander and Labrador City in Newfoundland and Labrador—were retired because the core population of each dropped below 10,000.

Several factors, including total population, population of the urban core and commuting flows, determine when a CA is promoted to a CMA. One reason that the number of large urban centres increased in 2006 is that the delineation rules for defining a CMA changed.

As of March 2003, a CA is no longer required to have an urban core population of 100,000 to be promoted to the status of a CMA. Instead, a CA assumes the status of a CMA if it attains a total population of at least 100,000 of which 50,000 or more must live in the urban core.

Together, CMAs and CAs contain 80% of Canada's population, although they cover only 4% of the land area—a sign that we are growing more urbanized.

Population of the six new CMAs, 2006

	number
Barrie, Ontario	177,061
Kelowna, British Columbia	162,276
Guelph, Ontario	127,009
Moncton, New Brunswick	126,424
Brantford, Ontario	124,607
Peterborough, Ontario	116,570

Source: Statistics Canada, 2006 Census of Population.

A planning tool

Statistics Canada's official classification for geographical areas in Canada is the Standard Geographical Classification (SGC). The geographical areas in the SGC—provinces and territories, counties and municipalities—were chosen because Canadians know them and because these entities are significant users of statistics when they plan programs that involve spending public funds.

The 10 provinces and 3 territories—the primary political subdivision of Canada—are at the top of the SGC hierarchy. Next are census divisions, which the SGC defines as a group of neighbouring municipalities. Usually, they exist for regional planning and managing common services, such as policing.

Chart 15.1
Population growth, by province

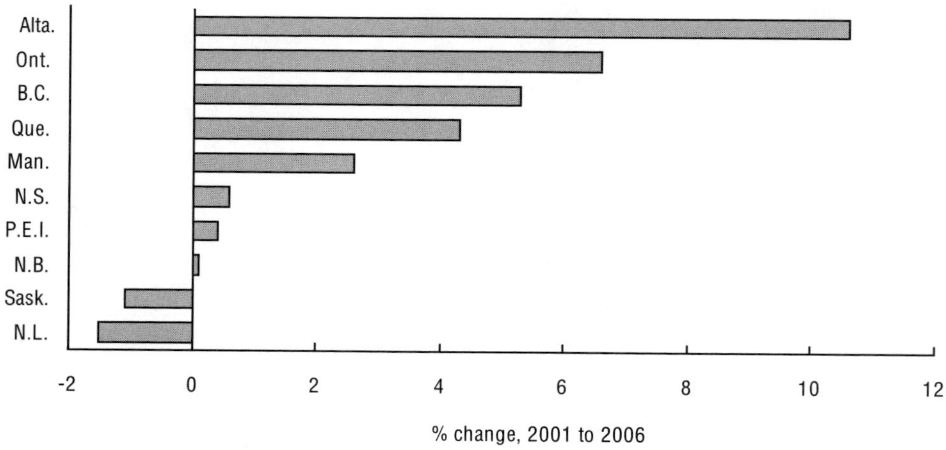

% change, 2001 to 2006

Source: Statistics Canada, 2006 Census of Population.

Often, a census division will correspond to a county or a regional district.

Census divisions are relatively stable geographic areas, which makes it easier to follow trends over time. For the 2006 Census, Statistics Canada delineated 288 census divisions in Canada, unchanged from the 1996 and 2001 censuses.

Census subdivisions are the smallest geographic area in the SGC. Generally, a census subdivision is a single municipality or its equivalent for statistical purposes, such as an Indian reserve. Census subdivisions can change, however, because of municipal restructuring or amalgamation. For the 2006 Census, there were 5,418 census subdivisions, compared with 5,600 in 2001.

Zones and regions

Like peering through a microscope, the SGC allows demographers to look at Canada from the widest focus—national, provincial and territorial data—right down to the narrowest focus—data from a census subdivision's suburbs, exurbs and neighbourhoods.

Chart 15.2
Population aged 15 and younger and aged 65 and older, by area type, 2006

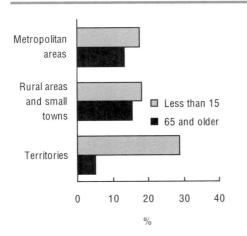

Source: Statistics Canada, 2006 Census of Population.

A recent concept in geography, the metropolitan-influenced zone (MIZ), uses data on Canadians' commuting flows to and from work to reveal patterns and degrees of social and economic integration between urban areas and the census subdivisions not included in any CMA or CA—these non-CMA/CA census subdivisions are sometimes described as 'rural and small town Canada.'

The influence of any nearby CMA or CA on rural and small town Canada can be either strong, moderate, weak or not at all. For example, a student might use the MIZ concept to closely compare the population characteristics of a rural area near Toronto with the population characteristics of the rural outskirts of Whitehorse, Yukon—perhaps comparing to what degree rents or unemployment rates are influenced by the two very different nearby CMAs.

Economic Regions (ERs) are another way to look at Canada's geography—they are made by grouping census divisions. As the name implies, Canada's 76 ERs describe regional economic activity. The ER is a geographic unit small enough to permit regional analysis, yet large enough to include enough respondents so that a broad range of economic statistics can be collected—for example, the Labour Force Survey uses economic regions in some provinces when collecting its data.

Selected sources

Statistics Canada

- *Agriculture and Rural Working Paper Series.* Occasional. 21-601-MIE

- *Geography Working Paper Series.* Occasional. 92F0138MIE

- *Rural and Small Town Canada Analysis Bulletin.* Occasional. 21-006-XIE

- *Standard Geographical Classification.* Occasional. 12-571-XWE

Regional context of community growth

Some regions have boomed in recent years, while some communities within those regions have experienced demographic decline.

One in three communities was in continuous demographic decline from 1981 to 2001, and most of those (65%) were also in regions with a shrinking population. In 2001, 9% of Canada's population lived in these declining communities.

A recent study took standard geographic units—census divisions to represent regions and census consolidated sub-divisions to represent communities—and analysed community population trends in relation to regional population trends and regional context. Demographic decline means the population fell in at least three of the four censuses taken from 1981 to 2001.

Regional context matters. In 2001, 43% of the population of Newfoundland and

Labrador resided in declining communities within declining regions. Communities in rural regions not adjacent to metropolitan areas and in rural northern regions are not as likely to be growing. In Canada's rural north, nearly two out of three communities are located in regions showing demographic decline.

But not all communities mirror the pattern of their region. For example, even though only 20% of the communities in the rural north are in a growing region, 29% of them are growing, due in part to the rising Aboriginal population.

Declining communities have a high share of their work force in primary industries, such as agriculture, and in manufacturing related to natural resources. Both are substituting machinery for labour and shedding jobs, which contributes to the demographic decline of these communities.

Map 15.2
Canada's growing/declining communities in growing/declining regions, 1981 to 2001

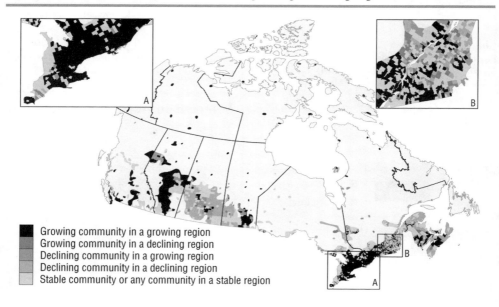

Growing community in a growing region
Growing community in a declining region
Declining community in a growing region
Declining community in a declining region
Stable community or any community in a stable region

Source: Statistics Canada, Census of Population.

Where might manure affect us?

Manure is a prime source of fertilizer for crops, one of the world's oldest examples of recycling waste products. However, if not managed properly, manure can be a source of pollution. It is important to know not only where manure is produced, but also how it affects the surrounding drainage area.

Analysts determine this connection by using the geographic unit known as the sub-sub-drainage area (SSDA) to map livestock manure production, which they estimate from Census of Agriculture livestock numbers, to the surrounding catchment area.

The SSDA is valuable because it reflects fixed physical features of the land, rather than changing political or administrative boundaries. It also presents local information that is environmentally relevant. There are 978 SSDAs in Canada. In 2001, livestock production occurred in fewer than 400.

Manure production is concentrated in five major areas: central and southern Alberta, southern Manitoba, southern Ontario, southeastern Quebec and Prince Edward Island. Two other significant areas are the Lower Fraser Valley in British Columbia and the Annapolis area in Nova Scotia.

Ontario was home to the three highest manure-producing SSDAs in 2001. A high number of SSDAs in Alberta had the largest increases in manure production from 1981 to 2001. One-third of the manure produced in 2001 came from beef cows.

As part of a natural cycle, nitrogen in manure turns into a nitrate form, which can compromise drinking water and lead to human health problems. Phosphorus in manure can cause excessive algae growth in our lakes and streams, leaving them uninhabitable for fish and other aquatic life.

Map 15.3
Western Canada, livestock manure production, by sub-sub-drainage area, 2001

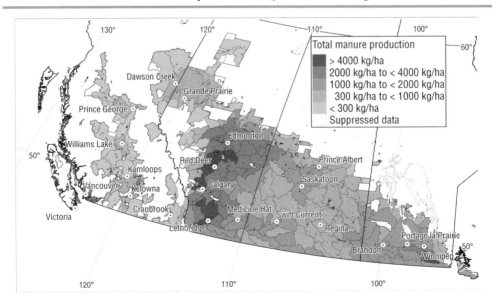

Note: Kilograms per hectare.
Source: Statistics Canada, Census of Agriculture.

Watershed pressures

A boil-water advisory surprised millions of Vancouverites in 2006 and contaminated drinking water killed seven and sickened hundreds in Walkerton, Ontario in 2000. Such events have generated debate about how best to manage our watersheds.

A watershed is a region of interconnected waterways that function as a single system—upstream activities may affect downstream quantity and quality. Geographers have defined 164 geographic units in Canada called sub-basins. These watersheds are the drainage areas of the smaller rivers that flow into Canada's major rivers.

In 2001, 10 million people resided in six watersheds, making them our most urban watersheds. These cover just 3% of Canada's land area. From 1981 to 2001, the population of these watersheds grew 45%, or by three million people. This reflects the

urban character of Canada's population and underlines the pressure on specific fresh water sources and the infrastructures that supply and treat freshwater.

Ontario stands out—six million people reside in just one watershed, covering the greater Toronto area, the Golden Horseshoe and the Niagara Peninsula. In British Columbia, 2.3 million people live in two watersheds covering Greater Vancouver and the Fraser Valley. Another one million reside in very highly urbanized watersheds in Calgary and Fort McMurray, where the oil and gas industry's water use is raising concerns.

Only 19% of Canada's entire rural population lives in a watershed where rural residents are the majority. This highlights a challenge facing rural and urban Canadians as they negotiate water-management solutions.

Map 15.4
Canada's watersheds, by the degree of rurality of the population, 2001

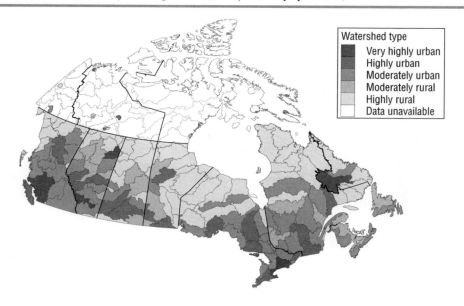

Watershed type
- Very highly urban
- Highly urban
- Moderately urban
- Moderately rural
- Highly rural
- Data unavailable

Source: Statistics Canada, Census of Population..

Mapping the data patterns

Statistics Canada gathers an enormous amount of data about our population, society and culture when it conducts its many surveys and, every five years, the census. Analysts use not only tables, charts and plain language writing to convey their findings from all that census data, they also use maps and mapping tools—available for everyone to use free at www.statcan.ca under Maps and geography. These include reference maps, thematic maps and interactive maps.

Reference maps show the location of the geographic areas using census geography. These maps display boundaries, names and statistical codes of standard geographic areas. Reference maps show the major visible features, such as roads, railroads, coastlines, lakes and rivers.

Thematic maps make data easier to understand. They let users see the data's

spatial patterns. Geographers use data from the census and surveys to create thematic maps for a range of subjects, such as land cover by major drainage areas, the proportion of the population by level of education and by census division, and the proportion of obese people by health region.

Interactive maps show places on a map and give the latest trove of census and other data for those places. Statistics Canada maintains 10 categories of interactive mapping tools, including Community Profiles, Crop Conditions, Federal Electoral Districts and a mapping tool called GeoSearch, which makes it easy to see basic geographic and census data for any place in Canada.

All these mapping tools transform data into pictures to help us better understand what the numbers mean and who we are as a nation.

Map 15.5
Adult obesity, by health region, 2005

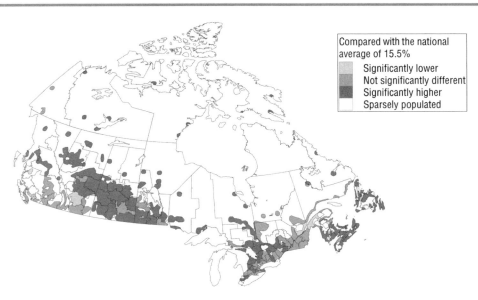

Compared with the national average of 15.5%
- Significantly lower
- Not significantly different
- Significantly higher
- Sparsely populated

Note: Proportion of the population aged 18 and older with body mass index classified as obese.
Source: Statistics Canada, Canadian Community Health Survey.

Table 15.1 Weather conditions, by selected urban centres

	Extreme maximum temperature		Extreme minimum temperature		Rainfall[1]	Snowfall[1,2]	Precipitation[2,3]
	degrees Celsius	years	degrees Celsius	years	millimetres	centimetres	millimetres
St. John's	31.5	1983	-23.8	1986	1,191.0	322.3	1,513.7
Charlottetown	34.4	1944	-30.5	1982	880.4	311.9	1,173.3
Halifax	35.0	1995	-28.5	1993	1,238.9	230.5	1,452.2
Saint John	34.4	1976	-36.7	1948	1,147.9	256.9	1,390.3
Fredericton	37.2	1975	-37.2	1962	885.5	276.5	1,143.3
Québec	35.6	1953	-36.1	1962	923.8	315.9	1,230.3
Sherbrooke	33.7	1983	-40.0	1979	873.9	294.3	1,144.1
Trois-Rivières	36.1	1975	-41.1	1976	858.6	241.4	1,099.8
Montréal	35.6	1955	-37.2	1933	819.7	220.5	1,046.2
Ottawa	37.8	1944	-36.1	1943	732.0	235.7	943.5
Kingston	34.3	1983	-34.5	1981	794.6	181.0	968.4
Oshawa	36.5	1988	-30.5	1981	759.5	118.4	877.9
Toronto	38.3	1948	-31.3	1981	684.6	115.4	792.7
Hamilton	37.4	1988	-28.0	1994	764.8	161.8	910.1
St. Catharines	37.4	1988	-25.7	1979	745.7	136.6	873.6
London	38.2	1988	-31.7	1970	817.9	202.4	987.1
Windsor	40.2	1988	-29.1	1994	805.2	126.6	918.3
Greater Sudbury / Grand Sudbury	38.3	1975	-39.3	1982	656.5	274.4	899.3
Thunder Bay	40.3	1983	-41.1	1951	559.0	187.6	711.6
Winnipeg	40.6	1949	-45.0	1966	415.6	110.6	513.7
Regina	43.3	1937	-50.0	1885	304.4	105.9	388.1
Saskatoon	40.6	1988	-50.0	1893	265.2	97.2	350.0
Edmonton	34.5	1998	-48.3	1938	365.7	123.5	476.9
Calgary	36.1	1919	-45.0	1893	320.6	126.7	412.6
Abbotsford	37.8	1958	-21.1	1950	1,507.5	63.5	1,573.2
Vancouver	33.3	1960	-17.8	1950	1,154.7	48.2	1,199.0
Victoria	36.1	1941	-15.6	1950	841.4	43.8	883.3
Whitehorse	34.4	1969	-52.2	1947	163.1	145.0	267.4
Yellowknife	32.5	1989	-51.2	1947	164.5	151.8	280.7
Iqaluit	25.8	2001	-45.6	1967	198.3	235.8	412.1

1. Annual average.

2. On average, one centimetre of snow equals one millimetre of rain.

3. Totals may not add up because of different densities of snow.

Source: Environment Canada, Climate Normals and Averages, 1971 to 2001.

Table 15.2 Major sea islands, by region

	Area square kilometres		Area square kilometres
Baffin Island	507,451	**Arctic islands south of Queen Elizabeth Islands**	
Queen Elizabeth Islands		**(but north of the Arctic Circle)[1] (concluded)**	
Ellesmere	196,236	Richards	2,165
Devon	55,247	Air Force	1,720
Axel Heiberg	43,178	Wales	1,137
Melville	42,149	Rowley	1,090
Bathurst	16,042	**Northwest Territories and Nunavut south of**	
Prince Patrick	15,848	**the Arctic Circle**	
Ellef Ringnes	11,295	Southampton[2]	41,214
Cornwallis	6,995	Coats[2]	5,498
Amund Ringnes	5,255	Mansel[2]	3,180
Mackenzie King	5,048	Akimiski[2]	3,001
Borden	2,794	Flaherty[2]	1,585
Cornwall	2,358	Nottingham[3]	1,372
Eglinton	1,541	Resolution[3]	1,015
Graham	1,378	**Pacific Coast**	
Lougheed	1,308	Vancouver	31,285
Byam Martin	1,150	Graham	6,361
Île Vanier	1,126	Moresby	2,608
Cameron	1,059	Princess Royal	2,251
Arctic islands south of Queen Elizabeth		Pitt	1,375
Islands (but north of the Arctic Circle)[1]		**Atlantic Coast and Gulf of St. Lawrence**	
Victoria	217,291	Newfoundland and Labrador (main island)	108,860
Banks	70,028	**Gulf of St. Lawrence**	
Prince of Wales	33,339	Cape Breton	10,311
Somerset	24,786	Anticosti	7,941
King William	13,111	Prince Edward	5,620
Bylot	11,067	**Bay of Fundy**	
Prince Charles	9,521	Grand Manan	137
Stefansson	4,463		

Note: A major island has a land area greater than 130 square kilometres.
1. There are no islands over 130 square kilometres in Yukon.
2. Formerly the District of Keewatin.
3. Formerly the District of Franklin.
Source: Natural Resources Canada, *Atlas of Canada*.

Table 15.3 Principal heights, by province and territory

	Elevation metres		Elevation metres
Newfoundland and Labrador		**Quebec** (concluded)	
Torngat Mountains		Monts Otish	
Mount Caubvik[1,2] (on N.L.–Que. boundary)	1,652	Unnamed peak (52°19', 71°27')	1,135
Cirque Mountain	1,568	Collines Montérégiennes	
Mount Cladonia	1,453	Mont Brome	533
Mount Eliot	1,356	**Ontario**	
Mount Tetragona	1,356	Ishpatina Ridge[2]	693
Quartzite Mountain	1,186	Ogidaki Mountain	665
Blow Me Down Mountain	1,183	Batchawana Mountain	653
Mealy Mountains		Tip Top Mountain	640
Unnamed peak (53°37', 58°33')	1,176	Niagara Escarpment	600
Kaumajet Mountains		Blue Mountains	541
Bishops Mitre	1,113	Osler Bluff	526
Long Range Mountains		Caledon Mountain	427
Lewis Hills	814	**Manitoba**	
Gros Morne	806	Baldy Mountain[2]	832
Prince Edward Island		Highest point in Porcupine Hills	823
Queen's County (46°20', 63°25')[2]	142	Riding Mountain	610
Nova Scotia		**Saskatchewan**	
Cape Breton Highlands (46°42', 60°36')[2]	532	Cypress Hills[2]	1,468
New Brunswick		Wood Mountain	1,013
Mount Carleton[2]	817	Vermilion Hills	785
Wilkinson Mountain	785	**Alberta**	
Quebec		Rocky Mountains	
Monts Torngat		Mount Columbia[2] (on Alta.–B.C. boundary)	3,747
Mont D'Iberville[1,2] (on N.L.–Que. boundary)	1,652	North Twin	3,733
Les Appalaches		Mount Alberta	3,620
Mont Jacques-Cartier	1,268	Mount Assiniboine (on Alta.–B.C. boundary)	3,618
Mont Gosford	1,192	Mount Forbes	3,612
Mont Richardson	1,185	South Twin	3,581
Mont Mégantic	1,105	Mount Temple	3,547
Les Laurentides		Mount Brazeau	3,525
Unnamed peak (47°19', 70°50')	1,166	Snow Dome (on Alta.–B.C. boundary)	3,520
Mont Tremblant	968	Mount Lyell (on Alta.–B.C. boundary)	3,504
Mont Sainte-Anne	800	Hungabee Mountain (on Alta.–B.C. boundary)	3,492
Mont Sir-Wilfrid	783	Mount Athabasca	3,491

See notes and source at the end of this table.

	Elevation			Elevation
	metres			metres
Alberta (concluded)			**Yukon** (concluded)	
Mount King Edward (on Alta.–B.C. boundary)	3,490		Mount Lucania	5,226
Mount Kitchener	3,490		King Peak	5,173
British Columbia			Mount Steele	5,067
St. Elias Mountains			Mount Wood	4,838
Fairweather Mountain[2] (on Alaska–B.C. boundary)	4,663		Mount Vancouver (on Alaska–Yukon boundary)	4,785
Mount Quincy Adams (on Alaska–B.C. boundary)	4,133		Mount Macaulay	4,663
Mount Root (on Alaska–B.C. boundary)	3,901		Mount Slaggard	4,663
Coast Mountains			Mount Hubbard (on Alaska–Yukon boundary)	4,577
Mount Waddington	4,016		**Northwest Territories**	
Mount Tiedemann	3,848		Mackenzie Mountains	
Combatant Mountain	3,756		Unnamed peak (61°52', 127°42')[2]	2,773
Asperity	3,716		Mount Sir James MacBrien	2,762
Serra Peaks	3,642		Franklin Mountains	
Monarch Mountain	3,459		Cap Mountain	1,577
Rocky Mountains			Mount Clark	1,462
Mount Robson	3,954		Pointed Mountain	1,405
Mount Columbia (on Alta.–B.C. boundary)	3,747		Nahanni Butte	1,396
Mount Clemenceau	3,642		Melville Island	
Mount Assiniboine (on Alta.–B.C. boundary)	3,618		Unnamed peak (75°25', 114°47')	776
Mount Goodsir, North Tower	3,581		Banks Island	
Mount Goodsir, South Tower	3,520		Durham Heights	732
Snow Dome (on Alta.–B.C. boundary)	3,520		Victoria Island	
Mount Bryce	3,507		Unnamed peak (71°51', 112°36')	655
Selkirk Mountains			**Nunavut**	
Mount Sir Sandford	3,522		Axel Heiberg Island	
Cariboo Mountains			Outlook Peak	2,210
Mount Sir Wilfrid Laurier	3,520		Baffin Island	
Purcell Mountains			Mount Odin	2,147
Mount Farnham	3,481		Devon Island	
Monashee Mountains			Summit Devon Ice Cap	1,908
Torii Mountain	3,429		Ellesmere Island	
Yukon			Barbeau Peak[2]	2,616
St. Elias Mountains				
Mount Logan[2,3]	5,959			
Mount St. Elias (on Alaska–Yukon boundary)	5,489			

1. Known as Mont D'Iberville in Quebec and as Mount Caubvik in Newfoundland and Labrador.

2. Highest point in province or territory.

3. Highest point in Canada.

Source: Natural Resources Canada, *Atlas of Canada*.

Table 15.4 Principal rivers and their tributaries

	Drainage area	Length		Drainage area	Length
	square kilometres	kilo- metres		square kilometres	kilo- metres
Flowing into the Pacific Ocean			**Flowing into the Arctic Ocean**		
Yukon (mouth to head of Nisutlin)	..	3,185	(concluded)		
(International boundary to head			Liard	277,100	1,115
of Nisutlin)	323,800	1,149	South Nahanni	36,300	563
Porcupine	61,400	721	Fort Nelson (to head of Sikanni Chief)	55,900	517
Stewart	51,000	644	Petitot	..	404
Pelly	51,000	608	Hay	48,200	702
Teslin	35,500	393	Peel (mouth of west Channel		
White	38,000	265	to head of Ogilvie)	73,600	684
Columbia (mouth to head			Arctic Red	..	499
of Columbia Lake)	..	2,000	Slave (from Peace River to		
(International boundary to head			Great Slave Lake)	616,400	415
of Columbia Lake)	102,800	801	Fond du Lac (to outlet of		
Kootenay	37,700	780	Wollaston Lake)	66,800	277
Kettle (to head of Holmes Lake)	4,700	336	Back (to outlet of Muskox Lake)	106,500	974
Okanagan (to head of			Coppermine	..	845
Okanagan Lake)	21,600	314	Anderson	..	692
Fraser	232,300	1,370	Horton	..	618
Thompson (to head of			**Flowing into Hudson Bay and**		
North Thompson)	55,400	489	**Hudson Strait**		
North Thompson	20,700	338	Nelson (to head of Bow)	892,300	2,575
South Thompson (to head of Shuswap)	17,800	332	Nelson (to outlet of Lake Winnipeg)	802,900	644
Nechako (to head of Eutsuk Lake)	47,100	462	Saskatchewan (to head of Bow)	334,100	1,939
Stuart (to head of Driftwood)	16,200	415	South Saskatchewan		
Skeena	54,400	579	(to head of Bow)	144,300	1,392
Stikine	49,800	539	Red Deer	45,100	724
Nass	21,100	380	Bow	26,200	587
Flowing into the Arctic Ocean			Oldman	26,700	362
Mackenzie (to head of Finlay)	1,805,200	4,241	North Saskatchewan	12,800	1,287
Peace (to head of Finlay)	302,500	1,923	Battle (to head of Pigeon Lake)	30,300	570
Smoky	51,300	492	Red (to head of Sheyenne)	138,600	877
Athabasca	95,300	1,231	Assiniboine	160,600	1,070
Pembina	12,900	547	Winnipeg (to head of Firesteel)	106,500	813

See source at the end of this table.

	Drainage area	Length		Drainage area	Length
	square kilometres	kilo- metres		square kilometres	kilo- metres
Flowing into Hudson Bay and			**Flowing into Hudson Bay and**		
Hudson Strait (continued)			**Hudson Strait** (concluded)		
English	52,300	615	Innuksuac	11,400	385
Fairford (to head of Manitoba Red Deer)	80,300	684	Petite rivière de la Baleine	15,900	380
Churchill (to head of Churchill Lake)	281,300	1,609	Arnaud	49,500	377
Beaver (to outlet of Beaver Lake)	..	491	Nastapoca	13,400	360
Severn (to head of Black Birch)	102,800	982	Kogaluc	11,600	304
Albany (to head of Cat)	135,200	982	**Flowing into the Atlantic Ocean**		
Thelon	142,400	904	St. Lawrence River	839,200	3,058
Dubawnt	57,500	842	Nipigon (to head of Ombabika)	25,400	209
La Grande-Rivière (Fort George River)	97,600	893	Spanish	14,000	338
Koksoak (to head of Caniapiscau)	133,400	874	Trent (to head of Irondale)	12,400	402
Nottaway (via Bell to head			Ottawa River	146,300	1,271
of Mégiscane)	65,800	776	Gatineau	23,700	386
Rupert (to head of Témiscamie)	43,400	763	du Lièvre	..	330
Eastmain	46,400	756	Saguenay (to head of Péribonca)	88,000	698
Attawapiskat (to head of			Péribonca	28,200	451
Bow Lake)	50,500	748	Mistassini	21,900	298
Kazan (to head of Ennadai Lake)	71,500	732	Chamouchouane	..	266
Grande rivière de la Baleine	42,700	724	Saint-Maurice	43,300	563
George	41,700	565	Manicouagan (to head	45,800	560
Moose (to head of Mattagami)	108,500	547	Mouchalagane)		
Abitibi (to head of Louis Lake)	29,500	547	aux Outardes	19,000	499
Mattagami (to head of			Romaine	14,350	496
Minisinakwa Lake)	37,000	443	Betsiamites (to head of Manouanis)	18,700	444
Missinaibi	23,500	426	Moisie	19,200	410
Harricana/Harricanaw	29,300	533	St-Augustin	9,900	233
Hayes	108,000	483	Richelieu (to mouth of	3,800	171
aux Feuilles	42,500	480	Lake Champlain)		
Winisk	67,300	475	Churchill (to head of Ashuanipi)	79,800	856
Broadback	20,800	450	Saint John	35,500	673
à la Baleine	31,900	428	Little Mecatina	19,600	547
de Povungnituk	28,500	389	Natashquan	16,100	410

Source: Natural Resources Canada, *Atlas of Canada*.

Table 15.5 Principal lakes, elevation and area, by province and territory

	Elevation	Area		Elevation	Area
	metres	square kilometres		metres	square kilometres
The Great Lakes[1]			**Ontario** (concluded)		
Superior	184	28,700	Lake Abitibi[3]	265	931
Michigan	176	0	Lake Nipissing	196	832
Huron	177	36,000	Lake Simcoe	219	744
Erie	174	12,800	Rainy Lake[3]	338	741
Ontario	75	10,000	Big Trout Lake	213	661
Newfoundland and Labrador			Lake St. Clair	175	490
Smallwood Reservoir	471	6,527	**Manitoba**		
Melville Lake	tidal[2]	3,069	Lake Winnipeg	217	24,387
Nova Scotia			Lake Winnipegosis	254	5,374
Bras d'Or Lake	tidal[2]	1,099	Lake Manitoba	248	4,624
Quebec			Southern Indian Lake	254	2,247
Lac Mistassini	372	2,335	Cedar Lake	253	1,353
Réservoir Manicouagan	360	1,942	Island Lake	227	1,223
Réservoir Gouin	404	1,570	Gods Lake	178	1,151
Lac à l'Eau-Claire	241	1,383	Cross Lake	207	755
Lac Bienville	426	1,249	Playgreen Lake	217	657
Lac Saint-Jean	98	1,003	**Saskatchewan**		
Réservoir Pipmuacan	396	978	Lake Athabasca[3]	213	7,935
Lac Minto	168	761	Reindeer Lake[3]	337	6,650
Réservoir Cabonga	361	677	Wollaston Lake	398	2,681
Ontario			Cree Lake	487	1,434
Lake Nipigon	260	4,848	Lac La Rouge	364	1,413
Lake of the Woods[3]	323	3,150	Peter Pond Lake	421	778
Lac Seul	357	1,657	Doré Lake	459	640

See notes and source at the end of this table.

	Elevation	Area		Elevation	Area
	metres	square kilometres		metres	square kilometres
Alberta			**Nunavut** (concluded)		
Lake Clair	213	1,436	Dubawnt Lake	236	3,833
Lesser Slave Lake	577	1,168	Amadjuak Lake	113	3,115
British Columbia			Nueltin Lake[3]	278	2,279
Williston Lake	671	1,761	Baker Lake	2	1,887
Atlin Lake[3]	668	775	Yathkyed Lake	140	1,449
Yukon			Aberdeen Lake	80	1,100
Kluane Lake	781	409	Napaktulik Lake	381	1,080
Northwest Territories			Garry Lake	148	976
Great Bear Lake[3]	156	31,328	Contwoyto Lake	564	957
Great Slave Lake	156	28,568	Ennadai Lake	311	681
Lac la Martre	265	1,776	Tulemalu Lake	279	668
Kasba Lake	336	1,341	Kamilukuak Lake	266	638
MacKay Lake	431	1,061	Kaminak Lake	53	600
Hottah Lake	180	918			
Aylmer Lake	375	847			
Nonacho Lake	354	784			
Clinton-Colden Lake	375	737			
Selwyn Lake	398	717			
Point Lake	375	701			
Wholdaia Lake	364	678			
Lac de Gras	396	633			
Buffalo Lake	265	612			
Nunavut					
Nettilling Lake	30	5,542			

Notes: A principal lake has an area larger than 400 square kilometres.

New Brunswick and Prince Edward Island have no principle lakes.

1. Data for the Great Lakes represent the area on the Canadian side of the Canada–U.S. border only.

2. Daily, monthly and seasonal variations in the time and heights of tides.

3. Spans provincial or territorial boundary. Listed under province or territory containing larger portion.

Source: Natural Resources Canada, *Atlas of Canada.*

Table 15.6 Land and freshwater area, Canada and selected countries

	Area	Land	Fresh water
	square kilometres		
Russia	17,075,200	16,995,800	79,400
Canada	9,984,670	9,093,507	891,163
United States	9,826,630	9,161,923	664,707
China	9,596,960	9,326,410	270,550
Brazil	8,511,965	8,456,510	55,455
Australia	7,686,850	7,617,930	68,920
India	3,287,590	2,973,190	314,400
Argentina	2,766,890	2,736,690	30,200
Kazakhstan	2,717,300	2,669,800	47,500
Sudan	2,505,810	2,376,000	129,810
Algeria	2,381,740	2,381,740	0
Democratic Republic of the Congo	2,345,410	2,267,600	77,810
Saudi Arabia	2,149,690	2,149,690	0
Mexico	1,972,550	1,923,040	49,510
Indonesia	1,919,440	1,826,440	93,000
Libya	1,759,540	1,759,540	0
Iran	1,648,000	1,636,000	12,000
Mongolia	1,564,116	1,564,116	0
Peru	1,285,220	1,280,000	5,220
Chad	1,284,000	1,259,200	24,800

Source: *The World Factbook 2007*, Washington D.C., Central Intelligence Agency, Office of Public Affairs, 2007.

Table 15.7 Land and freshwater area, by province and territory

	Area	Area	Land	Fresh water
	%	square kilometres		
Canada	**100.0**	**9,984,670**	**9,093,507**	**891,163**
Newfoundland and Labrador	4.1	405,212	373,872	31,340
Prince Edward Island	0.1	5,660	5,660	0
Nova Scotia	0.6	55,284	53,338	1,946
New Brunswick	0.7	72,908	71,450	1,458
Quebec	15.4	1,542,056	1,365,128	176,928
Ontario	10.8	1,076,395	917,741	158,654
Manitoba	6.5	647,797	553,556	94,241
Saskatchewan	6.5	651,036	591,670	59,366
Alberta	6.6	661,848	642,317	19,531
British Columbia	9.5	944,735	925,186	19,549
Yukon	4.8	482,443	474,391	8,052
Northwest Territories	13.5	1,346,106	1,183,085	163,021
Nunavut	21.0	2,093,190	1,936,113	157,077

Source: Natural Resources Canada, *Atlas of Canada*.

Government

OVERVIEW

Our three levels of government provide Canadians with many services that cannot be easily provided by private companies—the federal government is responsible for national defence and international diplomacy, for example. The provinces and territories, meanwhile, ensure that Canadians have access to essential services such as health care and education. Local governments take care of keeping our streets clean and our communities safe.

The constitution spells out the responsibilities of each level of government. But governments' accounting books shows where their priorities lie and where they spend taxpayers' dollars. All told, in 2005/2006 our governments spent $516 .9 billion providing Canadians with goods and services.

In 2005/2006, on a per capita basis, the federal government spent $6,794 for every man, woman and child in the country, and the provincial, territorial and local governments spent another $10,839 per capita.

But these averages vary widely, particularly among the provinces and territories. The high cost of providing services in Canada's North means that Nunavut spent $38,859 per capita, while the provincial per capita spending ranged between $10,000 and $15,000.

Where the federal money goes

The single largest expense for the federal government is social assistance. In 2005/2006, social security payments, family allowances and income maintenance programs cost just over $57.4 billion, a 9.6% increase since 2001/2002.

Chart 16.1
Selected federal general government expenditures, 2006

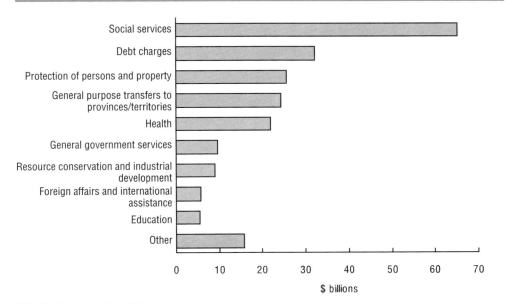

Note: Fiscal year ending March 31.
Source: Statistics Canada, CANSIM table 385-0002.

Federal expenditures for health care services jumped to $23.8 billion in 2004/2005 from $6.8 billion in 2003/2004. In 2005/2006, it was $21.8 billion. The increase in 2004/2005 was mainly because of the new Canada Health Transfer—a specific transfer payment for health care to the provinces and territories—which amounted to $14.0 billion in 2004/2005. Prior to 2004, the federal transfers for health care were part of a general purpose transfer called the Canada Health and Social Transfer. Accordingly, general purpose transfers declined from $29.6 billion in 2003/2004 to $21.0 billion in 2004/2005.

The protection of persons and property is another big-ticket spending item for the federal government—the military, federal policing, prisons and courts cost $25.5 billion in expenditures in 2005/2006.

Provincial and territorial spending

Providing hospital and medical care is the primary responsibility of the provinces and territories, and they collectively spent $93.8 billion on health care in 2005/2006. The combination of increased federal

Chart 16.2
Consolidated provincial and territorial government expenditures, 2006

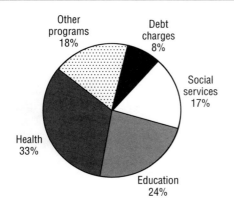

- Other programs 18%
- Debt charges 8%
- Social services 17%
- Education 24%
- Health 33%

Note: Fiscal year ending March 31.
Source: Statistics Canada, CANSIM table 385-0001.

Public sector employment, wages and salaries

	2005	2006
	number	
Employees	3,082,690	3,142,270
	$ thousands	
Wages and salaries	143,312,467	151,186,092

Source: Statistics Canada, CANSIM table 183-0002.

transfers for health care, an aging population and the rising cost of medical services has pushed spending in this area up by over one quarter since 2001/2002.

Schooling Canadians is the second largest expense for the provincial and territorial governments—to the tune of $70.6 billion in 2005/2006. Elementary, secondary and postsecondary education absorbs 96% of this spending.

The local level

Elementary and secondary education, keeping neighbourhoods clean and secure and providing local infrastructure are the biggest expenditures at the local level. In 2005, elementary and secondary education amounted to $40.1 billion. Municipal governments spent $10.5 billion on environmental programs—such as water purification and garbage collection—and another $9.8 billion on protection of persons and property.

Building and maintaining roads and streets and providing other transportation services cost local governments another $11.8 billion.

Taxes and other revenue sources

Running the country is expensive. Without collecting taxes from the population, our governments could not provide the services that Canadians have come to expect. In 2005/2006, all levels of government raised a total of $403.7 billion in taxes, about $70.0 billion more than in 2001/2002.

More than half of that total (56.3%) came from income taxes: personal income taxes totalled $169.2 billion and corporate income taxes amounted to $51.1 billion. Consumption taxes, such as gasoline taxes, customs duties and those on alcohol, tobacco and gambling—added another $108.0 billion; the provinces and territories collected more than half of these taxes. Property taxes totalled $49.6 billion—most of this money goes directly to local governments.

Governments also collect revenue from other sources. In 2005/2006, they collectively earned $45.3 billion from investment activities and sold $43.1 billion worth of goods and services—such as student tuition fees and municipal water.

Together, Canada's three levels of government and the Canada and Quebec Pension Plan accounts have pulled in more money than they have spent in every year since 1999/2000. This followed a string of deficits. However, much of this surplus is occurring at the federal level, in Alberta, and within the Canada and Quebec Pension Plan accounts.

Moreover, while the federal government has seen successive surpluses since 1997/1998, the 13 provincial and territorial governments together have posted only four surplus years during the last decade.

Public sector employees

Of Canada's 16.5 million workers in 2006, just over 3.1 million worked in the public sector. About 1.1 million of these public sector employees worked for the governments themselves, while 976,000 worked for educational institutions and 780,000 were employed with health care and social services providers.

Collectively, these public sector employees—our policemen, postal workers, diplomats, sanitation workers, health care workers, bureaucrats and other government service providers—earned $151.2 billion in wages in 2006. The public sector wage bill was flat or falling from 1994 to 1997, but then climbed by nearly 50% by the end of 2006.

Chart 16.3
Consolidated federal, provincial, territorial and local government revenue, 2006

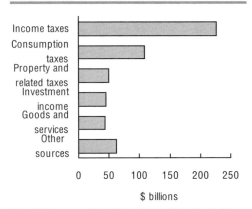

$ billions

Note: Data for consolidated federal, provincial and territorial governments are as at March 31.
Local government data are as at December 31.
Source: Statistics Canada, CANSIM table 385-0001.

Selected sources

Statistics Canada

- *Analysis in Brief.* Occasional. 11-621-MIE

- *Canada's Retirement Income Programs.* Irregular. 74-507-XCB

- *Labour Force Historical Review.* Annual. 71F0004XCB

- *Public Sector Statistics.* Annual. 68-213-XIE

- *The Control and Sale of Alcoholic Beverages in Canada.* Annual. 63-202-XIE

More Canadians choosing wine

Beer is by far the bestselling alcoholic beverage in Canada—$8.4 billion in sales or just more than half of all alcohol sold. But for the first time ever wine overtook spirits as the second bestseller in 2004/2005. Spirits and wine each account for about one-quarter of all alcohol sold.

Changing Canadian tastes are reflected in the growth of wine sales, which have consistently grown faster than those of beer and spirits in recent years. Wine sales rose 6.5% in 2004/2005 from the previous year, about twice the growth rate for beer and nearly three times that for spirits. Wine sales have grown at an annual average rate of 8.0% over the past decade.

Canadians also like sampling what the world has to offer and are increasingly buying imported drinks. Imported brands continue to expand their share of sales in Canada,

capturing 34% market share in 2004/2005, compared to 22% a decade earlier. Domestic brands—particularly in the beer market—have seen much slower sales growth than imported brands.

Canadians often purchase their alcohol at a government outlet. Government regulates the sale of alcohol in most provinces and territories. In 2004/2005, Canada's beer and liquor stores and agencies sold $16.8 billion worth of alcohol to consumers, bars, restaurants and other establishments.

Provincial and territorial liquor authorities collectively posted net income of $4.5 billion in 2004/2005. Net income increased most in British Columbia, 7.1%, and in Ontario, 6.7%. A three-month strike at Quebec's liquor authority resulted in a 4.4% decline there.

Chart 16.4
Sales of alcoholic beverages

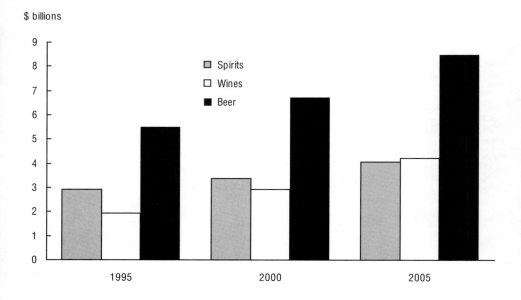

$ billions

Source: Statistics Canada, CANSIM table 183-0006.

Canada's government debt challenge

Despite the surpluses the three levels of government have collectively posted since the late 1990s, Canada still has a debt challenge to face. The government spending legacy from the 1970s to the mid-1990s has left Canadians shouldering a debt burden of $798.4 billion as of March 2004, or $25,044 for every person in the country.

The federal government has had the best success drawing down its debt. Yet it also carries the largest share of liabilities, $523.3 billion worth as of March 2005. On a per capita basis, net federal financial debt shrank from $18,850 to $16,270 in the decade since 1995.

In 2006, 15 cents of every dollar the federal government spends goes to interest charges on the debt. Still, this is an improvement over 1995, when Ottawa spent nearly 27 cents of every dollar on debt charges.

The provincial and territorial governments have had varying experiences managing their debt burdens. Over the past decade, Canada's biggest provinces—Quebec, Ontario and British Columbia—have also incurred the largest annual deficits, increasing their overall debt burden every year. However, Manitoba, Saskatchewan and New Brunswick have mostly seen annual surpluses and have been reducing their debt. Alberta has posted large surpluses in recent years and has completely eliminated its debt.

As of March 2004, all provinces except Alberta were carrying debt. Yukon and the Northwest Territories have been debt free over much of the past decade.

Canada's villages, towns and cities are also debtors, although they owe far less than the other levels of government—a net total of $11.4 billion in 2003.

Chart 16.5
Net financial debt per capita, by province and territory

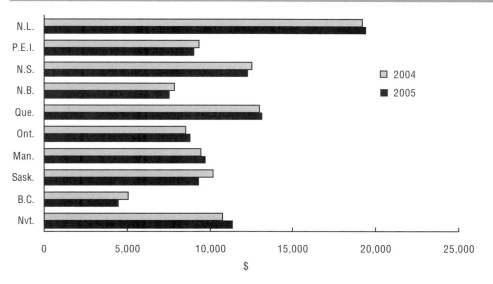

Notes: Does not include federal and local government debts.
Alberta, Yukon and the Northwest Territories are debt-free.
Population estimates as of April 1.
Source: Statistics Canada, CANSIM tables 051-0005 and 385-0014.

Investing in infrastructure

Imagine never re-investing in your home's infrastructure. After 15 years, your roof would need repairs. After 20 years, your furnace and air conditioning systems would begin breaking down, and plumbing and electrical networks start deteriorating. Soon enough, your house would be unliveable.

Governments face the same challenges with our public infrastructure—our roads, sewers, water treatment systems and bridges. Indeed, Canada's water treatment facilities, sewers and roads and highways are more than halfway through their expected useful lives. However, thanks to recent increases in government investment, the average age of Canada's public infrastructure dropped in 2003—the first decline since 1973.

Although Canadian drivers still curse potholes and summer construction, our road networks have been getting younger since 1995,

reaching an average age of 16.6 years in 2003. But roads and highways are expected to last about 28 years; this still puts them beyond the mid-point of their useful lives.

Since 1997, the average age of our municipal sewer systems has been getting younger. Huge investment by municipalities in sewer systems in recent years has helped triple the value of this category of infrastructure over the last 40 years, to $18.5 billion.

Of all infrastructure categories, wastewater treatment facilities are closest to the end of their service lives. Here too, municipal governments have been investing heavily, accounting for 95% of all investment from 1997 to 2003. Provincial investment has been lower, and the average age of their facilities has ballooned from 14.2 years to 22.1 years from 1963 to 2003.

**Chart 16.6
Age of public infrastructure**

average age in years

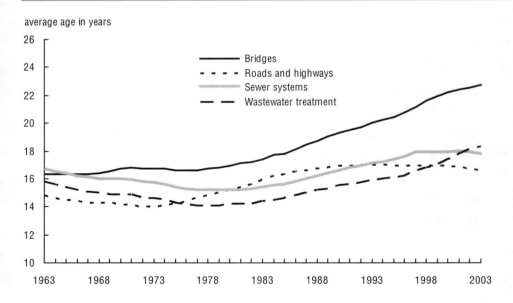

Source: Statistics Canada, Catalogue no. 11-621-MIE.

Public pension plans

Most Canadians look forward to retirement for many years—no more commuting to work, no more bosses and no more deadlines. But there's a flip side to all that freedom: regular paycheques stop coming in. While many have pensions they can draw on for income, all Canadians supplement their post-retirement income by receiving payments from government-run pension plans.

Established in 1966, the Canada Pension Plan (CPP) covers Canadians in all provinces and territories except Quebec, which runs its own plan—the Quebec Pension Plan (QPP). It is mandatory for nearly all employed persons to make contributions to these plans, which are heavily invested in bonds and investment funds. In March 2006, the combined financial assets of the two plans totalled just over $100.4 billion. The CPP accounted for $77.0 billion of this, and the QPP, $23.4 billion.

The two pension plans have grown tremendously since 2001, when their combined value was $64.1 billion. Despite shaky market conditions in the first years of the new century, concerns about declining balances in the CPP/QPP led to a change in the investment strategy for their growth. This, combined with rising contribution rates for both plans, has greatly improved their holdings.

Annual contributions to the CPP have grown by more than one-quarter from $23.5 billion in 2001/2002 to nearly $29.9 billion in 2005/2006. Coupled with pension payments growing at a slower pace (21%), and steady investment income, the CPP has generated strong surpluses over this period. The same trends are roughly mirrored in the QPP, although contributions to this plan have grown even faster, at 33%. CPP and QPP contribute almost one-fifth of total income for Canadians 65 and older.

Chart 16.7
Net financial wealth of public pension plans

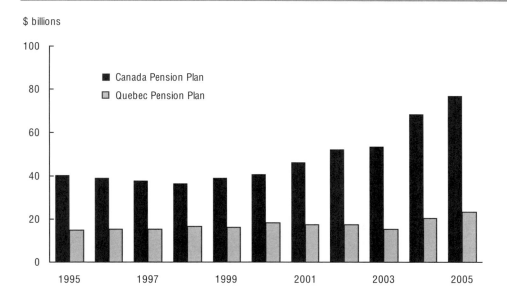

$ billions

Source: Statistics Canada, CANSIM table 385-0019.

Table 16.1 Consolidated federal, provincial, territorial and local government revenue and expenditures, 1992 to 2007

	1992	1993	1994	1995	1996	1997
	\$ millions					
Revenue	**293,731**	**299,232**	**305,105**	**321,073**	**337,869**	**351,459**
Income taxes	117,709	113,434	115,128	123,417	134,343	143,578
Personal income taxes	101,935	99,514	98,426	102,144	108,649	113,750
Corporation income taxes	14,417	12,606	15,240	19,525	23,604	26,758
Mining and logging taxes	96	123	191	308	479	223
Taxes on payments to non-residents	1,261	1,191	1,272	1,439	1,611	2,847
Consumption taxes	59,554	61,112	63,268	65,647	66,951	69,372
General sales tax	33,608	35,204	37,517	40,050	40,320	42,222
Alcoholic beverages and tobacco taxes	7,992	7,450	6,592	5,389	5,459	5,581
Amusement tax	248	270	208	309	351	411
Gasoline and motive fuel taxes	8,485	9,064	9,578	9,984	10,710	10,873
Custom duties	3,999	3,811	3,652	3,576	2,971	2,677
Liquor profits	2,428	2,402	2,408	2,356	2,658	2,519
Remitted gaming profits	1,495	1,739	2,158	2,814	3,200	3,517
Other consumption taxes	1,299	1,171	1,156	1,170	1,282	1,573
Property and related taxes	30,619	33,092	34,225	35,491	35,846	36,935
Other taxes	11,028	11,431	12,030	12,455	13,039	13,080
Health and drug insurance premiums	1,144	1,199	1,236	1,589	1,579	1,648
Contributions to social security plans	25,731	27,617	28,048	29,034	29,423	30,448
Sales of goods and services	22,413	23,094	24,082	25,208	25,993	28,036
Investment income	22,303	22,718	22,733	23,621	25,338	25,340
Other revenue from own sources	3,230	5,534	4,357	4,609	5,357	3,022
Expenditures	**356,372**	**365,336**	**368,752**	**373,760**	**381,158**	**371,693**
General government services	11,896	12,179	12,234	12,227	12,157	12,255
Protection of persons and property	27,569	28,195	29,538	29,248	29,330	28,501
Transportation and communication	18,588	18,133	17,156	18,150	19,680	17,422
Health	49,019	50,893	51,597	51,753	53,105	53,427
Social services	92,692	97,838	101,106	97,324	97,215	98,392
Education	51,193	54,125	54,268	55,644	55,602	54,269
Resource conservation and industrial development	18,987	16,685	15,777	15,473	15,029	13,072
Environment	7,263	7,441	7,849	8,398	8,666	8,381
Recreation and culture	8,805	9,077	8,832	8,906	9,189	9,010
Labour, employment and immigration	3,255	3,556	2,628	2,575	2,805	2,237
Housing	3,981	4,113	3,976	3,885	3,948	4,053
Foreign affairs and international assistance	3,862	4,128	3,600	4,634	3,954	3,761
Regional planning and development	1,594	1,671	1,514	1,564	1,558	1,527
Research establishments	1,655	1,932	1,904	2,135	1,933	1,623
Debt charges	55,671	55,119	56,079	61,409	66,432	63,232
Other expenditures	343	251	694	436	556	530
Surplus/deficit (-)	**-62,641**	**-66,104**	**-63,647**	**-52,687**	**-43,289**	**-20,234**

Notes: Data do not include Canada Pension Plan or Quebec Pension Plan.
Data for the federal, provincial and territorial governments are as of March 31 and the local government data are as of December 31.
Source: Statistics Canada, CANSIM table 385-0001.

1998	1999	2000	2001	2002	2003	2004	2005	2006	2007
				$ millions					
373,531	**385,460**	**414,170**	**446,959**	**437,288**	**447,861**	**468,557**	**499,072**	535,469	558,817
160,203	164,592	178,423	191,144	188,011	178,173	188,619	207,219	227,275	246,232
123,029	127,763	138,443	143,116	144,746	139,836	145,324	155,172	169,193	180,757
33,896	33,620	36,155	43,262	38,819	33,608	38,925	46,695	51,094	57,859
304	307	326	454	297	352	215	530	759	710
2,973	2,901	3,499	4,312	4,150	4,377	4,156	4,822	6,229	6,907
73,065	76,696	80,088	87,870	88,987	96,431	98,918	104,685	108,026	107,300
44,619	47,566	51,323	55,523	56,076	60,210	62,169	66,566	69,549	68,538
5,800	6,234	6,190	6,203	7,201	8,800	9,260	9,650	9,027	8,867
485	626	630	598	592	592	552	561	565	567
11,227	11,602	11,789	11,745	11,743	12,337	12,760	12,699	13,088	13,252
2,765	2,359	2,104	2,807	3,018	3,189	2,804	3,041	3,429	3,606
2,726	2,806	2,747	3,475	3,144	3,334	3,544	3,703	3,940	4,129
3,730	4,174	4,183	6,315	5,926	6,095	5,969	6,395	6,483	6,476
1,708	1,325	1,121	1,205	1,288	1,873	1,860	2,071	1,945	1,864
38,545	38,556	40,255	41,063	41,730	42,529	44,244	46,710	49,639	51,417
13,333	14,054	14,334	15,157	14,940	16,083	17,037	17,788	18,747	19,702
1,699	2,017	1,950	2,178	2,282	3,000	3,132	3,206	3,258	3,327
29,359	30,424	29,957	30,087	29,723	31,013	31,547	31,995	32,677	33,952
27,723	29,112	32,217	34,689	34,913	37,653	39,130	41,010	43,076	46,329
25,623	23,850	28,859	37,749	31,258	33,406	35,984	38,402	45,327	44,999
3,976	6,154	8,088	7,020	5,443	9,574	9,946	8,057	7,445	5,559
372,695	**387,438**	**401,520**	**424,557**	**437,568**	**455,442**	**474,712**	**487,552**	**516,910**	**540,339**
12,495	13,238	13,752	15,968	15,765	17,520	18,633	18,802	19,685	19,956
27,984	29,366	31,749	32,978	35,218	37,193	39,154	41,175	43,725	45,301
17,061	17,822	18,117	17,979	18,628	19,148	20,258	21,385	25,390	26,051
56,761	59,377	64,317	70,465	76,935	83,315	89,479	94,565	99,017	106,850
99,329	102,408	105,044	110,145	114,753	117,020	121,058	125,315	132,186	137,809
55,389	57,970	60,457	63,522	66,559	70,533	74,246	77,225	83,324	87,726
11,670	12,991	14,354	15,713	16,329	18,784	19,430	18,444	19,749	19,908
8,703	8,566	8,672	9,222	9,853	10,259	11,391	11,929	13,313	14,355
8,751	9,277	9,909	10,871	11,347	11,690	13,143	13,736	14,350	14,584
2,929	2,996	2,951	2,882	3,019	3,395	3,440	2,328	2,514	2,582
3,732	3,816	3,519	3,723	3,420	3,624	3,833	3,900	4,525	4,782
3,675	4,034	4,291	4,477	4,562	5,128	4,611	5,556	5,585	6,654
1,561	1,687	1,762	1,847	2,099	2,111	2,133	2,035	2,168	2,475
1,521	1,724	1,951	1,419	1,767	1,881	1,890	1,855	1,986	1,995
59,960	60,825	60,173	61,490	55,335	52,380	49,514	47,640	47,703	48,349
1,166	1,333	501	1,857	1,979	1,463	2,499	1,662	1,689	964
835	**-1,978**	**12,650**	**22,401**	**-280**	**-7,581**	**-6,156**	**11,520**	**18,559**	**18,477**

Table 16.2 Government transfer payments to individuals, 1991 to 2004

	1991	1992	1993	1994	1995	1996
	\$ millions					
All levels of government	**83,830**	**93,077**	**98,323**	**98,495**	**98,512**	**98,865**
Federal government	45,385	49,317	51,600	50,166	48,879	48,752
Family and youth allowances	2,824	2,870	37	37	38	39
Child Tax Benefit or Credit	598	658	5,252	5,259	5,214	5,228
Pensions (First and Second World Wars)	777	856	848	864	909	914
War veterans' allowances	439	443	441	417	397	383
Grants to Aboriginal people and organizations	2,376	2,573	2,886	3,027	3,566	3,564
Goods and Services Tax Credit	1,805	2,557	2,655	2,833	2,810	2,866
Employment Insurance benefits	17,323	18,648	17,591	15,012	12,889	11,859
Old Age Security payments	17,955	18,776	19,479	20,170	20,622	21,221
Scholarships and research grants	691	726	727	780	687	686
Miscellaneous and other transfers	597	1,210	1,684	1,767	1,747	1,992
Provincial governments	20,937	23,651	24,603	24,815	25,406	25,576
Social assistance, income maintenance	7,960	9,371	9,660	9,863	9,854	9,258
Social assistance, other	1,230	1,213	2,239	2,316	2,308	2,371
Workers' Compensation benefits	3,982	4,091	3,925	3,811	3,992	4,198
Grants to benevolent associations	5,571	6,848	5,506	5,577	5,962	6,123
Miscellaneous transfers	2,194	2,128	3,273	3,248	3,290	3,626
Local governments	2,700	3,410	3,899	3,949	3,738	2,950
Canada Pension Plan	11,298	12,808	14,058	15,132	15,777	16,559
Quebec Pension Plan	3,510	3,891	4,163	4,433	4,712	5,028

Source: Statistics Canada, CANSIM table 384-0009.

Table 16.3 Federal government debt, 1992 to 2006

	1992	1993	1994	1995	1996	1997
	\$ millions					
Gross federal debt	**476,104**	**514,357**	**557,604**	**595,877**	**634,939**	**651,124**
Unmatured debt	352,905	383,798	414,942	441,991	470,581	477,940
Marketable bonds	161,499	181,322	208,464	233,621	262,279	295,022
Treasury bills	152,300	162,050	166,000	164,450	166,100	135,400
Notes and loans	7	2,552	5,649	9,046	7,296	10,557
Canada Savings Bonds	35,598	34,369	31,331	31,386	31,428	33,493
Bonds issued to the Canada Pension Plan	3,501	3,505	3,498	3,488	3,478	3,468
Superannuation accounts	81,881	87,911	94,097	101,033	107,882	114,205
Dominion notes and coins in circulation	2,295	2,374	2,464	2,570	2,805	3,243
Other liabilities	39,023	40,274	46,101	50,283	53,671	55,736
Unmatured debt payable in foreign currencies	3,444	5,409	10,668	16,921	16,809	23,016
Financial assets	47,422	43,296	44,385	45,192	56,221	62,722
Net federal debt[1]	**428,682**	**471,061**	**513,219**	**550,685**	**578,718**	**588,402**

Note: Fiscal year ending March 31.

1. Net federal debt equals gross federal debt minus financial assets.

Source: Statistics Canada, CANSIM table 385-0010.

1997	1998	1999	2000	2001	2002	2003	2004
				$ millions			
100,431	104,558	106,006	110,487	117,633	121,047	124,738	129,956
49,234	50,739	51,575	53,479	57,965	60,857	62,949	65,436
43	58	84	99	116	133	140	157
5,310	5,600	5,939	6,577	7,379	7,824	8,051	8,549
921	918	910	973	1,196	1,398	1,463	1,527
387	387	414	404	267	212	223	266
3,730	4,447	4,271	4,511	4,448	4,800	4,951	5,191
2,905	2,924	2,943	2,974	3,099	3,140	3,264	3,346
10,874	10,713	10,150	9,615	11,361	12,837	13,361	13,269
21,798	22,398	22,907	23,790	24,789	25,747	26,931	27,992
700	519	519	531	560	585	612	668
2,566	2,775	3,438	4,005	4,750	4,181	3,953	4,471
25,945	26,717	27,170	28,574	29,662	29,781	30,039	31,021
8,723	8,050	7,048	6,538	6,547	6,603	6,642	6,739
2,408	2,241	2,546	2,906	2,966	2,936	3,130	3,229
4,067	3,886	4,073	4,434	4,840	5,150	5,034	5,117
6,714	7,196	7,322	7,953	8,406	8,500	8,593	8,868
4,033	5,344	6,181	6,743	6,903	6,592	6,640	7,068
2,640	3,523	2,990	3,248	3,641	2,637	2,737	2,870
17,327	18,054	18,540	19,183	20,023	21,076	21,986	23,129
5,285	5,525	5,731	6,003	6,342	6,696	7,027	7,500

1998	1999	2000	2001	2002	2003	2004	2005	2006
				$ millions				
645,725	648,389	648,212	644,900	640,526	629,638	628,830	626,217	619,701
468,024	461,004	457,331	447,741	444,058	441,366	437,946	432,996	428,354
309,256	315,421	315,854	316,651	314,685	303,689	292,145	276,676	269,577
112,300	96,950	99,850	88,700	94,201	104,600	113,400	127,200	131,600
12,533	16,353	11,302	12,570	7,765	7,124	7,720	6,705	6,740
30,479	28,217	26,899	26,416	24,021	22,584	21,330	19,080	17,342
3,456	4,063	3,426	3,404	3,386	3,369	3,351	3,335	3,095
117,456	122,407	128,346	129,185	126,921	125,708	127,560	129,579	131,062
3,346	3,428	3,601	3,763	3,914	4,122	4,193	4,310	4,533
56,899	61,550	58,934	64,211	65,633	58,442	59,131	59,332	55,752
27,183	36,000	32,589	33,664	27,547	21,603	20,827	16,543	14,333
64,144	73,921	86,479	99,600	105,836	103,146	105,182	102,873	105,609
581,581	574,468	561,733	545,300	534,690	526,492	523,648	523,344	514,089

Table 16.4 General local government revenue and expenditures, 1991 to 2005

	1991	1992	1993	1994	1995	1996
			$ thousands			
Revenue	**34,960,527**	**37,313,812**	**37,911,249**	**39,289,875**	**41,133,761**	**39,340,577**
Own-source revenue	26,270,406	27,609,032	28,277,839	29,310,874	30,582,415	30,515,429
Property and related taxes	16,806,435	17,936,420	18,500,589	19,055,608	19,158,680	19,545,258
Consumption taxes	71,049	60,916	46,897	50,055	51,119	53,752
Other taxes	324,040	349,796	341,474	374,643	368,840	388,478
Sales of goods and services	6,619,034	6,900,550	7,039,517	7,398,971	7,887,476	7,943,709
Investment income	2,094,570	1,988,056	1,941,689	1,988,419	2,691,690	2,153,561
Other revenue from own sources	355,278	373,294	407,673	443,178	424,610	430,671
Transfers	8,690,121	9,704,780	9,633,410	9,979,001	10,551,346	8,825,148
General-purpose transfers	1,737,648	1,916,222	1,504,938	1,405,870	1,358,395	1,520,974
Specific-purpose transfers	6,952,473	7,788,558	8,128,472	8,573,131	9,192,951	7,304,174
Federal government	200,258	213,794	214,862	326,895	560,015	497,538
Provincial and territorial governments	6,752,215	7,574,764	7,913,610	8,246,236	8,632,936	6,806,636
Expenditures	**36,700,754**	**38,388,959**	**39,175,489**	**39,830,832**	**41,422,310**	**39,531,850**
General government services	3,734,926	3,751,067	3,724,583	3,759,375	4,006,555	3,876,999
Protection of persons and property	5,379,143	5,625,165	5,759,405	5,849,975	6,049,580	6,113,280
Transportation and communications	7,364,948	7,603,564	7,727,202	7,970,965	8,415,181	7,936,934
Health	733,081	804,429	776,316	760,058	812,004	723,213
Social services	4,119,790	4,860,749	5,376,493	5,396,899	5,186,296	4,263,112
Education	180,069	151,561	149,150	149,669	148,372	148,294
Resource conservation and industrial development	795,391	765,319	757,393	812,597	808,144	720,586
Environment	5,303,036	5,560,787	5,627,471	5,957,365	6,419,277	6,299,724
Recreation and culture	4,237,428	4,453,275	4,382,103	4,474,516	4,821,431	4,846,078
Housing	777,657	735,781	664,941	634,745	575,561	550,909
Regional planning and development	693,106	701,830	662,301	624,732	693,551	623,945
Debt charges	3,083,493	3,220,211	3,364,485	3,197,402	3,219,343	3,109,192
Other expenditures	298,686	155,221	203,646	242,534	267,015	319,584
Surplus/deficit (-)	**-1,740,227**	**-1,075,147**	**-1,264,240**	**-540,957**	**-288,549**	**-191,273**

Note: Year ending December 31.
Source: Statistics Canada, CANSIM table 385-0004.

1997	1998	1999	2000	2001	2002	2003	2004	2005
				$ thousands				
39,830,426	**44,329,474**	**46,681,044**	**45,707,480**	**47,914,279**	**49,529,673**	**52,088,450**	**54,873,078**	**56,375,316**
31,612,035	35,447,971	37,514,492	38,470,120	40,344,645	41,427,165	43,459,745	45,711,851	46,714,178
20,156,358	23,202,176	24,166,067	24,347,710	25,216,004	26,066,057	27,561,288	28,936,177	29,705,281
54,984	57,688	77,824	83,450	91,430	96,387	102,279	97,668	101,099
439,999	457,849	511,083	513,055	555,742	619,738	631,634	693,747	721,902
8,497,302	9,131,215	10,006,389	10,503,975	11,217,092	11,641,456	11,804,220	12,311,861	12,515,841
2,017,827	2,108,481	2,206,737	2,363,079	2,535,109	2,260,957	2,545,493	2,864,104	2,858,336
445,565	490,562	546,392	658,851	729,268	742,570	814,831	808,294	811,719
8,218,391	8,881,503	9,166,552	7,237,360	7,569,634	8,102,508	8,628,705	9,161,227	9,661,138
1,238,912	1,424,893	1,183,535	1,165,153	1,335,653	1,474,235	1,540,818	1,617,394	1,618,974
6,979,479	7,456,610	7,983,017	6,072,207	6,233,981	6,628,273	7,087,887	7,543,833	8,042,164
369,127	292,967	225,439	207,188	331,767	645,828	647,329	729,673	841,009
6,610,352	7,163,643	7,757,578	5,865,019	5,902,214	5,982,445	6,440,558	6,814,160	7,201,155
40,005,727	**42,247,792**	**43,396,277**	**44,911,636**	**46,724,396**	**48,669,333**	**53,658,124**	**55,559,653**	**58,531,338**
4,014,048	4,237,621	4,711,618	3,836,904	4,359,578	5,165,139	5,688,639	5,719,359	6,062,095
6,195,067	6,767,336	6,819,085	7,194,115	7,707,272	8,096,465	8,632,608	9,225,001	9,665,621
8,390,914	8,492,782	8,822,465	8,918,128	9,094,338	9,245,703	10,078,677	10,980,749	11,545,112
674,411	860,300	763,441	914,879	1,142,819	1,248,668	1,358,072	1,468,330	1,517,110
4,213,551	5,171,253	4,982,959	5,532,077	5,187,874	5,285,551	5,510,649	5,704,180	5,493,263
182,891	183,812	176,403	190,711	223,890	202,385	202,342	205,221	198,149
796,395	813,459	912,009	940,118	970,859	937,830	1,054,767	1,124,402	1,152,578
6,442,329	6,250,761	6,388,056	6,797,043	7,168,290	7,432,848	8,351,000	8,981,743	10,135,087
4,649,903	4,741,202	5,003,778	5,538,033	5,846,720	5,751,152	6,472,763	7,015,622	7,050,286
558,536	1,098,613	1,142,914	1,481,658	1,721,882	1,901,034	2,005,897	1,879,764	1,958,357
648,769	696,463	742,136	780,654	859,517	903,391	877,434	989,182	1,066,274
2,908,177	2,803,772	2,668,034	2,448,319	2,328,317	2,291,318	2,207,397	2,215,020	2,196,839
330,736	130,418	263,379	338,997	113,040	207,849	1,217,879	51,080	490,567
-175,301	**2,081,682**	**3,284,767**	**795,844**	**1,189,883**	**860,340**	**-1,569,674**	**-686,575**	**-2,156,022**

Table 16.5 Public sector employment, wages and salaries, 2002 to 2006

	2002	2003	2004	2005	2006
			number		
Employment[1]	**2,953,012**	**3,024,090**	**3,038,693**	**3,082,690**	**3,142,270**
Government	2,689,111	2,756,850	2,773,734	2,819,229	2,879,547
Federal general government[2]	359,477	366,428	366,654	370,601	386,685
Provincial and territorial general government	333,193	345,684	344,384	347,828	350,756
Health and social service institutions, provincial and territorial	723,854	752,279	753,425	766,773	780,390
Universities, colleges, vocational and trade institutions, provincial and territorial	309,735	320,542	328,985	334,720	340,289
Local general government	359,271	367,627	368,123	377,603	385,621
Local school boards	603,581	604,290	612,162	621,703	635,806
Government business enterprises	263,901	267,240	264,958	263,461	262,723
Federal government business enterprises	88,429	88,366	87,911	87,502	87,138
Provincial and territorial government business enterprises	125,185	127,292	123,988	121,243	119,028
Local government business enterprises	50,287	51,582	53,060	54,717	56,558
			$ thousands		
Wages and salaries[3]	**126,127,906**	**132,087,438**	**136,860,265**	**143,312,467**	**151,186,092**
Government	113,719,389	119,301,395	123,990,420	130,297,376	137,984,277
Federal general government[2]	20,384,178	21,018,975	21,349,471	23,641,853	24,804,604
Provincial and territorial general government	16,126,533	17,047,909	17,284,858	17,718,811	18,689,994
Health and social service institutions, provincial and territorial	27,442,889	28,663,440	30,375,029	31,614,224	33,976,066
Universities, colleges, vocational and trade institutions, provincial and territorial	12,231,426	13,174,934	14,049,578	14,662,942	15,394,780
Local general government	13,831,226	14,826,207	15,468,000	16,328,820	17,173,727
Local school boards	23,703,134	24,569,925	25,463,486	26,330,725	27,945,103
Government business enterprises	12,408,518	12,786,045	12,869,841	13,015,090	13,201,815
Federal government business enterprises	3,720,828	3,776,196	3,831,447	3,909,689	3,990,372
Provincial and territorial government business enterprises	6,239,806	6,447,641	6,349,344	6,276,102	6,227,527
Local government business enterprises	2,447,884	2,562,206	2,689,052	2,829,299	2,983,915

Notes: As of August 24, 2005, minor revisions were brought to some estimates prior to 2005: the Nunavut general government data have been revised from 2000 on; the federal government business enterprise data for Nova Scotia and Manitoba have been revised from 2003 on; the Ontario provincial government business enterprise data have been revised from 2003 on. The corresponding totals have changed for total government, total government business enterprises and total public sector.
As at December 31.

1. Employment data are not in full-time equivalent and do not distinguish between full-time and part-time employees. Includes employees both in and outside of Canada.
2. Federal general government data includes reservists and full-time military personnel.
3. Wages and salaries data are an annual sum. Includes employees both in and outside of Canada.

Source: Statistics Canada, CANSIM table 183-0002.

Table 16.6 Military personnel and pay, 2002 to 2006

	2002	2003	2004	2005	2006
	average annual number of employees				
Canada and outside Canada	**82,217**	**83,766**	**84,059**	**85,706**	**87,728**
Newfoundland and Labrador	1,240	1,295	1,402	1,375	1,226
Prince Edward Island	263	262	266	284	213
Nova Scotia	10,526	10,598	10,696	10,830	10,520
New Brunswick	4,852	4,949	4,959	5,084	5,300
Quebec	15,569	15,384	15,402	16,121	17,663
Ontario	26,907	27,751	27,681	28,413	29,741
Manitoba	3,800	3,960	3,908	3,927	3,824
Saskatchewan	1,103	1,100	1,104	1,150	1,108
Alberta	8,887	9,052	9,209	9,078	9,090
British Columbia	7,461	7,741	7,776	7,793	7,298
Yukon	x	x	x	x	x
Northwest Territories	134	148	153	150	165
Nunavut	x	x	x	x	x
Outside Canada	1,470	1,521	1,496	1,494	1,577
	total annual wages and salaries ($ thousands)				
Canada and outside Canada	**3,949,221**	**4,072,576**	**4,131,026**	**4,635,783**	**4,862,433**
Newfoundland and Labrador	42,203	44,635	45,623	55,668	54,956
Prince Edward Island	4,722	4,516	4,838	6,299	4,643
Nova Scotia	560,373	571,509	577,835	645,756	651,303
New Brunswick	214,374	218,997	224,536	257,565	271,461
Quebec	652,574	667,067	691,186	777,348	868,205
Ontario	1,310,586	1,365,989	1,377,555	1,552,523	1,656,817
Manitoba	192,432	200,137	196,820	220,550	221,301
Saskatchewan	44,146	45,867	47,793	50,570	51,221
Alberta	417,826	426,726	433,678	483,977	504,057
British Columbia	387,656	399,413	406,287	448,902	424,966
Yukon	x	x	x	x	x
Northwest Territories	11,040	11,920	12,102	13,807	15,083
Nunavut	x	x	x	x	x
Outside Canada	111,003	115,550	112,388	122,103	137,954

Notes: Employment data are not in full-time equivalents and do not distinguish between full-time and part-time employees. Civilian employees are excluded.
Source: Statistics Canada, CANSIM table 183-0004.

Table 16.7 Health and social services institutions' revenue and expenditures, 2003 to 2007

	2003	2004	2005	2006	2007
			$ thousands		
Revenue	**53,363,118**	**57,163,948**	**60,362,742**	**63,712,802**	**69,039,362**
Own-source revenue	8,066,583	8,417,204	8,985,511	9,508,376	10,326,873
Sales of goods and services	6,742,844	7,236,310	7,748,671	8,202,267	8,909,139
Investment income	122,103	146,341	115,278	120,579	130,779
Other revenue from own sources	1,201,636	1,034,552	1,121,562	1,185,531	1,286,956
Transfers from all levels of government	45,296,535	48,746,744	51,377,231	54,204,425	58,712,489
Federal government	857	6,334	6,868	5,282	5,848
Provincial governments	45,105,809	48,475,693	51,148,536	53,962,320	58,449,620
Local governments	189,869	264,718	221,827	236,823	257,022
Expenditures	**55,064,854**	**59,121,941**	**61,907,633**	**63,972,758**	**69,301,721**
Health	48,856,865	52,582,587	55,037,326	56,800,899	61,568,320
Hospital care	25,624,256	27,357,155	28,647,459	30,126,928	32,716,547
Medical care	11,272,160	12,110,118	13,164,745	12,842,837	13,902,999
Preventive care	953,514	1,077,248	1,167,437	1,224,864	1,327,722
Other health services	11,006,935	12,038,066	12,057,686	12,606,270	13,621,052
Social services	5,998,135	6,315,931	6,641,924	6,938,575	7,484,622
Social assistance	58,051	47,541	41,312	4,471	4,906
Other social services	5,940,084	6,268,390	6,600,611	6,934,104	7,479,716
Debt charges	205,220	218,531	224,545	233,223	248,713
Housing	4,634	4,893	3,838	61	67
Surplus/deficit (-)	**-1,701,734**	**-1,957,994**	**-1,544,891**	**-259,957**	**-262,359**

Note: Fiscal year ending March 31.
Source: Statistics Canada, CANSIM table 385-0008.

Table 16.8 Distribution of House of Commons seats, 39th general election, 2006

	All seats	Conservative Party of Canada	Liberal Party of Canada	Bloc Québécois	New Democratic Party	Independent
				number		
Canada	**308**	**124**	**103**	**51**	**29**	**1**
Newfoundland and Labrador	7	3	4	0	0	0
Prince Edward Island	4	0	4	0	0	0
Nova Scotia	11	3	6	0	2	0
New Brunswick	10	3	6	0	1	0
Quebec	75	10	13	51	0	1
Ontario	106	40	54	0	12	0
Manitoba	14	8	3	0	3	0
Saskatchewan	14	12	2	0	0	0
Alberta	28	28	0	0	0	0
British Columbia	36	17	9	0	10	0
Yukon	1	0	1	0	0	0
Northwest Territories	1	0	0	0	1	0
Nunavut	1	0	1	0	0	0

Source: Elections Canada.

Health

17

OVERVIEW

Governments spent $99.0 billion on health services in 2006, up from $44.8 billion in 1991. Most public spending on health services pays for hospitals, drugs and physicians.

The health of Canadians has improved substantially in the last 100 years. Death rates have declined, life expectancy has climbed, many infectious diseases have been virtually eradicated and medical techniques have advanced. In recent surveys, 60% of Canadians said they were in very good or excellent health.

Proportionally more Canadians than in the past have adopted healthy lifestyles, such as exercising and not smoking. Canadians generally also enjoy better socio-economic conditions—such as higher incomes and higher levels of education—that promote better overall health.

Health status

Life expectancy at birth in Canada was 80.2 years in 2004, compared with 77.8 years in 1991. A girl born in 2004 can expect to live 82.6 years; a boy can expect to live 77.8 years. From 1979 to 2004, life expectancy rose 6.4 years for men and 3.8 years for women.

Most Canadians consider themselves to be in good health. In 2005, people aged 20 to 34 had the most positive opinion: 70% rated their health as excellent or very good. The higher their age, the less positive Canadians are about their health. Only 40% of people aged 65 and older regarded their health as good or excellent in 2005.

In the last quarter-century, the leading causes of death in Canada have been diseases of the circulatory system and cancer. Both are more

Chart 17.1
Life expectancy

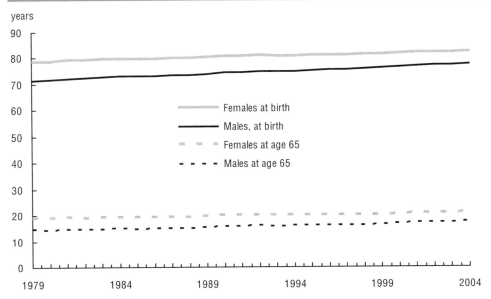

Note: Life expectancy is the estimated remaining years of life.
Source: Statistics Canada, CANSIM tables 102-0025 and 102-0511.

prevalent in an aging population. In 2003, these causes combined were responsible for 6 of every 10 deaths.

Many Canadians today live with chronic health problems, such as high blood pressure and cardiovascular disease. Asthma, diabetes and obesity are among the leading chronic conditions that threaten the health and well-being of a growing number of Canadians. Moreover, as the population ages, other chronic diseases are affecting more people, especially the elderly.

Healthy behaviours, better health

Behaviours such as regular exercise, good eating habits and not smoking are associated with better health. From 2001 to 2005, the proportion of Canadians aged 12 and older who were active or moderately active during their free time increased. In 2005, 51% of Canadians were active or moderately active during their free time, compared with 43% in 2000/2001. People aged 12 to 19 are the most active.

At the same time, the proportion of people who smoke daily declined. In 2005, 22% of

Health indicators, 2004

	Males	Females
Life expectancy at birth (years)	77.8	82.6
Infant mortality rate, (deaths per 1,000 live births)	5.5	5.0
Babies with low birth weight (%)	5.5	6.3
Total fertility rate, (number of live births per woman)	...	1.5
Daily smokers (%)[1]	18.2	14.9

1. Data for 2005.
Source: Statistics Canada, CANSIM tables 102-0506, 102-0511, 102-4505, 102-4511 and 105-0427.

Canadians aged 12 and older smoked, down from 26% in 2000/2001. The sharpest drop in smoking rates is among those aged 12 to 17.

Many Canadians do not have a balanced diet, according to the Canadian Community Health Survey. In 2004, 7 out of 10 children aged 4 to 8 were not eating the minimum number of fruit and vegetable servings recommended in *Canada's Food Guide*.

For one out of four Canadians aged 31 to 50, fat accounted for more than 35% of their total calories.

On the bright side, average daily calories eaten have increased little in the last three decades, and total fat consumed has declined

Chart 17.2
Leisure-time physical activity, by age group

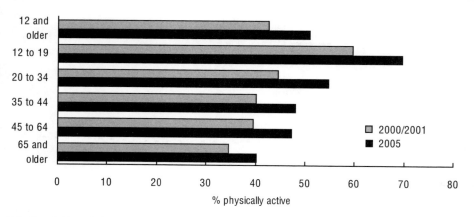

% physically active

Note: Household population who were physically active or moderately active in leisure time.
Source: Statistics Canada, CANSIM tables 105-0033 and 105-0433.

from 40% of Canadians' daily calories to 31%.

Access to health services

Although access to health care is guaranteed under the *Canada Health Act,* some Canadians have difficulty finding a physician—13.6% of the adult population, or 3.5 million Canadians, did not have a regular family doctor in 2005, down slightly from 13.7% in 2003.

A total of 2.8 million people aged 15 and older saw a specialist in 2005, and 19% who needed a specialist's services had trouble getting access. Long wait times remained the main obstacle. Median wait times for all specialist services varied from three to four weeks depending on the type; the figures were similar in 2003. In 2005, the proportion of Canadians who waited more than three months ranged from 10% for diagnostic tests to 19% for non-emergency surgery.

Progress on wait times has varied by province for certain specialist services. For example, median wait times for non-emergency surgery

have been halved in Quebec, dropping from nearly nine weeks in 2003 to four weeks in 2005. In Newfoundland and Labrador, however, median wait times for diagnostic tests have doubled, from two weeks to four weeks; in British Columbia, they increased from two weeks to three weeks.

Patients' perceptions of wait times were essentially unchanged from 2003 to 2005. Although 70% to 80% of patients consider wait times acceptable, some feel their wait times are unacceptable and have a negative effect on their lives.

The main negative effects that people report are anxiety, stress and worry for themselves, their friends and relatives. Some report they suffer pain and have trouble performing daily activities while they wait.

Selected sources

Statistics Canada

- *Access to Health Care Services in Canada.* Irregular. 82-575-XIE

- *Deaths.* Annual. 84F0211XWE

- *Health Indicators.* Semi-annual. 82-221-XIE

- *Health Reports.* Quarterly. 82-003-XIE

- *Health Reports – Supplement.* Annual. 82-003-SIE

- *Healthy Today, Healthy Tomorrow? Findings from the National Population Health Survey.* Occasional. 82-618-MWE

- *Mortality, Summary List of Causes.* Annual. 84F0209XWE

- *Nutrition: Findings from the Canadian Community Health Survey.* Occasional. 82-620-MWE

- *Your Community, Your Health: Findings from the Canadian Community Health Survey (CCHS).* Occasional. 82-621-XWE2006002

Chart 17.3
Waiting times for specialized medical services, 2005

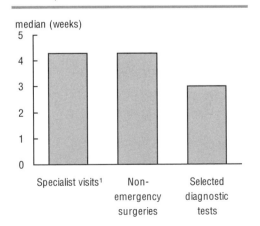

median (weeks)

1. For a new illness or condition.
Source: Statistics Canada, CANSIM table 105-3001.

Less exposure to second-hand smoke

Widespread smoking bans in public places appear to have reduced the proportion of smokers in Canada. An estimated 22% of Canadians smoked in 2005, down from 26% in 2000/2001. The sharpest decline is among youth aged 12 to 17 years—a growing proportion of young Canadians have never smoked.

As smoking bans in public places have become more common, exposure to second-hand smoke among non-smokers has also declined. The restrictions may have helped to change the behaviour of smokers in other places, such as homes and cars.

In 2005, 23% of non-smokers reported regular exposure to second-hand smoke in at least one of the following types of locations: public places, homes and private vehicles. This proportion is down from 29% two years earlier.

Even so, the most common location for exposure to second-hand smoke is public places. In 2005, 15% of non-smokers reported that public places are the location where they are most often exposed to second-hand smoke. The proportion of non-smokers exposed to second-hand smoke at home is 9%, and in private vehicles, 8%.

The risk of exposure to second-hand smoke in at least one type of location is highest among young people. In 2005, about 40% of non-smokers aged 12 to 17 reported regular exposure to second-hand smoke in at least one type of location. By comparison, the rate is 31% for those aged 18 to 34, 19% for those aged 35 to 64, and 11% for those 65 and older.

Chart 17.4
Current smokers, by province and territory

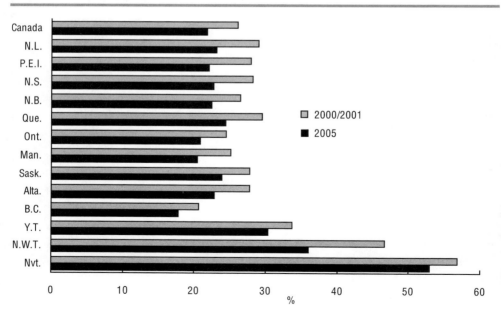

Note: Current smokers include daily and occasional smokers.
Source: Statistics Canada, Catalogue no. 82-621-XWE.

Health and well-being of nurses

Many nurses regularly work overtime and some have more than one job. This might suggest that they are more likely than the employed population as a whole to experience health problems.

However, the 2005 National Survey of the Work and Health of Nurses showed little correlation between poor health and factors such as shift work and long hours of work.

In general, nurses' health problems are more strongly associated with psychosocial factors, including stress at work, low autonomy and lack of respect. In addition, among the employed population nurses are more likely than other workers to experience a high level of job strain.

Job strain is strongly related to fair or poor physical and mental health and to lengthy or frequent absences from work for health-related reasons. For example, 17% of nurses who experienced high job strain reported 20 or more sick days in the year prior to the 2005 survey, compared with 12% of nurses who perceived less job strain.

Fifty-seven percent of nurses felt there had been no change in the quality of care in their workplace, but more nurses reported a deterioration in care than reported an improvement. Changes in staffing levels are a major factor in the quality of care question—27% of nurses who reported deterioration in patient care in 2005 mentioned a shortage of staff.

Of the 314,900 Canadians employed in 2005 as regulated nurses, 95% were women. The regulated nurses surveyed included registered nurses, licensed practical nurses and registered psychiatric nurses.

Chart 17.5
Nurses' work stress, by selected workplace characteristics, 2005

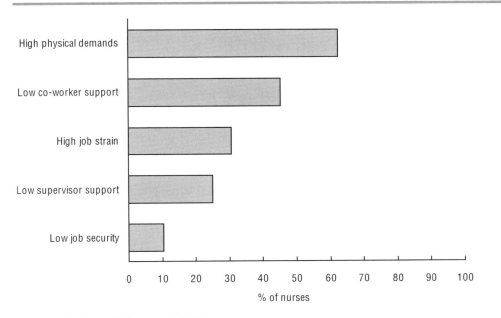

Source: Statistics Canada, Catalogue no. 83-003-XIE.

Depression and performance at work

While many people may feel depressed once in a while, they are still able to do their jobs. For some, however, depression can affect various aspects of their lives and have a serious impact on their performance at work.

About half a million Canadian workers aged 25 to 64 (4% of all such workers) experienced an episode of depression in the year preceding the 2002 Canadian Community Health Survey. Most of them felt that their symptoms had interfered with their ability to work.

Those at greatest risk of depression are white-collar workers and sales and service workers. As in the total population, depression is nearly twice as frequent among working women as among working men.

About four out of five workers who experienced depression during the year prior to the survey reported that their symptoms

affected their ability to work, at least to some extent. One out of five described their symptoms as very severe.

Workers who experienced depression said they were completely unable to work or perform their normal activities for an average of 32 days during the year prior to the 2002 survey. They were also more likely than workers with no history of depression to report a number of specific problems at work—including reduced activity at work because of a long-term health condition, at least one mental-health disability day in the previous two weeks, and absence from work in the previous week.

The survey found a correlation between worker depression and the presence of chronic health conditions, drug or alcohol dependency or anxiety disorders. But it did not find a correlation between excess weight and worker depression.

Chart 17.6
Employees with recent depression, by occupational category, 2002

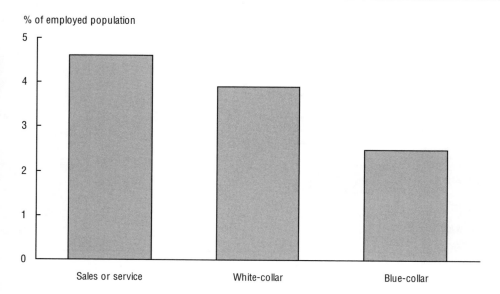

% of employed population

Note: Employed population aged 25 to 64 having experienced depression in the past 12 months.
Source: Statistics Canada, Catalogue no. 82-003-XWE.

Obesity less prevalent in large cities

Adults who live in large Canadian cities are far less likely to be obese than their counterparts living outside urban centres. Twenty percent of people aged 18 or older living in a census metropolitan area (CMA) in 2004 were obese, compared with 29% of those who lived outside a CMA. The national average is 23%.

The likelihood of being obese is smaller in cities with large populations. In CMAs with a population of at least two million—Toronto, Montréal and Vancouver—only 17% of adults were obese in 2004. By contrast, in CMAs with a population of 100,000 to 2 million, 24% of adults were obese. And in urban centres with populations of 10,000 to 100,000, 30% of adults were obese.

At the national level, this relationship between excess weight and urban/rural residence is not evident among children—

except in Alberta. In 2004, Albertans aged 2 to 17 who lived in CMAs were less likely to be overweight or obese than those who lived outside CMAs.

Among adults who do not live in urban centres, those who commute to a large city or even to a smaller urban centre are less likely to be obese. In municipalities where few residents commute to work in an urban centre, the obesity rate is almost twice the national average.

The growing prevalence of obesity among Canadians in recent years is a matter of some concern because obesity increases the higher risk of such health conditions as Type 2 diabetes, cardiovascular disease and high blood pressure. Functional limitations and disabilities are also associated with excess weight.

Chart 17.7
Adult obesity, by metropolitan zone, 2004

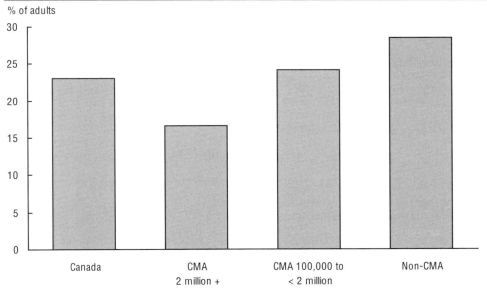

% of adults

Notes: Household population aged 18 and older with a measured body mass index of 30 or higher. Excludes the territories.
Source: Statistics Canada, Catalogue no. 82-003-XIE.

Table 17.1 Mortality rates, by selected causes and by sex, 2000 and 2004

	2000			2004		
	Both sexes	Males	Females	Both sexes	Males	Females
	rate per 100,000 population					
All causes of death	**615.5**	**778.3**	**493.2**	**571.9**	**710.0**	**465.6**
Septicaemia	**3.8**	4.6	3.3	**4.0**	4.6	3.6
Viral hepatitis	**0.4**	0.6	0.2	**1.0**	1.4	0.7
Human immunodeficiency virus	**1.6**	2.6	0.5	**1.2**	1.9	0.4
Malignant neoplasms	**180.4**	225.3	149.4	**173.7**	212.1	147.0
Colon, rectum and anus	**19.0**	24.0	15.1	**18.7**	23.5	15.0
Pancreas	**8.9**	10.1	7.8	**9.3**	10.4	8.2
Trachea, bronchus and lung	**47.1**	64.3	34.4	**46.6**	60.6	36.2
Breast	**13.9**	0.3	25.0	**12.8**	0.2	23.1
Prostate[1]	...	26.7	...	...	23.4	...
Diabetes mellitus	**18.9**	22.9	15.7	**19.6**	24.8	15.8
Alzheimer's disease	**13.2**	11.7	13.8	**12.7**	10.5	13.7
Heart diseases	**152.0**	202.9	113.4	**126.8**	168.1	94.6
Ischaemic heart diseases	**117.5**	163.1	82.9	**96.2**	133.3	67.6
Other heart diseases	**31.6**	37.3	27.3	**27.7**	32.0	24.1
Cerebrovascular diseases	**42.2**	46.4	38.8	**34.9**	37.9	32.4
Influenza and pneumonia	**13.2**	17.0	11.0	**13.4**	17.0	11.3
Influenza	**1.5**	1.6	1.4	**0.7**	0.8	0.6
Pneumonia	**11.7**	15.4	9.6	**12.7**	16.2	10.6
Chronic lower respiratory diseases	**27.2**	39.8	19.8	**24.8**	33.8	19.4
Chronic liver disease and cirrhosis	**6.5**	9.4	3.9	**6.0**	8.4	3.9
Alcoholic liver disease	**3.3**	5.2	1.5	**3.0**	4.5	1.6
Other chronic liver disease and cirrhosis	**3.2**	4.2	2.4	**3.0**	3.9	2.3
Renal failure	**8.4**	11.3	6.7	**8.3**	11.6	6.5
Certain conditions originating in the perinatal period	**3.9**	4.3	3.5	**4.3**	4.5	4.2
Congenital malformations, deformations and chromosomal abnormalities	**3.4**	3.7	3.1	**3.1**	3.1	3.1
Accidents (unintentional injuries)	**25.8**	35.8	16.6	**24.7**	33.8	16.0
Motor vehicle accidents	**8.6**	12.4	5.0	**8.7**	12.7	4.9
Falls	**4.3**	5.9	3.1	**5.4**	6.8	4.3
Accidental poisoning and exposure to noxious substances	**3.0**	4.3	1.7	**2.8**	4.1	1.6
Suicide	**11.4**	18.0	5.0	**10.8**	16.6	5.1
Homicide	**1.6**	2.3	0.8	**1.7**	2.4	0.9

Note: Rates are age standardized to the 1991 Census of Population.

1. A combined rate is not calculated for gender-specific causes of death.

Source: Statistics Canada, CANSIM table 102-0552.

Table 17.2 Life expectancy at birth, by sex and by province and territory, 2004

	Males	Females
	age in years	
Canada	**77.8**	**82.6**
Newfoundland and Labrador	75.8	81.3
Prince Edward Island	76.8	81.6
Nova Scotia	76.5	81.6
New Brunswick	77.0	82.2
Quebec	77.5	82.6
Ontario	78.3	82.7
Manitoba	76.4	81.4
Saskatchewan	76.6	82.1
Alberta	77.8	82.6
British Columbia	78.7	83.1
Yukon	74.5	78.6
Northwest Territories	78.4	81.7
Nunavut	66.8	74.2

Source: Statistics Canada, CANSIM table 102-0511.

Table 17.3 Residents of care facilities for the aged, by sex and by province and territory, 1999/2000 and 2004/2005

	1999/2000			2004/2005		
	Both sexes	**Males**	**Females**	**Both sexes**	**Males**	**Females**
	number					
Canada[1]	**168,911**	**38,469**	**97,605**	**189,325**	**44,748**	**106,146**
Newfoundland and Labrador	**3,785**	1,272	2,513	**4,225**	1,379	2,846
Prince Edward Island	**1,502**	443	1,059	**1,623**	494	1,129
Nova Scotia	**6,613**	1,737	4,876	**6,550**	1,772	4,778
New Brunswick	**5,814**	1,741	4,073	**6,206**	1,898	4,308
Quebec[1]	**32,837**	..	..	**38,431**	..	..
Ontario	**68,827**	18,656	50,171	**80,674**	23,001	57,673
Manitoba	**8,883**	2,515	6,368	**9,563**	2,856	6,707
Saskatchewan	**8,495**	2,632	5,863	**8,126**	2,568	5,558
Alberta	**13,382**	4,180	9,202	**14,185**	4,684	9,501
British Columbia	**18,582**	5,226	13,356	**19,528**	6,017	13,511
Territories[2]	**191**	67	124	**214**	79	135

Notes: Data are as of March 31.
　　　Care facilities in which the predominant group of residents are elderly; residents of these facilities are not exclusively the aged.

1. Data for Quebec are derived from administrative sources of the *Ministère de la santé et des services sociaux;* these sources do not provide the age and sex distribution of residents, therefore, the Canada totals for males and females exclude Quebec.

2. Includes data for Yukon, Northwest Territories and Nunavut.

Source: Statistics Canada, CANSIM table 107-5504.

Table 17.4 Self-rated health, by age group and sex, 2000/2001 and 2005

	2000/2001			2005		
	Very good or excellent	Good	Fair or poor	Very good or excellent	Good	Fair or poor
	%					
Both sexes	**61.4**	**26.6**	**12.0**	**60.1**	**28.7**	**11.2**
12 to 19	70.8	24.3	4.9	67.4	27.9	4.6
12 to 14	72.7	23.4	3.9	68.3	27.6	3.9
15 to 19	69.7	24.8	5.5	66.9	28.1	5.0
20 to 34	73.0	21.9	5.1	70.0	25.0	5.0
20 to 24	72.4	22.4	5.1	69.0	25.9	5.1
25 to 34	73.3	21.6	5.1	70.5	24.6	5.0
35 to 44	66.7	25.3	8.0	65.2	27.2	7.4
45 to 64	55.8	29.1	15.1	56.0	30.2	13.7
45 to 54	59.2	28.0	12.8	58.7	30.0	11.3
55 to 64	50.5	30.7	18.7	52.4	30.5	17.0
65 and older	36.4	33.8	29.7	39.5	34.0	26.2
Males	**63.0**	**25.8**	**11.2**	**60.6**	**28.7**	**10.7**
12 to 19	73.4	22.3	4.2	69.7	26.2	4.1
12 to 14	72.7	23.6	3.6	67.8	27.9	4.3
15 to 19	73.7	21.6	4.6	70.8	25.2	3.9
20 to 34	75.0	20.3	4.7	69.6	25.5	4.9
20 to 24	76.1	18.9	4.8	69.7	24.9	5.3
25 to 34	74.3	21.0	4.6	69.5	25.8	4.6
35 to 44	66.8	25.7	7.5	64.8	27.8	7.4
45 to 64	56.2	29.1	14.6	55.8	30.7	13.4
45 to 54	59.3	28.8	11.9	58.6	30.5	10.8
55 to 64	51.5	29.5	18.9	52.2	31.0	16.8
65 and older	36.7	33.0	30.2	39.9	33.6	26.2
Females	**59.9**	**27.4**	**12.7**	**59.6**	**28.7**	**11.7**
12 to 19	68.0	26.3	5.6	65.0	29.7	5.2
12 to 14	72.7	23.1	4.1	68.9	27.2	3.6
15 to 19	65.6	28.1	6.4	62.8	31.0	6.1
20 to 34	70.9	23.6	5.6	70.3	24.5	5.2
20 to 24	68.5	26.0	5.4	68.2	27.0	4.9
25 to 34	72.1	22.3	5.6	71.4	23.3	5.3
35 to 44	66.6	24.8	8.6	65.8	26.7	7.5
45 to 64	55.3	29.0	15.6	56.2	29.7	14.0
45 to 54	59.1	27.2	13.7	58.8	29.5	11.7
55 to 64	49.5	31.9	18.6	52.6	30.1	17.3
65 and older	36.2	34.4	29.3	39.1	34.3	26.3

Notes: Household population aged 12 and older who rate their own health status as being either excellent, very good, good, fair or poor.

Excludes the "Not stated" category.

Source: Statistics Canada, CANSIM tables 105-0022, 105-0222 and 105-0422.

Table 17.5 Fruit and vegetable consumption, by age group and sex, 2005

	Less than 5 times per day	5 to 10 times per day	More than 10 times per day	Not stated
		%		
Both sexes	**53.3**	**36.9**	**4.3**	**5.5**
12 to 19	47.7	38.8	7.1	6.5
12 to 14	43.0	40.7	8.3	8.0
15 to 19	50.7	37.5	6.3	5.6
20 to 34	55.3	35.9	5.3	3.5
20 to 24	56.1	34.1	5.9	3.9E
25 to 34	54.9	36.9	5.0	3.2
35 to 44	58.4	34.8	3.1	3.7
45 to 64	54.9	36.4	3.8	4.9
45 to 54	56.8	35.3	4.0	3.9
55 to 64	52.3	38.0	3.6	6.2
65 and older	44.7	40.6	3.2	11.6
Males	**60.0**	**30.4**	**3.6**	**6.0**
12 to 19	50.6	35.5	7.0	6.9
12 to 14	46.4	36.0	8.1E	9.5
15 to 19	53.5	35.1	6.3	5.1E
20 to 34	62.2	29.3	4.5	4.0
20 to 24	62.9	26.9	5.6E	4.6E
25 to 34	61.8	30.6	3.9	3.6
35 to 44	65.6	27.9	2.4	4.1
45 to 64	62.4	29.2	2.8	5.6
45 to 54	63.9	28.4	3.1E	4.6
55 to 64	60.5	30.3	2.3E	6.9
65 and older	51.2	33.7	2.2E	13.0
Females	**46.7**	**43.2**	**5.1**	**5.0**
12 to 19	44.5	42.2	7.2	6.1
12 to 14	39.3	45.8	8.5E	6.4E
15 to 19	47.8	39.9	6.3E	6.0
20 to 34	48.5	42.4	6.1	3.0
20 to 24	48.8	41.7	6.2E	3.2E
25 to 34	48.3	42.8	6.1	2.9E
35 to 44	50.9	41.9	3.8	3.4
45 to 64	47.5	43.5	4.8	4.2
45 to 54	50.1	41.8	4.8	3.3E
55 to 64	44.0	45.7	4.8	5.5
65 and older	39.4	46.1	4.0	10.5

Note: Household population aged 12 and older who reported the average number of times per day that they consume fruits and vegetables.

Source: Statistics Canada, CANSIM table 105-0449.

Table 17.6 Daily or occasional smokers, by sex and age group and by province and territory, 2005

	Canada	Newfoundland and Labrador	Prince Edward Island	Nova Scotia	New Brunswick
			%		
Both sexes	**21.7**	**23.1**	**22.2**	**22.6**	**22.5**
12 to 19	**12.1**	17.6	11.2E	9.5	9.8
20 to 34	**28.6**	32.3	29.3	30.8	32.2
35 to 44	**26.8**	29.2	21.8	32.9	29.2
45 to 64	**22.3**	20.6	27.6	21.6	22.8
65 and older	**10.5**	11.7	10.9E	12.2	9.6
Males	**23.6**	**23.4**	**25.4**	**23.7**	**24.8**
12 to 19	**11.9**	18.0E	10.6E	10.7E	11.4E
20 to 34	**32.1**	33.2	36.3	31.7	35.6
35 to 44	**29.6**	28.7	25.0E	36.8	31.9
45 to 64	**23.4**	19.1	29.1	22.0	24.5
65 and older	**11.1**	15.9	16.4E	11.2	10.2
Females	**19.8**	**22.8**	**19.1**	**21.6**	**20.3**
12 to 19	**12.3**	17.1E	11.7E	8.4E	8.2E
20 to 34	**25.0**	31.4	23.1	29.9	28.7
35 to 44	**23.9**	29.7	18.6E	29.3	26.6
45 to 64	**21.2**	22.0	26.2	21.2	21.2
65 and older	**10.1**	8.3	6.6E	12.9	9.2E

Note: Household population aged 12 and older who reported currently being a daily or occasional smoker.
Source: Statistics Canada, CANSIM table 105-0427.

Table 17.7 Exposure of non-smokers to second-hand smoke at home, by age group and by province and territory, 2005

	Canada	Newfoundland and Labrador	Prince Edward Island	Nova Scotia	New Brunswick
			%		
12 and older	**8.7**	**11.9**	**13.6**	**10.6**	**12.1**
12 to 14	**22.1**	35.2	28.7E	19.9	31.0
15 to 19	**20.8**	22.8	30.4E	23.7	25.8
20 to 24	**13.9**	16.4E	21.9E	17.7E	20.8E
25 to 34	**6.0**	5.4E	7.5E	6.8E	9.2E
35 to 44	**5.4**	10.6	11.0E	6.1E	8.5E
45 to 54	**6.9**	12.9	F	11.4E	9.0E
55 to 64	**6.9**	9.5E	13.0E	7.9E	10.2
65 to 74	**5.8**	3.5E	10.7E	7.9E	8.7E
75 and older	**4.4**	8.0E	F	5.1E	4.4E

Note: Non-smoking household population aged 12 and older who reported that at least one person smokes inside their home every day or almost every day.
Source: Statistics Canada, CANSIM table 105-0456.

Quebec	Ontario	Manitoba	Saskatchewan	Alberta	British Columbia	Yukon	Northwest Territories	Nunavut
					%			
24.4	20.7	20.4	23.8	22.7	17.8	30.4	36.0	52.8
16.6	10.6	9.9	13.1	10.9	10.0	15.2E	17.6	43.0
31.1	27.3	28.4	31.9	28.4	25.1	40.1	42.9	62.5
28.6	26.3	26.2	28.5	29.7	20.4	26.5E	46.6	57.5
25.3	21.4	21.4	27.0	22.8	17.8	35.0	31.8	45.6
12.6	9.3	8.6	11.4	12.0	9.3	18.7E	31.8E	F
25.3	23.3	21.7	24.8	25.5	19.6	32.6	33.7	52.8
15.1	10.9	10.5E	12.7	10.6	9.9	12.6E	19.8E	35.3
31.1	33.4	32.0	32.6	33.6	27.2	43.4E	42.6	65.1
31.2	28.8	25.9	30.2	33.8	25.0	33.0E	39.3	64.0
26.3	22.9	21.1	27.5	24.2	19.2	37.2	27.7E	40.4
13.5	9.7	10.8	12.6	12.4	9.1	F	34.1E	F
23.4	18.2	19.1	22.8	20.0	16.0	28.1	38.6	52.9
18.3	10.3	9.3E	13.4	11.1	10.0	18.1E	15.3E	50.9
31.0	21.5	24.9	31.2	23.1	23.0	37.3E	43.3	59.8
26.0	23.6	26.5	26.9	25.4	15.8	19.9E	54.4	51.2E
24.4	20.0	21.7	26.4	21.3	16.3	32.5	36.6E	50.9E
11.9	9.0	7.0	10.3	11.7	9.5	F	F	F

Quebec	Ontario	Manitoba	Saskatchewan	Alberta	British Columbia	Yukon	Northwest Territories	Nunavut
					%			
13.0	7.3	8.6	7.8	8.1	4.8	8.2E	19.0	17.0E
31.3	17.4	20.6	22.8	22.9	16.0	35.3E	43.4E	57.4
31.0	18.1	19.6	17.9	18.9	13.6	20.9E	37.4E	F
20.8	11.5	14.4E	7.8E	13.1	9.2	F	F	F
10.2	5.1	4.3E	3.7E	4.7	2.7E	F	F	F
8.7	4.2	5.3E	6.9E	4.4E	2.4E	F	F	F
10.7	5.3	7.0E	6.4E	5.9E	4.0E	F	F	F
10.6	5.6	7.9E	6.4E	5.8E	2.6E	F	F	F
7.9	5.7	5.8E	3.7E	4.8E	2.6E	F	F	F
6.3	4.4	4.2E	3.3E	4.6E	1.6E	F	F	F

Table 17.8 Health expenditures, 2002 to 2006

	2002	2003	2004	2005ᵖ	2006ᵖ
	\$ millions				
Health expenditures	**114,912.4**	**123,382.0**	**131,380.2**	**139,836.3**	**148,014.1**
Hospitals	34,887.5	37,162.1	39,863.8	42,098.8	44,131.3
Other institutions	10,751.1	11,501.9	12,326.1	13,204.3	13,962.2
Physicians	15,048.9	16,124.6	17,167.9	18,127.8	19,413.2
Other professionals	13,096.8	13,190.3	14,197.9	14,904.6	15,616.4
Dental services	8,264.8	8,447.1	8,983.1	9,486.1	9,943.3
Vision care services	2,792.1	2,675.0	3,054.2	3,117.5	3,247.7
Other	2,040.0	2,068.2	2,160.6	2,301.0	2,425.5
Drugs	18,441.3	20,139.3	21,829.0	23,721.6	25,155.4
Prescribed drugs	14,839.9	16,482.7	18,009.8	19,735.8	21,090.3
Non-prescribed drugs	3,601.4	3,656.6	3,819.1	3,985.8	4,065.1
Other expenditures	22,686.6	25,263.8	25,995.5	27,779.1	29,735.4
	% of gross domestic product				
Health expenditures	**10.0**	**10.1**	**10.2**	**10.2**	**10.3**

Note: Health expenditures include spending by federal, provincial, territorial and local governments, Workers' Compensation boards and the private sector.
Source: Canadian Institute for Health Information.

Table 17.9 Average weekly earnings of workers in the health care and social assistance sector, selected groups, 1996, 2001 and 2006

	1996	2001	2006
	\$		
All health care and social assistance	**536.84**	**580.66**	**678.91**
Ambulatory health care services	493.18	532.95	683.14
Offices of physicians	458.21	491.54	671.59
Offices of dentists	493.93	535.85	701.57
Hospitals	641.68	688.10	770.46
Nursing and residential care facilities	452.13	519.67	613.00
Social assistance	395.67	459.75	537.24
Child daycare services	345.58	409.10	472.99

Note: Data include overtime.
Source: Statistics Canada, CANSIM table 281-0027.

Table 17.10 Capital and repair expenditures by the health care and social assistance sector, by province and territory, 1995, 2000 and 2005

	1995	2000	2005ᵖ
		$ millions	
Canada	**2,814.4**	**4,658.8**	**8,035.2**
Newfoundland and Labrador	27.0	130.3	80.2
Prince Edward Island	6.9	16.0	17.0
Nova Scotia	87.6	75.7	123.0
New Brunswick	118.2	56.9	194.3
Quebec	x	982.9	1,709.8
Ontario	1,204.5	1,835.4	3,185.9
Manitoba	70.9	227.1	295.7
Saskatchewan	93.4	156.3	190.4
Alberta	123.8	557.2	1,011.2
British Columbia	370.6	602.3	1,189.8
Yukon	11.2	5.8	5.5
Northwest Territories (including Nunavut)	14.4	..	..
Northwest Territories	..	6.9	14.6
Nunavut	..	6.0	17.7

Source: Statistics Canada, CANSIM table 029-0005.

Table 17.11 Access to specialized health services, by type of service and difficulties experienced, 2003 and 2005

	2003	2005
	millions	
Individuals who accessed care		
Specialist visits	2.9	2.8
Non-emergency surgeries	1.6	1.6
Diagnostic tests	1.9	2.2
	%	
Individuals who accessed care		
Specialist visits	11.6	10.9
Non-emergency surgeries	6.2	6.0
Diagnostic tests	7.5	8.5
Individuals who experienced difficulties accessing care[1]		
Specialist visits	20.9	18.7
Non-emergency surgeries	12.9	12.5
Diagnostic tests	15.9	13.4

Notes: Household population aged 15 and older.

"Specialized services" includes specialist visits for a new illness or condition, non-emergency surgery other than dental surgery, and selected diagnostic tests (non-emergency MRIs, CT scans and angiographies).

1. Based on population accessing specialized service in past 12 months.

Source: Statistics Canada, Catalogue no. 82-575-XIE.

Table 17.12 Barriers to accessing specialized health services, by type of services, 2003 and 2005

	2003	2005
	%	
Specialist visits		
Waited too long for an appointment	67.8	67.8
Difficulty getting an appointment	24.5	32.2
Non-emergency surgeries		
Waited too long for an appointment	61.7	65.6
Difficulty getting an appointment	23.6E	22.9
Diagnostic tests		
Waited too long for an appointment	55.0	58.8
Waited too long for test	33.5	36.2
Difficulty getting an appointment	21.8E	17.8E

Notes: "Specialized services" includes specialist visits for a new illness or condition, non-emergency surgery other than dental surgery, and selected diagnostic tests (non-emergency MRIs, CT scans, and angiographies).
Household population aged 15 and older.
Because multiple responses were allowed, totals may exceed 100%.
Based on population accessing specialized service in past 12 months. Analysis excludes non-response ("I don't know," "not stated" and "refusal").
Source: Statistics Canada, Catalogue no. 82-575-XIE.

Table 17.13 Waiting times for specialized health services, by type of health service, 2003 and 2005

	2003	2005
	%	
Specialist visits		
Less than 1 month	47.9	46.0
1 to 3 months	40.7	41.1
Longer than 3 months	11.4	12.9
Non-emergency surgeries		
Less than 1 month	40.5	40.3
1 to 3 months	42.1	40.7
Longer than 3 months	17.4	19.1
Diagnostic tests		
Less than 1 month	57.5	56.4
1 to 3 months	31.1	33.3
Longer than 3 months	11.5	10.2

Notes: "Specialized services" includes specialist visits for a new illness or condition, non-emergency surgery other than dental surgery, and selected diagnostic tests (non-emergency MRIs, CT scans and angiographies).
Household population aged 15 and older.
Based on population reporting waiting times for specialized services accessed in the last 12 months. Analysis excludes non-response ("I don't know," "not stated" and "refusal").
Source: Statistics Canada, CANSIM tables 105-3002, 105-3003 and 105-3004.

Income, pensions, spending and wealth

18

OVERVIEW

The last decade of strong economic growth has benefited most Canadian families. Incomes have grown, while pensions, savings and retirement plans have grown strongly. Bigger incomes have enabled families to spend more and accrue wealth. By 2006, Canadians' wealth was at a near-record high.

Canada has many types of families, and each makes a living in a different way. In 2005, two-parent families with children had the highest median market income, at $72,800— market income is earnings from employment, investments and private pensions. But they also paid the most in taxes and received modest government transfers, bringing their median after-tax income to $65,700.

Single people had the lowest median market income, at $18,100. Female lone-parent families had low incomes on average, but they received significant government

transfers, so their median after-tax income was $30,400.

Senior families made little by way of market income in 2005; however, their median government transfers totalled $22,000, and they paid lower taxes. So senior families collected a median $40,400 in after-tax income in 2005.

Median after-tax income for all families with two or more people rose 1.6% from 2004 to $56,000, after adjusting for inflation. This gain in after-tax income came on the heels of a 1.3% gain in 2004 as strong economic growth created jobs and boosted earnings.

Proportion with low income has fallen considerably

Thanks to economic conditions over the past decade, the percentage of Canadians below

Chart 18.1
Low income rates, by family type

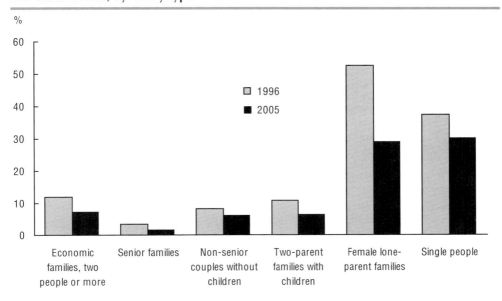

Note: After-tax income 1992 base.
Source: Statistics Canada, Catalogue no. 75-202-XIE.

the low-income cutoff rate—the threshold below which a larger share of income than average is devoted to the necessities of food, shelter and clothing—has decreased considerably. Among all family types, the proportion fell from a high of 12.1% in 1996 to 7.4% in 2005.

From 1996 to 2005, the percentage of female lone-parent families living in low income dropped from 52.7% to 29.1%, partly because more lone parents are earning income. The share of seniors with low income hit a low of 1.6% in 2005. Also, the proportion of children aged 18 and younger living in low-income families stood at 11.7%, down from a peak of 18.6% in 1996.

Income levels vary widely by province

Income levels vary widely from province to province. In 2005, for the second consecutive year, economic families of two or more people in Alberta had the highest median market income in the country, at $70,300. Ontario families were next, at $63,600. Only Alberta and Ontario families had median

Chart 18.2
Family median after-tax income, by province, 2005

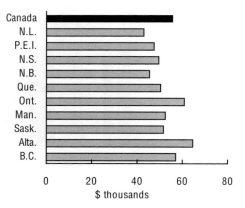

Note: Measured in 2005 constant dollars; economic families of two or more people.
Source: Statistics Canada, Catalogue no. 75-202-XIE.

Average household spending, selected expenditures, 2005

	$
Personal taxes	13,698
Shelter	12,614
Transportation	9,073
Food	7,135
Household operation	3,091
Clothing	2,588
Health care	1,799
Personal care	1,094

Source: Statistics Canada, CANSIM table 203-2001.

market incomes above the national median of $57,700 in 2005.

In Atlantic Canada, families' median market incomes ranged between $36,900 in Newfoundland and Labrador and $49,100 in Nova Scotia. In Quebec, families earned a median market income of $50,100.

Households have been spending more

With wallets generally getting fatter over the past five years, Canadian households have increased their spending as well. In 2000, households spent an average of $55,614 on food, shelter, clothing, transportation, taxes and other things; by 2005, this total had climbed to $66,857.

Where you live helps determine how much you spend—rural households spent an average $12,210 less than urban ones in 2005. Home ownership also affects household spending—annual expenditures of homeowners are almost double those of renters. Also, couples with children spend far more than single people.

Of the average $66,857 in household spending in 2005, about 20% went to taxes at the federal, provincial and municipal levels. Most of the rest was spent on shelter and household operation (23%), transportation (14%) and food (11%). Other components of after-tax household spending included recreation (6%), tobacco products and alcoholic beverages (2%), and personal care (2%).

Personal insurance and retirement plans are also major expenditures for most Canadian families. Among those who regularly set aside money for the future, the average in 2005 was $3,921.

Households spend money partly according to how much they earn. For example, among the richest fifth of Canadian households, 29% of their budget went to taxes and 15% to shelter costs. By contrast, among the poorest fifth of households, less than 4% went to taxes, but 30% was spent on shelter. As a proportion of the total household budget, the poorest families also spent more than twice as much as the richest families on food. Clothing and transportation took up roughly equal proportions among all income groups.

Assets and debts have both increased

Some household spending is entirely consumed or used, such as money spent on food, fuel or recreational activities. A

considerable amount also goes toward building equity in property and accumulating financial or non-financial assets. In 2005, the total value of Canadian families' assets climbed to $5.6 trillion, up from $3.9 trillion in 1999. For Canadian households, the roof above their heads is their single biggest asset, and the value of their homes has increased by half from 1999 to 2005.

The increase in household assets has been accompanied by a roughly similar increase in household debt. From 2001 to 2005, the value of Canadians' assets grew 25.9%. During this period, their liabilities also swelled, by 23.5%, as building those assets has required some borrowing. As a result, households were spending about 8% of their disposable income to pay the interest on borrowed funds in 2005.

Selected sources

Statistics Canada

- *Analytical Studies Branch Research Paper Series.* Occasional. 11F0019MIE2007294

- *Canada's Retirement Income Programs.* Irregular. 74-507-XCB

- *Canadian Economic Accounts Quarterly Review.* Quarterly. 13-010-XWE

- *Household Expenditures Research Paper Series.* Occasional. 62F0026MIE2006001

- *Income in Canada.* Annual. 75-202-XIE

- *Income Trends in Canada.* Annual. 13F0022XIE

- *National Balance Sheet Accounts, Quarterly Estimates.* Quarterly. 13-214-XWE

- *Pension and Wealth Research Paper Series.* Occasional. 13F0026MIE2006001

- *Perspectives on Labour and Income.* Monthly. 75-001-XWE

- *Spending Patterns in Canada.* Annual. 62-202-XWE

Chart 18.3
Average annual expenditures, by selected household type, 2005

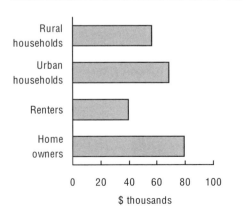

$ thousands

Source: Statistics Canada, Catalogue no. 67-202-XWE.

Net worth as a measure of security

Financial security means different things to each of us. Most often, we measure it by net worth—comparing our assets to our debts. Canadians' net worth has grown considerably after years of strong economic growth and an explosive real estate market. In 2005, Canada's 13.3 million families had a median net worth of $148,350.

The total value of all assets held by Canadian families rose 42.4% from 1999 to 2005, due in large part to the rapid rise in real estate prices. Canadians collectively owned $2.36 trillion worth of real estate in 2005.

Canadians have also seen their net worth rise thanks to the performance of private pension assets and financial, non-pension assets. Pension assets—such as employer-sponsored registered pension plans (RPPs) and personal registered retirement savings plans (RRSPs)—rose 41.7% from 1999 to 2005.

Financial assets such as mutual funds, investment funds, stocks and bonds have grown at a slower pace of 20.0%, in part because of fluctuations in the stock markets in the first years of the new century. The value of Canadians' stock holdings as a whole was virtually unchanged from 1999 to 2005.

Debts are the other side of the financial security equation. While Canadian families' assets were increasing tremendously in value from 1999 to 2005, their debts were also accumulating—their total amount of debt swelled by 47.5%. Mortgages accounted for three-quarters of all their debts, although lines of credit, credit cards and car loans were also major sources of debt.

But even though debts have grown at a slightly faster pace than assets, the financial security of the average Canadian family is still fairly strong.

Chart 18.4
Family assets

% of total assets

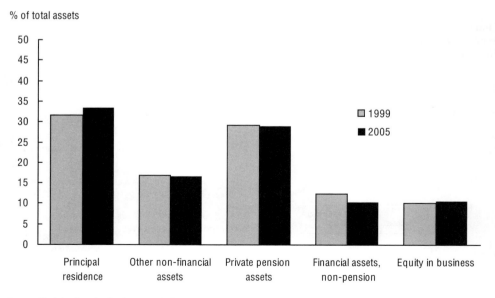

Source: Statistics Canada, Catalogue no. 13F0026MIE.

Low income among new immigrants

Imagine starting a new life in a new country. You leave family, friends and everything familiar behind. You step off the plane and begin looking for a place to call home. Perhaps you need to learn the language. You also need to find a source of income.

While many families begin earning a solid income soon after their arrival, some have a quite different experience. Canada has attracted more highly skilled and educated immigrants: despite this, the economic situation of new immigrant families has improved little since 2000. Immigrants who have been in Canada for less than two years seem to have difficulty adjusting over the short term, according to a study on the income of immigrants who arrived from 1992 to 2004. In 2004, low-income rates among immigrants during their first full year in Canada were 3.2 times higher than those of Canadian-born people.

The probability that an immigrant would enter a period of low income during their first year in Canada was high, ranging from 34% to 46% in the years studied. However, between 34% and 41% of those in low income during their first year escaped low income after just one year. In fact, if arriving immigrants escaped low income during their first full year in Canada, their chances of staying out of it were high.

Another 18.5% of recent immigrants remained in low income for at least four of their first five years in Canada.

In 1993, the selection system for immigrants was changed to attract those with more education and specific skills. As a result, the proportion of immigrants aged 15 and older with university degrees and marketable skills has risen dramatically.

Chart 18.5
Low-income rates for total population and immigrants

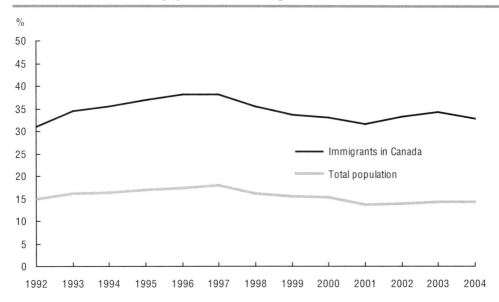

Note: Persons age 20 and older; immigrants in Canada 1 to 10 complete years.
Source: Statistics Canada, Catalogue no. 11F0019MIE.

Our growing nest eggs

Canadians' assets in registered pension plans (RPPs), registered retirement savings plans (RRSPs) and the Canada/Quebec Pension Plans (C/QPP) have doubled in value since 1990 (taking inflation into account). By 2003, Canadians had more than $1.3 trillion saved in these accounts for their senior years.

RPPs account for the biggest chunk of this total, at about 63%. These plans are established by companies to provide pension benefits for their employees when they retire. RRSPs account for 30%. They are personal retirement savings plans offered by financial institutions. The government-run C/QPP retirement plans account for about 6%.

Pension funds are heavily invested in stocks and equity investment funds, so the strong performance of the stock market over the 1990s was a major factor driving their growth. Weaker market conditions in the

first years of the new century have made it difficult for RPPs and RRSPs to regain the levels they reached in 2000. But over the longer term, the growth has been strong.

As of January 2004, there were 14,777 active registered pension plans in Canada, covering 5.6 million working Canadians. The share of people covered by an RPP, however, has been shrinking over the past three decades, from 46% in 1977 to 39% in 2003.

In addition to RPPs, Canadians can turn to other retirement savings programs, such as RRSPs. In 2004, about 5.6 million Canadians—or about 38% of all eligible taxfilers aged 25 to 64—made RRSP contributions with a value of $25.2 billion. This proportion was up slightly from 36% in 1992. In 2004, 1.4 million Canadians withdrew about $7 billion from their RRSP accounts—an average of $4,905 per person.

Chart 18.6
Pension savings

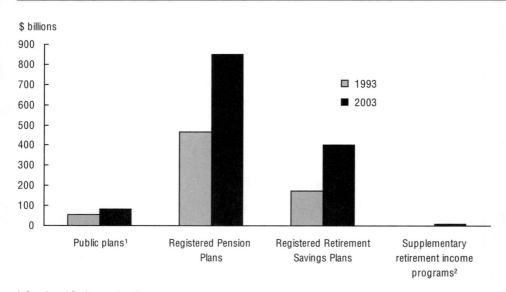

$ billions

1. Canada and Quebec pension plans.
2. Executive pension plans known as 'retirement compensation arrangements.'
Source: Statistics Canada, Catalogue no. 74-507-XIE.

Rising tide of wealth

In many ways the rich do get richer. From 1984 to 2005, the richest Canadian families enjoyed the strongest growth in wealth (excluding growth in pension accounts), as the average net worth of the richest fifth of families increased by 64% and the second richest fifth by 48%.

At the same time, families with the lowest net worth saw virtually no growth in wealth at all over that period. The second poorest actually saw their net worth decrease 11%.

The net worth of the middle group of Canadian families has risen at a steady pace over the past twenty years, climbing from $67,300 in 1984 to $74,400 in 1999 and to $84,800 in 2005—up 26% over the period.

Part of the growth in net worth can be attributed to Canada's aging population. The

higher average age of Canadians means that most people are in their prime earning years.

Another driving force is the hot housing market. Since most families in the top fifth own a house, this group gained significantly from the real estate boom—from 1999 to 2005, these families saw the median value of their principal residence rise by $75,000. However, since very few of the poorest families owned a residence, this group has gained little benefit from the rise in housing prices.

In terms of actual wealth, the gap between top and bottom is even starker—the median wealth of the richest families was $551,000, whereas the poorest owed about $1,000. The second poorest fifth of Canadian families were little better off, having an average net worth of just $12,500.

Chart 18.7
Family wealth

% of total wealth

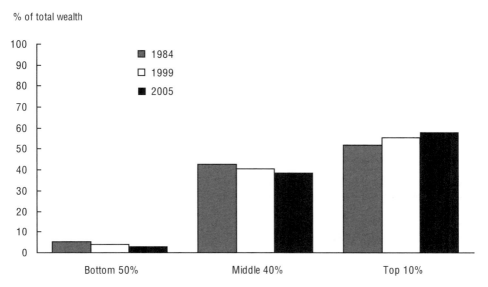

Note: Excluding the value of Registered Pension Plans.
Source: Statistics Canada, Catalogue no. 75-001-XIE.

Table 18.1 Average total income, by economic family type, 1991 to 2005

	1991	1992	1993	1994	1995	1996
			$ 2005 constant			
Economic families	**67,500**	**67,000**	**65,900**	**66,600**	**67,000**	**67,200**
Elderly families[1]	51,300	49,600	50,300	50,000	52,500	48,200
Married couples	45,800	44,800	46,300	46,000	47,000	47,000
Other elderly families	63,700	60,100	58,900	59,300	65,300	52,100
Non-elderly families[2]	70,300	70,100	68,700	69,600	69,600	70,200
Married couples	66,700	68,800	66,800	64,800	66,000	68,900
No earner	32,200	31,600	30,400	31,300	29,100	33,300
One earner	52,600	53,200	53,500	54,000	53,900	53,200
Two earners	76,300	79,200	78,000	74,800	76,400	81,500
Two-parent families with children[3]	75,400	75,800	74,000	75,300	75,100	75,000
No earner	21,400	21,500	23,200	22,300	20,700	22,700
One earner	55,800	55,700	54,500	56,900	54,200	57,800
Two earners	76,600	78,000	76,300	78,100	78,500	78,400
Three or more earners	95,700	94,300	95,700	95,800	95,700	97,000
Married couples with other relatives	93,000	92,300	92,500	93,500	92,000	96,600
Lone-parent families[3]	30,900	32,100	30,300	31,300	32,000	31,200
Male lone-parent families	48,600	49,900	43,100	43,200	43,900	48,200
Female lone-parent families	28,400	29,800	28,400	29,400	30,200	28,600
No earner	17,000	17,500	18,300	17,900	18,400	17,100
One earner	31,100	33,000	31,600	32,600	33,100	33,600
Two or more earners	45,700	46,600	43,600	48,400	50,600	46,300
Other non-elderly families	55,500	49,900	53,700	54,100	53,500	60,700
Unattached individuals	**27,800**	**28,000**	**28,000**	**27,800**	**28,200**	**27,500**
Elderly male	25,400	27,600	25,500	29,500	28,200	29,200
Non-earner	24,000	27,200	24,200	25,900	25,900	26,600
Earner	38,900	32,200	37,700	61,200	49,600	49,900E
Elderly female	22,400	22,100	20,900	21,200	22,800	23,700
Non-earner	22,000	21,600	20,400	20,800	22,400	23,100
Earner	33,900	29,400	36,600	32,600	35,600	40,500
Non-elderly male	31,900	31,700	32,100	32,400	31,700	31,000
Non-earner	13,200	13,400	13,300	13,900	12,900	11,600
Earner	36,200	35,800	37,700	37,200	36,400	36,000
Non-elderly female	26,700	26,900	27,800	25,800	27,200	24,800
Non-earner	14,100	14,100	13,800	16,000	14,100	11,300
Earner	30,500	31,300	32,500	29,900	31,800	30,100

Note: "Average total income" refers to income from all sources, including government transfers and before deduction of federal and provincial income taxes. It may also be called 'income before tax' (but after transfers).

1. Families in which the major income earner is 65 years of age and older; for data prior to 1996, the head of family is 65 years of age or older.
2. Families in which the major income earner is less than 65 years of age.
3. Families with children less than 18 years of age.
Source: Statistics Canada, CANSIM table 202-0403.

1997	1998	1999	2000	2001	2002	2003	2004	2005
				$ 2005 constant				
68,700	**71,200**	**72,700**	**75,400**	**76,600**	**76,400**	**75,900**	**77,700**	**78,400**
48,500	49,200	51,100	51,400	51,600	52,300	52,100	53,000	55,100
47,300	48,100	50,400	49,900	50,700	50,700	51,100	52,800	53,400
52,400	53,000	53,600	57,000	55,100	58,300	55,800	53,900	61,700
72,000	74,800	76,300	79,400	80,700	80,300	79,900	82,000	82,400
72,100	73,200	72,400	73,400	77,900	76,400	74,300	75,100	77,800
34,900	33,000	34,700	35,700	40,800	37,400	35,600	35,300	35,600
56,700	58,100	60,300	58,800	63,900	58,400	59,200	62,700	64,900
83,200	85,700	83,300	83,600	87,700	87,700	84,000	83,700	87,300
77,500	81,200	83,200	86,300	87,500	88,100	89,100	92,400	89,500
24,800	23,900	23,200	23,000	25,300	25,600	23,400	24,800	21,500
56,900	64,100	63,200	63,200	64,400	68,100	69,900	67,600	64,200
80,500	83,500	84,800	88,200	88,600	88,800	89,300	92,500	90,900
99,600	99,600	103,100	107,400	109,900	107,400	108,800	115,200	111,200
96,100	98,300	102,900	110,000	105,900	105,100	105,300	108,100	113,700
31,300	34,100	35,300	38,400	39,200	37,400	38,200	38,200	44,500
47,700	50,800	51,700	56,400	53,000	53,300	57,700	53,800	64,200
28,600	31,200	32,200	34,800	36,300	33,600	33,800	34,700	40,100
16,200	16,700	17,700	16,700	17,600	16,800	16,600	17,900	17,800
32,200	33,300	33,700	34,700	36,100	34,000	33,400	34,800	41,300
48,700	51,700	50,900	56,100	58,200	50,800	53,300	50,600	53,000
59,300	64,000	64,700	67,300	67,500	69,300	64,000	67,300	65,500
27,400	**28,200**	**30,000**	**30,000**	**30,800**	**31,400**	**32,000**	**31,800**	**32,300**
29,500	30,500	29,200	28,000	29,800	29,500	30,800	30,200	31,200
27,000	27,000	27,400	26,100	27,900	26,800	27,000	28,100	26,800
44,300	51,700E	41,200	38,500	40,900	41,200	44,300	38,300	48,600
24,300	23,900	23,900	24,500	25,500	26,000	25,800	26,900	25,900
23,300	23,000	23,200	23,700	24,300	25,400	24,900	25,700	24,800
38,300	36,700	35,200	35,900	40,200	33,300	33,200	36,800	36,500
30,500	31,600	33,300	34,600	35,100	35,300	36,300	35,400	36,800
10,900	10,900	10,600	10,500	12,400	12,200	12,900	12,500	12,900
36,200	37,100	38,000	39,100	39,500	40,100	41,200	39,800	42,000
24,700	25,600	29,300	27,500	28,300	29,800	30,100	30,000	29,800
12,200	11,400	11,300	11,200	12,600	12,500	13,500	13,400	15,200
29,800	31,400	35,800	33,100	33,500	35,200	34,900	35,000	33,700

Table 18.2 Average total income, by economic family type and by province, 2005

	Canada	Newfoundland and Labrador	Prince Edward Island	Nova Scotia
	\$ 2005 constant			
Economic families	**78,400**	**60,200**	**62,600**	**68,000**
Elderly families[1]	**55,100**	38,500	45,700	47,600
Married couples	**53,400**	37,000	45,800	48,100
Other elderly families	**61,700**	41,900	F	46,300
Non-elderly families[2]	**82,400**	64,400	65,800	72,100
Married couples	**77,800**	58,300	63,600	67,400
No earner	**35,600**	27,400[E]	F	39,500
One earner	**64,900**	48,900	50,800	57,700
Two earners	**87,300**	70,200	70,100	75,700
Two-parent families with children[3]	**89,500**	72,400	72,700	76,300
No earner	**21,500**	F	F	F
One earner	**64,200**	44,500	F	51,000
Two earners	**90,900**	77,000	70,800	75,500
Three or more earners	**111,200**	84,700	81,500	94,700
Married couples with other relatives	**113,700**	86,900	85,300	101,100
Lone-parent families[3]	**44,500**	35,300	32,300	35,600
Male lone-parent families	**64,200**	F	F	F
Female lone-parent families	**40,100**	31,100	31,200	31,500
No earner	**17,800**	F	F	F
One earner	**41,300**	31,800	29,800	30,400
Two or more earners	**53,000**	F	F	F
Other non-elderly families	**65,500**	52,900	52,200	72,800
Unattached individuals	**32,300**	**24,800**	**23,700**	**25,400**
Elderly male	**31,200**	20,800	F	24,700
Non-earner	**26,800**	20,400	F	24,800
Earner	**48,600**	F	F	F
Elderly female	**25,900**	19,700	22,400	24,500
Non-earner	**24,800**	19,700	22,600	24,400
Earner	**36,500**	F	F	F
Non-elderly male	**36,800**	28,000	22,300	26,200
Non-earner	**12,900**	F	F	11,800[E]
Earner	**42,000**	36,700	26,300	30,900
Non-elderly female	**29,800**	25,300	26,400	25,300
Non-earner	**15,200**	F	F	13,900
Earner	**33,700**	29,300	30,000	29,000

Note: "Average total income" refers to income from all sources, including government transfers and before deduction of federal and provincial income taxes. It may also be called "income before tax" (but after transfers).

1. Families in which the major income earner is 65 years of age and older.
2. Families in which the major income earner is less than 65 years of age.
3. Families with children less than 18 years of age.
Source: Statistics Canada, CANSIM table 202-0403.

New Brunswick	Quebec	Ontario	Manitoba	Saskatchewan	Alberta	British Columbia
			$ 2005 constant			
61,700	**69,800**	**85,700**	**71,600**	**70,700**	**88,100**	**77,100**
43,400	46,700	60,400	52,500	48,000	56,000	63,400
41,400	46,000	56,800	49,900	48,000	55,000	62,700
50,400	48,800	73,300	64,200	48,200	61,100E	66,700
65,100	73,700	90,100	75,000	75,100	92,800	79,500
58,900	68,500	84,700	68,100	73,400	94,900	80,400
30,300	37,400	34,500	F	F	F	39,800E
57,100	61,700	68,700	53,100	53,100	85,600E	60,200
64,900	75,600	97,700	75,100	80,600	99,300	91,600
74,500	83,800	94,400	81,300	82,900	98,400	87,800
F	F	F	F	F	F	F
44,600	64,100	64,000	62,400	54,200	83,000	58,900
75,400	85,500	97,900	78,600	79,000	92,000	94,200
92,400	100,800	115,600	105,900	107,800	126,000	108,800
90,400	96,800	130,800	107,200	106,800	127,900	91,300
32,400	45,600	48,700	37,700	32,200	46,500	39,500
F	70,800E	66,000	45,500	42,900	68,200	50,300E
30,000	37,600	45,400	36,000	30,500	41,000	37,500
F	17,100	19,000	F	F	F	F
28,800	36,900	49,300	34,500	29,200	39,300	38,200
F	54,700	56,100	F	F	50,700	F
48,800	57,100	70,300	69,500	58,700	67,500	66,000
23,700	**28,200**	**36,000**	**28,200**	**27,100**	**38,100**	**32,600**
22,900	26,300	38,100	28,100	27,400	33,600	29,400
20,500	23,200	30,700	24,400	25,400	33,800	26,100
F	F	60,100	F	F	F	F
22,300	22,100	29,500	23,700	22,800	26,100	28,400
21,700	21,300	28,200	22,700	21,900	23,900	27,000
F	32,800	40,400	29,200	29,300	37,200E	38,000
26,800	31,700	40,400	32,100	31,900	44,200	37,700
7,100	11,000	14,000	11,900E	10,800E	F	15,900E
31,800	36,800	46,600	34,900	35,500	46,300	43,400
20,700	27,300	33,200	26,000	24,300	34,200	28,000
13,500E	13,800	17,700	13,200E	10,500E	12,700E	15,900E
22,700	32,200	37,400	29,200	27,500	37,200	29,900

Table 18.3 Average income after tax, by economic family type, 1991 to 2005

	1991	1992	1993	1994	1995	1996
	\$ 2005 constant					
Economic families	**54,100**	**54,100**	**53,200**	**53,600**	**53,700**	**54,000**
Elderly families[1]	44,100	43,300	43,700	43,400	45,100	41,300
Married couples	39,700	39,400	40,300	40,000	40,600	40,100
Other elderly families	54,200	51,900	51,000	51,300	55,600	45,500
Non-elderly families[2]	55,900	56,100	54,900	55,400	55,300	56,000
Married couples	52,200	54,200	52,300	51,100	51,800	53,800
No earner	27,500	27,900	26,500	27,700	25,900	28,400
One earner	41,700	43,200	42,900	43,100	42,700	42,300
Two earners	59,200	61,500	60,200	58,200	59,300	62,900
Two-parent families with children[3]	59,500	60,100	58,900	59,400	59,100	59,300
No earner	20,900	21,200	22,700	21,900	20,400	22,200
One earner	44,200	44,400	44,200	45,100	43,500	45,400
Two earners	60,200	61,400	60,100	61,100	61,100	61,700
Three or more earners	75,800	75,300	76,300	76,100	75,700	77,100
Married couples with other relatives	74,400	74,200	74,200	74,500	73,100	76,900
Lone-parent families[3]	27,000	28,200	27,200	27,600	28,100	27,900
Male lone-parent families	38,200	40,000	36,100	35,000	35,700	39,800
Female lone-parent families	25,400	26,600	25,800	26,500	26,900	26,000
No earner	16,900	17,300	18,200	17,700	18,100	17,000
One earner	27,300	28,900	27,900	28,700	28,900	29,700
Two or more earners	38,600	40,000	38,400	41,700	43,000	40,800
Other non-elderly families	46,400	42,300	44,700	45,100	44,700	50,900
Unattached individuals	**23,000**	**23,200**	**23,100**	**22,900**	**23,200**	**22,800**
Elderly male	22,300	24,100	22,600	25,000	24,400	24,900
Non-earner	21,400	23,800	21,700	22,900	23,000	23,100
Earner	31,200	27,200	31,000	43,500	37,400	38,900
Elderly female	20,200	20,100	19,200	19,600	20,500	21,100
Non-earner	19,900	19,800	18,900	19,300	20,200	20,600
Earner	28,800	25,500	29,500	27,300	29,000	32,400
Non-elderly male	25,400	25,400	25,400	25,500	25,100	24,700
Non-earner	12,200	12,500	12,400	12,900	12,000	10,800
Earner	28,500	28,400	29,300	28,800	28,400	28,300
Non-elderly female	21,800	22,000	22,600	21,200	22,200	20,500
Non-earner	12,800	12,800	12,700	14,400	13,000	10,600
Earner	24,500	25,300	25,900	24,100	25,400	24,500

Note: "Average income after tax" refers to total income, which includes government transfers, minus income tax.

1. Families in which the major income earner is 65 years of age and older; for data prior to 1996, the head of family is 65 or older.
2. Families in which the major income earner is less than 65 years of age.
3. Families with children less than 18 years of age.
Source: Statistics Canada, CANSIM table 202-0603.

1997	1998	1999	2000	2001	2002	2003	2004	2005
				$ 2005 constant				
55,100	**56,900**	**58,600**	**60,400**	**62,900**	**62,900**	**62,400**	**63,900**	**64,800**
41,700	42,000	43,900	43,500	45,000	45,600	45,400	46,300	48,200
40,400	40,800	42,900	42,200	43,900	44,200	44,400	45,800	46,300
46,000	46,400	47,200	48,200	49,200	50,900	49,200	48,000	54,900
57,200	59,300	61,100	63,200	65,800	65,700	65,300	67,000	67,600
55,900	56,800	56,700	57,500	62,100	61,300	59,700	60,300	62,700
29,300	28,300	29,100	29,800	34,200	30,700	30,800	29,200	30,600
45,000	45,800	47,500	46,600	51,500	47,900	47,800	50,300	52,300
63,800	65,700	64,800	65,100	69,400	69,800	67,100	67,100	70,200
61,000	63,800	65,900	68,300	70,700	71,500	72,000	74,600	73,000
24,100	23,200	22,800	22,200	25,000	24,900	23,200	24,500	21,200
43,900	49,100	49,800	49,900	51,900	54,500	55,400	54,600	52,700
63,200	65,400	66,700	69,300	71,300	71,700	71,900	74,400	73,700
79,400	79,300	82,800	86,200	89,500	88,500	88,900	93,600	91,600
76,700	78,200	82,700	87,600	87,200	86,400	86,800	88,800	92,900
27,900	30,200	31,300	33,800	35,100	33,500	34,100	34,300	38,800
39,300	41,800	41,800	45,100	43,900	44,500	47,400	45,100	51,500
26,000	28,200	29,300	31,500	33,200	30,900	31,200	31,900	36,000
16,100	16,500	17,100	16,700	17,600	16,800	16,500	17,800	17,700
28,700	29,600	30,300	31,200	32,800	31,100	30,900	31,800	36,300
42,900	45,900	46,000	50,100	52,300	45,800	47,700	45,900	48,300
50,000	53,300	54,400	54,800	57,800	59,200	55,100	57,800	56,500
22,800	**23,200**	**24,400**	**24,600**	**25,700**	**26,300**	**26,600**	**26,500**	**27,000**
25,200	26,000	25,100	24,100	25,900	25,800	26,600	26,200	27,000
23,600	23,600	24,000	23,000	24,600	24,000	23,900	25,000	24,000
35,000	40,400	32,400	30,600	33,700	33,500	35,900	30,800	38,800
21,500	21,300	21,300	21,600	22,900	23,400	22,900	23,800	23,200
20,800	20,700	20,800	21,100	22,100	23,000	22,400	23,000	22,300
30,500	29,700	28,300	29,400	34,300	28,400	27,200	30,900	30,800
24,500	25,200	26,500	27,600	28,500	28,900	29,400	28,800	29,900
10,200	10,300	9,900	9,800	11,600	11,300	11,900	11,400	11,600
28,700	29,200	29,900	30,900	31,700	32,500	33,100	32,200	33,900
20,500	21,100	23,400	22,400	23,600	24,800	24,900	24,800	25,200
11,300	10,600	10,100	10,100	11,700	11,500	12,300	12,300	13,800
24,300	25,400	28,100	26,600	27,600	28,800	28,500	28,600	28,200

Table 18.4 Average income after tax, by economic family type, by province, 2005

	Canada	Newfoundland and Labrador	Prince Edward Island	Nova Scotia
	$ 2005 constant			
Economic families	**64,800**	**50,300**	**53,200**	**56,800**
Elderly families[1]	**48,200**	35,100	40,900	42,100
Married couples	**46,300**	33,600	40,800	41,800
Other elderly families	**54,900**	38,300	F	42,900
Non-elderly families[2]	**67,600**	53,300	55,500	59,700
Married couples	**62,700**	47,600	52,600	54,600
No earner	**30,600**	24,200	F	34,200
One earner	**52,300**	40,500	43,000	46,600
Two earners	**70,200**	56,600	57,500	61,100
Two-parent families with children[3]	**73,000**	58,700	60,800	63,100
No earner	**21,200**	F	F	F
One earner	**52,700**	38,600	F	43,300
Two earners	**73,700**	61,900	58,200	62,000
Three or more earners	**91,600**	68,600	69,600	78,500
Married couples with other relatives	**92,900**	72,700	72,700	84,800
Lone-parent families[3]	**38,800**	31,200	29,700	31,900
Male lone-parent families	**51,500**	F	F	F
Female lone-parent families	**36,000**	28,900	29,000	29,400
No earner	**17,700**	F	F	F
One earner	**36,300**	29,100	28,000	28,100
Two or more earners	**48,300**	F	F	F
Other non-elderly families	**56,500**	46,600	46,600	60,700
Unattached individuals	**27,000**	**21,400**	**20,800**	**21,800**
Elderly male	**27,000**	19,100	F	22,200
Non-earner	**24,000**	19,000	F	22,200
Earner	**38,800**	F	F	F
Elderly female	**23,200**	18,500	20,200	22,000
Non-earner	**22,300**	18,500	20,300	21,900
Earner	**30,800**	F	F	F
Non-elderly male	**29,900**	23,300	19,500	21,900
Non-earner	**11,600**	F	F	10,400[E]
Earner	**33,900**	30,000	22,600	25,700
Non-elderly female	**25,200**	21,400	22,700	21,400
Non-earner	**13,800**	F	F	12,700
Earner	**28,200**	24,400	25,600	24,300

Note: "Average income after tax" refers to total income, which includes government transfers, minus income tax.

1. Families in which the major income earner is 65 years of age and older.

2. Families in which the major income earner is less than 65 of age.

3. Families with children less than 18 years of age.

Source: Statistics Canada, CANSIM table 202-0603.

New Brunswick	Quebec	Ontario	Manitoba	Saskatchewan	Alberta	British Columbia
			$ 2005 constant			
52,300	**57,000**	**70,400**	**59,300**	**59,100**	**73,200**	**65,000**
39,200	40,500	52,400	45,900	42,900	50,000	55,200
37,500	39,500	49,000	43,800	42,700	48,700	54,400
45,200	44,100	64,300	55,200	43,500	56,500E	59,100
54,700	59,800	73,500	61,600	62,300	76,700	66,800
49,000	54,500	67,600	55,700	59,600	77,100	66,200
26,900	32,300	29,700	F	F	F	35,100
46,100	49,000	54,400	43,800	43,500	69,600E	51,100
54,000	59,900	77,900	61,200	65,300	80,700	74,800
61,800	67,600	76,800	66,100	68,400	81,000	72,600
F	F	F	F	F	F	F
39,400	52,000	52,500	50,000	45,800	65,900	50,000
61,900	68,700	79,100	64,200	65,100	76,200	76,700
77,000	81,600	95,200	85,000	88,600	104,000	91,600
76,000	78,700	105,300	87,800	88,700	105,200	78,600
29,700	39,000	42,000	33,500	29,900	41,200	36,000
F	53,700	54,600	36,900	36,700	56,700	42,800E
28,000	34,300	39,500	32,700	28,800	37,300	34,700
F	17,000	19,000	F	F	F	F
26,900	33,400	41,500	31,300	27,700	35,500	35,200
F	49,700	50,900	F	F	46,700	F
43,400	48,500	60,600	59,100	51,300	59,100	57,900
20,700	**23,500**	**29,800**	**23,900**	**23,200**	**31,900**	**27,600**
21,100	23,500	31,600	24,500	24,000	30,000	26,100
19,400	21,200	26,800	22,200	22,400	30,500	23,700
F	F	46,000	F	F	F	F
20,900	20,100	26,000	21,600	20,700	24,000	24,700
20,400	19,500	25,000	20,900	20,100	22,500	23,500
F	26,800	33,700	25,500	25,600	31,900E	33,000
22,600	25,400	32,700	26,100	26,300	35,900	31,100
7,000	10,100	12,400	10,500E	9,900E	F	13,900E
26,600	29,200	37,500	28,300	29,100	37,600	35,600
18,000	23,000	27,700	22,200	20,900	29,100	24,100
12,300	12,400	16,200	11,900E	9,500E	12,100E	14,600E
19,600	26,900	30,800	24,700	23,500	31,500	25,600

Table 18.5 People in low income after tax, by age group, sex and economic family type 1991 to 2005

	1991	1992	1993	1994	1995	1996
			%			
Both sexes	**13.2**	**13.3**	**14.3**	**13.7**	**14.6**	**15.7**
0 to 17 years	15.0	14.9	16.7	15.8	17.6	18.6
18 to 64 years	12.8	13.2	13.8	13.9	14.6	15.7
65 and older	11.1	9.8	11.5	8.6	8.6	9.8
Males	12.1	12.2	13.1	12.5	13.6	14.9
0 to 17 years	15.2	15.1	16.4	15.4	17.3	19.1
18 to 64 years	11.7	12.2	12.8	12.7	13.7	14.8
65 and older	6.6	5.1	7.1	4.1	3.8	5.6
Females	14.2	14.3	15.4	14.9	15.6	16.5
0 to 17 years	14.7	14.8	17.1	16.3	17.9	18.1
18 to 64 years	13.9	14.2	14.9	15.0	15.4	16.6
65 and older	14.5	13.4	14.8	11.9	12.2	13.0
Economic families	**9.9**	**10.1**	**11.2**	**10.6**	**11.6**	**12.5**
Males	9.2	9.2	10.1	9.6	10.7	11.8
Females	10.7	11.0	12.3	11.6	12.4	13.2
0 to 17 years	15.0	14.9	16.7	15.8	17.6	18.6
Two-parent families	9.3	9.1	10.7	10.2	11.8	12.4
Female lone-parent families	54.5	49.0	50.3	50.4	53.5	55.8
Other economic families	16.1	19.3	19.1	25.2	21.5	20.4
18 to 64 years	8.7	9.0	9.8	9.5	10.3	11.2
Males	7.3	7.4	8.0	8.0	9.0	9.8
Females	10.0	10.5	11.4	10.8	11.5	12.5
65 and older	2.8	2.6	3.5	2.3	1.9	2.8ᴱ
Males	2.8	2.5	3.7	2.1	1.9	2.5ᴱ
Females	2.7	2.7	3.3	2.5	1.9	3.1ᴱ
Unattached individuals	**35.4**	**35.1**	**35.4**	**35.0**	**35.0**	**37.3**
Males	33.2	33.4	34.1	32.5	33.8	35.8
Females	37.3	36.6	36.7	37.4	36.1	38.8
0 to 64 years	37.7	38.5	38.3	39.9	39.6	41.9
Males	34.8	36.0	36.3	35.7	37.5	38.4
Females	41.5	41.9	41.3	45.7	42.5	46.9
65 and older	29.1	25.9	28.1	22.3	23.1	25.4
Males	23.8	16.9	21.3	13.1	12.1	19.8
Females	30.8	28.8	30.4	25.3	26.7	27.3

Note: Prevalence of low-income shows the proportion of people living below the low-income cut-offs within a given group; these cut-offs were determined from an analysis of the 1992 Family Expenditure Survey data.
Source: Statistics Canada, CANSIM table 202-0802.

1997	1998	1999	2000	2001	2002	2003	2004	2005
				%				
15.3	**13.7**	**13.0**	**12.5**	**11.2**	**11.6**	**11.6**	**11.4**	**10.8**
17.8	15.5	14.4	13.8	12.1	12.2	12.5	13.0	11.7
15.5	13.9	13.4	12.9	11.7	12.1	12.2	11.9	11.4
9.1	8.6	7.8	7.6	6.7	7.6	6.8	5.6	6.1
14.3	12.8	12.4	11.4	10.3	10.7	11.0	10.8	10.5
18.0	16.0	14.7	13.4	12.0	12.7	12.8	13.1	12.2
14.3	12.9	12.7	11.8	10.6	11.0	11.5	11.3	11.1
5.6	5.4	4.7	4.6	4.6	4.9	4.4	3.5	3.2
16.3	14.5	13.6	13.6	12.1	12.4	12.2	11.9	11.2
17.5	14.9	14.1	14.2	12.2	11.8	12.2	12.8	11.1
16.7	15.0	14.0	14.1	12.8	13.1	12.9	12.6	11.8
11.8	11.1	10.3	10.0	8.3	9.7	8.7	7.3	8.4
11.9	**10.4**	**9.7**	**9.3**	**8.1**	**8.6**	**8.6**	**8.2**	**7.5**
10.9	9.6	9.1	8.4	7.4	8.0	8.1	7.7	7.1
12.8	11.1	10.2	10.0	8.7	9.2	9.2	8.8	7.9
17.8	15.5	14.4	13.8	12.1	12.2	12.5	13.0	11.7
11.6	9.9	9.4	9.5	8.3	7.3	7.9	8.4	7.8
53.2	46.1	41.9	40.1	37.4	43.0	41.2	40.4	33.4
23.6	20.0	21.4	12.8	8.9[E]	9.1[E]	12.2[E]	13.0[E]	11.8[E]
10.6	9.2	8.8	8.4	7.3	8.1	8.1	7.5	6.9
8.9	7.8	7.8	7.4	6.3	7.0	7.2	6.4	6.0
12.1	10.6	9.8	9.5	8.3	9.2	9.0	8.4	7.7
3.4[E]	3.3[E]	2.2[E]	2.1[E]	1.9[E]	2.4	2.2	1.6[E]	1.2[E]
3.0[E]	2.7[E]	2.0[E]	1.7[E]	1.9[E]	2.3[E]	2.0[E]	1.7[E]	1.1[E]
3.8[E]	3.9[E]	2.3[E]	2.5[E]	1.9[E]	2.4[E]	2.3[E]	1.6[E]	1.3[E]
37.9	**35.1**	**34.0**	**32.9**	**30.8**	**29.5**	**29.6**	**30.1**	**30.4**
36.6	33.8	32.9	30.0	28.4	27.1	28.4	29.2	29.8
39.2	36.4	35.1	35.6	33.2	32.0	30.8	31.0	31.0
43.8	40.4	38.7	37.3	35.3	33.2	33.8	35.0	34.3
39.8	36.5	35.4	32.1	30.3	29.0	30.7	32.0	32.3
49.5	45.8	43.4	44.3	42.1	39.0	38.0	39.3	37.1
22.0	20.8	21.0	20.6	18.1	19.4	17.7	15.4	18.4
17.2	17.5	17.2	17.6	16.8	15.9	14.7	11.5	13.4
23.7	22.0	22.3	21.6	18.6	20.7	18.9	16.9	20.3

Table 18.6 Average household expenditures, by province and territory, 2005

	Canada	Newfoundland and Labrador	Prince Edward Island	Nova Scotia	New Brunswick
			$		
Total expenditures	**66,857**	**52,612**	**53,007**	**56,105**	**53,714**
Total current consumption	**47,484**	38,250	38,887	41,038	39,370
Food	**7,135**	6,270	6,230	6,403	6,135
Shelter	**12,614**	8,415	9,652	10,097	9,074
Household operation	**3,091**	2,742	2,887	3,081	2,931
Household furnishings and equipment	**1,969**	1,810	1,619	1,607	1,632
Clothing	**2,588**	2,330	2,068	2,087	2,034
Transportation	**9,073**	7,635	7,209	7,922	8,335
Health care	**1,799**	1,524	1,820	1,693	1,772
Personal care	**1,094**	994	957	965	916
Recreation	**3,918**	3,263	2,794	3,219	3,279
Reading materials and other printed matter	**284**	199	269	263	232
Education	**1,219**	867	983	1,012	755
Tobacco products and alcoholic beverages	**1,422**	1,332	1,453	1,468	1,350
Games of chance (net amount)	**278**	270	273	320	239
Miscellaneous	**1,001**	599	672	901	688
Personal income taxes	**13,698**	10,123	9,356	10,207	9,865
Personal insurance payments and pension contributions	**3,921**	3,106	3,339	3,388	3,314
Gifts of money and contributions	**1,753**	1,133	1,424	1,471	1,165

Source: Statistics Canada, CANSIM table 203-0001.

Quebec	Ontario	Manitoba	Saskatchewan	Alberta	British Columbia	Yukon	Northwest Territories	Nunavut
					$			
55,348	75,920	60,181	57,734	75,346	68,231	64,477	89,729	64,225
39,418	52,926	41,579	41,337	53,019	51,002	45,660	62,201	46,327
6,900	7,431	6,351	5,854	7,390	7,502	7,350	10,002	12,819
9,715	15,135	9,997	9,924	13,137	13,899	11,428	17,692	10,027
2,420	3,452	2,810	2,879	3,569	3,228	3,010	3,820	3,082
1,623	2,160	1,705	1,772	2,432	2,057	1,559	1,944	1,916
2,189	2,936	2,179	2,231	2,889	2,611	2,120	3,564	2,739
7,132	10,351	8,253	8,387	10,301	9,366	9,390	10,503	4,607
1,861	1,587	1,558	1,712	2,130	2,185	949	1,373	735
1,022	1,167	977	989	1,236	1,058	877	1,277	902
3,235	4,089	3,859	3,998	5,100	4,246	4,905	6,166	5,347
232	325	279	244	303	288	362	327	136
650	1,620	964	843	1,348	1,453	477	591	235
1,365	1,288	1,298	1,330	1,759	1,693	2,185	3,182	2,771
230	301	360	252	295	274	327	638	407
845	1,083	989	919	1,132	1,143	720	1,121	606
11,464	16,308	12,571	10,792	16,094	11,921	13,411	20,949	13,467
3,634	4,388	3,819	3,742	4,043	3,492	3,850	5,299	3,246
831	2,299	2,211	1,863	2,190	1,816	1,557	1,279	1,186

Table 18.7 Assets and debts held by family units, 1999 and 2005

	1999			2005		
	$ 2005 constant	thousands of family units	% holding assets and debts	$ 2005 constant	thousands of family units	% holding assets and debts
Assets	**184,622**	**12,216**	**100.0**	**229,930**	**13,348**	**100.0**
Private pension assets[1]	57,602	8,511	69.7	68,020	9,417	70.6
RRSPs, LIRAs, RRIFs and other[2]	23,041	7,197	58.9	30,000	7,748	58.0
EPPs[3]	56,214	5,611	45.9	68,305	6,490	48.6
Financial assets, non-pension	5,299	10,965	89.8	6,100	11,932	89.4
Deposits in financial institutions	2,880	10,685	87.5	3,600	11,613	87.0
Mutual funds, investment funds and income trusts	14,976	1,706	14.0	24,200	1,641	12.3
Stocks	10,368	1,207	9.9	11,500	1,321	9.9
Bonds (savings and other)	2,880	1,715	14.0	2,500	1,394	10.4
Other financial assets[4]	5,530	1,615	13.2	6,000	2,329	17.5
Non-financial assets	115,204	12,216	100.0	141,700	13,348	100.0
Principal residence	144,005	7,278	59.6	180,000	8,265	61.9
Other real estate	72,578	1,987	16.3	85,000	2,142	16.1
Vehicles	10,368	9,346	76.5	11,557	10,062	75.4
Other non-financial assets[5]	11,520	12,216	100.0	10,000	13,348	100.0
Equity in business	10,368	2,325	19.0	15,794	2,221	16.6
Debts	**32,257**	**8,215**	**67.3**	**44,500**	**9,263**	**69.4**
Mortgages	79,490	4,191	34.3	93,000	4,870	36.5
Principal residence	76,610	3,908	32.0	90,000	4,557	34.1
Other real estate	69,122	563	4.6	90,000	624	4.7
Line of credit	5,760	1,880	15.4	9,000	3,323	24.9
Credit card and installment debt[6]	2,074	4,648	38.0	2,400	5,252	39.3
Student loans	8,295	1,435	11.7	9,000	1,574	11.8
Vehicle loans	10,368	2,541	20.8	11,000	3,449	25.8
Other debt	4,608	1,983	16.2	6,000	1,878	14.1
Net worth (assets less debts)[7]	**120,451**	**12,209**	**99.9**	**148,350**	**13,342**	**100.0**

Notes: Family units include economic families.
Median amounts.

1. Excludes public plans administered or sponsored by governments: Old Age Security including the Guaranteed Income Supplement and the Spouse's Allowance, as well as the Canada Pension Plan/Quebec Pension Plan.
2. Registered Retirement Savings Plans (RRSPs), Locked-in-Retirement Accounts (LIRAs), Registered Retirement Income Funds (RRIFs). Other includes Deferred Profit Sharing Plans (DPSPs), annuities and other miscellaneous pension assets.
3. Employer-sponsored Registered Pension Plans (EPPs). Valued on a termination basis. Only plan membership to the time of the Survey of Financial Security was considered. Interest rates are assumed based on current market rates.
4. Includes Registered Education Savings Plans (RESPs), treasury bills, mortgage-backed securities, money held in trust, money owed to the respondent and other miscellaneous financial assets, including shares of privately-held companies.
5. The value of the contents of the respondent's principal residence, valuables and collectibles, copyrights and patents, etc.
6. Includes major credit cards and retail store cards, gasoline station cards, etc. Instalment debt is the total amount owing on deferred payment or instalment plans where the purchased item is to be paid for over a period of time.
7. For net worth, the median has been calculated based on all applicable family units, not just those with net worth greater or less than $0. The number and percentage of family units with net worth, however, are those with net worth greater or less than $0.

Source: Statistics Canada, Survey of Financial Security.

Table 18.8 Assets and debts held by family units, by education level, 1999 and 2005

	1999		2005	
	$ 2005 constant	thousands of family units	$ 2005 constant	thousands of family units
All education levels[1]				
Assets[2]	184,622	12,216	229,930	13,348
Debts	32,257	8,215	44,500	9,263
Net worth (assets less debts)	120,451	12,209	148,350	13,342
Less than high school				
Assets[2]	118,660	3,375	114,198	2,813
Debts	13,248	1,723	14,400	1,408
Net worth (assets less debts)	87,901	3,370	92,433	2,806
Graduated high school				
Assets[2]	168,773	2,869	202,000	3,508
Debts	32,031	2,007	42,073	2,470
Net worth (assets less debts)	103,039	2,868	120,007	3,508
Non-university postsecondary certificate				
Assets[2]	191,579	3,434	251,125	3,737
Debts	38,017	2,579	45,500	2,907
Net worth (assets less debts)	117,841	3,432	171,000	3,737
University degree or certificate				
Assets[2]	313,354	2,539	370,500	3,290
Debts	54,155	1,907	78,130	2,478
Net worth (assets less debts)	**220,161**	**2,539**	**237,400**	**3,290**

Notes: Family units include economic families.

Median amounts.

1. "Education level" refers to the education level of an unattached individual or, for families, the major income recipient.

2. Includes Employer-sponsored Registered Pension Plans. These plans were valued on a termination basis. Only plan membership to the time of the Survey of Financial Security was considered. Interest rates are assumed based on current market rates. Excludes public plans administered or sponsored by governments: Old Age Security including the Guaranteed Income Supplement and the Spouse's Allowance, as well as the Canada Pension Plan/Quebec Pension Plan.

Source: Statistics Canada, Survey of Financial Security.

Table 18.9 Net worth of family units, by sex and age group, 2005

	Family units	Net worth[1]		
	%	%	$ 2005 constant[2]	debt-to-asset ratio
Both sexes, all ages[2]	**100.0**	**100.0**	**148,350**	**0.14**
Less than 65	82.0	76.0	120,200	0.17
Less than 35	25.0	5.3	18,750	0.39
35 to 44	21.8	18.2	135,408	0.24
45 to 54	20.7	26.6	231,900	0.13
55 to 64	14.5	25.9	407,417	0.07
65 and older	18.0	24.0	303,167	0.02
Males, all ages	**100.0**	**100.0**	**184,964**	**0.14**
Less than 65	83.4	75.9	151,471	0.17
Less than 35	23.9	5.2	28,203	0.41
35 to 44	22.5	18.1	150,225	0.25
45 to 54	21.7	25.9	273,483	0.13
55 to 64	15.3	26.8	448,795	0.07
65 and older	16.6	24.1	405,000	0.02
Females, all ages	**100.0**	**100.0**	**105,470**	**0.13**
Less than 65	79.9	76.2	76,499	0.16
Less than 35	26.6	5.6	9,900	0.37
35 to 44	20.7	18.6	96,856	0.22
45 to 54	19.2	28.1	178,650	0.14
55 to 64	13.4	24.0	345,877	0.07
65 and older	20.1	23.8	204,833	F

Notes: Family units include economic families.

Sex and age groups refer to an unattached individual or, for families, the major income recipient.

1. Net worth includes employer-sponsored registered pension plans valued on a termination basis.
2. Median amount.

Source: Statistics Canada, Survey of Financial Security.

Table 18.10 Family units and net worth, by net worth group, 2005

	Family units		Net worth[1]	
	thousands	%	$ millions 2005 constant	%
All family units' net worth groups[2]	**13,348**	**100.0**	**4,862,486**	**100.0**
Negative net worth	872	6.5	-12,751	-0.3
Less than $5,000	1,220	9.1	2,068	0.0
$5,000 to $14,999	854	6.4	7,762	0.2
$15,000 to $29,999	791	5.9	17,149	0.4
$30,000 to $49,999	602	4.5	23,235	0.5
$50,000 to $74,999	760	5.7	46,275	1.0
$75,000 to $99,999	583	4.4	51,702	1.1
$100,000 to $149,999	1,020	7.6	127,010	2.6
$150,000 to $249,999	1,487	11.1	293,647	6.0
$250,000 to $499,999	2,253	16.9	813,922	16.7
$500,000 to $999,999	1,807	13.5	1,233,616	25.4
$1,000,000 and over	1,098	8.2	2,258,851	46.5

Note: Family units include economic families.

1. Net worth includes employer-sponsored registered pension plans valued on a termination basis.
2. Includes family units with net worth of $0.

Source: Statistics Canada, Survey of Financial Security.

Table 18.11 Retirement savings through Registered Retirement Savings Plans and Registered Pension Plans, 2004

	Taxfilers[1] who save	Average savings[2]	Share of savings in RRSP[2]	Share of savings in RPP[2]	Share of income[3] saved
	thousands	$	%		
Both sexes	**7,941**	**6,402**	**49.6**	**50.4**	**10.9**
Under $10,000	147	1,314	45.4	54.6	24.7
$10,000 to $19,999	508	1,596	69.3	30.7	10.1
$20,000 to $29,999	991	2,370	59.1	40.9	9.3
$30,000 to $39,999	1,396	3,523	50.8	49.2	10.1
$40,000 to $59,999	2,325	5,785	44.4	55.6	11.8
$60,000 to $79,999	1,343	9,180	41.1	58.9	13.3
$80,000 and over	1,231	13,638	57.4	42.6	9.4
Men	**4,202**	**7,293**	**51.7**	**48.3**	**10.4**
Under $10,000	42	1,533	41.1	58.9	30.7
$10,000 to $19,999	145	1,795	75.1	24.9	11.4
$20,000 to $29,999	338	2,370	68.3	31.7	9.3
$30,000 to $39,999	584	3,306	57.8	42.2	9.4
$40,000 to $59,999	1,282	5,522	47.0	53.0	11.1
$60,000 to $79,999	877	8,823	42.8	57.3	12.8
$80,000 and over	935	13,657	57.4	42.6	9.1
Women	**3,740**	**5,400**	**46.4**	**53.6**	**11.8**
Under $10,000	106	1,228	47.5	52.5	22.5
$10,000 to $19,999	364	1,517	66.5	33.5	9.6
$20,000 to $29,999	653	2,371	54.4	45.6	9.3
$30,000 to $39,999	812	3,680	46.4	53.6	10.5
$40,000 to $59,999	1,043	6,107	41.5	58.5	12.6
$60,000 to $79,999	466	9,852	38.4	61.6	14.4
$80,000 and over	296	13,576	57.3	42.8	10.7

1. Includes taxfilers aged 25 to 64 as of December 31, 2004.

2. Savings refer to Registered Retirement Savings Plan (RRSP) contributions and pension adjustment as reported for the 2004 tax year. The pension adjustment is used to estimate retirement savings through Registered Pension Plans (RPPs).

3. Income as reported on line 150 of the income tax return.

Source: Statistics Canada, Catalogue no. 74-507-XCB.

Table 18.12 Private pension assets of family units, by selected family characteristics, 1999 and 2005

	1999			2005		
	All family units	Family units with private pension assets[1]		All family units	Family units with private pension assets[1]	
	%	%	$ 2005 constant[2]	%	%	$ 2005 constant[2]
All ages	**100.0**	**100.0**	**57,602**	**100.0**	**100.0**	**68,020**
Less than 35	25.4	4.8	11,515	25.0	3.1	10,421
35 to 44	25.2	14.4	40,545	21.8	11.8	47,000
45 to 54	19.1	25.8	97,923	20.7	26.4	121,052
55 to 64	11.9	27.8	188,632	14.5	32.8	242,547
65 and older	18.4	27.2	131,781	18.0	25.9	156,613
All after-tax income groups	**100.0**	**100.0**	**57,602**	**100.0**	**100.0**	**68,020**
Less than $20,000	23.5	4.5	16,179	21.0	2.6	F
$20,000 to $29,999	15.6	7.2	28,801	15.8	6.4	30,000
$30,000 to $39,999	15.0	11.6	34,561	13.8	8.7	40,000
$40,000 to $49,999	12.2	12.7	45,230	11.2	10.8	58,201
$50,000 to $74,999	19.3	27.0	66,568	19.6	27.5	69,567
$75,000 and more	14.2	37.0	150,124	18.6	44.1	187,275
All education levels	**100.0**	**100.0**	**57,602**	**100.0**	**100.0**	**68,020**
Less than high school	27.6	17.1	53,789	21.1	12.2	75,000
Graduated high school	23.5	20.5	48,197	26.3	21.9	60,000
Non-university postsecondary certificate	28.1	23.9	46,081	28.0	26.1	62,116
University degree or certificate	20.8	38.5	95,619	24.6	39.8	90,000
Employment status	**100.0**	**100.0**	**57,602**	**100.0**	**100.0**	**68,020**
Paid worker	56.2	48.0	42,169	58.1	52.6	52,486
Self-employed	10.2	11.0	50,114	9.8	9.1	60,000
Unpaid or not employed	33.6	41.1	121,230	32.0	38.3	149,512
Home ownership status	**100.0**	**100.0**	**57,602**	**100.0**	**100.0**	**68,020**
Own with mortgage	32.0	32.2	51,842	34.1	33.0	57,516
Own without mortgage	27.6	56.6	144,274	27.8	57.6	200,841
Do not own	40.4	11.2	16,772	38.1	9.4	15,000

Notes: Family units include economic families.

Characteristics refer to an unattached individual or, for families, the major income recipient.

Excludes public plans administered or sponsored by governments: Old Age Security including the Guaranteed Income Supplement and the Spouse's Allowance, as well as the Canada Pension Plan/Quebec Pension Plan.

1. The percentage of family units and median amounts include those with private pension assets other than Employer-sponsored Registered Pension Plans, Registered Retirement Savings Plans and Registered Retirement Income Funds. The aggregate amount in other pension assets is relatively small (about 5% of total private pension assets) and includes such things as annuities and Deferred Profit Sharing Plans.

2. Median amounts.

Source: Statistics Canada, Survey of Financial Security.

Information and communications technology

19

OVERVIEW

Information and communications technologies (ICTs) play a major role in Canadians' daily lives. Technologies such as wireless networks, software and the Internet have transformed the way we communicate and access information at home, work, school and on our daily commutes.

In 2005, almost 17 million adult Canadians, or 68% of the population age 18 and older, used the Internet for personal, non-business reasons. About 90% of them, 15 million, accessed it from home.

The vast majority of home users, 91%, went online to send and receive e-mail, and 84% used the Internet for general browsing. Gathering information and conducting personal business took precedence over entertainment, such as playing games or listening to the radio online. Roughly 6 out of 10 adult Internet users accessed weather or road reports, viewed news and sports, searched for medical or health-related information, obtained travel information and made bookings, and did personal banking.

About 50% of those using the Internet from home in 2005 did so via a cable connection; 44% used a telephone line. Over 80% of all home Internet users had a high-speed connection. Internet use is concentrated in urban areas, among adults under 45, people with postsecondary education, in households with children and in high-income households.

Businesses also use the Internet to their advantage. Private sector businesses' online sales surged 42% in 2006 from the year before to $46.5 billion. Most of these transactions, $31.4 billion worth, were business-to-business sales. In 2006, 45% of Canadian firms made purchases online. The

Chart 19.1
Selected Internet activities of adult home users, 2005

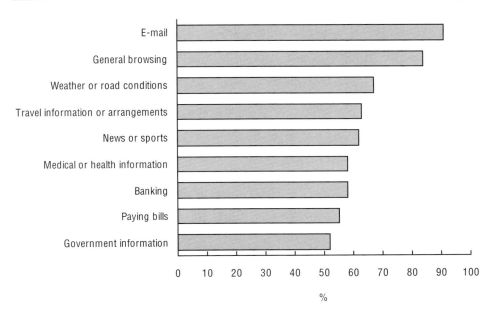

Source: Statistics Canada, CANSIM table 358-0130.

principal benefits of conducting business over the Internet were reaching new customers (36% of firms) and better coordination with suppliers, customers or partners (35%). Only 27% reported that conducting business over the Internet lowered costs.

Households spending more on technologies

Canadians spent more on Internet access, cell phone and other wireless services, computer hardware, and satellite and cable television subscriptions in 2005 than in 2004. In contrast, household spending on telephone land-line, or wireline, services continued to decline.

Annual spending on cell phone and other wireless services reached an average $410 per household in 2005, up more than 21% from 2004, whereas annual spending on wireline telephone service fell 3% to an average $680. Households spent 8% more on computer hardware in 2005, averaging $290 and almost matching the peak set in 2000.

Households also upped their spending on Internet access 15% in 2005, from 2004,

Chart 19.2
Households with only a cell phone, December 2005

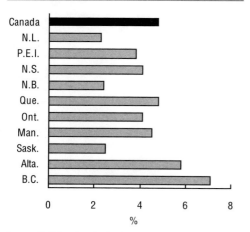

Source: Statistics Canada, Catalogue no. 56M0001XCB.

Internet users, by sex and age group, 2005

	Men	Women
	%	
18 to 34	88.2	89.7
35 to 54	72.6	77.4
55 to 64	52.0	55.6
65 and older	28.7	19.8

Source: Statistics Canada, CANSIM table 358-0124.

to an average $240. The proportion of households having high-speed Internet access grew to 50% in 2005, up from 43% in 2004.

One in five households owned a satellite television receiver in 2005, about the same proportion as in 2004. However, in 2005 average annual household spending on satellite subscriptions rose 17% from the year before to $138. More than three in five households subscribed to cable television in 2005: spending on these services rose only 1% from 2004, to $348.

Wireless is winning

Wireless communications technology again gained market share in 2006, and was the telecommunications industry's most profitable segment, with operating profit margins of almost 32%. The wireline providers' profit margins were half that, 16%.

Wireless telephone subscriptions rose above the 18-million mark in 2006, whereas the number of residential telephone wirelines fell to just over 11 million. The loss of residential telephone customers lowered the operating profits for providers of traditional wireline systems by 14% in 2006 to $3.5 billion.

Not only has the wireless industry continued to attract more subscribers, but it has also persuaded subscribers to make greater use of their devices and to spend more on services. At the end of 2006, operating revenue per subscriber had risen 7.2% to $190 per subscriber, compared with $177 in 2005.

But the most striking change in the wireless market is the convergence in usage rates with traditional phone services. At the end of 2006, Canada had 55.1 mobile subscribers per 100 inhabitants and 55.3 traditional wireline access lines per 100 inhabitants. That compares with 18.7 wireless subscribers per 100 inhabitants and 64.4 traditional wireline access lines per 100 inhabitants at the end of the first quarter of 1999. Clearly, more and more Canadians are adopting the technology as their principal telephone.

Sector maintains strength

The ICT sector contributed $65.0 billion in 2006 to Canada's gross domestic product (GDP), accounting for 6% of total GDP—the same proportion as the year before. ICT services account for the majority of this sector's revenues, 82% in 2006. ICT manufacturing accounted for 31% of this sector's GDP at its peak in 2000. However, their contribution was halved to 16% by 2002, a level ICT manufacturing still held in 2006.

Research and development (R&D) investment by the ICT sector in 2006 was over $5.7 billion, about the same as in 2005. Annual R&D expenditures reached a high of $6.6

billion in 2001, but dropped to $5.3 billion in 2002 as the high-tech downturn took hold. Investment in R&D by the ICT sector accounted for 39% of total private sector R&D expenditures in 2006.

ICT manufacturing industries are among the most innovative in the manufacturing sector. Eighty percent of ICT manufacturing plants introduced a new or significantly improved product or production process to the market from 2002 to 2004. The top two ICT manufacturing industries were computer and peripheral equipment manufacturing, and radio and television broadcasting and wireless communications equipment manufacturing, in which 89% of plants were innovative.

Selected sources

Statistics Canada

- *Broadcasting and Telecommunications.* Irregular. 56-001-XIE

- *Canadian Internet Use Survey - Public Use Microdata File.* Biennial. 56M0003XCB

- *Connectedness Series.* Occasional. 56F0004MIE

- *The Digital Divide in Canada.* Occasional. 56F0009XIE

- *Innovation Analysis Bulletin.* Irregular. 88-003-XIE

- *Quarterly Telecommunications Statistics.* Quarterly. 56-002-XIE

- *Residential Telephone Service Survey.* Semi-annual. 56M0001XCB

Other

- Canada Post Annual Report 2006. Annual.

Chart 19.3
Research and development expenditures

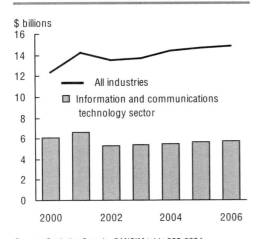

Source: Statistics Canada, CANSIM table 358-0024.

Who's using open-source software?

Just 14% of Canada's private sector firms reported using open-source software in 2006. 'Open source' means that the software's source code—the instructions that make the application run—is in the public domain. Anyone can view, modify and redistribute the software without paying royalties or licensing fees; the code evolves through collaboration. Open-source software can be updated much more quickly than conventional commercial software, whose source code is proprietary, meaning it is not released to the public for use or modification.

The public sector adopts new ICTs more rapidly than the private sector does, and open-source software is no exception: 51% of public sector firms were using this software in 2006.

The private sector's reluctance to adopt open-source software contrasts with its stronger connections to the Internet. In 2006, 45% of private firms purchased goods and services online, and 40% had a website.

Large private firms are more likely to use and be early adopters of advanced and innovative technologies: 34% of large firms used open-source software in 2006; only 13% of small firms did.

Firms using open-source software are seeing its benefits. In the past, concerns about stability and features prevented its widespread adoption. Today, open-source software enables firms to adapt quickly to their changing ICT needs.

Firms in information and cultural industries are most likely to use open-source software: 43% of them did so in 2006, as did 25% of utilities and educational services firms and 25% of professional, scientific and technical services firms.

Chart 19.4
Use of open-source software, by sector

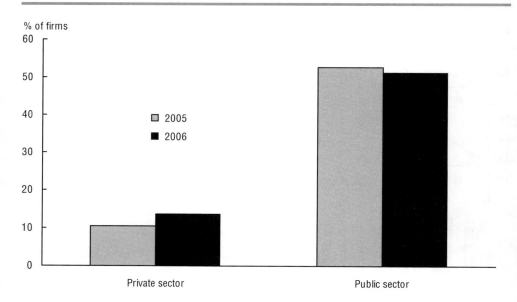

% of firms

2005
2006

Private sector

Public sector

Source: Statistics Canada, CANSIM table 358-0121.

Who's shopping on the Internet?

Over 9 million Canadians aged 18 and older window-shopped on the Internet in 2005. Nearly 7 million of us—about 41% of all adults who used the Internet that year—bought something online.

Whether browsing an online bookshop, comparing new car specifications and pricing at various dealers, or ordering new furniture, it is all called Internet shopping. Canadians might choose to shop online for the 24-hour convenience, the ease of comparing vendors' prices or access to merchants regardless of distance.

Canadian adults used the Internet to order $7.9 billion worth of goods and services for personal and household consumption in 2005. They placed almost 50 million orders online. However, e-commerce—the value of orders placed on the Internet—is still a small fraction of the $761 billion in personal

expenditures on goods and services that Canadians made in 2005.

The most popular online purchases Canadians made were travel services, such as hotel reservations and car rentals, followed closely by books and magazines. Entertainment items, such as concert tickets, as well as clothing, jewellery and accessories are also commonly bought online. The most popular items for window shopping are consumer electronics, housewares such as appliances and furniture, clothing, accessories and jewellery, and travel services.

About three-quarters of adults who placed an Internet order in 2005 paid directly online with a credit or debit card. However, security concerns may hinder e-commerce growth: 48% of Internet window shoppers who made purchases after searching online said they were very concerned about credit card security on the Internet..

Chart 19.5
Internet orders, average value per person, by vendor location, 2005

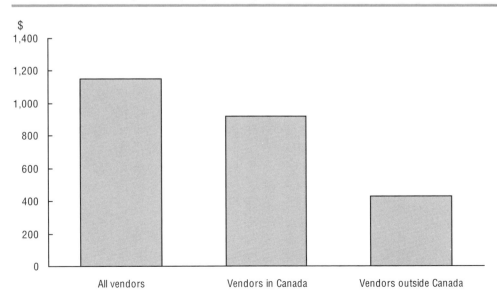

Note: Electronic orders for personal or household consumption.
Source: Statistics Canada, CANSIM table 358-0137.

Convergence and the cable industry

ICTs are not only changing the lives of people, they are also changing the way businesses operate. The transformation of the cable television industry is a good example.

In the late 1990s and early 2000s, the cable television industry invested heavily in ICTs to modernize its networks. These investments enabled the industry to offer Internet and telephone services and to provide digital television services comparable with those offered by satellite television operators. These investments drastically changed the industry.

Less than 10 years after introducing Internet services by cable in a few test markets, the cable television industry signed up its three-millionth Internet customer in 2005. At the end of August 2005, it had close to one Internet subscriber for every two television subscribers.

Cable companies were slower to launch telephone service, but a few major cable operators entered that market in 2005. Together they had slightly more than 200,000 clients as of August 31 of that year.

Consequently, the industry relies less and less on revenues from its traditional television services. Internet and telephony generated $1.4 billion in revenue in 2005, or just over 28% of the industry's total subscription revenues. Five years earlier, non-traditional services accounted for less than 8% of their revenues.

Digital technology has also enabled traditional telephone companies to offer television services via telephone land lines, pushing convergence of the telephone and cable television industries to another level.

Chart 19.6
Subscribers to Internet through cable companies

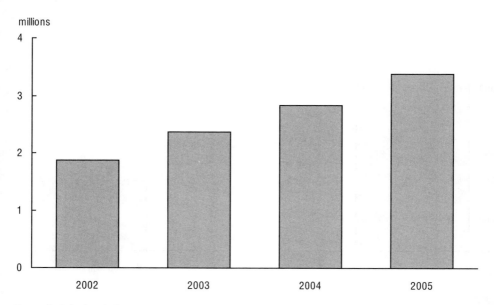

Source: Statistics Canada, Catalogue no. 56-001-XIE.

Life in digital times

The introduction of digital technology brought predictions of a paperless society and the end of traditional mail. Neither of these predictions has yet come true, but the widespread use of ICTs have brought about some interesting shifts in behaviour.

The arrival of the personal computer was supposed to lead to the paperless office. However, from 1985 to 2005, estimated consumption of printing and writing paper in Canada increased 73%, and most of that growth occurred from 1985 to 1995.

The volume of postal mail has also been rising. In 2006, Canada Post delivered 11.6 billion pieces of mail and parcels, including about 9 million Census forms for Statistics Canada. Couriers and local messengers are proliferating, even with the high usage of Internet and e-mail.

One extremely visible outcome of ICTs is

that the information society is a talkative society. Canadians have never spoken on the telephone more, despite also sending and receiving massive amounts of e-mail and other electronic communications. As people communicate more and in different ways, they are choosing to expand their associations, moving from geographically defined communities to communities of interest.

They are also willing to pay for their choices, as consumer spending patterns show. From 1997 to 2005, average annual spending by households on Internet services rose from $30 to $241. In the same period, spending on wireline telephone services dropped from $725 to $640.

Chart 19.7
Telephone use indicators

billions of minutes

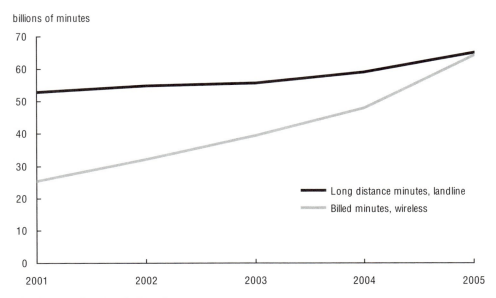

Long distance minutes, landline
Billed minutes, wireless

1. Data include local and long distance calls.
Sources: Statistics Canada, Catalogue no. 56-002-XIE; CRTC Telecommunications Monitoring Report, July 2006.

Table 19.1 Gross domestic product at basic prices, information and cultural industries, 1992 to 2006

	1992	1993	1994	1995	1996	1997
	\$ millions 1997 constant					
Information and cultural industries	**22,206**	**22,269**	**22,985**	**23,786**	**24,130**	**27,979**
Publishing industries, information services and data processing services	4,406	4,214	4,284	4,366	4,364	7,748
Publishing industries	..	..	..	..	..	6,211
Information services and data processing services	..	..	..	..	..	1,537
Motion picture and sound recording industries	1,201	1,411	1,460	1,595	1,671	1,718
Broadcasting and telecommunications	16,585	16,628	17,215	17,800	18,067	18,513
Special aggregations						
All information and communication technology industries	..	..	..	..	..	32,707
Manufacturing of information and communication technology	..	..	..	..	..	8,233
Services in information and communication technology	..	..	..	..	..	24,474

Note: North American Industry Classification System (NAICS), 2002.
Source: Statistics Canada, CANSIM tables 379-0017 and 379-0020.

Table 19.2 Employment, information and cultural industries, 1993 to 2006

	1993	1994	1995	1996	1997
	number				
Information and cultural industries	**279,504**	**279,777**	**284,566**	**283,051**	**288,372**
Publishing industries	71,566	68,555	68,679	69,542	72,250
Newspaper, periodical, book and database publishers	64,382	60,559	59,939	59,531	60,229
Software publishers	7,184	7,996	8,740	10,010	12,021
Motion picture and sound recording industries	24,456	25,210	25,234	26,895	29,912
Motion picture and video industries	22,778	23,552	23,488	24,944	27,791
Sound recording industries	1,678	1,657	1,746	1,950	2,121
Broadcasting (excluding Internet)	36,318	36,051	36,381	37,064	37,008
Radio and television broadcasting	35,378	35,071	35,429	36,098	36,074
Pay and specialty television	940	980	953	966	934
Internet publishing and broadcasting	..	..	..	..	..
Telecommunications	114,896	116,554	120,488	114,248	113,820
Wired telecommunications carriers	70,704	71,542	73,418	68,960	68,789
Wireless telecommunications carriers (excluding satellite)	22,089	22,734	23,567	22,339	22,355
Telecommunications resellers	5,788	6,188	6,614	5,743	5,423
Satellite telecommunications	2,504	2,560	2,606	2,425	2,502
Cable and other program distribution	13,403	13,121	13,857	14,343	14,316
Other telecommunications	407	409	427	438	435
Internet service providers, web search portals, and data processing services	x	x	x	x	x
Internet service providers, web search portals	x	x	x	x	x
Data processing, hosting, and related services	4,186	4,728	5,304	5,905	7,033
Other information services	x	x	x	x	x

Note: North American Industry Classification System (NAICS), 2002.
Source: Statistics Canada, CANSIM table 281-0024.

1998	1999	2000	2001	2002	2003	2004	2005	2006
				$ millions 1997 constant				
29,866	**33,658**	**36,356**	**39,232**	**41,017**	**41,924**	**42,534**	**44,258**	**45,311**
8,534	9,420	9,716	10,568	10,679	10,908	10,802	11,296	11,628
7,011	7,674	7,828	8,463	8,404	8,470	8,303	8,767	9,020
1,523	1,746	1,888	2,105	2,275	2,438	2,499	2,529	2,608
1,915	2,072	2,114	2,204	2,315	2,168	2,118	2,135	2,051
19,417	22,166	24,526	26,460	28,023	28,848	29,614	30,827	31,632
37,744	48,037	56,811	53,404	53,492	57,085	59,076	62,343	65,354
9,788	13,678	18,101	11,255	9,291	10,294	10,783	11,665	12,156
27,956	34,359	38,710	42,149	44,201	46,791	48,293	50,678	53,198

1998	1999	2000	2001	2002	2003	2004	2005	2006
				number				
297,503	**304,067**	**318,783**	**328,509**	**329,770**	**335,202**	**335,136**	**341,786**	**349,519**
75,475	76,656	83,152	85,653	86,087	x	82,512	85,371	85,787
61,348	59,589	62,964	63,030	62,694	x	59,546	60,252	58,638
14,127	17,066	20,188	22,623	23,393	22,526	22,966	25,119	27,148
32,735	34,306	36,622	38,228	38,694	37,872	35,549	36,065	34,037
30,430	31,954	34,213	35,872	36,260	35,256	32,659	33,023	31,346
2,305	2,351	2,409	2,356	2,434	2,616	2,890	3,041	2,691
37,837	37,453	37,634	37,436	37,822	39,006	39,888	39,103	42,369
36,897	36,550	36,764	35,975	36,125	37,005	37,775	37,035	40,122
941	902	870	1,460	1,698	2,000	2,113	2,068	2,247
..	..	..	0	x	x	434	1,006	1,583
115,881	116,265	118,426	119,036	119,764	125,999	130,441	134,758	139,228
70,457	70,740	72,257	71,344	72,297	76,811	78,991	80,415	80,788
22,367	22,257	22,837	23,176	22,661	23,206	23,142	23,351	24,689
5,527	5,457	5,562	6,294	6,072	5,266	5,732	6,276	7,041
2,574	2,571	2,641	3,300	3,759	4,883	5,731	6,202	6,792
14,545	14,863	14,734	14,616	14,720	15,614	16,580	18,251	19,516
410	377	395	306	256	218	264	264	401
x	x	x	x	x	x	19,860	19,125	19,368
x	x	x	x	x	x	6,146	5,969	5,635
8,248	10,233	11,939	14,344	13,963	13,628	13,715	13,156	13,733
x	x	x	x	x	x	26,452	26,358	27,148

Table 19.3 Time spent watching television, by selected age groups and by province, 2004

	Population aged 2 and older	Children aged 2 to 11	Adolescents aged 12 to 17	Population aged 18 and older	
				Men	Women
			average hours per week		
Canada	**21.4**	**14.1**	**12.9**	**20.9**	**25.6**
Newfoundland and Labrador	22.7	18.9	12.3	21.3	26.8
Prince Edward Island	20.0	14.5	12.3	19.8	23.5
Nova Scotia	22.7	12.9	13.8	22.4	27.2
New Brunswick	23.7	14.7	12.6	23.2	28.4
Quebec[1]	23.3	14.3	13.5	22.4	28.5
Anglophones	20.6	14.2	13.4	19.8	24.2
Francophones	23.8	14.3	13.7	22.9	29.2
Ontario	20.6	13.5	13.2	20.1	24.7
Manitoba	22.1	15.5	13.0	22.0	26.4
Saskatchewan	21.2	15.2	12.7	20.5	25.7
Alberta	19.4	14.1	12.4	18.2	23.9
British Columbia	20.7	14.4	11.7	21.5	23.4

Note: Data are collected over the fall period (four weeks of November).

1. For Quebec, the language classification is based on the language spoken at home. For Quebec as a total, respondents who did not reply to this question or who indicated a language other than English or French are included.

Source: Statistics Canada, CANSIM tables 502-0002 and 502-0003.

Table 19.4 Time spent watching television, by type of program, 2004

	Canadian and foreign programs	Canadian programs	Foreign programs
	% of hours		
All program types	**100.0**	**37.2**	**62.8**
News and public affairs	**24.4**	18.4	6.0
Documentary	**3.2**	1.3	1.9
Academic instruction	**3.2**	1.7	1.5
Social and/or recreational instruction	**1.1**	0.4	0.6
Religion	**0.3**	0.2	0.1
Sports	**6.5**	2.9	3.6
Variety and games	**15.2**	4.6	10.7
Music and dance	**1.0**	0.8	0.2
Comedy	**10.0**	1.6	8.4
Drama	**27.3**	5.3	22.1
Recorded program (VCR/DVD)	**4.9**	0.0	4.9
Other television programs	**2.9**	0.0	2.9

Notes: Data are collected over the fall period (four weeks of November).
Population aged 2 and older.

Source: Statistics Canada, CANSIM table 502-0004.

Table 19.5 Internet use at home by individuals, by type of activity, 2005

	All Canadians[1]	Internet users at home[2]
	%	
E-mail	55.6	91.3
Participating in chat groups or using a messenger	23.1	37.9
Searching for information on Canadian municipal, provincial or federal government	31.7	52.0
Communicating with Canadian municipal, provincial or federal government	13.8	22.6
Searching for medical or health related information	35.3	57.9
Education, training or school work	26.1	42.9
Travel information or making travel arrangements	38.5	63.1
Paying bills	33.5	55.0
Electronic banking	35.2	57.8
Researching investments	16.0	26.2
Playing games	23.5	38.7
Obtaining or saving music	22.3	36.6
Obtaining or saving software	19.4	31.8
Viewing the news or sports	37.6	61.7
Obtaining weather reports or road conditions	40.5	66.6
Listening to the radio over the Internet	15.9	26.1
Downloading or watching television	5.2	8.5
Downloading or watching a movie	5.0	8.3
Researching community events	25.8	42.3
General browsing (surfing)	51.2	84.0
Other Internet activity	6.7	10.9

1. Percentage of all individuals aged 18 and older.
2. Percentage of all individuals aged 18 and older who responded that they had used the Internet in the previous 12 months for personal non-business use from home.
Source: Statistics Canada, CANSIM table 358-0130.

Table 19.6 Internet use by individuals, by location of access, 2005

	%[1]
All locations[2]	**67.9**
Home	60.9
Work	26.3
School	11.7
Public library	10.2
Other location	20.3

1. Percentage of all individuals aged 18 and older who responded that they had used the Internet in the previous 12 months for personal non-business use from any location.
2. Includes use from home, school, work, public library or other location, and counts an individual only once, regardless of use from multiple locations.
Source: Statistics Canada, CANSIM table 358-0122.

Table 19.7 Cable and other program distribution industries, financial and operating statistics, 2001 to 2005

	2001	2002	2003	2004	2005
	$ millions				
Operating revenue	**4,606.0**	**5,215.7**	**5,818.8**	**6,350.4**	**6,818.0**
Cable television	3,926.6	4,268.9	4,615.2	4,995.8	5,347.8
Satellite and other wireless television[1]	679.4	946.8	1,203.6	1,354.7	1,470.2
Operating expenses	**4,268.9**	**4,728.8**	**5,066.8**	**5,245.2**	**5,445.7**
Cable television	3,279.1	3,536.1	3,753.1	3,797.6	4,018.1
Satellite and other wireless television[1]	989.8	1,192.7	1,313.8	1,447.5	1,427.6
Salaries and other staff benefits	**726.6**	**743.8**	**717.7**	**768.5**	**868.0**
Cable television	625.7	631.4	612.9	657.4	729.8
Satellite and other wireless television[1]	100.9	112.4	104.7	111.1	138.1
	thousands				
Subscribers to television programming services	**9,457**	**9,644**	**9,779**	**9,935**	**10,106**
Cable television	7,848	7,626	7,574	7,611	7,612
Satellite and other wireless television[1]	1,609	2,019	2,205	2,325	2,495

Note: North American Industry Classification System (NAICS), 2002.

1. Paid services similar to cable services but provided with wireless technologies. Does not include free television.

Source: Statistics Canada, CANSIM table 353-0003.

Table 19.8 Private radio and private conventional television, financial and operating statistics, 2001 to 2005

	2001	2002	2003	2004	2005
	$ millions				
Private radio					
Operating revenue	1,074.8	1,105.8	1,196.5	1,234.7	1,345.7
Advertising revenues	1,051.5	1,084.1	1,175.0	1,214.2	1,319.4
Operating expenses	902.9	932.8	969.2	1,011.8	1,068.5
Salaries and benefits	468.2	485.8	509.8	535.2	559.1
Profit before interest and taxes	171.9	173.1	227.3	222.9	277.3
Private conventional television					
Operating revenue	1,910.9	1,900.9	2,102.8	2,122.1	2,207.1
Advertising revenues	1,790.1	1,760.7	1,932.6	1,943.0	2,017.8
Operating expenses	1,669.2	1,722.2	1,802.5	1,889.6	1,964.4
Salaries and benefits	495.3	521.3	542.4	559.0	569.9
Profit before interest and taxes	241.6	178.6	300.3	232.5	242.7

Notes: North American Industry Classification System (NAICS), 2002.

Excludes television channels dedicated to sports, news or movies that are only available to those who subscribe to cable or satellite television.

Excludes channels largely financed by public funds or fund-raising activities.

Source: Statistics Canada, CANSIM table 357-0001.

International merchandise trade

20

If you want to see Canada's international trade in action, a good vantage point is Vancouver's Lions Gate Bridge. Looking east toward the Port of Vancouver, you'll see freighters move toward their berths; looking west, other ships sit moored at the mouth of Howe Sound, waiting their turn to dock.

Vancouver is our busiest port. Most of the commodities passing through it are headed offshore, mainly to Asia. However, Canada's trade travels by many other modes, such as truck, rail, air, pipeline and power line.

Canada exports more than it imports: in 2006, we exported $458.2 billion in goods, up 1.1% from 2005, and imported $404.5 billion, up 4.2% from 2005. We've posted a trade surplus every year since 1976.

In 2006, the value and volume of both our imports and exports reached record highs. This fits into a larger trend: world trade has

grown as much since 1990 as it did in the prior 100 years, the result of international trade agreements, falling transportation costs, and the free flow of information, ideas and product orders.

The United States remains our foremost trading partner by far, with China as our second largest trading partner. Trade flows to other countries shift over time. China surpassed Japan in 2003.

Our trade with China—Canada's fourth largest export market and second-largest source for imports—has been expanding significantly. China has become a major importer and consumer of our raw materials and an exporting powerhouse. Lately, China's manufacturers have shifted to making higher-value capital goods, such as computers and electronics equipment. Since 2003, Canada has imported more and more of these

Chart 20.1
Merchandise imports and exports

annual % change

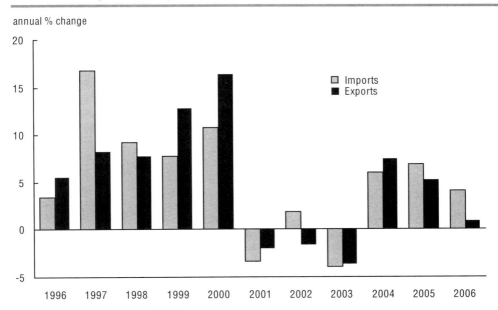

Note: Data are on a balance of payments basis.
Source: Statistics Canada, CANSIM table 228-0003.

higher-value items from China than lower-value items, such as clothing and shoes.

As an exporter, Canada has benefited directly and indirectly from China's industrial revolution. Indirectly, China's demand for all sorts of industrial raw materials, especially energy and metals, has pushed up world prices. As a major raw materials producer, Canada has enjoyed these higher prices, whether we sell those commodities to China or to another nation.

In 2006, the United Kingdom edged out Japan as Canada's second largest export market. Growth in exports to Japan remained subdued, but climbing metal prices—a trend in recent years—pushed up the value of exports of gold, uranium and nickel to the United Kingdom.

What goes out: Commodities are still key

Before there was a Canada, there was the fur and timber trade. Britain's Royal Navy used Canadian timber for the masts of the ships it built to fight Napoleon in the early 1800s. Until the start of the Second World War in

Canada's international trade partners, 2006

	Imports	Exports
	$ billions	
Total	**396.5**	**440.2**
United States	217.6	359.3
China	34.5	7.7
Japan	15.3	9.4
Mexico	16.0	4.4
United Kingdom	10.8	10.1
Other European Union countries	38.1	18.7
Other countries	64.2	42.7

Note: Data are on a customs basis.
Source: Statistics Canada, CANSIM table 228-0003 and catalogue no. 65-208-XIE.

1939, two-thirds of Canada's exports were grain and lumber.

Resources are still critical to our trade. Agricultural, fish and forestry products, energy, metals, chemicals and fertilizers accounted for about half our exports in 2006. Companies engaged in natural resources extraction flourished last year, save for those in lumber, an industry dogged by a slump in U.S. housing.

In Western Canada, higher export receipts for crude petroleum and metal products yielded unprecedented prosperity; in Quebec and Ontario, strong metal exports offset losses in the forestry and automotive sectors. Newfoundland and Labrador's exports rose because of higher iron ore and energy products shipments.

Metal and metal ore exports led the gain in exports in 2006, climbing to $45 billion. Prices for copper, zinc, gold, aluminum, nickel, potash and uranium all advanced in 2006. The United Kingdom was the largest market for Canadian metals outside of the United States, followed by China, Japan, Norway, South Korea and the Netherlands.

Crude petroleum exports were also up in 2006, reaching a new record of $39 billion, no small feat given the spike in prices in the fourth quarter of 2005 following the hurricanes in the Gulf of Mexico. In contrast, exports of forestry products fell in 2006 for

Chart 20.2
Merchandise trade with the United States

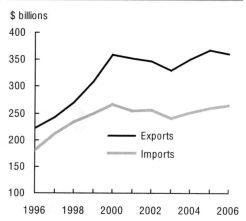

$ billions

Note: Data are on a balance of payments basis.
Source: Statistics Canada, CANSIM table 228-0003.

the second consecutive year, to $33.5 billion. This was down from $40 billion in 2004, a year in which lumber prices skyrocketed.

Exports of automotive products have also dipped in recent years while auto imports from overseas have been rising. In 1999, the auto sector's trade surplus was second only to that of forestry products at $21 billion; by 2006, the auto sector's surplus was $3 billion.

What comes in: Capital goods and consumer goods

The boom in the Western provinces made headlines as oilsands construction expanded and people flooded in to capitalize on the higher wages brought about by a tight labour market. Higher profits for businesses and incomes for individuals brought about a rapid expansion in investment and consumer purchases. This heightened demand pushed up imports of machinery, electronics, cars and trucks, home furnishings and clothing.

Imports of industrial machinery poured into the Western provinces in 2006, contributing to the 3% gain to $114.7 billion in machinery

and equipment imports. The stronger dollar, which translated into lower import prices, combined with high crude oil and metal prices, drove business profits up and encouraged this inflow of capital goods.

The rise in household incomes stimulated consumer spending in 2006, with Alberta in particular driving auto sales to their highest level ever. The increase in sales was concentrated in Japanese and German models manufactured outside of North America, raising automotive import values.

The renovation and design industry has become big business, and the imports tell the tale. In 2006, Canadians imported a record high value of home furnishings, totalling nearly $8.0 billion. In addition to redecorating with fabric and furniture, high definition televisions were in brisk demand. Over $1.3 billion worth of them, imported primarily from Mexico but also from China, made their way into Canadian electronics stores in 2006.

In addition to dressing the home, clothing imports have been on the rise in recent years, a result of the lifting of import limits. In 2006, imports were up 6.5% to $8.3 billion in spite of falling clothing prices. In real terms, i.e., adjusting for the price drop, clothing imports were up 11% to $9.6 billion. Demand was also higher for personal electronics equipment, mostly originating in China, South Korea and Malaysia—in particular, cellular phones and personal digital assistants, which are devices that make music, photos, e-mail and the internet available at our fingertips.

Chart 20.3
Exports of energy products and industrial goods

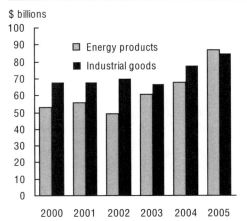

$ billions

Note: Data are on a balance of payments basis.
Source: Statistics Canada, Catalogue no. 65-208-XIE.

Ships as far as the eye can see

Most of the ship traffic passing under Vancouver's Lions Gate Bridge is picking up coal, grain and other Canadian commodities for shipment to Asia.

In 2004, Japan, China, South Korea, the United States and the Netherlands were the top five destinations for outbound Vancouver traffic as measured in metric tonnage. The leading points of origin for inbound traffic were China, the United States, South Korea, Hong Kong and Mexico.

The total amount of cargo handled at the port of Vancouver in 2004 was 75.0 million tonnes—65.9 million tonnes of cargo were loaded and 9.1 million tonnes were unloaded. Coal was the principal commodity moving through Vancouver.

Coal shipments out of Vancouver outpaced grains, the number two commodity exported from the port, by a ratio of almost 3 to 1 by

weight. Sulphur, potash and wood pulp were handled in significant quantities at the port. These goods are typically shipped in bulk.

Manufactured goods are usually shipped in containers, which can be in turn transferred onto freight trains. In 2004, Vancouver handled 45% of Canada's container traffic as well.

Other major ports have also seen traffic growth, both in bulk commodities and container traffic. In 2004, Canada's ports handled a record 452.3 million tonnes of cargo, up 2% from 2003—the third consecutive year that port activity surpassed 400 million tonnes. International cargo rose 3% to a record 314.6 million tonnes. Domestic cargo remained virtually unchanged at 137.8 million tonnes.

Chart 20.4
Tonnage shipped at the port of Vancouver, by principal trading economies, 2004

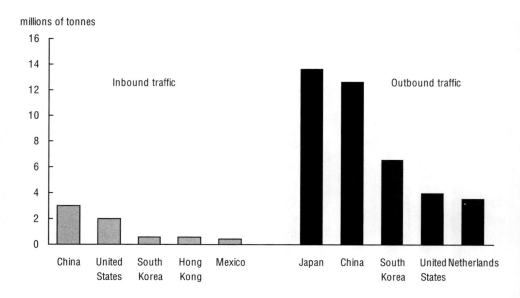

millions of tonnes

Inbound traffic / Outbound traffic

China, United States, South Korea, Hong Kong, Mexico / Japan, China, South Korea, United States, Netherlands

Source: Vancouver Port Authority.

Where's this made?

Our clothing, like other commodities we buy regularly, comes to us from an ever-shifting array of countries. Since 2002, China and Bangladesh have surged ahead as our number one and two sources of imported clothing.

It wasn't always this way. During the 1960s, most Canadians wore clothing manufactured in Canada and very little was imported. Although countries such as Taiwan, South Korea and Hong Kong were emerging as manufacturing powers, Canada and other Western countries negotiated a series of agreements that restricted clothing imports in the 1970s and 1980s.

A major shift came when Canada signed the Free Trade Agreement with the United States in 1989. As recently as 1998, that nation was our primary foreign clothing supplier: a surge in exports to the United States in those years revitalized our domestic industry.

Another shift began in 1995, when the World Trade Organization's Agreement on Textiles and Clothing led to a gradual lifting of quotas on clothing imports. Taiwan, South Korea, Hong Kong, Malaysia, Thailand, Pakistan, Sri Lanka, the Philippines and Macau were the first big beneficiaries of trade liberalization. Bangladesh started shipping into Canada tariff-free in 2003. China followed in 2004.

Canadian clothing manufacturers have by no means vanished: they supplied 32% of the domestic market in 2005. However, the industry is shrinking. From 2002 to 2005, employment in the clothing industry dropped from 94,000 to 60,000.

Consumers have also seen the impact of foreign competition. After rising steadily through the 1980s and 1990s, clothing prices began to fall. In 2005, consumer prices for clothing were 6% lower than in 2001.

Chart 20.5
Employment in clothing manufacturing

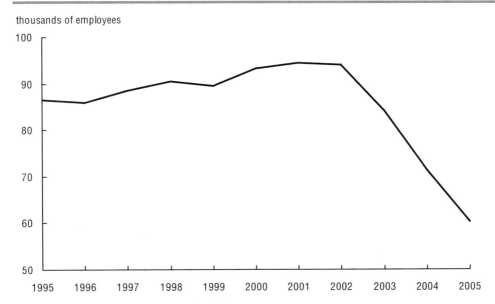

thousands of employees

Note: Data are annual and unadjusted for seasonal variation.
Source: Statistics Canada, CANSIM table 281-0024.

Diamonds in the ice

A century after the Klondike gold rush, the land of the midnight sun is yielding a different precious mineral: diamonds. Canada has quickly risen to third place in production on the list of diamond-producing countries, after Botswana and Russia.

A handful of adventurous mining companies are leading the exploration and mine development. The opening of diamond mines has been as dramatic for the economy of the North as the Klondike gold rush, particularly for the Northwest Territories.

From 1999—the first year of production—to 2005, per-capita gross domestic product in the Northwest Territories climbed at an average annual rate of 12.5%, compared with 1.7% before 1999. That 12.5% is about three times the rate for Canada as a whole.

In 2006, three mines were operating in the Northwest Territories, clustered northeast of

Yellowknife. A fourth mine is located just over the territorial boundary in Nunavut.

From 1998 to 2002, companies mined about 13.8 million carats of diamonds in Canada, worth $2.8 billion. This is roughly equal to 1,825 1.5-kilogram bags of ice, but worth $1.5 million each. Canadian diamonds are fetching top dollar. Their value averaged $228 per carat in 2001, third in the world behind Namibian and Angolan diamonds.

The value of diamond exports tripled from 1999 to 2005. Exports from the Northwest Territories were worth $1.7 billion in 2005. About 95% of Canada's exports, measured by value, are 'rough' diamonds, which have not yet been sorted, cut and polished. More than 90%, go to the world's two major diamond-trading centres: London, England and Antwerp, Belgium.

Chart 20.6
Diamond exports, by value, Canada and the Northwest Territories

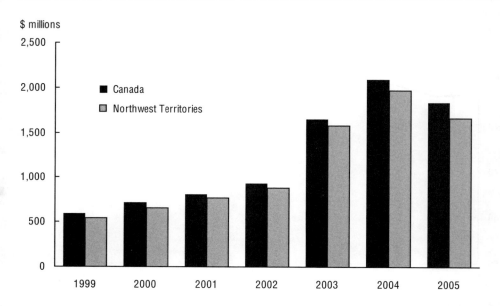

$ millions

Source: Statistics Canada, Catalogue no. 65-507-MWE.

Oil coming and going

Canada is both a major exporter and importer of crude oil. In 2005, we exported about 67% of our domestic oil production—primarily from Alberta to the United States. We imported about 55% of the oil we used that year: that oil flowed from an array of countries into Eastern Canada.

Crude oil exports were worth $30.2 billion in 2005, up from $25.0 billion in 2004 and almost four times the value posted in 1995.

However, the increase from 2004 to 2005 was the result of a 30% rise in prices: the volume of oil exports actually fell slightly. Imports equalled $21.9 billion in 2005.

Ninety-nine percent of Canada's crude oil exports in 2005 were shipped to the United States. Alberta produced 69% of total exports; Saskatchewan, nearly 21%; and the Atlantic provinces, 10%. British Columbia and Manitoba combined for less than 1%.

Alberta produced two-thirds of Canada's oil output in 2005; Saskatchewan provided 18%, and Newfoundland and Labrador's offshore fields, 13%. Ontario, Manitoba, British Columbia and the Northwest Territories combined for 3% of production.

In 2005, Canadian refineries processed 102.5 million cubic metres of crude oil, or 645 million barrels. Eastern Canada's refineries use a combination of Newfoundland and Labrador and imported crude oil to meet their refining needs; Central Canada's use eastern and western Canadian as well as imported crude. Western Canada's refineries process western Canadian production exclusively, including crude derived from oil sands.

Chart 20.7
Imports of crude oil from selected countries, 2005

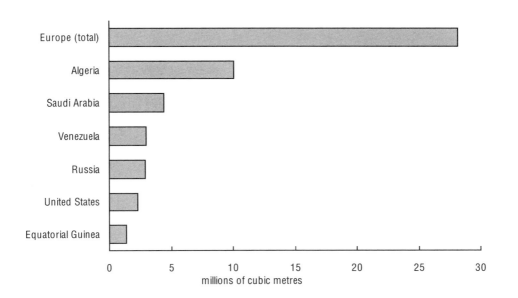

Source: Statistics Canada, Catalogue nº. 11-621-XIE.

Table 20.1 Merchandise imports, by commodity, 1992 to 2006

	1992	1993	1994	1995	1996	1997
	$ millions					
Imports, all merchandise	**154,429.6**	**177,123.2**	**207,872.5**	**229,936.5**	**237,688.6**	**277,726.5**
Live animals	150.8	174.0	215.4	188.3	171.1	183.8
Food, feed, beverages and tobacco	8,976.7	10,114.3	11,597.4	12,222.4	12,954.6	14,363.5
Meat and meat preparations	875.8	992.2	1,137.4	1,133.7	1,033.7	1,200.0
Fish and marine animals	776.6	996.1	1,126.4	1,286.5	1,469.6	1,434.0
Fresh fruits and berries	1,192.6	1,283.9	1,303.4	1,387.5	1,418.3	1,503.0
Dried fruits, fruits and fruit preparations	673.3	648.0	693.4	745.6	861.1	900.8
Fresh vegetables	827.3	944.7	949.6	1,054.4	971.7	1,112.5
Other vegetables and vegetable preparations	556.0	643.9	700.3	718.3	761.1	838.2
Cocoa, coffee, tea and other food preparations	1,229.3	1,452.9	2,089.3	2,056.9	2,131.7	2,589.7
Dairy produce, eggs and honey	212.5	245.2	265.5	276.1	352.0	355.0
Corn (maize), shelled	144.9	157.6	158.5	216.9	251.0	250.3
Other cereals and cereal preparations	568.7	632.9	750.1	805.1	891.1	998.0
Sugar and sugar preparations	677.0	759.7	866.5	879.4	970.7	1,035.6
Fodder and feed, except unmilled cereals	462.1	551.1	613.7	628.4	728.6	809.9
Beverages	720.3	746.2	872.8	959.4	1,015.3	1,214.7
Tobacco	60.4	60.0	70.4	74.2	98.6	121.6
Crude materials, inedible	8,180.0	9,143.2	9,898.0	11,531.4	13,048.1	14,171.5
Metals in ores, concentrates and scrap	1,676.2	1,983.6	2,326.2	2,989.1	2,863.0	2,950.2
Coal and other related products	661.2	476.9	548.0	591.6	751.4	910.3
Crude petroleum	4,174.9	4,687.9	4,609.3	4,833.2	6,707.8	7,189.4
Crude animal products	136.4	163.9	221.8	239.1	248.0	293.2
Crude vegetable products	528.7	638.4	663.1	815.2	843.9	949.6
Crude wood products	252.6	293.3	406.8	560.4	435.7	544.1
Cotton	80.2	86.8	101.6	149.2	168.3	154.0
Wool and man-made fibres	144.3	204.8	260.0	296.5	279.9	328.5
Crude non-metallic minerals	525.5	607.5	761.2	1,057.1	750.0	852.1
Fabricated materials, inedible	27,572.4	32,279.3	38,823.1	44,277.2	45,967.5	54,508.4
End products, inedible	99,297.1	114,407.5	136,993.1	151,331.7	153,330.6	181,930.0
Special transactions, trade	4,061.2	4,349.2	4,877.0	5,441.4	7,075.9	6,954.9
Other balance of payments adjustments	6,191.4	6,655.7	5,468.5	4,944.0	5,140.8	5,614.5

Note: On a balance of payments basis.
Source: Statistics Canada, CANSIM table 228-0003.

1998	1999	2000	2001	2002	2003	2004	2005	2006
				$ millions				
303,398.6	327,026.0	362,336.7	350,071.2	356,727.1	342,691.9	363,638.5	388,210.3	404,535.0
235.0	302.7	410.2	398.0	236.7	174.3	137.7	144.2	165.2
15,858.3	16,249.3	16,978.4	18,687.0	20,195.2	19,946.2	19,823.0	20,680.5	22,050.0
1,251.4	1,279.8	1,404.0	1,635.9	1,681.4	1,596.6	1,311.0	1,456.3	1,653.9
1,635.8	1,869.7	1,928.8	1,945.3	1,935.4	1,812.2	1,803.6	1,822.4	1,815.1
1,581.3	1,645.8	1,679.4	1,815.3	2,020.1	2,013.5	2,070.8	2,207.6	2,317.3
935.3	1,020.3	1,003.8	992.1	1,075.6	1,061.8	1,102.2	1,137.7	1,235.9
1,233.8	1,213.6	1,386.6	1,502.3	1,700.3	1,638.7	1,633.1	1,718.5	1,785.9
963.5	1,050.0	1,048.8	1,133.4	1,275.1	1,211.3	1,239.7	1,336.5	1,360.4
2,948.9	2,865.0	2,817.4	2,948.7	3,340.3	3,427.2	3,590.5	3,696.0	3,920.3
409.7	437.8	487.6	581.4	583.3	567.3	638.9	617.2	540.2
283.6	228.1	300.0	555.3	733.0	599.9	366.4	342.4	322.6
1,136.6	1,164.1	1,243.6	1,380.1	1,484.5	1,416.5	1,453.6	1,489.3	1,559.5
1,100.9	991.6	1,034.0	1,218.1	1,179.2	1,221.6	1,140.7	1,241.0	1,409.0
796.4	734.0	825.3	981.0	1,041.2	967.9	1,007.1	892.0	982.7
1,455.8	1,669.2	1,735.1	1,910.2	2,035.3	2,294.9	2,357.1	2,602.5	2,885.9
125.2	80.3	84.1	88.0	110.6	116.9	108.4	121.0	261.0
12,476.7	14,316.0	21,462.6	20,936.6	20,405.7	22,813.5	27,988.2	34,418.7	36,033.4
2,788.4	2,747.4	3,067.1	2,991.7	2,980.1	3,029.1	4,110.7	4,373.2	6,084.6
1,116.3	1,098.1	1,270.2	1,430.5	1,932.9	2,838.8	3,714.3	5,084.0	3,886.3
5,227.4	7,160.3	13,436.6	12,814.3	11,722.3	13,301.0	16,468.3	21,581.9	22,768.4
256.2	242.1	272.9	300.3	317.6	302.7	285.6	257.0	265.8
939.3	965.5	995.8	1,119.2	1,214.3	1,229.4	1,257.2	1,151.1	1,175.3
618.8	626.9	695.2	703.6	686.0	619.2	632.4	609.6	561.4
221.3	138.0	172.4	168.5	133.7	159.1	142.4	78.6	56.6
343.7	348.6	389.8	380.2	370.7	361.4	343.3	326.2	288.6
965.4	989.1	1,162.4	1,028.4	1,048.0	972.9	1,034.0	957.1	946.3
60,113.0	62,411.8	69,870.4	69,411.3	69,538.7	66,669.5	74,902.5	82,164.1	87,093.0
202,489.8	221,180.5	240,462.0	227,417.2	233,889.6	221,440.3	229,091.6	238,708.1	246,500.3
6,339.2	6,343.1	6,653.7	6,851.6	5,973.8	5,310.4	4,932.7	4,557.6	4,631.3
5,886.5	6,222.5	6,499.5	6,369.5	6,487.3	6,337.7	6,762.7	7,537.0	8,061.8

Table 20.2 Merchandise exports, by commodity, 1992 to 2006

	1992	1993	1994	1995	1996	1997
	$ millions					
Exports, all merchandise	**163,463.5**	**190,213.1**	**228,167.1**	**265,333.9**	**280,079.3**	**303,378.2**
Live animals	1,285.2	1,393.5	1,338.3	1,517.7	1,888.4	1,905.3
Food, feed, beverages and tobacco	12,873.1	13,233.3	14,890.6	17,014.1	18,884.6	20,380.4
Fish, fresh, frozen, preserved and canned	2,735.7	2,867.5	3,258.5	3,496.2	3,444.1	3,497.8
Barley	444.1	460.7	590.5	564.5	847.8	683.0
Wheat	3,835.8	2,952.4	3,547.3	4,325.2	4,658.6	5,051.5
Wheat flour	32.6	24.8	46.2	50.6	33.8	39.7
Other cereals, unmilled	186.1	220.3	250.9	318.6	432.5	489.8
Other cereal preparations	459.1	567.7	678.5	798.5	1,017.1	1,115.2
Meat and meat preparations	1,213.7	1,456.8	1,603.0	1,845.2	2,161.0	2,641.8
Alcoholic beverages	782.9	853.0	1,026.2	980.0	1,071.0	1,166.7
Other food, feed, beverages and tobacco	3,183.1	3,830.2	3,889.4	4,635.4	5,218.7	5,695.0
Crude materials, inedible	19,405.4	20,880.4	23,584.9	26,469.0	30,266.3	31,655.2
Rapeseed	573.7	735.1	1,571.5	1,265.3	1,158.0	1,126.1
Other crude vegetable products	606.7	790.3	1,013.2	1,169.0	1,236.7	1,362.1
Iron ores, concentrates and scrap	952.4	998.5	1,272.0	1,386.0	1,440.2	1,841.5
Copper in ores, concentrates and scrap	919.5	822.5	774.0	1,196.3	872.0	928.5
Nickel in ores, concentrates and scrap	666.3	618.0	592.9	981.5	1,117.7	907.3
Zinc in ores, concentrates and scrap	551.5	324.6	349.1	486.8	536.6	695.4
Other ores, concentrates and scrap	1,268.9	1,127.9	1,346.8	1,812.5	1,949.3	1,534.2
Crude petroleum	5,885.3	6,222.5	6,507.1	8,263.5	10,497.2	10,366.3
Natural gas	4,730.1	5,903.4	6,427.8	5,649.1	7,432.8	8,625.6
Coal and other crude bituminous substances	1,116.5	1,194.8	1,298.5	1,384.7	1,433.7	1,515.1
Unmanufactured asbestos	299.5	265.2	303.3	323.3	343.3	226.7
Other crude animal products	423.3	474.8	523.0	579.2	610.8	664.7
Other crude wood products	374.0	394.0	322.6	347.9	346.2	432.6
Other crude non-metallic minerals	500.2	484.5	625.9	714.1	694.5	652.9
Other crude materials, inedible	537.5	524.3	657.1	909.7	597.3	776.1
Fabricated materials, inedible	49,624.2	56,994.3	69,826.7	84,003.2	85,042.6	89,749.4
End products, inedible	74,463.3	91,064.8	110,410.1	127,264.6	134,806.7	149,130.3
Special transactions, trade	1,835.7	2,164.9	2,564.1	2,865.1	3,154.5	4,074.5
Other balance of payments adjustments	3,976.6	4,481.9	5,552.5	6,200.3	6,036.2	6,483.1

Note: On a balance of payments basis.
Source: Statistics Canada, CANSIM table 228-0003.

1998	1999	2000	2001	2002	2003	2004	2005	2006
				$ millions				
327,161.5	369,034.9	429,372.2	420,730.4	414,038.5	398,953.9	429,120.9	453,060.1	458,166.9
1,975.8	1,567.8	1,742.7	2,394.3	2,506.9	1,318.7	873.3	1,542.8	2,015.7
19,814.5	21,312.6	23,268.6	25,911.5	25,843.1	25,056.3	26,906.1	25,823.5	26,111.5
3,664.5	4,260.8	4,560.6	4,722.3	5,239.5	4,987.1	4,870.0	4,699.6	4,525.7
340.3	256.9	377.9	383.9	194.1	172.1	323.6	361.5	257.5
3,642.3	3,356.2	3,608.9	3,807.2	3,052.6	2,809.2	3,493.1	2,698.7	3,619.8
35.3	54.8	60.1	64.0	91.4	81.3	85.3	79.8	84.1
348.4	400.3	263.5	279.8	288.5	299.2	312.4	312.7	410.5
1,290.5	1,449.8	1,593.3	1,830.6	2,048.0	2,138.7	2,214.0	2,248.5	2,321.0
2,669.5	3,247.8	4,005.1	4,885.6	4,840.8	4,203.5	4,985.4	5,099.2	4,306.6
1,217.5	1,366.4	1,310.6	1,357.6	1,185.4	1,300.2	1,230.5	1,044.3	1,014.0
6,606.1	6,919.8	7,488.5	8,580.5	8,902.9	9,065.1	9,391.6	9,279.0	9,572.3
29,854.0	34,562.6	53,398.2	54,713.5	50,980.7	61,228.2	69,460.0	85,927.4	88,641.5
1,638.5	1,332.8	1,147.5	1,275.8	921.1	1,298.0	1,419.8	1,297.6	1,764.1
1,610.9	1,399.1	1,441.7	1,496.4	1,601.7	1,570.3	1,545.3	1,553.7	1,634.5
1,830.9	1,493.3	1,532.1	1,381.2	1,634.5	1,743.5	2,048.5	2,722.0	3,337.0
614.4	452.1	792.6	661.9	577.2	592.3	845.5	1,346.0	2,307.6
917.4	807.1	1,071.9	1,010.6	1,139.1	1,143.9	1,829.4	1,700.1	2,435.5
509.2	479.0	481.2	436.7	388.4	228.4	234.6	217.4	330.0
1,499.0	1,917.0	2,073.8	2,177.7	2,147.6	2,081.5	2,400.2	2,924.1	3,130.6
7,829.8	11,017.1	19,165.9	15,370.2	18,550.8	20,644.3	25,512.8	30,388.3	38,604.6
8,967.1	10,951.4	20,536.8	25,595.1	18,372.0	26,083.4	27,382.1	35,988.6	27,488.5
1,343.7	1,228.7	1,194.4	1,217.5	1,212.1	1,160.9	1,190.4	2,661.1	2,699.0
172.5	164.7	149.4	122.9	100.7	70.6	72.4	67.3	62.5
677.2	652.6	711.0	784.9	802.2	720.5	735.6	816.2	891.1
523.0	671.4	846.1	848.5	1,027.9	902.9	839.6	947.2	931.9
847.4	1,496.7	1,707.0	1,842.9	2,014.3	2,493.8	2,833.9	2,720.9	2,489.1
873.1	499.9	546.8	491.2	491.1	493.9	569.8	577.0	535.5
91,817.6	97,976.8	113,102.1	111,908.3	108,291.9	103,448.5	118,599.8	125,095.8	129,479.1
171,731.0	199,953.3	223,135.3	211,387.0	211,446.2	193,250.7	198,899.0	200,124.8	196,940.0
5,563.4	7,348.2	7,980.0	8,168.1	8,232.5	7,689.1	7,984.8	8,289.1	8,733.0
6,405.3	6,313.7	6,745.3	6,247.7	6,737.2	6,962.4	6,397.9	6,256.8	6,246.3

Table 20.3 Merchandise imports and exports, by origin and destination, 1992 to 2006

	All merchandise		United States[1]		United Kingdom	
	$ millions	% change from previous year	$ millions	% change from previous year	$ millions	% change from previous year
Imports						
1992	**154,429.6**	9.8	110,378.5	13.1	4,015.4	-7.0
1993	**177,123.2**	14.7	130,244.3	18.0	4,484.0	11.7
1994	**207,872.5**	17.4	155,661.3	19.5	4,854.4	8.3
1995	**229,936.5**	10.6	172,516.5	10.8	4,899.1	0.9
1996	**237,688.6**	3.4	180,010.1	4.3	5,581.1	13.9
1997	**277,726.5**	16.8	211,450.8	17.5	6,126.5	9.8
1998	**303,398.6**	9.2	233,777.6	10.6	6,083.1	-0.7
1999	**327,026.0**	7.8	249,485.3	6.7	7,685.4	26.3
2000	**362,336.7**	10.8	266,511.1	6.8	12,289.3	59.9
2001	**350,071.2**	-3.4	254,330.7	-4.6	11,954.1	-2.7
2002	**356,727.1**	1.9	255,232.5	0.4	10,181.3	-14.8
2003	**342,691.9**	-3.9	240,340.4	-5.8	9,180.9	-9.8
2004	**363,638.5**	6.1	250,515.6	4.2	9,466.3	3.1
2005	**388,210.3**	6.8	259,783.9	3.7	9,061.6	-4.3
2006	**404,535.0**	4.2	264,777.6	1.9	9,685.1	6.9
Exports						
1992	**163,463.5**	10.7	123,376.9	13.6	3,415.0	5.3
1993	**190,213.1**	16.4	149,099.7	20.8	3,211.5	-6.0
1994	**228,167.1**	20.0	181,049.3	21.4	3,677.1	14.5
1995	**265,333.9**	16.3	205,690.6	13.6	4,377.0	19.0
1996	**280,079.3**	5.6	222,461.3	8.2	4,608.5	5.3
1997	**303,378.2**	8.3	242,542.3	9.0	4,689.5	1.8
1998	**327,161.5**	7.8	269,318.9	11.0	5,323.3	13.5
1999	**369,034.9**	12.8	309,116.8	14.8	6,002.9	12.8
2000	**429,372.2**	16.4	359,021.2	16.1	7,273.3	21.2
2001	**420,730.4**	-2.0	352,165.0	-1.9	6,910.3	-5.0
2002	**414,038.5**	-1.6	347,051.8	-1.5	6,161.5	-10.8
2003	**398,953.9**	-3.6	329,000.3	-5.2	7,695.8	24.9
2004	**429,120.9**	7.6	350,751.0	6.6	9,425.2	22.5
2005	**453,060.1**	5.6	368,577.3	5.1	9,683.2	2.7
2006	**458,166.9**	1.1	361,308.7	-2.0	11,838.5	22.3

Note: On a balance of payments basis.

1. Includes Puerto Rico and Virgin Islands.

Source: Statistics Canada, CANSIM table 228-0003.

Japan		Other Organisation for Economic Co-operation and Development countries		Other countries		Other European Economic Community countries	
$ millions	% change from previous year	$ millions	% change from previous year	$ millions	% change from previous year	$ millions	% change from previous year
8,913.3	1.9	4,615.8	1.4	16,598.7	8.7	9,907.8	-2.8
8,477.4	-4.9	4,683.9	1.5	19,691.1	18.6	9,542.4	-3.7
8,315.4	-1.9	7,364.7	57.2	20,126.9	2.2	11,549.9	21.0
8,427.6	1.3	7,942.3	7.8	20,761.0	3.2	15,390.0	33.2
7,227.4	-14.2	9,040.6	13.8	20,834.6	0.4	14,994.7	-2.6
8,711.0	20.5	11,376.7	25.8	21,948.7	5.3	18,112.9	20.8
9,671.8	11.0	11,398.8	0.2	23,326.1	6.3	19,141.2	5.7
10,592.2	9.5	13,257.2	16.3	25,240.1	8.2	20,765.8	8.5
11,729.8	10.7	19,067.6	43.8	31,602.5	25.2	21,136.5	1.8
10,571.9	-9.9	18,649.8	-2.2	31,367.6	-0.7	23,197.1	9.7
11,732.6	11.0	19,686.6	5.6	34,027.1	8.5	25,867.0	11.5
10,645.1	-9.3	19,695.3	0.0	36,830.7	8.2	25,999.6	0.5
10,096.9	-5.1	22,254.1	13.0	44,293.2	20.3	27,012.3	3.9
11,214.3	11.1	24,308.8	9.2	54,556.1	23.2	29,285.6	8.4
11,877.1	5.9	23,724.5	-2.4	61,981.4	13.6	32,489.4	10.9
8,253.7	8.0	3,178.6	15.8	15,877.8	-1.3	9,361.5	0.2
9,184.5	11.3	3,361.7	5.8	16,557.6	4.3	8,798.0	-6.0
10,788.5	17.5	4,536.0	34.9	18,753.5	13.3	9,362.7	6.4
13,286.1	23.2	4,563.4	0.6	23,537.6	25.5	13,879.3	48.2
12,423.4	-6.5	5,087.8	11.5	22,702.0	-3.6	12,796.3	-7.8
11,925.5	-4.0	8,849.0	73.9	22,111.6	-2.6	13,260.4	3.6
9,745.8	-18.3	9,120.9	3.1	19,652.2	-11.1	14,000.5	5.6
10,125.9	3.9	9,947.2	9.1	19,458.4	-1.0	14,383.8	2.7
11,297.4	11.6	12,059.0	21.2	22,875.1	17.6	16,846.3	17.1
10,120.8	-10.4	12,172.5	0.9	22,672.9	-0.9	16,688.9	-0.9
10,115.0	-0.1	12,670.7	4.1	21,745.2	-4.1	16,294.3	-2.4
9,800.7	-3.1	12,751.1	0.6	23,291.5	7.1	16,414.5	0.7
9,950.6	1.5	14,399.1	12.9	27,243.1	17.0	17,351.9	5.7
10,470.5	5.2	15,245.5	5.9	29,876.9	9.7	19,206.8	10.7
10,760.8	2.8	18,379.2	20.6	34,160.6	14.3	21,719.0	13.1

Table 20.4 International trade in services, 1990 to 2005

	Receipts			
	1990	**1995**	**2000**	**2005**
	$ millions			
Travel	**7,398**	**10,819**	**15,997**	**16,460**
Business travel	1,549	1,988	2,920	2,793
Personal travel	5,849	8,831	13,077	13,667
Transportation	**4,920**	**7,207**	**11,196**	**11,632**
Water transport	1,524	1,994	2,317	3,278
Air transport	2,234	2,900	5,184	4,841
Land and other transport	1,162	2,313	3,695	3,513
Commercial services	**9,061**	**16,805**	**31,101**	**35,115**
Communications services	1,220	1,753	2,046	2,655
Construction services	52	131	323	167
Insurance services	1,957	3,096	2,877	3,716
Other financial services	490	866	1,304	2,131
Computer and information services	546	1,387	3,604	4,141
Royalties and license fees	173	513	3,353	4,206
Non-financial commissions	306	500	713	906
Equipment rentals	197	224	280	282
Management services	849	1,459	3,257	4,855
Advertising and related services	124	174	495	449
Research and development	700	1,463	4,230	2,910
Architectural, engineering and other technical services	549	2,000	2,654	4,077
Miscellaneous services to business	1,392	2,211	3,809	2,614
Audio-visual services	348	877	1,966	1,768
Personal, cultural and recreational services	157	150	188	240

Source: Statistics Canada, CANSIM tables 376-0031, 376-0032 and 376-0033.

	Payments				Balance		
1990	1995	2000	2005	1990	1995	2000	2005
			$ millions				
12,757	14,093	18,444	22,260	-5,359	-3,274	-2,447	-5,800
2,048	3,049	3,921	3,563	-498	-1,061	-1,001	-771
10,709	11,044	14,524	18,696	-4,860	-2,213	-1,447	-5,029
6,746	10,911	13,916	17,528	-1,826	-3,703	-2,719	-5,897
2,287	4,044	5,101	7,173	-763	-2,050	-2,784	-3,896
3,323	4,673	6,066	7,952	-1,089	-1,773	-882	-3,110
1,136	2,193	2,749	2,404	26	120	946	1,109
12,554	20,260	32,366	37,946	-3,493	-3,455	-1,265	-2,831
1,210	1,745	2,050	2,062	10	8	-4	592
35	266	119	134	17	-135	204	33
2,238	3,811	4,215	5,759	-281	-714	-1,338	-2,043
733	1,291	2,290	2,724	-244	-425	-987	-593
344	678	1,335	2,542	202	709	2,269	1,599
1,941	2,584	5,600	8,046	-1,768	-2,070	-2,247	-3,839
341	581	711	651	-35	-81	3	254
308	406	679	788	-111	-182	-398	-506
1,419	2,390	4,783	4,692	-570	-931	-1,526	163
211	448	536	666	-87	-274	-40	-217
483	861	1,711	1,105	217	602	2,520	1,805
439	848	1,546	2,531	110	1,152	1,108	1,545
2,018	2,979	4,341	3,887	-626	-769	-533	-1,274
709	1,228	2,283	2,146	-361	-352	-317	-379
123	143	166	211	34	7	23	28

Table 20.5 International trade, by province and territory, 1985 to 2005

	1985	1990	1995	2000	2005
	$ millions				
Imports to Canada	**126,077**	**174,624**	**276,618**	**428,754**	**467,673**
Newfoundland and Labrador	990	1,838	2,505	4,998	6,064
Prince Edward Island	220	267	438	782	973
Nova Scotia	2,868	4,037	5,209	8,502	9,921
New Brunswick	2,801	3,559	5,614	8,917	12,229
Quebec	27,896	39,385	55,139	89,999	95,688
Ontario	63,566	86,785	143,920	215,663	221,134
Manitoba	3,361	4,205	8,004	10,473	11,678
Saskatchewan	3,055	3,326	6,463	9,367	10,510
Alberta	9,722	12,820	19,521	40,419	53,327
British Columbia	10,789	17,297	28,786	38,240	44,290
Yukon	74	113	199	263	351
Northwest Territories (including Nunavut)	234	271	376	..	..
Northwest Territories	..	..	..	581	842
Nunavut	..	..	..	232	283
Outside Canada	501	721	444	318	382
Exports from Canada	**137,379**	**175,513**	**302,480**	**490,688**	**519,680**
Newfoundland and Labrador	1,825	2,638	3,069	5,899	8,344
Prince Edward Island	162	277	516	1,035	1,106
Nova Scotia	1,922	2,675	4,100	6,953	7,860
New Brunswick	2,670	3,609	5,385	8,441	11,981
Quebec	24,128	33,429	59,188	97,305	91,945
Ontario	64,657	82,739	148,030	237,395	231,957
Manitoba	3,169	4,485	6,888	10,471	12,487
Saskatchewan	5,141	5,302	9,739	14,684	17,428
Alberta	17,086	17,850	30,009	61,198	86,103
British Columbia	16,155	21,348	34,763	46,028	48,450
Yukon	102	574	240	210	191
Northwest Territories (including Nunavut)	251	443	533	..	..
Northwest Territories	..	..	..	804	1,785
Nunavut	..	..	..	261	42
Outside Canada	111	144	20	3	2

Note: Expenditure-based gross domestic product.
Source: Statistics Canada, CANSIM table 384-0002.

Labour

The monthly unemployment rate is one of Canada's most closely watched indicators of economic well-being. In 2006, the unemployment rate continued to be a good news story, as it hovered around a 30-year low, thanks largely to strength in industries such as mining and oil and gas extraction as well as construction.

The average unemployment rate over the course of 2006 was 6.3%, down from 6.8% in 2005. Employment rose 1.9% in 2006—the fourteenth straight year of job growth in Canada. As most Canadians receive most of their income from a job, paid work is a cornerstone of our society and economy, and having a job is a priority for many of us.

Six provinces set 30-year low unemployment rates in 2006. In all the western provinces, the rate was under 5.0%; it generally increased from Ontario (where it was 6.3%)

heading east, with the highest rate, 14.8%, in Newfoundland and Labrador.

Canada's labour force participation rate—the proportion of working-age Canadians who had a job or were looking for one—remained at 67.2% in 2006.

Women driving employment growth

The employment picture varies based on characteristics such as sex and age. For example, adult women (aged 25 and older) made strong gains in 2006. They accounted for nearly half of all employment growth that year. Over the course of 2006, the proportion of adult women who were working hit a record high of 58.3%, pushing their unemployment rate to 6.1%, below that of adult men (6.5%).

Chart 21.1
Unemployment rate, by province

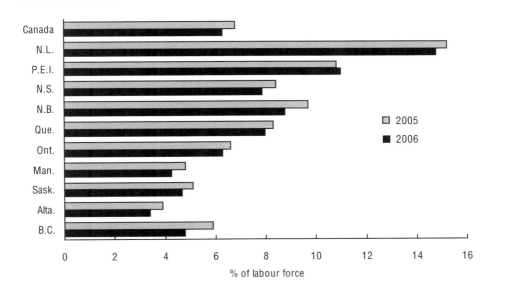

% of labour force

Source: Statistics Canada, CANSIM table 282-0002.

Youths, those aged 15 to 24, have also seen an improved labour market in recent years. Their unemployment rate fell to 11.6% in 2006, the lowest rate since 1989.

The effects of the baby boom are being seen in the participation rates of workers aged 55 and over, as more boomers reach that age. In 2006, 30.5% of Canadians in that age group had jobs, and their numbers increased 5.1% from 2005. The number of workers under 55 rose just 0.9%.

Aboriginal people have typically not fared as well in the labour force as non-Aboriginal people. In 2006, the unemployment rate for Aboriginal people living off reserves in the four western provinces was 9.8%, compared with 4.0% for the non-Aboriginal population.

Where the jobs are: Natural resources, the western provinces

Almost all industries gained jobs in 2006. The strongest proportional gains were posted in mining and oil and gas extraction, professional, scientific and technical services, business, building and other support services; finance, insurance, real estate and leasing;

Labour force characteristics, 2006

	Men	Women
	thousands	
Population age 15 and older	**12,882.7**	**13,302.5**
Labour force	9,335.4	8,257.3
Employment	8,727.1	7,757.2
Unemployment	608.3	500.1
Not in labour force	3,547.2	5,045.1
	%	
Unemployment rate	6.5	6.1
Participation rate	72.5	62.1
Employment rate	67.7	58.3

Source: Statistics Canada, CANSIM table 282-0002.

construction; educational services; health care and social assistance; and wholesale and retail trade. Only manufacturing and utilities lost jobs. Ontario continued to feel the loss of manufacturing jobs, which have declined by 130,000 in the province since the sector's peak in 2004. There were strong gains in mining, oil and gas extraction and construction in Alberta, Saskatchewan and British Columbia.

Manufacturing, despite recent job losses, is still the second-largest employer in Canada, behind the wholesale and retail trade industries. Nevertheless, a continuing

Chart 21.2
Job permanency

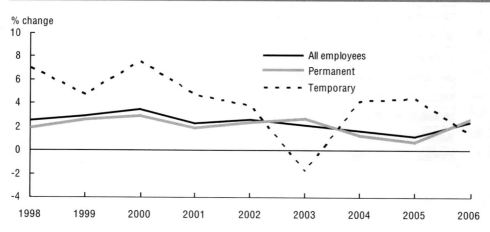

% change

Source: Statistics Canada, CANSIM table 282-0080.

shift away from jobs in the goods-producing industries to those in services is occurring.

As for occupations, the largest group of Canadian men work in trades or as transport or equipment operators. The most common occupations for women are in sales and services. The trend toward self-employment seems to have levelled off—reaching a peak of 17.1% of workers in 1997, but settling down to 15.2% in 2006.

Changing work hours

We have yet to reach the lives of leisure that some futurists predicted last century. In fact, after having declined steadily since 1994, the average work week for full-time employees rose in 2005 for a second straight year.

But the recent rise is not necessarily a bad thing—it is one indication that the hot labour market is almost at capacity. Employers unable to find more staff are giving more work to their existing employees.

Labour shortages may be one reason why the proportion of people working part time has been declining in recent years, reaching 18.0% in 2006, down from 18.8% in 2002.

Chart 21.3
Employment rate, by age group

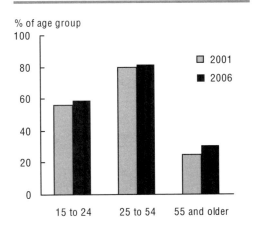

% of age group

☐ 2001
■ 2006

15 to 24   25 to 54   55 and older

Source: Statistics Canada, CANSIM table 282-0002.

Most job growth has been in full-time work. In 2006, over 9 out of 10 jobs created were full time. To meet their growing labour needs, some sectors have converted some part-time positions to full-time jobs. Among those working part time, most do so because they are attending school or out of personal preference.

Wages on the rise

The tightening labour market has pushed up wages. In 2006, total labour income grew by 6.1%, well above the inflation rate of 2.2%. Employees' average hourly wage was $19.72 in 2006, compared with $15.59 in 1997. When inflation is taken into account, that meant a 4.8% average increase.

Selected sources

Statistics Canada

- *Canadian Economic Observer.* Monthly. 11-010-XWB

- *The Canadian Labour Market at a Glance.* Irregular. 71-222-XWE

- *Canadian Social Trends. Irregular.* 11-008-XWE

- *Employment, Earnings and Hours.* Monthly. 72-002-XWE

- *General Social Survey on Time Use: Cycle 19.* Occasional. 89-622-XIE

- *Knowledge of Official Languages Among New Immigrants: How Important Is It in the Labour Market?.* Occasional. 89-624-XIE

- *Labour Force Historical Review.* Annual. 71F0004XCB

- *Labour Force Information.* Monthly. 71-001-XWE

- *Perspectives on Labour and Income.* Monthly. 75-001-XWE

Alberta's employment boom

Alberta's labour market is the tightest in North America, with the lowest proportion of jobless and the highest proportion of workers. Employment has been skyrocketing, thanks largely to the province's booming oil and gas and construction sectors.

The number of jobs in Alberta rose 6.0% in 2006, almost three times the national average. The 2006 unemployment rate averaged just 3.4% in Alberta, almost half the national rate of 6.3%. Alberta has had Canada's lowest rate since 2003.

Some 86,000 more people were working in Alberta in 2006, accounting for 27% of all employment growth in Canada that year, though only 1 in 10 working-age Canadians lives in the province.

The employment growth has brought with it wage increases. The average hourly wage rose 6.9% in 2006—more than double the

2.6% rise seen across Canada. Alberta's hourly wage rate, $21.62 an hour, was the highest in the country. Alberta had the lowest proportion of workers earning minimum wage or less—just 1.7%.

With more jobs available and at higher wages, more people are working in Alberta's largest cities. In 2006, Calgary and Edmonton ranked first and sixth, respectively, among Canadian cities with the highest employment rates. The job growth has also helped Aboriginal people—those living off reserves in Alberta have an employment rate close to the Canadian average.

However, the boom is not without its challenges. Alberta employers in some sectors are facing labour shortages. In 2005, for example, 42% of Alberta manufacturers reported being short of skilled workers.

Chart 21.4
Unemployment rate, Canada and Alberta

% of labour force

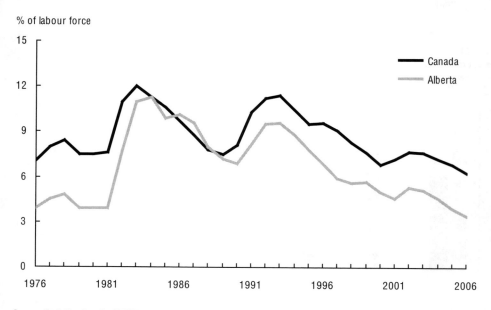

Source: Statistics Canada, CANSIM table 282-0002.

Immigrants' perspectives on employment

Most new immigrants are pleased to be living in Canada, and appreciate our social and political environment. However, their biggest difficulties, even after four years in the country, remain finding an adequate job and surmounting the language barrier.

A study of 25- to 44-year-old immigrants who arrived in Canada between April 2001 and March 2002 found that 62% of them were still looking for a job between 7 and 24 months after arrival. Fifty-three percent were still looking 25 to 48 months after arrival.

Most immigrant job-seekers reported difficulties searching for work. Cited most often were: the lack of Canadian work experience (50%); lack of contacts in the job market (37%); lack of recognition of either foreign experience (37%) or foreign qualifications (35%); and the language barrier (32%).

About 16% of the job-seekers cited language problems as their most serious difficulty. The 2001 Census shows that only 18% of immigrants who arrived in Canada between 1996 and 2001 spoke English or French as their mother tongue, down sharply from 40% of immigrants who arrived during the 1970s.

However, most eventually overcame these difficulties. The employment rate of the immigrants in this study rose from 51% six months after their arrival to 65% two years after arrival, then 75% after four years in Canada; the rate for Canadians in the 25-to-44 age group is 82%.

Immigrants' employment rates, and the quality of their employment—a job in their field, at a high skill level, and a good wage—improve with their ability to speak English. Employment rates were also better for immigrants who spoke French.

Chart 21.5
Immigrants' job search difficulties, 2005

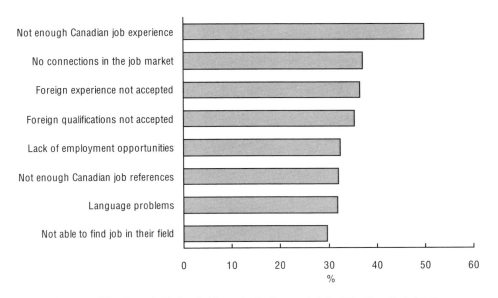

Note: Immigrants age 25 to 44 on arrival in Canada; job search difficulties reported after 25 to 48 months in Canada.
Source: Statistics Canada, Catalogue no. 11-008-XIE.

Attitudes toward commuting

We are spending more time commuting to work, and a 2005 survey of working Canadians shows that many of us enjoy our travel to work. For some, it is the only quiet time in a busy day, while for others it is a chance to catch up on work. Despite the negative impression that people have of commuting, many still prefer it to grocery shopping or doing home repairs.

Some 38% of commuters like their trip to and from work, including 16% who enjoy it a great deal. Only 30% say they dislike it. In addition, the more a person likes their job, the more likely they enjoy their daily commute and do not mind its frustrations.

Those who bike to work are the happiest commuters: 57% say they like or greatly like it. Those who combine a car ride with public transit are the most negative about their commute: 58% dislike or greatly dislike

it. Of those taking only public transit, 23% enjoy their commute, compared with 39% of drivers.

Commute times are getting longer. In 2005, we spent an average of 63 minutes a day travelling to and from work, which adds up to about 12 days a year for a full-time worker. This compares with 54 minutes a day in 1992 and 59 minutes in 1998.

Travel times vary by city. Among Canada's six largest cities, Toronto has the longest commute, at an average 79 minutes round trip in 2005, whereas Edmonton has the shortest, at 62 minutes.

We are travelling farther to work. From 1996 to 2001, the median commute increased from 7.0 kilometres to 7.2 kilometres.

Chart 21.6
Attitudes toward commuting, by type of transportation, 2005

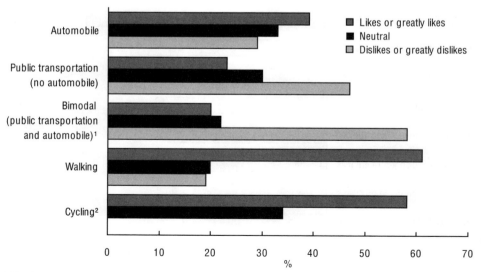

1. Use data with caution for Neutral and Likes or greatly likes.
2. Data too unreliable to be published for Dislikes or greatly dislikes.
Source: Statistics Canada, Catalogue no. 11-008-XIE.

Young pensioners: Few return to work

Generous employer pension benefits and other financial resources leave many 50-something retirees with little need to keep working.

About one in five Canadian taxfilers retire before they reach 60, the age when public pensions kick in. Fewer than 1% of workers collect an employer-sponsored pension at any age from 50 to 54. But 5% of men and 4% of women retire at age 55, which is when many employer pensions offer unrestricted benefits to long-term employees.

Once retired, it seems that very little can persuade these young pensioners to go back to work. Only half of them worked for some pay the year after they retired, and only 30% of early retirees earned more than $5,000. Seemingly content not to have a boss any longer, many of them did not even want to

be their own boss—fewer than 1 in 10 young pensioners reported self-employment income in the year after they retired. The likelihood of re-employment falls the older one is at retirement age.

Early retirement peaked in the mid-1990s when governments and other employers downsized and offered early retirement incentives. Early retirement has slowed as younger employees today are less likely to be covered by a pension.

On average, young pensioners' earnings a year before retirement were 50% higher than those who did not retire early. Early pensioners continue to earn about two-thirds of their pre-retirement income after they stop working. Employer pensions account for more than 60% of young pensioners' income.

Chart 21.7
Re-employment rates of young pensioners

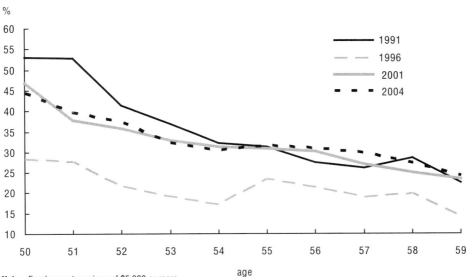

Notes: Employment earnings of $5,000 or more.
Pensioners aged 50 to 59.
Measured in 2004 constant dollars.
Source: Statistics Canada, Catalogue no. 75-001-XIE.

Table 21.1 Labour force characteristics, by sex and by province, 2006

	Canada	Newfoundland and Labrador	Prince Edward Island	Nova Scotia
	thousands			
Population				
Both sexes	26,185.1	427.7	112.3	762.8
Males	12,882.7	208.4	54.2	368.0
Females	13,302.5	219.3	58.1	394.8
Labour force				
Both sexes	17,592.8	253.1	77.1	480.0
Males	9,335.4	131.7	39.5	247.9
Females	8,257.3	121.4	37.6	232.0
Employed				
Both sexes	16,484.3	215.7	68.6	441.8
Males	8,727.1	109.8	34.4	224.8
Females	7,757.2	105.9	34.2	217.0
Unemployed				
Both sexes	1,108.4	37.5	8.5	38.1
Males	608.3	21.9	5.1	23.2
Females	500.1	15.6	3.5	15.0
Not in the labour force				
Both sexes	8,592.4	174.6	35.1	282.8
Males	3,547.2	76.7	14.7	120.1
Females	5,045.1	97.9	20.4	162.7
	%			
Participation rate				
Both sexes	67.2	59.2	68.7	62.9
Males	72.5	63.2	72.9	67.4
Females	62.1	55.4	64.7	58.8
Employment rate				
Both sexes	63.0	50.4	61.1	57.9
Males	67.7	52.7	63.5	61.1
Females	58.3	48.3	58.9	55.0
Unemployment rate				
Both sexes	6.3	14.8	11.0	7.9
Males	6.5	16.6	12.9	9.4
Females	6.1	12.9	9.3	6.5

Note: Population aged 15 and older.
Source: Statistics Canada, CANSIM table 282-0002.

New Brunswick	Quebec	Ontario	Manitoba	Saskatchewan	Alberta	British Columbia
			thousands			
611.3	6,251.5	10,229.0	892.0	746.4	2,641.3	3,511.0
298.3	3,073.4	5,016.1	438.5	368.0	1,329.6	1,728.1
313.0	3,178.1	5,212.9	453.4	378.4	1,311.7	1,782.8
389.6	4,094.2	6,927.3	613.5	515.6	1,937.5	2,305.1
203.8	2,184.3	3,650.3	326.6	275.9	1,058.2	1,217.2
185.7	1,909.9	3,277.0	286.8	239.6	879.3	1,087.9
355.4	3,765.4	6,492.7	587.0	491.6	1,870.7	2,195.5
182.9	1,998.4	3,418.4	312.0	262.4	1,023.1	1,160.9
172.5	1,767.0	3,074.3	275.0	229.2	847.6	1,034.5
34.2	328.7	434.6	26.5	24.0	66.8	109.6
21.0	185.8	231.9	14.7	13.5	35.1	56.2
13.2	142.9	202.7	11.8	10.5	31.7	53.4
221.7	2,157.3	3,301.7	278.5	230.9	703.8	1,205.9
94.4	889.1	1,365.8	111.9	92.1	271.4	510.9
127.3	1,268.2	1,935.9	166.6	138.8	432.4	694.9
			%			
63.7	65.5	67.7	68.8	69.1	73.4	65.7
68.3	71.1	72.8	74.5	75.0	79.6	70.4
59.3	60.1	62.9	63.3	63.3	67.0	61.0
58.1	60.2	63.5	65.8	65.9	70.8	62.5
61.3	65.0	68.1	71.2	71.3	76.9	67.2
55.1	55.6	59.0	60.7	60.6	64.6	58.0
8.8	8.0	6.3	4.3	4.7	3.4	4.8
10.3	8.5	6.4	4.5	4.9	3.3	4.6
7.1	7.5	6.2	4.1	4.4	3.6	4.9

Table 21.2 Labour force and participation rates, by sex and age group, 1981 to 2006

	Labour force			Participation rates		
	15 and older			15 and older		
	Both sexes	Males	Females	Both sexes	Males	Females
	thousands			%		
1981	12,235.8	7,269.2	4,966.7	65.0	78.4	52.0
1982	12,301.8	7,245.7	5,056.2	64.4	77.0	52.1
1983	12,527.6	7,319.8	5,207.8	64.7	76.9	53.0
1984	12,747.9	7,392.8	5,355.1	65.0	76.7	53.8
1985	13,012.4	7,478.9	5,533.5	65.6	76.7	54.9
1986	13,272.1	7,585.4	5,686.7	66.1	76.8	55.7
1987	13,526.0	7,680.2	5,845.8	66.5	76.8	56.5
1988	13,779.1	7,754.3	6,024.8	66.8	76.6	57.4
1989	14,057.0	7,872.4	6,184.6	67.3	76.8	58.1
1990	14,244.6	7,924.1	6,320.6	67.1	76.1	58.5
1991	14,336.3	7,924.6	6,411.8	66.6	75.0	58.4
1992	14,336.1	7,911.2	6,425.0	65.7	73.9	57.8
1993	14,435.0	7,943.2	6,491.9	65.3	73.3	57.7
1994	14,573.7	8,014.3	6,559.4	65.2	73.1	57.5
1995	14,689.2	8,049.5	6,639.8	64.8	72.5	57.5
1996	14,853.5	8,129.1	6,724.4	64.7	72.2	57.4
1997	15,079.1	8,233.8	6,845.3	64.8	72.2	57.8
1998	15,316.3	8,324.3	6,992.0	65.1	72.1	58.4
1999	15,588.3	8,457.6	7,130.7	65.5	72.4	58.9
2000	15,847.0	8,569.2	7,277.8	65.8	72.4	59.4
2001	16,109.8	8,690.9	7,418.9	65.9	72.3	59.7
2002	16,579.3	8,906.2	7,673.1	66.9	73.0	60.9
2003	16,958.5	9,067.7	7,890.9	67.5	73.4	61.9
2004	17,182.3	9,166.0	8,016.3	67.5	73.2	62.0
2005	17,342.6	9,243.7	8,098.8	67.2	72.8	61.8
2006	17,592.8	9,335.4	8,257.3	67.2	72.5	62.1

Source: Statistics Canada, CANSIM table 282-0002.

Participation rates							
15 to 24		25 to 44		45 and older		65 and older	
Males	Females	Males	Females	Males	Females	Males	Females
			%				
73.6	64.8	95.4	65.2	62.9	30.4	12.7	4.0
70.7	63.8	94.3	66.1	61.8	30.5	12.7	4.0
70.6	64.5	94.0	67.6	61.3	30.8	12.1	3.7
70.8	65.0	94.1	69.4	60.3	30.8	11.8	3.9
71.1	65.6	94.2	70.9	59.4	31.8	11.8	4.1
72.3	67.0	94.4	73.1	58.6	30.9	11.1	3.4
73.0	67.5	94.3	74.0	58.1	32.0	11.2	3.3
73.1	68.0	94.2	75.3	57.5	33.0	10.7	3.6
73.8	68.5	94.2	76.6	57.4	33.4	10.5	3.9
72.4	67.3	93.8	77.7	56.8	33.9	10.8	3.6
70.1	66.1	93.1	77.8	56.3	34.6	11.1	3.4
67.8	64.5	92.0	76.8	55.9	35.4	10.6	3.4
66.5	62.2	92.1	77.1	55.5	36.1	9.7	3.5
65.9	61.9	91.8	76.9	55.9	36.6	10.7	3.4
64.9	61.3	91.6	77.1	55.4	36.9	9.9	3.4
64.1	60.3	91.6	77.8	55.4	37.1	9.8	3.4
63.6	59.2	91.9	78.4	55.8	38.1	9.8	3.6
63.4	60.2	92.2	79.0	55.8	39.3	10.2	3.5
65.3	61.5	92.2	79.6	56.4	39.9	9.8	3.4
65.9	62.8	92.1	79.9	56.7	40.9	9.5	3.3
66.1	63.2	92.1	80.4	56.9	41.6	9.4	3.4
67.8	65.3	92.3	81.3	58.1	43.2	10.3	3.8
68.3	66.5	92.5	81.7	59.2	45.0	11.5	4.2
67.8	66.2	92.4	82.2	59.6	45.5	11.8	4.4
66.1	65.8	92.3	81.8	59.9	45.9	12.1	5.0
66.4	66.4	92.0	81.8	59.6	46.8	12.1	5.2

Table 21.3 Labour force characteristics, by sex and age group, 2006

	Population	Labour force	Employed	Unemployed	Participation rate	Employment rate	Unemployment rate
	thousands				%		
Both sexes	**26,185.1**	**17,592.8**	**16,484.3**	**1,108.4**	**67.2**	**63.0**	**6.3**
15 to 24	**4,320.6**	2,869.5	2,535.8	333.7	66.4	58.7	11.6
15 to 19	**2,113.1**	1,135.1	954.3	180.8	53.7	45.2	15.9
20 to 24	**2,207.5**	1,734.4	1,581.5	152.9	78.6	71.6	8.8
25 and older	**21,864.6**	14,723.2	13,948.5	774.7	67.3	63.8	5.3
25 to 44	**9,277.1**	8,063.8	7,610.7	453.0	86.9	82.0	5.6
25 to 34	**4,343.4**	3,748.8	3,528.0	220.8	86.3	81.2	5.9
35 to 44	**4,933.8**	4,315.0	4,082.7	232.3	87.5	82.7	5.4
45 to 64	**8,570.6**	6,327.7	6,020.7	307.0	73.8	70.2	4.9
45 to 54	**4,955.2**	4,205.2	4,008.9	196.3	84.9	80.9	4.7
55 to 64	**3,615.4**	2,122.5	2,011.8	110.7	58.7	55.6	5.2
55 and older	**7,632.2**	2,454.2	2,328.9	125.4	32.2	30.5	5.1
65 and older	**4,016.8**	331.8	317.1	14.7	8.3	7.9	4.4
Males	**12,882.7**	**9,335.4**	**8,727.1**	**608.3**	**72.5**	**67.7**	**6.5**
15 to 24	**2,205.1**	1,465.1	1,276.9	188.2	66.4	57.9	12.8
15 to 19	**1,080.8**	565.8	466.2	99.6	52.4	43.1	17.6
20 to 24	**1,124.3**	899.3	810.7	88.6	80.0	72.1	9.9
25 and older	**10,677.6**	7,870.4	7,450.2	420.2	73.7	69.8	5.3
25 to 44	**4,647.8**	4,278.2	4,035.3	242.9	92.0	86.8	5.7
25 to 34	**2,181.2**	1,992.8	1,871.7	121.2	91.4	85.8	6.1
35 to 44	**2,466.6**	2,285.3	2,163.6	121.7	92.6	87.7	5.3
45 to 64	**4,237.2**	3,375.6	3,208.3	167.3	79.7	75.7	5.0
45 to 54	**2,457.6**	2,195.8	2,091.4	104.4	89.3	85.1	4.8
55 to 64	**1,779.6**	1,179.8	1,116.9	62.9	66.3	62.8	5.3
55 and older	**3,572.1**	1,396.4	1,323.5	73.0	39.1	37.1	5.2
65 and older	**1,792.4**	216.6	206.6	10.0	12.1	11.5	4.6
Females	**13,302.5**	**8,257.3**	**7,757.2**	**500.1**	**62.1**	**58.3**	**6.1**
15 to 24	**2,115.5**	1,404.5	1,258.9	145.5	66.4	59.5	10.4
15 to 19	**1,032.3**	569.3	488.1	81.2	55.1	47.3	14.3
20 to 24	**1,083.2**	835.1	770.8	64.3	77.1	71.2	7.7
25 and older	**11,187.0**	6,852.9	6,498.3	354.6	61.3	58.1	5.2
25 to 44	**4,629.3**	3,785.6	3,575.4	210.2	81.8	77.2	5.6
25 to 34	**2,162.1**	1,756.0	1,656.4	99.5	81.2	76.6	5.7
35 to 44	**2,467.2**	2,029.6	1,919.0	110.6	82.3	77.8	5.4
45 to 64	**4,333.3**	2,952.2	2,812.3	139.7	68.1	64.9	4.7
45 to 54	**2,497.5**	2,009.5	1,917.4	91.9	80.5	76.8	4.6
55 to 64	**1,835.8**	942.7	894.9	47.8	51.4	48.7	5.1
55 and older	**4,060.1**	1,057.8	1,005.4	52.4	26.1	24.8	5.0
65 and older	**2,224.3**	115.2	110.5	4.6	5.2	5.0	4.0

Note: Population aged 15 and older.
Source: Statistics Canada, CANSIM table 282-0002.

Table 21.4 Labour force characteristics, by census metropolitan area, 2006

	Population	Labour force	Employed	Unemployed	Participation rate	Employment rate	Unemployment rate
	thousands				%		
St. John's	151.4	101.6	93.4	8.2	67.1	61.7	8.1
Halifax	311.3	215.7	204.8	10.8	69.3	65.8	5.0
Saint John	103.4	65.9	61.9	4.0	63.7	59.9	6.1
Saguenay	126.1	77.2	70.4	6.8	61.2	55.8	8.8
Québec	599.4	397.4	376.6	20.8	66.3	62.8	5.2
Sherbrooke	135.2	88.8	81.9	7.0	65.7	60.6	7.9
Trois-Rivières	119.3	73.2	67.3	5.9	61.4	56.4	8.1
Montréal	3,003.8	2,026.7	1,856.8	169.8	67.5	61.8	8.4
Ottawa–Gatineau	943.5	678.6	643.3	35.3	71.9	68.2	5.2
Quebec part	235.6	169.7	160.2	9.5	72.0	68.0	5.6
Ontario part	707.8	509.0	483.1	25.9	71.9	68.3	5.1
Kingston	125.7	82.4	77.3	5.1	65.6	61.5	6.2
Oshawa	274.5	189.7	177.3	12.4	69.1	64.6	6.5
Toronto	4,374.0	2,998.7	2,802.1	196.6	68.6	64.1	6.6
Hamilton	588.0	395.3	371.9	23.5	67.2	63.2	5.9
St. Catharines–Niagara	327.0	203.1	190.2	12.9	62.1	58.2	6.4
Kitchener	371.1	265.2	251.4	13.8	71.5	67.7	5.2
London	378.1	261.8	245.6	16.2	69.2	65.0	6.2
Windsor	270.5	181.3	165.1	16.3	67.0	61.0	9.0
Greater Sudbury / Grand Sudbury	132.6	84.2	78.1	6.1	63.5	58.9	7.2
Thunder Bay	104.3	66.5	61.5	5.0	63.8	59.0	7.5
Winnipeg	571.5	400.7	382.2	18.5	70.1	66.9	4.6
Regina	161.0	115.2	109.6	5.6	71.6	68.1	4.9
Saskatoon	188.2	133.9	128.0	5.9	71.1	68.0	4.4
Calgary	887.4	676.9	655.1	21.8	76.3	73.8	3.2
Edmonton	837.8	584.0	561.3	22.7	69.7	67.0	3.9
Abbotsford	128.2	86.3	82.3	3.9	67.3	64.2	4.5
Vancouver	1,862.2	1,241.9	1,187.1	54.8	66.7	63.7	4.4
Victoria	278.3	182.0	175.2	6.7	65.4	63.0	3.7

Note: Population aged 15 and older.
Source: Statistics Canada, CANSIM table 282-0053.

Table 21.5 Full-time and part-time employment, by sex and age group, 2001 to 2006

	2001	2002	2003	2004	2005	2006
			thousands			
Total employed, both sexes	**14,946.2**	**15,310.4**	**15,672.3**	**15,947.0**	**16,169.7**	**16,484.3**
15 to 24	2,324.6	2,399.1	2,449.4	2,461.0	2,472.5	2,535.8
25 to 44	7,570.8	7,575.6	7,571.5	7,594.0	7,597.5	7,610.7
45 and older	5,050.8	5,335.7	5,651.4	5,892.0	6,099.7	6,337.8
Full-time	12,242.5	12,439.3	12,705.3	12,998.1	13,206.2	13,509.7
15 to 24	1,314.8	1,323.1	1,344.3	1,361.4	1,370.2	1,419.8
25 to 44	6,637.5	6,627.0	6,624.7	6,671.2	6,684.7	6,730.9
45 and older	4,290.2	4,489.1	4,736.3	4,965.5	5,151.3	5,359.0
Part-time	2,703.7	2,871.1	2,967.0	2,948.9	2,963.5	2,974.7
15 to 24	1,009.8	1,076.0	1,105.1	1,099.6	1,102.3	1,116.0
25 to 44	933.3	948.5	946.8	922.8	912.8	879.9
45 and older	760.6	846.6	915.0	926.5	948.4	978.8
Total employed, males	**8,035.8**	**8,184.4**	**8,348.1**	**8,480.6**	**8,594.7**	**8,727.1**
15 to 24	1,192.6	1,224.3	1,243.2	1,248.3	1,239.0	1,276.9
25 to 44	4,044.9	4,028.4	4,029.0	4,023.8	4,032.1	4,035.3
45 and older	2,798.3	2,931.7	3,075.8	3,208.4	3,323.6	3,414.9
Full-time	7,195.3	7,287.9	7,423.0	7,559.3	7,664.0	7,781.0
15 to 24	753.3	763.9	774.9	781.2	782.5	809.2
25 to 44	3,855.2	3,831.1	3,832.2	3,834.1	3,832.6	3,845.6
45 and older	2,586.8	2,692.9	2,815.9	2,944.1	3,048.9	3,126.2
Part-time	840.5	896.5	925.0	921.3	930.7	946.1
15 to 24	439.3	460.4	468.3	467.1	456.5	467.7
25 to 44	189.7	197.4	196.9	189.8	199.5	189.7
45 and older	211.5	238.8	259.8	264.4	274.7	288.7
Total employed, females	**6,910.3**	**7,126.0**	**7,324.2**	**7,466.4**	**7,575.0**	**7,757.2**
15 to 24	1,132.0	1,174.8	1,206.2	1,212.6	1,233.5	1,258.9
25 to 44	3,525.9	3,547.1	3,542.5	3,570.2	3,565.4	3,575.4
45 and older	2,252.4	2,404.0	2,575.6	2,683.5	2,776.2	2,922.9
Full-time	5,047.1	5,151.4	5,282.3	5,438.8	5,542.3	5,728.7
15 to 24	561.5	559.2	569.4	580.2	587.8	610.5
25 to 44	2,782.3	2,796.0	2,792.5	2,837.2	2,852.1	2,885.3
45 and older	1,703.4	1,796.2	1,920.4	2,021.4	2,102.4	2,232.8
Part-time	1,863.2	1,974.6	2,041.9	2,027.6	2,032.8	2,028.5
15 to 24	570.5	615.6	636.8	632.4	645.8	648.4
25 to 44	743.6	751.2	749.9	733.0	713.3	690.1
45 and older	549.1	607.8	655.2	662.1	673.7	690.0

Source: Statistics Canada, CANSIM table 282-0002.

Table 21.6 Reasons for part-time work, by sex and age group, 2006

	All ages	15 to 24	25 to 44	45 and older
	thousands			
All persons employed part time	**2,974.7**	**1,116.0**	**879.9**	**978.8**
All males employed part time	**946.1**	467.7	189.7	288.7
All females employed part time	**2,028.5**	648.4	690.1	690.0
	%			
Both sexes				
Own illness	**3.1**	0.5	3.4	5.8
Caring for children	**10.3**	1.0	28.7	4.5
Other personal/family responsibilities	**2.9**	0.6	4.0	4.6
Going to school	**31.5**	75.0	10.4	0.9
Personal preference	**27.2**	5.8	20.0	58.2
Other voluntary	**0.8**	0.4	1.4	0.9
Involuntary (no full-time work available)	**24.1**	16.8	32.2	25.1
Males				
Own illness	**3.1**	0.6	5.1	6.0
Caring for children	**1.3**	x	4.0	1.4
Other personal/family responsibilities	**1.3**	0.6	2.0	2.1
Going to school	**41.7**	76.2	18.9	0.7
Personal preference	**25.4**	5.6	20.9	60.4
Other voluntary	**1.1**	0.4	2.5	1.3
Involuntary (no full-time work available)	**26.1**	16.5	46.8	28.2
Females				
Own illness	**3.0**	0.4	2.9	5.7
Caring for children	**14.6**	1.6	35.5	5.8
Other personal/family responsibilities	**3.7**	0.6	4.5	5.7
Going to school	**26.7**	74.1	8.0	0.9
Personal preference	**28.1**	5.9	19.8	57.3
Other voluntary	**0.7**	0.3	1.1	0.7
Involuntary (no full-time work available)	**23.2**	17.1	28.2	23.8

Notes: Expressed as a percentage of total part-time employment.
Population aged 15 and older.
Source: Statistics Canada, CANSIM table 282-0014.

Table 21.7 Employment, by sector, 1991 to 2006

	1991	1992	1993	1994	1995	1996	1997
				thousands			
All sectors	**12,857.4**	**12,730.9**	**12,792.7**	**13,058.7**	**13,295.4**	**13,421.4**	**13,706.0**
Goods-producing sector	3,518.8	3,390.6	3,325.2	3,397.5	3,467.6	3,476.0	3,561.0
Agriculture	448.9	439.4	445.5	437.2	419.3	422.5	417.0
Forestry, fishing, mining, oil and gas extraction	298.1	280.1	271.8	285.6	294.8	294.0	296.7
Utilities	142.8	143.5	137.4	127.0	123.5	124.1	115.3
Construction	738.9	713.1	691.2	724.6	726.4	709.7	721.0
Manufacturing	1,890.2	1,814.5	1,779.2	1,823.2	1,903.8	1,925.7	2,010.9
Services-producing sector	9,338.5	9,340.3	9,467.6	9,661.2	9,827.7	9,945.4	10,145.1
Trade	2,063.2	2,038.4	2,027.0	2,061.1	2,077.5	2,087.7	2,106.1
Transportation and warehousing	624.2	609.6	618.6	644.9	660.8	674.0	694.6
Finance, insurance, real estate and leasing	853.9	840.5	839.8	832.7	846.1	861.4	865.0
Professional, scientific and technical services	603.8	590.0	615.9	642.5	674.3	706.7	777.8
Business, building and other support services	319.2	322.8	342.8	365.4	402.5	420.8	441.8
Educational services	859.0	886.5	905.5	927.2	928.3	913.0	916.6
Health care and social assistance	1,310.0	1,326.9	1,348.5	1,364.2	1,388.6	1,390.9	1,388.4
Information, culture and recreation	499.1	492.9	503.2	537.4	567.7	579.1	603.5
Accommodation and food services	758.6	769.6	772.1	799.1	816.1	847.9	871.0
Public administration	852.0	865.0	861.7	834.8	818.6	807.8	797.2
Other services	595.6	598.0	632.5	651.9	647.2	656.0	683.0

Note: North American Industry Classification System (NAICS), 2002.
Source: Statistics Canada, CANSIM table 282-0008.

1998	1999	2000	2001	2002	2003	2004	2005	2006
				thousands				
14,046.2	14,406.7	14,764.2	14,946.2	15,310.4	15,672.3	15,947.0	16,169.7	16,484.3
3,657.9	3,742.5	3,822.0	3,779.9	3,878.6	3,925.7	3,989.8	4,002.4	3,985.9
424.2	406.0	372.1	323.3	325.4	332.4	326.0	343.7	346.4
293.5	263.8	275.4	278.9	270.3	281.6	286.6	306.4	330.1
114.7	114.3	114.9	124.4	131.9	130.5	133.3	125.3	122.0
731.9	766.9	810.1	824.3	865.2	906.0	951.7	1,019.5	1,069.7
2,093.5	2,191.5	2,249.4	2,229.0	2,285.9	2,275.2	2,292.1	2,207.4	2,117.7
10,388.4	10,664.3	10,942.2	11,166.2	11,431.8	11,746.6	11,957.2	12,167.3	12,498.4
2,125.4	2,218.2	2,293.3	2,363.3	2,409.3	2,467.8	2,507.1	2,574.6	2,633.5
712.7	737.0	772.3	775.8	760.7	790.9	799.4	793.6	802.2
847.9	859.9	857.9	876.7	895.1	917.0	960.6	987.8	1,040.5
849.8	900.7	932.2	986.5	987.1	1,003.6	1,018.3	1,050.0	1,089.9
478.1	504.7	537.0	537.2	579.6	608.7	630.2	654.4	690.0
930.0	970.7	974.1	981.6	1,007.4	1,027.1	1,035.7	1,106.1	1,158.4
1,428.5	1,436.0	1,514.0	1,540.4	1,617.3	1,679.2	1,733.4	1,734.6	1,785.5
615.8	630.5	662.1	709.4	715.1	714.6	738.0	735.1	745.0
911.4	913.6	938.2	943.2	985.1	1,005.5	1,012.4	1,004.5	1,015.0
781.9	776.3	772.6	785.4	788.9	819.0	825.5	833.1	837.4
706.8	716.5	688.5	666.8	686.2	713.1	696.6	693.4	701.0

Table 21.8 Employment, by sector and by province, 2006

	Canada	Newfoundland and Labrador	Prince Edward Island	Nova Scotia
		thousands		
All sectors	**16,484.3**	**215.7**	**68.6**	**441.8**
Goods-producing sector	**3,985.9**	49.1	18.9	85.7
Agriculture	**346.4**	1.9	3.9	4.7
Forestry, fishing, mining, oil and gas extraction	**330.1**	16.4	2.4	12.7
Utilities	**122.0**	2.2	0.3	1.8
Construction	**1,069.7**	12.9	5.7	27.3
Manufacturing	**2,117.7**	15.7	6.6	39.1
Services-producing sector	**12,498.4**	166.6	49.7	356.2
Trade	**2,633.5**	37.7	9.9	78.2
Transportation and warehousing	**802.2**	11.6	2.2	18.7
Finance, insurance, real estate and leasing	**1,040.5**	6.5	2.1	22.3
Professional, scientific and technical services	**1,089.9**	6.7	2.8	18.4
Business, building and other support services	**690.0**	8.5	2.8	28.8
Educational services	**1,158.4**	16.6	4.6	34.7
Health care and social assistance	**1,785.5**	30.1	7.9	59.1
Information, culture and recreation	**745.0**	8.8	2.6	16.3
Accommodation and food services	**1,015.0**	13.4	5.6	29.8
Public administration	**837.4**	15.3	6.3	29.2
Other services	**701.0**	11.3	2.9	20.7

Note: North American Industry Classification System (NAICS), 2002.
Source: Statistics Canada, CANSIM table 282-0008.

New Brunswick	Quebec	Ontario	Manitoba	Saskatchewan	Alberta	British Columbia
			thousands			
355.4	**3,765.4**	**6,492.7**	**587.0**	**491.6**	**1,870.7**	**2,195.5**
77.1	901.1	1,600.5	138.1	132.8	518.9	463.9
6.2	65.1	100.4	29.4	47.8	52.3	34.7
9.9	38.8	38.7	6.5	21.5	139.3	43.8
3.1	29.7	49.0	5.6	4.5	17.1	8.6
21.1	186.1	405.2	29.9	29.6	172.6	179.3
36.9	581.3	1,007.2	66.6	29.3	137.5	197.5
278.3	2,864.4	4,892.2	448.9	358.8	1,351.8	1,731.6
56.8	628.5	1,015.7	91.3	79.2	282.4	353.7
19.9	167.2	296.1	35.1	25.7	106.2	119.5
16.4	222.3	476.8	34.2	25.7	96.2	138.0
14.5	241.7	453.8	23.4	18.9	142.2	167.6
21.8	139.8	295.8	18.3	12.6	62.7	98.8
27.2	260.9	444.5	45.5	38.1	130.4	156.0
45.3	454.1	638.2	79.6	59.5	179.5	232.2
11.9	160.4	319.6	23.7	20.2	68.3	113.2
25.0	214.8	373.2	37.5	30.2	114.9	170.5
21.7	215.6	314.5	35.0	27.5	81.1	91.3
17.7	159.1	264.0	25.4	21.2	87.9	90.8

Table 21.9 Employment and average weekly earnings, public administration and all industries, 1993 to 2006

	1993	1994	1995	1996	1997
	thousands				
All industries[1]	**10,817.4**	**10,980.6**	**11,214.7**	**11,298.9**	**11,632.4**
Public administration	767.2	760.5	746.8	722.7	707.6
Federal administration[2]	279.8	278.1	265.0	251.9	236.8
Provincial and territorial administration	229.8	224.5	222.6	208.9	202.7
Local administration	226.6	227.2	228.4	230.1	234.8
	average weekly earnings ($)				
All industries[1]	**583.15**	**593.15**	**598.90**	**611.26**	**623.63**
Public administration	727.81	732.69	729.83	725.35	729.12
Federal administration[2]	800.45	803.86	804.63	801.01	813.34
Provincial and territorial administration	722.87	723.31	721.99	728.45	741.41
Local administration	672.67	683.45	678.67	670.12	666.15

Notes: North American Industry Classification System (NAICS), 2002.

Data include overtime.

Excludes owners or partners of unincorporated businesses and professional practices, the self-employed, unpaid family workers, people working outside of Canada, military personnel and casual workers for whom a T4 is not required.

1. Excludes agriculture, fishing and trapping, private household services, religious organizations and the military.

2. Excludes the military.

Source: Statistics Canada, CANSIM tables 281-0024 and 281-0027.

1998	1999	2000	2001	2002	2003	2004	2005	2006
				thousands				
11,894.0	**12,066.3**	**12,474.6**	**12,787.7**	**12,980.7**	**13,244.5**	**13,439.7**	**13,702.2**	**14,041.3**
702.3	705.0	713.0	743.7	746.7	782.1	785.0	795.3	813.7
234.7	237.9	240.9	247.5	248.0	258.0	257.0	257.5	269.2
202.1	206.1	208.0	208.4	207.0	222.5	224.4	226.3	229.7
231.5	226.6	229.9	252.8	255.5	260.9	261.6	268.4	272.9
				average weekly earnings ($)				
632.93	**640.71**	**655.91**	**665.30**	**679.32**	**688.31**	**702.87**	**725.51**	**747.08**
734.05	761.05	781.15	787.87	829.32	855.15	872.05	899.05	930.85
830.71	886.01	926.60	931.57	1,014.45	1,043.49	1,066.43	1,110.61	1,165.74
750.14	758.82	767.44	780.45	804.34	833.63	846.09	862.93	890.59
657.34	671.37	680.57	688.62	710.44	732.21	747.87	767.95	776.45

Table 21.10 Average hourly wages of employees, by selected characteristics and professions, 2005 and 2006

	2005		2006		2005 to 2006
	thousands	average hourly wage ($)	thousands	average hourly wage ($)	% change in average hourly wage
All employed people[1]	**13,658.2**	**19.09**	**13,986.3**	**19.72**	**3.3**
Age 15 to 24	2,373.5	10.87	2,443.4	11.36	4.5
Age 25 to 54	9,708.3	20.80	9,863.9	21.49	3.3
Age 55 and older	1,576.4	20.95	1,679.0	21.50	2.6
Males	6,949.1	20.74	7,105.7	21.43	3.3
Females	6,709.1	17.38	6,880.6	17.96	3.3
Full-time workers	11,224.5	20.31	11,526.9	20.99	3.4
Part-time workers	2,433.6	13.45	2,459.4	13.80	2.6
Union coverage[2]	4,374.4	22.15	4,428.6	22.73	2.6
No union coverage[3]	9,283.8	17.65	9,557.7	18.33	3.9
Permanent job[4]	11,860.6	19.73	12,163.1	20.38	3.3
Temporary job[5]	1,797.6	14.91	1,823.2	15.30	2.6
Management occupations	947.3	29.86	1,005.9	31.13	4.3
Business, finance and administrative occupations	2,649.3	18.23	2,729.8	18.79	3.1
Natural and applied sciences and related occupations	959.3	26.91	1,001.0	27.78	3.2
Health occupations	840.7	22.45	860.3	23.11	2.9
Occupations in social science, education, public administration and religion	1,182.7	25.04	1,239.6	25.64	2.4
Occupations in art, culture, recreation and sport	322.8	19.63	323.0	19.71	0.4
Sales and service occupations	3,453.4	12.82	3,514.2	13.10	2.2
Trade, transport and equipment operators and related occupations	1,982.8	18.91	2,032.4	19.52	3.2
Occupations unique to primary industry	282.8	15.63	299.6	16.20	3.7
Occupations unique to processing, manufacturing and utilities	1,037.1	16.71	980.8	17.18	2.8

Note: Data are not seasonally adjusted.

1. Those who work as employees of a private firm or business or the public sector.

2. Employees who are members of a union and employees who are not members of a union, but who are covered by a collective agreement or a union contract.

3. Employees who are not members of a union or not covered by a collective agreement or a union contract.

4. A job that is expected to last as long as the employee wants it (given that business conditions permit) and has no predetermined end date.

5. A job that has a predetermined end date or will end as soon as a specified project is completed. This includes seasonal jobs; temporary, term or contract jobs, including work done through a temporary help agency; casual jobs; and other temporary work.

Source: Statistics Canada, CANSIM tables 282-0069 and 282-0073.

Table 21.11 Average earnings, by sex and work pattern, 1990 to 2004

	All earners			Full-year, full-time workers		
	Females	Males	Earnings ratio[1]	Females	Males	Earnings ratio[1]
	$ 2004 constant		%	$ 2004 constant		%
1990	22,100	37,800	58.4	33,000	49,300	66.8
1991	22,100	36,700	60.1	33,700	49,000	68.7
1992	22,500	36,300	61.9	34,800	49,500	70.3
1993	22,700	36,400	62.5	34,900	49,000	71.3
1994	22,600	37,300	60.5	34,200	49,900	68.5
1995	23,300	36,800	63.4	35,500	49,100	72.4
1996	23,200	36,700	63.1	34,900	48,300	72.3
1997	23,300	37,700	61.9	34,600	50,700	68.3
1998	24,400	38,800	62.8	37,100	51,700	71.9
1999	24,800	39,500	62.6	35,700	52,200	68.4
2000	25,200	40,800	61.7	36,900	52,200	70.6
2001	25,300	40,700	62.1	37,200	53,300	69.9
2002	25,600	40,800	62.8	37,500	53,400	70.2
2003	25,300	40,200	62.9	37,300	53,200	70.2
2004	25,600	40,300	63.5	38,400	54,900	69.9

1. Represents female-to-male earnings ratio.
Source: Statistics Canada, CANSIM table 202-0102.

Table 21.12 Earners, by sex and work pattern, 1990 to 2004

	All earners			Full-year, full-time workers		
	Both sexes	Females	Males	Both sexes	Females	Males
	thousands					
1990	**15,239**	6,891	8,348	8,835	3,398	5,437
1991	**15,011**	6,804	8,207	8,564	3,352	5,212
1992	**15,048**	6,867	8,181	8,405	3,305	5,100
1993	**14,905**	6,795	8,110	8,461	3,347	5,114
1994	**15,006**	6,800	8,206	8,654	3,349	5,305
1995	**15,346**	6,993	8,352	8,843	3,478	5,365
1996	**15,187**	6,880	8,307	7,881	3,044	4,837
1997	**15,577**	7,122	8,455	8,008	3,135	4,873
1998	**15,896**	7,298	8,599	8,178	3,239	4,939
1999	**16,403**	7,590	8,813	8,497	3,431	5,066
2000	**16,858**	7,830	9,028	8,305	3,349	4,956
2001	**17,226**	8,004	9,221	8,713	3,518	5,194
2002	**17,445**	8,121	9,324	8,483	3,477	5,006
2003	**17,830**	8,336	9,494	8,725	3,650	5,075
2004	**18,302**	8,539	9,763	9,064	3,778	5,286

Note: Data before 1996 are taken from the Survey of Consumer Finances (SCF) and data from 1996 on are taken from the Survey of Labour and Income Dynamics (SLID). The surveys use different definitions and, as a result, the number of people working full year, full time in the SLID is smaller than in the SCF.
Source: Statistics Canada, CANSIM table 202-0101.

Table 21.13 Effective wage increases in collective agreements, by industry sector and bargaining unit, 2001 to 2006

	2001	2002	2003	2004	2005	2006
			%			
Industry sectors	**3.3**	**3.0**	**2.5**	**2.0**	**2.4**	**2.4**
Primary industries	2.6	..	..	..	2.2	..
Manufacturing	2.6	3.3	2.5	2.7	2.4	2.2
Utilities	2.4	2.6	2.8	..	2.5	2.6
Construction	3.1	..	..	2.7	..	..
Wholesale and retail trade	1.5	1.9	..	1.7	2.0	..
Transportation	2.6	3.4	1.9	1.6	2.8	2.5
Information and culture	3.1	..	2.1	2.6	2.3	1.8
Finance, real estate and management services	1.9	1.7	2.8	..	..	2.5
Education, health and social services	3.6	3.2	3.5	1.6	2.4	2.6
Entertainment and hospitality	..	1.8	2.6	..	..	2.9
Public administration	3.1	2.7	2.4	2.6	2.4	2.8
Private and public sector bargaining units						
Private sector	2.8	2.6	1.6	2.2	2.4	2.2
Public sector	3.4	3.1	2.8	1.6	2.4	2.6
Federal administration	3.7	3.2	..	2.6	2.4	2.6
Federal crown corporations	..	..	3.1	..	..	2.6
Provincial administration	3.5	2.3	..	..	2.1	2.6
Local administration	2.7	3.1	2.8	2.6	3.1	3.4
Education, health and welfare	3.7	3.2	3.5	1.6	2.4	2.6
Public utilities	2.8	2.9	2.7	..	2.0	..

Note: North American Industry Classification System (NAICS), 2002.
Source: Statistics Canada, CANSIM table 278-0007.

Table 21.14 Self-employment, by sex, 1976 to 2006

	Both sexes	Males	Females
	thousands		
1976	1,185.0	873.4	311.6
1977	1,210.3	880.4	329.8
1978	1,263.4	910.3	353.1
1979	1,324.7	944.6	380.1
1980	1,363.6	971.9	391.7
1981	1,425.2	1,020.6	404.6
1982	1,483.2	1,056.7	426.5
1983	1,543.2	1,094.5	448.7
1984	1,569.7	1,096.4	473.3
1985	1,726.0	1,188.9	537.2
1986	1,674.2	1,175.6	498.5
1987	1,699.1	1,185.8	513.3
1988	1,774.1	1,233.1	541.0
1989	1,800.3	1,240.7	559.6
1990	1,836.6	1,263.6	573.0
1991	1,895.8	1,313.2	582.6
1992	1,927.5	1,316.7	610.8
1993	2,011.1	1,361.7	649.4
1994	2,028.5	1,351.7	676.7
1995	2,083.1	1,381.8	701.3
1996	2,171.6	1,426.8	744.8
1997	2,349.4	1,522.2	827.2
1998	2,405.7	1,550.6	855.1
1999	2,433.0	1,582.8	850.2
2000	2,373.7	1,538.7	835.1
2001	2,276.7	1,503.3	773.4
2002	2,314.5	1,499.7	814.7
2003	2,401.8	1,571.1	830.7
2004	2,453.4	1,614.5	838.9
2005	2,511.6	1,645.6	866.0
2006	2,498.0	1,621.4	876.6

Source: Statistics Canada, CANSIM table 282-0012.

Table 21.15 Employment rate, by educational attainment, age group and sex, 2000 and 2006

	2000			2006		
	Both sexes	Males	Females	Both sexes	Males	Females
			%			
All education levels	61.3	67.3	55.4	63.0	67.7	58.3
15 to 24	56.3	56.8	55.7	58.7	57.9	59.5
25 to 44	80.8	86.5	75.1	82.0	86.8	77.2
45 and older	45.9	53.8	38.7	50.4	56.6	44.6
Less than Grade 9	21.9	30.4	14.3	21.5	29.5	14.5
15 to 24	25.1	29.6	19.0	26.5	30.9	20.9
25 to 44	52.0	62.7	39.5	52.1	64.6	36.3
45 and older	17.3	25.1	10.9	17.3	24.1	11.9
Some high school	45.3	53.1	37.4	44.9	51.3	38.3
15 to 24	41.9	43.2	40.5	43.4	43.5	43.3
25 to 44	67.8	76.5	56.7	66.8	75.6	55.2
45 and older	35.0	46.0	26.2	37.1	46.3	29.0
High school graduate	65.9	73.9	58.9	65.2	72.0	59.0
15 to 24	69.0	72.1	65.4	69.4	69.8	68.9
25 to 44	80.2	87.5	73.2	79.7	85.9	72.9
45 and older	50.5	58.9	44.4	53.6	61.1	47.9
Some postsecondary	63.6	67.3	60.0	64.0	66.6	61.3
15 to 24	58.6	58.7	58.6	60.6	59.0	62.0
25 to 44	77.0	82.7	71.5	78.0	81.7	73.8
45 and older	52.8	58.7	47.4	54.6	60.2	49.1
Postsecondary certificate or diploma[1]	72.9	78.0	67.8	72.7	76.5	69.0
15 to 24	75.7	75.5	75.9	78.0	77.5	78.5
25 to 44	85.2	90.2	80.2	86.1	90.1	82.2
45 and older	57.2	63.6	51.0	59.6	63.9	55.5
Bachelor's degree	78.1	80.9	75.5	76.8	79.4	74.5
15 to 24	75.1	74.6	75.5	74.7	73.0	75.6
25 to 44	86.4	91.0	82.6	85.9	90.3	82.4
45 and older	65.8	68.3	63.1	65.1	67.7	62.2
Above bachelor's degree	78.9	79.2	78.6	77.1	78.4	75.5
15 to 24	73.7	79.5	69.8	65.7	62.4	67.7
25 to 44	87.5	90.5	84.2	86.4	90.6	81.9
45 and older	70.7	70.3	71.3	69.0	69.3	68.5

1. Includes trades certificate.
Source: Statistics Canada, CANSIM table 282-0004.

Table 21.16 Days lost annually per worker, by sector, 2001 to 2006

	2001	2002	2003	2004	2005	2006
	average number					
Goods-producing sector	**8.5**	**9.2**	**9.3**	**9.1**	**9.3**	**9.6**
Primary industries	8.5	8.3	7.9	7.9	7.6	8.3
Utilities	7.9	8.3	10.0	10.2	9.1	12.4
Construction	8.4	9.2	8.6	7.2	8.3	9.5
Manufacturing	8.6	9.4	9.7	9.9	9.9	9.7
Services-producing sector	**8.5**	**9.1**	**9.2**	**9.2**	**9.8**	**9.8**
Trade	7.5	7.4	8.1	7.6	8.2	8.5
Transportation and warehousing	10.1	10.2	11.4	11.1	12.2	11.6
Finance, insurance, real estate and leasing	7.5	8.0	8.8	7.8	8.9	7.5
Professional, scientific and technical services	5.0	6.1	5.3	5.6	5.3	5.6
Business, building and other support services	8.1	9.1	8.7	9.6	11.0	11.5
Educational services	8.6	9.8	9.5	8.8	9.8	10.7
Health care and social assistance	12.8	13.7	13.0	14.4	14.2	14.4
Information, culture and recreation	7.5	8.2	7.6	7.9	8.5	8.7
Accommodation and food services	7.3	7.7	7.8	7.9	9.1	8.2
Public administration	10.2	11.1	10.9	10.9	12.2	12.0
Other services	6.5	6.7	7.0	7.5	6.8	7.3

Notes: North American Industry Classification System (NAICS), 2002.
Includes full-time paid workers only, who were not at work because of illness, disability or personal or family responsibility.
Source: Statistics Canada, CANSIM table 279-0030.

Table 21.17 Days lost annually per worker, by province, 2001 to 2006

	2001	2002	2003	2004	2005	2006
	average number					
Canada	**8.5**	**9.1**	**9.2**	**9.2**	**9.6**	**9.7**
Newfoundland and Labrador	8.7	8.6	10.5	10.3	9.5	9.7
Prince Edward Island	7.7	8.5	7.7	7.6	8.6	8.5
Nova Scotia	9.7	10.4	9.8	11.0	10.8	10.7
New Brunswick	10.2	9.7	10.2	9.6	10.3	11.5
Quebec	9.1	9.9	10.8	10.8	11.2	11.5
Ontario	7.6	8.4	8.3	8.5	8.6	8.8
Manitoba	9.4	10.1	9.4	9.8	9.9	10.1
Saskatchewan	10.0	10.3	10.4	10.3	11.1	11.0
Alberta	8.2	8.5	8.0	7.5	8.6	9.0
British Columbia	9.7	9.5	9.9	8.8	10.3	9.4

Note: Includes full-time paid workers only.
Source: Statistics Canada, CANSIM table 279-0029.

Table 21.18 Days lost annually per worker because of illness or disability, by province, 2001 to 2006

	2001	2002	2003	2004	2005	2006
	average number					
Canada	**7.0**	**7.4**	**7.5**	**7.5**	**7.8**	**7.6**
Newfoundland and Labrador	7.4	6.9	9.1	8.8	8.1	8.2
Prince Edward Island	6.5	6.9	6.4	6.0	6.9	6.9
Nova Scotia	8.3	8.8	8.1	9.1	9.0	8.9
New Brunswick	8.8	8.4	8.8	8.0	8.5	9.7
Quebec	7.9	8.4	9.3	9.4	9.6	9.3
Ontario	6.0	6.6	6.5	6.7	6.7	6.6
Manitoba	7.7	8.4	7.8	8.0	7.9	8.1
Saskatchewan	8.1	8.3	8.6	8.1	8.9	8.7
Alberta	6.5	6.7	6.2	5.6	6.5	6.6
British Columbia	8.3	7.8	8.1	7.3	8.5	7.6

Note: Includes full-time paid workers only.
Source: Statistics Canada, CANSIM table 279-0029.

Table 21.19 Labour force and paid workers covered by a Registered Pension Plan, by sex, 1984 to 2004

	1984	1989	1994	1999	2004
	number				
Registered pension plan[1] members					
Both sexes	**4,564,623**	**5,109,363**	**5,169,644**	**5,267,894**	**5,669,858**
Males	3,039,449	3,128,225	2,929,968	2,904,921	2,976,708
Females	1,525,174	1,981,138	2,239,676	2,362,973	2,693,150
	%				
Labour force covered by registered pension plans					
Both sexes	**35.9**	**35.8**	**35.1**	**33.5**	**32.8**
Males	40.8	38.9	36.0	34.0	32.2
Females	29.1	31.8	34.0	33.0	33.5
Paid workers[2] covered by registered pension plans					
Both sexes	**45.4**	**42.8**	**44.0**	**41.0**	**39.0**
Males	52.3	46.9	45.8	42.1	38.9
Females	35.8	37.4	41.6	39.6	39.0

Note: The data used from the Labour Force Survey (labour force and paid workers) are annual averages to which the number of Canadian Forces members was added.

1. Plans are established by either employers or unions to provide retirement income to employees.

2. Refers to employees in the public and private sector and includes self-employed workers in incorporated business (with and without paid help).

Source: Statistics Canada, Pension Plans in Canada and Labour Force Survey.

Languages

22

OVERVIEW

In the 2001 Census, English was the mother tongue for 59% of Canadians, unchanged from 1951, and French was the mother tongue for 23% of us, a decline from 29% in 1951. A mother tongue is the first language learned at home in childhood and still understood.

More than 100 other languages are spoken in Canada, and they can be heard on television and radio, at work, at school, on buses and at the local mall. So words such as donair, siesta, and ciao have found their way into our everyday speech.

After English and French, Chinese is the most commonly spoken language in Canada, followed by Italian and German. In 1971, German was third followed by Italian and Ukrainian. Arabic, Spanish and Punjabi are becoming more common, reflecting Canada's growing diversity and expanding trade.

Many factors influence how Canadians' use of language evolves: immigration, interprovincial migration, cross-cultural marriages, fertility rates, legislation and the languages spoken at home and at work.

Language usage and transfer

For most immigrants, English or French soon becomes the language used most often at school or work, even as many strive to maintain their ancestral languages. In the long run, children and grandchildren of immigrants tend to acquire English or French as their mother tongue.

Language transfer—the tendency to speak a language other than the mother tongue at home—can signal a change in the language that will be passed down to future generations within a family.

Chart 22.1
Mother tongue, Canada and Quebec, 1951 and 2001

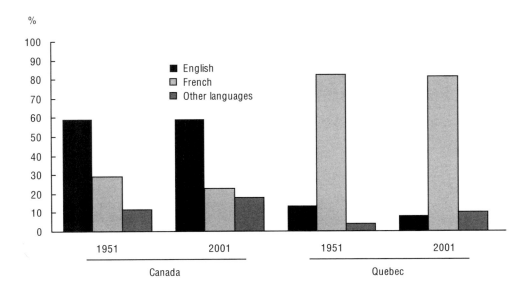

Source: Statistics Canada, Census of Population, 1951 and 2001.

For example, there has been an increase in language transfer among francophone minorities outside Quebec. In 1971, 30% of francophones outside Quebec spoke a language other than French, usually English, at home. By 2001, this increased to 38%. The transfer rate for francophones varied across the country from 11% for those living in New Brunswick to a rate of 75% in Saskatchewan.

Among Quebec's anglophone minority, the rate of language transfer was 10% in 2001, an increase from 8% in 1971.

In 2001, one out of six Canadians, more than 5.2 million people, were allophones; that is, their mother tongue was neither English nor French. They represented 18% of the population, up from 12% in 1951.

In Quebec these days, more allophones than in the past are learning and switching to French: 46% transferred to French in 2001, compared with 39% in 1996. In 2001, 73% of allophones could conduct a conversation in French, compared with 69% in 1996. About 54% transferred to English in 2001, compared with 61% in 1996.

The majority of allophones live in Ontario, British Columbia, Quebec and Alberta. Most

Top eight allophone groups

1971		2001[1]	
thousands			
German	559.0	Chinese	872.4
Italian	538.8	Italian	494.0
Ukrainian	309.9	German	455.5
Dutch[2]	146.7	Punjabi	284.8
Polish	136.5	Spanish	260.8
Greek	103.7	Portuguese	222.9
Chinese	95.9	Arabic	220.5
Magyar (Hungarian)	87.5	Polish	215.0

1. Includes all responses where these non-official languages are mentioned.
2. Includes respondents who reported Flemish or Frisian.
Source: Statistics Canada, Census of Population, 1971 and 2001.

live in our large cities. Chinese is the main non-official language in Vancouver, Toronto, Calgary, Ottawa and Edmonton. Italian is the main non-official language in Montréal and Windsor. In Winnipeg and Kitchener, it is German. In Abbotsford, British Columbia, Punjabi became the main non-official language in 2001.

Preserving mother tongues

Many immigrants believe that teaching their mother tongue to their Canadian-born children is important. Aside from the cultural

Chart 22.2
Allophone population, by province and territory, 2001

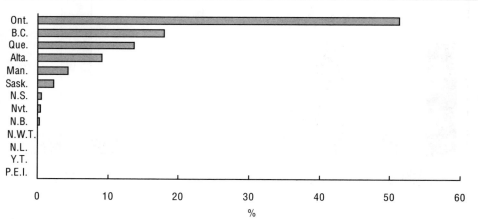

Note: Allophones are people whose mother tongue is neither English nor French.
Source: Statistics Canada, 2001 Census of Population.

value, it provides children with knowledge of another language, strong ethnic identity and enables participation in ethnic businesses and social life.

In the 2002 Ethnic Diversity Study, 64% of adults said they learned their parents' ancestral language in childhood and 74% of this group could still use it to carry on a conversation. Children were most likely to regularly use their parents' mother tongue at home if they acquired it early.

As adults, 32% used their parents' mother tongue regularly in the home. Outside the home, 16% of grown children of recent immigrants spoke their ancestral language regularly with their friends, while 12% of those in the labour market used it regularly in the workplace.

Parents whose mother tongue was Punjabi, Spanish, Cantonese, Korean or Greek were most likely to have children who learned these languages as their mother tongue. Individuals who were part of earlier immigrant groups—including Dutch, Scandinavian, German, Filipino, Semitic and Nigerian-Congolese—were the least likely to

pass along their languages to their Canadian-born children.

More of us are bilingual

In the 2001 Census, 18% of the population, or 5.2 million people, said they were bilingual in English and French, up from 17%, or 4.8 million, five years earlier. Nationally, 44% of francophones said they were bilingual in 2001, compared with 9% of anglophones.

Bilingualism is on the rise in Quebec. In 2001, 41% of Quebecers reported being bilingual, compared with 38% in 1996 and 35% in 1991. Anglophones in Quebec have the highest rate of bilingualism of all groups in Canada, and their bilingualism rate has risen, from 63% in 1996 to 67% in 2001. However, the proportion of anglophones has declined from 14% of Quebec's population in 1951 to 8% in 2001.

In the rest of Canada, however, the rate of bilingualism increased to 10% in 2001, compared with 8% in 1971.

Chart 22.3
English–French bilingualism, by province and territory, 2001

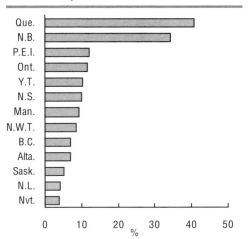

Source: Statistics Canada, 2001 Census of Population.

Selected sources

Statistics Canada

- *Canadian Social Trends*. Irregular. 11-008-XWE

- *Languages in Canada: 2001 Census.* Canadian Heritage/Statistics Canada, 2004, 96-326-XIE.

- *Profile of Languages in Canada: English, French and Many Others, 2001 Census.* Every 5 years. 96F0030XIE2001005

- *The Canadian Component of the 2003 International Adult Literacy and Skills Survey (IALSS): The Situation of Official Language Minorities.* Irregular. 89-552-MIE2006015

- *Use of English and French at Work, 2001 Census.* Every 5 years. 96F0030XIE2001011

Mother tongue, literacy and numeracy

Results of the 2003 International Adult Literacy and Skills Survey indicated major differences in literacy and numeracy levels among anglophone, francophone and allophone Canadians.

Fewer differences were found among the younger people in the survey and differences almost disappeared when education levels were taken into account. So level of schooling—not language—is strongly linked to the literacy skills required to process written information, be it words or numbers.

In the survey, people whose mother tongue was English scored higher than the other two linguistic groups in various literacy and numeracy tests. Almost 21% of anglophones obtained the highest level of competency in reading comprehension of narrative texts such as editorials, news articles or brochures.

By contrast, 13% of francophones and 10% of allophones scored at the highest level. Scores were similar in reading documents such as job applications, pay stubs, transport schedules, road maps, tables and charts.

According to the survey, 42% of the adult population aged 16 to 65 did not obtain at least a Level 3 in reading comprehension, which is seen as the minimum competency for responding to the demands of today's information-based society.

Literacy varies by province. For example, in New Brunswick, 66% of francophones did not achieve the minimum competency level for narrative texts, compared with 55% of francophones who did not in Quebec, Ontario and Manitoba. New Brunswick also had the highest proportion of anglophones who did not achieve the minimum levels.

Chart 22.4
Literacy and numeracy proficiency, Level 3 and higher, population aged 16 to 65, by mother tongue, 2003

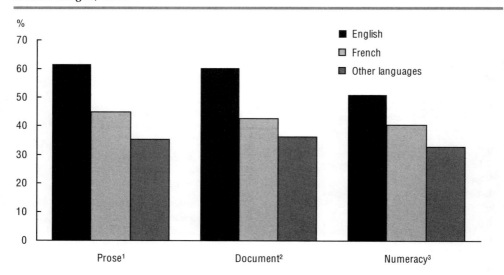

Note: Level 3 is considered the minimum threshold for using and understanding information in increasingly difficult texts and tasks.
1. The knowledge and skills needed to understand and use information from narrative texts.
2. The knowledge and skills required to locate and use information in various formats, such as maps, tables, charts and schedules.
3. The knowledge and skills required to effectively manage mathematical demands in daily life.
Source: Statistics Canada, Catalogue no. 89-617-MIE.

Evolution of Aboriginal languages

While the number of fluent speakers of some Aboriginal languages is declining, other languages are growing in use. Comparing Aboriginal communities counted in the 1996 Census with their status in 2001, Inuktituk is gaining fluent speakers. In 2001, 31,945 people reported that they could carry on a conversation in Inuktitut, up 8.7% from 29,400 in 1996. The number of speakers of Dene and Montagnais-Naskapi rose 10.2%.

However, fewer Aboriginal people reported having an Aboriginal language as a mother tongue: 198,595 in 2001, down almost 4% from 205,800 in 1996. A mother tongue is the first language learned in childhood and still understood.

The number of people whose mother tongue is Cree slipped 3% from 1996, whereas the number speaking Ojibway declined 6%. Among the Aboriginal languages reported

as a mother tongue in 2001, the three most common were Cree (80,000 people), Inuktitut (29,700) and Ojibway (23,500).

A good indicator of language retention in a community is the language spoken by children aged 14 and younger. In 2001, 64% of Inuit children used an Aboriginal language as their mother tongue, compared with 17% of First Nations children. Among Métis children, 2% spoke an Aboriginal language as their mother tongue.

In 2001, 71% of Inuit reported knowledge of their ancestral language, compared with almost 30% of First Nations members and 5% of Métis. In 2001, 24% of Aboriginal people said they could converse in their language, down from 29% in 1996. People living in the North and on reserves and settlements are more likely to maintain their Aboriginal language than those living in urban areas.

Chart 22.5
Mother tongue, selected Aboriginal languages, 2001

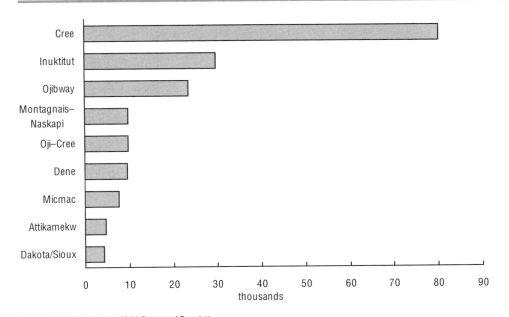

Source: Statistics Canada, 2001 Census of Population.

Chinese as a mother tongue

Chinese has been growing rapidly as a mother tongue in Canada since the 1980s, due to increased immigration, particularly from Hong Kong, the People's Republic of China and Taiwan.

Of all the languages spoken in Canada, Chinese is the most spoken language after English and French. In the 2001 Census, 853,700 people reported Chinese as their mother tongue—the first language learned and still understood. Among those whose mother tongue is Chinese, the most common dialects are Cantonese (322,300) and Mandarin (101,800).

Most immigrants settle in our biggest cities. Vancouver is a magnet for Chinese immigrants. In 2001, one in six residents of Vancouver spoke Chinese as their mother tongue. Among the city's allophone workers (people whose mother tongue is neither French nor English), 37% had Chinese as their mother tongue. Of this group, 53% use Chinese at work.

In Toronto, 18% of allophone workers have Chinese as their mother tongue and 40% of them use Chinese at work. In Montréal, 6% of allophone workers report Chinese as a mother tongue and 39% of them use Chinese at work.

In 2001, 85% of the Chinese in Canada— both Canadian- and foreign-born—had conversational knowledge of English or French. About 790,500 reported speaking a Chinese language at home regularly, 81,900 fewer than those who reported a Chinese mother tongue. This suggests some language transfer has occurred, mainly among those born in Canada who learned Chinese as a child but may not speak it regularly or do not use it as their main language at home.

Chart 22.6
Population with Chinese mother tongue, selected census metropolitan areas, 2001

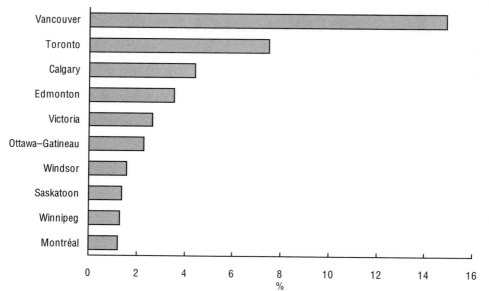

Note: Respondents who reported only one language as their mother tongue.
Source: Statistics Canada, 2001 Census of Population.

Language services

Canadians speak more than 100 languages besides French and English. Depending on the community, a visitor might hear Chinese, Italian, German, Punjabi, Inuktituk or Cree.

Not surprisingly, firms involved in supplying language services have a strong market in Canada. In 2004, more than 14,000 people worked as translators, language teachers and interpreters, either as permanent or contract workers, in the 600 private firms that make up the language services industry.

Together, these firms earned $404.1 million in revenues. Classroom and online training accounted for almost half of revenues or $193.2 million. Translation services revenues reached $154.1 million, while interpretation totalled $8.7 million. Accommodation fees associated with language study earned another $23.1 million, and a range of other services accounted for $25.0 million.

Nearly 200,000 people were enrolled in language training in 2004. Of the schools surveyed, 84% were private language schools, 9% were non-profit schools and another 7% were colleges, universities and other educational institutions.

The industry employed 7,405 permanent employees, split evenly between full-time and part-time workers. Among these workers, 2,557 were English-language instructors, 628 taught French and 1,033 were translators. Another 6,954 worked on contract.

Two-thirds of schools offered training to foreign students. Students from Asia made up the majority of foreign students, followed by students from Mexico, South and Central America and Europe. One-third of translation and interpretation firms exported goods and services—81% exported to the United States, while 38% exported to Europe.

Chart 22.7
Employment in the language services industry, by occupation, 2004

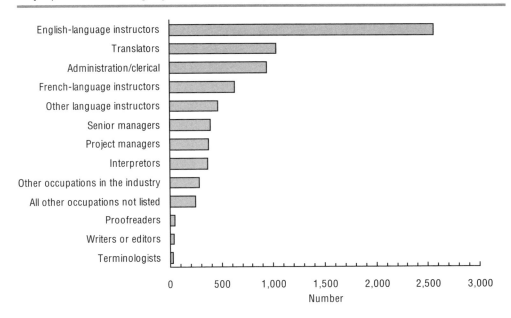

Source: Industry Canada.

Table 22.1 Population, by mother tongue and by province and territory, 2001

	Canada	Newfoundland and Labrador	Prince Edward Island	Nova Scotia	New Brunswick
			number		
Population	**29,639,035**	**508,080**	**133,385**	**897,570**	**719,710**
Mother tongue, single response[1]	29,257,885	507,425	132,855	893,195	713,770
English	17,352,315	499,750	125,125	832,660	465,170
French	6,703,325	2,110	5,665	34,025	236,665
Non-official languages	5,202,245	5,495	2,065	26,510	11,935
Chinese	853,745	520	130	2,125	1,215
Cantonese	322,315	50	0	425	190
Mandarin	101,790	25	20	115	105
Hakka	4,565	0	0	15	10
Chinese (not otherwise specified)	425,085	445	115	1,505	915
Italian	469,485	115	60	865	510
German	438,080	340	190	3,015	1,420
Polish	208,375	75	65	960	220
Spanish	245,495	55	55	700	510
Portuguese	213,815	105	15	355	150
Punjabi	271,220	90	0	275	80
Ukrainian	148,085	20	20	320	105
Arabic	199,940	215	145	4,035	535
Dutch	128,670	90	480	1,980	855
Tagalog (Pilipino)	174,060	130	20	335	150
Greek	120,360	35	0	1,110	165
Vietnamese	122,055	60	10	480	110
Cree	72,885	0	0	30	10
Inuktitut (Inuit)	29,010	550	10	10	15
Other non-official languages	1,506,965	3,090	860	9,930	5,815
Mother tongue, multiple responses[2]	381,145	650	530	4,375	5,940
English and French	112,575	330	440	2,555	5,255
English and non-official language	219,860	310	85	1,660	550
French and non-official language	38,630	0	0	125	105
English, French and non-official language	10,085	10	0	35	35

1. The respondent reported only one language as a mother tongue.
2. The respondent reported more than one language as a mother tongue.
Source: Statistics Canada, 2001 Census of Population.

Quebec	Ontario	Manitoba	Saskatchewan	Alberta	British Columbia	Yukon	Northwest Territories	Nunavut
				number				
7,125,580	**11,285,550**	**1,103,695**	**963,150**	**2,941,150**	**3,868,875**	**28,520**	**37,105**	**26,670**
7,028,225	11,122,935	1,087,415	953,500	2,907,380	3,820,125	28,190	36,660	26,210
557,040	7,965,225	823,910	817,955	2,379,515	2,825,780	24,590	28,650	6,940
5,761,765	485,630	44,340	17,775	58,645	54,400	890	950	395
709,420 '	2,672,085	219,160	117,765	469,220	939,945	2,705	7,065	18,875
43,745	404,250	9,115	6,010	78,205	307,990	175	160	25
6,140	158,035	2,530	1,430	26,255	127,160	30	65	10
4,050	41,845	700	395	5,580	48,880	10	10	0
70	2,245	15	20	570	1,625	0	0	0
33,490	202,125	5,945	4,170	45,795	130,330	150	90	10
124,695	295,205	4,945	890	13,935	28,165	30	60	15
17,690	156,080	63,215	32,515	78,040	84,605	725	215	25
17,155	138,940	9,910	3,015	20,635	17,320	20	40	10
70,095	111,690	5,210	1,970	19,820	28,240	75	60	15
33,355	152,115	7,005	405	6,110	14,155	0	15	10
9,900	110,540	5,420	535	22,535	121,740	70	20	0
5,125	48,620	26,540	19,650	33,970	13,600	55	50	15
76,285	94,640	1,280	1,085	15,390	6,235	10	70	0
3,220	69,655	3,975	1,930	19,575	26,740	100	65	0
9,550	88,870	11,385	1,545	11,705	35,940	100	300	25
41,980	65,285	1,315	975	2,770	6,680	10	25	0
21,640	55,240	2,950	1,390	16,680	23,215	65	160	0
11,810	4,405	11,110	22,055	15,105	1,115	20	155	10
8,620	160	70	50	95	50	15	765	18,605
214,550	869,400	41,645	23,730	107,635	224,070	1,215	4,910	105
7,350	162,605	16,285	9,650	33,770	48,750	335	440	455
50,060	37,135	2,675	1,375	5,780	6,780	85	85	20
15,045	114,275	13,070	7,910	26,420	39,525	250	335	430
26,890	8,000	435	255	1,090	1,705	0	15	10
5,355	3,200	110	115	475	745	0	10	10

Table 22.2 Population reporting an Aboriginal identity, by mother tongue and by province and territory, 2001

	Canada	Newfoundland and Labrador	Prince Edward Island	Nova Scotia	New Brunswick
			number		
Aboriginal identity population	**976,305**	**18,775**	**1,345**	**17,010**	**16,990**
Mother tongue, single response[1]	**956,240**	18,685	1,320	16,805	16,565
English	**704,770**	16,595	1,105	11,975	9,165
French	**64,130**	50	25	785	4,385
Non-official languages	**187,340**	2,040	195	4,050	3,020
Aboriginal languages	**186,835**	2,040	195	4,045	3,005
Cree	**72,680**	10	0	30	10
Inuktitut	**29,005**	545	10	10	20
Ojibway	**20,890**	0	0	10	10
Montagnais–Naskapi	**9,655**	1,470	0	0	0
Micmac	**7,230**	10	185	3,995	2,265
Dakota/Sioux	**3,880**	0	0	0	0
Blackfoot	**2,740**	0	0	0	0
Salish languages	**2,590**	0	0	0	0
South Slave	**1,380**	0	0	0	0
Dogrib	**1,860**	0	0	0	0
Carrier	**1,225**	0	0	0	0
Wakashan languages	**1,275**	0	0	0	0
Chipewyan	**575**	0	0	0	0
Other Aboriginal languages	**31,840**	0	0	15	715
Non-Aboriginal languages	**505**	0	0	0	15
Mother tongue, multiple responses[2]	**20,070**	90	20	205	425
Multiple Aboriginal and non-Aboriginal responses	**15,470**	75	10	135	190
English and Aboriginal language(s)	**14,130**	75	10	135	175
French and Aboriginal language(s)	**1,010**	0	0	0	15
English, French and Aboriginal language(s)	**330**	0	0	0	0
Other multiple responses	**4,600**	15	10	70	235

1. The respondent reported only one language as a mother tongue.

2. The respondent reported more than one language as a mother tongue.

Source: Statistics Canada, 2001 Census of Population.

Quebec	Ontario	Manitoba	Saskatchewan	Alberta	British Columbia	Yukon	Northwest Territories	Nunavut
				number				
79,400	**188,310**	**150,040**	**130,190**	**156,220**	**170,025**	**6,545**	**18,725**	**22,720**
77,560	185,010	145,845	127,125	153,000	167,240	6,360	18,440	22,290
9,180	151,320	106,050	95,095	127,505	154,640	5,540	12,965	3,640
32,900	13,560	6,400	1,585	2,050	2,180	60	135	25
35,480	20,125	33,395	30,445	23,445	10,420	755	5,340	18,625
35,455	19,970	33,315	30,405	23,380	10,315	755	5,340	18,615
11,810	4,385	18,090	22,020	15,010	1,160	15	155	0
8,620	160	70	50	100	50	20	760	18,605
20	9,670	8,840	1,370	625	275	10	65	0
8,180	0	0	0	0	0	0	0	0
690	60	0	20	0	15	0	0	0
0	10	730	350	2,765	25	0	0	0
10	25	25	15	2,630	35	10	0	0
0	0	0	0	0	2,570	10	0	0
0	0	0	0	250	100	20	1,005	0
0	10	0	10	10	20	0	1,830	0
0	0	0	0	0	1,215	0	0	0
0	0	0	0	0	1,270	0	0	0
0	10	20	0	225	10	10	300	10
6,130	5,640	5,540	6,570	1,760	3,570	675	1,215	0
30	155	75	45	70	105	0	0	10
1,845	3,300	4,200	3,065	3,215	2,790	195	290	445
970	1,605	3,645	2,845	2,915	2,225	160	270	435
325	1,485	3,520	2,695	2,770	2,100	150	260	425
565	65	95	95	90	70	0	10	10
80	55	30	55	55	55	10	0	0
875	1,695	555	220	300	565	35	20	10

Table 22.3 Selected languages spoken at home, by frequency of use, 2001

	Total frequency	Only language spoken	Most often[1]	Equally often[2]	Regularly[3]
			number		
English	21,863,015	18,267,825	1,506,980	478,760	1,609,450
French	7,214,280	5,861,130	586,455	172,880	593,815
Chinese (not otherwise specified)	392,950	199,995	109,250	20,265	63,440
Italian	371,200	110,275	76,275	30,515	154,135
Cantonese	345,730	189,430	95,645	13,245	47,410
Punjabi	280,535	132,380	71,660	29,220	47,275
Spanish	258,465	70,355	78,235	28,860	81,015
German	220,685	48,075	60,420	13,940	98,250
Arabic	209,240	58,115	57,235	32,635	61,255
Portuguese	187,475	63,890	46,670	15,355	61,560
Tagalog (Pilipino)	185,420	36,710	53,705	41,915	53,090
Polish	163,745	53,320	54,050	15,115	41,260
Vietnamese	130,280	64,665	35,865	9,555	20,195
Greek	114,955	33,515	30,385	10,255	40,800
Mandarin	110,710	54,060	36,335	3,660	16,655
Tamil	97,345	45,860	29,745	9,460	12,280
Persian (Farsi)	92,025	41,970	28,005	7,600	14,450
Urdu	89,370	30,760	27,845	12,200	18,565
Russian	87,080	37,905	28,025	5,150	16,000
Korean	83,020	44,255	23,600	3,165	12,000
Cree	71,955	20,585	21,730	7,440	22,200
Ukrainian	67,665	14,325	14,515	5,385	33,440
Hindi	65,895	14,175	16,075	9,090	26,555
Gujarati	60,105	18,305	16,830	7,180	17,790
Creoles	49,905	7,845	8,135	10,445	23,480
Dutch	45,780	3,700	8,010	3,260	30,810
Romanian	44,975	16,320	14,945	3,760	9,950
Croatian	44,605	10,645	13,635	4,135	16,190
Hungarian	44,590	11,575	11,810	3,940	17,265
Serbian	39,965	16,725	14,275	2,435	6,530
Japanese	30,565	10,255	6,865	1,775	11,670
Bengali	29,705	12,840	9,615	2,780	4,470
Inuktitut (Eskimo)	29,615	14,415	9,535	405	5,260
Somali	27,800	10,915	7,930	4,335	4,620
Armenian	26,215	10,395	9,045	1,875	4,900
Serbo-Croatian	24,530	9,630	8,840	1,850	4,210
Ojibway	18,540	4,930	3,250	2,385	7,975
Turkish	16,560	5,945	4,650	1,380	4,585
Khmer (Cambodian)	16,435	6,235	4,545	2,075	3,580
Malayo-Polynesian languages (not included elsewhere)	16,430	3,475	4,720	3,090	5,145
Hebrew	15,645	2,350	3,300	1,485	8,510
Czech	15,245	2,695	5,065	1,500	5,985
Macedonian	14,410	3,585	4,085	1,320	5,420
Lao	13,525	5,005	3,720	2,030	2,770

1. Language is spoken most often at home; at least one other language is spoken on a regular basis.
2. Language is reported with another language as being spoken most often at home.
3. Language is spoken on a regular basis at home; another language is spoken most often.
Source: Statistics Canada, Catalogue no. 97F0007XCB2001004.

Table 22.4 Selected languages spoken at home, by census metropolitan area, 2001

	English	French	Chinese[1]	Italian	Cantonese	Punjabi	Aboriginal languages[2]
				number			
Canada	**21,863,015**	**7,214,280**	**392,950**	**371,200**	**345,730**	**280,535**	**63,315**
St. John's	170,520	1,105	210	45	60	45	0
Halifax	350,575	10,255	1,135	370	265	195	50
Saint John	120,015	4,755	300	155	20	20	20
Saguenay	3,495	152,505	125	0	0	0	45
Québec	28,235	667,410	480	290	55	0	240
Sherbrooke	15,055	143,320	100	145	0	0	0
Trois-Rivières	4,005	134,115	0	65	0	0	45
Montréal	886,050	2,638,915	31,640	101,650	6,390	10,200	445
Ottawa–Gatineau	759,310	377,960	14,415	8,140	5,115	2,545	460
Quebec part	72,570	222,655	485	215	105	140	100
Ontario part	686,740	155,305	13,930	7,940	5,010	2,415	335
Kingston	139,225	4,720	675	630	225	140	20
Oshawa	287,165	6,420	680	2,435	530	475	0
Toronto	3,940,275	81,855	155,000	162,415	159,085	99,000	350
Hamilton	615,530	10,520	4,560	17,460	1,765	4,120	170
St. Catharines–Niagara	359,750	12,465	1,355	9,845	195	210	25
Kitchener	384,170	5,480	2,845	1,280	1,085	2,500	40
London	409,010	5,860	2,325	2,955	635	685	40
Windsor	282,575	11,255	3,215	9,540	865	1,605	0
Greater Sudbury / Grand Sudbury	139,380	42,980	300	2,280	50	45	345
Thunder Bay	117,755	2,625	170	2,795	15	25	690
Winnipeg	629,765	26,405	5,190	3,660	2,460	5,335	3,625
Regina	187,105	2,610	1,130	370	405	340	320
Saskatoon	218,340	3,180	1,985	115	745	190	1,670
Calgary	884,990	15,570	21,955	4,790	15,145	13,565	585
Edmonton	881,160	18,945	17,995	4,280	11,945	9,695	2,165
Abbotsford	132,560	1,590	585	155	380	16,300	10
Vancouver	1,663,185	29,515	109,575	13,235	129,695	91,210	680
Victoria	298,950	5,370	3,350	780	2,930	2,765	180

Note: Language spoken at home (total frequencies).

1. Not otherwise specified.

2. Total of all Aboriginal languages ranks twelfth in frequency for Canada.

Source: Statistics Canada, Catalogue no. 97F0007XCB2001004.

Table 22.5 Language of work, by frequency of use, 2001

	Total frequency	Only language spoken	Most often[1]	Equally often[2]	Regularly[3]
			number		
English	14,371,770	11,918,110	1,015,235	367,300	1,071,125
French	4,355,930	2,433,570	981,525	289,890	650,945
Chinese (not otherwise specified)	108,260	31,505	19,760	11,515	45,480
Cantonese	74,720	22,740	14,625	6,170	31,185
Punjabi	49,835	11,265	5,240	8,345	24,985
German	59,030	7,365	10,330	5,095	36,240
Mandarin	25,425	6,635	4,820	2,225	11,745
Portuguese	38,205	5,775	5,415	4,750	22,265
Spanish	63,820	5,380	4,980	9,325	44,135
Vietnamese	17,905	3,525	2,205	2,185	9,990
Korean	15,470	3,110	3,135	1,425	7,800
Italian	64,590	3,075	4,330	11,200	45,985
Other languages	271,240	27,535	36,585	39,415	167,705

1. Language is spoken most often at work; at least one other language is spoken on a regular basis.
2. Language is reported with another language as being spoken most often at work.
3. Language is spoken on a regular basis at work; another language is spoken most often.
Source: Statistics Canada, 2001 Census of Population.

Table 22.6 Selected languages of work, by selected census metropolitan area, 2001

	English	French	Chinese[1]	Cantonese	Italian	Spanish
			number			
Canada	14,371,770	4,355,930	108,260	74,720	64,590	63,820
St. John's	96,300	1,280	15	0	15	55
Halifax	210,255	8,810	260	60	55	280
Saint John	66,365	4,005	55	0	10	160
Saguenay	7,845	77,245	0	0	0	105
Québec	77,320	383,470	165	10	85	1,805
Sherbrooke	25,870	83,020	40	0	40	300
Trois-Rivières	9,480	69,825	10	0	0	110
Montréal	1,068,440	1,729,840	7,275	1,020	18,165	16,860
Ottawa–Gatineau	578,270	270,310	2,250	725	1,370	2,815
Oshawa	169,920	4,080	125	165	300	230
Toronto	2,692,890	70,150	42,565	33,375	32,285	18,780
Hamilton	366,415	7,110	715	220	2,450	1,040
St. Catharines–Niagara	205,050	6,070	285	55	1,340	440
Kitchener	246,690	3,830	340	95	140	775
London	245,305	3,965	435	90	280	1,035
Windsor	168,165	4,645	530	125	1,495	270
Winnipeg	390,385	15,060	935	430	360	885
Regina	113,630	1,635	195	60	30	145
Saskatoon	131,945	1,345	285	185	0	165
Calgary	605,165	9,005	5,380	2,730	500	2,395
Edmonton	570,510	9,425	3,770	2,040	440	1,365
Vancouver	1,112,005	17,470	38,215	31,475	1,580	5,390
Victoria	178,375	3,790	770	450	55	410

Note: Language spoken at work (total frequencies).
1. Not otherwise specified.
Source: Statistics Canada, Catalogue no. 97F0016XCB2001006.

Manufacturing

23

Nearly two million Canadians work in manufacturing. They transform raw materials into the finished products that line our store shelves and are exported for consumers around the world. Traditionally one of Canada's strongest industries, manufacturing is still a cornerstone of hundreds of communities large and small.

But our economy has been changing quickly. In the face of lower-priced global competition, a stronger Canadian dollar, and the robust growth of the services sector, the manufacturing sector is in a period of decline.

Factories thinning out

Employment in manufacturing has been shrinking. According to the Annual Survey of Manufacturers, there were 1.3 million manufacturing production workers in 2005, a drop from 1.4 million in 2003. Many of these jobs were lost in Ontario and Quebec.

During the mid- to late-1990s, manufacturing was a major source of new jobs. By 2001, however, the high-tech sector began to collapse and many production workers were laid off. By the end of 2002, employees were being swept from factory floors in droves. Another challenge hit manufacturers when the Canadian dollar rose to a 14-year high in the fourth quarter of 2005. The higher exchange rate made Canadian products more expensive abroad and slowed sales.

The decline in manufacturing jobs that followed is the sharpest since the recession of the early 1990s, when factory jobs vanished at twice the current rate. Quebec and Ontario have seen 90% of the manufacturing job losses nationwide since 2002.

Chart 23.1
Employment in manufacturing, by province

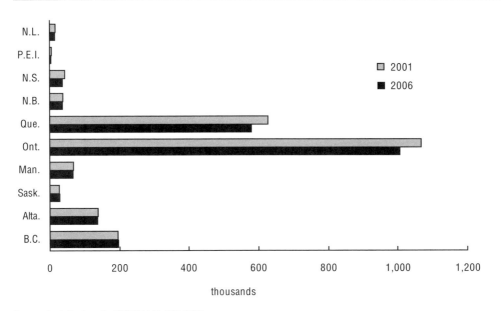

thousands

Source: Statistics Canada, CANSIM table 282-0008.

Shipping it out

Nevertheless, manufacturing remains a significant economic driving force in this country. The sector accounts for about 16% of Canada's gross domestic product and is the economic lifeblood of many communities and provinces.

Canada's largest manufacturing industry is transportation equipment. Automobile and automobile parts manufacturing play a major role in this sector and account for about one-third of Ontario's manufacturing output. Transportation equipment generated 21% of the $591 billion worth of goods manufactured in 2005. Food manufacturing was the second largest component of this total, accounting for 11% of the value of all shipped goods.

As the hub of Canada's manufacturing activity, Ontario and Quebec are responsible for close to three-quarters of the country's manufacturing shipments. However, of these two manufacturing powerhouses, Ontario has been losing strength relative to the country as a whole. In Ontario, industries such as petroleum and coal product manufacturing

Chart 23.2
Manufacturing shipments, selected industries, 2006

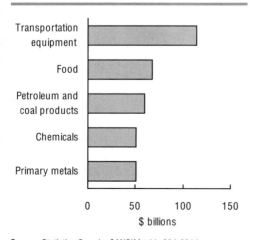

Source: Statistics Canada, CANSIM table 304-0014.

Manufacturing shipments, by region, 2006

	$ billions	% of total
Atlantic provinces	27.7	4.7
Quebec	141.1	24.0
Ontario	287.6	49.0
Prairies	88.9	15.1
British Columbia	42.0	7.1

Note: Data for the territories represent less than 1% of the total.
Source: Statistics Canada, CANSIM table 304-0015.

have done well, but a downturn in auto making has pulled down the overall level and value of the province's shipments. Quebec, however, has strengthened in recent years, with petroleum refining, aerospace and chemical products buoying the sector there. In fact, the transportation equipment industry has become Quebec's second-largest source of manufacturing shipments, after primary metals.

Growth in the manufacturing sector made a noticeable shift westward in 2005. Shipments in British Columbia, Alberta and Saskatchewan have been increasing at a faster pace than in Central Canada. In particular, manufacturers in Alberta and Saskatchewan have made dramatic gains, mostly because of resource-based production of petroleum products and primary metals. The four Western provinces accounted for 21% of all Canadian manufacturing shipments in 2005, compared with 18% in 2000.

Atlantic Canada has a strong food manufacturing industry and accounts for almost 5% of the country's manufacturing shipments.

Overall, though, Canada's manufacturers have maintained consistent shipment volumes over the past couple of years. Yet they are becoming more concerned about their ability to boost production in the face of a few developments: the stronger loonie, particularly against the U.S. dollar—the United States is their principal trading partner; higher costs for raw materials; competition from cheaper foreign imports, notably from Asia; and shortages of skilled labour, especially in Western Canada. Labour shortages affected one-fifth of manufacturers in Alberta in 2005.

Profits drop in some industries

These pressures on the sector have translated into substantially lower operating profits for manufacturing companies. Their total profits had reached $49 billion in 2004, after an exceptional gain of 34% over 2003. However, by the end of 2005, their total operating profits fell to $42 billion.

Ten of the 13 manufacturing industries lost ground in 2005, and in 2006 profits remained essentially flat. Most notably, declining North American demand, rising fuel prices, foreign competition and high marketing and restructuring costs all combined to hit the auto and auto parts manufacturers hard—their profits plunged 83% from $9.0 billion in 2000 to $1.5 billion in 2006.

Change is also giving rise to new challenges for other manufacturers. For instance, the shift to electronic media and shrinking newsprint markets have contributed to a 58% drop in operating profits for wood and paper

producers in the past six years, from a high of $7.8 billion in 2000 to $3.3 billion in 2006.

Elsewhere, greater demand for petroleum and coal is helping operating profits in those industries to surge—profits climbed to $11.7 billion in 2005 from less than half that in 2000. Also over the past few years, computers and electronics manufacturers—a group which includes communications, audio and video equipment—have been profiting from high consumer demand for their products. Though they have not yet reached the high-tech boom levels of 2000, these manufacturers have been enjoying growth in their operating profits since 2003.

Selected sources

Statistics Canada

- *Analysis in Brief.* Occasional. 11-621-MIE

- *Canadian Economic Observer.* Monthly. 11-010-XWB

- *Economic Analysis (EA) Research Paper Series.* Occasional. 11F0027MIE

- *Gross Domestic Product by Industry.* Monthly. 15-001-XIE

- *Labour Force Information.* Monthly. 71-001-XIE

- *Perspectives on Labour and Income.* Monthly. 75-001-XIE

- *Update on Economic Analysis.* Irregular. 11-623-XIE

Chart 23.3
Operating profits, selected manufacturing industries

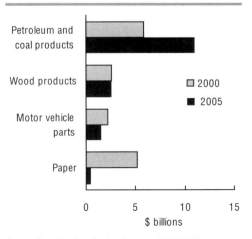

Source: Statistics Canada, Catalogue no. 62-219-XIE.

Productivity and Canadian manufacturing

Productivity is fuel for economic growth. Doing more with less—by training higher-skilled workers, using less expensive materials, or introducing new technologies— enables factories to be more efficient. This reduces costs, leaving more dollars to create even more products, raise wages or lower prices for consumers.

Productivity growth is so important that it has accounted for more than half of the growth in Canada's gross domestic product over the past 40 years. It matters for individual Canadians as well: over the past four decades, the rise in hourly wages has closely followed the rise in labour productivity.

Unfortunately for Canadian manufacturers, one of the major economic developments in 2006 was the slowdown in productivity growth for goods-producing industries. After

brisk 3.6% growth in 2005, productivity stalled in 2006, edging up just 0.1%.

Falling productivity in 2006 was driven by a decline in output per employee: each employee in manufacturing produced, on average, less in 2006 than in the previous year. This lowered the 'capacity utilization' of Canada's factories—how close they were running to their full potential. At year-end, Canadian industries were operating at just 82.5% of their capacity, a drop of 1.2% from 2005.

In fact, so far this decade, factories have not come close to matching their stellar productivity gains during the high-tech boom in the late 1990s. The sudden productivity downturn in 2006 was particularly notable in industries not normally considered high-tech, such as textiles, clothing and furniture. Many factories in these industries closed in 2006.

Chart 23.4
Industrial capacity utilization rates, selected industries

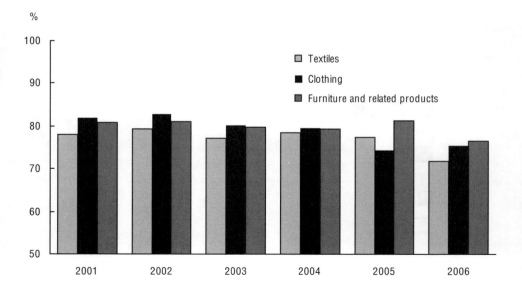

Source: Statistics Canada, CANSIM table 028-0002.

Manufacturing plants have short lives

Manufacturing plants have a life expectancy like humans do. But unlike humans, whose lifespan is rising over time in many countries, manufacturing plants have relatively short lives—most expire early; others may be weak yet cling to life for a time.

Over half of new manufacturing plants shut down by the time they are six years old. By the age of 15, fewer than 20% are still functioning. The average new manufacturing plant in Canada operates for only nine years; 14% of new plants close in their first year.

How long a plant survives varies by industry. The longest lifespan is 13 years, in the primary metals and paper and allied products industries. The shortest is less than eight years in the wood and furniture industries.

The high rate of plant closures means that a person working at one production facility is not likely to have a job that lasts a lifetime.

When shutdowns occur, they might be relocated to other plants within the same firm.

However, when the firm goes out of business, employees often face periods of unemployment. In many cases, they have no alternative except to take up a new position that often pays less than the job they left.

Manufacturing plants that introduce technological innovations to their manufacturing processes have a higher survival rate than those that put their efforts into changing their products.

Innovation also increases the likelihood that a firm will see higher rates of productivity growth. Though it is the new smaller plants that tend to fold most rapidly, failing to innovate will lead to early death—even for larger plants.

Chart 23.5
Life of new manufacturing plants, by selected industries

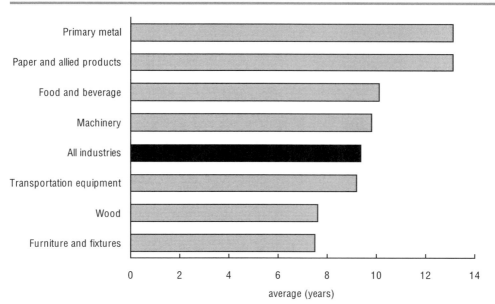

Note: The closure rate is based on data from 1960 to 1999 for new plants in the Canadian manufacturing sector.
Source: Statistics Canada, Catalogue no. 11F0027MIE.

Competitiveness and the exchange rate

Over the past 40 years, the value of the Canadian dollar, or loonie, against the U.S. dollar has ranged from a high of US$1.04 in October 1959 to a low of US$0.62 in January 2002. In December 2006, CAN$1.00 was worth US$0.90. What do these exchange rate fluctuations mean for Canadian manufacturers?

We export 43% of the machinery, autos and consumer goods we manufacture. Thus, the ups and downs of the loonie can strongly influence how competitive our products are on the global market.

In the mid-1990s, a low loonie boosted demand for Canadian-made goods in other countries. Since 2002, however, the loonie—and thus the prices of Canadian-made goods—has been rising, making other countries' products more competitive against ours.

Two other factors that affect Canadian competitiveness are productivity growth and production costs, such as labour, energy and materials. When productivity is growing faster in Canada than in the United States, our goods are generally cheaper, giving Canadian manufacturers an edge selling their products in the global marketplace.

But when production costs are higher in Canada than in the United States, our products are more expensive than American ones, and so Canadian manufacturers have a tougher time competing. However, the exchange rate can also affect these factors.

Many export-oriented industries—such as motor vehicles, machinery, pulp, paper and wood products—have been able to adjust their profit margins rapidly, reducing the effects of exchange rate fluctuations.

Chart 23.6
Exchange rate, United States dollar to Canadian dollar

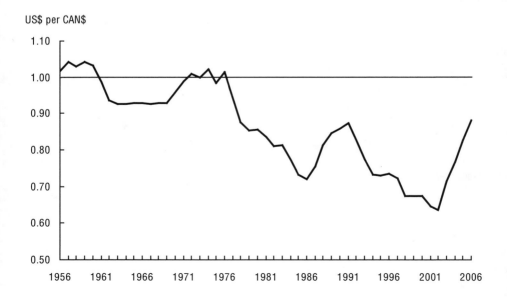

Source: Statistics Canada, CANSIM table 176-0064.

Autos driving Canada's economy

The auto industry is one that drives the Canadian economy. It is concentrated in Ontario, and is vital to the province's economy. Auto manufacturing employs 42,000 people in Ontario, comprises 24% of all sales of manufactured goods and drives other industries, such as automotive parts.

Over the past 30 years, the automotive sector has had its ups and downs, thanks to factors such as changes in what consumers demand, more competition from countries outside North America, and an oversupply of certain models. Energy-conscious consumers are also reassessing their need for large vehicles, so demand for SUVs and other gas-guzzlers has fallen off in North America. In 2005, layoffs, temporary shutdowns of assembly lines and permanent plant closures hit the industry.

All three North American automakers—General Motors, Ford and DaimlerChrysler—

have lost retail sales because of competition from innovative, foreign-owned automakers. In 2005, these three companies accounted for 75% of Canadian auto assembly, down from 85% just five years earlier.

Nevertheless, Canadians continued to buy trucks and SUVs in increasing numbers in 2005. Truck sales were especially high in Alberta, and remained strong in British Columbia and Ontario and Quebec.

The good news for the industry is that auto manufacturing in Canada may be revving up. Several of the world's biggest players have announced billions of dollars in new investment in Canada over the next few years, and many car manufacturers are re-engineering their product lines to meet changing consumer demand.

Chart 23.7
Sales of new motor vehicles, by type

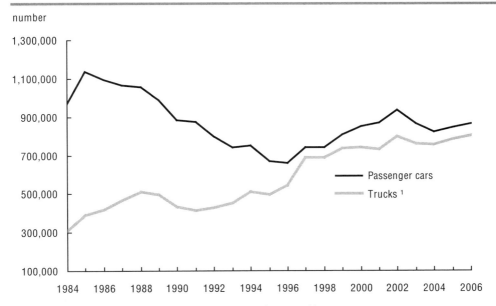

number

1. Trucks include minivans, sport-utility vehicles, light and heavy trucks, vans and buses.
Source: Statistics Canada, Catalogue no. 63-007-XIE.

Table 23.1 Gross domestic product at basic prices, by manufacturing subsector, 1998 to 2006

	1998	1999	2000
	chained (1997) $ millions		
Manufacturing sector	**149,314**	**161,634**	**177,618**
Food	14,520	14,883	15,499
Beverage and tobacco products	5,186	4,729	4,896
Textile mills and textile product mills	2,431	2,458	2,703
Clothing	3,266	3,164	3,778
Leather and allied products	388	371	437
Paper	10,559	11,606	12,035
Printing and related support activities	4,313	4,411	5,042
Petroleum and coal products	1,805	1,737	1,741
Chemicals	12,958	13,470	14,926
Plastics and rubber products	7,343	7,989	9,138
Wood products	9,669	10,390	11,524
Non-metallic mineral products	4,121	4,152	4,566
Primary metals and fabricated metal products	20,186	21,300	24,815
Machinery	10,111	9,938	11,383
Computer and electronic products	8,841	12,384	14,963
Electrical equipment, appliances and components	3,625	3,803	4,573
Transportation equipment	23,181	27,779	28,104
Furniture and related products	4,102	4,487	5,241
Miscellaneous manufacturing	2,768	2,734	3,142

Note: North American Industry Classification System (NAICS), 2002.
Source: Statistics Canada, CANSIM table 379-0017.

2001	2002	2003	2004	2005	2006
		chained (1997) $ millions			
170,247	**171,800**	**170,465**	**173,726**	**174,987**	**172,706**
16,627	16,528	16,316	16,665	16,879	17,041
4,690	4,679	4,478	4,593	4,706	4,140
2,555	2,539	2,211	2,153	1,993	1,723
3,655	3,419	3,290	3,054	2,758	2,617
372	362	310	248	179	173
11,430	12,007	12,101	12,077	11,711	10,940
5,608	5,252	5,106	5,023	4,979	4,861
1,950	1,981	2,002	2,044	1,987	1,999
15,307	16,052	16,473	17,109	17,202	17,400
9,123	9,845	9,772	9,643	9,349	8,814
11,016	12,281	12,482	13,280	13,488	13,219
4,772	4,869	5,120	5,145	5,149	5,158
24,135	24,875	24,309	24,430	24,932	25,000
11,184	10,896	10,605	10,686	10,983	11,365
8,854	7,620	8,731	8,915	9,496	9,734
4,519	3,825	3,340	3,288	3,236	3,160
25,345	25,241	25,196	26,736	27,342	26,947
5,461	5,405	4,954	4,952	5,031	4,800
3,123	3,479	3,500	3,480	3,470	3,657

Table 23.2 Manufacturing shipments, by manufacturing subsector, 1994 to 2006

	1994	1995	1996	1997	1998
			$ millions		
Manufacturing sector	**346,940.8**	**389,779.5**	**400,085.1**	**426,519.4**	**441,152.6**
Food	43,075.3	45,170.0	48,246.0	50,513.4	51,468.6
Beverage and tobacco products	9,175.8	9,317.9	9,610.4	10,154.4	11,190.5
Textile mills and textile products mills	5,303.5	5,558.6	5,621.5	5,960.2	6,371.0
Clothing	6,229.0	6,568.4	6,677.7	6,947.0	6,967.6
Leather and allied products	1,005.0	985.9	942.8	1,001.3	944.2
Paper	25,226.4	36,013.7	30,663.2	29,761.6	29,790.5
Printing and related support activities	7,641.3	8,447.9	8,841.4	8,961.8	9,341.9
Petroleum and coal products	16,677.2	17,969.3	20,688.6	20,932.8	16,325.6
Chemicals	27,822.1	30,074.0	30,252.6	32,486.3	31,374.1
Plastics and rubber products	12,504.8	14,048.1	15,045.3	16,504.1	17,362.1
Wood products	22,274.8	22,621.5	24,000.3	25,960.2	25,994.4
Non-metallic mineral products	6,794.4	7,220.7	7,851.9	8,487.7	8,930.3
Primary metals	24,019.4	26,178.1	26,781.9	28,743.2	29,596.9
Fabricated metal products	15,391.5	17,505.8	19,174.5	21,082.6	22,850.8
Machinery	15,407.3	18,060.8	19,548.5	21,835.9	23,097.3
Computer and electronic products	18,122.7	22,845.0	22,072.9	23,154.3	25,356.4
Electrical equipment, appliances and components	6,889.0	7,587.9	7,834.5	8,085.3	8,486.9
Transportation equipment	73,392.3	82,992.4	84,548.0	92,822.9	101,064.1
Furniture and related products	5,664.9	6,140.3	6,839.8	7,892.6	9,013.0
Miscellaneous manufacturing	4,324.3	4,473.0	4,843.2	5,231.8	5,626.2

Note: North American Industry Classification System (NAICS), 2002.
Source: Statistics Canada, CANSIM table 304-0014.

1999	2000	2001	2002	2003	2004	2005	2006
			$ millions				
510,549.9	561,300.9	543,272.0	559,902.7	562,551.7	586,105.8	591,086.0	587,642.6
55,104.9	57,278.7	61,609.3	64,089.5	67,065.8	68,163.7	65,814.5	67,587.2
11,250.8	11,625.5	11,699.1	12,074.4	12,191.5	12,428.2	12,607.1	11,762.9
6,602.4	6,966.1	6,848.8	7,211.0	6,672.8	6,167.6	5,514.5	4,936.8
7,429.3	7,936.6	7,685.0	8,024.4	7,893.8	6,482.3	4,980.1	4,793.2
967.1	956.4	967.2	933.6	849.6	668.2	475.1	452.5
33,236.4	38,213.2	35,852.9	34,284.4	33,359.4	33,894.4	33,241.8	31,753.2
10,436.0	11,079.3	11,633.8	12,155.3	12,435.5	11,948.7	11,717.1	11,455.3
21,347.3	33,918.0	33,407.5	33,690.1	37,585.3	45,736.2	56,278.3	59,282.3
34,194.7	37,205.8	38,391.4	40,469.2	43,088.5	47,425.1	50,177.5	51,081.3
21,108.8	21,858.0	22,986.9	25,286.6	26,464.1	26,069.6	26,130.8	25,460.9
31,214.5	31,669.8	30,074.1	32,801.6	32,360.0	35,913.6	31,811.5	28,229.5
9,653.4	9,926.8	10,324.3	11,630.8	12,029.4	12,272.2	12,315.7	12,799.1
30,755.1	36,352.2	34,115.3	36,074.9	36,812.6	43,249.5	44,160.2	50,523.0
27,625.0	29,685.8	30,189.5	32,210.5	33,080.6	33,032.4	32,707.8	32,900.7
24,284.6	26,283.4	26,422.0	27,448.5	28,070.2	28,833.2	30,015.2	31,449.4
27,295.3	37,273.3	27,040.1	22,656.3	20,826.3	20,195.8	18,630.4	17,250.5
10,488.1	11,595.5	11,637.6	10,135.9	9,482.2	9,534.2	9,554.6	9,872.0
130,037.5	132,252.5	122,560.4	126,451.6	119,935.1	122,745.9	123,079.7	113,895.1
10,995.4	12,608.2	13,054.9	13,916.5	13,719.5	13,349.2	12,786.5	12,622.8
6,523.2	6,615.9	6,771.9	8,357.6	8,702.3	8,525.2	9,087.7	9,534.7

Table 23.3 Employment, by manufacturing subsector, 1994 to 2006

	1994	1995	1996	1997
	number			
Manufacturing sector	**1,716,245**	**1,748,443**	**1,788,952**	**1,855,391**
Food	210,941	209,853	217,599	219,833
Beverage and tobacco products	33,371	32,984	29,736	32,068
Textile mills	26,357	26,992	27,278	28,594
Textile product mills	17,863	16,507	17,885	19,840
Clothing	85,610	86,515	85,886	88,574
Leather and allied products	12,238	12,396	12,459	12,656
Paper	104,779	104,450	103,394	104,098
Printing and related support activities	75,309	80,375	76,787	76,948
Petroleum and coal products	21,622	19,770	20,397	19,875
Chemicals	89,019	88,054	86,874	88,774
Plastics and rubber products	94,081	96,920	104,370	111,773
Wood products	109,790	108,431	116,544	124,299
Non-metallic mineral products	43,880	47,077	45,687	48,554
Primary metals	102,587	102,127	101,727	98,828
Fabricated metal products	134,821	139,590	146,910	157,630
Machinery	108,524	116,421	124,531	131,837
Computer and electronic products	79,622	87,969	87,403	91,747
Electrical equipment, appliances and components	52,507	46,669	45,178	45,477
Transportation equipment	198,701	204,515	214,514	215,733
Furniture and related products	67,232	68,425	70,346	80,754
Miscellaneous manufacturing	47,390	52,402	53,447	57,498

Notes: North American Industry Classification System (NAICS), 2002.
Annual number of salaried and hourly employees on payroll.
Source: Statistics Canada, CANSIM table 281-0024.

Table 23.4 Manufacturing sector establishments and workers, by province and territory, 2004 and 2005

	Canada	Newfoundland and Labrador	Prince Edward Island	Nova Scotia	New Brunswick
	number				
Establishments					
2004	**32,657**	387	204	747	656
2005	**32,582**	369	196	707	631
Production workers					
2004	**1,317,711**	14,957	5,164	30,208	29,386
2005	**1,312,484**	14,136	4,973	29,867	28,028

Note: The number of establishments represents a count of locations that perform manufacturing activities and normally correspond to a plant, factory or mill. It excludes sales offices and warehouses that support manufacturing activities.
Source: Statistics Canada, CANSIM table 301-0006.

1998	1999	2000	2001	2002	2003	2004	2005	2006
				number				
1,916,170	1,955,914	2,047,798	2,008,877	1,968,314	1,950,380	1,909,124	1,872,657	1,854,475
226,471	228,779	238,354	237,652	241,948	244,954	246,537	241,232	240,828
34,255	33,791	35,424	36,594	37,214	34,396	33,004	29,105	29,038
29,793	29,834	30,365	30,336	30,222	30,350	26,482	21,897	18,136
20,495	20,411	20,923	19,707	19,020	18,412	18,071	17,681	16,474
90,427	89,471	93,351	87,287	81,190	75,697	66,558	55,288	49,166
11,775	11,561	12,566	12,842	14,846	14,799	12,868	11,413	10,253
100,821	103,110	110,144	103,835	95,981	97,039	94,093	88,316	84,437
79,810	82,459	85,537	83,529	79,678	78,593	73,774	72,829	73,148
20,377	22,876	25,110	23,217	21,238	20,896	20,499	21,296	22,608
89,227	91,385	95,493	93,535	92,285	92,803	92,765	92,828	90,168
115,544	117,708	123,490	125,996	127,801	128,875	129,969	127,967	127,374
127,559	134,177	141,872	134,714	132,267	131,707	135,115	133,721	128,887
52,166	53,286	56,440	53,719	52,547	53,351	53,307	53,066	55,521
100,957	100,529	104,253	91,936	90,322	85,394	79,703	78,297	79,740
165,626	173,072	183,246	187,521	183,980	183,364	178,988	178,727	184,311
134,385	132,451	136,361	134,877	137,296	137,130	136,007	140,369	144,433
95,685	98,444	101,877	98,889	88,788	83,349	81,651	79,718	80,158
45,898	48,538	53,780	50,375	47,002	46,362	43,898	43,044	43,157
229,457	235,528	244,176	242,698	233,576	231,248	229,222	229,313	222,773
85,247	87,844	93,489	98,154	99,033	98,660	93,770	94,879	90,918
60,192	60,661	61,544	61,465	62,079	63,004	62,842	61,673	62,946

Quebec	Ontario	Manitoba	Saskatchewan	Alberta	British Columbia	Yukon	Northwest Territories	Nunavut
				number				
8,058	13,533	1,034	760	3,088	4,129	32	18	11
8,059	13,451	995	767	3,100	4,241	35	20	11
351,649	612,078	46,357	18,513	93,685	115,329	128	170	87
342,379	609,718	46,432	20,071	99,697	116,737	159	204	83

Table 23.5 Industrial capacity utilization rates, 2006

	1st quarter	2nd quarter	3rd quarter	4th quarter
	%			
All industries	**85.8**	**84.5**	**83.4**	**82.5**
Manufacturing	84.6	83.2	82.2	81.4
Food	81.9	81.1	80.8	80.3
Beverage and tobacco products	72.7	73.8	76.9	77.7
Textile mills and textile products	74.1	70.5	69.5	73.0
Clothing	75.9	81.0	74.9	70.3
Leather and allied products	76.0	76.3	73.6	68.6
Paper	86.2	86.7	88.0	88.5
Printing and related support activities	78.2	77.0	72.1	71.9
Petroleum and coal products	87.4	85.8	88.5	84.4
Chemical	82.3	83.2	82.8	83.0
Plastics and rubber products	81.9	78.0	76.4	73.4
Wood products	89.7	84.7	82.6	78.5
Non-metallic mineral products	88.8	82.4	79.4	79.1
Primary metals	94.1	94.5	93.6	89.3
Fabricated metal products	84.4	80.0	79.3	78.1
Machinery	87.9	80.9	81.2	81.7
Computer and electronic products	88.2	87.8	87.7	91.2
Electrical equipment, appliances and components	77.8	77.6	77.3	80.1
Transportation equipment	86.5	87.0	84.4	83.1
Furniture and related products	76.2	76.3	77.7	76.3
Miscellaneous manufacturing	83.0	80.8	79.3	82.5

Note: North American Industry Classification System (NAICS), 2002.
Source: Statistics Canada, CANSIM table 028-0002.

Population and demography

24

OVERVIEW

Canada's population grew slightly over the past few years, despite an aging population and low fertility among women. On July 1, 2006, it reached the 32.6 million mark.

In large part, Canada depends on immigration for its population growth. From July 2005 to June 2006, two-thirds of the country's population increase was due to immigration, as Canada welcomed 254,400 immigrants. That's slightly above the annual average of 225,000 since the early 1990s. At the same time, the natural increase—births minus deaths—continued to drop. The most recent estimates show a drop from 210,500 people in 1990/1991 to 108,600 in 2005/2006.

Most of the Canadian population lives in a narrow corridor at the southern part of the country, near the American border. On July 1, 2006, 62% of the population lived in Quebec and Ontario, the two largest provinces.

The vast polar expanses of the Northwest Territories, Yukon and Nunavut represent 40% of the continental mass of Canada and are much less populated. Their inhabitants make up just 0.3% of the population.

Lower fertility

Many Canadian couples wait to start a family, mainly because they are completing their studies and marrying in their late twenties. The average age of women who gave birth in 2004 was 29.7 years, a slight increase compared with 29.6 years in 2003. This continues a 30-year trend toward having children later in life.

By delaying pregnancy, couples often have fewer children. Over the past two decades, fertility among Canadian women has generally declined. The total fertility rate was

Chart 24.1
Population growth

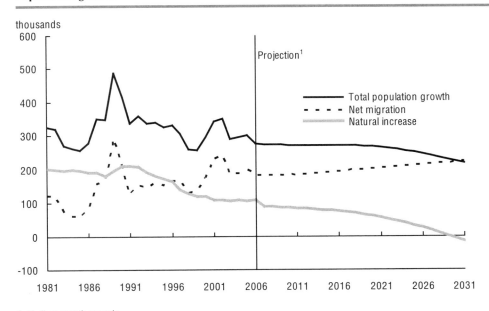

thousands

Projection[1]

— Total population growth
- - - Net migration
— Natural increase

1. Medium growth scenario.
Source: Statistics Canada, CANSIM tables 051-0004 and 052-0004.

1.49 children per woman in 2000, down from 1.65 in 1981. Since then, it has risen slightly to 1.53 in 2003 and 2004.

Canada's total fertility rate is similar to that of other industrialized countries, but lower than that of the United States, where the rate for many years has been very close to the replacement level of 2.1 children per woman. U.S. population growth depends more on natural increase than in Canada, where two-thirds of our growth is due to immigration.

According to the 2001 Census, the total fertility rate of immigrants who came to Canada from 1996 to 2001 was 3.1 children per woman, higher than that of other Canadian women. However, the longer an immigrant woman resides in Canada, the more closely her fertility resembles that of other Canadian women.

Our population is aging quickly

Although Canada has one of the highest life expectancies of industrialized countries, the number of deaths has continued to rise since the beginning of the decade, due to an increasing and aging population.

Chart 24.2
Total fertility rate

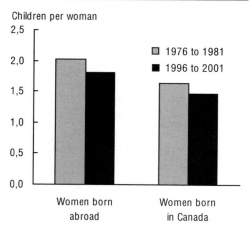

Children per woman

Legend:
- ☐ 1976 to 1981
- ■ 1996 to 2001

X-axis categories: Women born abroad, Women born in Canada

Source: Statistics Canada, Catalogue no. 91-209-XIE.

Selected components of population growth

	1990/1991	2005/2006
	number	
Births	402,929	343,517
Deaths	192,439	234,914
Immigrants	221,382	254,359
Emigrants	43,692	38,551

Note: Period from July 1 to June 30.
Source: Statistics Canada, CANSIM table 051-0004.

In 2005/2006, 234,914 people died in Canada, up from 219,114 deaths recorded in 2000/2001.

While life expectancy is increasing and fertility remains relatively stable, the population is aging quickly. On July 1, 2006, the median age of the Canadian population was 39 years, up from 31 years in 1985.

The elderly represented 13% of the population, almost twice the proportion of 7% at the start of the baby boom in 1946. Over the same period, the proportion of people aged 20 to 64 rose from 56% to 63%.

At the same time, the proportion of children and young people fell considerably. On July 1, 2006, the group aged 19 and younger represented 24% of the population, versus 37% in 1946. This trend is expected to continue over the next 50 years.

Since men do not tend to live as long as women, there are fewer men in older age groups. In 2005/2006, there were 91 men for every 100 women in the 65-to-74 age group. In the 90-and-over group, the ratio was 36 men for every 100 women. However, in the 19-and-under population, there were 105 boys for every 100 girls.

Unequal growth

In 2005/2006, only three provinces and one territory experienced higher population growth than the 10.0 people per 1,000 inhabitants recorded in Canada as a whole: Alberta (29.5 per 1,000), British Columbia (12.3 per 1,000), Ontario (10.2 per 1,000) and Nunavut (24.4 per 1,000).

For the fourteenth consecutive year, Newfoundland and Labrador saw its population fall in 2005/2006, resulting in a negative growth rate (-8.4 per 1,000). The growth rates of the other provinces ranged from -4.6 people per 1,000 inhabitants in Saskatchewan to 7.1 per 1,000 in Quebec.

Migration fuels growth

Alberta, the province that has experienced the greatest population growth since 1997, owes this growth to a combination of relatively high natural increase compared with the other provinces, and a considerable increase in interprovincial migration and, to a lesser extent, international migration.

Like most Canadian provinces, the population growth of Ontario and British Columbia depends largely on immigration, whereas the population growth of Nunavut is due primarily to a total fertility rate of three children per woman, around twice that of the national rate. Meanwhile, from July 2005 to June 2006, Newfoundland and Labrador was the first province where it was estimated that deaths exceeded births in the course of one year.

Chart 24.3
Top six fastest-growing census metropolitan areas

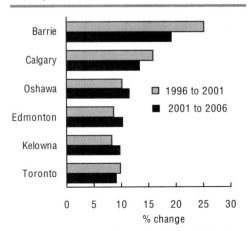

Source: Statistics Canada, Census of Population, 1996, 2001 and 2006.

Most Canadians continue to live in urban areas. According to the 2006 Census, 25.6 million people, more than 80% of Canada's population, live in cities and the majority, 21.5 million people, live in one of our 33 census metropolitan areas (CMAs).

Six CMAs have a population of more than one million people—Toronto, Montréal, Vancouver and Ottawa–Gatineau and, for the first time, Calgary and Edmonton. Combined, these six urban areas are home to 14.1 million people, or 45% of the population.

Collectively, Canada's CMAs grew at a faster rate than the national average. From 2001 to 2006, the six largest gained 6.9%; the rest of the country grew 5.4%. Fifteen CMAs had a higher rate of population growth than the national average. Of these, six are in Southern Ontario's Greater Golden Horseshoe region—Barrie, Oshawa, Toronto, Kitchener, Guelph and Brantford.

The fastest growing CMA in 2006 was Barrie, which grew 19% to 177,061. It was followed by Calgary, which gained 13% to 1.1 million. From 2001 to 2006, the population of Canada's small towns and rural areas rose 1%. The 2006 Census reported that just under 20% of Canadians, about 6 million people, live in small towns and rural areas.

Selected sources

Statistics Canada

- *Annual Demographic Statistics.* Annual. 91-213-XIB

- *Births.* Semi-annual. 84F0210XIE

- *Canadian Social Trends.* Quarterly. 11-008-XIE

- *Population Projections for Canada, Provinces and Territories.* Occasional. 91-520-XWE

- *Quarterly Demographic Statistics.* Quarterly. 91-002-XWE

Canada's population future

According to the most recent projections, the Canadian population—which rose to 32.6 million in 2006—is expected to reach 36 to 42 million people by 2031. Moreover, it is projected that deaths will outnumber births from the years 2020 to 2046, and that net international migration will become the primary source of population growth.

In 2005, Canada's population was one of the youngest among the G8 countries. However, it is expected to age more quickly in the coming years, in large part due to low fertility and increased longevity. Over the next two decades, baby boomers, who make up the largest segment of the population, will be turning 65, accelerating this aging.

Around the year 2015, for the first time in Canada's history, there could be more people aged 65 and older than children under

the age of 15. In 2031, 8.9 to 9.4 million Canadians will be aged 65 and older, whereas the number of children is expected to be around 4.8 million to 6.6 million.

In the coming decades, the proportion of elderly people will increase and could reach from 23% to 25% of the population in 2031, twice the current proportion of 13%. The proportion of people aged 80 and older is expected to increase more rapidly than the proportion aged 65 and older. One Canadian in 10 will be over the age of 80 by 2056, compared with 1 in 30 in 2005.

The aging of the baby boom generation will have repercussions on the labour force. Canadians of working age (aged 15 to 64) currently represent 70% of the population. This proportion could fall to 62% by the early 2030s and stabilize thereafter at around 60%.

Chart 24.4
Population projections, children and seniors

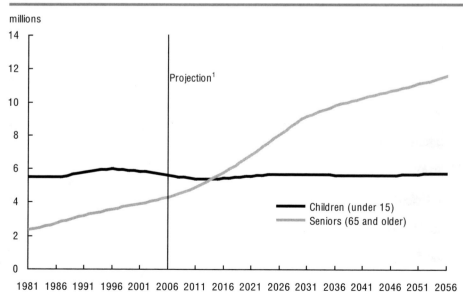

1. Medium growth scenario.
Source: Statistics Canada, CANSIM tables 051-0001 and 052-0004.

Second fastest growth in the G8

Canada had one of the fastest population growth rates in the industrialized world from 1994 to 2004. It was twice as fast as the average growth rate of the European G8 countries. During this period only the United States had faster population growth than Canada.

However, in recent years Canada's population has grown only slightly faster than that of its southern neighbour. In 2004/2005, Canada's population grew by 9.6 people for every 1,000 inhabitants, compared with 9.3 people per 1,000 inhabitants in the United States.

What distinguishes Canada's population growth is the large contribution of immigration. From 1994 to 2004, the net international migration rate in Canada was 0.61%—the highest among the G8 countries. The United States was second with a rate of 0.52%. Japan at 0.01% and France at 0.07% had the lowest migration growth rates.

While the net migration rate continues to boost Canada's population, growth in the United States is due primarily to natural increase. From 1994 to 2004, the natural increase rate in Canada was 0.39%, whereas in the United States it was 0.58%.

Canada ranks fourth among the G8 countries for total fertility rate (1.5 children per woman in 2004), and life expectancy here is similar to the G8 level. These factors resulted in Canada's natural rate of increase remaining relatively high in 2004 compared with other G8 countries. Only the United States had a higher rate of natural population increase.

Compared with other G8 countries, Canada has one of the youngest populations. Only the United States, where the median age is 36.3 years, and the Russian Federation, where it is 37.9 years, have populations younger than Canada, where the median age is 38.3 years.

Chart 24.5
Population growth rates of G8 countries, annual average, 1994 to 2004

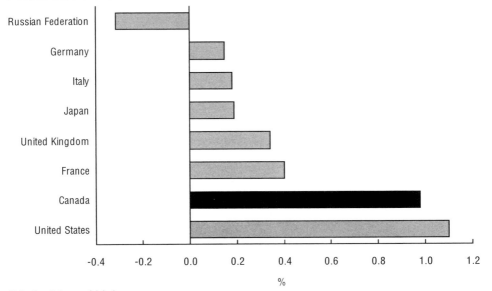

Note: Population as of July 1.
Sources: Statistics Canada; US Census Bureau; Eurostat; UK Office of National Statistics; Statistics Bureau of Japan; and Russian Federal State Statistics Service.

Alberta's population boom

Alberta's economy is undergoing an unprecedented growth. It is therefore not surprising that its population has grown considerably in the past few years. From July 2005 to June 2006, Alberta's population grew by 29.5 per 1,000 inhabitants, three times the national rate. According to estimates, the Alberta population on July 1, 2006 was 3.4 million.

An abundance of jobs, high salaries, budget surpluses and low taxes have been attracting migrants from other Canadian provinces. From July 2005 to June 2006, Alberta had a record 57,100 people migrate from other provinces, an increase of 22,700 over the previous year. Interprovincial net migration was responsible for 58% of the province's population growth. Additionally, Alberta's natural increase remained the highest among the provinces, with the number of births rising each year since 2000.

The pull of Alberta has primarily been felt in British Columbia, Saskatchewan and the Northwest Territories; more than half of migrants from these areas chose Alberta in 2005/2006. In the same year, 27,961 migrants from Ontario—one out of every three people leaving the province—also chose to move to Alberta. Meanwhile, 48% of migrants who left Newfoundland and Labrador, 7,103 people, moved to Alberta.

A lack of affordable housing and a labour shortage are considerable challenges stemming from Alberta's rapid growth. Despite an increase in housing starts, the demand for housing jumped 17% in 2005, which sent the prices of new houses skyrocketing in 2006. According to the 2005 Business Conditions Survey, 25% of Alberta manufacturers reported a shortage of unskilled workers; in 2003, just 2% reported a shortage.

Chart 24.6
Population growth rates, by province and territory

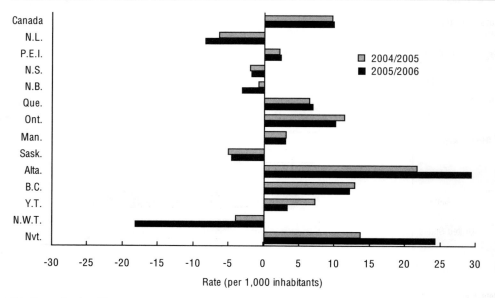

Note: Year ending June 30.
Source: Statistics Canada, Catalogue no. 91-215-XIE.

Migration influencing birth trends

Each year, many Canadians pack up and move to a different province or territory. This interprovincial migration is one of the major factors behind the variations in birth rates among the provinces, as is immigration from other countries. These migrants have children in a province or territory other than where they were born, changing Canada's demographic picture.

Many young people in their child-bearing years leave Newfoundland and Labrador for other provinces and the result is fewer births in that province. In 2004, women living in Newfoundland and Labrador gave birth to 4,598 babies—about half the 8,929 babies born in 1983.

The population of Newfoundland and Labrador has a low population replacement rate. The number of people leaving the province is greater than the number of people

settling there. In 2004, Newfoundland and Labrador had the lowest proportion of births to women born outside Canada (less than 1 birth in 100) or born elsewhere in Canada (9 births in 100).

Alberta was the only province with an increase in births for a fourth consecutive year in 2004. Alberta's baby boom is largely attributable to many young people moving in from other parts of the country. In Alberta, 29 babies out of 100 were born to women from other parts of Canada, and 20 babies out of 100 were born to immigrants.

Ontario has a much higher proportion of babies born to immigrant women. Just 8 of 100 babies were born to women who were born elsewhere in Canada, 56 out of 100 babies in the province were born to women who were born in Ontario, and 36 of 100 babies were born to immigrant women.

Chart 24.7
Births, by place of birth of mother and child, Canada and selected provinces, 2004

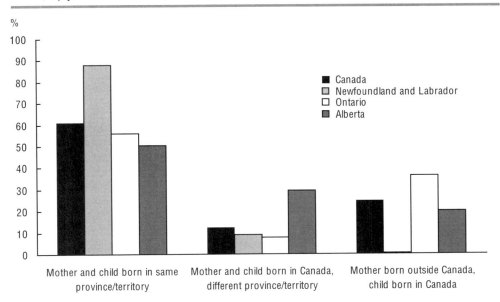

Legend:
- Canada
- Newfoundland and Labrador
- Ontario
- Alberta

Categories:
- Mother and child born in same province/territory
- Mother and child born in Canada, different province/territory
- Mother born outside Canada, child born in Canada

Note: Data reflect child's province/territory of residence at time of birth.
Source: Statistics Canada, Catalogue no. 84F0210XIE.

Table 24.1 Population, by province and territory, census years 1861 to 2006

	1861	1871	1881	1891	1901	1911	1921
				number			
Canada[1]	**3,229,633**	**3,689,257**	**4,324,810**	**4,833,239**	**5,371,315**	**7,206,643**	**8,787,949[2]**
Newfoundland and Labrador	..	..	..	..	..	..	..
Prince Edward Island	80,857	94,021	108,891	109,078	103,259	93,728	88,615
Nova Scotia	330,857	387,800	440,572	450,396	459,574	492,338	523,837
New Brunswick	252,047	285,594	321,233	321,263	331,120	351,889	387,876
Quebec	1,111,566	1,191,516	1,359,027	1,488,535	1,648,898	2,005,776	2,360,510
Ontario	1,396,091	1,620,851	1,926,922	2,114,321	2,182,947	2,527,292	2,933,662
Manitoba	..[3]	25,228	62,260	152,506	255,211	461,394	610,118
Saskatchewan	..[3]	..[3]	..[3]	..[3]	91,279	492,432	757,510
Alberta	..[3]	..[3]	..[3]	..[3]	73,022	374,295	588,454
British Columbia	51,524	36,247	49,459	98,173	178,657	392,480	524,582
Yukon	..	..	..	..	27,219	8,512	4,157
Northwest Territories (including Nunavut)	6,691	48,000	56,446	98,967	20,129	6,507	8,143
Northwest Territories[4]	..	..	..	..	..	..	..
Nunavut[4]	..	..	..	..	..	..	..

Note: Prior to 1961, data are as of Census Day; from 1961 on, data are as of July 1.
1. Beginning in 1951, Newfoundland and Labrador is included in Canada total.
2. Includes 485 members of the Royal Canadian Navy whose province of residence is not known.
3. Included with Northwest Territories.
4. Prior to July 1, 1991, only data for Northwest Territories and Nunavut combined are available.
Source: Statistics Canada, CANSIM table 051-0001 and Catalogue no. 11-516-XIE.

Table 24.2 Population, by sex and age group and by province and territory, 2006

	Both sexes			
	All ages	0 to 14	15 to 64	65 and older
	thousands			
Canada	**32,623.5**	**5,644.6**	**22,664.6**	**4,314.2**
Newfoundland and Labrador	**509.7**	78.3	362.4	69.0
Prince Edward Island	**138.5**	24.0	94.6	19.9
Nova Scotia	**934.4**	147.7	650.7	136.0
New Brunswick	**749.2**	118.2	524.4	106.6
Quebec	**7,651.5**	1,241.6	5,334.5	1,075.3
Ontario	**12,687.0**	2,262.9	8,782.6	1,641.5
Manitoba	**1,177.8**	228.0	790.0	159.8
Saskatchewan	**985.4**	190.0	648.3	147.0
Alberta	**3,375.8**	637.4	2,386.0	352.3
British Columbia	**4,310.5**	690.2	3,018.7	601.5
Yukon	**31.2**	5.6	23.3	2.3
Northwest Territories	**41.9**	10.2	29.7	2.0
Nunavut	**30.8**	10.4	19.5	0.9

Note: Population as of July 1, 2006.
Source: Statistics Canada, CANSIM table 051-0001.

1931	1941	1951	1961	1971	1981	1991	2001	2006
				number				
10,376,786	**11,506,655**	**14,009,429**	**18,238,247**	**21,961,999**	**24,820,393**	**28,031,394**	**31,021,251**	**32,623,490**
..	..	361,416	457,853	530,851	574,775	579,518	521,986	509,677
88,038	95,047	98,429	104,629	112,591	123,741	130,306	136,672	138,519
512,846	577,962	642,584	737,007	797,291	854,646	915,102	932,389	934,405
408,219	457,401	515,697	597,936	642,469	706,325	745,528	749,890	749,168
2,874,662	3,331,882	4,055,681	5,259,211	6,137,306	6,547,705	7,064,586	7,396,990	7,651,531
3,431,683	3,787,655	4,597,542	6,236,092	7,849,002	8,811,312	10,428,132	11,897,647	12,686,952
700,139	729,744	776,541	921,686	998,874	1,036,433	1,109,614	1,151,285	1,177,765
921,785	895,992	831,728	925,181	932,037	975,867	1,002,686	1,000,134	985,386
731,605	796,169	939,501	1,331,944	1,665,717	2,294,198	2,592,626	3,056,739	3,375,763
694,263	817,861	1,165,210	1,629,082	2,240,472	2,823,933	3,373,464	4,078,447	4,310,452
4,230	4,914	9,096	14,628	18,991	23,903	28,907	30,129	31,229
9,316	12,028	16,004	22,998	36,398	47,555	..	..	..
..	..	..	..	..	..	38,746	40,822	41,861
..	..	..	..	..	..	22,179	28,121	30,782

Males				Females			
All ages	0 to 14	15 to 64	65 and older	All ages	0 to 14	15 to 64	65 and older
			thousands				
16,155.5	**2,890.9**	**11,382.6**	**1,882.0**	**16,468.0**	**2,753.7**	**11,282.0**	**2,432.3**
250.1	40.3	178.9	30.9	259.6	38.0	183.5	38.1
67.4	12.3	46.4	8.6	71.2	11.7	48.1	11.3
456.9	74.8	323.1	58.9	477.5	72.9	327.6	77.1
369.5	60.5	263.1	45.8	379.7	57.7	261.3	60.7
3,777.3	636.1	2,687.4	453.8	3,874.2	605.6	2,647.2	621.5
6,262.1	1,156.3	4,387.8	718.0	6,424.8	1,106.6	4,394.8	923.4
585.4	117.0	400.0	68.4	592.4	111.0	390.0	91.4
489.7	97.7	328.0	64.0	495.7	92.4	320.2	83.1
1,707.0	327.3	1,221.9	157.8	1,668.8	310.1	1,164.2	194.5
2,136.9	355.1	1,508.9	272.8	2,173.6	335.1	1,509.8	328.7
15.7	2.8	11.7	1.2	15.5	2.9	11.5	1.1
21.6	5.2	15.4	1.0	20.2	5.0	14.3	1.0
15.9	5.4	10.0	0.5	14.8	5.0	9.5	0.4

Table 24.3 Population and dwelling counts, by census metropolitan area, census years 1996, 2001 and 2006

	1996	2001	2006
		number	
St. John's	174,051	172,918	181,113
Halifax	342,966[1]	359,183	372,858
Moncton	..	118,678[1]	126,424
Saint John	125,705	122,678	122,389
Saguenay	160,454	154,938	151,643
Québec[2]	671,889	686,569[1]	715,515
Sherbrooke	149,569[1]	175,950[1]	186,952
Trois-Rivières	139,956	137,507	141,529
Montréal[2]	3,326,447[1]	3,451,027[1]	3,635,571
Ottawa–Gatineau	998,718[1]	1,067,800[1]	1,130,761
Kingston	144,528[1]	146,838	152,358
Peterborough	..	110,876[1]	116,570
Oshawa	268,773	296,298	330,594
Toronto	4,263,759[1]	4,682,897	5,113,149
Hamilton	624,360	662,401	692,911
St. Catharines–Niagara	372,406	377,009	390,317
Kitchener	382,940	414,284	451,235
Brantford[2]	..	118,086[1]	124,607
Guelph	..	117,344	127,009
London	416,546[1]	435,600[1]	457,720
Windsor	286,811[1]	307,877	323,342
Barrie	..	148,480	177,061
Greater Sudbury / Grand Sudbury	165,618[1]	155,601	158,258
Thunder Bay	126,643[1]	121,986	122,907
Winnipeg	667,093[1]	676,594[1]	694,668
Regina	193,652	192,800	194,971
Saskatoon	219,056	225,927	233,923
Calgary[2]	821,628	951,494[1]	1,079,310
Edmonton	862,597	937,845	1,034,945
Kelowna	..	147,739	162,276
Abbotsford	136,480	147,370	159,020
Vancouver	1,831,665	1,986,965	2,116,581
Victoria[2]	304,287	311,902	330,088

1. Figure adjusted because of boundary change.
2. Excludes census data for one or more incompletely enumerated Indian reserves or Indian settlements.
Source: Statistics Canada, Census of Population, 1996, 2001 and 2006.

Table 24.4 Mid-size urban centres with the fastest population growth from 2001 to 2006

	2001	2006	Growth
	number		%
Okotoks, Alberta	11,689	17,145	46.7
Wood Buffalo, Alberta	42,581	52,643	23.6
Grande Prairie, Alberta	58,787	71,868	22.3
Red Deer, Alberta	67,829	82,772	22.0
Yellowknife, Northwest Territories	16,541	18,700	13.1
Lloydminster, Saskatchewan/Alberta	23,964	27,023	12.8
Canmore, Alberta	10,792	12,039	11.6
Medicine Hat, Alberta	61,735	68,822	11.5
Saint-Jean-sur-Richelieu, Quebec	79,600	87,492	9.9
Joliette, Quebec	39,720	43,595	9.8
Chilliwack, British Columbia	74,003	80,892	9.3
Fort St. John, British Columbia	23,007	25,136	9.3
Parksville, British Columbia	24,285	26,518	9.2
Lethbridge, Alberta	87,388	95,196	8.9
Courtenay, British Columbia	45,205	49,214	8.9
Granby, Quebec	63,069	68,352	8.4
Nanaimo, British Columbia	85,664	92,361	7.8
Collingwood, Ontario	16,039	17,290	7.8
Kawartha Lakes, Ontario	69,179	74,561	7.8
Vernon, British Columbia	51,530	55,418	7.5

Source: Statistics Canada, Census of Population, 2001 and 2006.

Table 24.5 Mid-size urban centres with the most significant population decline from 2001 to 2006

	2001	2006	Decline
	number		%
Kitimat, British Columbia	10,285	8,987	12.6
Prince Rupert, British Columbia	15,302	13,392	12.5
Quesnel, British Columbia	24,426	22,449	8.1
Terrace, British Columbia	19,980	18,581	7.0
Williams Lake, British Columbia	19,768	18,760	5.1
Campbellton, New Brunswick / Quebec	18,820	17,888	5.0
North Battleford, Saskatchewan	18,590	17,765	4.4
Kenora, Ontario	15,838	15,177	4.2
Elliot Lake, Ontario	11,956	11,549	3.4
Bathurst, New Brunswick	32,523	31,424	3.4
Edmundston, New Brunswick	22,173	21,442	3.3
Cape Breton, Nova Scotia	109,330	105,928	3.1
La Tuque, Quebec	15,725	15,293	2.7
Thetford Mines, Quebec	26,721	26,107	2.3
Dolbeau-Mistassini, Quebec	14,879	14,546	2.2
Prince George, British Columbia	85,035	83,225	2.1
Miramichi, New Brunswick	25,274	24,737	2.1
Amos, Quebec	18,302	17,918	2.1
Baie-Comeau, Quebec	30,401	29,808	2.0
Prince Albert, Saskatchewan	41,460	40,766	1.7

Source: Statistics Canada, Census of Population, 2001 and 2006.

Table 24.6 Components of population growth, 1861 to 2006

	1861 to 1871	1871 to 1881	1881 to 1891	1891 to 1901	1901 to 1911	1911 to 1921	1921 to 1931	1931 to 1941
				thousands				
Census population at end of period[2]	3,689	4,325	4,833	5,371	7,207	8,788	10,377	11,507
Total population growth[3]	459	636	508	538	1,836	1,581	1,589	1,130
Births	1,370	1,480	1,524	1,548	1,925	2,340	2,415	2,294
Deaths	760	790	870	880	900	1,070	1,055	1,072
Immigration[2]	260	350	680	250	1,550	1,400	1,200	149
Emigration[2]	410	404	826	380	740	1,089	970	241

1. Beginning in 1951, Newfoundland and Labrador is included.
2. Population based on census counts prior to 1971; from 1971 on, based on adjusted population estimates.
3. The change in population numbers between two censuses.
Source: Statistics Canada, Census of Population, CANSIM tables 051-0001, 051-0004 and 071-0001, and Catalogue no. 11-516-XIE.

Table 24.7 Components of population growth, by province and territory, 2005/2006

	Canada	Newfoundland and Labrador	Prince Edward Island	Nova Scotia	New Brunswick
			number		
Births	343,517	4,368	1,393	8,617	6,837
Deaths	234,914	4,494	1,231	8,446	6,585
Immigration	254,359	450	343	2,199	1,387
Emigration	38,551	140	139	784	337
Net temporary emigration	25,562	105	33	375	223
Returning emigrants	20,505	66	61	386	330
Net non-permanent residents	4,640	-62	76	608	66
Net interprovincial migration	...	-4,368	-127	-3,930	-3,788

Notes: Period from July 1, 2005 to June 30, 2006.
Preliminary data.
Source: Statistics Canada, CANSIM table 051-0004.

Table 24.8 Population growth rate for Canada, provinces and territories, 1956 to 2006

	Canada	Newfoundland and Labrador	Prince Edward Island	Nova Scotia	New Brunswick
			%		
1956 to 1961	13.4	10.3	5.4	6.1	7.8
1961 to 1966	9.7	7.8	3.7	2.6	3.2
1966 to 1971	7.8	5.8	2.9	4.4	2.9
1971 to 1976	6.6	6.8	5.9	5.0	6.7
1976 to 1981	5.9	1.8	3.6	2.3	2.8
1981 to 1986	4.0	0.1	3.4	3.0	1.9
1986 to 1991	7.9	0.0	2.5	3.1	2.0
1991 to 1996	5.7	-2.9	3.7	1.0	2.0
1996 to 2001	4.0	-7.0	0.5	-0.1	-1.2
2001 to 2006	5.4	-1.5	0.4	0.6	0.1

1. Prior to July 1, 1991, data for Northwest Territories include Nunavut.
Source: Statistics Canada, Census of Population, 1956 to 2006.

1941 to 1951[1]	1951 to 1956	1956 to 1961	1961 to 1966	1966 to 1971	1971 to 1976	1976 to 1981	1981 to 1986	1986 to 1991	1991 to 1996	1996 to 2001	2001 to 2006
					thousands						
13,648	16,081	18,238	20,015	21,568	23,450	24,820	26,101	28,031	29,611	31,021	32,623
2,141	2,433	2,157	1,777	1,553	1,488	1,371	1,281	1,930	1,579	1,410	1,602
3,186	2,106	2,362	2,249	1,856	1,760	1,820	1,872	1,933	1,936	1,705	1,679
1,214	633	687	731	766	824	843	885	946	1,024	1,089	1,143
548	783	760	539	890	1,053	771	678	1,164	1,118	1,217	1,384
379	185	278	280	427	358	278	278	213	338	376	317

Quebec	Ontario	Manitoba	Saskatchewan	Alberta	British Columbia	Yukon	Northwest Territories	Nunavut
				number				
78,450	133,170	13,915	12,031	41,989	40,926	365	686	770
52,900	90,945	10,226	9,250	20,310	30,028	149	214	136
41,983	133,116	8,884	2,112	19,869	43,858	76	73	9
6,139	16,643	1,370	522	5,311	7,116	15	20	15
4,074	10,627	560	513	2,932	6,068	24	18	10
3,343	9,046	795	376	3,026	3,062	7	4	3
1,255	-7,443	814	268	4,745	4,206	42	48	17
-8,155	-21,391	-8,635	-9,073	57,105	3,779	-194	-1,327	104

Quebec	Ontario	Manitoba	Saskatchewan	Alberta	British Columbia	Yukon	Northwest Territories[1]	Nunavut[1]
				%				
13.6	15.4	8.4	5.1	18.6	16.5	20.0	19.1	...
9.9	11.6	4.5	3.3	9.9	15.0	-1.7	25.0	...
4.3	10.7	2.6	-3.0	11.3	16.6	27.9	21.1	...
3.4	7.3	3.4	-0.5	12.9	12.9	18.7	22.4	...
3.3	4.4	0.5	5.1	21.7	11.3	6.0	7.3	...
1.5	5.5	3.6	4.3	5.7	5.1	1.5	14.2	...
5.6	10.8	2.7	-2.0	7.6	13.8	18.3	10.4	...
3.5	6.6	2.0	0.1	5.9	13.5	10.7	9.0	16.4
1.4	6.1	0.5	-1.1	10.3	4.9	-6.8	-5.8	8.1
4.3	6.6	2.6	-1.1	10.6	5.3	5.9	11.0	10.2

Table 24.9 Births, by province and territory, 2000 to 2006

	2000 to 2001	2001 to 2002	2002 to 2003	2003 to 2004	2004 to 2005	2005 to 2006p
	number					
Canada	**327,107**	**328,155**	**330,523**	**337,762**	**338,894**	**343,517**
Newfoundland and Labrador	4,732	4,636	4,596	4,598	4,451	4,368
Prince Edward Island	1,381	1,313	1,374	1,403	1,390	1,393
Nova Scotia	8,922	8,693	8,635	8,713	8,700	8,617
New Brunswick	7,202	6,971	7,104	7,072	6,924	6,837
Quebec	71,825	72,602	72,273	74,364	75,347	78,450
Ontario	127,741	128,947	129,256	132,874	132,769	133,170
Manitoba	13,939	13,746	13,765	13,981	13,864	13,915
Saskatchewan	12,084	11,996	11,794	12,121	12,012	12,031
Alberta	37,197	37,602	39,450	40,635	41,056	41,989
British Columbia	40,367	39,932	40,534	40,205	40,565	40,926
Yukon	348	344	322	374	364	365
Northwest Territories	656	651	658	697	698	686
Nunavut	713	722	762	725	754	770

Note: Period from July 1 to June 30.
Source: Statistics Canada, CANSIM table 051-0004.

Table 24.10 Birth rate, by province and territory, 2000 to 2006

	2000 to 2001	2001 to 2002	2002 to 2003	2003 to 2004	2004 to 2005	2005 to 2006p
	rate per 1,000 population					
Canada	**10.6**	**10.5**	**10.5**	**10.6**	**10.5**	**10.6**
Newfoundland and Labrador	9.0	8.9	8.9	8.9	8.6	8.5
Prince Edward Island	10.1	9.6	10.0	10.2	10.1	10.1
Nova Scotia	9.6	9.3	9.2	9.3	9.3	9.2
New Brunswick	9.6	9.3	9.5	9.4	9.2	9.1
Quebec	9.7	9.8	9.7	9.9	9.9	10.3
Ontario	10.8	10.7	10.6	10.8	10.6	10.5
Manitoba	12.1	11.9	11.9	12.0	11.8	11.8
Saskatchewan	12.0	12.0	11.8	12.2	12.1	12.2
Alberta	12.3	12.2	12.6	12.8	12.7	12.6
British Columbia	9.9	9.7	9.8	9.6	9.6	9.6
Yukon	11.5	11.4	10.6	12.2	11.7	11.7
Northwest Territories	16.1	15.8	15.7	16.4	16.3	16.2
Nunavut	25.6	25.4	26.3	24.7	25.3	25.3

Note: Period from July 1 to June 30.
Source: Statistics Canada, CANSIM tables 051-0001 and 051-0004.

Table 24.11 Deaths, by province and territory, 2000 to 2006

	2000 to 2001	2001 to 2002	2002 to 2003	2003 to 2004	2004 to 2005	2005 to 2006p
	number					
Canada	**219,114**	**220,494**	**223,905**	**230,092**	**233,749**	**234,914**
Newfoundland and Labrador	4,233	4,126	4,276	4,318	4,405	4,494
Prince Edward Island	1,209	1,205	1,217	1,190	1,208	1,231
Nova Scotia	7,847	7,922	7,944	8,146	8,305	8,446
New Brunswick	5,972	6,065	6,181	6,325	6,461	6,585
Quebec	54,017	54,735	54,896	56,475	55,800	52,900
Ontario	81,119	80,993	83,410	85,524	88,196	90,945
Manitoba	9,873	9,720	9,852	9,940	10,096	10,226
Saskatchewan	9,001	8,650	8,880	9,061	9,172	9,250
Alberta	17,590	17,937	18,098	18,888	19,517	20,310
British Columbia	27,815	28,697	28,694	29,752	30,103	30,028
Yukon	135	150	145	136	141	149
Northwest Territories	175	164	183	205	212	214
Nunavut	128	130	129	132	133	136

Note: Period from July 1 to June 30.
Source: Statistics Canada, CANSIM table 051-0004.

Table 24.12 Death rate, by province and territory, 2000 to 2006

	2000 to 2001	2001 to 2002	2002 to 2003	2003 to 2004	2004 to 2005	2005 to 2006p
	rate per 1,000 population					
Canada	**7.1**	**7.1**	**7.1**	**7.2**	**7.3**	**7.2**
Newfoundland and Labrador	8.1	7.9	8.2	8.3	8.5	8.8
Prince Edward Island	8.9	8.8	8.9	8.6	8.8	8.9
Nova Scotia	8.4	8.5	8.5	8.7	8.9	9.0
New Brunswick	8.0	8.1	8.2	8.4	8.6	8.8
Quebec	7.3	7.4	7.3	7.5	7.4	6.9
Ontario	6.9	6.7	6.8	6.9	7.1	7.2
Manitoba	8.6	8.4	8.5	8.5	8.6	8.7
Saskatchewan	9.0	8.7	8.9	9.1	9.2	9.4
Alberta	5.8	5.8	5.8	5.9	6.0	6.1
British Columbia	6.9	7.0	6.9	7.1	7.1	7.0
Yukon	4.5	5.0	4.8	4.4	4.5	4.8
Northwest Territories	7.0	7.0	7.3	7.9	5.0	5.1
Nunavut	4.4	4.5	4.4	4.4	4.4	4.5

Note: Period from July 1 to June 30.
Source: Statistics Canada, CANSIM tables 051-0001 and 051-0004.

Table 24.13 Interprovincial migrants, by province or territory of origin and destination, 2005/2006

	Destination			
	Newfoundland and Labrador	Prince Edward Island	Nova Scotia	New Brunswick
	number			
Net migration	**-4,368**	**-127**	**-3,930**	**-3,788**
In-migrants[1]	10,544	3,356	16,486	12,116
Out-migrants[1]	14,912	3,483	20,416	15,904
Origin				
Newfoundland and Labrador	.	181	1,384	614
Prince Edward Island	162	.	737	427
Nova Scotia	1,644	788	.	2,505
New Brunswick	701	471	2,724	.
Quebec	277	275	846	2,267
Ontario	4,713	1,139	6,601	3,942
Manitoba	138	57	413	314
Saskatchewan	91	75	184	125
Alberta	2,112	205	1,971	1,145
British Columbia	398	133	1,496	690
Yukon	28	26	40	19
Northwest Territories	197	0	56	23
Nunavut	83	6	34	45

Note: Period from July 1, 2005 to June 30, 2006.
1. Excludes moves between census divisions within the province or territory.
Source: Statistics Canada, Catalogue no. 91-215-XIE.

Table 24.14 Interprovincial migrants, by age group and by province and territory, 2005/2006

	Newfoundland and Labrador	Prince Edward Island	Nova Scotia	New Brunswick
	number			
In-migrants, all ages	**10,544**	**3,356**	**16,486**	**12,116**
0 to 17	2,342	680	3,296	2,642
18 to 24	1,669	562	3,095	2,099
25 to 44	4,381	1,269	6,940	5,049
45 to 64	1,828	665	2,424	1,805
65 and older	324	180	731	521
Out-migrants, all ages	**14,912**	**3,483**	**20,416**	**15,904**
0 to 17	2,652	597	4,201	3,257
18 to 24	4,563	1,032	4,519	3,920
25 to 44	5,348	1,255	8,475	6,287
45 to 64	2,015	448	2,542	1,920
65 and older	334	151	679	520
Total net migrants, all ages	**-4,368**	**-127**	**-3,930**	**-3,788**
0 to 17	-310	83	-905	-615
18 to 24	-2,894	-470	-1,424	-1,821
25 to 44	-967	14	-1,535	-1,238
45 to 64	-187	217	-118	-115
65 and older	-10	29	52	1

Note: Period from July 1, 2005 to June 30, 2006.
Source: Statistics Canada, CANSIM table 051-0012.

				Destination				
Quebec	Ontario	Manitoba	Saskatchewan	Alberta	British Columbia	Yukon	Northwest Territories	Nunavut
				number				
-8,155	-21,391	-8,635	-9,073	57,105	3,779	-194	-1,327	104
25,627	64,236	14,215	16,031	109,686	55,759	1,494	2,230	1,066
33,782	85,627	22,850	25,104	52,581	51,980	1,688	3,557	962
198	4,104	249	91	7,103	587	17	195	189
256	858	36	54	734	209	3	7	0
784	6,366	347	236	6,133	1,442	62	91	18
2,420	3,870	278	120	4,260	1,001	23	31	5
.	19,585	357	545	5,953	3,390	110	114	63
16,234	.	4,921	1,953	27,961	17,326	183	346	308
526	5,389	.	2,565	9,018	4,196	35	79	120
472	2,139	2,353	.	15,758	3,718	50	102	37
2,074	9,839	3,364	7,942	.	22,745	269	765	150
2,452	11,377	2,055	2,233	30,225	.	583	294	44
46	109	37	52	578	639	.	89	25
65	396	127	177	1,789	461	159	.	107
100	204	91	63	174	45	0	117	.

Quebec	Ontario	Manitoba	Saskatchewan	Alberta	British Columbia	Yukon	Northwest Territories	Nunavut
				number				
25,627	64,236	14,215	16,031	109,686	55,759	1,494	2,230	1,066
5,046	13,407	3,521	4,298	24,858	10,057	332	497	221
4,383	10,837	2,597	3,051	24,779	9,897	221	434	168
11,083	27,749	5,501	5,849	42,572	21,458	644	936	464
3,878	8,920	1,887	2,114	13,292	10,571	245	335	200
1,237	3,323	709	719	4,185	3,776	52	28	13
33,782	85,627	22,850	25,104	52,581	51,980	1,688	3,557	962
6,984	18,252	5,524	5,930	11,270	11,081	365	853	231
4,903	13,654	4,172	6,017	9,578	10,437	329	571	97
15,495	36,230	8,903	8,711	20,770	20,023	601	1,391	406
4,481	13,172	3,135	3,152	8,665	7,378	348	690	218
1,919	4,319	1,116	1,294	2,298	3,061	45	52	10
-8,155	-21,391	-8,635	-9,073	57,105	3,779	-194	-1,327	104
-1,938	-4,845	-2,003	-1,632	13,588	-1,024	-33	-356	-10
-520	-2,817	-1,575	-2,966	15,201	-540	-108	-137	71
-4,412	-8,481	-3,402	-2,862	21,802	1,435	43	-455	58
-603	-4,252	-1,248	-1,038	4,627	3,193	-103	-355	-18
-682	-996	-407	-575	1,887	715	7	-24	3

Table 24.15 Population projections, by age group, selected years from 2006 to 2031

	2006	2011	2016	2021	2026	2031
			thousands			
All ages[1]	**32,547.2**	**33,909.7**	**35,266.8**	**36,608.5**	**37,882.7**	**39,029.4**
0 to 4	1,697.5	1,724.7	1,781.9	1,816.8	1,812.8	1,781.3
5 to 9	1,842.6	1,780.8	1,810.7	1,871.9	1,910.9	1,910.9
10 to 14	2,084.6	1,916.4	1,858.1	1,892.0	1,956.8	1,999.4
15 to 19	2,164.8	2,170.4	2,006.4	1,952.7	1,990.3	2,058.4
20 to 24	2,252.9	2,295.3	2,304.1	2,145.8	2,096.8	2,138.2
25 to 29	2,226.1	2,330.2	2,376.7	2,391.9	2,241.4	2,198.8
30 to 34	2,222.6	2,354.8	2,462.8	2,518.1	2,542.1	2,402.7
35 to 39	2,351.1	2,327.1	2,462.6	2,576.9	2,639.6	2,671.1
40 to 44	2,698.3	2,409.3	2,390.6	2,530.6	2,649.3	2,717.1
45 to 49	2,671.5	2,711.2	2,431.6	2,418.6	2,561.7	2,683.3
50 to 54	2,363.9	2,651.5	2,695.4	2,425.9	2,417.8	2,563.0
55 to 59	2,082.5	2,327.4	2,614.1	2,662.9	2,404.5	2,401.4
60 to 64	1,583.3	2,027.9	2,272.3	2,557.8	2,612.4	2,367.8
65 to 69	1,227.3	1,513.1	1,942.1	2,184.7	2,466.6	2,527.6
70 to 74	1,044.2	1,130.8	1,401.5	1,806.8	2,044.1	2,318.2
75 to 79	878.0	907.6	993.3	1,241.0	1,610.8	1,837.3
80 to 84	638.3	692.2	724.3	804.0	1,016.1	1,332.1
85 to 89	342.8	422.2	465.5	494.6	560.3	719.8
90 to 94	137.3	169.2	211.2	237.4	257.2	299.2
95 to 99	33.1	42.4	54.4	68.6	79.0	87.4
100 and older	4.7	5.4	7.1	9.5	12.1	14.4

Note: Of the six population projection scenarios, based on population estimates as of July 1, 2005, results from scenario 3 medium growth and medium migration trends are presented in this table.
1. Figures may not add to totals because of rounding.
Source: Statistics Canada, CANSIM table 052-0004.

Table 24.16 Population projections, by province and territory, selected years from 2006 to 2031

	2006	2011	2016	2021	2026	2031
			thousands			
Canada	**32,547.2**	**33,909.7**	**35,266.8**	**36,608.5**	**37,882.7**	**39,029.4**
Newfoundland and Labrador	515.2	512.5	511.3	510.7	509.1	505.6
Prince Edward Island	138.7	141.2	143.7	146.1	148.2	149.5
Nova Scotia	939.6	948.5	958.4	968.2	975.8	979.4
New Brunswick	752.9	757.4	762.2	766.4	768.5	767.2
Quebec	7,641.6	7,841.4	8,018.7	8,176.8	8,306.8	8,396.4
Ontario	12,682.0	13,374.7	14,071.4	14,776.6	15,472.0	16,130.4
Manitoba	1,183.1	1,214.8	1,250.9	1,288.1	1,323.7	1,355.7
Saskatchewan	991.5	982.0	978.2	977.4	977.0	975.8
Alberta	3,295.0	3,483.2	3,667.1	3,841.9	4,002.2	4,144.9
British Columbia	4,302.9	4,545.0	4,792.0	5,040.0	5,280.0	5,502.9
Yukon	31.1	31.6	32.1	32.7	33.4	34.0
Northwest Territories	43.6	46.4	48.9	51.1	52.9	54.4
Nunavut	30.2	31.1	31.9	32.5	33.0	33.3

Note: Of the six population projection scenarios, based on population estimates as of July 1, 2005, results from scenario 3 medium growth and medium migration trends are presented in this table.
Source: Statistics Canada, CANSIM table 052-0004.

Prices and price indexes

25

OVERVIEW

Everybody loves a deal, and when it comes to spending our hard-earned dollars, we sometimes go to great lengths to find the best price possible. Whether driving from one gas station to the next seeking a half-cent discount on a litre of unleaded, browsing online 'e-tailers,' or waiting for the big sales, Canadians make many of their purchasing decisions based on price. And for virtually every good and service that we buy, Statistics Canada has a tool for tracking its price.

These tools include price indexes that track very specific goods and services, such as machinery and equipment, new housing, couriers and messengers, exports and imports, farm products and commercial software. These very specific indexes are used by companies and industry analysts to make business decisions, to set prices and to negotiate contracts.

The price-tracking toolbox also contains more general price indexes that measure prices for goods and services that average Canadians buy regularly. The most widely used of these is the Consumer Price Index (CPI), which tracks the cost of a 'basket' of goods and services bought by Canadian consumers.

The Consumer Price Index

The CPI was introduced in the early 1900s. Its basket then included 29 food items, 5 fuel and lighting items, and the cost of rent in some 60 cities. Today, the CPI reflects prices for virtually every single good and service Canadians can buy, right across the country.

Since the early 1900s, prices have gone up dramatically. Using average price increases as measured by the CPI and 1992 dollars as the

Chart 25.1
Consumer Price Index

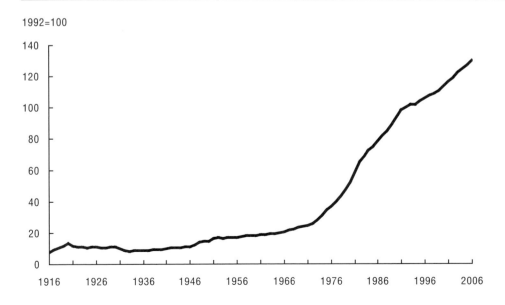

1992=100

Source: Statistics Canada, CANSIM table 326-0002.

benchmark, a $3.00 carton of orange juice cost roughly $0.22 in 1914, about $0.33 in 1945, and $0.78 in 1972.

This gradual rise in prices picked up steam over the 1970s, so that just 10 years later, in 1982, that same carton of juice cost $1.96. Strong price growth continued until about 1992, but slowed thereafter. In 2006, that $3.00 carton cost $3.90. This persistent rise in prices is called inflation, and the primary tool for measuring it is the CPI.

What the CPI's major components show

The CPI measures the average change in retail prices encountered by all consumers in Canada—no one consumer buys all of the goods and services included in the CPI's basket. Moreover, items in the CPI are weighted to account for typical spending patterns (for example, food accounts for 17% of spending) and how often consumers buy certain items (appliances are replaced only rarely). The CPI is also continually updated to be as comprehensive and representative as possible.

Selected special aggregates, goods and services

	1986	2006
	1992=100	
Goods and services	78.1	129.9
Goods	80.7	124.0
Services	75.2	136.4

Source: Statistics Canada, CANSIM table 326-0002.

In January 2007, the All-items CPI was at 130.3, compared with 1992. This means that the cost of the basket of goods and services bought by Canadians has risen 30% since 1992. Shelter costs, the single largest component of the CPI and comprising nearly 27% of all spending, rose at the same rate.

However, the prices of other major components have increased much faster since 1992. Transportation costs have jumped more than 50% and food prices are up about 33%, while recreation, education and reading costs have increased just 25%. Generally, the prices of services have climbed much faster than the prices of goods. Only one major component of the CPI has actually seen prices fall—clothing and footwear is 1% cheaper today than in 1992.

Chart 25.2
Consumer Price Index, all-items and energy

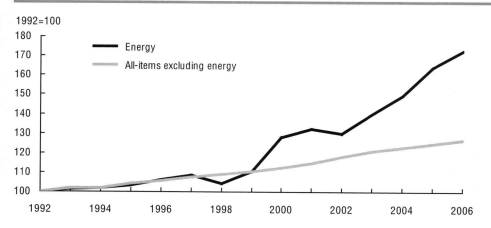

Source: Statistics Canada, CANSIM table 326-0002.

The component showing the greatest price increase has been energy—from 1992 to January 2007, it climbed 62%. But, as anyone with a car knows, the price of fuel can swing wildly from one month to the next. In 2006 alone, the price of a litre of regular unleaded at full-service stations in Vancouver saw a high of $1.19 in May and a low of $0.91 in February.

The prices of fuel and items such as fruits, vegetables, mortgage interest costs and inter-city transportation, are highly volatile. To account for this, Statistics Canada measures data for different CPI baskets, such as the 'All-items CPI excluding food and energy,' and the 'Core CPI,' which exclude the CPI's eight most volatile components.

Price changes can vary widely across the country

The CPI is also compiled for Canada's provinces and some major cities. Price changes can vary quite widely across the country. On the CPI scale, most provinces fit nicely in the middle, having a CPI that ranges from 128 to 132.

Chart 25.3
Consumer Price Index, shelter, selected CMAs, 2006

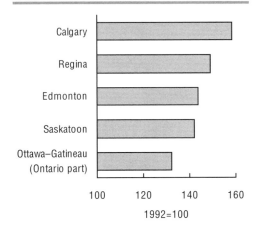

Source: Statistics Canada, CANSIM table 326-0002.

Even Ontario and British Columbia—long regarded as the most expensive parts of the country—fit in this range. But the exceptions are notable. Alberta, at 142.4, has seen prices rise the most since 1992. By contrast, prices have grown the least in Quebec, at 125.7.

The price indexes for Canada's major urban centres may make you think twice before taking that job in Calgary, Edmonton or Regina, where prices have risen faster than all other Canadian cities. Since 1992, shelter costs alone in Calgary have risen 71%, compared with the national average of 31%. At the other end of the scale, prices for rented and owned accommodation have moved little since 1992 in Thunder Bay.

Selected sources

Statistics Canada

- *Capital Expenditure Price Statistics.* Quarterly. 62-007-XIE

- *Farm Product Price Index.* Monthly. 21-007-XWE

- *Income and Expenditure Accounts Technical Series.* Occasional. 13-604-MIE

- *Industry Price Indexes.* Monthly. 62-011-XWE

- *The Consumer Price Index.* Monthly. 62-001-XWB

Other

- "Purchasing Power Parities: Comparative Price Levels." Main Economic Indicators. OECD, May 2007

Heavy metals

While prices rise for many reasons, a major force behind inflation is the rising cost of the materials that go into the products we buy—the raw materials and industrial products manufacturers use to make their own products. In recent years, metals prices have pushed up commodity prices.

Manufacturers of metal products start production by buying unprocessed ferrous or non-ferrous metals that are mined or extracted from the ground. The Raw Materials Price Index (RMPI), which tracks prices paid by manufacturers for key raw materials such as metals, shows that the cost of metals has gone through the roof since 2001.

In 2006, while prices for unprocessed ferrous metal—in other words, iron ore—have risen 39 % since 1997 (the current base year of the RMPI), the most dramatic price growth has been in the non-ferrous metals category

(96%). Canada's uranium miners—many of which are found in Saskatchewan—have seen prices of radioactive concentrates nearly quadruple. Prices for copper, nickel and zinc concentrates have also risen sharply: copper theft from residential homes has become a strange but growing trend. Precious metals such as gold and palladium have also seen strong price growth since 1997.

Raw metals are in turn transformed into commercial products. And as the Industrial Product Price Index (IPPI) suggests, dearer metals translates into higher prices for metal products coming out of the factory gate.

The overall IPPI is up about 14% since 1997; by comparison, prices for primary metal products sold to other manufacturers for making appliances, cars or other metal products have climbed 39%. As a result, the price of these fabricated metal products has increased about 23% since 1997.

Chart 25.4
Raw Materials Price Index, selected commodities

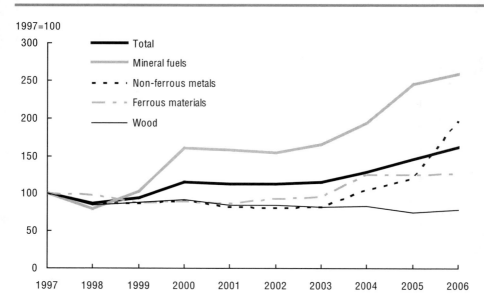

1997=100

Source: Statistics Canada, CANSIM table 330-0006.

Flat prices at the farm gate

All Canadians are affected by price changes, but few feel it as directly as our farmers. Farmers are particularly vulnerable to Mother Nature, which can dramatically affect prices for crops and livestock and make the difference between profit and loss. Agriculture as an industry has not seen prices rise as much as have most others. In many cases, the prices that farmers receive today are lower than they were in 1997.

The Farm Product Price Index (FPPI) tracks prices for crops and livestock sold directly from the farm, and specifically excludes expenses such as transportation beyond the farm gate and storage costs. The index reflects the prices farmers actually receive when they sell their goods.

The trend in recent years has not been positive: At the end of 2006, the FPPI was at 98.9 against 1997 dollars. This means that

overall prices for farm products in Canada fell by about 1% from 1997 prices. Over this period, the index peaked at 111.6 at the start of 2003. At the end of 2006, crop prices were at 98.6; livestock prices were roughly what they were in 1997, at 99.5.

Some of the hardest hit farm sectors are grains, oilseeds and hogs. The prices farmers received for grains such as corn, wheat, oats and barley at the end of 2006 fell by more than 10% from 1997. Hog prices also dropped by about one-third and oilseed prices were down 15%.

There were a few bright spots for some farmers, however. As of the end of 2006, potato farmers had seen prices increase by more than half since 1997, and dairy farmers were receiving one-third higher prices for dairy products. Vegetable farmers saw growth of about 19% in their prices.

Chart 25.5
Farm Product Price Index, selected commodities

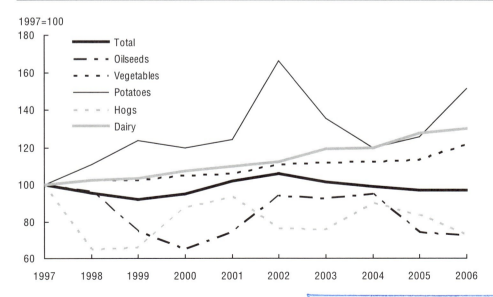

1997=100

Legend:
- Total
- Oilseeds
- Vegetables
- Potatoes
- Hogs
- Dairy

Note: Vegetables excludes potatoes.
Source: Statistics Canada, CANSIM table 002-0022.

Going like a house on fire

A strong economy, a steady influx of immigrants, and baby boomers spending more and more of their inheritance money has heated up the Canadian housing market over the last few years. As a result, the average cost of new homes has increased by nearly half since 1997.

The booming economy in Alberta and strong markets in the other prairie provinces account for a large part of the overall price rise. The New Housing Price Index (NHPI), which measures changes in contractors' selling prices for new residential houses, shows that, as of December 2006, housing prices in Calgary and Edmonton had more than doubled since 1997, the base year of the index. New house prices in Regina, Winnipeg and Saskatoon have grown by half or more over that same period.

The NHPI (1997=100) for Canada was at 147.5 in December 2006—not quite matching the boom in Alberta but a 48% jump in prices over 10 years nonetheless. Montréal, Ottawa–Gatineau and St. Catharines–Niagara all roughly tracked with this national average.

But the heat in some regions has not been felt in others. New house prices in Prince Edward Island and New Brunswick have climbed around 15% since 1997, and prices have edged up just 4% in Windsor, Ont., which has seen a downturn in its economy because of the slumping automotive sector.

Besides continued strong demand for new houses, the NHPI has been pushed up by steadily growing costs of building materials, such as copper, drywall, concrete and windows, as well as labour and land costs.

Chart 25.6
New Housing Price Index, selected census metropolitan areas

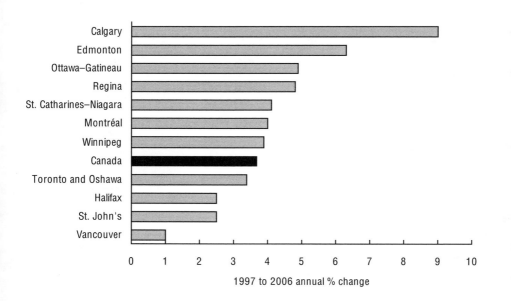

1997 to 2006 annual % change

Source: Statistics Canada, CANSIM table 327-0005.

Purchasing power parities

Would a cup of coffee cost more in Paris than at your favourite local drive-through? A statistical tool called purchasing power parities (PPP) helps to answer this and similar questions because it compares the purchasing power of different countries' currencies.

For example, if the price of a coffee is 2 euros in France and $3 in Canada, then the PPP between the two countries would be $3 divided by 2—in other words, for every euro needed to buy a coffee in France, you would need $1.50 in Canada.

In reality, though, many more goods and services are exchanged in an economy than just cups of coffee. That is why PPP estimates in practice cover a wide-ranging basket of more than 3,000 goods and services.

The Organisation for Economic Co-operation and Development (OECD) calculated 2006 PPP estimates for Canada. These showed

that $CAN1.23 in Canada has the same purchasing power as $US1.00 in the United States or 0.89 euros in France—the U.S. dollar is the reference currency.

Other interesting economic statistics can be derived from PPPs, such as comparative price levels. For instance, an index of 107 for Canada would mean that the same basket of goods and services cost 7% more in Canada in 2006 compared with the OECD average, which is set at 100.

PPPs can also be used to make meaningful comparisons of countries' economic output. For instance, the PPP-adjusted estimate of gross domestic product per person of 118 for Canada in 2006 means that Canadians produce 18% more goods and services per person than the OECD average.

Chart 25.7
Comparative price levels, selected countries, 2006

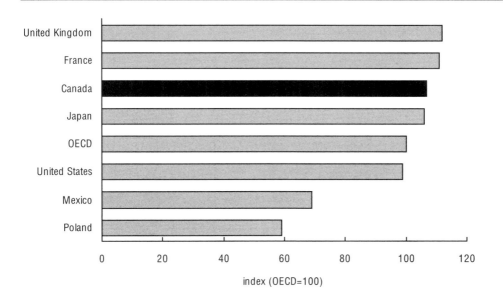

index (OECD=100)

Source: Organization for Economic Co-operation and Development.

Table 25.1 Consumer Price Index, 1987 to 2006

	1987	1988	1989	1990	1991	1992	1993
				1992=100			
All-items	**81.5**	**84.8**	**89.0**	**93.3**	**98.5**	**100.0**	**101.8**
Food	86.4	88.7	92.0	95.8	100.4	100.0	101.7
Shelter	80.3	84.0	88.9	93.9	98.2	100.0	101.4
Household operations and furnishings	87.3	90.6	93.8	95.8	99.5	100.0	101.0
Clothing and footwear	80.5	84.7	88.1	90.6	99.1	100.0	101.0
Transportation	85.1	86.7	91.2	96.3	98.0	100.0	103.2
Health and personal care	80.0	83.5	87.1	91.4	97.8	100.0	102.7
Recreation, education and reading	80.4	84.9	88.8	92.5	98.9	100.0	102.4
Alcoholic beverages and tobacco products	63.1	67.8	74.1	80.6	94.4	100.0	101.6
Special aggregates							
All-items excluding food	80.5	84.0	88.4	92.8	98.2	100.0	101.9
All-items excluding energy	81.4	84.9	89.2	93.2	98.4	100.0	101.9
				% change from previous year			
All-items	**4.4**	**4.0**	**5.0**	**4.8**	**5.6**	**1.5**	**1.8**
Food	4.3	2.7	3.7	4.1	4.8	-0.4	1.7
Shelter	4.6	4.6	5.8	5.6	4.6	1.8	1.4
Household operations and furnishings	2.9	3.8	3.5	2.1	3.9	0.5	1.0
Clothing and footwear	4.3	5.2	4.0	2.8	9.4	0.9	1.0
Transportation	3.7	1.9	5.2	5.6	1.8	2.0	3.2
Health and personal care	5.1	4.4	4.3	4.9	7.0	2.2	2.7
Recreation, education and reading	5.0	5.6	4.6	4.2	6.9	1.1	2.4
Alcoholic beverages and tobacco products	6.6	7.4	9.3	8.8	17.1	5.9	1.6
Special aggregates							
All-items excluding food	4.4	4.3	5.2	5.0	5.8	1.8	1.9
All-items excluding energy	4.6	4.3	5.1	4.5	5.6	1.6	1.9

Note: Annual average indexes are obtained by averaging the indexes for the 12 months of the calendar year.
Source: Statistics Canada, CANSIM table 326-0002.

1994	1995	1996	1997	1998	1999	2000	2001	2002	2003	2004	2005	2006
						1992=100						
102.0	**104.2**	**105.9**	**107.6**	**108.6**	**110.5**	**113.5**	**116.4**	**119.0**	**122.3**	**124.6**	**127.3**	**129.9**
102.1	104.5	105.9	107.6	109.3	110.7	112.2	117.2	120.3	122.4	124.9	128.0	131.0
101.8	102.9	103.1	103.3	103.7	105.1	108.8	112.8	113.8	117.5	120.5	124.2	128.7
101.2	103.1	105.3	106.6	108.2	109.0	110.0	112.2	113.8	114.6	115.2	115.8	116.2
101.8	101.7	101.4	102.7	103.9	105.3	105.5	106.0	105.2	103.3	103.1	102.6	100.8
107.8	113.4	117.8	121.5	120.5	124.5	130.7	130.8	134.4	141.4	144.8	150.7	154.8
103.6	103.5	104.1	105.9	108.1	110.2	112.0	114.2	115.5	117.0	118.8	120.8	122.3
105.5	109.5	112.1	114.9	117.5	119.6	122.5	124.3	126.3	127.3	127.7	127.4	127.1
85.0	84.9	86.6	89.3	92.6	94.5	97.6	105.1	123.6	136.0	143.3	147.2	150.4
102.0	104.2	105.9	107.6	108.6	110.5	113.9	116.3	118.8	122.4	124.5	127.3	129.7
102.0	104.3	105.9	107.5	109.0	110.5	112.2	114.9	118.1	120.9	122.6	124.5	126.6
						% change from previous year						
0.2	**2.2**	**1.6**	**1.6**	**0.9**	**1.7**	**2.7**	**2.6**	**2.2**	**2.8**	**1.9**	**2.2**	**2.0**
0.4	2.4	1.3	1.6	1.6	1.3	1.4	4.5	2.6	1.7	2.0	2.5	2.3
0.4	1.1	0.2	0.2	0.4	1.4	3.5	3.7	0.9	3.3	2.6	3.1	3.6
0.2	1.9	2.1	1.2	1.5	0.7	0.9	2.0	1.4	0.7	0.5	0.5	0.3
0.8	-0.1	-0.3	1.3	1.2	1.3	0.2	0.5	-0.8	-1.8	-0.2	-0.5	-1.8
4.5	5.2	3.9	3.1	-0.8	3.3	5.0	0.1	2.8	5.2	2.4	4.1	2.7
0.9	-0.1	0.6	1.7	2.1	1.9	1.6	2.0	1.1	1.3	1.5	1.7	1.2
3.0	3.8	2.4	2.5	2.3	1.8	2.4	1.5	1.6	0.8	0.3	-0.2	-0.2
-16.3	-0.1	2.0	3.1	3.7	2.1	3.3	7.7	17.6	10.0	5.4	2.7	2.2
0.1	2.2	1.6	1.6	0.9	1.7	3.1	2.1	2.1	3.0	1.7	2.2	1.9
0.1	2.3	1.5	1.5	1.4	1.4	1.5	2.4	2.8	2.4	1.4	1.5	1.7

Table 25.2 Consumer Price Index, all-items, by province, 1977 to 2006

	1977 to 1981	1982 to 1986	1987 to 1991	1992 to 1996	1997 to 2001	2002 to 2006
			1992=100			
Canada	**48.5**	**71.9**	**89.4**	**102.8**	**111.3**	**124.6**
Newfoundland and Labrador	..	75.9	90.4	103.0	110.9	123.1
Prince Edward Island	..	74.0	89.1	102.4	109.2	124.8
Nova Scotia	..	73.6	89.9	102.6	111.4	126.3
New Brunswick	..	73.5	89.9	102.3	110.2	124.5
Quebec	..	71.2	88.5	101.3	108.6	120.7
Ontario	..	71.0	90.1	102.8	111.9	125.6
Manitoba	..	72.5	90.0	104.6	115.8	128.2
Saskatchewan	..	73.4	90.4	104.7	114.6	129.3
Alberta	..	74.2	89.3	103.2	114.2	131.8
British Columbia	..	73.5	88.5	105.2	111.9	122.8
			five-year average % change			
Canada	**9.7**	**5.8**	**4.8**	**1.5**	**1.9**	**2.2**
Newfoundland and Labrador	..	5.7	3.9	1.4	1.6	2.3
Prince Edward Island	..	4.9	4.7	1.2	1.7	2.8
Nova Scotia	..	5.6	4.5	1.2	2.0	2.6
New Brunswick	..	5.8	4.4	1.1	1.8	2.5
Quebec	..	6.1	4.8	1.0	1.8	2.1
Ontario	..	6.1	5.0	1.4	2.1	2.1
Manitoba	..	5.6	4.6	2.1	2.1	2.0
Saskatchewan	..	5.2	4.7	1.9	2.0	2.3
Alberta	..	5.1	4.5	1.7	2.3	3.0
British Columbia	..	5.2	4.4	2.3	1.1	2.0

Note: Annual average indexes are obtained by averaging the indexes for the 12 months of the calendar year.
Source: Statistics Canada, CANSIM table 326-0002.

Table 25.3 Composite Leading Index, February 2006 to February 2007

	February 2006	January 2007	February 2007	January 2007 to February 2007
				% change
Composite Leading Indicator (1992=100)	**211.9**	**222.1**	**223.7**	**0.7**
Housing Index (1992=100)[1]	146.7	143.3	144.3	0.7
Business and personal services employment (thousands)	2,684	2,794	2,805	0.4
Stock Price Index, Toronto Stock Exchange 300 (1975=1,000)	11,223	12,565	12,817	2.0
M1, Money Supply ($ millions 1992)[2]	142,883	159,525	162,079	1.6
U.S. Conference Board Leading Indicator (1992=100)[3]	126.5	126.8	127.1	0.2
Manufacturing				
Average work week (hours)	38.1	38.4	38.4	0.0
New orders, durables ($ millions 1992)[4]	26,906	25,943	26,407	1.8
Shipments to inventory ratio of finished goods[4]	1.9	1.8	1.8	-0.6
Retail trade				
Furniture and appliance sales ($ millions 1992)[4]	2,346	2,614	2,631	0.7
Other durable goods sales ($ millions 1992)[4]	8,058	8,800	8,859	0.7
Unsmoothed composite (1992=100)	**214.9**	**225.3**	**226.5**	**0.5**

1. Composite index of housing starts (units) and house sales (Multiple Listing Service).
2. Deflated by the Consumer Price Index for all-items.
3. Data reflect findings published in the month indicated, but the data themselves refer to the month immediately preceding.
4. Data reflect findings published in the month indicated, but the data themselves refer to two months prior.
Source: Statistics Canada, CANSIM table 377-0003.

Table 25.4 Raw Material Price Index, 2000 to 2006

	2000	2001	2002	2003	2004	2005	2006
				1997=100			
All raw materials	**114.7**	**113.2**	**112.6**	**114.8**	**128.3**	**145.3**	**161.6**
Mineral fuels	160.2	157.5	154.5	165.6	193.9	244.7	258.7
Vegetable products	78.7	84.8	97.7	92.2	88.8	80.3	84.6
Animals and animal products	103.9	108.9	103.6	100.3	101.4	104.6	104.3
Wood	91.9	85.0	83.9	82.2	83.0	75.1	77.8
Ferrous materials	88.8	87.0	92.8	95.9	125.0	125.0	125.7
Non-ferrous metals	90.4	82.0	81.3	82.0	104.8	119.7	195.7
Non-metallic minerals	108.1	109.0	110.5	116.4	122.6	133.9	141.1
All raw materials excluding mineral fuels	93.6	92.7	93.2	91.4	97.9	99.3	116.8

Note: Annual average indexes are obtained by averaging the indexes for the 12 months of the calendar year.
Source: Statistics Canada, CANSIM table 330-0006.

Table 25.5 Consumer Price Index, food, 2002 to 2006

	2002	2003	2004	2005	2006
	1992=100				
All-items	**119.0**	**122.3**	**124.6**	**127.3**	**129.9**
Food	120.3	122.4	124.9	128.0	131.0
Food purchased from stores	119.8	121.6	123.7	126.6	129.4
Meat	127.0	129.3	134.9	137.5	137.1
Fresh or frozen meat (excluding poultry)	129.9	131.0	136.4	138.9	137.4
Fresh or frozen poultry meat	118.5	124.2	133.0	134.0	134.4
Processed meat	127.0	127.8	130.9	135.1	135.5
Fish and other seafood	123.2	122.8	122.0	122.1	120.7
Fish	119.9	119.3	119.2	120.4	120.3
Other seafood	132.3	132.6	130.0	126.7	121.7
Dairy products and eggs	120.1	123.9	127.0	133.3	138.7
Dairy products	118.8	122.3	125.3	132.0	137.5
Eggs	133.9	140.4	144.3	146.1	149.9
Bakery and other cereal products	121.4	126.6	129.9	133.3	137.9
Bakery products	119.2	126.1	130.3	134.8	140.9
Other cereal grains and cereal products	126.9	128.9	130.4	131.8	133.7
Fruit, fruit preparations and nuts	109.4	107.4	108.6	108.1	110.8
Fresh fruit	113.1	109.1	110.7	108.8	111.2
Preserved fruit and fruit preparations	103.7	104.6	105.0	106.3	109.8
Nuts	110.0	109.3	111.7	113.3	113.8
Vegetables and vegetable preparations	117.6	110.8	108.3	110.0	115.7
Fresh vegetables	122.3	112.7	108.7	109.9	116.5
Preserved vegetables and vegetable preparations	104.5	106.3	108.0	111.5	114.1
Other food products	117.0	120.9	122.2	125.3	127.5
Sugar and confectionery	142.0	150.5	152.7	153.0	159.1
Fats and oils	126.1	130.8	134.7	136.8	139.1
Coffee and tea	124.2	125.2	127.6	131.8	136.3
Condiments, spices and vinegars	118.7	119.4	119.7	122.2	123.3
Other food preparations	111.9	117.2	119.3	122.1	124.4
Non-alcoholic beverages	101.2	100.6	100.4	104.6	105.0
Food purchased from restaurants	122.1	125.1	128.4	132.1	135.6

Note: Annual average indexes are obtained by averaging the indexes for the 12 months of the calendar year.
Source: Statistics Canada, CANSIM table 326-0002.

Table 25.6 Farm Input Price Index, Eastern and Western Canada, 1999 to 2005

	1999	2000	2001	2002	2003	2004	2005
				1992=100			
Canada							
Farm inputs	**117.0**	**124.1**	**129.5**	**128.5**	**132.8**	**129.6**	**134.8**
Building and fencing	123.1	119.8	120.0	122.8	122.4	137.7	136.2
Machinery and motor vehicles	125.6	137.7	143.7	143.5	157.0	155.3	163.6
Crop production	121.6	121.5	137.6	135.7	154.7	151.1	156.1
Animal production	117.5	127.8	135.1	132.3	128.2	114.4	124.2
Supplies and services	112.0	118.4	121.1	120.7	127.5	126.9	129.8
Hired farm labour	113.3	119.5	125.4	128.2	129.0	135.4	137.7
Property taxes	113.8	114.1	112.6	118.9	126.4	129.5	133.2
Interest	87.6	96.1	90.5	84.9	83.9	80.7	80.8
Farm rent	120.5	113.8	113.8	121.8	131.9	135.8	129.4
Eastern Canada							
Farm inputs	**115.0**	**121.6**	**126.6**	**126.2**	**129.0**	**127.5**	**131.3**
Building and fencing	122.9	121.2	121.9	124.3	124.2	136.2	138.6
Machinery and motor vehicles	126.4	139.4	144.4	145.9	159.3	156.4	163.6
Crop production	120.4	119.1	130.1	128.3	137.0	139.8	148.0
Animal production	114.7	122.1	129.3	128.0	125.4	117.6	120.4
Supplies and services	111.8	120.4	123.4	121.8	129.8	129.1	132.9
Hired farm labour	115.6	121.8	127.2	130.4	128.9	135.2	137.8
Property taxes	76.4	74.6	79.7	84.8	90.0	93.8	97.7
Interest	88.6	98.0	92.6	86.7	85.8	83.2	83.7
Farm rent	85.9	81.2	85.2	93.5	97.8	101.4	102.4
Western Canada							
Farm inputs	**119.0**	**126.7**	**132.9**	**130.9**	**137.5**	**131.6**	**138.9**
Building and fencing	123.2	118.6	118.5	121.6	120.9	138.8	134.2
Machinery and motor vehicles	125.0	136.0	143.3	140.7	154.4	154.3	164.1
Crop production	122.4	123.1	142.7	140.6	167.1	158.4	161.0
Animal production	120.3	133.6	141.0	136.6	131.0	111.4	127.3
Supplies and services	112.3	116.2	118.6	119.6	125.0	124.4	126.5
Hired farm labour	111.0	117.1	123.8	126.0	129.9	136.5	138.3
Property taxes	124.6	126.1	121.4	127.9	136.0	138.7	142.2
Interest	86.9	95.0	89.2	83.7	82.7	79.1	79.0
Farm rent	138.4	130.6	128.0	135.6	148.9	152.8	142.2

Note: The Farm Input Price Index measures the change through time in the prices received for agricultural commodities at the first transaction point. The prices used in computing the index are, as closely as can be determined, the transaction prices received by farmers when ownership first changes hands. These prices include any bonuses and premiums that can be attributed to specific commodities, but they exclude any storage, transportation, processing and handling charges, which are deducted before the farmer is paid.

Source: Statistics Canada, CANSIM table 328-0014.

Table 25.7 Industrial Product Price Index, 1987 to 2006

	1987	1988	1989	1990	1991	1992	1993
				1997=100			
All industrial products	**78.9**	**82.3**	**84.0**	**84.2**	**83.3**	**83.8**	**86.8**
Intermediate goods	79.2	84.5	86.1	85.1	82.6	82.2	85.1
First-stage intermediate goods	81.6	95.2	97.3	90.5	81.8	79.5	76.2
Second-stage intermediate goods	78.2	81.1	82.6	83.2	82.5	82.6	86.5
Finished goods	78.4	78.9	80.7	82.9	84.4	86.1	89.4
Finished foods and feeds	80.0	81.9	84.6	87.1	88.9	89.8	91.4
Capital equipment	76.6	77.0	78.8	80.6	82.0	84.8	89.1
All other finished goods	78.5	78.5	79.8	82.1	83.4	85.0	88.6
Aggregation, by commodities							
Meat, fish and dairy products	78.7	79.1	79.7	82.0	82.8	83.7	88.3
Fruits, vegetables, feeds, other food products	77.8	83.3	86.4	86.6	86.3	87.4	88.6
Beverages	76.4	79.3	84.0	86.5	89.5	90.8	92.2
Tobacco, tobacco products	56.0	58.3	61.2	66.2	73.4	78.9	84.1
Rubber, leather, plastic fabricated products	79.7	85.9	88.9	89.3	89.0	88.1	87.7
Textile products	85.4	88.5	90.3	91.4	91.4	91.2	92.3
Knitted products and clothing	84.2	86.6	88.9	91.1	92.2	92.6	92.8
Lumber, other wood products	62.3	63.4	65.9	65.5	64.4	69.8	87.1
Furniture and fixtures	78.0	81.0	84.4	87.4	88.4	87.9	89.8
Pulp and paper products	82.6	90.5	93.4	91.9	83.0	79.7	77.3
Printing and publishing	65.1	69.2	72.7	74.8	77.4	79.1	82.9
Primary metal products	82.7	98.1	97.8	88.6	81.2	79.0	78.2
Metal fabricated products	77.0	80.6	83.3	84.0	83.9	83.7	85.6
Machinery and equipment	78.8	81.6	85.5	87.4	88.7	90.0	92.8
Motor vehicles and other transport equipment	78.8	76.6	76.3	76.7	78.2	82.3	87.8
Electrical and communications products	86.9	90.6	93.8	94.0	93.6	94.4	97.0
Non-metallic mineral products	85.3	89.1	90.5	91.5	90.8	90.3	91.0
Petroleum and coal products	91.5	84.7	86.4	97.3	94.0	86.7	85.8
Chemicals and chemical products	77.5	86.5	87.7	85.4	86.5	85.3	87.0
Miscellaneous manufactured products	79.9	82.3	84.1	85.1	86.6	86.9	90.0
Miscellaneous non-manufactured products	119.4	123.7	104.6	95.0	84.5	83.2	91.3

Note: Annual average indexes are obtained by averaging the indexes for the 12 months of the calendar year.

Source: Statistics Canada, CANSIM tables 329-0039, 329-0040, 329-0041, 329-0042, 329-0044, 329-0045, 329-0046 and 329-0048.

1994	1995	1996	1997	1998	1999	2000	2001	2002	2003	2004	2005	2006
						1997=100						
92.0	**98.9**	**99.3**	**100.0**	**100.4**	**102.2**	**106.5**	**107.6**	**107.6**	**106.2**	**109.5**	**111.2**	**113.8**
91.8	101.1	100.1	100.0	98.4	99.9	105.3	105.0	104.2	103.8	109.9	112.8	117.5
92.1	118.5	100.1	100.0	93.8	96.5	111.9	104.5	101.8	105.6	118.0	123.1	141.8
91.7	98.3	100.1	100.0	99.0	100.4	104.3	105.1	104.6	103.5	108.7	111.2	113.9
92.5	95.4	98.0	100.0	103.4	105.6	108.3	111.3	112.6	109.7	108.9	108.7	108.1
93.7	95.9	98.2	100.0	100.9	102.2	104.3	106.4	108.0	110.3	112.0	112.1	113.4
92.7	96.0	98.0	100.0	104.9	106.6	107.3	110.7	112.6	107.1	104.5	102.5	100.2
91.8	95.0	97.9	100.0	103.5	106.4	110.7	113.8	114.7	111.1	110.3	111.0	110.6
90.3	92.5	97.0	100.0	98.7	100.4	104.6	107.7	107.2	108.5	109.7	107.1	107.2
93.0	95.8	99.6	100.0	97.9	95.6	95.6	98.2	101.6	103.6	104.9	102.8	104.6
92.8	94.9	97.4	100.0	102.4	105.6	109.0	111.4	114.6	117.7	120.4	121.3	122.4
86.9	89.6	93.4	100.0	103.8	109.4	114.2	127.4	139.5	162.7	169.3	176.3	189.9
91.4	100.2	99.4	100.0	99.8	100.2	105.2	106.1	105.0	106.2	108.1	114.3	118.4
94.1	97.8	99.2	100.0	101.2	99.6	99.1	100.5	100.4	99.4	98.9	99.9	100.3
94.2	96.7	99.0	100.0	101.6	102.2	102.8	103.2	103.8	104.1	104.5	104.3	104.7
97.8	94.0	99.3	100.0	95.9	105.1	95.9	94.6	94.0	90.3	101.1	92.5	87.1
92.1	98.3	99.3	100.0	101.1	102.3	104.8	106.3	107.5	109.2	111.8	115.1	118.2
85.8	119.5	105.7	100.0	103.5	101.7	115.2	115.0	106.0	102.8	104.1	103.5	105.1
87.7	98.6	99.4	100.0	103.5	105.8	109.2	111.8	114.1	113.0	114.0	115.3	115.5
92.4	105.4	97.9	100.0	96.0	95.2	100.6	94.4	96.3	96.2	113.4	116.5	138.6
89.1	96.4	98.5	100.0	102.6	103.0	104.7	104.9	106.5	107.2	117.0	121.5	123.1
95.6	97.6	99.2	100.0	102.3	103.7	104.8	105.9	106.9	105.9	106.0	107.3	107.1
92.2	94.9	97.5	100.0	107.1	108.5	109.0	113.5	115.1	106.3	101.2	96.5	92.4
99.8	102.2	101.1	100.0	100.1	100.2	98.5	99.4	101.3	95.8	94.7	93.7	93.7
94.5	98.9	100.1	100.0	100.2	102.0	105.2	107.4	108.7	109.7	111.6	114.9	119.6
85.6	90.4	100.5	100.0	82.3	96.1	140.3	133.7	125.5	138.4	161.8	199.9	218.1
93.2	101.8	99.8	100.0	96.9	98.6	104.8	107.4	107.3	110.4	113.8	121.0	122.9
95.8	98.7	100.0	100.0	101.4	103.0	104.3	105.5	107.5	107.2	109.6	110.7	112.9
102.9	120.3	111.1	100.0	90.3	90.3	86.4	86.6	90.8	95.8	125.1	163.7	248.1

Table 25.8 Purchasing power parities for GDP and OECD countries, national currency per U.S. dollar, 2001 to 2006

	2001	2002	2003	2004	2005	2006
	per U.S. dollar					
Pacific group						
Canada (Canadian dollar)	1.22	1.23	1.24	1.25	1.25	1.23
Mexico (peso)	6.33	6.58	7.00	7.31	7.48	7.57
United States (U.S. dollar)	1.00	1.00	1.00	1.00	1.00	1.00
Japan (yen)	149	144	138	133	128	124
Korea (won)	761	779	783	782	756	744
Australia (Australian dollar)	1.33	1.34	1.35	1.36	1.38	1.39
New Zealand (N.Z. dollar)	1.47	1.47	1.46	1.47	1.46	1.47
European countries						
Austria (euro)	0.92	0.91	0.88	0.87	0.87	0.86
Belgium (euro)	0.90	0.88	0.87	0.87	0.86	0.86
Czech Republic (koruna)	14.57	14.27	13.89	14.03	14.08	14.15
Denmark (krone)	8.33	8.43	8.47	8.40	8.40	8.37
Finland (euro)	0.97	0.97	1.00	0.97	0.97	0.96
France (euro)	0.90	0.90	0.93	0.92	0.90	0.89
Germany (euro)	0.97	0.96	0.91	0.89	0.88	0.88
Greece (euro)	0.69	0.68	0.68	0.70	0.70	0.70
Hungary (forint)	109.89	114.72	119.60	124.05	124.90	127.83
Iceland (krona)	88.65	92.18	93.41	94.02	94.55	95.56
Ireland (euro)	0.98	1.00	1.01	1.00	1.00	1.00
Italy (euro)	0.82	0.83	0.85	0.86	0.86	0.86
Luxembourg (euro)	1.00	0.98	0.94	0.92	0.92	0.92
Netherlands (euro)	0.92	0.92	0.92	0.90	0.88	0.87
Norway (krone)	9.10	9.14	9.03	8.93	8.73	8.68
Poland (zloty)	1.84	1.83	1.83	1.85	1.85	1.84
Portugal (euro)	0.66	0.66	0.70	0.71	0.70	0.70
Slovak republic (koruna)	16.26	16.21	16.59	17.19	17.09	17.24
Spain (euro)	0.75	0.74	0.75	0.76	0.76	0.77
Sweden (krona)	9.32	9.36	9.25	9.18	9.21	9.17
Switzerland (franc)	1.89	1.80	1.76	1.73	1.70	1.68
Turkey (lira)	0.42	0.61	0.76	0.83	0.88	0.92
United Kingdom (pound sterling)	0.62	0.61	0.62	0.62	0.62	0.62

Source: Statistics Canada, Organisation for Economic Co-operation and Development, 2007.

Retail and wholesale trade

26

OVERVIEW

Buying and selling goods—manufacturers and importers selling to wholesalers, wholesalers selling to retailers and retailers to consumers—is a big part of the Canadian economy. Combined, retail and wholesale trade employ the largest number of workers in the country.

In 2005, some 1.7 million people worked in retail, comprising 12% of all employment, while 607,100 people worked in wholesale. That year, retail and wholesale each generated about 6% of Canada's economy.

But these industries are vulnerable to economic shifts. Temporary declines and increases in revenue are sometimes also due to changing wholesale prices of items, such as gasoline.

Retail sales are often seasonal—clothing sales can fall in October after the back-to-school rush, while December revenues in many categories increase because of holiday gift-buying.

Retail trade

From 2004 to 2005, retail revenues on the whole rose steadily in Canada. In 2005, retailers—including both brick-and-mortar and non-store retailers, such as those selling exclusively through e-commerce, mail order or catalogues—posted operating revenues of $403.6 billion, up 5% from the year before. Consumers opened their wallets wider in part because of higher gasoline prices and more purchases at home furnishing stores.

Alberta led the country in retail sales gains from 2000 to 2005, thanks to the energy boom. Growth there was nearly double that of the next province, British Columbia, where retailers profited from a hot housing market.

Chart 26.1
GDP of retail and wholesale trade

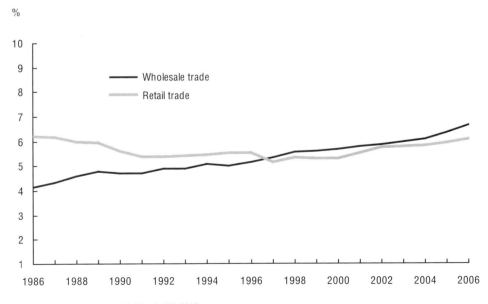

%

Source: Statistics Canada, CANSIM table 379-0017.

The total gross margin—the difference between total operating revenues and the cost of goods—for all store retailers rose 6% in 2005. The highest gains in margins were in furniture stores (13% growth over 2004), home furnishing stores (10%) and gasoline stations (10%).

Another measure of a retailer's health is its operating profit—total operating revenues minus total operating expenses and the cost of goods sold. In 2005, operating profits for store retailers rose 6% from the year before, while they increased 10% for non-store retailers.

Other ways to shop

Gone are the days when your only retail choice was to walk into a store, pay cash and leave with an item. Today, Canadians have many shopping choices, as the Internet continues to change the face of retail. Surveys of retailers do not give a breakdown for online sales, nor do they account for people who browse online for product information but then purchase an item on the phone, by mail or in a store. Yet we do know a bit about

Chart 26.2
Non-store retail operating revenues, by industry group, 2005

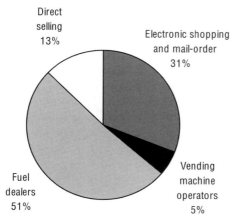

Direct selling 13%

Electronic shopping and mail-order 31%

Vending machine operators 5%

Fuel dealers 51%

Note: Percentage share.
Source: Statistics Canada, CANSIM table 080-0012.

Internet shopping by selected type of product and service, 2005

	%
Travel arrangements	36.4
Books, magazines and online newspapers	35.4
Clothing, jewellery and accessories	24.8
Computer software	20.2
Sports equipment	6.6
Food, condiments and beverages	3.4

Source: Statistics Canada, CANSIM table 358-0136.

consumers' online shopping habits from the Canadian Internet Use Survey conducted in November 2005.

In the 12 months prior to November 2005, some seven million Canadians aged 18 and older ordered $7.9 billion worth of goods and services for personal use online—this includes booking travel arrangements and concert tickets, which are not considered retail sales. Nearly two-thirds (63%) of the value of these Internet orders went to suppliers based in Canada.

The most popular online retail items are books, magazines and online newspapers, bought by 35% of Canadian Internet shoppers, followed by clothing, jewellery and accessories (25%), computer software (20%), music (16%), consumer electronics (16%), and videos and DVDs (13%).

Even how we pay for things in traditional stores is changing. The proportion of retailers offering gift cards that can be redeemed for merchandise is ballooning. From December 2003 to December 2005, the proportion of stores owned by large retailers that offered gift cards rose 29 percentage points to 82%. By the 2005 holiday shopping season, all the major home electronics and appliance retailers in Canada offered gift cards, while 79% of large clothing stores (including shoe stores) and 70% of supermarkets sold gift cards.

Consumers enjoy the convenience of giving and receiving gift cards, while retailers like the cards because they can build store loyalty and increase sales, especially in January—

since most gift card recipients buy more in their stores than the face value of the cards.

Wholesale trade

Most consumers do not see wholesalers, who distribute goods to retailers and other businesses, but they are the key link between manufacturers and the marketplace. Wholesalers' operating revenues grew 8% in 2005 from the year before, to $626.5 billion.

The largest gains were in the petroleum industry—revenues climbed 25% from the year before, mainly because of price increases for crude oil—in metal products (up 17%) and in machinery and equipment wholesalers (up 15%). In 2005, 5 of 17 industry groups saw revenues decline: farm products, alcohol and tobacco, motor vehicles, lumber and millwork, and agents and brokers.

Wholesale prices of goods also affect sales figures for this industry and are subject to economic factors. For example, the rising Canadian dollar has lowered prices on some goods coming from the United States. In 2005, demand for imported products

continued to grow, which is important to the industry—roughly 40% of all imports are brought into Canada through wholesalers.

The gross margin as a proportion of operating revenue for all wholesalers decreased one percentage point to 17% in 2005. Operating profit margins as a percentage of total operating revenue also declined one percentage point in 2005, to 5%.

Selected sources

Statistics Canada

- *Analysis in Brief.* Occasional. 11-621-MIE

- *Canadian Economic Accounts Quarterly Review.* Quarterly. 13-010-XWE

- *The Canadian Labour Market at a Glance.* Irregular. 71-222-XIE

- *New Motor Vehicle Sales.* Monthly. 63-007-XIE

- *Retail Trade.* Monthly. 63-005-XIE

- *Wholesale Trade.* Monthly. 63-008-XWE

Chart 26.3
Operating revenue, wholesale trade

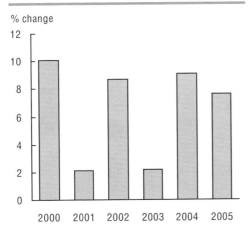

% change

Source: Statistics Canada, CANSIM table 081-0005.

Traditional stores blur the lines

We used to go to the grocery store to buy groceries, the drugstore to pick up prescription drugs and the department store to get clothing. Today, however, we can get virtually all these things at any of these stores, as retailers compete in each other's traditional territories to become 'one-stop shops' for busy consumers.

Food stores are expanding in size and product lines, while some drugstore chains are also opening larger stores and selling food. The discount department stores are also selling food. They are all trying to take market shares away from each other. The percentages may be slight, but retail is a multibillion-dollar industry, so the effects can be significant.

In 1998, Canadians made 82% of all food and beverage purchases in a food store. By 2004, that dropped to 77%—a loss of 5 percentage points in market share for these products. Food stores partly compensated by gaining 2 percentage points of market share in health and personal care products—typically the domain of drugstores and general merchandise stores—and 3 percentage points in other non-food products.

Over those six years, general merchandise stores gained 1 percentage point of market share in food and beverages and 3 percentage points in health and personal care products. But they lost 4 percentage points of market share in other non-food products.

Pharmacies, meanwhile, are losing market share of prescription and over-the-counter drugs to these other stores. In 1998, they accounted for 84% of drug sales; by 2005, this fell to 77%.

Chart 26.4
Food and general merchandise stores, selected product sales

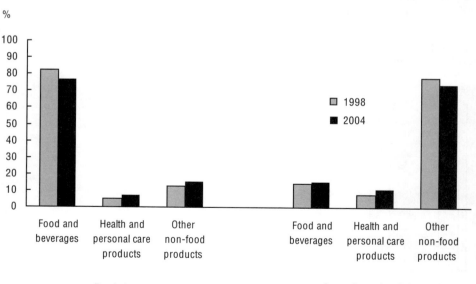

Source: Statistics Canada, Catalogue no. 11-621-MIE.

Auto sales strong

Sales of cars, trucks, recreational and other vehicles were strong in 2006, despite higher gasoline prices. Apart from consumer demand, many businesses buy vehicles for their operations regardless of the cost of gas.

A total of 1,666,327 new vehicles were sold in 2006, the second-highest annual number ever in Canada. Sales totalled a record-high $54.3 billion, up 4% from 2005. Buyer incentives partly boosted sales in 2006.

Sales of trucks, which includes minivans, sport-utility vehicles, light and heavy trucks, vans and buses, reached a record-high 803,166 vehicles in 2006, up 2% from 2005.

Demand was also high for recreational vehicles. Dealers' sales of new and used recreational vehicles climbed 39% in 2006 to $3.1 billion. Nearly one-third of that was in Alberta, where sales totalled $1.0 billion—a massive 69% increase from 2005.

Recreational vehicles are popular in Alberta, partly because of the housing shortage in the booming oil patch. Some workers there are temporarily living in recreational vehicles. At the national level, the increase could be partly explained by the growing number of retirees buying a home on wheels.

For consumers, their vehicles make up the largest portion of their retail spending. In 2005, they spent 20 cents of every retail dollar on motor vehicles, parts and services, and another 9 cents for fuels, oils and additives.

Many who are not buying a vehicle are at least dreaming of doing so. In 2005, 25% of Canadians who shopped online used the Internet to look at automotive products.

Chart 26.5
New motor vehicle sales, by province, 2006

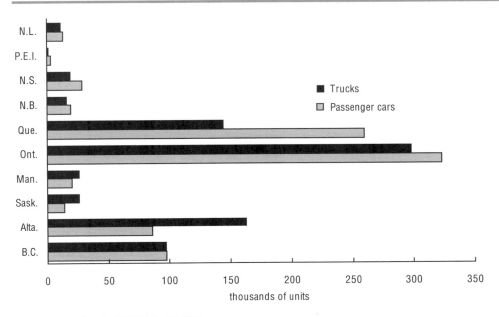

Source: Statistics Canada, CANSIM table 079-0001.

Western wholesalers enjoying the ride

Distributors of wholesale goods to retailers and other businesses are cashing in on Western Canada's economic boom. From 2002 to 2005, wholesalers based in Manitoba, Saskatchewan, Alberta and British Columbia recorded the strongest growth among wholesalers in Canada. In those three years, sales of Western-based wholesalers rose at an average annual rate of 10%, double the 5% average for all of Canada.

The economic and demographic boom is pushing up demand for machinery and electronic equipment and for building materials—these two categories showed the strongest growth in Western Canada.

Among the Western-based wholesalers, those in Alberta and British Columbia accounted for nearly 90% of the growth since 2002. In 2005, Alberta's wholesalers sold nearly

$54.6 billion worth of merchandise, up 16% from 2004. In British Columbia, wholesalers' sales rose 9% to $47.3 billion.

Oil companies have accelerated their investments in machinery, benefiting Alberta's machinery wholesalers. British Columbia's lumber wholesalers saw volumes increase, partly thanks to exports to feed construction in the United States. However, lumber sales values dropped because of lower prices.

The largest growth rate among wholesalers in any province was in Alberta, where the most notable gain occurred in the machinery and electronic equipment category.

In Saskatchewan, firms selling farm products saw revenues rise 27% in 2005, largely because of the reopening of the U.S. border in July to Canadian cattle under 30 months of age.

Chart 26.6
Wholesalers' sales growth rate, by province, 2004 to 2005

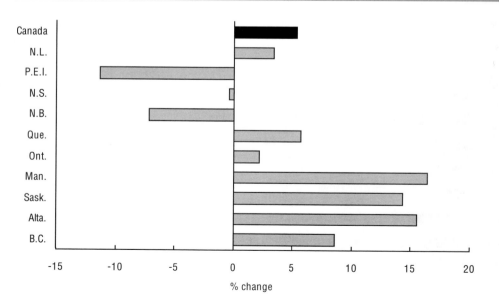

Source: Statistics Canada, CANSIM table 081-0007.

Shopping outside the box

We all do some shopping outside the four walls of a retail store. In 2005, Canadians bought $12.8 billion worth of goods and services from 'non-store retailers'—these include mail-order, online catalogues, door-to-door sales, TV infomercials and vending machines. Non-store retailers account for just 3% of retail sales in Canada, but this sector is enjoying strong growth.

In 2005, these retailers posted 8% sales growth from the year before, compared with 5% for brick-and-mortar stores. Fuel dealers accounted for 51% of non-store operating revenues—the lion's share in 2005. Fuel dealers' revenues surged 18% and their profits rose 8%.

Electronic shopping and mail-order businesses are the second largest group—they generated 31% of non-store revenues in 2005. Their sales growth was less than 1%

above 2004, but some of these retailers are eroding the sales of their brick-and-mortar competitors. For example, computer and software stores struggled in 2005; revenue rose just 2% from 2004. But computer software sales by electronic shopping and mail-order establishments soared 121%.

Vending machine operators and direct selling businesses saw sales drop 4% and 5%, respectively in 2005. However, lower revenues were more than offset by lower operating expenses. As a result, these two groups saw the strongest profit growth—22% for vending machine operators and 30% for direct sellers.

Of the products sold by non-store retailers, services, such as meals and lunches, repairs, rental and leasing, saw the sharpest sales growth, up 20% to $376.8 million in 2005.

Chart 26.7
Gross margins, non-store retail industries

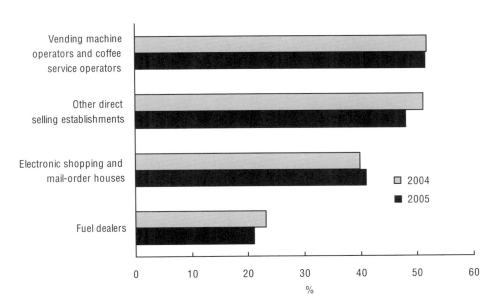

Source: Statistics Canada, CANSIM table 080-0012.

Table 26.1 Interprovincial trade, by province and territory, 2006

	All goods and services	Goods	Services
	$ millions		
Imports to provinces	**281,646**	.	.
Newfoundland and Labrador	6,724	3,173	3,551
Prince Edward Island	2,103	1,039	1,064
Nova Scotia	10,396	5,418	4,978
New Brunswick	11,066	6,316	4,750
Quebec	58,591	32,520	26,071
Ontario	78,200	48,989	29,211
Manitoba	15,537	8,931	6,606
Saskatchewan	16,828	8,462	8,366
Alberta	43,292	23,340	19,952
British Columbia	35,449	18,097	17,352
Yukon	656	265	391
Northwest Territories	1,847	856	991
Nunavut	756	303	453
Outside Canada	201	146	55
Exports from provinces	**281,646**	.	.
Newfoundland and Labrador	6,440	5,476	964
Prince Edward Island	974	555	419
Nova Scotia	6,635	3,991	2,644
New Brunswick	8,331	5,748	2,583
Quebec	55,967	34,122	21,845
Ontario	100,462	44,698	55,764
Manitoba	12,553	6,143	6,410
Saskatchewan	12,767	9,742	3,025
Alberta	49,150	33,743	15,407
British Columbia	27,124	13,034	14,090
Yukon	215	77	138
Northwest Territories	888	518	370
Nunavut	132	9	123
Outside Canada	7	0	7

Note: Expenditure-based gross domestic product.
Source: Statistics Canada, CANSIM table 384-0002.

Table 26.2 Wholesale trade, sales by trade group, 2002 to 2006

	2002	2003	2004	2005	2006
	\$ millions				
All trade groups	**409,927.7**	**418,810.2**	**444,913.5**	**468,043.0**	**497,397.6**
Farm products	4,723.3	4,759.5	5,104.1	5,548.8	5,247.1
Food products	76,873.3	78,038.4	78,240.6	79,308.5	82,974.7
Alcohol and tobacco	6,974.3	7,538.4	7,743.3	7,558.0	7,888.6
Apparel	8,746.5	9,102.2	8,634.9	8,923.1	9,015.1
Home and personal products	23,678.1	23,960.6	25,330.9	27,747.6	31,320.0
Pharmaceuticals	22,531.0	24,829.0	28,551.0	30,205.4	32,059.7
Motor vehicles	73,643.4	73,235.4	72,902.6	71,919.8	75,854.9
Motor vehicle parts and accessories	15,690.7	15,462.5	18,268.2	18,499.6	18,611.7
Building supplies	30,582.5	30,814.8	35,331.4	39,302.5	42,658.3
Metal products	9,721.4	9,497.8	12,663.9	13,566.2	15,120.3
Lumber and millwork	10,110.7	10,458.5	12,947.5	13,264.8	12,711.9
Machinery and equipment	34,102.8	35,108.4	38,925.4	45,240.1	49,420.7
Computers and other electronic equipment	28,839.0	27,561.6	27,259.0	28,606.3	31,479.5
Office and professional equipment	20,615.6	19,992.7	20,516.7	21,687.3	23,887.4
Other products	43,095.2	48,450.3	52,494.0	56,665.1	59,147.7

Note: North American Industry Classification System (NAICS), 2002.
Source: Statistics Canada, CANSIM table 081-0007.

Table 26.3 Wholesale trade, sales by province and territory, 2002 to 2006

	2002	2003	2004	2005	2006
	\$ millions				
Canada	**409,927.7**	**418,810.2**	**444,913.5**	**468,043.0**	**497,397.6**
Newfoundland and Labrador	2,517.8	2,514.6	2,504.5	2,588.2	2,766.0
Prince Edward Island	489.1	543.2	591.7	524.8	432.7
Nova Scotia	6,651.4	6,854.3	6,256.5	6,241.8	6,472.3
New Brunswick	5,374.7	5,282.0	5,234.5	4,863.8	4,908.9
Quebec	79,113.0	79,635.4	85,613.6	90,627.6	93,697.3
Ontario	216,669.2	219,780.9	230,987.7	235,850.0	250,920.5
Manitoba	10,040.9	10,608.4	10,838.6	11,547.1	11,901.5
Saskatchewan	11,656.2	11,760.4	11,920.1	13,644.7	13,556.4
Alberta	38,758.1	41,868.0	47,163.1	54,550.6	61,644.8
British Columbia	38,228.9	39,658.9	43,497.7	47,277.0	50,724.8
Yukon	86.9	83.3	85.9	95.1	119.1
Northwest Territories	301.4	198.8	192.7	207.6	229.5
Nunavut	40.0	21.9	27.0	24.8	23.7

Source: Statistics Canada, CANSIM table 081-0007.

Table 26.4 Retail store sales, by selected commodities, 2001 to 2006

	2001	2002	2003	2004	2005	2006
	\$ thousands					
Total commodities	**301,221,201**	**320,372,749**	**332,027,040**	**347,703,971**	**368,840,320**	**392,383,358**
Food (exclude pet food, meals and lunches)	49,960,489	51,657,937	53,903,751	56,652,229	59,886,997	61,988,503
Non-alcoholic beverages	3,937,096	3,983,295	4,171,140	4,487,664	4,690,359	4,996,518
Alcoholic beverages	13,530,245	14,408,373	15,208,713	15,728,696	16,441,560	17,318,455
Personal care, health and beauty products (non-electric)[1]	7,348,008	8,005,008	8,243,691	9,136,351	9,414,283	9,954,328
Eyewear, prescription and non-prescription	1,194,276	1,234,260	1,220,881	1,299,106	1,374,389	1,470,314
Drugs (prescription and over-the-counter), vitamins and other health supplements	14,615,318	16,258,706	17,689,289	18,847,652	20,007,650	22,060,709
Luggage and jewellery	2,514,320	2,669,784	2,729,653	2,922,966	2,987,334	3,333,074
Clothing and accessories	20,947,535	21,064,469	21,330,150	22,193,535	23,074,904	24,462,809
Footwear	3,860,406	4,015,217	4,096,491	4,089,528	4,358,938	4,738,369
Furniture (indoor), household appliances and electronics	19,335,333	20,830,879	21,968,969	23,216,362	24,360,169	26,258,607
Home furnishings	6,924,673	7,615,669	7,905,124	8,388,694	8,837,044	9,672,991
New automotive vehicles	39,082,958	42,609,510	42,110,185	42,135,933	44,504,086	46,348,067
Used automotive vehicles	19,647,076	20,921,130	19,211,016	18,939,461	19,216,268	20,417,572
Automotive parts and accessories, labour receipts and rental receipts	13,299,379	13,904,854	14,949,971	15,524,002	16,991,122	17,968,047
Automotive fuels	22,189,024	22,963,371	24,498,428	28,204,465	33,307,031	36,603,086
Automotive oils and additives	749,950	756,394	826,626	811,850	855,827	971,098
Tableware, kitchenware, cookware and bakeware	1,447,901	1,592,461	1,630,403	1,748,933	1,790,832	1,948,572
Household cleaning supplies, chemicals and paper products	3,068,739	3,266,793	3,385,810	3,464,650	3,574,421	3,667,577
Other household supplies	1,711,239	1,918,349	2,022,554	2,073,350	2,120,387	2,266,021
Hardware and home renovation products	13,150,607	14,816,055	16,609,941	18,369,582	19,821,803	21,707,980
Lawn and garden products, equipment and plants	3,609,879	3,996,625	4,388,176	4,819,370	5,322,215	5,766,409
Sporting goods	3,649,056	3,836,514	3,881,883	3,844,770	4,009,702	4,326,360
Toys, games and hobby supplies (include electronic games)	2,403,394	2,531,502	2,595,763	2,642,719	2,797,759	3,052,072
Fabrics, yarns, sewing supplies and notions	741,439	735,625	722,810	740,717	696,441	675,078
Craft and artists' supplies	353,440	340,664	348,376	382,897	381,630	403,734
Prerecorded media[2]	1,638,959	1,757,464	1,830,651	1,940,899	2,056,302	2,064,746
Books, newspapers and other periodicals	2,547,702	2,596,982	2,658,077	2,740,443	2,897,746	2,944,384
Musical instruments, parts, accessories and supplies	475,161	461,840	469,330	502,270	496,088	460,386
Recreational vehicles	5,706,758	5,920,353	6,078,357	5,826,704	6,016,296	6,786,682
Pet food, supplies and accessories	1,315,402	1,447,161	1,606,080	1,767,702	1,953,193	2,031,854
Tobacco products and supplies	6,926,104	8,091,879	8,882,966	8,844,281	8,578,727	8,492,866
Giftware, novelties and souvenirs	1,651,751	1,555,145	1,401,010	1,297,702	1,200,625	1,347,595
Stationery, office supplies, cards, gift wrap and party supplies	2,763,797	2,814,674	3,105,829	3,329,898	3,357,798	3,454,584
Used and second-hand merchandise and antiques	1,159,228	1,353,210	1,400,177	1,394,336	1,455,556	1,687,320
Meals and lunches	673,584	764,193	831,503	889,098	947,065	1,053,721

1. Includes home health care sick room equipment and supplies.

2. Includes compact discs (CDs), digital video discs (DVDs) and video and audio tapes (excluding rentals).

Source: Statistics Canada, CANSIM table 080-0018.

Table 26.5 Retail trade, sales by trade group, 2002 to 2006

	2002	2003	2004	2005	2006
			$ millions		
All trade groups	**319,525.4**	**331,143.4**	**346,721.5**	**366,170.7**	**389,567.4**
New car dealers	69,161.0	68,183.6	68,141.1	71,515.6	74,663.2
Used and recreational motor vehicle and parts dealers	14,303.0	14,393.9	14,559.2	15,301.4	17,380.5
Gasoline stations	28,138.4	29,951.3	33,363.8	38,356.8	41,606.9
Furniture stores	7,467.3	7,923.8	8,506.5	8,914.4	9,585.5
Home furnishings stores	3,701.2	3,971.6	4,438.9	4,686.3	5,339.9
Computer and software stores	1,967.7	1,883.9	1,581.8	1,557.5	1,517.6
Home electronics and appliance stores	8,361.1	9,089.7	9,443.1	10,164.8	11,157.0
Home centres and hardware stores	12,517.4	14,595.2	16,597.8	18,220.7	20,126.5
Specialized building materials and garden stores	4,234.1	4,316.0	4,372.8	4,340.4	4,627.9
Supermarkets	54,343.6	56,874.1	59,760.9	62,196.3	63,512.5
Convenience and specialty food stores	7,694.4	8,371.4	8,806.9	9,128.6	9,356.4
Beer, wine and liquor stores	12,696.7	13,293.7	13,789.8	14,343.9	15,160.3
Pharmacies and personal care stores	20,410.4	21,266.6	22,769.3	23,642.7	26,070.3
Clothing stores	14,220.0	14,567.1	15,311.6	16,069.3	17,248.5
Shoe, clothing accessories and jewellery stores	4,925.6	4,903.8	4,876.8	4,981.3	5,400.3
General merchandise stores	38,419.5	40,011.0	42,123.7	43,758.4	46,518.3
Department stores	20,112.5	20,800.8	21,849.9	x	..
Other general merchandise stores[1]	18,307.0	19,210.2	20,273.8	x	..
Sporting goods, hobby, music and book stores	8,501.2	8,676.1	8,831.4	9,379.3	10,003.1
Miscellaneous store retailers[2]	8,462.8	8,870.7	9,446.1	9,613.1	10,292.8

Note: North American Industry Classification System (NAICS), 2002.

1. Includes warehouse clubs and superstores and all other general merchandise stores.

2. Includes florists; office supply and stationary stores; gift, novelty and souvenir stores; used merchandise stores; pet and pet supply stores; art dealers; mobile home dealers; and all other miscellaneous store retailers.

Source: Statistics Canada, CANSIM table 080-0014.

Table 26.6 Retail trade, by province and territory, 2002 to 2006

	2002	2003	2004	2005	2006
	\$ millions				
Canada	**319,525.4**	**331,143.4**	**346,721.5**	**366,170.7**	**389,567.4**
Newfoundland and Labrador	5,407.0	5,736.3	5,755.5	5,825.9	6,042.4
Prince Edward Island	1,369.0	1,382.6	1,384.7	1,423.9	1,481.3
Nova Scotia	9,839.5	10,014.9	10,296.5	10,526.9	11,191.8
New Brunswick	7,786.8	7,826.8	7,962.7	8,326.1	8,834.8
Quebec	72,099.0	75,325.7	78,517.9	82,532.5	86,762.8
Ontario	120,992.0	125,122.5	129,085.8	135,320.6	140,835.4
Manitoba	10,569.5	10,953.2	11,691.6	12,381.3	12,938.3
Saskatchewan	9,388.8	9,858.1	10,259.4	10,796.1	11,494.7
Alberta	37,662.7	39,317.8	43,371.6	48,493.0	56,046.6
British Columbia	43,265.0	44,421.0	47,216.6	49,286.3	52,626.9
Yukon	413.9	421.6	414.0	433.9	451.1
Northwest Territories	505.0	529.9	532.1	574.8	599.6
Nunavut	227.2	232.9	233.2	249.2	261.8

Source: Statistics Canada, CANSIM table 080-0014.

Table 26.7 Non-store retailers, financial estimates, by trade group, 2005

	All non-store retailers	Electronic shopping and mail-order houses	Vending machine operators and coffee service operators	Fuel dealers	Other direct selling establishments
	\$ thousands				
Total operating revenue	**12,767,494**	3,953,575	651,293	6,520,859	1,641,767
Sales of goods for resale	**11,999,059**	3,666,871	626,708	6,292,204	1,413,276
Opening inventory	**596,065**	356,814	40,190	100,796	98,265
Purchases	**8,556,557**	2,330,999	290,643	5,092,030	842,886
Closing inventory	**679,224**	409,465	38,477	101,620	129,662
Cost of goods sold	**8,638,117**	2,333,111	314,697	5,137,750	852,558
Total operating expenses	**3,190,329**	1,323,694	292,653	898,196	675,786
Total labour remuneration	**1,080,116**	352,130	119,244	367,560	241,183

Note: North American Industry Classification System (NAICS), 2002.
Source: Statistics Canada, CANSIM table 080-0012.

Science and technology

27

OVERVIEW

Science fiction is not what it used to be. In our technology-dependent world, it is no longer part of an inaccessible dream world—science is central to daily Canadian life.

Biotechnology and chemistry deliver new drugs, high-tech firms release the newest must-have gadgets at an unprecedented pace, and research programs regularly generate leading-edge innovations in artificial intelligence, nanotechnology, robotics, photonics, geomatics and aeronautics.

Less noticeable in daily life are the ways that industry uses science to improve how our resources are extracted, refined, delivered and sustained. In a world where science has drastically changed our understanding of our impact on the environment, science also helps us to develop alternative energy sources, more sustainable growth and healthier products.

The impact of science is huge. It improves our quality of life, boosts our economy and strengthens our industries. Today, hundreds of thousands of talented Canadians across the country—in private industry, government labs and university research programs—are pushing science in new directions.

Who funds science?

Canada invests significantly in scientific research and development (R&D). In 2006, Canadian universities, hospitals, government laboratories and businesses planned to spend $28.4 billion on R&D, more than double the spending of a decade earlier. This total—the gross domestic expenditures on research and development (GERD)—refers to all money spent on R&D performed within the country in a given year.

Chart 27.1
Gross domestic expenditures on research and development, by sector

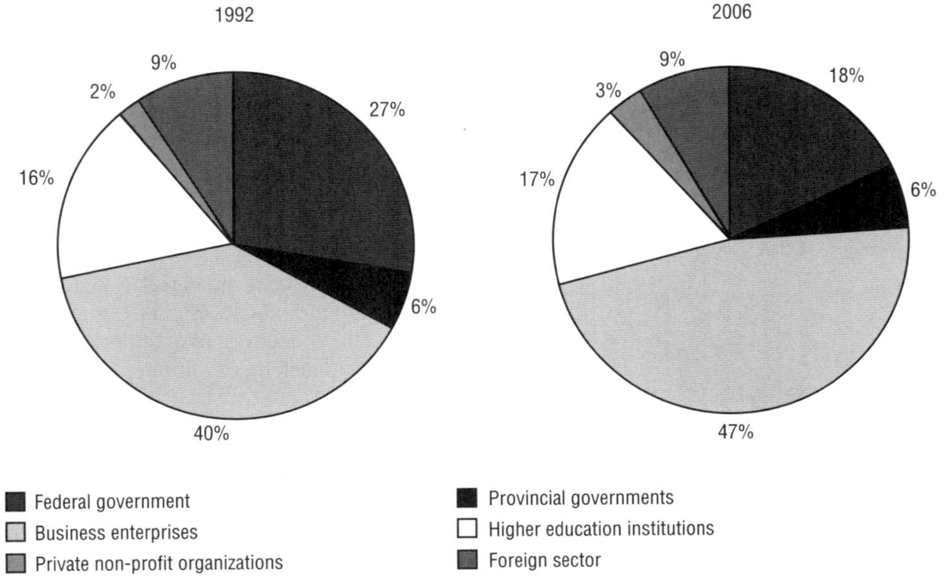

1992
9%
2%
27%
16%
6%
40%
2006
9%
3%
18%
17%
6%
47%
Federal government
Business enterprises
Private non-profit organizations
Provincial governments
Higher education institutions
Foreign sector

Source: Statistics Canada, CANSIM table 358-0001.

GERD represents the total spending on R&D performed within a country from all funding sources, as well as funding from abroad. It excludes payments sent abroad for R&D performed in other countries.

GERD is a key benchmark for determining the research intensity in a given country and for making national and international comparisons. More GERD funding generally reflects the creation of more scientific knowledge.

In 2006, business enterprises were expected to account for $13.2 billion, or nearly half of total planned funding of GERD. The federal government was projected to fund $5.2 billion, and higher education institutions, $4.9 billion. Another $900 million was anticipated from private, non-profit organizations, a sector that has increased its R&D funding almost 300% since 1992. The remaining funding was expected to come from provincial governments ($1.6 billion) and from abroad ($2.4 billion).

In 2004, Canada ranked 12 out of 30 member countries of the Organisation of Economic Co-operation and Development

Biotechnology revenues and research and development expenditures by sector, 2005

	Firms	Revenues	Research and development expenditures
	number	$ millions	
All innovative biotech firms	**532**	**4,191**	**1,703**
Human Health	303	2,955	1,486
Agriculture and food processing	130	1,075	157
Environment	54	121	34
Other	45	41	27

Source: Statistics Canada, Catalogue no. 88-003-XIE.

(OECD) in terms of the percentage of gross domestic product (GDP) spent on R&D. Canada spent 2.0% of its GDP, compared with an OECD average of 2.3%. Some of the biggest spenders were Finland at 3.5% and Japan at 3.1%.

In the 2006/2007 fiscal year, the federal government planned to spend $9.2 billion on science and technology (S&T), including $5.7 billion on research and experimental development.

Spending grows

The share of federal science and technology (S&T) spending allocated to the natural sciences and engineering was $6.9 billion in 2006/2007, or 74% of total spending, down from a high of 78% in 2002/2003. Only 30% of the $2.4 billion allocated to the social sciences is allocated to R&D, with the rest going to related scientific activities, such as data collection, maintaining national standards and testing, feasibility studies and policy research.

From 2000/2001 to 2006/2007, Canadian federal government spending on S&T advanced 39% (in current dollars). Most of this gain came in 2001/2002, when the federal government invested an additional $1.5 billion, up 22% from the previous fiscal year.

Chart 27.2
Federal spending on science and technology activities

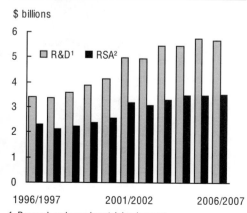

$ billions

☐ R&D[1] ■ RSA[2]

1996/1997   2001/2002   2006/2007

1. Research and experimental development.
2. Related scientific activities.
Source: Statistics Canada, Catalogue no. 88-001-XIE.

University institutions and research hospitals are also expanding funding of their science programs. In 2000, higher education was responsible for 14% of GERD; by 2006, their share was 17%. During the same period, the business sector increased its share of GERD from 45% to 47%.

Who's minding the lab?

More than 36,000 full-time federal government jobs were devoted to science and technology (S&T) activities in 2006/2007, 3% more than in 2005/2006. Sixty-one percent of those jobs were involved in related scientific activities in 2006/2007.

The natural sciences and engineering field accounted for 68% of the estimated total personnel spending in 2006/2007, of which 54% were engaged in R&D. Personnel in the social sciences and humanities accounted for 32% of the total, of which only 7% were engaged in R&D.

Canadian scientists are also pushing the frontiers of knowledge and are major players in cutting-edge sciences such as biotechnology, where they develop

virus-resistant crops or produce new burn treatments.

In 2005, more than 13,400 Canadians were involved in biotechnology activities at 532 innovative biotech firms in Canada—firms that are developing new products or processes. More than three out of four of these companies are in the three provinces that account for more than 90% of biotechnology revenues: Quebec, Ontario and British Columbia.

Altogether, Canada's biotech firms generated $4.2 billion in 2005 and spent $1.7 billion on R&D. Most are fairly small, employing fewer than 50 people. However, the 50 largest companies—those with at least 150 employees—accounted for more than two-thirds of the revenues.

Biotechnology related to human health remains the most significant biotechnology sector in terms of number of firms, employment, R&D and revenues.

Selected sources

Statistics Canada

- *Federal Scientific Activities.* Annual. 88-204-XIE

- *Innovation Analysis Bulletin.* Irregular. 88-003-XIE

- *Science, Innovation and Electronic Information Division Research Papers.* Irregular. 88F0017MIE

- *Science, Innovation and Electronic Information Division Working Papers.* Occasional. 88F0006XIE

- *Science Statistics.* Irregular. 88-001-XIE

Chart 27.3
Biotechnology firms, by size, 2005

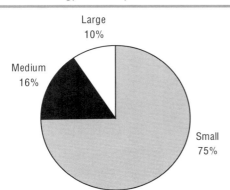

Large
10%

Medium
16%

Small
75%

Notes: Small (0 to 50 employees)
Medium (50 to 149 employees)
Large (more than 150 employees)
Percentages may not add to 100 due to rounding.
Source: Statistics Canada, Catalogue no. 88-003-XWE.

Functional foods and nutraceuticals

As Canadians age and face rising health care costs, many are considering the link between health and diet. The functional food and nutraceutical industry is seizing the opportunity—389 firms in Canada generated $2.9 billion in revenues from these products in 2004/2005 and employed 13,000 people.

These firms develop products—which are taken as foods or supplements—directly from natural sources to benefit human health. Of those total revenues, $1.6 billion came from companies selling just nutraceuticals, $824 million was from firms specializing in functional foods and $443 million from companies selling both.

Today, 10,000 functional foods and nutraceutical products are available on store shelves, and R&D is expanding the product line. The industry spent $75 million in 2004 on R&D specifically for functional foods or

nutraceuticals. This amounted to 46% of the total funds these firms spent on R&D.

The share of funds devoted to functional foods and nutraceuticals R&D was lowest, 39%, among firms that only sell nutraceuticals. Yet these firms also had the highest share of sales from functional foods and nutraceuticals, 57%. This indicates that most nutraceutical products are already on the market and generating revenues.

The number of Canadian firms producing functional foods or nutraceuticals grew from 294 in 2002 to 389 in 2004. These products pose not just a domestic opportunity but also a chance for international growth. The United States is a major market for the $545 million worth of functional foods and nutraceutical products these firms export.

Chart 27.4
Firms with functional food or nutraceutical-related activities, 2004

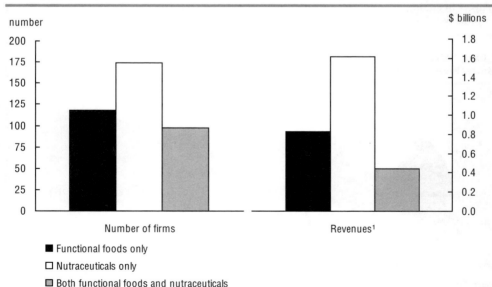

1. The estimate for revenues for firms with both functional food and nutraceutical-related activities should be used with caution.
Source: Statistics Canada, Catalogue no. 88-003-XIE.

Persistence pays off

Every year, thousands of companies across Canada take on R&D projects to advance science and develop new products and services. But according to the Research and Development in Canadian Industry Survey, only a minority of these companies maintain R&D programs over long periods.

Of the 31,200 companies doing some form of R&D from 1994 to 2002, only 5% (1,700 firms) were 'persistent' R&D performers. The survey grouped firms according to their annual R&D spending—a gauge of the strength of a firm's R&D program. It found that the R&D spending group a firm belonged to influenced their persistence with R&D. Firms that spent $10 million or more on R&D in 1994 had longer-lasting programs than firms that spent less than $100,000 that year. Nearly one-third of

the highest annual spenders reported R&D activity in all nine years from 1994 to 2002; only 3% of the lowest spending group—less than $100,000—reported undertaking R&D for that long. This pattern reflects different R&D approaches firms take—large spenders view R&D as a program, whereas small spenders see it as a short-term project.

Average annual R&D spending by all firms was $1.7 million in 2001 and $1.6 million in 2002—a reflection of the market setbacks in the 'dot-com' and telecommunications equipment sectors. Still, this was nearly triple the average annual spending in 1994. Moreover, the total spent on R&D by industry was projected to reach $14.8 billion in 2006, 86% more than in 1996. From 1994 to 2002, the number of firms spending $10 million or more per year on R&D nearly doubled.

Chart 27.5
Persistence of R&D performance, by selected amount of expenditures, 1994 to 2002

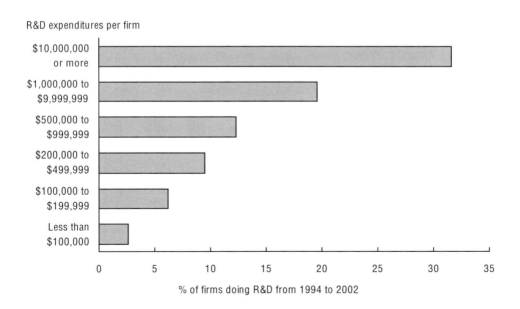

R&D expenditures per firm

% of firms doing R&D from 1994 to 2002

Source: Statistics Canada, Catalogue no. 88-003-XIE.

The researchers and developers

Scientific researchers and technicians are in demand. From 1980 to 2004, the number of full-time researchers, technicians and support staff engaged in R&D in Canada grew 140%, from 83,000 to 199,000. The number of researchers more than tripled; the number of technicians nearly doubled.

Canada has 7.2 researchers per 1,000 workers—above the OECD average of 6.9. The United States has 9.6 per 1,000 workers, and Japan has the highest, 10.4 per 1,000.

Natural sciences and engineering attract by far the most R&D employees—almost 90% of researchers, technicians and support staff in 2004. Business enterprises employed 73%, higher education institutions, 18% and federal and provincial governments, 9%.

At postsecondary institutions, R&D spending climbed from $5.1 billion in 1999 to $9.0 billion in 2004. The number of R&D

personnel in higher education surged 6% from 2003 to 2004. Since 2002, Canada's ranks of R&D personnel in higher education have grown slightly faster than in many OECD countries.

The concentration of R&D personnel across Canada reflects regional spending patterns. Ontario and Quebec are home to most of Canada's research facilities. These provinces accounted for 76% of all R&D personnel in 2004. About 10% of R&D personnel worked in British Columbia that year, while another 7% worked in Alberta.

In Newfoundland and Labrador, two out of three R&D personnel work in the higher education and private non-profit sectors, as do one out of two in Nova Scotia and New Brunswick. The majority (62% to 70%) of R&D personnel in Quebec, Ontario and British Columbia work in the business sector.

Chart 27.6
Employment in research and development

number of employees

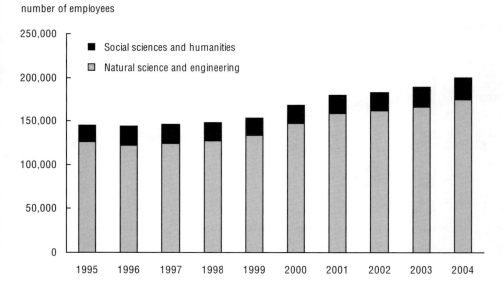

Source: Statistics Canada, Catalogue no. 88-001-XIE.

Unveiling the inventions

Canadian universities and research hospitals are commercializing more of the inventions coming from their laboratories. They are also capitalizing on those with the highest potential via spin-off companies, creating 50 of them in 2003 and 2004 alone.

Universities and research hospitals unveiled 1,432 inventions in 2004, up 26% from 2003. They also received nearly 400 patents for these new technologies. At the end of 2004, 50% of the patents they held in Canada had been licensed, assigned or otherwise commercialized, compared with 35% at the end of 2003.

As of the end of 2004, universities and their research hospitals had created 968 spin-off firms. They cover many industries and focus on high-tech inventions such as engineering and medical devices manufacturing and

computer systems design. One in three spin-offs was incorporated from 1995 to 1999; 64% of them are still going concerns in their early active stages. In 2004, 33 universities and hospitals provided space to 87 start-up companies. In 2003, 25 institutions provided space to 74 start-ups.

Sponsored research funding totalled $5.0 billion in 2004, of which 68% went to institutions in Ontario and Quebec. Those two provinces accounted for 57% of the inventions disclosed in 2004.

Prairie universities received 18% of sponsored research dollars, unveiled 21% of the nation's inventions and accounted for 26% of patents issued. British Columbia's institutions also overachieved, using 10% of total research funding and generating 17% of all inventions. Atlantic Canada's institutions account for 7% of all spin-off companies created to date.

Chart 27.7
Universities and teaching hospitals' share of research funding and inventions, by region, 2004

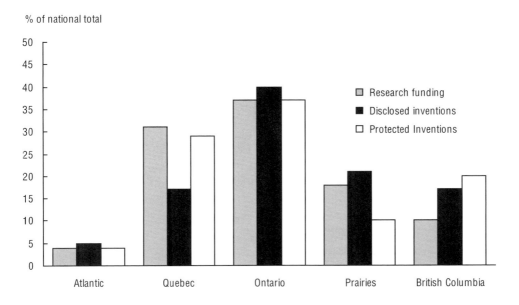

% of national total

Source: Statistics Canada, Catalogue no. 88F0006XIE.

Table 27.1 Federal expenditures on science and technology, by province and territory, 1999/2000 to 2004/2005

	1999/2000	2000/2001	2001/2002	2002/2003	2003/2004	2004/2005
	\$ millions					
Canada (including the National Capital Region)	**5,640**	**6,084**	**7,476**	**7,300**	**7,976**	**8,156**
National Capital Region[1]	1,981	2,130	2,603	2,608	2,642	2,708
Canada (excluding the National Capital Region)	**3,659**	**3,954**	**4,873**	**4,692**	**5,333**	**5,448**
Newfoundland and Labrador	87	101	95	117	121	137
Prince Edward Island	20	29	26	24	33	39
Nova Scotia	197	220	225	247	257	294
New Brunswick	72	68	82	102	100	122
Quebec[2]	833	1,017	1,381	1,243	1,328	1,352
Ontario[2]	1,309	1,347	1,653	1,582	2,038	1,967
Manitoba	161	190	211	214	194	226
Saskatchewan	131	148	165	151	159	157
Alberta	301	327	476	395	469	474
British Columbia	528	479	525	582	588	645
Yukon, Northwest Territories and Nunavut	20	28	34	35	46	35

1. Federal intramural expenditures only.
2. Includes extramural expenditures of the National Capital Region executed within the province.
Source: Statistics Canada, Catalogue no. 88-001-XIE.

Table 27.2 Federal expenditures on research and development, by activity, 2001/2002 to 2006/2007

	2001/2002	2002/2003	2003/2004	2004/2005	2005/2006p	2006/2007p
	\$ millions					
Research and development and related scientific activities	**8,169**	**8,014**	**8,765**	**8,935**	**9,228**	**9,185**
Research and development	4,989	4,927	5,462	5,455	5,751	5,663
Current expenditures	4,571	4,492	5,033	5,033	5,314	5,259
Administration of extramural programs	213	227	257	269	282	275
Capital expenditures	205	208	172	152	154	128
Related scientific activities	3,180	3,087	3,303	3,480	3,477	3,523
Data collection	1,611	1,498	1,618	1,702	1,699	1,717
Information services	618	679	663	679	708	717
Special services and studies	513	588	615	666	644	655
Education support	286[1]	177	206	230	253	267
Administration of extramural programs	49	54	56	58	58	61
Capital expenditures	103	91	145	146	115	106

1. Includes a \$125 million grant to the Pierre Elliott Trudeau Foundation.
Source: Statistics Canada, Catalogue no. 88-001-XIE.

Table 27.3 Gross domestic expenditures on research and development, by the performing and funding sectors, 1990 to 2006

	Total[1]	Federal government	Provincial governments	Business enterprises	Higher education	Foreign sources
	\$ millions					
Performing sector						
1990	**10,260**	1,654	302	5,169	3,033	...
1991	**10,770**	1,685	328	5,355	3,292	...
1992	**11,338**	1,716	293	5,742[2]	3,519	...
1993	**12,184**	1,757	269	6,424	3,660	...
1994	**13,341**	1,753	260	7,567[2]	3,675	...
1995	**13,754**	1,727	254	7,991	3,691	...
1996	**13,817**	1,792	242	7,997	3,697	...
1997	**14,634**	1,720	214	8,739	3,879	...
1998	**16,088**	1,743	216	9,682	4,370	...
1999	**17,637**	1,859	233	10,400	5,082	...
2000	**20,580**	2,080	255	12,395	5,793	...
2001	**23,169**	2,103	307	14,272	6,424	...
2002	**23,539**	2,190	315	13,516	7,455	...
2003	**24,337**	2,083	315	13,704	8,143	...
2004	**26,003**	2,083	326	14,441	9,037	...
2005p	**27,174**	2,162	336	14,655	9,900	...
2006p	**28,357**	2,145	345	14,850	10,890	...
Funding sector						
1990	**10,260**	2,859	641	3,960	1,618	949
1991	**10,770**	2,946	696	4,113	1,735	1,013
1992	**11,338**	3,109	644	4,445[2]	1,867	1,049
1993	**12,184**	3,156	665	5,025	1,892	1,170
1994	**13,341**	3,094	663	5,874[2]	1,914	1,498
1995	**13,754**	2,989	652	6,288	1,926	1,590
1996	**13,817**	2,815	629	6,396	1,905	1,714
1997	**14,634**	2,813	658	7,031	1,971	1,794
1998	**16,088**	2,831	639	7,354	2,339	2,553
1999	**17,637**	3,216	770	7,917	2,649	2,705
2000	**20,580**	3,560	878	9,224	2,892	3,580
2001	**23,169**	4,096	1,048	11,643	2,928	2,918
2002	**23,539**	4,254	1,185	12,086	3,462	1,924
2003	**24,337**	4,533	1,396	12,057	3,589	2,125
2004	**26,003**	4,666	1,407	12,743	4,126	2,332
2005p	**27,174**	4,978	1,520	13,004	4,498	2,375
2006p	**28,357**	5,227	1,644	13,245	4,948	2,416

1. Includes private non-profit organizations.
2. Estimates, as a complete survey was not conducted.
Source: Statistics Canada, Catalogue no. 88-001-XIE.

Table 27.4 Federal expenditures on research and development, by the performing and funding provinces, 1990 to 2004

	Canada[1]	National Capital Region	Canada[2]	Newfoundland and Labrador	Prince Edward Island	Nova Scotia
			$ millions			
Performing province						
1990	1,654	711	943	35	10	81
1991	1,685	733	952	35	10	81
1992	1,716	753	963	35	9	73
1993	1,757	774	983	36	11	75
1994	1,753	789	964	33	11	84
1995	1,727	805	922	27	9	77
1996	1,792	771	1,021	25	10	79
1997	1,720	757	963	23	10	70
1998	1,743	812	931	26	10	77
1999	1,859	808	1,051	25	12	72
2000	2,080	889	1,191	30	16	88
2001	2,103	926	1,177	27	16	70
2002	2,190	1,015	1,175	32	8	76
2003	2,083	999	1,084	23	12	65
2004	2,083	960	1,123	23	10	81
Funding province						
1990	2,859	711	2,148	56	11	133
1991	2,946	733	2,213	54	12	135
1992	3,109	748	2,361	62	10	125
1993	3,156	767	2,388	59	12	120
1994	3,094	784	2,310	52	12	127
1995	2,989	796	2,193	42	11	113
1996	2,815	755	2,060	42	12	112
1997	2,813	740	2,073	40	11	107
1998	2,831	798	2,033	44	12	113
1999	3,216	796	2,420	48	14	113
2000	3,560	872	2,688	54	19	129
2001	4,096	907	3,189	52	20	121
2002	4,254	994	3,260	63	13	134
2003	4,533	983	3,550	59	20	132
2004	4,666	945	3,721	60	19	157

1. Includes the National Capital Region, Yukon, Northwest Territories and Nunavut.
2. Includes the Yukon, Northwest Territories and Nunavut; excludes the National Capital Region.
3. Quebec and Ontario figures exclude federal government expenditures performed in the National Capital Region.
Source: Statistics Canada, Catalogue no. 88-001-XIE.

New Brunswick	Quebec[3]	Ontario[3]	Manitoba	Saskatchewan	Alberta	British Columbia
			$ millions			
36	215	249	94	50	77	95
37	217	251	95	51	78	96
36	234	274	81	56	78	86
33	250	276	83	54	75	88
28	225	253	79	48	93	103
29	218	259	71	52	98	81
32	226	348	77	47	94	78
29	212	302	59	74	96	83
31	226	276	49	54	94	85
32	250	322	58	60	108	106
27	350	314	69	62	116	111
26	373	328	77	63	98	96
46	370	324	72	53	92	99
30	314	351	63	54	87	80
26	320	329	73	54	110	91
56	550	730	131	78	162	240
54	568	746	133	84	168	258
54	634	848	119	89	167	252
63	660	849	121	87	164	251
60	592	799	119	82	190	270
60	580	756	108	81	207	234
44	546	719	108	75	191	206
41	547	741	88	96	195	200
44	540	737	82	77	183	198
49	665	868	98	103	218	238
42	806	899	113	121	234	263
45	999	1,126	126	123	284	290
68	994	1,118	132	113	282	340
61	1,056	1,289	132	121	325	349
58	1,057	1,327	148	124	339	427

Table 27.5 Gross domestic expenditure on research and development, by province, 1992, 1996, 2000 and 2004

	1992	1996	2000	2004
	\$ millions			
Canada (including the National Capital Region)[1]	11,338	13,817	20,580	26,003
National Capital Region	753	771	889	960
Canada (excluding the National Capital Region)[1]	10,585	13,046	19,691	25,043
Newfoundland and Labrador	110	103	138	169
Prince Edward Island	14	17	36	40
Nova Scotia	233	257	363	446
New Brunswick	122	150	161	222
Quebec[2]	3,113	3,801	5,680	7,161
Ontario[2]	4,818	6,176	9,564	11,720
Manitoba	281	295	412	519
Saskatchewan	235	233	376	422
Alberta	779	1,007	1,337	2,053
British Columbia	879	1,002	1,616	2,282

1. Includes the Yukon, Northwest Territories and Nunavut.
2. Quebec and Ontario figures exclude federal government expenditures performed in the National Capital Region.
Source: Statistics Canada, Catalogue no. 88-001-XIE.

Table 27.6 Gross domestic expenditures on research and development, health sector compared with all sectors, 1988 to 2005

	All sectors	Health sector		
	\$ millions	\$ millions	% of all sectors	\$ per capita
1988	9,045	1,221	13.5	46
1989	9,516	1,365	14.3	50
1990	10,260	1,551	15.1	56
1991	10,767	1,665	15.5	59
1992	11,338	1,783	15.7	63
1993	12,184	2,006	16.5	70
1994	13,342	2,105	15.8	73
1995	13,754	2,196	16.0	75
1996	13,816	2,317	16.8	78
1997	14,634	2,447	16.7	82
1998	16,088	2,692	16.7	89
1999	17,637	2,967	16.8	98
2000	20,635	3,560	17.3	116
2001	23,206	4,159	17.9	134
2002	23,382	5,050	21.6	161
2003	23,992	5,234	21.8	165
2004	25,259	5,574	22.1	174
2005p	26,268	5,953	22.7	184

Source: Statistics Canada, CANSIM tables 051-0001, 358-0001 and 384-0036, and Catalogue no. 88-001-XIE.

Table 27.7 Business enterprises' research and development expenditures, by province and territory, 1999 to 2004

	1999	2000	2001	2002	2003	2004
	\$ millions					
Canada	**10,400**	**12,395**	**14,272**	**13,516**	**13,704**	**14,441**
Newfoundland and Labrador	18	20	21	21	26	26
Prince Edward Island	3	5	6	4	7	6
Nova Scotia	62	67	91	95	77	89
New Brunswick	39	40	45	64	62	75
Quebec	3,047	3,642	4,158	4,131	4,154	4,308
Ontario	5,799	6,856	7,900	7,064	7,241	7,457
Manitoba	148	133	173	150	136	165
Saskatchewan	78	76	87	112	84	111
Alberta	490	583	710	782	790	892
British Columbia	714	973	1,080	1,092	1,127	1,309
Yukon, Northwest Territories and Nunavut	2	0	1	0	1	3

Note: Expenditures on performing research and development.
Source: Statistics Canada, Catalogue no. 88-001-XIE.

Table 27.8 Intellectual property management at universities and research hospitals, 1999 to 2005

	1999	2001	2003	2004	2005P
	%				
Institutions engaged in intellectual property management	61	66	72	76	..
	number				
Full-time equivalent employees engaged in intellectual property management	178	221	255	280	..
Research contracts	5,748	8,247	11,432	14,324	..
Invention disclosures	893	1,105	1,133	1,432	1,475
Inventions protected[1]	549	682	527	629	744
Inventions declined by the institution	..	..	256	355	323
Patent applications	656	932	1,252	1,264	1,427
Patents issued	349	381	347	397	374
Patents held	1,915	2,133	3,047	3,827	3,953
New licences and options	232	354	422	494	577
Active licences and options	1,165	1,424	1,756	2,022	2,216
	\$ thousands				
Operational expenditures for intellectual property management	22,018	28,505	36,419	36,927	..
Value of research contracts	393,358	527,051	810,431	940,993	..
Income from intellectual property	24,745	52,510	55,525	51,210	55,127
Value of remaining equity held by the institution in publicly traded spin-offs	54,560	45,120	52,351	49,872	..
Investment in spin-offs raised with the assistance of the institution	..	..	54,640	56,421	..

Note: Data were not collected for 2000 and 2002 since the Survey of Intellectual Property Commercialization in the Higher Education Sector was conducted on an occasional basis from 1998 to 2003.
1. Resulted in protection activity.
Source: Statistics Canada, CANSIM table 358-0025.

Table 27.9 University enrolment in natural and applied science and technology programs, by sex, 2000/2001 to 2004/2005

	2000/2001	2001/2002	2002/2003	2003/2004	2004/2005
	number				
All instructional programs					
Both sexes[1]	**850,572**	**886,605**	**933,870**	**993,246**	**1,014,486**
Men	362,271	376,884	397,167	419,463	429,006
Women	488,145	509,586	536,640	573,531	585,249
Physical and life sciences and technologies					
Both sexes[1]	**79,140**	**80,553**	**83,616**	**91,719**	**96,441**
Men	35,766	36,396	37,329	40,692	42,738
Women	43,368	44,154	46,284	51,015	53,697
Mathematics, computer and information sciences					
Both sexes[1]	**43,527**	**46,377**	**45,897**	**44,190**	**40,929**
Men	30,801	32,958	33,165	32,304	29,880
Women	12,723	13,419	12,732	11,865	11,004
Architecture, engineering and related technologies					
Both sexes[1]	**70,023**	**74,817**	**81,087**	**85,776**	**86,451**
Men	53,640	57,432	62,376	66,522	67,332
Women	16,380	17,385	18,708	19,242	19,116
Agriculture, natural resources and conservation					
Both sexes[1]	**15,420**	**14,841**	**14,487**	**14,613**	**14,640**
Men	7,491	6,930	6,666	6,579	6,588
Women	7,929	7,908	7,821	8,028	8,052

Notes: Figures are rounded to the nearest five.

Historical data coded with the University Student Information System classification have been converted to the Classification of Instructional Programs 2000.

1. Figures may not add up to the totals because of the exclusion of the 'sex unknown' category in the table or because of rounding.

Source: Statistics Canada, CANSIM table 477-0013.

Seniors

28

OVERVIEW

Like most industrialized countries, Canada is seeing an increase in its senior population. In recent decades, the Canadian population aged 65 and older has grown—it totalled 4.3 million in 2006.

Seniors comprised 13% of Canada's population in 2006, compared with 10% in 1981 and only 5% in 1921. By 2056, the share of the population aged 65 and older may reach 27%. Women are the majority among seniors—56% of persons aged 65 and older and 64% of those 80 and older in 2006.

The most rapid growth is in the older age groups. In 2006, 3.6% of the population was aged 80 and older—this figure could reach 10% by 2056.

The percentage of seniors varies greatly from one census metropolitan area to another. In 2006, St. Catharines–Niagara and Victoria had the largest shares, followed by Trois-

Rivières and Thunder Bay. Proportionally fewer seniors live in Calgary, St. John's, Oshawa, Edmonton and Ottawa–Gatineau. From 1986 to 2004, the share of seniors grew the most in Saguenay, Trois-Rivières and Greater Sudbury.

Family status

In 2001, 93% of seniors lived in private households and 7% in collective dwellings— primarily health care institutions such as nursing homes and hospitals. The proportion of seniors living in an institution ranged between 2% for those aged 65 to 74 and 32% for those aged 85 and older.

In all age groups, a larger proportion of seniors lived with a spouse in 2001 than in 1981: 54% of seniors aged 65 to 74 lived with a spouse, up from 51% in 1981. The gap

Chart 28.1
Population projections, 65 years and older

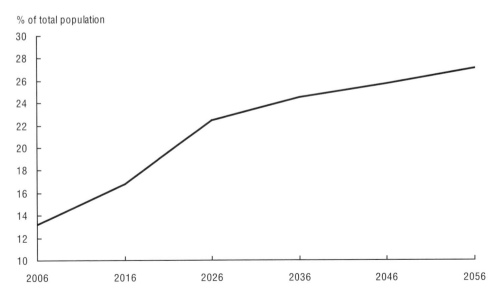

% of total population

Note: Medium growth scenario.
Source: Statistics Canada, Catalogue no. 91-520-XIE.

in life expectancy between men and women has narrowed since the late 1970s.

In 2001, most seniors living with their spouse had marriage as their form of union, since most had gotten together when legal marriage was the only socially acceptable option. Thus, only 2% of seniors lived common-law in 2001, compared with 14% of couples aged 25 to 54.

The share of seniors aged 85 and older who live alone has changed dramatically: 22% of them lived alone in 1981, compared with 34% in 2001. The share of seniors aged 65 to 74 living alone has remained stable at 22%.

Senior women were twice as likely as senior men to live alone in 2001. Women's longer life expectancy helps explain this, as does men's tendency to marry younger women. Since women enjoy a greater probability of outliving their spouse, they are more likely to be living alone late in life.

Financial status

Canadian seniors' financial status has improved significantly over the last 25 years.

Chart 28.2
Median income of seniors, by family type and sex

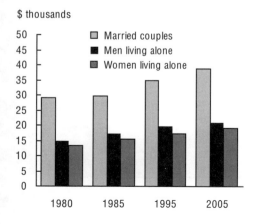

$ thousands

Source: Statistics Canada, CANSIM table 202-0605.

Seniors' income, by source, 2005

	number of seniors	$ thousands
Total employment income	**790,360**	**14,494,560**
Investment income	2,385,030	13,660,905
Total government transfers	4,095,270	52,657,997
Private pensions	2,415,010	35,800,725
Registered Retirement Savings Plans	415,630	2,595,343
Other income	1,082,520	4,549,203

Note: Population aged 65 and older.
Source: Statistics Canada, CANSIM table 111-0035.

The median after-tax income of elderly married couples in 2005 dollars rose from $29,000 in 1980 to $38,900 in 2005, an increase of 34%. Across the provinces, their median after-tax income ranged from $28,700 in Newfoundland and Labrador to $44,100 in Ontario. The incomes of seniors not living with family members rose by even higher percentages in this period.

Greater access to the Canada and Quebec pension plans has done much to improve seniors' financial status, as has the expanded coverage of private employer-sponsored pension plans. Also, a greater proportion of seniors are now eligible to collect benefits from the Canada and Quebec pension plans. This has helped substantially lower the percentage of seniors in low income—in 2005, that percentage was lower in Canada than in most industrialized countries. This is a marked change from the 1970s, when the percentage of low income seniors in Canada was among the highest of the industrialized countries.

Seniors are now getting a smaller proportion of their total income from government transfers such as Old Age Security benefits, the Guaranteed Income Supplement and the Spouse's Allowance than in the early 1980s. Still, 97% of seniors received income from one or more of these sources in 2005, and these sources accounted for 32% of senior women's income.

From 1980 to 1992, the share of men aged 65 and older with employment earnings dropped from 24% to 13%. By 2005, it had rebounded to 24%.

Health status

During the twentieth century, life expectancy at 65 in Canada increased dramatically. In 1901, a 65-year-old could expect to live an additional 11 years; by 2001, this had increased to 19 years.

Cancer and heart disease are the leading causes of death for those 65 and older, followed by stroke and respiratory diseases. According to a study of factors associated with death in seniors over an eight-year period, psychological distress strongly predicted death in women, as did widowhood in men.

Arthritis (or rheumatism) and high blood pressure were the chronic health conditions most often reported by seniors in 2005, especially women. The frequency of these two chronic conditions may rise in the future, since obesity—a factor closely linked to the probability of developing each of these disorders—has been rising in recent years.

Nevertheless, many seniors still fare very well, even though aging tends to be associated with a decline in general health and the onset of various activity limitations. In the 2003 Canadian Community Health Survey (CCHS), more than 7 seniors in 10 had good functional health, were independent in the activities of daily living and had a positive perception of their general health.

However, the proportion of seniors in good functional health declines sharply with age. In 2003, 80% of seniors aged 65 to 74 either had no disabilities or had fully-corrected disabilities (wearing glasses, for example). This was true of only 37% of seniors aged 85 and older. Declines by age are steepest for mobility and cognition.

The 2003 CCHS data showed that exercising occasionally or frequently, drinking moderately, eating fruit and vegetables often, having a normal body weight, having low stress levels and feeling connected to the community all play an important role in seniors' overall health. An eight-year follow-up of seniors surveyed in 1994/1995 showed that avoiding smoking, obesity, inactivity and heavy drinking helped seniors to stay healthy and increased their chances of recovering after an illness.

Chart 28.3
Older adults and seniors in good health, 2003

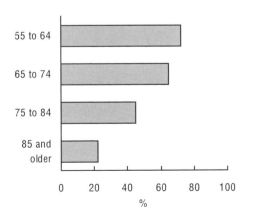

Source: Statistics Canada, Catalogue no. 82-003-SIE.

Selected sources

Statistics Canada

- *Analysis in Brief.* Occasional. 11-621-MIE

- *A Portrait of Seniors in Canada.* Occasional. 89-519-XWE

- *General Social Survey on Time Use: Cycle 19.* Occasional. 89-622-XIE

- *Health Reports - Supplement.* Annual. 82-003-SIE

- *Population Projections for Canada, Provinces and Territories.* Occasional. 91-520-XIE

Seniors are more educated now

Senior Canadians are much more educated than were previous generations. Their education levels have increased considerably over the past decade—a change that is expected to continue in the coming years.

From 1990 to 2006, the share of men aged 65 and older with less than high school completion dropped from 63% to 46% and the percentage of postsecondary graduates increased. The same trends are evident among women aged 65 and older.

The higher educational attainment is especially striking among Canadians 55 to 64. The share of men in this age group with less than a high school education fell from 53% in 1990 to 24% in 2006, while the share with a university degree jumped from 10% to 22%. Even more striking, the share of women in this age group with a university degree tripled, from 5% to 17%.

These are the first baby boomers to reach their senior years. During the 1960s, they were the first generation to benefit when postsecondary education became accessible to a wider population than in the past. As successive waves of baby boomers enter their sixties, the proportion of seniors with a postsecondary education will continue to grow, and the overall education level of seniors will also continue to rise.

Education level is clearly associated with particular behaviours and socioeconomic conditions, according to a recent study. For example, people—of all ages—with more education tend to have better health, are less likely to have a low income and are less likely to be socially isolated.

Chart 28.4
Education attainment of adults aged 55 and older

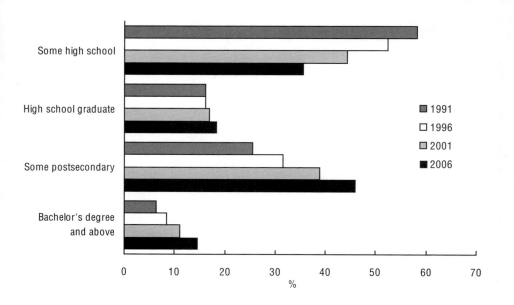

Source: Statistics Canada, CANSIM table 282-0004.

Seniors satisfied with their lives

Four million Canadians have reached the official retirement age—and aging for them is not necessarily synonymous with illness, dependency, poverty, inactivity or social withdrawal. Seniors aged 65 to 74 today devote less time to paid work than when they were aged 55 to 64, and more time to unpaid work in the home and leisure activities.

Canadians aged 65 to 74 engaged in leisure activities for most of their day—7.8 hours for men and 7.2 hours for women in 2005. Men aged 75 and older spent even more time—8.0 hours a day—on leisure; women spent 7.9 hours. Retired women spend more time than men on domestic chores, yet leisure activities still take up more of their day.

Both men and women aged 65 to 74 in 2005 devoted more time on average to active leisure—such as physical exercise, reading and going out and socializing—than to

passive leisure—such as watching television, listening to music or to the radio. Men aged 75 and older spent the same number of hours on active leisure as on passive leisure. But active leisure continues to predominate later in life for women aged 75 and older.

Women aged 65 to 74 spent more time than men that age doing unpaid work in 2005. On average, they also devoted the same number of hours to unpaid work as younger women. Men aged 65 to 74 spent, on average, more hours on unpaid work than those in the youngest age group.

Seniors, especially those aged 65 to 74, are more satisfied with their life than those 25 to 64. Whatever their age, the seniors who are the least healthy and the least satisfied are those who spend the most time on passive leisure.

Chart 28.5
Time spent on leisure by adults aged 55 and older, 2005

average hours per day

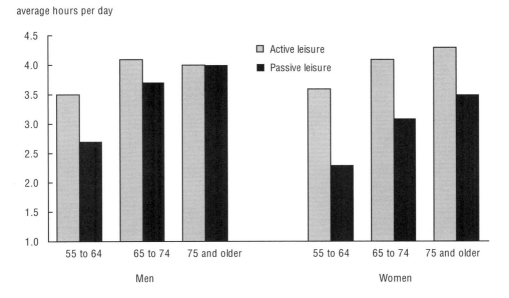

Source: Statistics Canada, Catalogue no. 89-622-XIE.

Most seniors able to get around

Most seniors in Canada have access to either private or public transportation for getting around—for shopping, getting to appointments, visiting family and friends or taking part in leisure activities.

In 2005, 98% of men and 95% of women aged 65 to 74 had access either to a vehicle in their household or to public transit. Although access to both these types of transportation is lower among seniors in older age groups, 86% of those aged 85 and older had such access in 2005.

Public transit is a satisfactory option for many people of all ages, especially those who live downtown. However, access to a private vehicle does make it much easier to get around, especially in an emergency. In 2005, 80% of all seniors had access to a household vehicle, compared with 91% of Canadians aged 55 to 64, while 71% of seniors aged 65

and older were able to drive a vehicle. Yet, proportionally fewer women aged 75 and older are able to drive.

Seniors who have a valid driver's licence and own a vehicle are the most likely to leave their home at least once each day. In fact, they are two times less likely to remain at home all day on any given day than those who do not have access to a household vehicle or public transit. Seniors with access to their own vehicle are also more likely to do volunteer work.

Very few seniors were completely without a means of transportation in 2005. However, people 85 and older, women, and seniors in rural areas are more likely to have limited transportation options.

Chart 28.6
Seniors' access to a household vehicle or public transportation, 2005

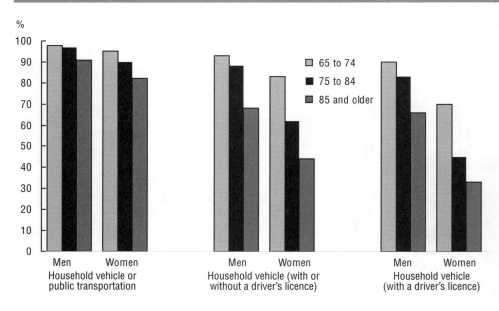

Source: Statistics Canada, Catalogue no. 11-008-XIE.

Does inflation affect seniors more?

Senior households have very different spending patterns than other households. However, inflation is not much different for seniors—prices rose 26.1% for their households from January 1992 to February 2004, compared with 24.4% for other households.

Seniors spend proportionally more on travel, recreation and sports services. The prices of some of their preferred forms of recreation have increased, such as cable subscriptions and travel. This pattern may contribute to higher inflation for senior households.

However, seniors tend to spend proportionally less on transportation items, such as new cars and gasoline, clothing and footwear, and alcohol and tobacco products. So they are less affected by changes in the prices of these products. However, the steady decline in electronic equipment prices has

done less to lower the inflation rate for senior households than for households in general. Non-senior households spend more of their income on the latest electronic gadgetry, so the ongoing price declines have helped to moderate increases in the Consumer Price Index more for all households than for senior households.

Whether seniors are homeowners or renters affects their inflation rate. From 1992 to 2004, the national rate of inflation for seniors who were renters was 22.7%, compared with 28.1% for seniors who owned their own homes.

The average inflation rate for seniors during this period ranged from 21.2% in Quebec to 32.0% in Alberta. Seniors coped with inflation at or above the national average in Nova Scotia, Ontario, Manitoba, Saskatchewan and Alberta.

Chart 28.7
Inflation rates, senior and non-senior households, by selected characteristics

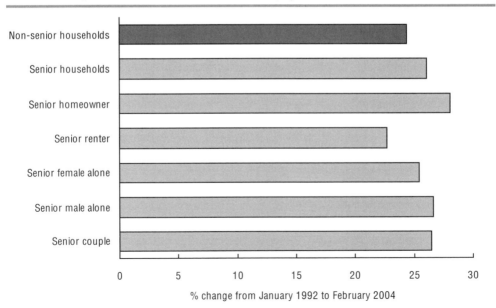

% change from January 1992 to February 2004

Source: Statistics Canada, Catalogue no. 11-621-XIE.

Table 28.1 Population estimates and projections, by age group and by province and territory, selected years from 1981 to 2026

	1981			1991		
	0 to 14	15 to 64	65 and older	0 to 14	15 to 64	65 and older
	thousands					
Canada	**5,532.4**	**16,910.7**	**2,377.3**	**5,789.8**	**19,024.3**	**3,217.3**
Newfoundland and Labrador	168.0	362.7	44.1	128.4	395.4	55.7
Prince Edward Island	30.6	78.2	15.0	29.4	83.8	17.1
Nova Scotia	199.0	562.7	92.9	185.9	614.9	114.3
New Brunswick	174.7	460.7	71.0	154.2	501.8	89.5
Quebec	1,407.7	4,566.8	573.2	1,396.7	4,885.6	782.3
Ontario	1,904.5	6,032.7	874.1	2,099.3	7,123.5	1,205.3
Manitoba	239.2	675.0	122.2	242.5	719.4	147.7
Saskatchewan	239.5	619.8	116.5	239.2	622.4	141.1
Alberta	548.8	1,580.4	165.0	611.2	1,748.6	232.9
British Columbia	598.0	1,924.7	301.2	676.4	2,268.4	428.7
Yukon	6.2	16.9	0.8	7.0	20.7	1.1
Northwest Territories (including Nunavut)	16.2	30.0	1.4	..	..	..
Northwest Territories	..	..	..	11.0	26.5	1.2
Nunavut	..	..	..	8.5	13.2	0.4
	%					
Canada	**22.3**	**68.1**	**9.6**	**20.7**	**67.9**	**11.5**
Newfoundland and Labrador	29.2	63.1	7.7	22.2	68.2	9.6
Prince Edward Island	24.7	63.2	12.1	22.5	64.3	13.1
Nova Scotia	23.3	65.8	10.9	20.3	67.2	12.5
New Brunswick	24.7	65.2	10.0	20.7	67.3	12.0
Quebec	21.5	69.7	8.8	19.8	69.2	11.1
Ontario	21.6	68.5	9.9	20.1	68.3	11.6
Manitoba	23.1	65.1	11.8	21.9	64.8	13.3
Saskatchewan	24.5	63.5	11.9	23.9	62.1	14.1
Alberta	23.9	68.9	7.2	23.6	67.4	9.0
British Columbia	21.2	68.2	10.7	20.1	67.2	12.7
Yukon	25.9	70.9	3.3	24.3	71.8	3.9
Northwest Territories (including Nunavut)	34.1	63.0	3.0	..	..	..
Northwest Territories	..	..	..	28.4	68.5	3.1
Nunavut	..	..	..	38.5	59.6	2.0

Source: Statistics Canada, CANSIM table 051-0001.

	2001			2006			2026	
0 to 14	15 to 64	65 and older	0 to 14	15 to 64	65 and older	0 to 14	15 to 64	65 and older
				thousands				
5,854.5	**21,243.7**	**3,923.1**	**5,644.6**	**22,664.6**	**4,314.2**	**5,680.5**	**24,155.9**	**8,046.2**
89.3	369.4	63.3	78.3	362.4	69.0	63.0	310.9	135.2
26.7	91.4	18.6	24.0	94.6	19.9	21.3	91.2	35.5
166.6	638.3	127.5	147.7	650.7	136.0	127.9	601.4	246.6
131.5	518.8	99.6	118.2	524.4	106.6	98.9	472.5	196.9
1,305.1	5,126.7	965.2	1,241.6	5,334.5	1,075.3	1,169.7	5,214.7	1,922.6
2,309.0	8,099.3	1,489.3	2,262.9	8,782.6	1,641.5	2,365.6	10,027.1	3,079.1
238.2	755.9	157.2	228.0	790.0	159.8	231.1	829.7	263.2
209.7	642.4	148.1	190.0	648.3	147.0	166.5	589.6	220.9
626.6	2,119.6	310.5	637.4	2,386.0	352.3	663.5	2,571.7	767.0
724.6	2,814.2	539.6	690.2	3,018.7	601.5	745.8	3,370.1	1,164.0
6.2	22.1	1.8	5.6	23.3	2.3	5.5	21.8	6.0
..	..	..	..	..	..	..	..	..
10.8	28.3	1.7	10.2	29.7	2.0	11.0	35.0	6.8
10.3	17.3	0.6	10.4	19.5	0.9	10.6	20.5	1.8
				%				
18.9	**68.5**	**12.6**	**17.3**	**69.5**	**13.2**	**15.0**	**63.8**	**21.2**
17.1	70.8	12.1	15.4	71.1	13.5	12.4	61.1	26.6
19.5	66.9	13.6	17.3	68.3	14.4	14.4	61.5	24.0
17.9	68.5	13.7	15.8	69.6	14.6	13.1	61.6	25.3
17.5	69.2	13.3	15.8	70.0	14.2	12.9	61.5	25.6
17.6	69.3	13.0	16.2	69.7	14.1	14.1	62.8	23.1
19.4	68.1	12.5	17.8	69.2	12.9	15.3	64.8	19.9
20.7	65.7	13.7	19.4	67.1	13.6	17.5	62.7	19.9
21.0	64.2	14.8	19.3	65.8	14.9	17.0	60.3	22.6
20.5	69.3	10.2	18.9	70.7	10.4	16.6	64.3	19.2
17.8	69.0	13.2	16.0	70.0	14.0	14.1	63.8	22.0
20.7	73.5	5.9	18.0	74.5	7.5	16.5	65.3	18.0
..	..	..	..	..	..	..	..	..
26.5	69.3	4.1	24.2	70.9	4.8	20.8	66.2	12.9
36.5	61.4	2.2	33.9	63.2	2.9	32.1	62.1	5.5

Table 28.2 Senior population proportion, by selected census metropolitan area, selected years from 1986 to 2006

	1986	1991	1996	2001	2006
			%		
All census metropolitan areas	**10.0**	**10.8**	**11.5**	**11.9**	**12.3**
St. John's	9.6	9.2	9.9	10.5	10.9
Halifax	8.9	9.6	10.1	10.8	11.5
Saint John	12.1	12.2	12.5	12.9	13.3
Québec	9.4	10.6	11.5	12.9	14.1
Sherbrooke	10.4	11.4	12.1	13.0	13.9
Montréal	10.1	11.1	12.0	12.7	13.4
Ottawa–Gatineau	8.8	9.4	10.1	10.5	11.3
Toronto	9.5	10.2	10.8	10.9	11.2
Thunder Bay	10.4	13.1	13.8	14.6	15.6
Winnipeg	12.1	12.7	13.2	13.4	13.3
Regina	10.4	10.8	11.6	12.3	12.8
Calgary	6.9	7.7	8.6	8.8	9.1
Vancouver	11.8	12.0	11.6	11.8	12.2
Victoria	17.9	18.3	17.5	17.2	17.2

Note: Seniors are people aged 65 and older.
Source: Statistics Canada, CANSIM table 051-0036.

Table 28.3 Life expectancy at birth and at age 65, by sex, selected years from 1921 to 2004

	Life expectancy at birth			Life expectancy at age 65		
	Both sexes	**Males**	**Females**	**Both sexes**	**Males**	**Females**
			years			
1921	59.7	58.8	60.6	13.3	13.0	13.6
1931	61.0	60.0	62.1	13.3	13.0	13.7
1941	64.6	63.0	66.3	13.4	12.8	14.1
1951	68.5	66.4	70.9	14.1	13.3	15.0
1961	71.1	68.4	74.3	14.8	13.6	16.1
1971	72.7	69.4	76.5	15.7	13.8	17.6
1981	75.4	71.9	79.1	16.8	14.6	18.9
1991	77.8	74.6	80.9	18.0	15.8	19.9
2001	79.6	77.0	82.1	19.0	17.1	20.6
2002	79.7	77.2	82.1	19.1	17.2	20.6
2003	79.9	77.4	82.4	19.2	17.4	20.8
2004	80.2	77.8	82.6	19.5	17.7	21.0

Notes: Life expectancy estimates for 1921 to 1981 are based on complete life tables.
Newfoundland and Labrador is not included in the 1921 to 1946 life expectancy estimates.
Quebec is not included in the 1921 estimates.
Source: Statistics Canada, CANSIM table 102-0511 and Catalogue no. 89-506-XPB.

Table 28.4 Income of seniors, by sex and selected income sources, selected years from 1980 to 2005

	1980	1985	1990	1995	2000	2005
			%			
Males						
Earnings	24.2	16.4	14.3	13.9	20.8	24.3
Investment income	67.4	61.7	64.9	54.9	59.2	55.1
Retirement income	39.8	45.3	53.7	56.9	68.3	69.8
Old Age Security and Guaranteed Income Supplement, Spouse's Allowance	96.0	96.8	99.0	97.4	95.1	95.7
Canada Pension Plan and Quebec Pension Plan benefits	68.6	77.7	85.3	90.2	94.1	94.3
	aggregate income in $ millions 2005 constant					
Earnings	5,909	3,802	3,433	4,084	3,574	5,633
Investment income	5,964	6,151	7,131	5,810	5,770	5,997
Retirement income	4,191	5,829	9,135	13,100	18,388	22,546
Old Age Security and Guaranteed Income Supplement, Spouse's Allowance	5,924	7,442	8,489	9,351	9,633	10,809
Canada Pension Plan and Quebec Pension Plan benefits	2,700	4,416	6,921	8,988	10,385	11,383
	average income in $ millions 2005 constant					
Earnings	25,900	21,800	19,100	20,700	10,800	13,100
Investment income	9,400	9,400	8,800	7,500	6,200	6,100
Retirement income	11,200	12,200	13,500	16,200	17,000	18,200
Old Age Security and Guaranteed Income Supplement, Spouse's Allowance	6,500	7,300	6,800	6,800	6,400	6,400
Canada Pension Plan and Quebec Pension Plan benefits	4,200	5,400	6,500	7,000	7,000	6,800
			%			
Females						
Earnings	8.7	6.2	5.1	5.2	7.9	10.8
Investment income	56.5	53.6	61.0	51.6	59.6	57.0
Retirement income	19.7	21.1	26.9	33.6	47.9	53.1
Old Age Security and Guaranteed Income Supplement, Spouse's Allowance	96.7	97.9	98.9	97.3	97.2	98.1
Canada Pension Plan and Quebec Pension Plan benefits	34.8	44.2	61.8	70.8	80.5	82.7
	aggregate income in $ millions 2005 constant					
Earnings	1,308	1,052	1,383	1,404	1,359	1,789
Investment income	5,262	6,793	9,213	6,922	6,043	5,568
Retirement income	1,683	2,180	3,888	6,113	9,660	13,034
Old Age Security and Guaranteed Income Supplement, Spouse's Allowance	8,212	10,948	12,612	13,499	13,960	15,249
Canada Pension Plan and Quebec Pension Plan benefits	1,353	2,451	4,599	6,779	8,315	9,617
	average income in $ millions 2005 constant					
Earnings	12,500	12,100	16,400	14,600	8,500	7,600
Investment income	7,800	9,000	9,100	7,200	5,000	4,400
Retirement income	7,100	7,400	8,700	9,800	10,000	11,100
Old Age Security and Guaranteed Income Supplement, Spouse's Allowance	7,100	8,000	7,700	7,500	7,100	7,100
Canada Pension Plan and Quebec Pension Plan benefits	3,300	3,900	4,500	5,200	5,100	5,300

Note: Seniors are people age 65 and older.
Source: Statistics Canada, CANSIM table 202-0407.

Table 28.5 Impact of pain on activities of older adults, by age group and sex, 2003 and 2005

	Pain or discomfort prevents a few or some activities		Pain or discomfort prevents most activities	
	2003	2005	2003	2005
	%			
Both sexes				
55 to 64	11.2	11.4	4.1	4.8
65 and older	12.7	13.1	5.0	5.8
65 to 74	11.5	12.2	4.5	4.3
75 and older	14.6	14.3	5.8	7.8
Males				
55 to 64	7.9	7.8	4.0	5.1
65 and older	8.5	8.1	4.3	4.9
65 to 74	7.4	8.5	4.0ᴱ	3.3ᴱ
75 and older	10.3	7.4	4.8ᴱ	7.5
Females				
55 to 64	14.6	15.1	4.1	4.5
65 and older	16.1	17.1	5.6	6.4
65 to 74	15.1	15.7	4.9	5.2
75 and older	17.3	18.7	6.5	7.9

Note: Pain includes discomfort.
Source: Statistics Canada, CANSIM table 105-0203.

Table 28.6 Selected chronic conditions in older adults, by age group and sex, 2005

	Arthritis or rheumatism	Asthma	High blood pressure	Diabetes
	%			
Both sexes				
45 to 64	23.5	7.1	21.7	6.9
65 and older	45.9	7.4	44.1	14.6
65 to 74	42.5	7.6	42.3	14.6
75 and older	50.5	7.2	46.6	14.6
Males				
45 to 64	18.2	5.0	22.0	7.9
65 and older	36.4	6.7	39.4	17.1
65 to 74	33.3	6.5	38.8	17.3
75 and older	41.2	7.0	40.3	16.8
Females				
45 to 64	28.7	9.2	21.3	5.9
65 and older	53.6	8.0	47.9	12.6
65 to 74	50.8	8.6	45.4	12.3
75 and older	56.8	7.3	50.8	13.1

Note: Population who reported that they have been diagnosed by a health professional as having the condition.
Source: Statistics Canada, CANSIM tables 105-0401, 105-0402, 105-0410 and 105-0411.

Table 28.7 Seniors' death rates, by selected causes of death, age group and sex, 2000 and 2004

	65 to 74		75 to 84		85 and older	
	2000	2004	2000	2004	2000	2004
	age-specific mortality rate per 100,000 population					
Both sexes						
All causes of death	4,111.4	3,684.4	10,852.9	9,972.2	32,286.4	31,269.3
Malignant neoplasms	1,674.9	1,592.4	2,917.5	2,917.6	4,172.9	4,202.3
Alzheimer's disease	36.5	32.7	306.8	284.1	1,507.8	1,539.4
Ischaemic heart diseases	807.6	612.7	2,372.5	1,873.9	7,198.4	6,524.7
Cerebrovascular diseases	216.5	168.3	938.0	758.2	3,481.2	3,033.5
Influenza and pneumonia	45.3	45.6	243.1	233.7	1,563.2	1,608.5
Chronic lower respiratory diseases	205.1	178.9	668.8	603.4	1,440.3	1,416.8
Falls	19.3	22.4	73.5	96.2	361.5	467.5
Males						
All causes of death	5,336.3	4,646.1	14,207.0	12,676.0	37,640.5	36,347.1
Malignant neoplasms	2,102.8	1,931.4	4,013.7	3,855.5	6,150.4	6,216.9
Alzheimer's disease	38.1	30.2	296.7	249.7	1,158.6	1,129.6
Ischaemic heart diseases	1,186.3	896.1	3,274.1	2,559.0	8,564.8	7,861.2
Cerebrovascular diseases	264.5	202.1	1,078.8	860.6	3,287.1	2,925.6
Influenza and pneumonia	58.7	56.1	326.9	304.2	1,952.5	2,025.7
Chronic lower respiratory diseases	260.4	217.2	1,004.6	817.8	2,554.2	2,294.6
Falls	28.8	29.1	98.0	118.6	470.4	527.5
Females						
All causes of death	3,046.8	2,821.7	8,713.8	8,147.8	30,056.8	29,133.8
Malignant neoplasms	1,304.5	1,289.0	2,216.6	2,282.2	3,366.4	3,372.5
Alzheimer's disease	35.0	34.9	312.4	306.3	1,638.8	1,692.0
Ischaemic heart diseases	477.2	358.0	1,795.0	1,411.6	6,625.3	5,959.7
Cerebrovascular diseases	175.0	138.1	847.4	688.8	3,543.6	3,072.0
Influenza and pneumonia	33.9	36.3	190.9	187.1	1,409.5	1,445.3
Chronic lower respiratory diseases	157.4	144.8	457.1	460.7	996.3	1,062.0
Falls	10.9	16.4	57.8	81.1	322.3	443.7

Notes: Age at time of death.
Seniors are people aged 65 and older.
Source: Statistics Canada, CANSIM table 102-0551.

Table 28.8 Time use of seniors, by type of activity and life satisfaction, age group and sex, 2005

	Men				Women			
	Healthy and satisfied	Less healthy and satisfied	Healthy and less satisfied	Less healthy and less satisfied	Healthy and satisfied	Less healthy and satisfied	Healthy and less satisfied	Less healthy and less satisfied
	hours per day							
Aged 65 to 74								
Paid work	F	F	F	F	F	F	F	F
Unpaid work	4.4	3.9	4.1	3.5	5.3	4.6	5.0	4.5
Self-care	11.1	11.0	11.0	11.8	11.2	11.9	11.2	12.1
Passive leisure	3.1	4.5	3.4	4.0	2.8	3.0	2.8	3.4
Cognitive leisure	2.0	1.8	1.5	1.6	2.2	1.6	2.0	1.8
Social leisure	1.7	1.7	2.0	1.4	1.7	2.3	1.7	1.8
Physical leisure	0.9	F	0.9	0.6	0.4	F	0.6	0.3
Aged 75 and older								
Paid work	F	F	F	F	F	F	F	F
Unpaid work	3.4	3.2	3.8	3.3	3.7	3.9	3.9	3.6
Self-care	12.0	12.9	11.9	12.5	12.1	12.3	12.1	12.5
Passive leisure	3.3	4.0	4.0	4.2	3.2	3.5	3.5	3.6
Cognitive leisure	1.9	1.5	1.9	1.9	2.9	2.1	2.2	1.9
Social leisure	F	1.4	F	1.3	1.7	2.0	1.8	2.1
Physical leisure	F	F	F	F	F	F	0.3	0.2

Notes: Seniors are people aged 65 years and older.
Satisfied refers to life satisfaction.
Source: Statistics Canada, Catalogue no. 89-622-XIE.

Table 28.9 Living arrangements of seniors, by age group, census years 1981, 1991 and 2001

	65 to 74			75 to 84			85 and older		
	1981	1991	2001	1981	1991	2001	1981	1991	2001
	%								
All living arrangements	100.0	100.0	100.0	100.0	100.0	100.0	100.0	100.0	100.0
Institutional	3.4	3.0	2.2	12.2	10.9	8.2	37.5	37.4	31.6
Spouse	50.9	53.3	54.4	33.6	37.3	39.9	12.7	13.6	16.2
Children or grandchildren	17.8	16.3	18.9	17.0	12.8	16.0	21.1	15.1	15.8
Alone	21.7	21.7	21.5	30.0	32.6	33.0	22.4	27.6	33.7
Others	6.2	5.7	2.9	7.2	6.5	2.8	6.3	6.3	2.6

Source: Statistics Canada, Census of Population, 1981, 1991 and 2001.

Society and community

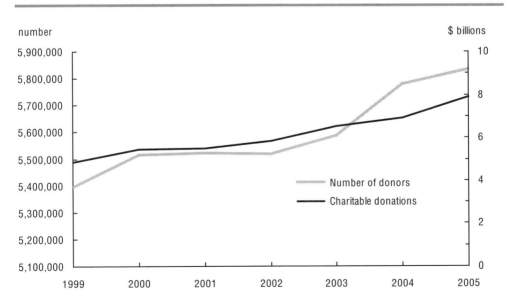

29

Social, economic and demographic changes are reshaping Canadian society. People are seeing less of their families and friends on workdays, and spending much more time alone.

Yet Canadians can generally be described as involved citizens, generous with their money and their time. Most also like to stay well informed. They consume a considerable amount of news and current affairs information. Similarly, they tend to be more involved in political activities other than voting, such as attending public meetings, searching for information on political issues, volunteering for a political party, or expressing their point of view by contacting a newspaper or politician, by signing a petition or by participating in a march or demonstration.

Charitable donations

Canadians continued in 2005 to give generously to registered charities and non-profit organizations. Over 5.8 million Canadian taxfilers donated a record $7.9 billion to charities that provide official tax receipts—almost 1% more donors, and 13.8% more in total donations compared with 2004.

Donations rose in all provinces and territories. The strongest increases were 21.1% in Alberta, 18.5% in Nova Scotia and 17.7% in Manitoba. The number of donors also grew everywhere except Saskatchewan and Newfoundland and Labrador. In those two provinces, the number of donors slipped, but not the dollars donated.

At the national level, the median total income of donors in 2005 was $45,400, up 3.9%

Chart 29.1
Charitable donors and donations, by number and amount

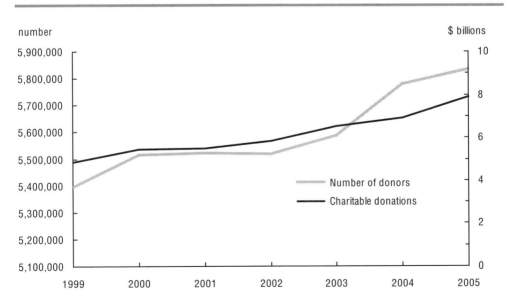

Source: Statistics Canada, CANSIM table 111-0001.

from 2004. The median donation rose 4.3% from $230 to $240.

Nunavut's donors had the highest median income in 2005, at $77,100, as well as the highest median donation, at $400. But Alberta reported the largest growth in donors' median income, 6.1%, and a 3.6% rise in median donation, from $280 to $290.

The average age of donors across the country in 2005 was 52 years, unchanged from 2004. Donors in Nova Scotia were the oldest, on average, at 55 years of age; donors in Nunavut and the Northwest Territories had the youngest average age of charitable donors, at 44 years.

Volunteering and civic participation

About 34% of Canadians said they did volunteer work in 2003. Rural residents are more likely than urban residents to do volunteering—even when factors like age, gender, household income, level of education, place of birth, province of residence and marital status are taken into account.

Sense of belonging to local community, household population aged 12 and older, 2005

	Men	Women
	%	
Very strong or somewhat strong sense of belonging	61.7	62.9
Somewhat weak sense of belonging	25.5	24.9
Very weak sense of belonging	9.2	9.4
Sense of belonging not stated	3.6	2.9

Source: Statistics Canada, CANSIM table 105-0490.

Differences between rural and urban residents narrow when it comes to involvement or membership in different types of organizations, such as professional associations, sports or recreation organizations, religious groups, or service clubs and fraternal organizations. Yet, in 2003, rural residents were more likely than urban dwellers to be involved in service clubs and fraternal organizations. Citizen involvement in the political process, such as attendance at public meetings on local affairs, is more frequent in rural areas and small towns than in large cities. In 2003, the larger the place, the lower the proportion of individuals who said that they attended a public meeting.

Chart 29.2
Selected types of organizations with which Canadians are involved, 2003

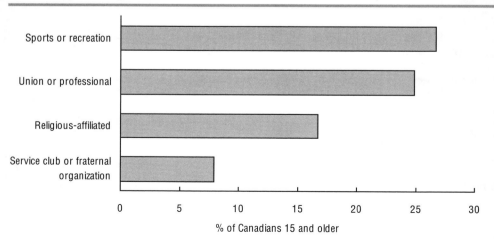

% of Canadians 15 and older

Source: Statistics Canada, Catalogue no. 89-598-XIE.

Social networks in urban and rural Canada

Many people believe that residents of large urban areas are more likely to be socially isolated or to see friends less often than those living in rural communities. That is not the case in Canada.

Granted, the social networks of Canada's urban dwellers do include a smaller slice of family and neighbours. However, their networks also include a larger slice of friends and acquaintances. Rural residents, by contrast, have a larger share of neighbours and family members in their close social networks, but the share of friends is smaller.

Isolation from family

Rural residents are no more or less likely than urban dwellers to be isolated from family. Among the Canadian-born population in 2003, an equal proportion of rural residents and urban dwellers had not seen their relatives in a month. However, the proportion of rural residents who saw their relatives a few times a week or every day was higher.

Canadians living in rural areas are just as likely as Canadians living in the country's largest census metropolitan areas (CMAs) to say they do not have any close friends. Also, rural residents are very similar to urban dwellers when it comes to the kind of help they give their friends, neighbours and relatives.

People living in Canada's large CMAs are perhaps less likely to help with transportation or domestic chores, because this kind of help is less important for people in their social networks. They are also slightly less likely than rural residents to help others in their circle with child care. However, in 2003, urban dwellers were just as likely as residents of any other area to provide emotional support, teach, coach or give practical advice, or to help a person in some other way.

Selected sources

Statistics Canada

- *Canadian Social Trends.* Irregular. 11-008-XWE

- *Perspectives on Labour and Income.* Monthly. 75-001-XIE

- *Rural and Small Town Canada Analysis Bulletin.* Occasional. 21-006-XIE

Chart 29.3
Social involvement by type of activity, 2004

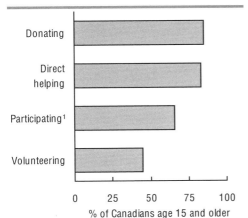

% of Canadians age 15 and older

1. Participating defined as belonging to a group or organization.
Source: Statistics Canada, Catalogue no. 71-542-XIE.

News consumption and good citizenship

Frequent news followers are more likely to be politically engaged than those who are not. Most Canadians follow the news and current affairs at least several times a week, which is an important indicator of a thriving society.

The 2003 General Social Survey found that 89% of Canadians follow news daily or several times a week. Seniors aged 65 and older are more likely to follow news on a frequent basis than young adults aged 19 to 24.

Television is the number one choice—91% of frequent users tune in. It is the top choice for women, Quebecers and those with household income below $60,000 annually.

As a news source, newspapers are chosen by 70% of frequent news followers. Reading a newspaper is most common among men and those with an income above $60,000.

Radio is the third most common news source for frequent news followers—53% listen to it. Seniors listen to the radio at a much higher rate of 83%.

The Internet is especially popular among young people: 42% of them use it, compared with 9% of seniors and 30% of all frequent news followers. Men are more likely to turn to the Internet for news, as are higher-income Canadians. Immigrants are also more likely to turn to it, as coverage is more likely to be deeper and available in their preferred language.

Canadians who follow news via several media are more likely to engage in other political activities in addition to voting—for example, attending a public meeting or volunteering for a political party. Those who choose television as their only news source tend to participate less.

Chart 29.4
Main sources of news for frequent news followers, 2003

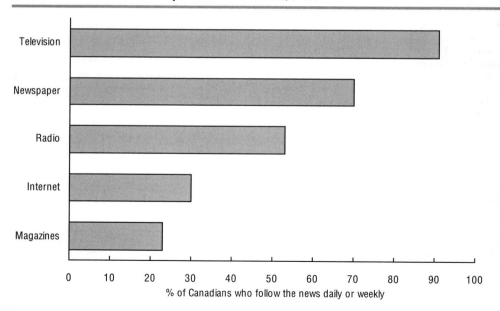

Note: Canadians aged 19 and older.
Source: Statistics Canada, Catalogue no. 11-008-XIE.

Converging gender roles

Canadian women participate in the labour force at a rate nearly equal to men. In fact, their participation rate for paid work is one of the highest in the world. But does that mean that their partners are sharing more of the housework?

Today's couples aged 25 to 54 have a more equal partnership in the sharing of financial, child care and household responsibilities. However, gender differences in the division of labour are still evident, if diminishing.

Women continue to do significantly more housework than men. In 1986, 54% of men did some housework daily; by 2005, 69% did so. Women's participation in daily housework remained steady at around 90%. Men's involvement in child care has also grown.

Interestingly, although more people are doing housework and the trend is toward larger homes, the time they spend doing housework

has decreased. One reason could be today's services-oriented economy. Canadians are hiring others to do housecleaning, snow removal and groundskeeping, and are availing themselves of time-saving appliances, pre-packaged foods and take-out meals. As well, housework standards appear to have relaxed as people's priorities have shifted.

In dual-earner families, men's participation in housework has grown from 70% in 1992 to 74% in 2005, whereas women's has dropped from 94% to 90%.

Dual-earner couples feel more time-stressed—particularly the women in these couples. However, despite the pressures of trying to maintain a work–life balance, most dual-earner couples in Canada are satisfied with their life as a whole.

Chart 29.5
Time spent on paid work and housework in dual-earner families, by type of work

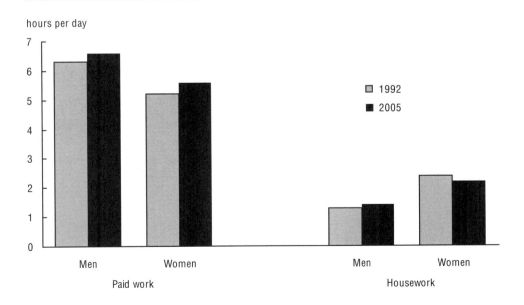

Source: Statistics Canada, Catalogue no. 75-001-XIE.

Less family time

Working Canadians are spending less time with family, and the decrease is widespread. It affects men, women, workers living with a spouse only and those living with children, workers with a college degree and those who have not completed high school. Workers living with one child under five spend the most time with family; lone parents living with a youth or young adult spend the least.

From 1986 to 2005, the average time workers spent with family members on a typical workday dropped from 250 minutes per day to 206 minutes per day. And workers are not replacing family time with friends—that also dropped, from 44 minutes to 19 minutes.

Average time devoted to paid employment has risen significantly, from 506 minutes to 536 minutes. As well, workers are spending more time alone—an average 174 minutes per day in solitary activities in 2005,

compared with 133 minutes per day in 1986. Nevertheless, in 2005, about one in three workers said they would like more time alone. Time alone does not count solitary time on the job.

Five trends have cut into family time since 1986. First, workers are far more likely to have at least one meal, snack or coffee alone—27% in 2005 compared with only 17% in 1986. Second, the average time spent at meals outside work hours has decreased from 60 minutes to 45 minutes. Third, more workers are watching television alone—27% in 2005 versus 17% in 1986. Fourth, workers are spending more time on personal care, such as washing, dressing and sleeping, rather than with family. And fifth, workers are spending less than half the time they did in 1986 on social activities outside the home.

Chart 29.6
Average time spent with family, by age group

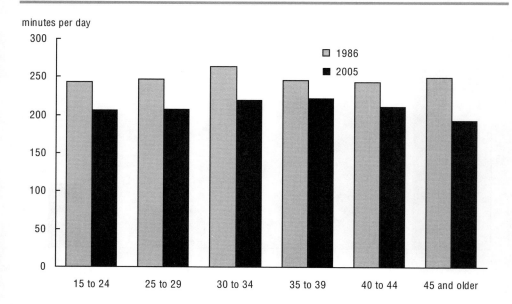

minutes per day

Source: Statistics Canada, Catalogue no. 11-008-XIE.

Interreligious unions on the rise

Interreligious unions are on the rise in Canada — not a surprise given the country's increasing cultural diversity and declining religious affiliation. Still, four out of five couples are made up of partners from the same religious group.

In 1981, just 15% of Canadians in couples had an interreligious union, either marriage or common-law. By 2001, interreligious unions had grown to 19% of couples—of the 14.1 million Canadians in couples, 2.7 million had a partner from a different broad religious group.

Half of all interreligious unions, or 1.3 million, are between Catholics and Protestants, the two largest religious groups in Canada. These unions are not evenly distributed geographically, as the availability of same-faith partners tends to lower the frequency of interreligious unions. For

example, 83% of the population in Quebec is Catholic and 5% is Protestant: only 2% of Catholics are in Catholic/Protestant interreligious unions. In Ontario, where there are nearly equal numbers of Catholics and Protestants, 18% of Catholics in couples are in interreligious unions with a Protestant.

Highly religious people and those with more traditional doctrine are less likely to have an interreligious union. For instance, only 13% of conservative Protestants have one, whereas 23% of mainline Protestants do.

Orthodox Christians are more likely today to be in interreligious unions, especially with Catholics. Jews, meanwhile, are tending toward more interreligious unions, particularly with Catholics and Protestants. For Buddhists, the most frequent interreligious union is with a partner who has no religion. Sikhs, Muslims and Hindus are least likely to be in interreligious unions.

Chart 29.7
People in interreligious unions, by age group

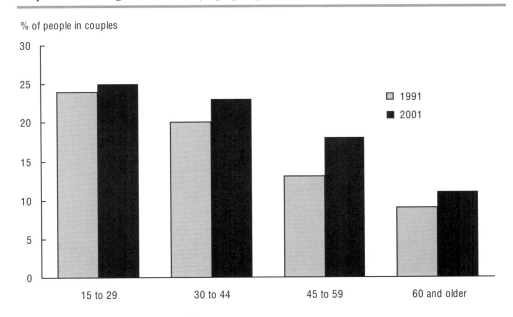

% of people in couples

Source: Statistics Canada, Catalogue 11-008-XIE.

Table 29.1 Charitable giving, by selected characteristics of donors and by province and territory, 2005

	Canada	Newfoundland and Labrador	Prince Edward Island	Nova Scotia	New Brunswick
	number				
All taxfilers[1]	23,311,690	390,770	102,870	685,500	563,240
All donors	5,833,930	83,420	27,030	162,830	130,620
	%				
Males					
Taxfilers[1]	48	49	48	48	49
Donors	56	60	54	55	56
Females					
Taxfilers[1]	52	51	52	52	51
Donors	44	40	46	45	44
	years				
Average age of donors[2]	52	54	54	55	54
	%				
Age group of donors[2]					
0 to 24	3	1	2	2	2
25 to 34	12	9	10	9	11
35 to 44	20	18	18	17	18
45 to 54	23	24	23	23	23
55 to 64	18	23	21	21	21
65 and older	24	23	25	28	25
	$				
Average donation by age group of donors[2]					
0 to 24	490	330	240	290	410
25 to 34	820	480	390	540	600
35 to 44	1,200	620	680	850	870
45 to 54	1,400	860	800	1,100	1,100
55 to 64	1,500	990	1,000	1,200	1,300
65 and older	1,700	1,000	1,600	1,600	1,500
Median total income of donors[3,4]	45,400	34,400	36,700	40,800	38,000
Median donation, both sexes[4]	240	320	340	280	280
Males	260	340	390	310	320
Females	210	280	290	260	240
	$ thousands				
Total charitable donations	7,879,588	69,933	26,256	184,297	148,430
Males	5,293,624	47,615	15,439	119,708	95,883
Females	2,585,965	22,317	10,817	64,588	52,547

Notes: Charitable giving is the allowable portion of total donations, as reported on the income tax return.

A donor is defined as a taxfiler reporting a charitable donation amount on line 340 of the personal income tax form.

1. Taxfilers are people who filed a tax return for the reference year and were alive at the end of the year.

2. Characteristics such as age are as of December 31 of the reference year.

3. Total income is income from all sources. Median income is rounded to the nearest hundred dollars.

4. Zero values are not included in the calculation of medians for individuals.

Source: Statistics Canada, CANSIM tables 111-0001 and 111-0002.

Quebec	Ontario	Manitoba	Saskatchewan	Alberta	British Columbia	Yukon	Northwest Territories	Nunavut
				number				
5,766,410	8,804,910	832,510	706,360	2,375,330	3,019,590	21,630	27,050	15,520
1,290,340	2,389,140	236,620	185,660	601,180	715,940	4,680	4,760	1,710
				%				
49	48	48	48	49	48	50	51	50
58	56	55	55	58	54	46	52	49
51	52	52	52	51	52	50	49	50
42	44	45	45	42	46	54	48	51
				years				
53	52	52	54	50	53	49	44	44
				%				
3	3	4	3	4	3	2	4	5
11	13	12	11	15	11	13	20	23
19	20	19	17	21	19	22	27	23
25	23	23	23	25	23	31	28	26
19	17	17	17	16	19	20	15	18
24	24	25	29	20	26	12	5	6
				$				
150	600	640	680	630	570	290	240	430
290	1,000	970	750	980	880	550	690	790
500	1,500	1,500	1,100	1,500	1,300	700	920	1,200
560	1,800	1,800	1,300	2,100	1,600	1,100	1,300	1,800
600	1,800	1,800	1,400	2,300	1,600	1,300	1,700	1,800
810	1,900	1,800	1,500	2,600	1,900	1,300	1,600	980
42,700	48,600	40,000	40,300	50,300	44,800	56,000	73,800	77,100
120	300	300	300	290	300	220	210	400
140	330	350	330	340	340	260	250	420
100	270	260	270	250	260	200	180	370
				$ thousands				
738,774	3,869,951	376,491	235,751	1,116,053	1,101,549	4,595	5,216	2,292
495,270	2,587,602	257,472	151,460	794,400	721,916	2,594	3,031	1,232
243,504	1,282,348	119,019	84,291	321,653	379,632	2,001	2,185	1,060

Table 29.2 Charitable giving, by selected characteristics of donors, 2000 to 2005

	2000	2001	2002	2003	2004	2005
	number					
All taxfilers[1]	21,611,830	21,886,860	21,979,210	22,465,770	22,725,310	23,311,690
All donors	5,516,420	5,521,780	5,520,560	5,588,590	5,781,250	5,833,930
	%					
Males						
Taxfilers[1]	49	49	49	49	48	48
Donors	57	57	57	57	56	56
Females						
Taxfilers[1]	51	51	51	51	52	52
Donors	43	43	43	43	44	44
	years					
Average age of donors[2]	52	52	52	52	52	52
	%					
Age group of donors[2]						
0 to 24	3	3	3	3	3	3
25 to 34	13	12	12	12	12	12
35 to 44	22	22	21	21	20	20
45 to 54	23	23	23	23	23	23
55 to 64	15	16	16	17	18	18
65 and older	24	24	24	24	24	24
	$					
Average donations by age group of donors[2]						
0 to 24	340	360	380	470	460	490
25 to 34	510	520	590	700	700	820
35 to 44	840	860	940	1,000	1,000	1,200
45 to 54	1,000	1,100	1,100	1,200	1,300	1,400
55 to 64	1,100	1,100	1,200	1,300	1,300	1,500
65 and older	1,300	1,300	1,300	1,400	1,500	1,700
Median total income of donors[3,4]	39,300	40,300	41,200	42,400	43,700	45,400
Total median donations, both sexes[4]	190	200	210	220	230	240
Males	210	220	230	240	250	260
Females	170	180	180	200	200	210
	$ thousands					
Total charitable donations	5,438,672	5,514,371	5,847,068	6,513,013	6,922,616	7,879,588
Males	3,636,560	3,715,250	3,940,147	4,389,106	4,591,471	5,293,624
Females	1,802,112	1,799,121	1,906,921	2,123,908	2,331,145	2,585,965

Notes: Charitable giving is the allowable portion of total donations, as reported on the income tax return.

A donor is defined as a taxfiler reporting a charitable donation amount on line 340 of the personal income tax form.

1. Taxfilers are people who filed a tax return for the reference year and were alive at the end of the year.

2. Characteristics such as age are as of December 31 of the reference year.

3. Total income is income from all sources.

4. Median income is rounded to the nearest hundred dollars. Zero values are not included in the calculation of medians for individuals.

Source: Statistics Canada, CANSIM tables 111-0001 and 111-0002.

Table 29.3 Average time spent with family by workers on a typical work day, by selected characteristics of workers, 1986 and 2005

	1986	2005	Change from 1986 to 2005
	minutes		
All workers	250	206	-44
Age			
15 to 24	243	207	n.s.[1]
25 to 29	247	208	-39
30 to 34	264	220	-44
35 to 39	246	223	-23
40 to 44	243	212	-31
45 and older	249	194	-54
Sex			
Women	248	209	-39
Men	250	205	-45
Region of residence			
Atlantic Canada	258	220	-38
Quebec	237	209	-28
Ontario	254	205	-50
Prairies	255	207	-48
British Columbia	250	201	-49
Family structure			
Spouse, no children	231	191	-40
Spouse, youngest child under 5	274	244	-30
Spouse, youngest child aged 5 to 12	271	227	-44
Spouse, youngest child aged 13 to 24	247	198	-49
Lone parent, youngest child under 5	346	251	-95
Lone parent, youngest child aged 5 to 12	243	196	n.s.[1]
Lone parent, youngest child aged 13 to 24	150	132	n.s.[1]
Highest level of schooling			
Elementary school	252	210	-42
Secondary diploma	254	203	-50
College or trade school diploma or certificate	243	205	-38
University degree	241	211	-30

1. n.s. indicates that the change from 1986 to 2005 is not statistically significant at the $p < 0.01$ threshold.
Source: Statistics Canada, Catalogue no. 11-008-XIE.

Table 29.4 Average time spent with family by workers on typical workdays, by selected activities of workers, 1986 and 2005

	Average time spent with the family		
	1986	2005	Change from 1986 to 2005
		minutes	
All workers	250	206	-44
Time spent on work and work-related activities			
3 to 5 hours	379	345	n.s.[1]
5 to 6 hours	341	307	n.s.[1]
6 to 7 hours	279	270	n.s.[1]
7 to 8 hours	270	236	34
8 to 9 hours	260	219	41
9 to 10 hours	220	202	18
10 to 11 hours	206	164	42
11 hours or more	118	107	n.s.[1]
Time spent on personal care including sleep			
Less than 7 hours	303	244	-58
7 to 8 hours	257	216	-40
8 to 9 hours	250	213	-37
9 to 10 hours	228	185	-43
10 to 11 hours	208	179	n.s.[1]
11 hours or more	189	143	n.s.[1]
Time for meals at home, snacks, coffee			
Did not eat at home	169	200	n.s.[1]
1 to 24 minutes	233	183	-51
25 to 44 minutes	227	196	-31
45 to 64 minutes	245	211	-35
65 minutes or more	285	233	-53
Trips by car or public transport			
No trips either by car or public transport	242	201	-42
1 to 60 minutes	248	196	-52
61 to 120 minutes	246	216	-30
121 minutes or more	273	221	-52
Time spent watching television, including watching videos or DVDs			
No television	218	184	-34
1 to 60 minutes	236	193	-43
61 to 120 minutes	241	216	-25
121 to 180 minutes	260	228	-32
181 minutes or more	323	256	-67

1. n.s. indicates that the change from 1986 to 2005 is not statistically significant at the p < 0.01 threshold.
Source: Statistics Canada, Catalogue no. 11-008-XIE.

Table 29.5 Disability-related work limitations, 2001

	Total employed	Degree of disability		
		Mild	Moderate	Severe / very severe
		thousands		
Total disabled people	817.0	379.8	242.7	194.5
		%		
Disability affects work or school				
Sometimes	33.5	32.7	41.1	25.5
Often	25.4	8.0	28.0	56.4
Never	34.5	53.0	26.6	8.2
Not applicable	5.9	5.4E	3.7E	9.5
Changes made at work because of disability				
Change type of work	33.5	22.3	40.3	46.9
Change amount of work	42.9	29.2	47.6	63.6
Change job	28.2	19.6	32.6	39.3
Disability limits duties at work	51.4	34.9	56.7	77.0
Attitude concerning disability				
Consider self to be disadvantaged in employment	34.3	17.2	41.0	59.1
Considered disadvantaged by employer	35.4	19.3	41.3	59.5
Disability makes it difficult to change jobs or advance				
Very difficult	20.9	8.0	20.0	47.4
Difficult	23.0	15.9	31.9	25.6
Not difficult	49.3	68.8	41.2	21.3
Lost opportunities because of disability, in the previous five years				
Refused employment	10.6	4.3	12.5	20.8
Refused a promotion	5.9	2.6E	7.0	11.0
Refused access to training	2.8	1.2E	2.0E	6.9
Terminated from job	6.6	3.6E	7.0	12.0

Note: Population aged 15 to 64.

Table 29.6 Average time spent on selected activities by workers on a typical workday, 1986, 1992, 1998 and 2005

	1986	1992	1998	2005
	minutes			
Work and work-related activities	506	523	528	536
Personal care including sleep	491	484	488	500
Meals at home, snacks, coffee	60	52	44	45
Trips by car or public transport	66	68	72	73
Trips by foot	5	5	5	3
Social activities outside the home	23	16	14	11
Reading books, magazines, newspapers	18	17	15	10
Watching television, watching videos or DVDs	95	89	84	79

Source: Statistics Canada, Catalogue no. 11-008-XIE.

Table 29.7 Interreligious couples, by selected religious faith groups, 1981, 1991 and 2001

	Both sexes			Men	Women
	1981	1991	2001	2001	
	%				
All religious faith groups	**15**	**17**	**19**	**19**	**19**
Catholic	12	14	16	15	17
Protestant	14	17	21	19	23
Mainline Protestant[1]	15	19	23	21	25
Conservative Protestant[2]	9	11	13	11	15
Other Protestant	15	22	25	23	27
Orthodox Christian	23	25	26	27	24
Other Christian religions	19	18	18	15	20
Muslim	13	11	9	11	6
Jewish	9	12	17	19	16
Buddhist	19	16	19	16	22
Hindu	11	10	9	9	8
Sikh	4	4	3	4	3
Other Eastern religions	26	24	27	25	29
Other religions[3]	41	41	46	40	50
No religion	38	27	25	32	17

Note: Interreligious couples are people who are married to or living in a common-law union with a spouse who belongs to a different religious faith group.

1. Mainline Protestant includes Anglican, Lutheran, Presbyterian and United Church.
2. Conservative Protestant includes Baptist, Pentecostal, Nazarene, Evangelical Free, Mennonite, Salvation Army, Reformed, Christian and Missionary Alliance and other small protestant groups.
3. Other religions includes New Age, Aboriginal Spirituality, Pagan, Scientology, Satanist, Wicca, Gnostic, Rastafarian, Unity, New Thought, Pantheist and other small religious groups.

Source: Statistics Canada, Catalogue no. 11-008-XIE.

Table 29.8 Participation in, and time spent on, paid work, housework and other unpaid work, by activity and by sex, 1992, 1998 and 2005

	Men aged 25 to 54			Women aged 25 to 54		
	1992	1998	2005	1992	1998	2005
	average number of hours per day[1], participants[2] and non-participants					
Total paid and unpaid work	**8.6**	**8.9**	**8.8**	**8.4**	**8.5**	**8.8**
Paid work and related activities	6.1	6.3	6.3	3.6	4.0	4.4
Work	5.1	5.1	5.3	3.0	3.2	3.7
Related activities	0.6	0.6	0.4	0.3	0.4	0.3
Commute	0.5	0.5	0.6	0.3	0.3	0.4
Housework	1.4	1.4	1.4	2.9	2.6	2.4
Core	0.5	0.7	0.7	2.3	2.2	1.9
Non-core	0.9	0.7	0.7	0.6	0.5	0.5
Other unpaid	1.1	1.2	1.1	1.9	2.0	1.9
Child care	0.4	0.5	0.5	1.0	1.0	1.0
Shopping and services	0.6	0.7	0.6	0.9	1.0	0.9
	average hours per day[1], participants[2]					
Total paid and unpaid work	**8.9**	**9.1**	**9.2**	**8.5**	**8.6**	**8.9**
Paid work and related activities	9.4	9.5	9.7	8.0	8.2	8.5
Work	8.1	8.1	8.5	6.9	7.1	7.5
Related activities	1.2	1.3	1.1	1.0	1.0	1.1
Commute	0.8	0.9	1.0	0.7	0.8	0.9
Housework	2.0	1.8	2.1	3.1	2.8	2.8
Core	1.0	1.0	1.2	2.6	2.4	2.3
Non-core	2.3	2.2	2.5	1.6	1.4	1.8
Other unpaid	2.1	2.1	2.2	2.8	2.8	2.9
Child care	1.6	1.8	1.8	2.2	2.3	2.5
Shopping and services	1.8	1.7	1.9	2.0	1.9	2.0
	% of population who did the work or activity					
Total paid and unpaid work	**96**	**98**	**96**	**99**	**99**	**98**
Paid work and related activities	65	67	65	45	48	51
Work	63	63	62	43	46	49
Related activities	48	51	39	33	36	30
Commute	57	59	58	40	43	46
Housework	67	77	69	93	94	89
Core	52	69	59	91	92	85
Non-core	38	36	31	37	42	35
Other unpaid	51	56	49	68	71	66
Child care	28	30	27	44	43	39
Shopping and services	33	39	31	47	51	45

1. Time averaged over seven days; numbers may not add because of rounding.

2. Includes only those who actually did the work activity.

Source: Statistics Canada, Catalogue no. 75-001-XIE.

Table 29.9 Characteristics of Canadians who follow the news frequently, by media source, 2003

	All media sources	Television	Radio	Newspaper	Magazines	Internet	Average number of sources used
				%			
All frequent news users[1]	89	91	53	70	23	30	2.67
Age group							
19 to 24	79	86	41	66	20	42	2.55
25 to 44	87	89	54	67	21	38	2.70
45 to 64	93	92	57	73	25	27	2.73
65 and older	95	95	83	74	24	9	2.55
Sex							
Women	88	92	52	68	22	24	2.58
Men	91	90	54	73	24	36	2.76
Marital status							
Married/common-law	91	91	56	72	23	30	2.71
Other	86	89	49	68	21	30	2.58
Highest level of education							
No postsecondary	87	93	47	64	16	12	2.32
Some postsecondary	91	89	57	73	26	39	2.81
Occupation type							
Professional/manager	93	91	60	75	30	48	3.04
Other occupations	88	88	52	69	21	24	2.58
Household Income							
Less than $29,999	87	93	48	61	18	20	2.40
$30,000 to $59,999	89	91	53	68	21	27	2.59
$60,000 and more	92	87	59	76	28	41	2.92
Not stated	87	92	49	69	19	21	2.50
Born in Canada							
Yes	89	91	54	71	23	28	2.67
No	90	90	52	67	20	36	2.68
Language used at home							
English	89	89	57	75	25	32	2.79
French	91	94	44	61	19	21	2.39
Other	87	90	49	62	18	34	2.53
Region							
Atlantic	88	91	58	67	17	24	2.57
Quebec	91	94	46	62	19	23	2.44
Ontario	90	89	55	74	24	34	2.75
Prairies	88	90	56	74	24	29	2.73
British Columbia	88	89	57	75	27	36	2.81
Urban/rural area							
Montréal	91	93	48	63	21	29	2.53
Toronto	92	90	55	73	24	39	2.80
Vancouver	89	88	57	74	25	39	2.83
Other census metropolitan areas	89	89	54	73	24	32	2.73
Census agglomerations	88	92	53	74	23	26	2.67
Rural	87	92	54	64	20	19	2.48

Note: Population age 19 and older; excludes the territories.

1. Those who follow the news and current affairs at least several times a week.

Source: Statistics Canada, Catalogue no. 11-008-XIE.

Transportation

Canada is a large country geographically, has a wealth of natural resources and is highly urbanized. So Canadians must rely on many modes of transportation to ship raw materials and finished goods around the country and to markets abroad.

Our system has more than 1.4 million kilometres of roads, 10 major international airports, 300 smaller airports, 72,093 kilometres of functioning railroad track, and more than 300 commercial ports and harbours that provide access to three oceans, the Great Lakes and the St. Lawrence Seaway.

Despite a jump in fuel prices in 2005, demand for transportation services in Canada increased. A strong economy prompted a recovery of trucking and rail in 2004. Air transportation turned around in 2005, following three consecutive years of decline after the attacks of September 11, 2001.

Shipments from overseas have also played a role in boosting the transportation industry. Port activity surged in 2004 thanks to increased demand for goods, particularly for products made in Asia.

Trucking makes gains

A healthy economy and higher wholesale and retail sales drove the demand for trucking services in 2005, which grew despite rising fuel costs. More than one-third of the gross domestic product (GDP) generated by transportation in 2005 came from trucking.

Trucking of goods within provinces accounted for more than two-thirds of the trucking industry's growth in 2005 and more than half its growth since 2002. From 1990 to 2003, the amount of freight carried by for-hire trucking grew nearly three times faster

Chart 30.1
Freight carried, by mode of transport, 2003

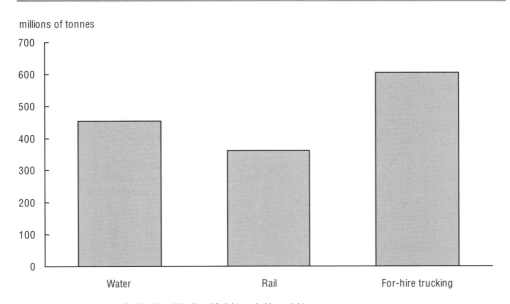

millions of tonnes

	Water	Rail	For-hire trucking

Note: Air transport accounts for less than 1% of total freight carried by weight.
Source: Statistics Canada, CANSIM tables 404-0016 and 403-0001, and Catalogue no. 16-201-XIE.

than that carried by all other transportation modes combined.

For-hire trucking contributed most of the growth in 2005, generating $27 billion in revenues. From 2002 to 2005, for-hire trucking companies based in Canada saw their revenues increase an average 9.8% a year. During that same period, manufacturing output increased 3.6%, wholesale trade, 4.7% and retail trade, 4.8%.

In 2005, fuel made up 11.6% of total operating expenditures, only a slight increase compared with 2004. However, the fleet owners' most costly expenditure was labour.

Rail loads increase

The rail industry posted gains for a second consecutive year in 2005, moving the largest total freight tonnage since 2000. Rising demand in Canada for manufactured goods from China and other Asian countries increased the tonnage carried by rail from Canada's ports.

Export shipments of lumber, iron ore concentrates and coal rose, whereas wheat

Chart 30.2
Railway container cargo shipments

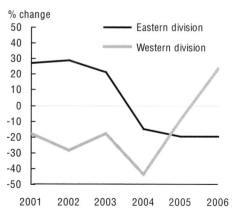

% change

Eastern division
Western division

Note: The Eastern and Western Divisions are separated by an imaginary line running from Thunder Bay to Armstrong, Ontario.
Source: Statistics Canada, CANSIM table 404-0002.

GDP of the transportation industries by mode of transport, 2005

	Share of transportation GDP	Growth rate from 2004
	%	
Total	**100**	**5**
Air	9	12
Rail	13	5
Water	3	3
Truck	35	4
Transit and ground passenger	12	3
Pipeline	11	3
Scenic and sightseeing transportation and support activities	17	3

Source: Statistics Canada, CANSIM table 379-0017.

and potash shipments fell. In 2005, railways loaded more than 288.6 million tonnes of goods, an increase of 3.6% or 10.1 million tonnes compared with 2004.

Western Canada's containerized cargo shipments rose faster than those of the provinces east of Manitoba, due in part to growing shipments to and from the Far East.

Ports are booming

Traffic through Canadian ports increased in 2004. Ports handled an estimated 452.3 million tonnes of goods, up from 443.8 million in 2003. Marine transportation carried 48% of the value of Canadian international trade and was the main mode for shipping freight overseas.

Cross-border marine traffic between Canada and the United States totalled 123.3 million tonnes, virtually unchanged from 2003. Shipping activity with foreign countries (excluding the United States) rose to 191.3 million tonnes, a rise of 4.3% from 2003.

Marine trade between Canada and foreign countries (excluding the United States) was $101.2 billion in 2004, with exports accounting for $40 billion of this amount and imports accounting for $61 billion.

Most Canadian exports in 2004, as measured by weight, were destined for the United States, Asia and Europe, and were predominantly iron ore and concentrates, crude petroleum and coal. The majority of cargo brought into Canada came from the United States and Europe. The bulk of these shipments were coal, crude petroleum and iron ore and concentrates.

The five most active ports in 2004 were, by weight of shipments handled: Vancouver, Come by Chance, N.L., Saint John, N.B., Port Hawkesbury, N.S. and Montréal/Contrecoeur.

Air traffic grows

The commercial air transport industry grew in 2005, ending three years of decline that followed the events of September 11, 2001. Following a 7.9% gain in 2004, the air transport industry's GDP jumped 11.8% in 2005, and generated nearly $4.2 billion. That was slightly below the $4.3 billion in 2000.

There were more commercial domestic flights in 2005 than in 2000. Available seats fell to 63.5 million in 2005, down from 71.4 million in 1995. The loss of two small carriers—one

in 2004 and the other in 2005—contributed to the decrease in seats and, possibly, to a rise in fares.

The increase in flights and decrease in seats resulted from major changes in the air carriers' fleets. They have been replacing larger aircraft with greater seating capacities with smaller, more fuel-efficient planes. At the same time, the major Canadian airlines are increasing the number of passengers carried by flying with higher load factors, that is, a greater number of passengers per flight.

The airports in Canada with the greatest number of flights in 2005 were:

- Lester B. Pearson International Airport, Toronto, more than 411,000 flights;
- Vancouver International Airport, 323,000;
- Calgary International Airport, 229,000;
- Pierre Elliott Trudeau Airport in Montréal, 208,000.

Selected sources

Statistics Canada

- *An Analysis of the Transportation Industry in 2005.* Occasional. 11-621-MWE

- *Aviation Service Bulletin.* Irregular. 51-004-XIB

- *Human Activity and the Environment: Annual Statistics.* Annual. 16-201-XWE

- *Perspectives on Labour and Income.* Quarterly. 75-001-XIE.

- *Trucking in Canada.* Annual. 53-222-XIE

Other

- Transport Canada

Chart 30.3
Air passengers

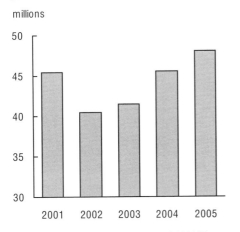

millions

Source: Statistics Canada, Catalogue no. 51-004-XIE.

Help wanted: truck drivers

The trucking industry has grown steadily since the late 1980s, a result of the 1989 Canada–U.S. Free Trade Agreement. However, the increasing demand for truck transportation, an aging work force and a waning interest in the occupation by young people are contributing to a potential shortage of qualified drivers.

In 2004, there were 271,000 people working as truckers in Canada, up 28% from 1987. Approximately 80% are salaried employees and the others are owner-operators. Men make up 97% of the trucker population. They tend to be less educated than men in the work force in general. Still, full-time truckers in 2004 had average earnings of $41,100 per year, more than the average $40,500 for all workers in Canada. But it was only slightly more than the truck drivers' 1998 salary figures, when adjusted for inflation.

Stagnant earnings growth aside, trucking is appealing less to younger workers possibly because of its long hours, irregular schedules, fewer benefits and the attractiveness of competing jobs. Adding to recruitment problems are minimum age regulations on trucking licences and higher insurance premiums for male drivers under 25.

In 1987, the average age of a trucker was 37; by 2004, it was 42 for wage-earning truckers and 45 for owner-operators. In 2004, for the first time, truckers aged 55 and over outnumbered those under 30. In addition, 18% of truckers are over 55 compared with 13% of the general work force.

A 2003 industry study estimated that an average of 37,300 new drivers are needed annually until 2008 to keep up with industry growth, retirements and other people leaving the industry.

Chart 30.4
Distribution of workers, all occupations and truckers by age group, 2004

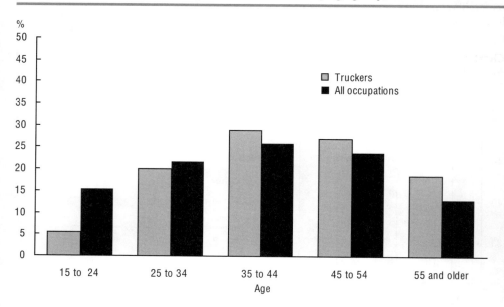

Source: Statistics Canada, Catalogue no. 75-001-XIE.

Transportation's economic importance

Much of the transportation industry is 'for hire': the driver and vehicle are hired to move goods from factory to store or to move a family's possessions across the country. There is also 'own-account' transportation, where a company uses its own vehicles to carry, for example, produce from a main terminal to a grocery store.

In 2000, for-hire transportation services accounted for 3.7% of Canada's economic output. When own-account services are included, the economic importance of transportation rises to 6.3%. In total, the transportation industry contributes $64 billion to the economy, of which own-account services account for $27 billion.

However, even including own-account services, the industry represents a smaller share of the Canadian economy than manufacturing or public administration.

Firms that provide their own-account transportation spend 89% of their costs on trucks and delivery vans. The remaining 11% goes to spending on air, rail, water, bus and other ground transportation. Only 45% of for-hire transportation costs go to trucks and delivery vans.

The remaining for-hire spending is a complex intermodal mix: other transportation services (including freight forwarders, customs brokers, packing and crating), 22%; air, 13%; rail, 11%; urban, interurban and other ground transportation, 7%; and water, 2%.

Nationally, industries spent an estimated 3.4 cents on transportation for every dollar of output in 2000. Wholesalers have the highest demand for transportation services, spending 10.3 cents on transport for every dollar of output. Retailers follow at 7.6 cents.

Chart 30.5
Share of GDP, selected industries, 2000

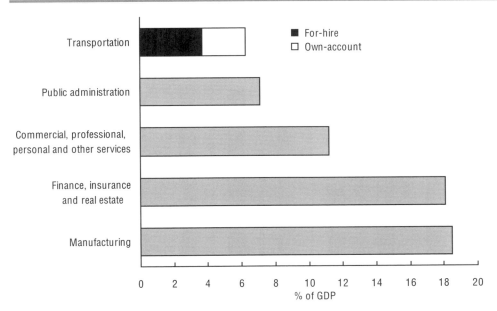

Source: Statistics Canada, Catalogue no. 13-597-XIE.

Gas consumption and the price of gas

Canadian motorists took a hit at the pumps in 2005. They could blame conflict in the Middle East, hurricanes Katrina and Rita in the Gulf of Mexico, and an aging northern pipeline for the higher gas prices.

The higher prices coincided with lower consumption, as drivers bought less gas for their vehicles—the first major decline in gross gasoline sales since 1994. Exceptions were Prince Edward Island, where the provincial government controls the price of gas, and Alberta, where there is no provincial sales tax.

Gasoline prices across Canada peaked in September 2005. In Montréal, they averaged 118.5 cents a litre for regular unleaded gas at self-service stations. Prices averaged 107.2 cents in Toronto and 102.2 cents in Edmonton. By contrast, prices in August 2002 averaged 75.3 cents a litre in Montréal, 70.3 cents in Toronto and 68.8 cents in Edmonton.

In 2005, drivers bought 39.8 billion litres of gasoline, down 1.4% from 40.3 billion litres in 2004. A 0.1% dip occurred in 2001, when the attacks of September 11 disrupted the transportation industry.

Gas sales increased in 2005 in two provinces: sales rose 4.1% in Prince Edward Island and 0.6% in Alberta. However, if growth of vehicle registrations is factored in, gas sales per vehicle decreased 3.5% in Alberta by from 1,563 litres per vehicle in 2004 to 1,509 litres in 2005.

The biggest drop in gross sales per vehicle occurred in Saskatchewan—down 16.7% from 2,038 litres per vehicle to 1,697 litres. Gross gas sales decreased 3.0% in Ontario and 2.8% in Quebec. In 1999, Ontario and Quebec had the highest gross gasoline sales, whereas Prince Edward Island, the Northwest Territories and Yukon had significantly higher gas sales per vehicle.

Chart 30.6
Average retail price of gasoline, selected census metropolitan areas

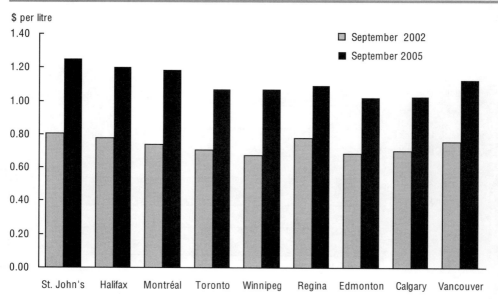

Note: Regular unleaded gasoline at self-service filling stations.
Source: Statistics Canada, CANSIM table 326-0009.

Moving cargo by rail

Every day, freight trains chug through our communities, hauling long lines of boxcars and containers of consumer and industrial goods from sources around the world.

These containers form part of a freight transport system that spans the globe. It is an intermodal system because it uses more than one transportation mode—ships, trucks or rail cars—to move freight. Given Canada's vast distances, rail is central to getting the containers to their final destination.

Intermodal rail transport made steady gains from 2000 to 2005, growing an average 4.9% per year, while loads increased from 21.9 million tonnes to 27.8 million tonnes. The Western provinces accounted for most of this growth, with a yearly average increase of 11.6%, much greater than the 3.2% increase for the provinces east of Manitoba.

Shipping goods via standardized containers reduces cargo handling, making it faster, more cost effective, secure and reliable, while reducing damage and loss. Most of the containers drivers see on trains are carrying goods made in Asia or the United States destined for Canada's retail stores.

Raw materials are not typically transported in cargo containers. Such non-intermodal transport is still dominant in Canada, accounting for about 90% of rail tonnage. In 2005, this totalled 260.8 million tonnes. The growth in tonnage has been strong—rising 6.9% in 2004 and 3.8% in 2005—and was largely increased shipments of coal, lumber and iron ore, which together made up more than one-third of non-intermodal railway carloadings in 2005. Non-intermodal traffic grew by 2.4% over the 2000 to 2005 period, from 254.7 to 260.7 million tonnes.

Chart 30.7
Railway freight traffic, annual growth rates

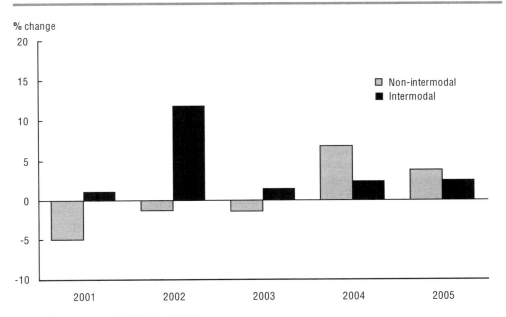

% change

Source: Statistics Canada, CANSIM table 404-0002.

Table 30.1 Gross domestic product at basic prices for transportation and warehousing, by selected subsectors, 2001 to 2006

	2001	2002	2003	2004	2005	2006
	chained (1997) $ millions					
Transportation and warehousing	**47,014**	**46,911**	**47,517**	**49,528**	**51,241**	**52,789**
Air transportation	4,017	3,657	3,563	3,848	4,262	4,659
Rail transportation	5,259	5,343	5,401	5,743	5,885	5,898
Water transportation	1,220	1,237	1,315	1,432	1,451	1,522
Truck transportation	13,263	13,451	13,607	14,212	14,744	15,116
Transit and ground passenger transportation	4,909	5,228	5,140	5,277	5,438	5,509
Pipeline transportation	4,572	4,691	4,800	4,912	5,044	5,102
Postal service	3,096	2,886	3,093	3,074	3,090	3,144
Couriers and messengers	2,279	2,290	2,324	2,373	2,454	2,501
Warehousing and storage	1,453	1,438	1,484	1,694	1,791	1,912

Source: Statistics Canada, CANSIM table 379-0017.

Table 30.2 Operating statistics of Canadian railway carriers, 2000 to 2005

	2000	2001	2002	2003	2004	2005
	$ thousands					
Operating revenue	**8,100,542**	**8,149,560**	**8,192,924**	**8,287,268**	**8,861,767**	**9,823,178**
Freight revenue	7,196,857	7,216,866	7,236,765	7,336,846	7,879,379	8,760,228
Passenger revenue	247,338	268,504	287,196	255,822	265,192	282,881
All other operating revenue	656,347	664,190	668,963	694,600	717,194	780,069
Operating expenses	**6,421,478**	**6,587,940**	**6,593,880**	**6,691,897**	**6,951,895**	**7,507,357**
Ways and structures expenses	1,230,377	1,209,088	1,227,811	1,218,878	1,283,774	1,311,699
Equipment expenses	1,420,580	1,465,863	1,389,300	1,428,561	1,371,147	1,441,080
Rail operating expenses	2,676,069	2,793,077	2,710,634	2,765,619	2,929,148	3,216,557
General expenses	1,094,452	1,119,912	1,266,135	1,278,837	1,367,826	1,538,021
	thousands					
Transportation and other cost-generating sources						
Tonnes of freight transported	352,203	345,795	333,974	338,036	361,606	369,719
Tonne-kilometres of freight transported	321,894,342	321,291,130	318,314,680	317,932,601	338,897,938	352,133,353
Passengers transported	4,160	4,179	4,251	3,958	4,048	4,257
Passenger-kilometres of passengers transported	1,532,715	1,553,059	1,596,947	1,426,367	1,420,804	1,472,781
Litres of diesel oil consumed for all trains	1,987,610	2,002,327	2,019,167	2,050,764	2,097,070	2,130,224
	number					
Employees	40,983	39,475	37,246	36,276	35,591	34,995

Source: Statistics Canada, CANSIM tables 404-0004, 404-0005, 404-0013, 404-0016 and 404-0019.

Table 30.3 Shipping activities at Canadian ports, tonnage loaded and unloaded, 1994 to 2004

	Total	Domestic	International		
			Total	United States	Other
	thousands of tonnes				
Total handled					
1994	**351,316**	104,368	246,948	78,801	168,147
1995	**360,455**	100,740	259,715	85,198	174,518
1996	**357,513**	97,649	259,863	88,484	171,379
1997	**376,067**	93,418	282,650	94,313	188,337
1998	**376,032**	96,607	279,425	100,060	179,364
1999	**385,597**	104,398	281,199	101,983	179,216
2000	**402,783**	109,020	293,762	108,794	184,969
2001	**394,701**	107,842	286,859	107,955	178,904
2002	**408,141**	125,407	282,734	114,310	168,424
2003	**443,779**	137,079	306,700	123,366	183,335
2004	**452,328**	137,768	314,560	123,280	191,280
Loaded					
1994	**222,222**	52,184	170,038	49,520	120,518
1995	**226,910**	50,370	176,540	49,939	126,601
1996	**223,096**	48,825	174,272	52,399	121,873
1997	**234,653**	46,709	187,945	56,891	131,054
1998	**227,346**	48,304	179,042	58,872	120,171
1999	**231,847**	52,199	179,648	59,727	119,921
2000	**242,351**	54,507	187,843	64,744	123,099
2001	**228,663**	53,939	174,724	62,038	112,685
2002	**237,051**	62,780	174,270	72,867	101,404
2003	**259,872**	68,485	191,387	81,180	110,207
2004	**264,999**	68,897	196,102	83,792	112,310
Unloaded					
1994	**129,094**	52,184	76,910	29,282	47,629
1995	**133,546**	50,370	83,176	35,259	47,917
1996	**134,416**	48,825	85,592	36,085	49,506
1997	**141,414**	46,709	94,705	37,423	57,283
1998	**148,686**	48,304	100,382	41,189	59,194
1999	**153,750**	52,199	101,551	42,256	59,295
2000	**160,432**	54,513	105,919	44,050	61,869
2001	**166,038**	53,903	112,135	45,917	66,219
2002	**171,091**	62,626	108,464	41,444	67,020
2003	**183,908**	68,594	115,314	42,186	73,128
2004	**187,330**	68,871	118,458	39,488	78,971

Source: Statistics Canada, Catalogue no. 54-205-XIE.

Table 30.4 Employment in transportation and warehousing, by selected subsector, 1992 to 2006

	1992	1993	1994	1995	1996	1997
			number			
Transportation and warehousing	**544,935**	**548,415**	**548,374**	**552,170**	**555,010**	**567,099**
Air transportation	47,534	45,386	45,660	48,634	50,059	55,863
Rail transportation	58,566	55,924	53,619	50,971	48,349	46,614
Water transportation	10,487	10,765	11,088	12,827	13,209	11,683
Truck transportation	132,311	133,101	137,754	141,304	145,125	155,044
Transit and ground passenger transportation	103,507	103,087	95,453	91,245	91,752	91,173
Pipeline transportation	5,776	5,483	5,310	5,086	4,842	4,943
Scenic and sightseeing transportation	1,645	1,735	1,791	1,931	1,872	1,786
Support activities for transportation	67,195	68,431	69,741	69,385	66,534	68,732
Couriers and messengers	33,060	34,904	36,070	36,815	37,047	38,160
Warehousing and storage	23,873	25,653	25,949	25,568	27,584	27,144

Note: North American Industry Classification System, 2002.
Source: Statistics Canada, CANSIM table 281-0024.

Table 30.5 Operating statistics of major Canadian airlines, 1991 to 2005

	1991	1992	1993	1994	1995	1996
			thousands			
Passengers transported	21,000	21,261	21,947	19,126	21,428	23,164
Passenger-kilometres	43,626,433	45,414,285	44,806,137	45,281,336	51,798,045	57,015,549
Kilograms of goods transported	390,819	392,514	419,838	395,674	386,560	405,975
Tonne-kilometres of goods transported	1,315,448	1,331,586	1,463,995	1,537,977	1,728,762	1,882,803
Hours flown	774	783	746	638	723	785
Litres of turbo fuel consumed	3,208,912	3,157,922	3,035,245	3,055,616	3,417,802	3,349,814

Source: Statistics Canada, CANSIM table 401-0001.

Table 30.6 For-hire trucking, 1990 to 2004

	1990	1991	1992	1993	1994	1995	1996
				thousands			
Tonnes of freight transported	174,245	150,605	149,499	173,400	195,587	210,941	228,974
Tonne-kilometres of freight transported	77,770,738	70,624,205	72,947,210	84,613,287	101,783,711	110,010,665	121,133,146
Shipments (units)	29,953	29,082	27,636	27,930	30,474	32,341	35,181

1. The Trucking Commodity Origin and Destination Survey's scope expanded in 2004 to include local shipments of long-distance carriers and all shipments of local carriers.
Source: Statistics Canada, CANSIM table 403-0001 and Catalogue no. 53-222-XIE.

1998	1999	2000	2001	2002	2003	2004	2005	2006
				number				
584,948	**591,979**	**603,483**	**615,404**	**614,210**	**608,616**	**614,272**	**622,719**	**633,516**
62,040	64,694	65,120	62,568	56,746	57,809	57,435	57,636	57,808
47,059	47,240	49,144	50,376	49,703	44,936	43,145	43,612	42,427
10,965	11,580	12,705	14,439	14,783	x	x	x	x
156,256	156,415	157,328	160,389	163,043	162,665	166,735	171,077	172,847
91,776	93,039	97,161	98,157	101,115	100,199	99,275	99,389	100,687
4,694	4,653	4,949	4,989	5,012	x	x	x	x
1,780	1,903	2,051	2,855	2,879	x	x	x	x
71,285	76,532	78,978	83,520	83,862	84,857	84,378	83,565	86,602
39,215	38,501	38,271	39,766	39,978	40,549	41,561	43,034	44,103
28,350	29,033	29,436	30,842	30,950	30,820	33,284	34,650	39,043

1997	1998	1999	2000	2001	2002	2003	2004	2005
				thousands				
24,363	24,571	24,047	24,480	23,414	23,430	20,042	28,159	32,091
62,479,410	64,426,065	65,711,146	68,516,738	67,018,521	69,254,337	59,508,960	76,122,855	83,909,440
449,828	431,150	451,801	407,876	361,834	355,493	298,990	297,246	268,947
2,058,953	2,340,594	2,016,503	1,934,683	1,725,325	1,800,415	1,419,988	1,478,716	1,378,548
826	843	904	921	856	806	703	926	981
3,631,436	3,855,178	3,571,445	3,871,274	3,678,966	3,453,486	2,999,282	3,660,671	3,855,953

1997	1998	1999	2000	2001	2002	2003	2004[1]
				thousands			
223,313	233,931	269,285	278,442	287,975	293,644	305,153	604,273
130,853,651	138,090,023	158,656,177	164,981,978	170,936,593	177,215,621	184,963,662	225,608,043
32,076	33,832	36,410	35,561	36,917	38,492	40,259	65,884

Table 30.7 Vehicle registrations, 2001 to 2006

	2001	2002	2003	2004	2005	2006
	number					
All vehicle registrations	**23,427,184**	**24,198,219**	**24,687,511**	**25,196,428**	**25,838,309**	**26,684,822**
Road motor vehicle registrations	18,101,675	18,617,413	18,883,584	19,156,055	19,515,295	20,065,171
Vehicles weighing less than 4,500 kilograms	17,054,798	17,543,659	17,768,773	17,989,919	18,275,275	18,738,941
Vehicles weighing from 4,500 kilograms to 14,999 kilograms	387,330	366,962	379,079	393,528	415,764	442,607
Vehicles weighing 15,000 kilograms or more	267,129	277,339	282,420	285,942	301,574	318,272
Buses	74,086	79,364	79,948	77,842	78,962	80,447
Motorcyles and mopeds	318,330	350,088	373,362	408,822	443,718	484,903
Trailers	4,023,215	4,161,491	4,315,996	4,513,641	4,722,563	4,961,184
Off-road, construction and farm vehicles	1,302,295	1,419,305	1,487,930	1,526,731	1,600,450	1,658,466

Source: Statistics Canada, CANSIM table 405-0004.

Table 30.8 Road motor vehicle fuel sales, 2000 to 2005

	2000	2001	2002	2003	2004	2005
	thousands of litres					
Net sales of gasoline	36,375,338	36,552,556	37,949,600	38,421,608	39,103,552	38,499,830
Gross sales of gasoline	38,176,681	38,126,164	39,205,669	39,797,315	40,337,720	39,784,265
Net sales of diesel oil	13,179,694	13,336,346	13,737,648	14,720,634	15,678,724	16,219,913
Net sales of liquefied petroleum gas[1]	461,641	415,355	323,935	313,019	324,238	F

Note: Gross is the total volume sold and net is the volume on which taxes were paid.
1. Data for British Columbia are not included.
Source: Statistics Canada, CANSIM table 405-0002.

Travel and tourism

OVERVIEW

Most Canadians are active travellers. Business people travel overseas frequently to buy and sell goods and services, Canadians regularly visit relatives in other parts of the world, and the backpacking tour of Europe or Australia is a tradition for thousands of students every year. For many of the same reasons, Canada has long been a popular destination for foreign tourists.

The Canadian dollar gained value against the American dollar and no major crises—such as the outbreak of severe acute respiratory syndrome (SARS) in 2003—arose to stall Canadians' wanderlust in 2004. So they travelled more than the year before: this strengthened tourism by 2.6% with 216.9 million trips.

Yet Canadians vacationed closer to home in 2004. Four-fifths of those trips, or 175.1 million, were taken within the country.

This marked a small recovery from 2003, when the number of trips taken in Canada dropped.

Domestic travellers boost tourism industry

The most popular destination for inter-provincial travel in 2004 was Ontario. Canadians made 65.2 million trips to Ontario, and 48.5 million trips to Quebec. Alberta and British Columbia, meanwhile, were the destination for close to 16 million trips. Nevertheless, intraprovincial travel—trips within one's home province—accounted for almost 9 out of 10 domestic trips in 2004.

Travelling is significant for the economy—Canadians spent nearly $43 billion in 2005 on domestic travel, according to the National Tourism Indicators. Domestic spending was

Chart 31.1
Provinces visited by Canadians, 2004

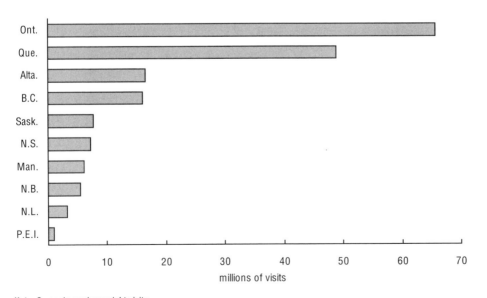

millions of visits

Note: Same-day and overnight visits.
Source: Statistics Canada, CANSIM table 426-0004.

the only source of growth in the Canadian travel and tourism industry in 2005.

Canadian tourists boosted their travel spending in Canada by 5.9% in 2005, the largest annual gain since 2000. International visitors to Canada, meanwhile, spent slightly less while travelling here after a 9.0% increase in 2004. A downturn in visitors from the United States drove this decline, likely a result of the stronger loonie—it climbed 7.4% against the American dollar in 2005.

Airlines were the big winner in the travel industry in 2005, as spending on air transportation soared 8.6%, which accounted for one-third of the travel industry's annual growth.

Other segments of the industry did not fare so well. Spending on fuel for vehicles rose only very slightly, as drivers were discouraged by higher prices at the gas pumps. Accommodation and food and beverage services also saw only slightly higher spending. And travel services companies were pinched by low-cost online travel bookings, though travel services spending increased 3.2%.

Chart 31.2
Top three countries visited by Canadians, 2005

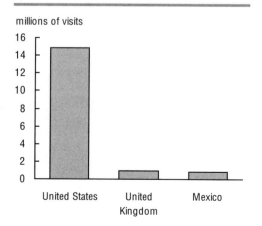

millions of visits

Note: Visits of one night or more.
Source: Statistics Canada, International Travel Survey, 2005.

Travel arrangement and reservation services, financial characteristics

	2004	2005
	\$ millions	
Operating revenue	1,501.1	1592.3
Operating expenses	1,414.7	1509.0
	%	
Operating profit margin	5.8	5.2
	number	
Active establishments	4,997	4,785

Source: Statistics Canada, CANSIM : table 351-0003.

In 2005, the increase in domestic spending led travel and tourism's gross domestic product to rise 4.0%—faster than the overall economy's growth of 2.9%. The rise came on the heels of a similar gain the previous year. Employment in travel and tourism rose 1.7% to 626,000 jobs, the largest increase since 2000.

Canadians travelling abroad

Canadian residents made 44 million same-day and overnight trips abroad in 2005, spending \$20.2 billion doing so. Almost half of these, or 21.1 million trips, were overnight trips outside the country. About 6.2 million of these overnight trips were to overseas destinations (not the United States), with more than half of them to Europe. Canadians spent \$9.4 billion on overseas travel in 2005.

Still, Canadians' top destination continues to be the United States—Canadians made nearly 15 million overnight visits and spent \$9.5 billion there in 2005.

Their second most popular destination was the United Kingdom, with 898,000 overnight visits, followed by Mexico, with 794,000 visits. Rounding out Canadians' top five international travel destinations were France, with 616,000 visits, and Cuba, with 518,000 visits.

Italy had the biggest jump in Canadian travellers in 2005, as visits there surged by half from the previous year.

Overnight travel to Asia totalled 1.1 million visits, up only 8.3% from 2004. Nevertheless, Canadian travel to Asia has soared 60.6% since 2000, possibly due to a rise in immigration to Canada from China and increased trade between the two countries.

Tourism to Canada

In 2005, non-resident visitors made 36 million same-day and overnight trips to Canada, spending $14 billion doing so. Following three consecutive declines, travel to Canada from overseas nations rose for a second year in a row.

Trips originating in the United States—the most important market for tourism to Canada—declined in 2005. Americans' number of overnight trips fell 4.6% to 14.4 million, and they spent about $7.5 billion, 8.6% less than the year before.

The number of overnight trips to Canada from countries other than the United States increased 7.1% to 4.2 million trips. These overseas visitors spent $5.8 billion in Canada in 2005, up 7.0% from 2004.

Chart 31.3
Top three countries of origin of travellers to Canada, 2005

The most important overseas market for tourism to Canada is still the United Kingdom. The number of trips to Canada from the United Kingdom in 2005 reached 888,000, a 10.8% gain from the previous year.

After the United States and the United Kingdom, the top countries of origin for travellers to Canada in 2005 were Japan, France and Germany. China had the largest annual percentage increase in 2005 among the top 12 markets for travel to Canada—Chinese residents made 113,000 trips here that year.

Selected sources

Statistics Canada

- *Analytical Paper Series - Service Industries Division.* Occasional. 63F0002XIE

- *Canadian Travel Survey: Domestic Travel.* Annual. 87-212-XIE

- *International Travel: Advance Information.* Monthly. 66-001-PIE

- *National Tourism Indicators, Quarterly Estimates.* Quarterly. 13-009-XIB

- *Travel-log (Touriscope).* Quarterly. 87-003-XIE

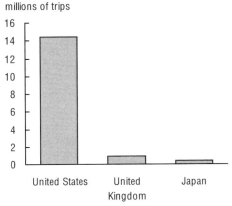

millions of trips

Note: Overnight trips.
Source: Statistics Canada, International Travel Survey, 2005.

Changing times for cross-border travellers

Sharing the world's longest unprotected border has advantages for Canadian and American travellers. One-day shopping trips and overnight stays north or south of the border have become time-honoured traditions. But longer waits at border crossings, stricter security policies and higher gas prices are changing those traditions for both Canadian and American travellers.

In 2004, Americans made 34.6 million same-day and overnight trips to Canada, down 2.5% from the previous year. Their same-day travel fell 8% to 19.5 million trips, but their overnight travel increased 6% to 15.1 million trips. Americans' overnight trips to Canada have gone up every year since 1996.

Americans visiting Canada on overnight trips spent $8.2 billion here in 2004, up 12% from 2003. Visitors averaged about four nights per trip, and spent $541 per trip.

Cross-border traffic heading south was also busy in 2004. Canadians took 22.2 million same-day trips to the United States, a 3% increase from 2003, and the first increase since 1991. Meanwhile, Canadians' overnight travel to the United States rose 9% to 13.9 million trips.

Among Canadians heading south, driving the family car has become an increasingly popular option—perhaps due to the costs and difficulties of air travel. In 2004, overnight car travel to the United States from Canada climbed to its highest level since 1997, reaching 8.1 million trips.

Canadian travellers stayed more than 107 million nights in the United States in 2004. And they spent $8.7 billion, or an average of $625 per trip, which is more than what Americans spent while travelling in Canada.

Chart 31.4
Travel between Canada and the United States

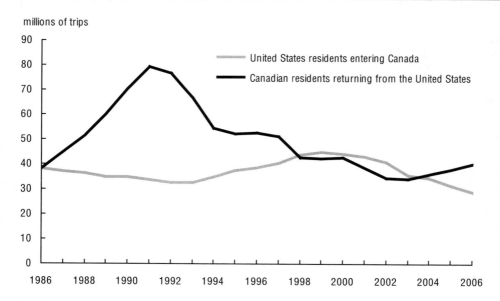

millions of trips

United States residents entering Canada

Canadian residents returning from the United States

Note: Same-day and overnight trips.
Source: Statistics Canada, CANSIM table 427-0001.

2003: A bad year for tourism

Canada's natural beauty and popular attractions have long made it one of the world's most popular tourist destinations—and that means income for Canada's tourism industry. So when events occur that make travel less attractive, Canada is particularly affected. In 2003, lingering fears from September 11, the Iraq conflict and the unexpected SARS outbreak in Canada all combined to dampen tourism worldwide—making that year one of the most painful in recent memory for Canada's tourism industry.

The largest single drop in tourism over the past two decades occurred in 2001, with Asian and North American travellers in particular accounting for a large part of the overall decline. When the Iraq conflict began in March 2003 and the SARS outbreak hit its peak in April and May, the tourism industry—especially in Toronto and Vancouver—was hit hard.

By May 2003, the total number of trips to Canada from overseas countries excluding the United States tumbled 33% from the previous year. Travel from Asia between April and May 2003 alone dropped 32%, likely because of the SARS epidemic.

Visits from Taiwan suffered the biggest decline, plunging nearly 94% from December 2002 to May 2003. Trips from Japan, China, Hong Kong and South Korea were down anywhere from 40% to 73%. All these countries had been on Canada's list of top-12 overseas tourism markets in December 2002.

Travel to Canada did not rebound until 2004. That year, Canada registered 1.3 million trips from China, Hong Kong, Japan, Thailand and other Asian countries, up from 923,000 in 2003. Moreover, spending by travellers from these countries also increased, from $1.2 billion in 2003 to $1.6 billion in 2004.

Chart 31.5
International travellers

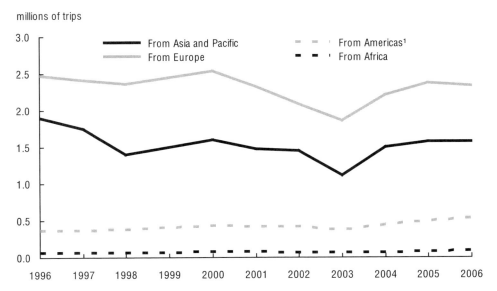

millions of trips

Legend: From Asia and Pacific — From Europe — From Americas[1] — From Africa

Note: Same-day and overnight trips.
    1. Excludes travellers from United States.
Source: Statistics Canada, CANSIM table 387-0004.

International travel deficit highest ever

Tourism like other major sectors of the economy that involve trade, is measured in surpluses and deficits. For example, when Canadians spend more abroad than foreign visitors spend here, the international travel account posts a deficit and vice versa for a surplus.

The international travel deficit in 2006 reached $6.7 billion—an all-time high. The major cause was Canadians' record spending in the United States and overseas, $23.3 billion, a 5.7% increase from the previous high in 2005. Meanwhile, foreigners travelling in Canada spent slightly less than in 2005, $16.6 billion.

Still, foreign spending in Canada reached its fourth highest level in 2006. Prior to 2005, foreign spending in Canada had risen every year since 1987—except in 2003, when the SARS outbreak cut travel to Canada.

Canada's travel deficit with the United States climbed to $4.3 billion in 2006, the highest since 1993. While a nine-year low in overnight travel from the United States cut American spending in Canada, Canadian spending south of the border climbed to a record $12.9 billion.

Travelling overseas is a growing passion among Canadians. This continues to expand Canada's travel deficit with overseas countries, which has nearly tripled in the last five years, to $2.5 billion in 2006. Over the past 25 years, Canadian spending overseas has actually decreased only once—in 1991. Travellers from overseas spent $7.9 billion or 2.8% more here in 2006.

Canada's international travel deficit with all countries more than quadrupled from 2002 to 2006.

Chart 31.6
International travel account

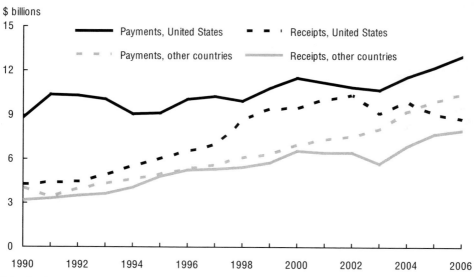

$ billions

Legend: Payments, United States · Receipts, United States · Payments, other countries · Receipts, other countries

Notes: Receipts represent spending by foreigners travelling in Canada, including education spending and medical spending.
Payments represent spending by Canadian residents travelling abroad, including education spending and medical spending.
Source: Statistics Canada, CANSIM table 376-0001.

Vacation travel on the rise

Many Canadians book time off work to putter around the house or to enjoy the weather. But today more and more Canadians are using their annual leave to travel.

According to the Travel Activities and Motivation Survey, 74% of all adult Canadians—about 18 million people—travelled for vacation or pleasure sometime from 2004 to 2006. This compares with 73% of adults from 1997 to 1999.

More Canadians are vacationing overseas—28% of the population in 2006, compared with 20% in 1999. Meanwhile, 35% took a vacation to the United States, compared with 29% previously, and 41% took a vacation in Canada outside their home province, up from 36%. The share of Canadians vacationing in their home province rose from 48% to 59%.

Younger adults and those in a household with above-average income took more overnight

vacations than older adults and people in lower-income households. From 2004 to 2006, 80% of Canadians aged 18 to 34 took at least one out-of-town, overnight vacation. Only 66% of those aged 55 and older took similar trips.

Interestingly, adults born in Canada take proportionally more overnight vacations than those born outside the country. However, those born outside Canada are almost twice as likely to take an international vacation as their Canadian-born counterparts.

Sixty percent of adults who took an overnight vacation from 2004 to 2006 say the decision about where to travel was very or extremely important. Their top consideration in choosing a destination was feeling safe.

Chart 31.7
Domestic and international travel by Canadians

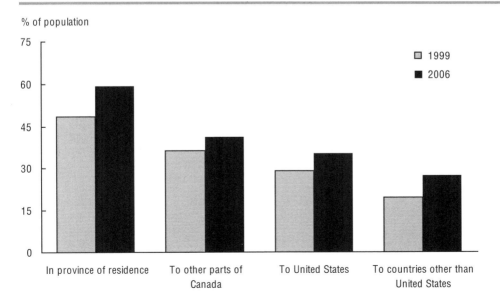

% of population

1999
2006

In province of residence | To other parts of Canada | To United States | To countries other than United States

Note: Population reporting at least one overnight, out-of-town vacation in the past two years
Source: Statistics Canada, Travel Activities and Motivation Survey.

Table 31.1 Canadians travelling in Canada, by province and territory of destination, 1999 to 2004

	1999	2000	2001	2002	2003	2004
	thousands					
Canada	**177,461**	**178,628**	**182,092**	**187,890**	**172,244**	**175,084**
Newfoundland and Labrador	3,975	3,955	3,902	3,784	3,236	3,107
Prince Edward Island	864	977	966	1,125	897	911
Nova Scotia	7,006	7,034	7,019	8,287	7,164	7,066
New Brunswick	5,376	4,794	5,344	6,075	5,613	5,038
Quebec	38,745	40,842	40,608	45,928	47,216	48,484
Ontario	63,282	65,220	67,160	70,257	62,168	65,290
Manitoba	6,895	6,542	6,621	6,265	5,938	6,009
Saskatchewan	9,043	8,222	8,139	8,029	7,413	7,451
Alberta	20,998	20,022	21,256	19,186	15,775	15,890
British Columbia	21,183	20,893	20,984	18,842	16,742	15,738
Yukon, Northwest Territories and Nunavut	F	F	92E	113E	83E	99E

Note: Trips of 80 kilometres or more.
Source: Statistics Canada, CANSIM table 426-0001.

Table 31.2 Canadians travelling in Canada, by selected census metropolitan area of destination, 1999 to 2004

	1999	2000	2001	2002	2003	2004
	thousands					
St. John's	1,574	1,416	1,357	1,068	1,018	1,129
Halifax	2,786	2,905	2,999	3,513	2,769	2,870
Saint John	662	738	815	770	802	619
Saguenay	653	609	713	770	652	773
Québec	5,610	6,256	6,087	7,114	6,836	7,075
Sherbrooke	1,332	1,274	1,746	1,992	1,521	1,654
Trois-Rivières	1,151	1,188	985	1,293	1,434	1,512
Montréal	8,465	9,470	10,117	10,913	11,023	11,000
Ottawa–Gatineau	5,422	5,487	5,924	5,936	6,110	6,194
Toronto	13,752	14,708	14,144	13,894	12,706	13,738
Hamilton	1,968	1,712	2,308	1,966	1,675	1,766
St. Catharines–Niagara	3,010	4,110	4,056	3,949	3,806	4,157
Kitchener	1,858	2,618	2,371	2,833	2,031	2,337
London	3,647	3,124	3,107	3,478	3,282	3,341
Windsor	1,188	1,243	1,033	851	864	1,067
Greater Sudbury / Grand Sudbury	643	927E	1,164	1,002	965	1,005
Winnipeg	2,346	2,395	2,533	2,297	2,305	2,294
Regina	1,329	1,289	1,422	1,357	1,305	1,447
Saskatoon	2,321	1,991	1,980	1,951	1,888	1,854
Calgary	3,734	3,535	3,734	3,701	2,976	2,963
Edmonton	5,043	4,450	4,813	4,448	3,782	3,564
Vancouver	4,275	3,942	3,904	3,437	3,029	2,765
Victoria	1,776	1,800	1,630	1,801	1,568	1,599

Note: Trips of 80 kilometres or more.
Source: Statistics Canada, CANSIM table 426-0001.

Table 31.3 Expenditures by Canadians on trips in Canada, by province and territory of destination, 1999 to 2004

	1999	2000	2001	2002	2003	2004
	\$ thousands					
Canada	**23,764,527**	**26,845,970**	**29,692,470**	**30,926,146**	**28,454,953**	**29,708,136**
Newfoundland and Labrador	629,831	745,069	795,488	812,691	791,499	722,995
Prince Edward Island	209,213	245,001	249,143	254,211	240,243	239,427
Nova Scotia	904,459	983,217	1,177,481	1,309,866	1,260,350	1,206,290
New Brunswick	748,223	798,979	856,011	970,911	842,605	812,595
Quebec	4,665,194	5,146,754	5,581,632	6,652,815	6,476,795	6,782,331
Ontario	7,483,373	9,241,261	10,497,261	10,246,161	9,541,466	10,154,235
Manitoba	871,953	865,858	1,033,426	905,212	919,443	967,300
Saskatchewan	942,592	1,024,053	1,151,025	1,112,872	1,076,599	1,120,068
Alberta	3,135,557	3,414,852	3,895,231	4,068,107	3,071,985	3,466,705
British Columbia	4,136,020	4,278,782	4,407,321	4,525,894	4,162,907	4,162,189
Yukon, Northwest Territories and Nunavut	F	F	F	67,405E	F	F

Note: Trips of 80 kilometres or more.
Source: Statistics Canada, CANSIM table 426-0001.

Table 31.4 Travel by Canadians to foreign countries, by selected destinations, 2000 and 2005

	2000			2005		
	Visits	Nights	Spending in country	Visits	Nights	Spending in country
	thousands		CAN\$ millions	thousands		CAN\$ millions
Austria	97	579	74	128	640	79
China	92	1,868	175	161	2,996	304
Cuba	260	2,290	206	518	4,574	470
Dominican Republic	187	1,714	150	506	4,488	457
France	461	4,918	583	616	7,770	829
Germany	284	2,573	238	317	3,205	276
Hong Kong	97	1,449	103	151	2,793	209
Italy	232	2,967	340	383	4,860	616
Japan	119	1,874	182	143	1,866	220
Mexico	692	7,470	691	794	8,780	910
Netherlands	155	1,389	107	197	1,601	132
Spain	142	2,069	173	170	2,300	223
Switzerland	145	996	109	139	937	122
United Kingdom	797	10,438	976	898	11,376	1,091
United States	14,666	109,062	9,191	14,862	117,164	9,537

Note: Visits of one night or more.
Source: Statistics Canada, International Travel Survey.

Table 31.5 Travel by Canadians to the United States, by selected destinations, 2000 and 2005

	2000			2005		
	Visits	Nights	Spending in state	Visits	Nights	Spending in state
	thousands		CAN$ millions	thousands		CAN$ millions
California	1,036	8,591	950	1,008	8,641	861
Florida	2,042	36,232	2,227	2,038	38,802	2,348
Maine	682	2,255	155	734	2,359	182
Massachusetts	473	2,043	204	505	2,183	204
Michigan	1,237	3,142	228	1,239	3,257	252
Minnesota	511	1,343	134	593	1,663	162
Nevada	811	3,761	592	931	4,354	777
New York	2,314	6,358	628	2,344	6,914	658
Ohio	508	1,297	114	511	1,589	116
Pennsylvania	648	1,680	146	646	1,533	125
Vermont	608	1,729	100	644	1,757	108
Washington	1,581	4,567	257	1,612	4,588	310

Note: Visits of one night or more.
Source: Statistics Canada, International Travel Survey.

Table 31.6 Travel to Canada, by selected countries of origin, 2000 and 2005

	2000			2005		
	Visits	Nights	Spending in Canada	Visits	Nights	Spending in Canada
	thousands		CAN$ millions	thousands		CAN$ millions
Australia	173	2,099	231	179	2,447	287
China	74	1,561	120	113	3,723	219
France	402	6,052	480	351	5,836	463
Germany	380	5,770	498	311	4,900	410
Hong Kong	138	1,894	167	109	2,161	151
India	66	1,398	79	94	1,771	82
Italy	110	1,609	135	91	1,061	95
Japan	493	4,628	687	398	4,750	557
Mexico	140	1,788	174	179	3,149	240
Netherlands	131	1,767	139	118	1,580	131
South Korea	129	3,507	221	173	4,466	247
Switzerland	105	1,851	154	97	1,684	163
Taiwan	163	2,043	239	98	1,536	110
United Kingdom	862	10,261	1,074	888	11,882	1,246
United States	15,188	58,447	7,321	14,390	57,331	7,463

Note: Visits of one night or more.
Source: Statistics Canada, International Travel Survey.

Table 31.7 Travel to Canada from the United States, by selected states of origin, 2000 and 2005

	2000			2005		
	Visits	Nights	Spending in Canada	Visits	Nights	Spending in Canada
	thousands		CAN$ millions	thousands		CAN$ millions
California	1,011	5,160	820	877	4,348	611
Florida	353	2,467	277	466	2,815	338
Illinois	520	2,139	331	477	2,038	308
Maine	264	878	87	284	1,074	123
Massachusetts	678	2,448	306	554	2,078	265
Michigan	1,821	4,895	527	1,689	4,794	589
Minnesota	540	2,075	256	545	2,389	257
New Jersey	356	1,422	218	417	1,629	238
New York	1,907	6,197	654	1,771	5,833	680
Ohio	816	2,669	350	698	2,377	285
Pennsylvania	629	2,612	312	642	2,751	361
Texas	415	1,972	332	419	2,018	325
Washington	1,644	5,443	523	1,464	4,914	496
Wisconsin	308	1,431	162	328	1,549	200

Note: Visits of one night or more.
Source: Statistics Canada, International Travel Survey.

Table 31.8 Financial characteristics of the travel arrangement industry, 2000 to 2005

	2000	2001	2002	2003	2004	2005
	$ millions					
Operating revenue						
Accommodation services	11,804.6	12,165.4	12,780.2	12,314.6	13,220.9	14,311.6
Hotels, motor hotels and motels	10,421.0	10,755.4	11,291.0	10,902.6	11,528.4	12,431.5
Other accommodation industries	1,383.6	1,410.0	1,489.2	1,412.0	1,692.5	1,880.1
Travel agencies	1,782.6	1,518.3	1,542.1	1,480.0	1,501.1	1,592.3
Tour operators	5,418.9	5,738.1	5,735.4	6,105.8	6,288.0	7,019.0
Other travel arrangement and reservation services	222.6	218.4	216.5	229.5	240.7	264.7
Operating expenses						
Accommodation services	10,301.7	10,682.7	11,231.0	10,993.6	11,267.9	12,124.4
Hotels, motor hotels and motels	9,050.5	9,372.9	9,875.3	9,710.0	9,860.1	10,525.9
Other accommodation industries	1,251.2	1,309.8	1,355.8	1,283.5	1,407.7	1,598.5
Travel agencies	1,660.2	1,421.2	1,435.7	1,455.6	1,414.7	1,509.0
Tour operators	5,141.0	5,691.7	5,684.7	6,130.9	6,188.6	6,942.2
Other travel arrangement and reservation services	205.3	201.4	199.1	211.2	221.7	243.8
	%					
Operating profit margin						
Accommodation services	12.7	12.2	12.1	10.7	14.8	15.3
Hotels, motor hotels and motels	13.2	12.9	12.5	10.9	14.5	15.3
Other accommodation industries	9.6	7.1	9.0	9.1	16.8	15.0
Travel agencies	6.9	6.4	6.9	1.6	5.8	5.2
Tour operators	5.1	0.8	0.9	-0.4	1.6	1.1
Other travel arrangement and reservation services	8.5	8.0	8.0	8.0	7.9	7.9
	number					
Active establishments						
Accommodation services	16,924	16,330	16,407	16,355	15,463	16,630
Hotels, motor hotels and motels	9,419	9,015	8,814	8,624	8,026	8,538
Other accommodation industries	7,505	7,315	7,593	7,731	7,437	8,092
Travel agencies	4,962	5,341	5,362	5,364	4,997	4,785
Tour operators	1,117	1,147	1,207	1,237	1,238	1,238
Other travel arrangement and reservation services	295	281	282	294	306	338

Source: Statistics Canada, CANSIM tables 351-0002 and 351-0003.

List of maps, charts and tables

Maps

Charts

Tables

Glossary

Aboriginal identity: People who identify with at least one Aboriginal group (i.e., North American Indian, Métis or Inuit), who are Treaty Indians, Registered Indians as defined by the Indian Act, or who are members of an Indian Band or First Nation.

Age-specific fertility rate: Number of live births per 1,000 women in a specific age group. *See also* Fertility rate *and* Total fertility rate.

Allophones: People whose mother tongue is neither English nor French.

Anglophones: People whose mother tongue is English.

Balance of payments (BOP): A statistical statement that systematically summarizes, for a specific time period, the economic transactions of a country with the rest of the world.

Blue-collar: Of or relating to manual or industrial labourers, usually paid wages rather than salary. *See also* White-collar.

BMI: *See* Body Mass Index.

Body Mass Index (BMI): Overweight and obesity are based on BMI, which is a measure of an individual's weight in relation to his or her height. BMI is highly correlated with body fat and is widely used to indicate health risks. According to new Canadian guidelines, aligned with those of the World Health Organization, BMI is classified into six categories, each representing a different level of risk: 'Underweight' is less than 18.5 BMI; 'Normal weight' is from 18.5 to 24.9 BMI; 'Overweight' is from 25.0 to 29.9 BMI; 'Obese Class I' is from 30.0 to 34.9 BMI; 'Obese Class II' is from 35.0 to 39.9 BMI; and 'Obese Class III' is greater than or equal to 40.0 BMI.

BOP: *See* Balance of payments.

Bovine spongiform encephalopathy (BSE): Fatal disease of cattle that affects the central nervous system. Sometimes called 'mad cow disease,' BSE was identified in England in 1986, where it was attributed to the practice of feeding cattle a meat-and-bone meal supplement made from either bovines already infected with BSE or from scrapie-infected sheep.

BSE: *See* Bovine spongiform encephalopathy.

Building permit: Permit required in most jurisdictions for new construction, or adding onto pre-existing structures, and in some cases for major renovations. Generally, the new construction must be inspected to ensure compliance with national, regional, and local building codes. Failure to obtain a permit can result in significant fines and penalties, and even demolition of unauthorised construction if it cannot be made to meet code.

CA: *See* Census agglomeration.

Canada Pension Plan (CPP): Contributory, earnings-related social insurance program that provides a stable and dependable pension that can be build on for retirement. It also provides people and their dependants with basic financial protection in the event of disability or death.

CANSIM (Canadian Socio-economic Information Management System): Database that contains more than 26 million time series (observations for a given subject at regular intervals) regrouped in over 2,400 tables containing data on labour, manufacturing, investment, international trade and much more; CANSIM enables users to track trends in virtually every aspect of Canadian life.

Capital investment: Includes all expenditures on buildings, engineering construction and machinery and equipment. Gross fixed capital formation on buildings includes transfer costs on the sale of existing fixed assets (e.g., real estate commissions). Gross capital formation in machinery and equipment includes imports of new and used machinery and equipment. The latter are included, as they constitute additions to domestic capital stock.

Census: Any survey that includes all units in a population (persons, events, businesses, etc.).

Census of Agriculture: Survey conducted every five years to produce data on the agriculture industry, such as number and type of agricultural operations, farm operator characteristics, business operating arrangements, land management practices, planted or seeded areas, number of livestock and poultry, farm business capital, operating expenses and receipts, and farm machinery and equipment.

Census agglomeration (CA): An area with an urban core population of at least 10,000.

Census family: A married couple (with or without children of either or both spouses), a couple living common-law (with or without children of either or both partners) or a lone parent of any marital status, with at least one child living in the same dwelling. A couple may be of opposite or same sex. Children in a census family include grandchildren living with their grandparent(s) but with no parents present.

Census metropolitan area (CMA): Area consisting of one or more adjacent municipalities situated around a major urban core. The urban core must have a population of at least 100,000.

Census of Population: Survey conducted every five years to produce data on the population and dwelling counts for Canada, each province and territory, and smaller geographic units such as cities or districts within cities. Questionnaires are distributed to all Canadian households and on Indian reserves and include questions concerning age, sex, education, ethnic origin, mother tongue, marital status, religion, employment and housing.

CMA: *See* Census metropolitan area.

Conditional sentence: Community-based alternative to imprisonment introduced in the reforms to Bill C-41. If certain legal criteria are met, a judge may sentence an offender who would otherwise go to prison to a conditional term of imprisonment. The offender will serve the term of imprisonment in the community, provided that they abide by the conditions imposed by the court as part of the conditional sentence order. If the offender violates these conditions, they may be sent to prison to serve the balance of that sentence.

Constant dollars: Dollars of a particular base year that are not adjusted (by inflation or deflation) to show changes in the purchasing power of the dollar. Note that the terms 'uninflated dollars' and 'deflated dollars' are often used as synonyms for 'constant dollars.'

Consumer Price Index (CPI): Measure of the percentage change over time in the average cost of a large basket of goods and services purchased by Canadians. The quantity and quality of the items in the basket are held constant. As a result, changes in the cost of the basket are due to pure price movements and not to changes in the composition of the basket.

CPI: *See* Consumer Price Index.

CPP: *See* Canada Pension Plan.

Custodial remand: *See* Remand.

Deficit: Amount by which government budgetary spending exceeds revenues in any given year.

Economic family: Group of two or more persons who live in the same dwelling and are related to each other by blood, marriage, common-law or adoption.

Ecozone: An area of the earth's surface that represents a large and very generalized ecological units which are characterized by interactive and adjusting abiotic and biotic factors. There are 15 terrestrial and 5 marine ecozones in Canada.

Educators: All employees of the public school system who are required to have teaching certification as a condition of their employment. This includes teaching staff, principals, vice-principals, professional non-teaching staff (e.g., pedagogical consultants, guidance counsellors and special education teachers) and excludes substitute/supply teachers, temporary replacement teachers, teachers on leave, student assistants and teaching assistants.

Electoral district: Area that one Member of Parliament (MP) is elected to represent in the House of Commons. Canada is divided into 308 federal electoral districts.

Employed: Persons who, during the Labour Force Survey reference week, did any work at all at a job or business, that is, paid work in the context of an employer–employee relationship, or self-employment (includes unpaid family work, which is defined as unpaid work contributing directly to the operation of a farm, business or professional practice owned and operated by a related member of the same household); or had a job, but were not at work because of factors such as own illness or disability, personal or family responsibilities, vacation, labour dispute or other reasons. Excludes persons on layoff, between casual jobs, and those with a job to start at a future date). *See also* Unemployed *and* Not in the labour force.

Ethnic origin: Ethnic or cultural group(s) to which the respondent's ancestors belong.

Exchange rate: Value of the Canadian dollar against the currencies of other countries.

Experienced workers: People who, during the week from Sunday to Saturday and prior to Census Day (May 15), were members of the labour force since January 1.

Farm Product Price Index (FPPI): Measures the change through time in prices received for agricultural commodities at the first transaction point.

Fertility rate: Number of live births occurring in a given time period relative to the number of women of childbearing age. *See also* Age-specific fertility rates *and* Total fertility rate.

Fine particulates: *See* Particulate.

Fossil fuel: Combustible substance derived from the decay of organic material over long periods of time and under high pressure. Examples are natural gas, oil, propane and coal.

FPPI: *See* Farm Product Price Index.

Francophones: People whose mother tongue is French.

G8: Top eight industrialized countries in the world: Canada, France, Germany, Italy, Japan, Russia, the United Kingdom and the United States.

General government: Administrative part of governments. Excludes units such as schools and hospitals directly engaged in the delivery of services.

GDP: *See* Gross domestic product.

GHGs: *See* Greenhouse gases.

Gigajoule: Unit of energy. A 30-litre gasoline fill-up contains about 1 gigajoule of energy.

Goods-producing sector: Sector of the economy that is comprised of agriculture, forestry, fishing and hunting; mining, oil and gas extraction; utilities (electric power, gas and water); construction; and manufacturing.

Greenhouse gases (GHGs): Group of chemical compounds that are responsible for the greenhouse effect. The most significant greenhouse gases produced by economic activity are: carbon dioxide (CO_2), methane (CH_4), nitrous oxide (N_2O) and chlorofluorocarbons (CFC).

Gross domestic product (GDP): Total unduplicated value of goods and services produced in the economic territory of a country or region during a given period. GDP can be measured in three ways: 1) as total income earned in current production; 2) as total final sales of current production; or 3) as total net values added in current production. However it is measured, GDP can be valued either at factor cost or at market prices.

Gross fixed capital formation: *See* Capital investment.

Ground-level ozone: Ozone (O_3) that occurs near the surface of the earth. It is a pollutant of concern in smog because of its toxic effects.

Heritage institution: Institution whose purpose is to acquire, preserve, study,

interpret, and make accessible to the public, for its instruction and enjoyment, objects, specimens, documents, buildings, and land areas of educational and cultural value, including artistic, scientific, historical, natural and technological material.

IIP: *See* International investment position.

International investment position (IIP): A country's balance sheet of the stock of financial assets and liabilities with the rest of the world. Together with the balance of payments transactions, the IIP constitutes a country's set of international accounts.

Industrial Product Price Index (IPPI): Measures price changes for major commodities sold by Canadian manufacturers.

Industry: *See* North American Industry Classification System.

Industry group: *See* North American Industry Classification System.

Inflation: Upward movement in the average level of prices or a persistent rise in the average price of goods and services; affects cost of living. The most widely used measure of inflation is the Consumer Price Index (CPI).

Intellectual property: Form of creative endeavour that can be protected through a trademark, patent, copyright, industrial design or integrated circuit topography.

Intermodal: Operations that involve more than one mode of transport to complete the movement of shipments. Goods are carried in a highway trailer or freight container, which is transferred between a rail car and some other mode, usually a truck or ship.

IPPI: *See* Industrial Product Price Index.

Kilowatt hour (kWh): Commercial unit of electric energy, which is 1,000 watt-hours. A kilowatt-hour can be described as the amount of electricity consumed by 10 light bulbs of 100 watts burning for 1 hour.

kWh: *See* Kilowatt hour.

Labour force: Civilian, non-institutional members of the population aged 15 and older who, during the Labour Force Survey reference week, were employed or unemployed.

Labour productivity: Real output per hours worked.

Longitudinal: A type of survey or study over time of the same variable or the same group of respondents.

Median: Value of the middle number of a series ranked in order of size. For example, a group of five children has the ages of 5, 4, 8, 3 and 10. To find their median age, first rearrange the series in order of size (i.e., 3, 4, 5, 8, and 10). The value of the middle number in the series (5) is the median age.

Mortality rate: Number of deaths for all causes per 100,000 population.

NAICS: *See* North American Industry Classification System.

National Population Health Survey (NPHS): Survey designed to enhance our understanding of the processes affecting health. The survey, which began in 1994/1995, is conducted every two years and collects data from over 17,000 respondents.

Net debt: *See* Net federal debt.

Net federal debt: Accumulated total of all past federal deficits and surpluses since Confederation. The net federal debt is the gross federal debt minus the federal government's financial assets such as loans, investments and foreign exchange accounts.

New Housing Price Index (NHPI): Measures changes over time in contractors' selling prices of new residential houses, where detailed specifications pertaining to each house remain the same between two consecutive periods.

NHPI: *See* New Housing Price Index.

Non-family households: Consists either of one person living alone or of two or more persons who share a dwelling, but do not constitute a family (e.g., a couple with or without children).

Non-family people: Household members who do not belong to a census family. They may be related to Person 1 (e.g., Person 1's sister, brother-in-law, cousin, grandparent), or unrelated to Person 1 (e.g., lodger, room-mate, employee). A person living alone is always a non-family person.

Non-profit organization: Organizations that are institutionally separate from governments, do not return any profits generated to their owners or directors, are independent and able to regulate their own activities, benefit to some degree from voluntary contributions of time or money, and are formally incorporated or registered under specific legislation with provincial/territorial or federal governments.

North American Industry Classification System (NAICS): Industry classification system developed to provide common definitions of the industrial structures of Canada, Mexico and the United States. Its hierarchical structure is composed of sectors (two-digit code), subsectors (three-digit code), industry groups (four-digit code), and industries (five-digit code).

Not in the labour force: People who, during the Labour Force Survey reference week, were unwilling or unable to offer or supply labour services under conditions existing in their labour markets (i.e., they were neither employed nor unemployed). *See also* Employed *and* Unemployed.

NPHS: *See* National Population Health Survey.

OAS: *See* Old Age Security.

Obesity: *See* Body Mass Index.

OECD: *See* Organisation for Economic Co-operation and Development.

Off reserve: Aboriginal people not living on a reserve.

Old Age Security (OAS): Monthly benefit available to most Canadians 65 years of age or older who have lived in Canada for at least 10 years. Low-income seniors may be eligible for other benefits as early as age 60.

Organic compounds: Compounds based on carbon and usually containing hydrogen, with or without oxygen, nitrogen, or other elements. Organic originally meant 'of plant or animal origin,' and it is still sometimes used in this way. For example, 'organic waste' can mean food scraps, manure, sewage, leaves, etc.; 'organic fertilizer' can mean manure; 'organic deposits' can mean peat or other plant material in soil; 'organic nutrients' can mean nutrients derived from decayed plant material. However, now that organic compounds are routinely created by people, the word 'organic' is also used to refer to synthetic organic compounds, as in 'organic pollution' (which can include toxic human-made organic compounds).

Organisation for Economic Co-operation and Development (OECD): A group of 30 member countries sharing a commitment to democratic government and the market economy. The OECD produces internationally agreed upon instruments, decisions and recommendations to promote rules in areas where multilateral agreement is necessary for individual countries to make progress in a globalized economy.

Overweight: *See* Body Mass Index.

Participation rate: Represents the labour force expressed as a percentage of the population of those 15 years of age and over. The participation rate for a particular group (age, sex, etc.) is the labour force in that group expressed as a percentage of the population for that group.

Particulate: Anything that can be filtered from the air. Large particles, such as road dust or pollen, can irritate the eyes, whereas smaller particles (often called 'fine particulates') from smoke and fumes can be inhaled into the lungs.

Passenger-kilometres: The movement of a passenger over a distance of one kilometre. derived by multiplying the number of passengers by distance travelled.

Per capita: For each person or per person.

Petajoule: One million gigajoules.

PAC: Pollution abatement and control.

Population density: Number of persons per square kilometre.

Productivity: *See* Labour productivity.

Public sector: Public administration at the federal, provincial or municipal levels of government, as well as Crown corporations, liquor control boards and other government institutions such as schools (including universities), hospitals and public libraries.

Raw Materials Price Indexes (RMPI): Measure price changes for the purchase of raw materials by Canadian industry. The term 'raw material' refers either to a commodity that is sold for the first time after being extracted from nature, or a substitutable recycled product (for example, metal scrap).

Recent immigrant: People who immigrated to Canada 5 years or less prior to the date of the Census. For example, in the case of the 1996 Census, recent immigrants refer to those who immigrated between 1991 and the first four months of 1996.

Recession: Two consecutive quarterly declines in real gross domestic product (GDP).

Registered Pension Plan (RPP): Pension plans for employees sponsored by employers or unions and usually funded through contributions by both employees and employers. RPPs must satisfy certain conditions and be registered for the purposes of the federal *Income Tax Act*.

Registered Retirement Savings Plan (RRSP): Program that allows savings for retirement to grow tax free in a special savings plan registered by the Canada Revenue Agency. Contributions to RRSPs can be made up to December 31 of the year the contributor turns 69.

Remand: Court order for a person to be held in custody while awaiting a further court appearance. The person has not been sentenced and can be held for a number of reasons (e.g., risk that they won't appear for their court date, danger to themselves or others, risk to re-offend).

Research and development (R&D): In general, R&D activities are conducted by specialized units or centres belonging to companies, universities and state agencies. R&D normally refers to future-oriented, longer-term activities in science or technology.

Riding: *See* Electoral district.

RMPI: *See* Raw Materials Price Indexes.

RPP: *See* Registered Pension Plan.

RRSP: *See* Registered Retirement Savings Plan.

R&D: *See* Research and development.

Sector: *See* North American Industry Classification System.

Services-producing sector: Sector of the economy comprised of the following: trade; transportation and warehousing; finance and insurance, real estate and renting and leasing and management of companies and enterprises; professional, scientific and technical services; information and cultural industries; arts, entertainment and recreation; administrative and support services; waste management and remediation services; educational services; health care and social assistance; information, culture and recreation; accommodation and food services; public administration; and other services.

Social assistance: Transfer payments (including refundable tax credits) to help individuals and families maintain a socially acceptable level of earnings.

SSDA: *See* Sub-sub-drainage area.

Subsector: *See* North American Industry Classification System.

Sub-sub-drainage area (SSDA): The smallest environmental geography unit that measures surface drainage catchment areas. There are 978 SSDAs in Canada.

Total fertility rate: Estimate of the average number of live births a woman can be expected to have in her lifetime, based on the age-specific fertility rates of a given year. *See also* Age-specific fertility rate *and* Fertility rate.

Trade deficit: If the country imports more goods than it exports, the trade balance is negative and there is a trade deficit.

Trade surplus: If the country exports more goods than it imports, the trade balance is positive and there is a trade surplus.

Unemployed: People who, during the Labour Force Survey reference week, were on temporary layoff with an expectation of recall and were available for work; were without work, had actively looked for work in the past four weeks, and were available for work; or had a new job to start within four weeks from the reference week, and were available for work. *See also* Employed *and* Not in the labour force.

Unemployment rate: Number of unemployed people, during the Labour Force Survey reference week, expressed as a percentage of the labour force (unemployed plus employed). The unemployment rate for a particular group (age, sex, province, etc.) is the number unemployed in that group expressed as a percentage of the labour force for that group.

Urban core: Large urban area around which a census metropolitan area or a census agglomeration is delineated. The urban core must have a population (based on the previous census) of at least 100,000 in the case of a census metropolitan area, or from 10,000 to 99,999 in the case of a census agglomeration.

Visible minority: Refers to the visible minority group to which the respondent belongs. The *Employment Equity Act* defines visible minorities as "persons, other than Aboriginal peoples, who are non-Caucasian in race or non-white in colour."

VOC: *See* Volatile organic compound.

Volatile organic compound (VOC): Any organic compound that has a high tendency to pass from the solid or liquid state to the vapour state under typical environmental conditions. Such compounds participate in a range of processes that lead to atmospheric pollution, including the formation of urban smog.

White-collar: Of or related to performing non-manual, especially clerical, administrative or professional, work. *See also* Blue-collar.

Index

Note: Page references in *italics* denote a chart or table. CMA stands for 'census metropolitan areas;' CPI, for 'Consumer Price Index;' GHG, for 'greenhouse gas;' ICT, for 'information and communications technologies;' SSDA, for 'sub-subdrainage area.'

sales/shipments, 365, *372-73*
spending on, 294
trade, 305-6
See also Internet
Construction industry
average weekly earnings, *47,* 87
bankruptcies, *54, 60-61*
in British Columbia, 130
building materials industry, 85, *92*
building permits, 81-82, *86, 88-89*
capital expenditures, by sector, *91*
collective agreements, *344*
corporate taxes, 59
days of work lost per worker, *347*
employment, *48-51,* 82, 84, *92,* 322, *336-39*
GDP contribution, 82, *131, 138-39*
GHG emissions, *190*
non-residential, 81-83, 86, *90*
operating profits, 58
residential, 81-82, 86, *88-89*
revenues, 53
Consumer Price Index (CPI)
All-items CPI, 396-97, *402-3*
changes, 395-97, *402-4, 406*
city differentials, 397
Core CPI, 396-97, *402-3*
energy, *176-77,* 396-97
food, 396-97, 399, *402-3, 406*
Correctional system, 93, 98, 108, 237, 238
Couriers/messengers, 299, 474, 476-77
Court cases, 93, 106-7
See also Crime; Justice system
CPP (Canada Pension Plan)
net worth and savings, 243, 274
payments, *246-47*
seniors' income and, 438, *447*
surpluses, 239
Credit card companies, 54
Credit cards, 297
Credit unions. *See* Finance and insurance
Crime
assaults, sexual and other, 93, *94,* 97, *100-103*
firearm use, 94-95, *104*
homicides, 93-95, 97, *100-105, 260*
persons charged, by type of offence, *103*
by province and territory, *100-101*
rates, 93-94
sentenced cases, *106-7*
stalking and spousal violence, 97

by type of offence, *94, 100-102*
violent crimes, 93-95
youth, 95
Culture and leisure. *See* Arts, entertainment and recreation; Information and cultural industries

D
Daycare, 69, 70
Deaths
causes, 68, *77,* 253-54, *260, 449*
child mortality rates, 68, *76, 254*
rates, *76,* 378, *391, 449*
by year and region, *388-89, 391*
Debt
corporate, 54-55
government, *237, 238,* 241, *244-49*
household, 271, 272, *288-89*
mortgage, 83, 272, *288*
Demography. *See* Population and demography
Depression and work performance, 258
Diabetes mellitus, 7, 18, 254, 260, 448
Diamond industry, 40, 189, 194, 310
Diet, 23, 68-69, 254, 263
Disabled persons, 463
Divorce, 96, 211, 215
Drug offences, 100-103
DVD players, 210, 218-19

E
E-commerce, 293-94, 297, 411-12
Earnings
Aboriginal women, 4
in Alberta, 324
average hourly wage, 323, *342*
collective agreements, *344*
goods-producing industries, 45, *47*
level *vs.* educational attainment, 152
lone parents, 213
second- and third-generation Canadians, 201
services sector, 45, *47*
by sex and profession, *342-43*
by sex and work pattern, *343*
See also Income; *and individual sectors*
Economic regions (ERs), 223
Economy
assets and liabilities, 128, *142-45*
balance of international payments, 129, *140-41*

days of work lost per worker, *347*
employment, *48-51*, 322, *336-39*
GDP contribution, *138-39*

V

Vancouver, British Columbia
  airport and port activity, 305, 308, 469
  ethnic diversity, 195, *204-5*
  gas prices, 172, *178-79, 472*
  home ownership by immigrants, 199
  house prices, 82
  immigrants, 195, 197, *202*
  languages spoken, 350, 354, *361-62*
  mixed-union couples, 198
  obesity in, 259
  population, 1-2, 379, *386*
  See also Census metropolitan areas
Video games, 69
Violence, family, 97
Violent crime, 93-95
Volunteering, 112, 452
Voter participation, 451, 454

W

Wages. *See* Earnings
Wait times for health care, 255, 267-68
Warehousing and storage, 48-51, 58, *138-39*,
  336-39, 474, *476-77*
Washing machines, 210, 218-19
Waste management and remediation services
  average weekly earnings, *47*
  bankruptcies, *60-61*
  GDP contribution, *138-39*
  GHG emissions, *190-91*
  growth of industry, 40
  pollution control spending, 187
  revenues, 57
  sewage, 242
  solid waste management, 188
Watersheds, 226
Weather, 228
Western Canada
  Aboriginal labour force, *14*
  construction boom, 81-83, 86-87
  containerized cargo shipments, 468, 473
  economic growth, 81-82, 86-87, 130
  export trade products, 306
  Farm Input Price Index, *407*
  unemployment rates, 321
  wholesalers growth rate, 416

Wheat, 20-21, 28-33
Wholesale trade. *See* Trade, retail and
  wholesale
Wind power, 170, 173
Windsor, Ontario, 350, 361-62
  See also Census metropolitan areas
Winnipeg, Manitoba
  Aboriginal population, 1, *2*
  gas prices, *172, 178-79, 472*
  house prices, 400
  non-official language use, 350, *361-62*
  wages in construction, 87
  See also Census metropolitan areas
Wireless technology, 294-95, 299
Women
  Aboriginal, 3, 4, *8-11*
  average earnings, *342-43*
  average income, *276-83*
  in care facilities, *261*
  charitable donations, *458-60*
  chronic conditions, *448*
  depression and work performance, 258
  earners/earnings by work pattern, *343*
  educational levels, *12, 154-55,* 201, *346,*
  440
  employment, 321, *328-32, 334, 346*
  family net worth, *290*
  fruit/vegetable consumption, 68-69, *263*
  full- and part-time work, *334-35*
  high blood pressure, *448*
  housework by, 455, *465*
  income of seniors, 438, *447*
  in labour force, 321, 323, *328-32*
  life expectancy, *253-54, 261,* 378, *446*
  living arrangements, 209, 438
  lone-parent income, 213, 269-70, *276-83*
  low-income families, 269-70, *284-85*
  maintenance enforcement programs, 96
  by marital status, *214*
  mortality rates, *260*
  news sources, 454, *466*
  participation rates, *328-32*
  with pension plans, *347*
  police officers, 99
  in population, 378
  retirement savings, *291*
  in science and technology, *436*
  self-employment, *345*
  self-rated health status, *262*
  seniors, *276-79, 437-38*
  seniors' access to transportation, 442